THE
LAST MOGUL
. . . .

ALSO BY DENNIS McDOUGAL

Angel of Darkness

In the Best of Families

Mother's Day

Fatal Subtraction: How Hollywood Really Does Business
(with Pierce O'Donnell)

THE
LAST MOGUL

······································

LEW WASSERMAN, MCA, AND THE HIDDEN HISTORY OF HOLLYWOOD

BY

DENNIS McDOUGAL

CROWN PUBLISHERS, INC., NEW YORK

Published by Crown Publishers, Inc., 201 East 50th Street, New York, New York 10022. Member of the Crown Publishing Group.

Random House, Inc. New York, Toronto, London, Sydney, Auckland
www.randomhouse.com

CROWN and colophon are trademarks of Crown Publishers, Inc.

Printed in the United States of America

Design by Lauren Dong

Library of Congress Cataloging-in-Publication Data
    McDougal, Dennis. The last mogul: Lew Wasserman, MCA, and the hidden history of Hollywood/ by Dennis McDougal. — 1st ed.
    Includes bibliographical references and index.
    1. Wasserman, Lew.   2. Chief executive officers — United States — Biography.
3. MCA Inc. — History. I. Title.
PN2287.W4525M34   1998
384'.8'092 — dc21
[b]   98-18739

ISBN 0-517-70464-1

10 9 8 7 6 5 4 3 2 1
First Edition

For Murph, for sure,

that's what friends are for…

CONTENTS

Preface   ix

Introduction   1

ACT I: MUSIC, 1896–1938

1   SOUTH BEND AND CHICAGO, 1896–1924   9

2   CHICAGO, 1925–1928   18

3   NEW YORK, 1927–1930   26

4   CHICAGO, 1930–1936   34

5   CLEVELAND, 1913–1931   45

6   CLEVELAND, 1932–1937   56

7   CHICAGO AND NEW YORK, 1937–1938   66

ACT II: CORPORATION, 1938–1960

8   HOLLYWOOD, 1938–1939   75

9   BETTE, BETTY, AND THE BIG TIME, 1940–1941   86

10   HOLLYWOOD CANTEEN, 1942–1944   95

11   BEVERLY HILLS AND BROADWAY, 1945   103

12   OCTOPUS, 1946   113

13   BEVERLY HILLS, MOSCOW, AND GANGLAND, USA,
     1947–1950   130

14   TV, TANTRUMS, AND THE DEAL THAT DOOMED
     THE MOGULS, 1950   149

15   LAUGHS AND LOOSE WOMEN, 1951–1952   167

16   THE WAIVER, 1952–1954   182

17   EQUITY, 1953–1954   192

18	BLONDES AND BIG SPENDERS, 1955–1956	209
19	OCTOPUS II, 1957–1958	224
20	UNIVERSAL, 1958–1959	241
21	MONOPOLY, 1960	256

ACT III: AMERICA, 1960–1995

22	KENNEDY JUSTICE, 1960–1961	273
23	USA *v.* MCA, 1962	289
24	BLIND AMBITION, 1963–1964	309
25	UNIVERSAL STUDIOS TOUR, 1965–1966	321
26	THE BLACK TOWER, 1967–1968	335
27	PALACE COUP, 1969	349
28	THE HEIR APPARENT, 1970–1973	362
29	THE HEIR UNAPPARENT, 1974–1976	376
30	THE ACTING PRESIDENT, 1977–1980	401
31	DEATH OF A SALESMAN, 1980–1982	416
32	THE LEGACY, 1983–1985	430
33	MCA AND THE MOB, 1986–1987	443
34	CASHING OUT, 1988–1990	460
35	BANZAI, 1990–1993	479
36	THE END, 1994–1995	494

EPILOGUE: 1995–1998

| THE LION IN WINTER | 513 |

Acknowledgments	528
Bibliography	531
Index	544

PREFACE

ew Wasserman did not want this book published, but then, Lew Wasserman never wanted *any* book published about him or MCA, the music-movie-media conglomerate that he and the late Dr. Jules Stein invented over sixty years ago.

The eighty-five-year-old chairman emeritus of Universal Studios has defeated every attempt to document his own life or that of Dr. Stein. The list of would-be MCA historians includes at least two veterans of the *New York Times* as well as the late Jacqueline Kennedy Onassis and one of Dr. Stein's oldest and most trusted colleagues. Lew Wasserman stopped them all for fear that the world would learn how and why MCA grew into the rapacious behemoth that gobbled up Universal Studios, Decca Records, G. P. Putnam's Sons, Columbia Savings and Loan, and dozens of other businesses. Only now that Wasserman's power has been exchanged for mere money and Dr. Stein's beloved MCA has itself been gobbled up — first by Matsushita Electric Industrial Company Limited and finally by the Seagram Corporation, which recently wiped out the name MCA altogether — can the remarkable story unfold.

Many would-be biographers quit long before they wrote a word. Only three succeeded in getting a book published.

In 1972, novelist-attorney Henry Denker wrote a roman à clef about Jules Stein and his role in creating presidential candidate Ronald Reagan.

"It was Jules Stein who got the idea that this guy had a future if he was used right," recalled Denker, himself a producer in the early days of television when MCA launched Reagan's political career as host of *General Electric Theater*. "People liked him, and they were willing to listen, willing to go with him. That's when it began."

Denker's stingingly melodramatic novel, *The Kingmaker*, sold modestly, then disappeared. A movie deal that Denker made for the book soured, then also disappeared.

"I was told that Lew had it killed," Denker told me. "Once I couldn't sell it as a picture, somebody got the idea to use the second half of that book as a blueprint for *The Candidate*. Remember at the end, where Robert Redford has just won the election and he says, 'What do we do now?' Go back to the end of *The Kingmaker* and you'll see that as they are coming down the statehouse steps, I've got my political expert character saying to the Jules Stein character: 'The thing about this business, defeat takes care of itself. Victory's what you've got to worry about.'

"Same concept as *The Candidate*: 'What do we do now?'"

Denker's novel reemerged as a paperback six years later, on the eve of Reagan's run for the presidency, but it never caught on. Denker moved on. He's written nearly one novel a year since.

Seven years after *The Kingmaker*, British journalist Michael Pye included a profile of Jules Stein in *Moguls: Inside the Business of Show Business*, a study of six show business titans. His study of Stein grew out of a 1973 interview that the MCA founder granted while Pye was still a business columnist for the *Sunday Times* of London.

"I suppose he believed a British journalist would be different, the way he believed everything British was somehow a cut above," said Pye. "He had this whole story concocted about growing up in South Bend and going to medical school and reluctantly getting into the band business and all of that. Rubbish! I thought to myself. When I began asking the hard questions, he shrank away and became very cold, very distant."

Though both Denker and Pye dealt with the myths and manipulations of Jules Stein, neither author touched much on Lew Wasserman or the others who created the Stein machine. That task was left to Dan Moldea, who overcame enormous obstacles to publish *Dark Victory: Ronald Reagan, MCA and the Mob*.

"Writing *Dark Victory* was the only time I ever really feared for my career," said Moldea, who has written extensively for more than twenty years about organized crime and its influence on politics (*The Killing of Robert Kennedy*), the Teamsters Union (*The Hoffa Wars*), and professional sports (*Interference*). "I felt raw power coming at me like a rifle shot."

Moldea maintains that he was followed and his phone lines tapped during the year he worked on the book. He is certain that Lew Wasserman targeted him for harassment. Wasserman's former son-in-law, Jack Myers, who was married to Lew's daughter from 1970 to 1982, confirmed that Moldea had a point. "I was in New York when *Dark Victory* first came out," Myers told me, "and it was in the windows of bookstores up and down Fifth Avenue, but Lew boasted that he actually kept it out of California altogether for quite a while. You simply couldn't find a copy."

Despite respectable reviews and a must-read reputation in Hollywood and Washington, D.C., *Dark Victory* never achieved a wide national readership, and its revelations about MCA's role in manufacturing the Ronald Reagan presidency were all but ignored by mainstream media.[1] During a late 1980s federal grand jury investigation of MCA's alleged complicity in a broad-based counterfeit record scheme,[2] however, one associate of a New Jersey organized crime family told the prosecutor questioning him, "You'll never get an indictment."

"And why is that?" asked the prosecutor.

"Because of this," said the witness, pulling a copy of *Dark Victory* from the satchel he had carried into the grand jury room with him.

Indeed, the grand jury was excused several months later without issuing a single indictment. A short time later the prosecutor was accused of being "overzealous" and was forced from Justice Department service, as were government lawyers and investigators involved in the MCA investigation.

One of Ronald Reagan's last official acts before he left office in 1989 was to disband the national Organized Crime Strike Force. The first person to pay a social call on the ex-president following his return to Los Angeles was Lew Wasserman.

—*◦◦◦*—

AMONG THOSE WHO wrote unpublished accounts of MCA was Karl Kramer, MCA secretary-treasurer and one of the handful of men who helped Jules Stein create the company nearly three-quarters of a century ago. While Stein liked the dozen or so chapters Kramer wrote, Wasserman did not. He found the account too specific about the agency's relations with bootlegging and the Chicago Mob. Kramer died in 1981 at the age of eighty-two without finishing his memoir.

Stein was determined to leave behind his own version of his life, however, and commissioned *New York Times* reporter Murray Schumach to ghostwrite his autobiography in 1974.

"At first, I said no," said Schumach. "Then [*New York Times* editor] Clifton Daniels called me in and told me I ought to do it. So I took a six-month leave from the paper. My office was next to Stein's, and we got to be very close. We ate at a place a block away from Fifty-seventh and Madison every day and always had the same thing: burger, apple pie, and coffee. We wouldn't talk about the book. We'd talk about football." Despite Stein's constant second-guessing—ordering him to

---

[1]   The book spent ten weeks on the *Los Angeles Times* best-seller list and *The Nation* editor Katrina vanden Heuvel cited *Dark Victory* as one of her favorite books of 1986. Vanden Heuvel is the daughter of Jean Stein and the granddaughter of Jules and Doris Stein.

[2]   Detailed in *Stiffed: A True Story of MCA, the Music Business and the Mafia* by William Knoedelseder, yet another book about MCA's link between show business and the underworld.

edit names, places, and events that might cast Stein in a bad light—Schumach finished the manuscript. Stein was so pleased that he gave Schumach a bonus.

"At the end, he said 'I have a present for you,'" said Schumach. "He gave me MCA stock." Over the years, Schumach's stock split repeatedly, always climbing in value. "By the time MCA was sold to Matsushita, my stock was worth more than I earned writing the book," he said, "and Stein made sure it was a tax-free gift."

If Stein was happy with the manuscript, Lew wasn't. It was never published.

At one point, while she was an editor at Doubleday, Jackie Onassis approached Wasserman about writing his memoirs, but he declined. He reportedly told the former first lady, "I don't want to write one, and besides, don't you know we own Putnam?"

—*◠◠◠*—

IN 1983 ANOTHER *New York Times* reporter tried to tell the story. As it turned out, his fiercest competition came from Stein's own daughter.

Jean Stein had twice teamed with author and New York literary lion George Plimpton to produce nonfiction best-sellers: *American Journey: The Times of Robert Kennedy* and *Edie,* the true tale of 1960s debutante Edie Sedgwick who plunged into Andy Warhol's culture of excess and died of drug abuse before she celebrated her thirtieth birthday. After a falling-out with Plimpton in the early 1980s over authorship of *Edie,*[3] Jean began her third oral history, an ambitious attempt to reconstruct the behind-the-scenes history of old Hollywood from the recollections of her father's friends, business associates, employees, and competitors, and her mother's memoirs. With a foreword by Jimmy Stewart, *We Just Kept Going—An American Clan Moves Forward* was to have been Doris Stein's swan song detailing her version of her life with Jules Stein and the rise of MCA during their fifty-three years of marriage.

To ensure absolute control, Doris turned over her memoirs to Harold Oppenheimer, her son by a previous marriage. A retired Marine Corps general and Kansas cattle rancher, Harold Oppenheimer had been publishing farming textbooks for years in Illinois. But *We Just Kept Going* was never published.

Publication was first delayed until after Reagan's 1984 reelection campaign because the book confirmed the truth of a widely reported rumor that Dr. Stein had masterminded a shady California real estate deal enabling Ronald Reagan, then governor of California, to run for president. But Doris died in April 1984, and

---

[3] Plimpton finally agreed to be identified as the book's editor while Jean Stein took author credit. Norman Mailer, who also helped sift through the 15,000 pages of transcripts of Stein's interviews, got no credit at all.

the frustrated editors at the Illinois publishing house could do nothing with the fragmentary manuscript that she had left behind. "If the book had been completed, they planned to release it the day after Reagan's election," said Ron McDaniel, the publishing company's marketing chief.

Any hope that *We Just Kept Going* would ever reach the bookstores evaporated in October 1985 when Harold Oppenheimer died. Jean decided to proceed in writing her own book, based in part on her mother's memoirs.

Meanwhile, the *New York Times* reporter who was writing a book about Jules Stein and MCA arranged a meeting with Jean. They shared a pleasant evening with Jean's guests John Gregory Dunne and Joan Didion at Jean's Manhattan apartment, but he got only her limited cooperation. While she gave the *Times* reporter no hint that she had any misgivings about his book, secretly she panicked. She saw him as competition.

It made little difference to the reporter. After more than two years of research, he had already learned a good deal about MCA's relations with organized crime in Chicago as well as a number of embarrassing stories about the sexual peccadilloes of the MCA brass. Jean began to believe her own promiscuity might be revealed, and that he would skewer her vanity in print for wresting the author's credit away from Plimpton on her previous books. She warned the Illinois publisher not to tell the *Times* reporter anything.

"We are aware that this will be a sensational type exposé and the family as well as Mr. Wasserman, the present chairman of the board of MCA, have refused to give him any information on the basis that it is competitive with Mother's book," Jean wrote to Ron McDaniel.

She need not have worried. When *Dark Victory* hit the bookstores, the *Times* reporter lost interest in the Stein story. His book was never completed.

Jean also declined to cooperate with me. In a September 25, 1997, letter to me she wrote: "I recognize that you have serious credentials as a writer, but the underlying reason for my silence is that I am a very private person and do not wish to be interviewed by anybody about my father and our family."

Jean did get her interview with Lew Wasserman, however, and planned to include it in her oral history, but she ultimately decided to shelve the project. For the sake of history, I urged her to resurrect her book, but heard nothing further from her.

I spoke with the *Times* reporter, too. He advised me about pitfalls, false trails, and deceptive sources. Perhaps the most valuable bit of advice he gave me when I started *The Last Mogul* back in the summer of 1994 was to pack a lunch. What did he mean by that? I asked.

"You're going to be on the road a long, long time," he said with a chuckle.

How right he was.

People in the East pretend to be interested in how pictures are made, but if you actually tell them anything, you find they are only interested in Colbert's clothes or Gable's private life. They never see the ventriloquist for the doll. Even the intellectuals, who ought to know better, like to hear about the pretensions, extravagances, and vulgarities.

F. Scott Fitzgerald, *The Last Tycoon*, 1940

INTRODUCTION

A copy of the March 31, 1995, edition of the *Wall Street Journal* lay on the Spartan desktop. The headline announced to the world what MCA-Universal Chairman Lew R. Wasserman had only just confirmed himself: MCA's parent corporation, Matsushita Electric Industrial Company, would sell MCA out from under him to Seagram's.

Wasserman, a tall, somber-looking man of eighty-two, leaned over the newspaper, rereading intently what he'd first read at home before dawn.

The MCA courier had rushed overnight mail and a half-dozen daily newspapers to Wasserman's front door as he did every business day. Lew had already been on the phone for hours—from home, from the car, and then from his fifteenth-floor office. Everyone wanted to know the same thing: was it true?

Lew had his answer on the front page of the *Journal*. For half a century he had made it his business to know other people's business before they did. Now the routine had been broken, and with shock force. The lead of the *Journal* story read: "Rumors have surfaced since last year of a separation between parent Matsushita and its Hollywood movie, record and theme park subsidiary, which the Japanese company bought five years ago for $6.5 billion."

Wasserman blinked. His hair was chalk white but not thinning, and it contrasted dramatically with his black-rimmed glasses and fading Palm Springs tan. His business suit was dark and well tailored, far from ostentatious. He wore his thin, simple tie drawn tight at the throat. Impeccable, as usual. A study in patrician power. Yet this was not the same Lew R. Wasserman that Jack Valenti, president of the Motion Picture Association of America, had once referred to as the Zeus of the Mount Olympus known as Hollywood. The years he'd fought off with such passion had begun to show. There was frailty behind the dour visage. He had bad knees. His eyes were weak. He might have been angry over the headlines, but even if he had thrown one of his notorious tantrums, it would have had no impact.

Ten years earlier this would not have happened. Wasserman was still a titan then. Known only vaguely, if at all, to the great audiences that bicoastal MCA executives contemptuously referred to as "flyover people," Lew Wasserman topped every Hollywood insider's list of the most powerful men in entertainment. Like the late Jules Stein, who had founded the Music Corporation of America in 1924, Lew Wasserman wielded his might silently, judiciously, without fanfare, but with dead aim and in dead earnest. To court Lew Wasserman successfully meant fame, influence, riches. To cross Lew Wasserman meant the end of your career.

Of course, if you believed the "100 Most Powerful People in the Industry" lists in *Premiere* or *Entertainment Weekly* magazines, Jim Carrey and Whoopi Goldberg had more clout in Hollywood than Lew Wasserman.

Lew Wasserman. Who knew his name outside the industry? Those who mattered, of course. Lew understood and exercised real power, not flash-in-the-pan glitz like Roseanne or Howard Stern. For more than a generation, he had mingled with sovereigns. When Pope John Paul II visited L.A., Lew was at his right hand throughout the stay. Men behind the throne—Henry Kissinger, Cyrus Vance, Robert Strauss, and Warren Christopher—returned Lew's phone calls immediately. Every president since Kennedy had paid him homage. It was widely acknowledged that Lew and Jules Stein helped create Ronald Reagan. Lady Bird Johnson still sent Lew and his wife, Edie, birthday greetings each year and insisted they come down to the ranch for barbecue whenever they were in Texas. He was benefactor and confidant to Jimmy Carter. Even Bill Clinton paid his respects to the Wassermans during his extended California visits.

Perhaps that is why it was not hard to imagine Wasserman grimacing as he read further into the *Wall Street Journal* article: "Seagram already owns a 15 percent stake in Time Warner Inc., which has blocked any increase in ownership by the Bronfman family company. However, it is known that Seagram Chief Executive Officer Edgar Bronfman Jr. would like to extend his interest in the entertainment industry."

The sale of yet another movie studio to yet another rich interloper was nothing new. In the 1960s, billionaire auto salvage tycoon Charles Bluhdorn had bought Paramount Pictures. In the 1970s, Denver oilman Marvin Davis had snapped up Twentieth Century Fox. Both men were at least as interested in rubbing shoulders with the stars and amusing themselves with the mysteries of moviemaking as they were in turning a profit.

It made sense that Edgar Bronfman Jr., the bearded young pup taking aim at MCA, would be cast from that same billion-dollar dilettante's mold. Twenty-two years earlier, Bronfman had made his first venture into Hollywood, using his father's money to finance a forgettable teen love story briefly released in 1971 under the title *Melody*. Bronfman had been all of seventeen at the time. Ever since, he'd been angling to move into movies permanently. That was why he'd encouraged Seagram to buy up Time Warner. That was why he now sought MCA. In addition to a moviemaking wanna-be, Bronfman fancied himself a ladies' man in the same league as Warren Beatty, and as a creative artist with a talent for writing lyrics and music. Hollywood was perfect for him.

Still, there was more to this Seagram bid than the satisfaction of a rich kid's desire for an ego trip. If Seagram consumed the MCA-Universal empire, Wasserman certainly wouldn't enjoy the autonomy he had under Matsushita. Bronfman would most likely loosen Lew's grip on the MCA reins and ease him out. It would mark the end of a dynasty. The end of an era. Maybe the end of MCA.

Funny that Lew Wasserman, of all people, apparently hadn't seen it coming. The Japanese had kept him in the dark for months about their plans. In a sense, MCA was already dead, had been ever since Wasserman and his board of directors agreed to sell control to Matsushita in November of 1990.

Wasserman had assured his associates that dealing with the Japanese would be different. He counted on them to be as much of a visionary as he had been. Matsushita had the money. Lew learned quickly that the company he and Jules Stein had carefully built since 1938 into the most powerful engine in Hollywood would function as a wholly owned subsidiary of its Asian overlord. It was a bitter pill to swallow for a man accustomed to having his own way for half a century.

Wasserman himself had once been the overlord. From his windows atop Universal's legendary Black Tower, the tall, snowy-haired patriarch could still see much of what he had built during his fifty-nine-year tenure with MCA. Down below, the Universal Studios Tour trams snaked through the make-believe street scenes on the 300-acre back lot, transformed over thirty years into one of the most successful theme parks on the planet. As an actual movie studio, Universal's output had slowed considerably since its mass-production heyday in the 1960s, but the studio still cranked out a few TV dramas and sitcoms each week, including ABC's high-rated *Coach* and the venerable Angela Lansbury series *Murder, She Wrote* on CBS. The studio was also good for at least a couple dozen big-budget films a year. At the moment, Universal was taking a drubbing for having produced the most expensive movie ever made: *Waterworld*, starring Kevin Costner and Dennis Hopper and featuring the most disaster-prone sets ever built. One of them sank in Hawaii before Costner as prima donna director was able to shoot a single can of film. The price tag reported for the movie was $165 million and still climbing.

But one year's bomb gave way to the next year's bonanza, as it always had in the movie business. Amid the deluge of doomsday reporting about *Waterworld*, everyone seemed to forget that just two years earlier Universal had sponsored Steven Spielberg's *Jurassic Park*, one of the most successful films of all time. Movies were crap shoots, but if you were a savvy lifelong gambler like Lew and you knew when to roll the dice, you never lost in the long run. Lew understood that, but he couldn't convince the Japanese. They read the *Wall Street Journal*.

In the same way, the Japanese trusted Mike Ovitz, the smarmy young tyrant of Creative Artists Agency, which dominated Hollywood in the eighties and nineties the way MCA had in the forties and fifties. It was Ovitz who had engineered the sale of MCA to the Japanese and who appeared to be brokering this latest deal with Bronfman. Ovitz had never made it a secret that he both admired and envied Lew. He seemed to seek ways to top the legend of Lew the way Wasserman himself had once tried to top Jules Stein. The difference was that Ovitz didn't have the same respect for those who had gone before him. MCA may have been ruthless, but at its heart were tradition and teamwork among a brain trust that was as close-knit as any Mafia family.

From where Lew sat, Creative Artists more closely resembled a street gang with Ovitz as chief thug.

On this day before April Fool's Day 1995, the skies were clear. From atop the Black Tower that Lew had constructed when MCA bought Universal, Wasserman could almost pick out the old Beverly Hills headquarters of Music Corporation of America. Stein had the old MCA building erected the same year the Wassermans arrived in southern California. By the time MCA merged with Universal twenty-five years later, Jules Stein was the semiretired chairman of the board, Lew was president, and the company was no longer privately held by Dr. Stein and his family. It was publicly traded on the New York Stock Exchange, though most of the stock was still closely held. Lew was among its largest shareholders, along with a cabal of about a dozen other executives whom Dr. Stein had plucked from obscurity or hired away from other agencies. There was Lew's chief rival, Taft Schreiber, who helped create the political careers of Richard Nixon and Ronald Reagan, and Sonny Werblin, who left the company to reinvent a flagging pro football team called the New York Titans, which he renamed the New York Jets. There was razor-sharp Berle Adams, whose executive brilliance at the dawn of the TV age pushed MCA to new levels of power, but who turned out to be Brutus to Wasserman's Julius Caesar. There was Leland Hayward, a bon vivant talent wizard who sold his agency to Wasserman and solidified MCA's position as the most powerful engine in Hollywood.

There was tiny, tough Mickey Rockford; long, tall Herb Rosenthal, who worked for Werblin in the New York office; and faithful, plodding Maurie Lipsey of Chicago. There was Karl Kramer, the numbers whiz from Detroit; George Campbell, who went mad after thirty-five years of loyally serving the company; Stein's older brother, Bill, who died a bachelor at fifty after spending a lifetime trying to sleep with seemingly every woman in the United States; and Stein's brother-in-law, Charlie Miller, who joined MCA straight out of law school during the Roaring Twenties. And there was Sidney Korshak, the ultimate insider who never owned a single share of stock or attached his name to any movie, yet held more influence over the fortunes of the company than anyone other than Lew and Dr. Stein.

Most of them were gone now, and the original palatial headquarters had been sold to Litton Industries when MCA moved to Universal City. Nowadays the old headquarters building housed the offices of Western Atlas, the holding corporation that gobbled up Litton.

It seemed oddly ironic. When MCA pioneered the practice of gobbling up smaller companies, the Justice Department considered it some sort of unpatriotic sin. Since the mid-1940s, the government and press alike had nicknamed MCA "the Star-Spangled Octopus" because of Dr. Stein's propensity for wrapping himself in the flag whenever he reached out his tentacles and obliterated his competition. By 1960, MCA had become so successful at beating or buying every other agency in the world that the FBI revived a twenty-year-old antitrust investigation into the agency's practices. The charge: monopolizing the entertainment business. Only after MCA agreed to quit the agency business and concentrate strictly on TV, movie, and record production did Robert Kennedy's Justice Department back off.

MCA's mistake was being ahead of its time by thirty years. Had MCA-Universal been allowed to continue building itself into Hollywood's most powerful agency *and* the world's most prolific producer of TV shows and movies, Lew never would have needed Japanese money. The company would have dominated the entertainment industry in the 1990s.

The run-in with the Kennedys taught Lew one important lesson: real success on a grand scale had everything to do with political patronage. The important thing wasn't which party you chose. The important thing was to keep on top of lawmakers, contribute to both parties, and exact a quid pro quo in the form of tax breaks and legislation favorable to MCA in particular and the industry in general.

Lew was a staunch Democrat in matters of civil liberties and racial equality, but when it came to money and power, he was a pragmatist. Ronald Reagan's first stop following the 1988 inauguration of his White House successor was a private lunch with Lew Wasserman, who had been his first real Hollywood agent. The most revered Republican since Abraham Lincoln understood that being a Democrat meant about as much to Lew Wasserman as being a Jew: that was what he was and that was what he would always be, but it wasn't going to stop him from playing the right poker hand to take the whole pot on his own terms.

After all, Lew loved MCA the way the average man loves his family. In a way, MCA *was* his family. After their first few years together, Edie had become more of a social and business partner than a wife. *Time* magazine guessed in the 1950s that the Wassermans had ceased sleeping together. Edie got the bedroom. Lew slept in his study, where he could be up by 5:00 A.M. without disturbing Edie. He had always spent more time at work than at home. He was too busy figuring profit margins and box office grosses to bother with domestic trivia. He actually became more of a father to his only daughter, Lynne, *after* she grew up, went through a couple of divorces, and had two children of her own. Now whenever she hit the emotional skids, he was there for her in ways that he couldn't be when she was young. The company had always had first claim on his devotion. Universal City was his feudal domain. In one of her periodic piques, Edie snubbed Princess Grace of Monaco by pointing out that the Wassermans' kingdom was larger and more powerful than Rainier's puny 465-acre Mediterranean principality.

Edie may have been a princess, if not a queen, but Lew never did act much like a king. He still ate tuna fish for lunch from the studio commissary and dressed in his bland MCA uniform: white shirt, dark tie, dark suit. But Universal City was a kingdom of a sort—his kingdom, with its own police force, its own freeway off-ramp, its own zip code. From his office he could see Universal CityWalk, the latest addition. From dawn to past midnight nearly every day of the year, tourists packed its pricey boutiques. At the far southern end, Universal's Cineplex Odeon theater complex showed a dozen different feature films continuously in eighteen theaters, seven days and nights a week. They served cappuccino, croissants, and designer seltzer from the snack bar. A far cry from the Cleveland movie palaces of the 1920s, where Lew had started out showing patrons to their seats. He had been lucky in those days to eat a box of stale popcorn during his nine-hour shift.

The movies had been silent back then, mostly slapstick or melodrama. But they were movies. The men in white hats rode off into the sunset. The villains were hanged or went to jail, scowling. And in the end, the poor underdog of a hero triumphed to save the day, win the girl, get the pot of gold, and live happily ever after.

Born Louis Wasserman, the third son of immigrant Russian Jews, Lew was seduced by the silver screen the very first time he stepped into a dark movie theater. In a way, his life and the whole history of MCA were just like a movie. A movie with a beginning, a middle, and an end. Three acts, complete with plot twists, comic relief, and a denouement. A movie that wasn't over quite yet. A movie that had begun twenty years before he was born....

ACT I

MUSIC

1896–1938

Music oft hath such a charm

To make bad good, and good provoke to harm.

<small>WILLIAM SHAKESPEARE</small>

ONE

South Bend and Chicago

1896–1924

The man who created Lew Wasserman's beloved MCA—who, in fact, created Lew Wasserman—was born in 1896 in South Bend, Indiana. Julius Caesar Stein was the son of Lithuanian Jews who fled to Canada and then entered the United States in a wave of immigration that began in 1870 and didn't slow until the beginning of World War I.

Persecution in America wasn't as violent as it had been in Europe, but in the Midwest during the first half of the twentieth century, Jews were cursed. Jews—especially working-class Jews like the Stein family—were labeled Christ-killers, hebes, kikes. Indiana, which may have the dubious distinction of having given birth to the Ku Klux Klan, was a particularly difficult place in which to grow up Jewish. Still, the Steins found the people of South Bend less bigoted than most.

Louis Stein sold clothes, brooms, welcome mats, and other household items from Stein Dry Goods at the corner of West Washington Avenue and Walnut Street, just west of the well-to-do downtown area of South Bend. Their home was next door, where Louis and his wife, the former Rosa Cohen (née Kahanaski), raised three boys and two girls. Theirs was an arranged marriage—comfortable but not romantic or particularly warm, even after nearly fifty years together. The daughter of a rabbi and martyred newspaper publisher who had fought the czar's oppression in the old country, Rosa grew to resent her husband's simple, uncultured ways.

The Steins earned a living, but they were never rich. When Jules was four, Louis had to declare temporary bankruptcy after he was robbed of $4,010 during a business trip to Chicago. But he was an honorable and hardworking man. He paid his creditors and kept his store open. After several prosperous years, Rosa's buggy overturned in a freak accident three years after the birth of her last child. The horse kicked her, and she was paralyzed, wheelchair-bound for the rest of her life. Much of the Steins' income went to pay a full-time live-in servant and a Hungarian cook. But their neighbors were tolerant, and Louis and Rosa Stein never felt the urge to move. They lived out most of their lives in South Bend.

Not so with their second son. Unlike his parents and his more complaisant older brother, Billy—who started out to become a lawyer but wound up selling ladies' ready-to-wear clothing— Jules Stein hungered to succeed.

When he was eight, Rosa bought a mandolin and sixteen dollars' worth of lessons from a traveling salesman, and encouraged Jules to take up music. Three years later she bought him a violin. By the age of twelve, he played onstage between feature films at a downtown nickelodeon. At fifteen, Jules took up the saxophone and formed a six-piece neighborhood band that earned money playing at birthday parties.

Louis Stein was less indulgent with his son than Rosa was. Deeply religious (he was the first president of South Bend's Hebrew Orthodox Congregation), Louis demanded perfection. Shortly after Jules entered high school, he built a table in wood shop and proudly took it home to display to his father. "What is this garbage?" asked Louis, who cruelly tossed his boy's handiwork out into the snow. Jules was crushed. But his father became merely the first in a long line of older male authority figures who underestimated Jules's resolve. Years later, as one of the wealthiest men in America, Jules finally responded in his own way to his father's cruel disdain by obsessively collecting fine English antiques until he owned the greatest collection of Queen Anne furniture in the world.

Jules Stein was diminutive and thin, never athletic, but always a ladies' man. He stood five feet seven and weighed 140 pounds most of his life. Before he reached his mid-twenties, the thin black hair he parted in the middle of his high forehead had begun to recede. For several years early in his career, he sported a mustache, giving him the faintest resemblance to Charlie Chaplin. His brown eyes were as expressionless as his pursed mouth, revealing nothing of his secretive nature. But he could be a witty raconteur and carry on a conversation for hours if he liked someone...or if he believed he could get something out of him.

The usual adolescent preoccupations with sex, sports, and rebellion meant little to Jules. What intrigued him was success: getting beyond his Jewishness to become a power in upper-crust WASP society.

In 1911 he left home and enrolled in a college prep course at the new Winona Academy in the Indiana farm country, 50 miles southeast of South Bend, operated by Billy Sunday, the celebrated Chicago Cub–turned-evangelist. In addition to music, Jules studied the evangelist's hellfire-and-brimstone sales techniques and watched with keen interest as tent show audiences ponied up their tithes. From Winona Academy, Stein went to the University of West Virginia in Morgantown, where he learned that his tuition would be paid if he played in the school band. In 1913, the same year that his future protégé, Louis Wasserman, was born in Cleveland, the seventeen-year-old Stein moved on to the University of Chicago.

Musically, the timing for his arrival in Chicago couldn't have been better. During World War I, Chicago became the capital of dance-hall ragtime. While still an undergraduate, Jules organized dance bands to defray living costs. One of his earliest gigs was playing backup fiddle to a busty young vaudevillian from Brooklyn named Mary Jane West. Stein remembered her, even in 1913, as "voluptuous." She was one of the first white performers he'd ever seen stand on stage and shimmy her ample bosom like a hot young soul singer. Mary Jane let Jules accompany her to the South Side black joints where she could study hootchy-kootchy technique up close, but she never dated her fiddle player. She was too old for him, she teased. For the next sixty years, long after she'd changed her name to Mae West, she reminded Stein often about his missed chance.

In the years just prior to and during World War I, ragtime was in decline and a new kind of music was rising in Chicago. It was called jazz and it became synonymous with easy sex. When they shut down the New Orleans brothels where jazz was born, the pimps and whores moved north. So did the black musicians. And Chicago jazz was born.

After Jules took his bachelor's degree in 1915, he quit college to earn enough money as a musician to go to medical school. In the fall of 1917 he entered the University of Chicago's Rush Medical School as a scholarship student.

Meanwhile, Chicago entered the Roaring Twenties. Jules had nearly completed medical school when the Eighteenth Amendment banning alcohol became law. He and thousands of others marked the occasion on the night of January 15, 1920, by getting legally drunk for the last time. During the next decade, Chicago would become the hub of a national obsession with booze, blues, and big-money crime.

Everyone paid cash in the music business because no one trusted anyone. It wasn't unusual for Stein and his associates to carry several thousand dollars.

"Mr. Stein was friends with Al Capone," said Charles Harris, Stein's butler and confidant for the final forty years of his life. "Four or five of his bands played Capone's speakeasies." Though he would learn from their tactics and make deals with the devils who ran the nightclubs and brothels, Jules Stein maintained that he was neither a gangster nor a down-and-dirty bluesman. Jules had worked too long and too hard to be recognized as anything other than a respectable professional man, and that was the image he cultivated, even though he was increasingly forced to deal with gangsters. He had stumbled upon the band-booking business purely by accident. Only after years of booking weddings and bar mitzvahs did he venture into the netherworld of nightclubs.

Jules was never a great musician, but he had a head for organizing. He scheduled the gigs, negotiated the money, and paid each band member his share. One Saturday night while he was still an undergraduate, Jules mistakenly double-booked his band. Instead of canceling one gig, he found a second band and let them play the extra booking in exchange for paying him a 10 percent commission. That night Jules discovered the obvious: instead of organizing the band, rehearsing, paying the travel gas, blowing a saxophone, and bowing his fiddle for three or four hours, then divvying up the money five ways, Jules could earn almost as much by simply picking up the phone and scheduling some other band to do all the work.

Despite this lucrative discovery, Jules resisted the lure of booking bands full time. He put up $5,000 and became partners with a pair of brash young music promoters, Fred Hamm and Ernie Young, who were to run the day-to-day operations of a partnership Stein called the Music Corporation. Hamm and Young also contributed $5,000 each, and the trio rented a dingy one-room office at 20 East Jackson Boulevard on the east side of the Loop for ten dollars a month.

"Jules never liked to start a business by himself," said former MCA vice president Berle Adams, who later became a close Stein confidant. "He met with Ernie Young and said, 'I'd like to use your offices. So what if I become your partner?' He'd decided that if he could take a band on the road, they could make money by booking the ballrooms in the vicinity of Chicago."

Jules helped his partners, but he had loftier goals. He wanted to be a man of science, not a vaudevillian. Most of his grades were B's, but he was shrewd and fellow students recognized his exceptional focus and drive when he was still in his twenties. Printed below his picture in his 1921 college yearbook was a simple but dead-on summary of his personality: "He knows what is what."

—◈—

IN 1921, JULES graduated from medical school. He went to Europe the following year to study at the University of Vienna.[1] When he returned to Chicago, he landed an appointment as chief resident at Cook County Hospital, where he set a record for performing the most tonsillectomies in a single day. But when he tried the next logical step in his medical career—postgraduate study in ophthalmology at Harvard or Johns Hopkins—he was turned down.[2] He didn't have enough credits in organic chemistry, he was told. As a consolation prize, he accepted an apprenticeship with Dr. Harry S. Gradle, a highly regarded eye surgeon who practiced in downtown Chicago and lived in Highland Park, one of the tonier suburbs 26 miles north of the city. Stein was well on his way toward a brilliant medical career.

His older brother, meanwhile, was well on his way to oblivion. A failure as a lawyer, Bill Stein floundered in business and seduced as many women as he could

---

[1] During his brief European sojourn, Stein studied much more than medicine, according to intimates. He frequented cabarets, circuses, and sideshows, making the acquaintance of singers, musicians, and strippers he would eventually import into the United States.
[2] Stein once explained that ophthalmology and dermatology were the two most lucrative medical specialties because statistically they had the highest patient turnover in a single business day.

fit between his sheets. In addition, in 1925 he was diagnosed with rheumatic heart disease, a condition that would ruin his health and plague him for the rest of his life. "Jules was working for Dr. Gradle, and he had a fine position and he had no reason to leave the business, but he told me he had to find something for Bill to do," said Berle Adams.

Stein tried to turn Bill into a band booker, but his brother just didn't have the drive or talent. Jules was on the phone as much or more than Bill, cajoling road-house owners, nightclub managers, and wedding party coordinators into taking this band or that. "I'd have a patient in front of me, fitting him for eyeglasses, and I'd get a call," Stein recalled years later. Dr. Stein the ophthalmologist would adjust his patient's lenses while J. C. Stein the booker would whisper into the receiver: "Book the band in Lafayette!" As an agent and doctor, his life had become schizoid. Within a year, J. C. Stein the agent was earning ten times what Dr. Jules Stein did practicing medicine. J.C. signed up for a three-year correspon-dence course in business while Dr. Stein kept pace with the current literature on ophthalmology. The double life, however, could not continue indefinitely.

The Stein brothers called themselves the Kenneworth Music Company and shared office space in the Garrick Theater Building with the man who would later become Stein's first partner, Ernie Young. Jules dreamed of going head-to-head with Edgar Benson, Chicago's most successful music agent. He was the chief booker for the "sweet" bands that steered clear of honky-tonk and stuck to slower tempos. Benson often took one-third or more of the bands' earnings as his com-mission, so Jules undercut him by offering the same service for 10 percent on a weekly booking and 20 percent for a one-night stand.

The first band Jules sent on the road was King Joe Oliver's Creole Jazz Band, at a royal nightly guarantee of $125. Oliver was an unusual choice because he and his musicians—including a young cornet player named Louis Armstrong—were black. Most of the early 1920s "sweet" bands that Stein represented were the white orchestras that midwestern dance-hall owners and their top-dollar audiences demanded.

Stein needed one more ingredient to put the Stein brothers' agency ahead of the pack: broadcasting. On October 27, 1920, Westinghouse Electric established Pittsburgh's KDKA as the first commercial radio station in the nation. Three years later every major city had its own station. Stein first heard bands playing over the radio out of Kansas City, Missouri, via radio station WDAF. Crystal sets were sell-ing off the shelf. By 1924 the biggest problem facing new station owners was how to fill the airwaves with cheap round-the-clock programming to cash in on this new audience. One solution was to find a nightclub with a slick-sounding band and stick a microphone in front of the musicians.

In Kansas City in the mid-1920s, that band became the Coon Sanders Orches-tra, led jointly by snare drummer Carlton Coon and pianist Joe Sanders. They were nicknamed the Kansas City Night Hawks because their music originated from the ballroom of the Muehlbach Hotel in downtown Kansas City each evening at midnight.

What followed was an hour of the Coon Sanders Orchestra's clean, straight-ahead, commercial white jazz. The musicians had no idea how popular the new medium of radio had made them, but Stein did. "They didn't know who I was when they played a roadhouse called the Lincoln Tavern [near Chicago] in 1924," Jules said years later. "But I pestered them to go on a tour of one-night stands. They finally said, 'Okay, if you pay us $10,000.' I didn't have the $10,000. I went back to them and said, 'I'll give you $2,000 when you sign the contract and the rest when you go on tour.'"

Stein didn't have $2,000, let alone $10,000, so he had to work fast. He was betting that young people in every town from Kansas City to Chicago had heard the midnight broadcasts from the Muehlbach, just as Stein had, and dance-hall owners would pay just about anything to have the band in person. "My trick was to ask for 50 percent in advance when I booked them," Stein recalled. Thus he was able to pay off the band before they even played a note, and still collect the other half of the booking fee as pure profit once the gig was over. At the end of thirty days, he had earned $10,000, and the Coon Sanders Orchestra was ready to go anywhere Stein suggested. Despite his overwhelming success, Jules couldn't interest Ernie Young in coming in as his partner. "Ernie Young said, 'I want no part of it. I've got my own business and it's very good,'" Stein recalled.

That may have been the first time a business associate failed to appreciate the vision of Jules Stein. Stein and Young were an odd couple anyway. Fresh from a background of buttoned-down academe, Stein recoiled whenever Young bounded into the office like P. T. Barnum. Jules patterned himself after the young brokers who worked at the Chicago Stock Exchange: Oxford gray suits, crisp white shirts, and black ties became his uniform and that of everyone who worked for him. In Jules's estimation, a businessman's appearance was at least as important as his speech or behavior. If an agent dressed like a professional, Stein reasoned, he would be trusted as a professional. If he dressed like a clown, that's how clients would treat him.

But Ernie Young did have something Jules wanted. Young listed his businesses under several names in the trade magazine *Billboard*, and one of those names was Music Corporation of America — an elongated version of the partnership name that Young, Stein, and Fred Hamm had used. It was grandiose, even arrogant, but it was a name that Jules believed he could turn into cash during those early days of recorded music and radio, when David Sarnoff's hugely successful — and similarly named — Radio Corporation of America was just beginning to take the nation by storm.

Young told Stein if he paid him the $10,000 that Young and Hamm had originally invested, the Stein brothers could have the name. Jules forked over the $10,000 he'd earned on the first Coon Sanders tour, and the Music Corporation of America was born.

It was a corporation in name only. It became the real thing on May 24, 1924, when Stein hired a pair of Chicago lawyers to incorporate. In the articles of incorporation, he gave four reasons for going into business:

1. To carry on the business of providing, furnishing, arranging, and presenting public or private entertainments, exhibitions, concerts, and musical organizations of all kinds.
2. To provide, furnish, engage, and employ musicians and musical artists, orchestras, bands, and entertainers.
3. To buy, sell, lease, hold, own, and operate dance halls, amusements, enterprises, music halls, restaurants, cafés, and other places of public amusement, refreshment, and entertainment.
4. To buy, sell, trade in, and deal in musical instruments, music, and supplies and any and all other merchandise of whatsoever kind, nature, or description.

In the blank marked "Duration of the corporation," Jules filled in the word "perpetual." He named Bill and his own employer, Dr. Harry S. Gradle, as members of MCA's first board of directors, issuing them two shares each of MCA's initial 4,000 shares of stock. Jules held 196 shares, worth $5 each, and left the remaining 3,800 shares in the corporation.

—⌇⌇—

JULES AND HIS brother continued to share office space with Ernie Young, but the Music Corporation of America—or MCA, as it came to be known—operated independently.

Needing a partner as hungry as he was, Stein found one in a twenty-two-year-old medical student from the University of Illinois who gave up hope of a medical career when he failed German. In frustration, Billy Goodheart Jr. quit college and hooked up with "Doc" Stein, as Jules had come to be known in Chicago's dance halls and speakeasies. Billy Goodheart was six years younger than Jules, but due to a spinal condition, he was several inches shorter than Stein and looked older. Jules was thin and poised while Goodheart was built like a barrel. Goodheart was gruff, coarse, and loud whereas Jules was steely, soft-spoken, and cultured to the point of pretension. Jules liked to show off his money; Goodheart liked to show off his power. Jules believed in the accumulation of wealth; Goodheart believed in the accumulation of experience. Jules was a man of analysis; Billy Goodheart was a man of action.

They both loved the pursuit of the deal. They went at it with totally different styles, but Stein and Goodheart were equals at driving a hard bargain and telling as many versions of the truth as necessary to close a sale. On paper, Billy Stein remained an equal partner of Music Corporation of America, but Jules Stein's real partner at the birth of MCA was another Billy—and Billy Goodheart would remain Stein's equal for nearly twenty years.

⤙∿⤚

THE STATIONERY STEIN ordered for his new company featured a pencil sketch of the globe at the top center of the sheet with the North American continent featured prominently. Below the globe were the first three verses of "My Country, 'Tis of Thee" and the address of the new MCA offices, located in a two-room rented office next door to the Chicago Theater at 159 North State Street.

Jules remained ambivalent about the business. He wanted both the money that band booking offered and the prestige of being a man of medicine. He still went into Gradle's office every day. He wrote a well-received scientific paper that was reprinted by Zeiss Optical Company as an instructional manual for optometrists.

Chiefly through Billy Goodheart's efforts, MCA held its own, but competition remained cutthroat. One of MCA's innovations was band rotation—a simple idea that no one had exploited successfully until Goodheart and Stein. After Coon Sanders had played the Muehlbach Hotel for a while, Jules wanted to send them on the road to cash in on their new fame, but that left the Muehlbach without an orchestra. So Stein sent in Eddie Niebahr and his Seattle Harmony Kings, one of the bands MCA regularly booked on one-night stands around Chicago. This type of rotation worked well. Hotels liked it because guests always had fresh music, and bands liked it because the money was good and MCA took care of travel, lodging, meals, and publicity.

The only opposition came from unions, which didn't appreciate out-of-town musicians taking away their business. MCA orchestras had to deal with occasional threats, stink bombs, and hotel workers' strikes. When a union sought to fine Stein for booking nonunion talent in a Chinese restaurant called the Canton Tea Gardens, Jules refused to pay. Two days later the restaurant was bombed.

Unions were MCA's bane, with one notable exception. For years Stein proudly boasted that he held the number one charter membership in the Chicago local of the American Federation of Musicians. For a time he sat on the union's administrative council and attended its annual conventions. He kept up his dues and held on to his working musician's status long after he quit playing his violin. While he might have had to fight off union goons in Kansas City or Cleveland, Stein knew how to buy labor peace in Chicago: befriend the head man and keep him happy.

The head man was James Caesar Petrillo, the son of a West Side sewer digger. Petrillo, who had dropped out of school in the fourth grade, mangled the English language in a grating voice reminiscent of Jimmy Durante. Like many union leaders, he maintained his power through a combination of threats and promises to both recalcitrant club owners and dissident musicians. He eventually defeated the rival musicians' unions and, with the backing of the Mob, became the music czar of Chicago.

As Petrillo's power base spread across the country, MCA's rotating bands also moved to all corners of America. The symbiotic relationship between the AFM and MCA grew tighter. Petrillo granted MCA special dispensation that turned the band-booking agency into a Big Band supermarket. Musicians and rival bookers cried foul, alleging that Stein must have bribed Petrillo for his favor, but no one was ever able to prove anything more between the two than friendship.

Unlike any other band booker, Stein could demand that his orchestras deliver $1 million in commissions to MCA before he allowed them out of their contracts. Some bandleaders, like Tommy Dorsey and Benny Goodman, later complained bitterly that Stein had the same power over musicians that a plantation owner had over his slaves, because a band was forced to work only for MCA until it earned $10 million—an unimaginable figure. Eventually, even Petrillo had to recognize the inequity and ordered the $1 million contract banned.

"They make me so mad I could cut their throats, but I've got to play ball with them," Dorsey said. Like every other MCA bandleader, Dorsey had to pay his own expenses *after* delivering MCA its commission, and he had to play when and where MCA told him to play. More than once he tried to fight back. Once, Dorsey even showed up in Goodheart's office with his lawyer. Billy was waiting for him. The agent sat on the edge of his desk, stopping them dead before either of them could open their mouths. "Tommy, if you continue this bullshit, making everybody miserable, you see these balls?"—at which point he grabbed his own scrotum—"I'm gonna cut yours off. Not only won't you be working for MCA, you won't be working for anybody else for maybe the rest of your life. You have something to say, put it in writing. Now get the fuck out of here. You irritate me."

The exclusive contract became both a lure and a weapon: if an orchestra signed with MCA, it was guaranteed work. But if the bandleader crossed Stein, the shrewd ophthalmologist with the owlish stare and pursed lips could punish the band by withholding bookings, sending the musicians on grueling road tours, or relegating them to some backwater dance hall. And the bandleaders could do nothing about it. The contracts were perfectly legal. Only five orchestras ever earned their way out of an MCA contract: Goodman, Dorsey, Guy Lombardo, Ted Fiorito, and Horace Heidt. Every other band worked exclusively for MCA—or it didn't work at all.

TWO

Chicago

1925–1928

MCA's first trade journal ad was a full page in *Billboard* magazine on May 15, 1926, proclaiming the agency to be the originator of "The Circuit of Orchestras." Whether the boast was true or not, Stein and Goodheart listed twelve of the Midwest's top bands as clients:

MAKE YOUR DANCES PAY THROUGH THE MCA

COON SANDERS	ZEZ CONFREY
TED WEEMS	CHARLIE STRAIGHT
JACK CRAWFORD	ROSS REYNOLDS
ISHAM JONES	BENNY KRUEGER
DON BESTOR	CARL FENTON
EARL HOFFMAN	EGYPTIAN SERENADERS

Available for single engagements anywhere—guarantee and percentage basis. Guaranteed recognized novelty entertaining orchestras in units of eight on weekly charge at $600 per week. Daily circuit as low as $100 per engagement. Attractive advertising free with all orchestras. Special service for summer pavilions and resorts

(one sheets–window cards–heralds–newspaper stories–cuts–photographs–tickets–et cetera)

One of the first long-term Chicago bookings that MCA landed for the Kansas City Night Hawks was, appropriately, the Blackhawk Restaurant, located beneath the El at the corner of Randolph Street and Wabash Avenue. Owned by Otto Roth and run by a gruff maître d' named Tully, the Blackhawk was a steak house turned nightclub, complete with floor show. During the Roaring Twenties it was one of the finer places to drink and gamble along Chicago's version of Tin Pan Alley. Roth liked Coon Sanders so much that he signed the band to an exclusive contract. Each time the musicians tried to move on, he persuaded them to stay. Their contract had a time limit, but contracts meant little if the club owner had any pull with — or acted as a front for — the Mob.

Louis Armstrong himself crossed a mobster by trying to leave a Chicago club once his engagement was over, just as his contract stipulated. He was told he wasn't going anywhere. He was packing them in, and the club owner ordered him to extend his stay. Armstrong wound up on the run, hiding out in New Orleans for a while and then playing jazz clubs in Europe for a couple of years until things cooled down. His longtime manager, Joe Glaser, who joined MCA briefly during the early 1930s before starting Associated Booking, told Satchmo he'd wind up dead if he tried playing anywhere in the United States. Coon Sanders wanted to go to New York, but remained a Blackhawk headliner for six years, with MCA collecting its percentage of every dime earned. MCA no longer just booked bands; it owned them and told them when and where to play.

Stein still wasn't satisfied. He saw more money to be made via radio. Chicago's version of WDAF was WGN, the radio arm of Colonel Robert McCormick's *Chicago Tribune* empire. Simultaneously with their opening at the Blackhawk, the Kansas City Night Hawks became Chicago's Coon Sanders Orchestra and WGN took over live broadcasting chores. Monday night became Night Hawk night on WGN. Eventually the station began a nationwide hookup with other stations, giving the Blackhawk's house band national network exposure. Stein saw no reason to give that kind of exposure away. For the next twenty years the Blackhawk Restaurant was famous for its evening broadcasts and WGN radio never missed a chance to plug the *Chicago Tribune* ("World's Greatest Newspaper"). Soon Coon Sanders began plugging other products, too, and Jules Stein made certain that MCA collected its share of the plug fees and other advertising revenues.

MCA signed most of the important white Chicago bands, including Wayne King, who took over the ritzy Aragon Ballroom about 1927, and Charlie Straight, whose ten-piece band played in a style that he later called the forerunner of swing. Ted Weems, another MCA client, became the nation's first million-selling recording star with his rendition of "Somebody Stole My Gal."

HARRY GRADLE WAS irritated. His assistant had turned thirty years old and still hadn't made up his mind. Was Jules going to be an ophthalmologist or an agent? Since MCA had moved to larger quarters, in an office building at 32 West Randolph Street, just a block from the Blackhawk Restaurant, Jules was spending less time at Gradle's office.

In addition to "Music Corporation of America," Jules was also calling his company the American Music Corporation so that its listing would be first in the Yellow Pages. MCA was growing. To handle the ever-increasing number of bands, Jules hired a publicist named Karl F. Kramer, a twenty-six-year-old from Detroit with a head for numbers and a knack for hype. He also hired an office boy named Bernard Taft Schreiber, a nineteen-year-old saxophonist and part-time shoe salesman from Waukegan.

Jules also brought in a couple of new agents to help Billy Goodheart sell the bands. By now Bill Stein had become more of a talent scout than a booker, touring clubs all over the Midwest in search of new orchestras. Goodheart needed help in finding places for the new talent to play.

Stein studied his rivals and identified the ones who were giving him the most serious competition. In Chicago it was a young piano player named Maurie Lipsey and an orchestra leader named Ray O'Hara. Like the Stein brothers and Goodheart, Lipsey and O'Hara first teamed up on the bandstand, but discovered it was far more lucrative to book the bands. In that business, the Lipsey-O'Hara Agency had an ethnicity edge: Maurie booked the bar mitzvahs and Ray took care of the Irish Catholic parish socials and the Chicago Park District dances controlled by Irish politicians.

Stein's rule then and for the next fifty years was "If you can't beat 'em, buy 'em." He hired a lawyer to make the offer to the rival agency. Lipsey accepted; O'Hara declined. Within a few years, O'Hara gave up his agency business and disappeared into obscurity as a second-rate orchestra leader. Lipsey took charge of MCA's Chicago operation while Jules and Billy Goodheart set up a new office in New York.

Jules dispatched another agent, George Campbell, to open a branch office in San Francisco, where Campbell took over the Winterland auditorium for Stein and oversaw MCA's entry into the business of ice shows. Twice, Campbell nearly died from ulcers that he earned while on the MCA payroll.

In hiring MCA's first in-house lawyer, Jules continued another lifelong tradition: nepotism. Although he strictly forbade anyone else in his company to hire relatives, Stein consistently put his own family on the payroll. A Memphis native and University of Tennessee graduate, twenty-four-year-old Charles R. Miller married Stein's younger sister, Adelaide, and went to work for MCA.

The final member of the MCA team during the early Chicago years was a munchkin of a man named Mickey Rockford. Billy hired him straight out of high school, at the age of seventeen. MCA was supposed to be a summer job before he went on to college, but Jules took a shine to Mickey and offered to put him through night school.

An altar boy with ties to Chicago's Italian and Irish communities, Rockford was expected to do for MCA what Ray O'Hara had done for the Lipsey-O'Hara Agency: bring in the Catholic business. He not only broke through the anti-Semitic barriers but also gave the Stein-Goodheart agency entrée into country club society and beyond. Rich WASP families like the Rockefellers and McCormicks began seeking out MCA to book bands for their social engagements.

Rockford kept a low profile throughout his MCA career, but he understood better than almost anyone how Jules Stein functioned and what was most impor-tant to him. He understood money—when to pay it in order to keep peace with a politician or a hoodlum, when to collect it to fatten the company bank account. In addition to his band-booking duties, Mickey Rockford often doubled as Stein's bodyguard.

Norton Styne, son of composer Jule Styne,[1] recalled the day in the late 1920s when his father happened to meet Stein and Rockford in La Salle, Illinois. The newly prosperous Stein wore a fur-collared coat, a muffler, and pince-nez and drove a late model car. When they stopped to chat on the street, Dr. Stein told the composer about his latest touring orchestra: "Would you believe that band made $30,000 in thirty nights? I made $3,000." And Rockford, who at five feet two was even shorter than his boss, proudly displayed a satchel full of cash. He also showed Styne the gun he was carrying.

For Jules Stein, the time had finally come to make his choice. He knew as well as Dr. Gradle what it would be, but he needed one last assurance that his Music Corporation of America was really going to last. His brother Bill found that assur-ance on a road trip to Cleveland in 1926. It was called Guy Lombardo and the Royal Canadians.

—◦◦◦—

"THE YEAR WAS 1927. The city, Chicago. The scene, an obscure, dimly lit night-club on the South Side," wrote Jules Stein in the introduction to Lombardo's 1975 autobiography, *Auld Acquaintance.* "Inside the café most of the tables were empty and the dance floor almost deserted. This was the first engagement of Guy Lom-bardo and his Royal Canadians in the Windy City, and it was booked by the Music Corporation of America."

Within a few months, Stein wrote, Lombardo's nine-piece orchestra was the toast of Chicago—hotter than the Coon Sanders Night Hawks. Like most overnight success stories, the phenomenon of the Royal Canadians had actually been shaped over the better part of a decade in Canada and on the U.S. side of

---

[1]   Jule Styne was born Julius Stein, but changed the spelling of his name because he was con-stantly being mistaken for Dr. Jules Stein.

Lake Erie in Ohio. When Lombardo's offer of a free daily one-hour show was accepted by Cleveland radio station WTAM, the response was phenomenal. By the following year, Guy Lombardo and the Royal Canadians ruled Cleveland. They moved to an exclusive lakefront club called the Blossom Heath, where they sold out virtually every performance for months.

A few weeks before the Royal Canadians were to end their Blossom Heath engagement and hit the road, Jules went to Cleveland. He summoned Guy Lombardo to his suite at the Statler, one of the finest hotels in the city. The man who met him at the door was dressed like no agent Lombardo had ever met. He looked more like a well-heeled stockbroker than he did a band booker. Guy was suitably impressed, but he wanted to know why MCA was so interested in his orchestra to the exclusion of dozens of others then traversing the Midwest.

"Guy, I want you to know one thing," said the sober, self-confident man who sat before him. "Bands aren't made. Bands just happen. And you have happened. Look, let's sign a contract for us to represent you. You can eliminate northern Ohio, where you've proven yourself. We'll represent you everywhere else."

Impressed or not, Lombardo still held out. His orchestra would do the tour, but they weren't ready to sign. Like an expert fisherman who senses the trout eyeing his fly, Stein shrugged and left Guy with one other thought. He told him that he was heading to New York where MCA was about to open its first branch outside of Chicago.

"We're just starting and it's going to take me a while to get the lay of the land," Stein said. "But the thing I have uppermost in my mind is that I'm going to bring Guy Lombardo and his Royal Canadians to New York as my big attraction. I think you guys are so good you're going to make it big, and the other bands are going to line up to be represented by MCA."

Better than the devil himself, Jules Stein understood pride, the first of the seven deadly sins. Within a week, Guy Lombardo took the train to New York to meet Jules in MCA's new Manhattan headquarters in the Paramount Theater Building at Forty-third and Broadway. By now the stakes had grown even higher. Maybe, Stein suggested, MCA could book the Royal Canadians on a tour of England. And, if not there, how about the Muehlbach Hotel in Kansas City, where the Coon Sanders Night Hawks became the single most popular band in America? Lombardo was hooked. He signed and sped back to Cleveland to tell the boys the good news.

When Lombardo arrived, unbeknownst to Jules, Billy Stein was waiting for him backstage, accompanied by a grizzly bear of a man in patent-leather shoes. Billy didn't bother to introduce him. "Al wants to hear the band," Billy said simply. Al Quodbach, a tall, loud club owner from Chicago's seedy South Side, stood well over six feet tall. He had the beat-up profile of a prizefighter and sported diamonds everywhere: on his cuff links, shirt studs, rings. "Al Quodbach owned the Granada

Café, one of three South Side gambling joints," Berle Adams recalled. The other two were the Venetian Gardens, a Capone enterprise, and the Dells, a converted farmhouse rumored to be owned by Sam "Golf Bag" Hunt, who got his nickname because he carried a shotgun in his golf bag during a rival's assassination.

"He's offering $1,600 a week and you only play nights," Billy whispered to Guy following their audition.

When Jules got wind of his brother's proposed deal, he went nuts. The American Federation of Music would never approve. "Billy ought to know that an out-of-town band can't go to work there without an okay from the union!" he told Lombardo. "And Jimmy Petrillo doesn't give that kind of okay unless the guy that owns the place is a friend of his." Apparently Al Quodbach was just such a friend.

The Granada Café wasn't New York City or London, or even the Muehlbach Hotel in Kansas City. It had a small casino upstairs and a pistol range in the basement where Quodbach and his pals practiced shooting. What was more, it was located across the street from a cemetery in a rough part of town. When Quodbach had trouble with one of his employees, including entertainers he booked into the club, he'd silently escort the miscreant to his sedan, drive around the cemetery, and take target practice on the headstones. Then he'd pull up in front of the Granada, turn to the quaking employee and ask: "Any questions?" Still, he was offering $300 a week more than the Royal Canadians had been earning up to that time in Cleveland. Lombardo agreed to go to Chicago.

WBBM had just gone on the air as WGN's rival in Chicago, and offered to broadcast the Royal Canadians live from the Granada Café for fifteen minutes each night if Lombardo would pay a $75-a-week hookup charge.[2] Quodbach, MCA, and Lombardo each agreed to pay $25 and the broadcasts began in November of 1927. By the end of the first week, the place was packed and they were soon doing turn-away business. The Granada Café and the Blackhawk Restaurant were now Chicago's top entertainment spots as well as rivals for the nighttime radio audience. Even in a blizzard, business poured into Quodbach's nightclub.

If there was any doubt that MCA's first booking for Lombardo was a Mob-run restaurant, it disappeared the night Al Jolson came to the Granada. Hot on the heels of his success in *The Jazz Singer*, Jolson showed up, only to be upstaged by a gangster. The Capone clientele had been coming for weeks, sitting up front and impressing their women by boasting that they were personal friends of Quodbach and Guy Lombardo himself, though Lombardo had met none of them. On the night Jolson was there, one of them stepped onstage and took the microphone

[2] According to one lifelong federal investigator, "The hookup charge was a bone given to Local 134 of the electricians' union, courtesy of Capone while ingratiating himself to the local's leader, Mike 'Umbrella' Boyle. From that time to the present, the Mob always had a couple of business agents on the 134 payroll."

away from Lombardo. Lombardo pushed him offstage, and he skidded into a heap at the base of Jolson's table.

The following day, Lombardo learned that the stage crasher had come close to plugging him. His name was George Maloney, a member of Bugs Moran's North Side Irish gang and a bitter rival of Capone's South Side syndicate. Quodbach told Guy that if Maloney hadn't left his pistol in his car, Lombardo would probably have been dead. Maloney returned a few nights later, but this time he had his gun with him. When a couple of Capone's goons began teasing him about the night a mere bandleader had tossed him off stage, Maloney shot one man in the head and one in the heart as three hundred Granada patrons watched in horror. Meanwhile, the Royal Canadians were on the air over WBBM, and Lombardo carried on as if everything were normal. He even sang the band off the air to the strains of "I've Got a Woman Crazy for Me, She's Funny That Way." The next morning's newspaper called the incident the first murder ever committed on live radio.

Lombardo had had enough. Like Coon Sanders, he and his Royal Canadians had been lassoed into a short engagement at a Chicago nightclub and wound up staying for two years. He called on Stein and demanded that he and Goodheart get them out of the Granada Café. After all, their contract had expired months earlier. It was time for Stein to finally make good on his promises of stardom.

In the meantime Stein had New York softened up for Lombardo. He had even negotiated a preliminary deal to air a Guy Lombardo show over the Columbia Broadcasting System, a new radio network that a young entrepreneur named William Paley had put together in New York. Robert Burns panatelas would be the show's sponsor, Stein told him, and the band would broadcast live from midtown Manhattan's Roosevelt Hotel.

But getting out of a Chicago contract, even an expired one, was a problem. It was not a matter that could be handled by Maurie Lipsey, the agent Jules and Goodheart had left in charge while they tackled the Big Apple. Stein himself would have to return from New York to explain the facts of life to Al Quodbach. "What kind of agent are you?" Quodbach shouted, pointing his finger at Stein. "Don't you know I have an option to renew on these boys?"

He didn't, of course. If Jules Stein knew anything, it was contracts, and he wielded them like a baseball bat against customer and client alike, with his chin jutting out and steely resolve in his eyes. Once he had Quodbach convinced that even his close association with influential thugs could not overcome the contract language or Stein's own formidable associations with men of influence, Quodbach got desperate. Lombardo recalled that Quodbach went to his desk drawer, pulled out a nickel-plated revolver, and started shooting at a picture of Stein that hung on his wall.

"You took away my band!" he shouted.

Stein didn't blink and didn't back down. Lombardo swallowed hard and told

Quodbach to put the gun down. "We're going to New York, Jules Stein or no and Al Quodbach or no," he said.

The match was over. Quodbach returned the gun to the drawer, put his head on his desk, and started to cry.

The Royal Canadians left for New York the next day. They preceded the Coon Sanders Night Hawks, who were still playing the Blackhawk Restaurant and still waiting for Stein to make good on his promise to get them out of Chicago.

THREE

New York

1927-1930

A short announcement of the marriage of Dr. Jules Stein appeared in the November 19, 1928, edition of the *South Bend Evening Tribune*, accompanied by a smoldering photo of Stein's dark-haired ice queen, with her penciled-in eyebrows and rosebud lips, and a single strand of rich white pearls draped around her regal neck.

"Mrs. Jules C. Stein before her marriage to Mr. Stein in New York City Friday was Miss Doris Jones Oppenheim, of Kansas City, Mo.," proclaimed the newspaper. "Mr. and Mrs. Stein sailed Friday night on the *Ile de France* for a tour of Europe, returning Dec. 24. Mr. Stein was formerly a resident of this city and is now president of the Music Corporation of America. They will reside in New York City."

All of which was true...except for the "Miss" in front of the new Mrs. Stein's maiden name. And the accuracy of her middle name. And the misspelling of her last name.

Just eighteen months earlier, Mrs. Doris Stein had been Mrs. Doris Oppenheimer.

Married to Kansas City Chrysler dealer and insurance executive Harold Oppenheimer, she had borne her first son before she turned eighteen, and she was eight months shy of her twenty-first birthday when she had her second son. Harold was well established and steady, the youngest of three brothers who founded a surety bonding firm that would evolve into one of Missouri's most successful insurance businesses. Harold was affluent, but he was twelve years older than Doris and certainly not involved in a profession that promised excitement, world travel, and social status.

Jules Stein, the young medical student whom Doris had met years earlier when she was a teenager, seemed to be just the opposite. He and his traveling band had played one summer at the Muehlbach Hotel, where Doris married Harold. Jules was the same age as her brother Larry, who also dreamed of becoming a doctor. Jules and Doris stayed in touch, even after she married the hometown insurance salesman and became mother to his two sons. Stein met another young woman at the Muehlbach that summer. That girl, whom he would later describe to close friends as his first true love, died while he was still in college. Jules was brokenhearted and poured himself into work over the next several years. Eventually he got back to dating, but he never grew so attached to a woman again.

During one of his Kansas City sojourns in the late 1920s with the Coon Sanders Orchestra, he made Doris's acquaintance once again. This time, however, she was another man's wife. "He drove a Stutz Bearcat. I think it was bright yellow or red," said Charles Harris, the Steins' butler from 1946 to 1986. "And he went after her. I'm sure she was two-timing Oppenheimer." Whether Stein's influence had anything to do with her decision to leave Harold Oppenheimer is as hazy as the question of Doris's fidelity to her husband. What is clear is that, at twenty-six, she decided that she had had enough of playing small-town housewife. Mrs. Doris Oppenheimer filed for divorce.

Doris was never meant to play wet nurse to a couple of boys and homemaker to a well-heeled rube of a car salesman. She was still young and vibrant, and she had far grander designs in mind for the rest of her life. Mrs. Oppenheimer was found by the courts to be the "innocent and injured party" in the July 5, 1927, divorce proceeding. Her husband drank, she said. She neglected to reveal to the court that she too liked a Scotch or two or three, before and after meals.

Thereafter, when she was asked who she had been before she became Mrs. Jules Stein, she either neglected to reveal that she had been married or simply discarded the "Oppenheimer" altogether, reverting instead to her maiden name, Doris Babette Jones. But the name Doris Jones wasn't exactly accurate either. Before her father met and married Doris's mother — a Louisianan named Blanche Dreyfus — he had changed his own name from Geoffrey Jonas to Geoffrey Jones. Like so many other European immigrants, Mr. Jonas switched to a WASP surname to avoid the taint of Judaism. Doris followed his example. Throughout her life, she skirted the religious issue, despite her parentage and the fact that a rabbi officiated at both of her weddings. Only those closest to her knew that she was, in fact, a cousin of the proudly Jewish entertainer George Jessel.

Jackson County Circuit Court ordered the hapless Harold Oppenheimer to give Doris a hefty settlement and pay $225 a month in alimony, plus $100 in child support — a considerable sum in 1927. In exchange, the court awarded Oppenheimer the right to see his sons "at all reasonable times."

Within two years it became clear that Doris needed somewhere semipermanent to park ten-year-old Harold and eight-year-old Gerald, while she launched a new life among the nouveau riche of Chicago, New York, and Los Angeles. Her provincial ex-husband and her own Kansas City relatives became the logical choice. Meanwhile, the Steins treated themselves to a life of travel, power, pleasure, and the highest society that money could buy.

Doris was somewhat gracious about the divorce. On January 12, 1932, she gave up her $225 a month alimony. By this time, Jules could certainly afford her. A Kansas City boy, Oppenheimer died there ten years later at fifty-three, unmarried and unmourned. By then Doris Stein's life was just revving up. To make her transformation from Doris Oppenheimer to Mrs. Jules Stein complete, Doris had her nose surgically reduced in size and her breasts enlarged, according to Charles Harris. After all, she was now a physician's wife, not the hausfrau of some Kansas City insurance salesman.

—◦◦◦—

THE STEINS DEPARTED for their European honeymoon from New York, not Chicago, because Jules had taken up residence in Manhattan. In Chicago the couple owned a lakefront mansion in the northern suburb of Highland Park where Harry Gradle lived, but in New York the Steins also bought their own apartment at 13 Sutton Place, on the upper East Side overlooking the East River. Much of the year, they considered themselves New Yorkers.

In only four years, MCA's fortunes had risen with the fame of the musicians that Jules and Billy Goodheart handpicked and groomed for stardom, like the Royal Canadians and the Night Hawks. Since their move to 32 West Randolph Street in 1926, MCA's business had expanded exponentially, leading Stein and Goodheart to decide that 1928 would be the year that they took their corporation national.

The fanfare outside of Chicago, however, was muted, to say the least. Stein sent twenty-one-year-old Taft Schreiber out to Los Angeles to see about busting into the West Coast market, and MCA was summarily ignored. For the first few years, Schreiber failed to make much headway in the L.A. market. Out west, all anyone could think about was the movies. Dance halls, nightclubs, and band bookings were picking up steam as popular diversions as the Depression set in, but not in the same way they were in the East.

New York was a different story. A year before Schreiber opened the branch office in the Oviatt Building in downtown Los Angeles, Stein dispatched his new brother-in-law, Charlie Miller, to help Billy Goodheart settle into the Paramount Building at West Forty-third Street and Broadway. Nightlife was flourishing in the hotels and the Mob-controlled clubs along Fifty-second Street, and the Stein-Goodheart team was determined to crack that market. MCA's soul might still be in Chicago, but it's heart was now beating in New York.

Stein himself couldn't resist the lure. He understood that conquering New York was the key to locking up the best bands and the best ballrooms in the rest of the nation. Eventually, MCA might open offices in Atlanta, Dallas, Miami, Denver, Seattle—even conquer L.A.—but first Stein had to win over New York. So he put Maurie Lipsey in charge of day-to-day operations in Chicago and joined the MCA invasion of Manhattan.

Business wasn't the only reason he loved New York. His bride was agog over the Fifth Avenue finery. Doris could also immerse herself in the kind of culture Kansas City never knew existed: the opera, the theater, the Metropolitan Museum of Art. Recalled Marguerite Madden, Billy Goodheart's eldest daughter, "The first time I remember the Steins coming to visit us, Doris opened all the closets and said, 'What! No minks?'"

Doris Stein found plenty of other nouveau riche wives to share her pretensions in New York, but the wife of her husband's business partner was not one of them. "I think Jules always felt my dad should have married someone more showy, but he married a good solid farm girl from Tolono, Illinois," said Madden's younger brother, Bill Goodheart III. "Jules was always after the theatrical, high-society types."

In matters of business, however, Stein and Goodheart remained a well-tuned team. They approached their New York campaign like a couple of Confederate generals slipping behind Yankee lines. Whenever they secured a one-night stand in Midtown for a band, they launched a word-of-mouth advertising onslaught, supplemented by trade paper ads and publicity gimmicks. Every smart band booker did those things. What gave MCA its edge was a willingness to gamble and a wily counterintelligence operation. They scoped out the competition, learning what hotel owners and nightclubs wanted, and giving it to them—for a premium price.

———

NEW YORK WAS the home of Broadway, Tin Pan Alley, and the emerging NBC radio networks that were wiring America and, in the process, creating a fortune in advertising. By 1931 radio would be generating $170 million a year in revenue, and Jules Stein wanted his 10 percent.

The moment they hit town, Stein and Goodheart began forming strategic alliances. By this time, the influence of Stein's old pal Jimmy Petrillo was being felt even in New York, and Stein used the favor that he had curried from the head of the musicians' union back in Chicago to keep his own MCA bands under control. Nightclub owners and band members who refused to obey the contractual demands of Stein and Goodheart had Petrillo to answer to. He was a lifelong hypochondriac, convinced that he would contract something and die at any moment. But when he trusted someone, he ceased to be a hard-nosed hypochondriac. With Stein, he was happy to bestow special favors. Those favors were a boon when MCA ran into problems with Petrillo's union rule forbidding out-of-town bands from performing for money on local radio stations. In one of the many rules that Petrillo waived for his good friend Jules Stein, MCA was allowed to put its Chicago bands on the radio in New York if it could find a radio booking for a New York band in Chicago. No other band booker enjoyed such a valuable union dispensation.

Stein also brought with him to New York what he had learned in Chicago about using radio: cozying up to station owners, advertising reps, and, most important of all, network programmers.

Finding good programming remained a struggle. While rival NBC produced slick shows featuring well-known talent in state-of-the-art studios, CBS could not afford Broadway stars like Eddie Cantor and Jimmy Durante. Encouraged by "Doc" Stein, the steely-eyed chief of the music agency located just downstairs, CBS's William Paley decided that one way to beat NBC at its own game was to do for New York and the rest of the nation what local radio powerhouses WGN and WBBM had done for Chicago: go directly to nightclubs and put live music on the air. When Stein informed Paley that MCA planned to import Guy Lombardo to play the Grill in the Roosevelt Hotel, Paley signed Lombardo to an exclusive CBS contract for a La Palina–sponsored show. Stein's schmoozing with junior magnates like Paley, coupled with his natural manipulative charm, proved to be key contributors to the early success of MCA in Manhattan. But Stein moved back and forth between Chicago and New York. MCA's permanent presence in New York was Billy Goodheart.

When Guy Lombardo needed a shoulder to cry on — as he did the day the stock market crashed and he and his brothers lost everything — it was invariably Billy's. Billy kept Lombardo and all the rest of MCA's bands working, even while other businesses were shutting down all over New York. And he kept them working at the highest prices the market would bear.

"Get me some theater dates at $6,000 quick, before it's too late," Lombardo whined when the stock market panic was at its highest pitch and banks were closing all over America.

"Don't be silly," said Goodheart. "The new price for your band is $10,000."

"But it says in *Variety* and *Billboard* —"

"The hell with what it says," snapped Goodheart. "They're desperate to fill their theaters and they'll have to pay."

Goodheart was right, of course. At the height of the worst economic disaster in U.S. history, Lombardo's band was grossing $1.2 million a year.

He also parlayed Lombardo's CBS connection into a regular weekly radio program featuring well-known dance bands in different major cities, sponsored by

Lucky Strike cigarettes.[1] A band that carried the MCA stamp of approval and got its shot on the weekly Lucky Strike hour could command top dollar wherever it played. The name MCA became as important a calling card for an orchestra as the *Good Housekeeping* Seal of Approval was for cereal.

Once the Royal Canadians were well established at the Roosevelt Hotel as a regular CBS attraction, Goodheart sent them on the road to cash in on their cosmopolitan popularity in the hinterlands. When the hotel owner's screaming died down, Billy delivered the good news: MCA had another band, just as good as Lombardo's, ready to take the stage. Though Jules took credit for it, Billy was the mastermind behind this "just-as-good-an-act" substitution, an MCA quid pro quo that would remain the company's hallmark long after it ceased representing big bands.

One such substitute orchestra leader was a stiff, bland accordion player from North Dakota who spoke with a thick, often indecipherable accent. When Goodheart presented the Roosevelt Hotel management with the odd North Dakotan, they absolutely refused to sign him or his band of corn-fed hicks. Goodheart threatened to withhold the Royal Canadians, once they returned to New York, so the Roosevelt had no choice. The hotel accepted Lawrence Welk and his Champagne Music Makers as the replacement orchestra while Lombardo was on the road.

MCA used this take-it-or-leave-it tactic shamelessly throughout the 1930s, threatening an MCA band boycott if a hotel owner, radio programmer, or advertiser refused to accept the musical act offered. "MCA did not handle black bands," said Bill Goodheart III. "If you handled white bands, you couldn't handle black bands, especially in the South. Dad was a good friend of Count Basie, but he couldn't book him."

The Lombardo brothers from London, Ontario, were Italian, but they were white-bread enough to finally give MCA a permanent foothold in New York. Billy Goodheart and Guy Lombardo got to be as close as brothers. Their birthdays were one day apart, and they celebrated together. Their wives became friends, and their families grew up together. They shared everything.

So when it came time for the Royal Canadians to hit the road, Billy loaned the Lombardos his own newly hired office boy to keep their books. This newest MCA employee was only six years younger than Billy, but Goodheart still got a kick out of calling him Sonny Boy—a nickname that stuck for the rest of his life. His real name was David, but for the rest of the century everyone called him Sonny Werblin.

---

[1]   It helped that Lucky Strike was an account handled by Stein's good friend Albert Lasker, who stood ready to help MCA whenever it needed a radio sponsor—this despite the irony that Lasker was tone-deaf and would not have been able to tell the difference between Guy Lombardo and the Egyptian Serenaders.

—◊◊◊—

ABRAHAM DAVID "SONNY" Werblin was born in Flatbush, Brooklyn, on Saint Patrick's Day 1908. He grew up in Brooklyn, played football and soccer in high school, and entered Rutgers University in 1927, graduating four years later with a B.A. in liberal arts and journalism.

Sonny loved sports, but lacking the build and the talent to play, he turned to sportswriting, stringing for seven different New York and New Jersey newspapers before graduating from college. He then worked as a sportswriter for the *Brooklyn Eagle* and, later, as a copyboy at the *New York Times*. Reporters, he quickly learned, earned spit, and copyboys earned a whole lot less than that. So when he heard of an office boy position at the Music Corporation of America—an outfit he thought might have something to do with the exploding and very affluent entertainment business—he applied. He won the job, but found that office boys had far more contact with eccentric tyrants than with entertainers.

Billy Goodheart would position his crippled five-foot-three-inch frame in a raised chair, so he could look down on all who entered his office. If someone asked for two minutes of his time, Billy would pull out a stopwatch and time them. Werblin apparently spoke quickly and well, because he passed muster. Billy offered him the job at $21 a week, and Werblin accepted.

Billy was driven and exacting, and he demanded the same of his subordinates.

"Goodheart drove us like a drill sergeant," recalled Irving "Swifty" Lazar, the legendary agent who worked briefly for MCA during the 1930s.[2]

The MCA office was growing, with a half dozen agents hustling talent: Harold Hackett, Al Gazley, Manie Sacks, Milton Pickman, Lou Mining, and Willard Alexander, Werblin's roommate at the Alrae Hotel. They were expected to troll for talent late into the night along Billy Rose's Broadway and Nicky Blair's Fifty-second Street and still be in the office by 8:30 A.M. Agents who showed up late often found Goodheart snooping through their desk drawers to find out what, if anything, they were doing to earn their keep. He accepted no excuses. If they couldn't get their commission any other way, Goodheart instructed his agents to lift it from the client's cash register. Failure was failure. Those who couldn't bring in the money got the boot.

Such was the boss Werblin hired on with. Goodheart told Werblin his morning duties began with making Goodheart's desk presentable. Billy needed a clean desktop to start each day. No loose papers. No spills. No extraneous memos. Sonny

---

[2] Humphrey Bogart dubbed Lazar "Swifty" during the 1940s after losing a bet that the agent could secure him three separate deals in less than twenty-four hours. Though Lazar smugly protested throughout his life that he was Irving, not Swifty, he secretly relished the nickname. In his *History of the World—Part I* (1981), Mel Brooks spoofs the world's first agent with a fanciful character named Swiftus Lazarus, played by Ron Carey.

complied meticulously. If Billy got off the Long Island train and the weather was not to his liking or he scuffed a shoe on his short walk from Grand Central Station to the Paramount Building, he'd arrive in the office and go into a rage, breaking pencil points, splashing ink, and tossing wads of paper all over. Then he'd summon Werblin and berate him in front of the others for not having brains enough to tidy up the boss's desk.

Theirs was a master-slave relationship that never quite evolved. Though Werblin was unable to bring himself to admit it, Billy's tyrannical ways eventually rubbed off on him. One person who knew both men described Werblin in later years as "very similar to Goodheart: like an objectionable city editor." Goodheart became a kind of dysfunctional father figure to Werblin, counseling Sonny—usually by shouting at him—in the fundamentals of becoming a successful agent. Appearing to be wealthy, even if you were dirt poor, was essential. If people *believed* you were prosperous, you were—and they'd line up to become your clients. One agent Werblin observed kept a gold cigarette lighter as a prop on his desk, near an open window in the thirtieth-floor office where he closed his sales. When the agent had a live one sitting in front of him, he'd rant and pace, lighting cigarette after cigarette, growing more and more animated with each puff. In one of his agitated lightings, he would absentmindedly toss the gold lighter through the open window and keep on talking without missing a beat. The clients never knew that the lighter landed on a ledge two stories down and that an office boy was sent to fetch it moments after the contract was signed.

Werblin learned firsthand what kind of a world he was up against. His MCA bosses might have appeared to be hard-nosed, cynical, and cheap, but they were operating in a business that was totally unregulated, among clients who were one step above cardsharps and carnival workers. Big band musicians were the bohemians of their day and carried a reputation of loose ethics and light fingers wherever they went.

"People feel today that we're falling by the wayside with our morals, but I don't think it's all that much different from the big band era," said Kathy Gazley, whose husband, Al Gazley, was hired as an MCA office boy with Werblin. "When my husband went on the road with them, he knew who was sleeping with whom and which band member was gay. The same things went on then that go on now. Celebrities are just more public about it today."

As the impoverished 1930s began, cash was king. Desperate businessmen were far more prone to cheating, chiseling, wholesale thievery, even murder, than they had been during the flush days of the Roaring Twenties, when MCA first clawed its way to prominence.

FOUR

Chicago

1930–1936

From Al Capone to John Gotti, Mob bosses who flaunt power, flash wealth, and bask in headlines invariably wind up in prison or dead. Gangsters, like talent agents, should never crow about their success. Those who keep quiet and skim their vigorish in silence usually remain alive and free. Hubris takes down more public enemies than bullets—an immutable truth that Jules Stein and Billy Goodheart took to heart early in MCA's history.

And so it was on June 5, 1931, that the IRS handed Al Capone a twenty-two-count indictment for income tax evasion: he owed the United States over $1 million, by Treasury Department calculations. If Capone laughed at the government's case, it wasn't for very long. His chief lieutenant, Frank Nitti, had done time for tax evasion, as had Syndicate treasurer Jake "Greasy Thumb" Guzik. Capone's own brother, Ralph, had gone to prison for not paying his taxes. These convictions were not indiscriminate. The Justice Department had been warming up for Capone himself.

By 1931 income tax evasion had become the government's favored tool for putting away those who could not be convicted of other felonies, either because they shrewdly left no fingerprints or because they had succeeded in bribing and intimidating judges and jurors. Though the income tax had been around for eighteen years, less than 7 percent of the total U.S. population earned enough to pay any tax at all, and fewer than .001 percent of those who did pay were caught cheating.

Jules Stein took notice. Throughout his life, he hated paying taxes. Jules and Doris crawled through every loophole they could find, from tax-free municipal bonds to the questionable practice of depreciating priceless antiques to a clever Kansas cattle tax shelter run by Doris's elder son, Harold Oppenheimer. Using family trusts and a myriad of interlinking corporations stretching from New York

34

to California, Stein paid the smallest possible personal income tax the law allowed—and sometimes, some would argue, what the law did *not* allow.

Stein made a habit of setting up new corporations, usually to keep taxes down. But as the years rolled on and MCA burrowed into different types of business, Stein created new corporations just as often to preserve trade secrets or to prevent government antitrust snoops from looking too closely at MCA's business. "The more corporations," he reasoned, "the more places to hide capital."

On March 18, 1938, Stein incorporated the parent company, Music Corporation of America, in Delaware—a state famous for protecting corporate secrecy and taxing lightly. By then MCA owned or operated corporations that handled everything from talent to real estate. Many began with, or were acronyms for, that original combination of magical letters: MCA.[1]

In a cash-and-carry business like band booking, keeping the IRS at bay required finesse. Jules entrusted the books to his sister Ruth, who personally watched over her brother's tax tightrope for half a century. As the years passed, MCA hired and fired dozens of accountants, but Stein himself had only one. Through motherhood and two marriages, Mrs. Ruth Stein Lowe Cogan kept the books.

"Ruth *always* worked for Jules, *never* for the company," stressed more than one person who grew up with MCA.

But Al Capone's evasion of taxes offered a tough lesson for the ostentatious Dr. Stein, who took great glee in dressing like a million bucks, crashing the highest society that money would permit, and tossing a leopard-skin blanket across the back seat of his Rolls-Royce and tooling down Michigan Avenue like a peacock. "He did it because it was the thing to do," Taft Schreiber recalled. "He was a modern guy, and he always kept up with the age." Showing off one's money was not smart, though. Sooner or later, Stein learned, if the gangs didn't get you, the IRS would.

The Capone that Jules knew was not nearly so bloodthirsty or so mean-spirited as the newspapers portrayed him. He was actually kind of a likable goof. The pudgy man in the gaudy clothes whom Jules Stein saw showing up each day at the courthouse on Dearborn Street for his tax trial resembled a puffy, well-fed Wall Street banker. Stein concluded that Al Capone's sins were not murder and mayhem. When Capone was convicted of tax evasion on October 17, 1931, Jules realized he was actually convicted of conspicuous consumption of wealth and an arrogant and public display of power. Jules understood the grave consequences of both.

He began lowering his profile.

---

[1]   Music Corporation of America, Management Corporation of America, Manufacturing Corporation of America, MCA Artists Ltd., MCA Holding Co., MCA Inc., Movie Corporation of America, MCA Enterprises, MCA Ltd., MCA TV Ltd., MCA Management Ltd., and so on.

"ALL THE BANDS got their big boost in '33 because of the World's Fair," recalled former agent Chuck Suber, one of Stein's youngest contemporaries in Depression-era Chicago. "That's when the wires came in for the remote radio broadcasts, and every hotel had a band, not just Chicago. All the surrounding cities too, across the Dakotas, clear up to Manitoba. It was the World's Fair and the end of Prohibition. It was the right time."

The Chicago World's Fair, "A Century of Progress," began as a boondoggle but wound up a bonanza, thanks to sex, booze, and big band music. According to the WPA Writers' Project manual of Chicago cultural history, the fair was supposed to be a vast and courageous display of applied sciences, demonstrating to a skeptical world just how far the United States had come despite the worst economic disaster in history. Instead, the "Century of Progress" exposition bled red ink and might have been forced to shut down early.

According to the WPA, "Hard times accounted in large part for the fact that the exposition was a financial disappointment in its first year, but Sally Rand and her fan dancers accomplished what applied science had failed to do, and the exposition closed in 1934 with a net profit, which was donated to participating cultural institutions, excluding Sally Rand."

Sally Rand, whose real name was Helen Gould Beck, had gone to Hollywood to become an actress in the early 1920s. But she landed only bit parts in extravaganzas like *King of Kings* and cheesecake characters in peekaboo productions like *Getting Gertie's Garter*. At the Chicago World's Fair she hit her stride as Sally Rand, Queen of the Fan Dancers, who dared to dance au naturel, with only a pair of huge feather fans separating her from her audience. Strain as they might, none of the thousands of male patrons who paid top dollar for a gape got to glimpse nipple, nook, or even so much as a single pubic hair. Sally was expert at exposing only enough skin to titillate, and to keep them coming back for more.

Sally also worked for the Capone organization—a fact that Jules Stein and his agents learned only after MCA, too, was persuaded to work with, rather than against, the Mob.

After witnessing Sally's success, Stein enlisted the services of a French-speaking entrepreneur named Clifford C. Fischer, who arranged to bring a little Gallic culture to Chicago's World's Fair. Outside of its bands, MCA's premier offering during the fair was the Folies-Bergère, second only to the Eiffel Tower as the most popular tourist attraction among Americans in Paris. But more important, the U.S. version featured topless showgirls for a midwestern audience a full generation before nudity became the *pièce de résistance* of Las Vegas showroom entertainment.

On opening night Stein invited his most favored agents and their wives to ogle the dancers from a reserved table next to the stage. While the wives giggled and would not look straight up at the bared bosoms, their husbands propped their chins in their hands and leered like teenagers. The only MCA man who didn't give more than a glance at the two dozen breasts bouncing not six feet away was George Campbell. He barely looked up from his plate, where he sawed his T-bone into bite-size pieces. The novelty of bare breasts coupled with top-quality food and bonded booze kept people coming back show after show. Within two weeks the Folies proved to be such a success that the waiters went out on strike. The workers who put the food on the tables wanted their share of the profits too, but not just their fair share. The waiters' union demanded $50,000 to return to work. As Karl Kramer remembered it, MCA was made a proposition that the union could not refuse.

At Stein's order, Kramer went to a Loop nightclub one evening where he was to meet with a union representative. When he entered, the maître d' showed Kramer to an unoccupied table next to the stage. He sat through the floor show and ate dinner, but still nobody came to his table. Finally, just before closing, a well-dressed, heavyset little man with bushy eyebrows and a deeply lined face too large for his body sat in the chair across from him. "Hello," he said. "I'm Alex Louis Greenberg."

Greenberg was a Russian emigrant who had come to Chicago in 1909, worked his way up in the restaurant business, and earned enough to buy his own West Side saloon when he was nineteen years old. He ran a finance company and a hotel before he turned thirty, dabbling in handbook gambling on the side, but with the advent of Prohibition, Louie—as he was affectionately known—became truly prosperous. He joined bootleggers Dion O'Banion and Hymie Weiss in buying the Manhattan brewery in southwest Chicago. After Capone hit men gunned down his two partners in the mid-1920s, Greenberg became sole owner. Kramer vaguely knew who Greenberg was, but he was not shaken. Louie asked if Karl was comfortable, if the food had been all right, and if he'd enjoyed the show. Karl assured him everything had been fine. When it came to discussion of the $50,000 contribution to the waiters' union, however, Kramer relayed Stein's message in a clear voice: MCA would not be blackmailed. Greenberg smiled and negotiated. Perhaps for a lesser contribution the waiters could be persuaded to return to work. Kramer didn't budge. Greenberg then switched tactics.

The people he represented owned Sally Rand, he said. How would Kramer and his boss like ringside seats to see her do her fan dance? Kramer politely refused. When it became apparent that they were at an impasse, Kramer excused himself. Greenberg made no threat, but suggested it was time Jules Stein himself got in touch.

The waiters ended their strike a short time later and were back at work at the Folies-Bergère. Stein never told Kramer what arrangement he'd made or how much, if anything, he wound up paying to Greenberg's union, but MCA had no further trouble. They earned a small fortune from the Folies-Bergère. And Sally Rand became an MCA client, hitting the road with Bob Crosby and his Bobcats, yet another band that Jules Stein launched at the Blackhawk Restaurant.

The following year, Stein was called before a Cook County grand jury investigating government and corrupt labor practices. According to Kramer, Stein testified that he'd had nothing to do with gangsters. That was not his style. Jules Stein was a businessman — a very successful, respectable businessman. He did what he had to in order to earn a profit, but he broke no laws. The grand jury excused Jules Stein but continued its investigation.

"I don't know what arrangement Stein had with the Mob, but he did offer to deal with them," said Suber, who worked for MCA's rival, General Artists Corporation, in the late 1930s. "You had to if you were going to stay in business. We all did."

The Mob brought order to anarchy. Its methods might have been brutal at times, but its leaders wisely recognized that murder and mayhem alone accomplished nothing. That was the central theme at a summit meeting held at the Waldorf-Astoria in New York City during April of 1934, when Chicago's Johnny Torrio invited top mobsters from across the nation to assemble for a peace conference.

They pledged to begin cooperating in every Mob enterprise from gambling to the construction trade. It was the only way for them to build their *own* monopoly, Torrio preached. Thus a restaurant built by Zwillman's construction company, on land that Lansky brokered, would have a back room serviced by Vogel's slot machines and a bar that served Greenberg's beer, Costello's Scotch whisky and Fusco's gin. Adonis would furnish the cigarette vending machines and Ralph Capone's jukebox company would furnish the music. One or more Mob-controlled unions would supply the manpower, and everyone would get his cut.

Torrio had made Ralph Capone's dream of owning a piece of every element in the nightclub business come true. Naturally, entertainment was as integral to the package as an olive in every martini.

IN 1924 WHEN he was first beginning to throw his weight around, Jimmy Petrillo of the American Federation of Musicians got a rude wake-up call. Federation members stopped a funeral procession being led by a band of nonunion musicians, and when Petrillo returned home from an evening out with his family, he found that his place had been firebombed. No one was hurt, but the incident firmly established in his own mind, and in those of his friends, just how deadly the entertainment business could be.

Ten years later, after the repeal of Prohibition, matters got worse, not better. During the Roaring Twenties gangsters were chiefly preoccupied with the illegal production, distribution, and sale of booze, but after December 6, 1933, anyone could sell alcohol. Hoods had to focus on new ways to make money, which made power brokers like Petrillo and his pal Jules Stein even more nervous than they had been during the 1920s.

In the 1930s, kidnapping for big ransoms, labor racketeering, and gambling had become the crimes du jour. Labor boss Petrillo was pulled from his automobile by armed thugs and held for $50,000 ransom. Afterward a handful of dissident musicians questioned whether Petrillo had merely used the kidnapping as a ruse to steal $50,000 from the union coffers as "ransom," which he then split with the gang that snatched him. But Chicago City Hall took the abduction seriously enough to guarantee Petrillo protection for the next twelve years, assigning two Chicago police officers as his full-time bodyguards.

Petrillo's kidnapping was reason enough for Jules to cringe when journalist Walter Davenport wrote the first national magazine story about the rich, reclusive Doc Stein. Published in the March 10, 1934, edition of *Collier's*, the article revealed a perfect target for a kidnapping:

> Under his energetic direction there arose what his puny rivals scold as the band trust—the Music Corporation of America, which, as I have told you, manages, books, routes and dictates the engagements of more than 90 percent of the dance bands in America....
>
> Since he was a gentleman with whom it was safe to deal, the restaurant, hotel and club managements found it convenient to buy all their entertainment from the one office rather than procure their bands here and their shows from hither and yon, dealing thereby with four or five agencies and managers who had a harassing way of not getting along together and whose performers were forever threatening to commit murder and suicide if somebody else's name wasn't taken out of the electric lights and their own substituted. For one price in one office, Dr. Stein attended to all of that and the performers, like the bands, worked under firm and unified management.

Of course, "firm and unified management" had not always been the case. Stein's success had come after years of trial and error. Despite outward appearances of prosperity, the agency showed no profit at all until 1931. At one point following the 1929 stock market crash, he'd grown so uneasy about his company's prospects that he even came close to selling when rival agent Ralph Wonders offered to buy him out. And as the Depression gained momentum, Stein's own personal fortune began to erode.

But MCA diversified and fought back. Stein and Goodheart sold dance teams, party favors, comedians, confetti, jugglers, chorus lines, napkins, swizzle sticks, and more. One lucrative gimmick involved wrapping up an ankle bracelet or a cut-glass pendant with a bow and party paper, planting it at a table where a woman was sitting, and tacking the price of the gift onto the dinner tab—all payable to MCA.

As Walter Davenport of *Collier's* discovered, MCA had become a full-service agency by the mid-1930s, packaging a nightclub's every need and taking a percentage of everything, down to the toothpicks in the martini olives. Jules even offered a discount linen service to the clubs that hired his bands. In addition to earning a little extra from the clubs, he would order a nightly count of the linen napkins to make sure that MCA wasn't being cheated on the house count.

Stein didn't give a second thought to the consequences of competing head-to-head with gangsters. With Kramer's warehouse full of premium whiskey, MCA's standard package deal now consisted of top name musical acts, advertising, radio promotion, and the best booze that money could buy.

The company Jules and Billy Stein had created with $1,000 in capital in 1924 was now clearing over $1 million a year—a fact that could mean trouble if the wrong people knew about it.

"If you live by publicity, you'll die by publicity," Mickey Rockford liked to recite to his fellow agents. Despite his penchant for living the high life, Stein had to agree.

Not long after Walter Davenport's story hit the newsstands Stein began getting kidnap threats against himself and his family. Years later he maintained that the threats came from Roger Touhy, the North Side gangster who was accused of abducting Petrillo, but Justice Department documents dispute that assertion. According to the documents, the kidnap threats against Stein came from the Capone mob.

Stein later said he had "the guts of a fool" when he refused to be intimidated. In response to strikes, threats, and nine firebombings of nightclubs where MCA bands were booked, Stein beefed up his own personal security and paid out a $5,000 premium to Lloyd's of London for a $75,000 kidnapping policy.

Stein also played hardball. He used an Indiana labor union racketeer named Fred "Bugs" Blacker to "take care of" nightclubs that refused to hire MCA bands by hurling stink bombs onto the premises, along with bags of roaches—hence the nickname "Bugs."

On November 26, 1937, Blacker and his wife stepped out of the Argo Theater in the Chicago suburb of Summit, where Blacker had been working as a projectionist under the assumed name of "James Brown." Three masked gunmen drove up. Two jumped out of the car. One held Mrs. Blacker by the arms while his partner shot Blacker in the chest. Then the gangster calmly walked up to the dying man and put a bullet through Blacker's brain while his horrified widow screamed.

The masked trio drove off in the direction of Chicago. The murder was never solved, but stink bombings ceased to be a problem in Midwest theaters.

———

JULES STEIN MADE more than his share of enemies, but his career kept rolling forward.

He sold insurance policies through an agency in which he had an interest; he sold houses from an MCA-controlled real estate firm; and he sold cars from General Motors and Rolls-Royce dealerships he owned. He played the stock market obsessively, claiming that his only pleasure reading was company prospectuses and initial public offerings.[2]

"I don't live on the golf course," Stein once explained. "I learned long ago how to study. I don't even read much fiction. I would rather deal with corporate tax problems and the intricacies of corporate structure. I relax that way."

His frequent market successes led acquaintances and even his own MCA agents to remark that a Jules Stein stock buy was rarely a gamble. Those MCA star clients who asked Jules to invest their surplus funds got a bonus. Bandleader Horace Heidt even had a clause written into his contract: if he didn't earn a 10 percent return each year, MCA lost its option on his contract. For years, MCA clients like Eddy Duchin, Ben Bernie, and the Lombardo brothers sought and gratefully accepted Stein's stock tips. When Wayne King played at a social gathering for the manufacturer of Lady Esther perfume, Stein urged the bandleader to take his salary in the form of stock. King became one of the company's largest stockholders — and retired on the proceeds.

By 1936, Jules was rich enough to write out a check for $139,000 for his own seat on the New York Stock Exchange. It was the highest amount any of the sixty-one new members paid that year, but Stein never had to pay another commission for his frequent stock trades.

After Doris had made him a father, he started a family trust fund in 1935 with 20,000 shares of Paramount Pictures stock. Stein bought at $11 a share, and as a stock exchange member, he paid no commission. Within ten years, the trust fund stock for which he paid $220,000 had grown to $1.5 million.

The Steins' first daughter, Jean, was born in 1934; Susan came along two years later. Doris consigned their upbringing to nannies. The Steins lived not in Chicago but in the affluent suburb of Highland Park, 20 miles north of the Loop

---

[2] Known on Wall Street as a Dow theorist, Stein followed a pattern of investing that closely tracked percentage rises and dips in each stock in his portfolio. If a stock rose 15 percent above or dropped 15 percent below his purchase price, he sold it.

via the Northwestern Railroad. Located along Lake Michigan's western shore, near the Wisconsin state line, Highland Park had been an exclusive upper-middle-class enclave for white Protestant families since the Civil War. It had no synagogue, but it did have a local chapter of the Covenant Club and the Conference of Jewish Women's Organizations. The Steins' palatial home in the Deere Park section of town was modeled after a French château, with hardwood forest on one side and the endless vista of Lake Michigan on the other. Occasionally, Jules invited relatives up from South Bend, but the servants, the silverware, and the French cuisine only made them ill at ease.

Stein's former mentor, Dr. Harry Gradle, still lived in Highland Park, though his Vine Avenue home near the center of town seemed modest in comparison to the Steins' lakefront estate. But what Harry lacked in wealth, he more than made up for in professional accolades and peer acceptance. In addition to serving as chief of staff at the Illinois Eye and Ear Infirmary and attending ophthalmologist at Michael Reese and Cook County hospitals, Gradle had made his mark internationally.

Whenever Dr. Gradle and his wife celebrated a birthday or returned from a trip abroad, the event was duly noted in the society columns of the *Highland Park Press*. When Jules and Doris traveled abroad or observed any kind of milestone in their lives, the *Press* reported nothing.

It was different in New York. There Doris regularly made the list of best-dressed women during the late 1930s and '40s. Anti-Semitism still existed among New York's class-conscious nouveau riche, but not nearly to the same degree as in America's heartland. In Manhattan, money mattered more than race or religion. Doris adored the trappings of wealth and class and shared her husband's passion for acceptance among the elite.

In 1933 she started Jules on his lifelong obsession with English antiques by giving him an antique desk and breakfront when he moved MCA headquarters from Randolph Street to new offices up the street in the Oriental Theater Building, nearer the center of Chicago's busy theater district. Until then MCA's offices in both Chicago and New York had been furnished in heavy, dark Spanish furniture and framed Viennese etchings that Jules had brought home from his studies in Austria. From that day forward, the Steins scoured London for old English hunting prints, Currier and Ives lithographs, and finely crafted Georgian and Queen Anne pieces, eventually accumulating the largest private collection of British antiques in the United States.

When Stein later bought a twenty-story Chicago headquarters building next door to the Wrigley Building on Michigan Avenue and directly across the street from the *Tribune*, at the northern edge of the Loop, he furnished every office with English antiques.

Each morning during good weather, Stein motored across the lake by private launch from his Highland Park estate to the mouth of the Chicago River, just steps from his new office. While he'd learned to be more conservative, Stein never totally muted his taste for grandiosity.

MCA, meanwhile, continued to expand on a grand scale. By 1936 it controlled every band of any consequence in America. Its biggest rival, the William Morris Agency, dominated the vaudeville circuit of big-name comics, singers, and variety acts, but it couldn't compare to the big band lineup that Stein and Goodheart had assembled. The agency packaged radio programs the same way it had nightclubs, supplying everything from the stars to the sponsor and taking its 10 percent off the top every time. For the first time since 1928, Jules talked about expanding, maybe even getting into the motion picture business.

The movies were booming and all signs pointed west, but Jules remained close to Chicago during the early thirties to be near his invalid mother. He moved her from South Bend to Chicago in 1932 and consulted the best doctors, but Rosa Stein died in September 1935 following a short bout with bronchial pneumonia. She was sixty-three. The cynical Dr. Stein took her death hard. Beneath his steely facade was a broken heart. Jules had abandoned medicine for music and music for money, but he had never forgotten his family, especially his mother. After he'd climbed to the top, he tried to please her by putting all of his brothers and sisters to work. Ruth was MCA's in-house accountant, Adelaide helped furnish and decorate the MCA offices in New York, and Billy and David both became agents, though neither was ever very good at it.

While Jules was still young and subject to the browbeating that his father never failed to deliver, Rosa Stein's faith and encouragement had kept him going. He owed her a debt he could never repay. In 1937, two years after he returned her casket to Indiana for burial, Jules bought an ornate 10-foot iron fence from an estate that was being demolished on Chicago's North Side and had it shipped to the Hebrew Orthodox Cemetery in South Bend where Rosa Stein was buried. Two bronze plaques still frame the cemetery's entryway.

For MCA, and the music business in general, it was an important time. Records, once a high-end consumer product available only to the well-to-do, were now mass-produced, making band music even more popular. "In '35, Jack and David Kapp, two brothers who had a music store on Randolph Street, came out with a 35-cent single, with a song on each side," recalled Chuck Suber. "They called their company Decca and within a year, you had Decca singles in jukeboxes all over the country."

It was also an important time for MCA in New York, and even in Los Angeles, where Taft Schreiber seemed finally to be making some headway in radio and band booking. A half dozen agents were now working for him, sewing up dance halls from Seattle to San Diego with exclusive contracts that guaranteed a steady stream of MCA bands as long as the dance-hall owners hired no talent from any other agency. Those same MCA bands—which the agents sold to stations in small and medium-size radio markets like Fresno and Sacramento, California, and Portland, Oregon—grew hotter as the dance hall–radio cycle fed upon itself. The public could not get enough.

It was an important time for MCA in Cleveland, too. The newly hired head of the office there, DeArv Barton, had just moved the agency to the Union Commerce Building at the center of town just ten blocks west of Playhouse Square, where Cleveland's theaters and night life spots were concentrated. MCA's agents could concentrate on signing the best new bands from the very city that had given MCA its first bona fide star, Guy Lombardo.

For his right-hand man, Barton hired musician Merle Jacobs, a bon vivant who knew the town better than Barton did and who had been sent down from Chicago to drum up business. Jacobs had played in bands in all the clubs along Playhouse Square, including a glitzy new place called the Mayfair Casino. Despite its chandeliers, crushed-velvet seating, and other posh trappings, the Mayfair had been struggling to stay out of bankruptcy. Even the slot machines and games of chance in the basement couldn't seem to keep the management out of the red.

So when the Mayfair's ambitious young publicist came to Jacobs with news that the club might be closing soon, Merle took pity on the kid. He talked it over with Barton, and they decided to see if Jules Stein might have a spot for him. Accordingly, during his next scouting trip through Cleveland, Billy Stein was formally introduced to the tall, coltish young press agent from the Mayfair. He talked fast, dressed like a Republican lawyer, and oozed a smooth clarity of purpose that made him seem far older than twenty-three. His mind bit into ideas and would not be shaken loose until he'd managed to get his way. He was like a moray eel. Billy reckoned that Jules would like that.

The young fellow gave his name as Lew Wasserman.

FIVE

Cleveland

1913–1931

While Jules Stein's whole life revolved around music, Lew Wasserman's was all about the movies. He had grown up watching Dusty Farnum, Pearl White, Rudolph Valentino, and the Keystone Kops at the same time that Jules was booking bands and conquering radio in the 1920s.

Wasserman was only seventeen years younger than Stein, but he was far more fascinated with what he saw on the screen than what he heard on the radio. The very year that Wasserman was born, the modern motion picture industry first planted its roots in California. The surprise movie hit was *The Squaw Man*, a film about an English dandy in the Old West, produced by a retired vaudevillian named Jesse Lasky who decided to shoot his epic on location in the West. Lasky wasn't as interested in the movie's authenticity as he was in ducking the licensing fees he would have to pay if he got caught making his movie in New York. Making movies, even then, was all about avoiding costs and collecting cash at the box office.

Lasky and his partner, former glove salesman Sam Goldfish, hired a gang of derelicts, called them Lasky's Famous Players, and put them on a westbound train. To bring some order to the enterprise, they put a Spanish-American War veteran named Cecil DeMille in charge and asked him to position the actors in front of the cameras.[1]

The Lasky film crew's original destination was Flagstaff, Arizona, but when the train arrived there and the crew saw nothing but thousands of square miles of desert, they got back on the train and kept going until they reached the Pacific

---

[1] Samuel Goldfish changed his name to Samuel Goldwyn at about the same time DeMille began using his middle initial, B., in the affected manner of East Coast politicians and West Coast studio moguls. Jesse Lasky remained Jesse Lasky until the day he died.

Ocean. DeMille's telegram to Lasky and Goldfish became one of the founding documents of movie history: "Have proceeded to California. Want authority to rent barn in a place called Hollywood for $75 a month. Regards to Sam."

Shot on a budget of $15,000, *The Squaw Man* was filmed entirely at the base of the Santa Monica Mountains in an arid southern California suburb known as Hollywood—so called, according to one story, because the wife of the original owner of the property had seen the name on a map of Scotland and thought it sounded quaint.

A huge success with eastern audiences, *The Squaw Man* sparked a land rush from the wet and windy East to oasislike Los Angeles. From 1914 on, American movies had a distinctly dry, warm California look about them.

———✺———

STRUGGLING IMMIGRANTS BECAME the first generation of movie moguls—men like furrier Adolph Zukor, junkman Louis B. Mayer, and a loud, brutish pool hustler from Manhattan's Lower East Side named Harry Cohn. Given their own origins, it was no surprise that the first moguls hired writers and directors who cranked out stories of working-class characters who struggled for riches.

It seemed to Wasserman that the movies told the story of his own life. He was the third son of Isaac and Minnie Weiserman, Russian Orthodox Jews who fled the czar in 1908, booked passage from Odessa to Bremen and on to Baltimore, where they caught a train to Ohio and settled among family and friends in the Lake Erie port town of Cleveland. Lou's parents, who spoke Yiddish, had virtually no money and arrived owning nothing.

In the old country, Isaac had been a bookbinder. But bookbinders—especially those who spoke little English—weren't much in demand in Ohio during the years leading up to and following World War I. He was more likely to find work clerking in a dry goods store. Isaac Weiserman was short (5 feet 5), thin (130 pounds), and as dapper as a man of modest means could hope to be. The one dream he pursued was operating a restaurant, but it was a dream that kept failing.

About two years before their third son was born, the Weisermans changed the spelling of their name to Wasserman, which in Russian meant "water carrier." The name also had a potent mythical connotation, associated with Aquarius, the first sign of the Zodiac. Wasserman was a *mazal*, or luck, name. In the Jewish community, Wassermans were seen as honest, forthright, tolerant, and visionary, often acting fifty years or more ahead of their time. But their high standards and dreamy dispositions could make them eccentric and unrealistic at times. They could become hypercritical, even vindictive.

Isaac Wasserman was all of those things—and unlucky in business. He went into the café business with an Austrian immigrant named Benjamin Mintz shortly after his arrival in Cleveland. The Mintz and Wasserman Restaurant was the first of several eateries that Isaac and Minnie would open along Woodland Avenue in Cleveland's shifting borscht belt. Over the years the addresses and names and partners would change—the Wasserman and Missman Restaurant at 4312 Woodland, the Missman and Wasserman Restaurant at 4957 Woodland, the Up-to-Date Restaurant at the same address a few years later—but the cuisine and cost of doing business would remain roughly the same. When Prohibition arrived, the Wassermans did a brisk business selling booze on the side, but the proceeds still barely covered the rent. Practically from the cradle, the Wassermans' youngest son witnessed on a daily basis the downside of Darwinian capitalism.

Louis Wasserman was born at 6:42 A.M. at the Wassermans' tiny home on Woodland Avenue on March 22, 1913, exactly eighteen days after Thomas Woodrow Wilson was sworn in as the twenty-seventh president of the United States.[2] While growing up, he watched his parents rise before dawn, toil until nightfall, and collapse into bed exhausted while their creditors—suppliers, wholesalers, landlords—constantly chased after them for money. The Wassermans had traded Russian servitude for a new kind of serfdom on the streets of Cleveland. Observing his parents' struggles, Lou learned early the power of ownership. His father had it half right: avoid being another man's employee. But if you must work for someone else, always get a piece of his action. Equity. Ownership. That became Lou's guiding corollary to the work ethic instilled in him by his father. Lou grew up an American, not just the son of Russian immigrants.

Until she married Isaac, Minnie's surname had been Chernick. Before she left her native Kiev, twenty-five-year-old Minnie Wasserman gave birth to her first son. Max Wasserman was born in 1906, and William Isaac Wasserman followed in 1908, after the Wassermans had arrived in America. Both William and Lou were American citizens, born on U.S. soil, but Max would officially remain a Russian immigrant throughout his sad, short life.

Diagnosed as an epileptic while still very young, Max was sent away at the age of seven to the Ohio Hospital for Epileptics, located in the small Ohio River town of Gallipolis. He returned home to Cleveland four months later, but his records were stamped "unimproved." When his poverty-stricken family could no longer care for him, Max returned to Gallipolis two years later and spent the last seven years of his life as one of 1,700 inmates in a state-funded asylum. He died on Octo-

---

2   When he was in high school, Wasserman began giving his birth date as March 15, 1913. Some of his later acquaintances speculated that he selected the ides of March because it had more mythic potency to it. Historically, it was the day that Brutus murdered Julius Caesar. March 15, 1915, was also the day that Hollywood mogul Carl Laemmle paid $135,000 for a chicken ranch located on 230 acres of hill property south of the Cahuenga Pass and founded Universal Studios.

ber 23, 1922, following two days of violent serial convulsions. He was only sixteen when his body was shipped back to Cleveland for burial. His youngest brother, Lou, was six months shy of his tenth birthday when he watched the brother he barely knew being lowered into the ground.

The two surviving boys worked from childhood on, but honest labor and long hours earned them the same rewards accorded their parents: cynicism and exhaustion. When they were old enough, both brothers welcomed the chance to seek jobs beyond the restaurant. By the time he was in junior high, William had found a job in a drugstore, and later on, he sold shoes. Lou worked in a dry goods store; in later years he boasted that he got his start in show business when he was just twelve, an eighth grade student at Patrick Henry Junior High, by selling candy in a burlesque house.

Burlesque was a Cleveland institution as old as the city itself. From its very beginnings, Lou Wasserman's Cleveland demanded that its newly landed European immigrants make believe just to survive. From its official founding in 1796, the town had always been home to knaves, fugitives, and fools. Before any school or any church was ever built, Cleveland knew how to keep itself drunk and happy. Bawdy houses and saloons lined the streets.

By the 1920s, burlesque houses on a one-block stretch in downtown Cleveland, called Short Vincent, were featuring jazz bands, scantily clad women who did Arabian dances with veils, and clownish characters in baggy pants who passed gas and told crude jokes. Workingmen who could pay a nickel got a few laughs. The hangouts and the strip joints, with names like the Theatrical Grill and the Roxy, were also known for parting fools from their money.

Lou understood the need to escape, but disciplined himself early not to slip into a bottle or fall under the spell of a woman. He fostered the fiction through much of his early adult life that he seldom drank anything stronger than an imported beer.[3] Even as a boy, he knew better than to plot his exit from Ohio — and poverty — by indulging in alcohol or fast women.

Lou bought his ticket out of Cleveland at the movies.

—⁓—

BEFORE HE WAS out of knickers, Lou was a fan of the movies and movie stars. A bright student who learned to read early, he was able to follow the antics of the stars and their keepers in the newspapers and fan magazines. He could write well enough, too. His grades in English were usually B's and seldom less than a C-plus

[3]   Once his conquest of Hollywood was well under way, Lew switched to a single vodka on the rocks as his beverage of choice at cocktail parties.

throughout junior high and high school. His performance was mediocre only in foreign languages, such as French and Latin.

He excelled in geometry, algebra, and trigonometry, however, and he could add and subtract more quickly in his head than he could with pencil and paper. He made change faster than salesmen twice his age. By the time he entered Glenville High School in 1927, his classmates observed, counting money and watching movies had become his twin passions.

After quitting his job at the burlesque house, Lou worked at Levinson's Dry Goods, selling women's dresses, underwear, and stockings. He was barely out of puberty when he quit the clothing business.

Minnie Wasserman used to throw her hands up in exasperation and trill to the neighbors: "My Louie! He gets funny ideas. Funny ideas, all day long. Why can't he get a good job like his brother Bill?"

John Royal, one of the regulars at the Wassermans' Up-to-Date Restaurant, managed a movie theater and had to listen to Minnie's complaints when he came in to drink on the weekends.

"Give him a job!" she'd harp, pointing at her Louie. "Get him out of the house!"

Royal obliged. Through Minnie's badgering, Lou finally went to work as an usher. He worked for a time at Keith's 105th Street Theater. The magnificent old three-story movie palace at the corner of 105th Street and Euclid Avenue.

As an usher, Lou wore a red uniform, replete with brass buttons, braid, and white gloves — an ensemble that proved impressive to girls as well as high school pals who wanted to sneak into the Saturday matinee.

Between movies, the theater management booked touring vaudeville acts, giving audiences and ushers firsthand exposure to many singers, comics, and musicians who would soon become stars on the emerging radio networks. Lou got to see Eddie Cantor, Sophie Tucker, Burns and Allen, Edgar Bergen and Charlie McCarthy, and a host of hoofers and jokesters before they became national commodities via NBC and CBS.

Backstage, the theater even offered billiards, so that its employees and visiting vaudevillians could get to know one another. One of the regulars who was shooting pool long before Lou was even out of grammar school was a transplanted Britisher named Leslie Townes Hope. Their paths didn't cross in Cleveland, but they would years later, after Lou had changed his name to Lew R. Wasserman and Leslie had changed his to Bob Hope.

Lew and his best friend, Derrick Caplan, worked every day from 3:00 P.M. to midnight, showing people to their seats and cleaning the aisles of popcorn and candy wrappers once the double feature was over. He earned $18 a week, most of which went to support his family.

It took discipline to rush to the theater right after school, put in a nine-hour shift, walk a mile back home to his parents' apartment at 839½ East 105th Street, and get up the next morning at 7:15 to walk the five miles to school and start the routine again. Lew claimed it was the daily grind of school and ushering that created the lifelong habit of getting by with little sleep. "I can't sleep and the reason is, when I was going to high school in Cleveland, I was too poor to sleep," he said in later years. Among his buddies, he was nicknamed "the Vampire."

"He always had the ability to be very serious and very effective in everything he did," remembered Al Setnick, whose family owned a shoe repair shop a block away from the Wassermans'. "Lew didn't spend any time with foolish things. Even way back when we were in high school, he was the man who ran the movies."

Once he had established himself, Lew wasn't satisfied simply showing people to their seats. First, he got himself promoted to chief usher. Then he moved on from Keith's 105th to Rappaport Exhibits, an advertising agency that created movie posters, lobby cards, and department store displays.

"Everything about him smelled theater," recalled Marianne Rose, who worked at the desk next to Lew's at the Rappaport agency. "He was bold and brash, but in a quiet sort of way. You had an instinct about him that he was going to get his way, legally, illegally, or however. I mean, he wasn't going to let little things get in the way of his objective."

Because Rappaport Exhibits worked closely with the Warner Brothers theater chain in Cleveland, Lew became acquainted with and began dating a young woman who was "high up in Warner Brothers," said Rose. He used that relationship to move into an advertising job at Warners' Hippodrome Theater in downtown Cleveland, where the vaudeville stage was big enough to support horse-riding acts and dancing elephants. There Lew ingratiated himself with the theater's manager who drank during working hours, according to Al Setnick. Within a short time, the nondrinking Wasserman rose to assistant manager, though he seemed to be more in charge than the manager. He found himself in a position to offer friends like Setnick a job.

"He was somehow connected with the management of the Hippodrome," said Setnick. "The manager allowed him to...well, actually, *he* did most of the managing. So I was walking upstairs to get a seat one night and I met him in the hallway and he says, 'What are you doing?' I says, 'Nothing.' And he says, 'How'd you like to go to work?' That was on a Friday, and I started working Monday."

By then Lew no longer wore a uniform. As quasi-manager, he had switched to suit and tie, shopping at Larry Symonds, an expensive tailor shop on Superior Avenue. He frequently got Setnick, who owned a car, to drive him to work, but if he had to, he took the streetcar from his home on the east side of town into central Cleveland. Lew watched the Euclid Avenue mansions through the windows of the streetcar—posh homes of the men who ran Western Union, the Standard Oil Trust, and the very company that operated the streetcar in which he was riding.

"He dressed like a professional man, because that's what he was," said Setnick. And he was barely out of high school. "Some of my other friends asked me what was his title, and I said I didn't know but that he just ran the whole thing."

—◦◦◦—

As CHAIRMAN OF the Motto Committee of the student House of Representatives, Lew helped come up with the slogan for the Glenville High class of 1930. It was taken from Hebrew scripture and translated into English as "Education teaches tolerance."

It was an apt description of Glenville High School, the home of scholars and second-generation Americans who sought tolerance as much as they taught it. During the early 1900s, the neighborhoods of Cleveland were gerrymandered by race and religion with each ethnic group isolated in its own schools. For Eastern European Jews, that school was Glenville.

"Somehow or other, the brightest and the best went there," said classmate Phil Bartok. "They were so competitive. Really!"

"It made for a very unique education," said Leonard Goldhammer, another classmate. "The faculty seemed to know that education was the key to success, and everybody was very hardworking and very motivated. Glenville didn't have much in the way of athletes, but it turned out a lot of people who went on to become very successful in their chosen field."

Graduates ranged from U.S. Senator Howard Metzenbaum to Caesar's Palace president Billy Weinberger to *Superman* creators Joe Shuster and Jerry Siegel to a former owner of the Cleveland Indians and the founder of the Stouffer's frozen food empire. Lew's classmates went on to become physicians, engineers, and attorneys, and Lou Wasserman went on to become the most successful of all.

In the Glenville High yearbook, the *Olympiad*, he was identified as a man behind the scenes. The editors voted Lew "Class Sales Person" and noted: "Funny how Lew always manages to handle the money end of a job."

Classmate Mollie Marshall remembers a resourceful Lew Wasserman showing movies each week during the lunch hour in the Glenville auditorium. She assumed he simply borrowed the two-reel silent comedies and melodramas from Keith's 105th Street Theater or the Hippodrome where he worked. But Lew didn't run the movies for forty-five minutes each noon just to be nice. He stood at the door and collected two cents' admission from every student.

Eddie Preisler, another classmate, remembered Lew lisping his sibilants, which turned his otherwise pleasant speaking voice into a parody of the cartoon character Sylvester the Cat—a speech problem that would crop up throughout his professional life, especially when he lost his temper and wound up sputtering so badly that he'd have to wipe the saliva from his chin.

"He had a speech impediment and that made him the butt of a lot of jokes," said Preisler. "But mostly, he was the kind of guy you could never really say anything bad about. The other side of that is that you couldn't find too much great to say about him either."

Lew's classmates all recall one thing that changed after 1930: Louis Wasserman ceased to exist, and Lewis Wasserman took his place.

—⁓—

BY SIMPLY READING the Cleveland newspapers, Wasserman got a dose of much more than Hollywood news. He read about politics, organized crime, and corruption, learning early and in dramatic fashion that money, politics, and mobsters were never far apart.

Lew was ideally situated to develop an early taste for politics. When his parents first came to Cleveland, it was home to former Mayor Mark Hanna, whose name remains synonymous with political corruption today, nearly a century after he left office. Though he did not hail from Cleveland himself, Ohio native Warren G. Harding ran what many historians still describe as the single most corrupt presidential administration in U.S. history, aided by several notable and nefarious Cleveland Republicans.[4]

One of President Harding's staunchest supporters was a bright young lawyer named Henry A. Beckerman. Young Wasserman was able to learn about Beckerman because his political string-pulling and shady business deals became regular fodder for the *News*, the *Press*, and the *Plain Dealer*.

Like Isaac and Minnie Wasserman, Henry Beckerman was a product of Eastern Europe. One of eight children of a German rabbi who emigrated to the United States, Henry graduated from law school, married a feisty young woman named Tillie Kline, also the child of a rabbi, and joined the practice of attorney Maurice Maschke, by far the most influential politician in northern Ohio during the 1920s.

[4.] Harding's postmaster general, Will Hays, for example, left Washington for Hollywood just as the Teapot Dome scandal broke. Hays was hired by the studios for $150,000 a year to act as czar of Hollywood's first self-censoring office, known thereafter as the Hays Office. Once he began banning sex and limiting violence in the movies, Hays successfully preempted a congressional drive to crack down on the business. He became such a well-known arbiter of movie morality that the pope granted him a private audience to discuss sin in Hollywood. Back in 1924, however, he lied to the U.S. Senate about $185,000 in shady contributions made to Harding's presidential campaign in connection with Teapot Dome.

As a member of the Republican National Committee, Maschke not only hand-picked Cleveland's elected officials but also decided who would occupy the governor's mansion in Columbus and who would go to Washington, D.C., as Ohio's senators and congressmen. During Harding's presidency, Maschke's Republicans ruled Cleveland.

And Henry Beckerman became his chief lieutenant. On the flip side of Maschke's political power were the political spoils, and Beckerman shared in those, too.

Edwin P. Strong, operator of Loew's Ohio Theater and another Maschke Republican, partnered with Beckerman in the Thistledown Race Track. One of the most successful experiments in legalized gambling in Ohio history, the track still operates today. Strong was a key link between respectable business and the underworld, and no freshman in the business of gambling. During the early 1920s, he helped notorious New York gambler Nicky Arnstein escape Mob vengeance, offering Arnstein refuge after he'd fenced $2 million in stolen securities.

With friends like Maschke and Strong, attorney Henry Beckerman became a millionaire by 1929, even though he never argued a case in court. He and his wife, Tillie, lived with their two sons and one daughter in Cleveland Heights, on a narrow tree-lined avenue of fine two-story estates, several miles up the hill from crowded 105th Street where the Wassermans and most other Cleveland Jews lived. Unlike Isaac and Minnie Wasserman, the immigrant Beckermans had already learned something about ownership, deal-making, and tapping into the American dream. Holding on to that dream meant passing on the secrets of success to the next generation.

One of the Beckermans' boys, Stanley, attended Harvard with Maurice Maschke Jr. while their younger son, Robert, also prepared for college. Edith, their fourteen-year-old daughter, was Henry's little princess. Though girls seldom aspired to college in those days, Edie had already learned what she needed to know. She dressed in fashionable outfits and bobbed her hair, as did her friends. Her mother, a crack bridge player, taught Edie to play cards. She was tiny, but confident — even shrill if she did not get her way. Edie knew how to pout, she could wheedle almost anything she wanted, and she played a fair game of golf before she entered high school.

But the Beckerman family's future was not cloudless. Following the stock market crash, many Republicans' fortunes hit the skids, and so did Henry Beckerman's. Even an expert behind-the-scenes player like Beckerman suffered in the plummeting economy and felt compelled to do whatever was necessary to maintain his family's lifestyle.

Early on the morning of November 30, 1931, a small fire was discovered and extinguished in a four-story warehouse at 7500 Stanton Avenue. But in the course of the cleanup, firemen discovered several barrels of gasoline connected by fuses designed to be ignited by an elaborate tangle of electric irons and toasters. Had the crude firebomb gone off, it would have blown up half a city block. Though its $325,000 mortgage was in default, the building had been insured for $800,000. The warehouse owner turned out to be Beth Realty, a company that was owned and controlled by Edward P. Strong and Henry A. Beckerman.

Following a lengthy investigation, the county prosecutor indicted Beckerman, his law partner, his law partner's brother, and an interior decorator from Detroit with ties to that city's notorious Purple Gang. The charge: attempted arson.

Beckerman proclaimed his innocence. A trial was repeatedly postponed while both sides prepared their cases. The cost of defending himself began mounting. Meanwhile, Edward Strong and Maurice Maschke distanced themselves from Beckerman. Even though they vowed support behind the scenes, Beckerman had to fend for himself in public. The price of protecting his integrity would rise.

The year following the arson arrests, the Cuyahoga County treasury wound up $500,000 short. Again, Maschke's name came up during the investigation, but Beckerman and four others were indicted for embezzlement. They were tried and acquitted, but the missing money never turned up.

Two years later, when the Stanton Avenue arson case finally came to trial, the judge called a halt to testimony after just three weeks. He told a shocked courtroom that two jurors reported they'd been approached with offers of business deals once the trial was over. The judge declared a mistrial and ordered a jury-tampering investigation. Nothing came of it, but the prosecutor, a Democrat, vowed to re-file the case against all four defendants, including Beckerman.

In the meantime, Henry's fortune continued to dwindle. He declared bankruptcy, claiming that his million-dollar empire had crumbled and he was penniless. Despite the fact that the Beckermans resided in the same well-kept Cleveland Heights home and continued to live in apparent affluence, the only real asset Beckerman professed to own was a $90,000 life insurance policy, which he said he was borrowing against in order to pay son Stanley's way through Harvard.

And still his legal troubles dragged on. Two more years passed before the arson case came to trial again. By then Henry's little princess had graduated from high school and been forced to take a job instead of going to college like her classmates and her brothers. The Beckermans' only daughter had to forgo her privileged existence and hire on as a salesclerk for the May Company at eighteen dollars a week.

Edith Beckerman took the Euclid Avenue streetcar to the ornate seven-story department store in downtown Cleveland, passing those same mansions that Lew Wasserman had seen through streetcar windows for years as he rode to his ushering job. Lew may have been "from the wrong side of the tracks, and I was from the right side," as Edie would remark in later years, but hard times and bad luck leveled the playing field. The only difference between the bourgeois Beckermans and the proletarian Wassermans was that—for a time, at least—Henry Beckerman's only daughter had actually lived the good life, which Lew could see only from a streetcar window.

SIX

Cleveland

1932–1937

I knew Lew," said Herman Pirchner, owner of the Mayfair Café in downtown Cleveland. "He was a tall skinny kid who went up and down Playhouse Square hustling, trying to get items in the [newspaper] columns."

Before he sold his restaurant in 1934 and the new management renamed it the Mayfair Casino, Pirchner frequently ran into the coltish young publicist who called himself Lew R. Wasserman.

Lew had been fired from his job at the Hippodrome after Nat Wolfe, the manager of the chain that owned the theater, accused him of corruption and ordered an audit of the Hippodrome's petty cash. Though no money was missing and no charges were brought against him, Lew was still out of a job. But he had learned a great deal about selling movies during his time as assistant manager.

"It was a big thing in our office, preparing the ad that was coming out for the weekend," recalled Maurice Englander, who also worked for the Hippodrome. "Lew took charge right away. He knew all about the picture before the picture came out. He knew all about the stars, and he knew how to promote the movie. He hired an illustrator and instructed him how to lay out the ad: 'Put in a breast over here and an eyelash over there.' That sort of thing."

After he was fired, Lew took his portfolio of successful ad campaigns to the manager of the Circle Theater and then to the venerable 3,500-seat Palace Theater, where he landed a position as publicity director, but it wasn't long after the Mayfair Casino opened that the young Wasserman became a fixture at Cleveland's biggest, flashiest, most exclusive nightclub. He was only twenty-two years old.

In later years Lew scorned the press and came to avoid journalists. But during his quick climb to the top rungs of Cleveland nightlife, Wasserman courted newspaper reporters—buying them drinks, partying with them at the Alcazar Hotel, escorting them home when they'd had a little too much, and generally currying their favor. In fact, he wrote their articles for them.

"He wrote some very good copy," said Pirchner. "As you know, columnists are a little bit lazy, and he would write the whole column for them. There was George Davis and Norman Siegel of the *Cleveland Press*, and William McDermott and Windsor French of the *Plain Dealer*, and George Condon and Arthur Spath of the *Cleveland News*, and Sidney Andorn who was all over the place. It was very competitive in Cleveland with three daily newspapers."

As a nightclub owner in the thick of Cleveland's Playhouse Square theater district, Pirchner was in a position to appreciate the fine distinction between bad publicity and the clever material churned out by a Lew Wasserman. The trick was to solicit free advertising in the entertainment columns about the fabulous chorus lines, amazingly cheap liquor, gourmet food, upbeat band music, and celebrity headliners, while at the same time discouraging the columnist from writing about high cover charges, watered-down drinks, illegal gambling, shabby service, and strong-arm bouncers who tossed patrons out on their ear if they were liquored up or disgruntled over what they got for their money.

Nightlife in Cleveland could be dangerous. From the days of Guy Lombardo's very first gig at the Claremont Tent, when Lew was only ten years old, Cleveland had been only slightly less rough-and-tumble than Jules Stein's Chicago. Cleveland's nightclubs were often underwritten by underworld figures who chose to conceal their stake in show business. Herman Pirchner learned this after Prohibition was repealed in 1933, when he was approached to sell out his interest in the Mayfair Café. The investment group that wanted to buy it planned to move the restaurant across the street to the old Ohio State Theater; redecorate the place with chandeliers, crimson velour, and sweeping staircases; and rename it the Mayfair Casino. Pirchner didn't care what they planned to do with his old restaurant. He knew what most likely would be going on in the back room while the band played out front, but dice and cards were not his style. He offered modestly priced dinners and family entertainment, so he took what the new owners paid him and opened another restaurant down the street called the Alpine Village, featuring oompah bands and schnitzel, but no slot machines or roulette tables.

The nominal owner of the new Mayfair Casino was ebullient Harry Propper, the late Louie Bleet's glad-handing partner in the nightclub business during Prohibition. According to Pirchner, however, jolly Harry Propper's actual stake in Cleveland's newest club venture was minimal.

"Harry Propper was a very polished gentleman, but he was the front man. I guess he had a piece of the action, but [the casino] was owned by the Syndicate: four Jewish gentlemen," said Pirchner.

The members of the Syndicate—Moe B. Dalitz, Lou Rothkopf, Morris Kleinman, and Sam Tucker—were all graduates of Cleveland's notorious Mayfield

Road Gang, an organization of immigrant Italian and Eastern European Jews who controlled most of the city's gambling, bootlegging, and prostitution in the wide-open east Cleveland suburbs during Prohibition.[1]

These four semiretired gangsters, the true owners of the new Mayfair Casino, were obsessed with remaining utterly out of sight. They would come to be known in northern Ohio and, much later, in the casinos of Las Vegas and in southern California's La Costa Country Club, as the Silent Syndicate. Even when subpoenaed in 1950 to testify before the Kefauver Committee on Organized Crime in Interstate Commerce, the quartet refused to answer most of the senators' questions about the murders, extortion, and bribery that had accompanied their rise to prosperity.

But during the Depression the group's operations were still concentrated in Cleveland. With the much-publicized inauguration of the Mayfair Casino on October 22, 1935, the Silent Syndicate hoped to convince the conservative city fathers that legalized gambling was not all bad. The argument was that a vibrant nightlife could reinvigorate Cleveland's depressed downtown and provide a boost for business. The Mayfair Casino would represent organized crime's perennial three-pronged solution for economic distress: top-notch entertainment, bonded whiskey, and games of chance.

And the newspapers never seemed to get wise. From opening night, the Mayfair had the cooperation of the Cleveland press corps.

To ferry free-spending revelers into downtown Cleveland from the suburbs, the Mayfair's owners paid seven dollars a load to an enterprising young limousine operator named Aladena Fratianno. Born the same year as Wasserman, Fratianno bought a two-year-old Marmon limousine and hired someone else at half the fee to do the driving for him when he grew tired of doing it himself. Some fifty years later, Fratianno would gain his own notoriety under his nickname "Jimmy the Weasel," when he became the first major Mafia assassin to turn on the Mob, testify against his former bosses, and finish out his life anonymously under the federal Witness Protection Program.

Inside the Mayfair, hotel operators mingled with newspaper executives; shipping magnates sat next to union leaders; movie theater owners shared tables with politicians. The mayor himself stood by with a highball while two ranking officers of Cleveland's police force swapped jokes with the business agent for Local 27 of the International Alliance of Theatrical Stage Employees.

The gaudy tomato-red, peach, and chartreuse lobby boasted an oval bar — the

---

[1]   According to court and property records, other Mayfair investors included Lake Erie bootlegger John O'Boyle; attorney Samuel T. Haas, a business partner of Edward Strong; John "King" Angersola; Alfred "Big Al" Polizzi; and Charles "Chuck" Polizzi — all identified in the Kefauver hearings as ranking members of the Cleveland Mafia who worked in lockstep with Dalitz, Kleinman, Rothkopf, and Tucker.

largest in the country, the world, or the universe, depending upon whose column you read — as well as a "sky bar" on the balcony, with a grand total of sixteen bartenders on duty. Both the ground floor and the balcony were terraced for dinner tables, and 112 waiters rushed back and forth from the $60,000 kitchen, located beneath the newly expanded stage, where no less than twenty acts — three bands, a chorus line, animal acts, jugglers, a torch singer, dance teams, a psychic, and more — performed for over two hours each evening.

Lew Wasserman, who would soon become Harry Propper's young protégé, would learn a thing or two from watching the masterful Propper turn a tidy profit while displaying savoir faire for swank-starved midwesterners. The Mayfair Casino was basically a large movie theater converted into a Parisian fantasy that existed for the most part only in the imaginations of its bejeweled and ingenuous patrons.

"Diners who weren't quite sure of what wine to drink with which course received expert advice from a 'wine steward' who moved from table to table," wrote columnist George Davis in his opening night review. "[The steward] wore a heavy chain to which was attached a big silver key. The key, which he admitted was just for show, would open the wine cellar, if the Mayfair Casino had a wine cellar. Mr. Propper said the wine steward was there to add 'the continental touch.'"

—◦◦◦◦—

SEVERAL BLOCKS UP Euclid Avenue at the Circle Theater, Lew Wasserman was the new publicity director, but despite his new job title, he knew he was little more than a movie plugger. The real action in Cleveland was no longer in the movie houses. The only thing anyone talked about was the Mayfair Casino. The excitement of live acts every night onstage made Lew's job pale by comparison.

According to Seymour Heller, a former MCA agent and a Wasserman intimate for more than sixty years, it was around this time that Lew finally decided he was ready for Hollywood. He quit his job at the Circle Theater and caught a train to California to work publicity at one of the movie studios. Within weeks, however, a slightly humbled Lew returned to Cleveland. He told Heller he would have made the grade in Tinseltown if he hadn't gotten sick.

"I never knew exactly what he had, but he was jaundiced, and from then on his complexion always had a yellow color to it," said Heller. "People didn't notice it that much after he came back to California with MCA because he spent a lot of time in Palm Springs. Most of the time he always had a tan that covered it up."

After Lew had recovered sufficiently, he insinuated himself into the splashy action at the Mayfair Casino, persuading Harry Propper that he needed a publicity director. One of the perks of his new job was simply hanging out every night in the club, looking important. After sucking up to newspaper columnists all day and making sure they had just the right spin on the latest stage act, Lew could dress up, run a comb through his straight black hair, and stroll through *his* nightclub, just like Harry Propper, shaking hands, introducing himself to movers and shakers, and ordering an occasional round of drinks for those he wanted to impress.

One such person was a petite dark-haired girl who was obviously underage but who showed up at the club anyway, accompanied by none other than Helen Maschke, daughter of Republican kingmaker Maurice Maschke.

"I knew Edie before Lew [met her]," said Merle Jacobs, a bandleader from the era who used to play at the Mayfair Casino. "I knew her and Stanley Beckerman too. Stanley was quite a sharp kid. Edie was a social climber."

Helen Maschke, the leader of Edie's clique, was a tease, according to Jacobs. Helen was brassy and notoriously loose with the boys, while Edie had developed a reputation around downtown nightspots as only slightly less flirtatious.

"She was a real live wire," said Eddie Walpaw, another of the young men Edie kept on a string. "She used to pick me up in this beautiful convertible that her father got for her, and we'd go dancing. In fact, she taught me how to dance, and we were out every night—the Statler Hotel, the Southern Tavern, fraternity parties."

"Edie was a kind of spoiled little girl, but very attractive and with an exceptionally effective voice," recalled Johnny Singer, another Cleveland bandleader from the era. "She was very clear when she spoke. She had perfect diction."

Edie Beckerman and her friends lusted after big band musicians the way teens idolize rock stars today, said Singer. "I dated her and so did a lot of other musicians," he said.

But not after she met Lew R. Wasserman.

The match between Edie and Lew was made by Sidney Andorn, who wrote the "Hollywood Lowdown" column for the *Town Crier*, a weekly magazine, and who knew that Edie and Helen were daughters of the chieftains of Cleveland's recently deposed but still politically potent Republican machine.

The fast-talking, fast-thinking Wasserman instantly hit it off with Henry Beckerman's starstruck but shrewd daughter by offering her free passes to the Circle Theater.

"I leaped at the offer, because he was a very attractive man," Edie recalled. "The passes launched our romance. I took a girlfriend with me, but I paid more attention to Lew than to the show. After that I chased him for a year, until he caught me."

Later in their courtship, he introduced her backstage at the Mayfair to as many performers and musicians as she liked. She was insatiable, feeding off Lew's access to the stars like a stage vampire. They became totally devoted to each other. On the rare occasions when he doubted himself and his ability to jump his success up another notch, Edie was behind him, shoving and shouting with all her might.

"Lew was from the wrong side of the tracks, and I was from the right side, and the twain met," she told author Dominick Dunne sixty years later.

"Everything in my life has had something to do with show business," she said. "My fascination with the industry was natural, since my father was an attorney for show business people, and I wanted to be a dancer. But when I was a little girl, dancing was not considered a proper career for a young lady."

Edie understood what she had in Lew. She earned barely enough at the May Company to keep herself in clothes, while her father continued to spend all of his money fighting the arson charges against him. Lew represented more than a good time and a backstage pass; he represented the future. When Edie introduced Lew to her family, there was a mesh, especially with Stanley Beckerman who gave his Harvard-educated approval to the young buck from 105th Street.

Henry liked his prospective son-in-law, too. They went to the racetrack and prizefights together, and Henry introduced Lew to people who could make a difference in the bright young man's show business career. But Henry was too preoccupied to plan his daughter's wedding. In the spring of 1936, Henry Beckerman finally got his day in court on the Stanton Avenue fire case.

—◈—

THE TRIAL BEGAN on June 11 and lasted just over two weeks. Two days into the trial, the jury revisited the crime scene. While photographers' flashbulbs popped, jurors solemnly paraded past the spot where Beckerman had allegedly ordered his henchmen to set off the firebomb.

Back in the courtroom, the case seemed to come down to the testimony of one witness: Beckerman's former law partner, H. H. "Bob" Felsman, whose younger brother, Max, had already been convicted of brokering the arson deal.

"You said that Henry Beckerman met you in New York about December 8, 1931, and told you he was responsible for setting the building on fire?" asked William Corrigan, Beckerman's defense counsel.

Felsman testified that he had indeed met Beckerman in his hotel room that morning, while both men were in New York on business, and that Beckerman had confessed to the arson while he was shaving.

"Did he quit shaving?" asked Corrigan.

"No," answered Felsman.

"As he shaved away, he told you he had planned to burn the building?"

"Not at all!" Felsman snapped. "I made no attempt to give you that picture. When I came into the room, Mr. Beckerman was shaving. He said: 'Bob, sit down. I want to tell you about the fire.' I said: 'Yes, I want to know all about it.' He said, 'Your brother is innocent—that's the first thing you'll want to hear.' I said: 'Yes, I'm grateful for that.'

"He said: 'I regret I had a silly crazy notion that that building could be fired. Your brother was innocently involved.' I said: 'How?'"

Felsman explained that his brother followed Beckerman's instructions, hiring a night watchman at the warehouse who would look the other way while a trio of torch men from Detroit sneaked in and set off the bomb.

"He [Beckerman] said he didn't know Max would be asked to do those things and was very sorry he was involved," said Felsman.

When Max Felsman took the stand, he repeated his brother's story and added that he had lied at his own trial in order to protect Beckerman. Eli Robinson, the Detroit interior decorator accused of hiring two other Detroit hoodlums to help set the fire, refused to testify at all and was jailed for contempt of court.

The Beckerman family sat behind Henry and his lawyer at the defense table virtually every day of the trial. Mrs. Tillie Beckerman barely kept her emotions in check as the testimony ground on. From time to time, a tall, handsome young man with a grim smile could be seen at the front of the courtroom, sitting next to Edie, patting her arm and holding her hand. Stanley Beckerman, who had recently taken the bar exam, sat with his father at the defense table, taking copious notes on legal pads.

Finally, on Friday, June 26, the case went to the jury. Deliberations lasted most of the day and on into the weekend. On Saturday, June 27, at 5:45 P.M., the verdict came in. It was reported Sunday morning on the front page of the *Plain Dealer*: "Henry A. Beckerman was acquitted of conspiracy in the Stanton Avenue warehouse arson plot by a jury of nine women and three men yesterday."

Exactly one week later, on July 5, 1936, Edith Beckerman became Mrs. Lew R. Wasserman and the couple moved in with the Beckermans.

—⁓—

"WHEN WE MARRIED, we didn't talk along the lines of wealth," Edie maintained. "We wanted success, certainly, and I knew he was ambitious. But I never thought of him as an empire builder. In the thirties all you worried about was where your next dollar was coming from."

From where the newlywed Wassermans sat, the next dollar did not look as if it would come from the Mayfair Casino. The nightclub was drowning in red ink.

"The Mayfair Casino only lasted two years," said Herman Pirchner. "The owners wanted to put in an actual casino, but gambling was illegal. They hoped that would change, because [the Mayfair] couldn't survive without gambling."

Behind the scenes at Cleveland City Hall, strings were pulled. Politicians and journalists were wined and dined without success. Six months after its opening, the Mayfair was facing receivership.

The week following the Wassermans' wedding, Lew's employer announced in the *Plain Dealer* that the Mayfair would shut down for the summer. Only its cocktail lounge would remain open.

"Sophie Tucker will end her current engagement at the Casino Sunday," read the announcement. "The following Friday Estelle Taylor, movie actress and former wife of Jack Dempsey, will inaugurate a new policy of guest stars in the cocktail room."

The plan, according to the newspaper, was to reopen the club the week following Labor Day with band leader Ted Lewis and his orchestra heading the bill. The contract with Lewis, an MCA client, had already been signed, according to the Mayfair's publicist. But the article could not disguise a note of desperation.

The summer passed, as did the week after Labor Day, and still the main room of the Mayfair Casino remained closed. Finally, on September 19, 1936, the Cleveland newspapers reported that the nightclub that had opened with such bombast just one year earlier would be back in business the following week.

A steady supply of MCA talent passed through the club over the next few weeks, but what turned out to be equally significant to Lew Wasserman was that the men who supplied that talent to the Mayfair and virtually every other club, dance hall, and theater in Cleveland, got to know the Mayfair's glad-handing young publicist.

One of them was the head of MCA's Cleveland operation: a shrewd young operator from Chicago named DeArv Barton. The son of an abusive Iowa preacher who literally beat his son out of the house, Barton had met and married a young woman who, like him, seemed to know instinctively how to survive by her wits. At the beginning of the Depression, when neither of them could find a job anywhere, even in the thriving fringes of Chicago, they took out an ad in the classified section of a suburban newspaper promising to analyze handwriting for a dime. Soon they were advertising in newspapers all over the Midwest and taking in hundreds of dimes each week. But personalizing each handwriting analysis got to be too much of a chore. DeArv went to the Loop, looking for an easier way to make a living.

Before entering the handwriting game, Barton had tried his hand at booking bands and knew a thing or two about the vaudeville circuit. He also knew that MCA was fast becoming the premier booking agency in the Midwest. Jules Stein liked Barton's handwriting scam, hired him, and dispatched the Bartons to Cleveland.[2]

DeArv provided MCA talent to the Silent Syndicate's Mounds Club, the downtown hotels, and the nightclubs in Playhouse Square. According to Dorothy Barton, it was her husband who came up with stage names for a host of MCA performers. A young barber named Pierino Como wanted to call himself Nick Perido

---

[2] Jules Stein came to believe passionately in graphology, insisting that each future MCA executive submit a handwriting sample for analysis before he or she could be hired.

when he joined the Sammy Watkins band as its lead singer, but Barton advised him to stick with Perry Como. Another young gambler who gave up cardsharping to become a singer with the Freddy DeCarlo orchestra, changed his name on DeArv's advice, too: Dino Crocetti became Dean Martin.

Barton was clever and resourceful. Unfortunately, said Dorothy, he was not Jewish. "DeArv took a lot of heat for working for a Jewish company," said Mrs. Barton.

Even in the 1930s, MCA developed a reputation for hiring and promoting talented young Jews. Though executives all the way up to Jules Stein himself vehemently denied any conspiracy to concentrate control of the company in the hands of Jews, longtime employees who were not Jewish, like Barton, maintained for decades that Gentiles could climb only so high on the corporate ladder. Barton worked for MCA his entire life and never entered the pantheon of MCA's chiefly Jewish ruling hierarchy.[3]

"The idea of some Jewish conspiracy was nonsense, at least while my father was there," said Marguerite Madden, Billy Goodheart's daughter. "He never had a prejudiced bone in his body."

Merle Jacobs, Barton's second-in-command in Cleveland, was a Jew, but he never climbed any higher in the agency, either. He said that was probably because he chose music-making over deal-making after forming his own orchestra in the mid-1930s. Jacobs spent a good deal of time at the Mayfair listening to new bands perform and grew to know Wasserman well. He watched how the twenty-three-year-old handled himself when trouble surfaced at the club.

In mid-November, the newspapers reported that the Mayfair would be sold to the owners of the similar but far more successful French Casino in New York. Five days after that announcement, however, on November 19, 1936, the Mayfair filed for bankruptcy. The single largest of the Mayfair's debtors was one Nate Weisenberg, known to law enforcement throughout northern Ohio as the Slot Machine King because he held a monopoly on the manufacture, repair, and distribution of nightclub slots, even though such gambling devices were technically illegal.[4] Another creditor—MCA—was stiffed for $2,321.50.

Upon the Mayfair's declaration of bankruptcy, Lew learned fast that the odds on holding the bag for gangsters were way too long for anyone with common sense

---

[3]   Besides Goodheart, three other founding MCA agents—George Campbell, Mickey Rockford, and Karl Kramer—were Gentiles. Ironically, Kramer was refused membership at Hillcrest, the Jewish community's answer to L.A.'s anti-Semitic country clubs, because he was a goy.

[4]   Nine years later Weisenberg wound up being a debtor to the Mob instead of a creditor, and paid his bill with a shotgun blast to the back of his head. On February 24, 1945, he was found slumped over the wheel of his Lincoln coupe, parked just a few blocks from the Cleveland Heights neighborhood where Edie Wasserman grew up. When police found his body, Weisenberg was still wearing a diamond pinky ring.

to play. Harry Propper suddenly left town with a health problem, according to the young man who had just as suddenly risen from the role of Mayfair's publicity director to the rank of acting manager. In addition to keeping creditors away, Lew was responsible for fending off his former pals in the media who smelled blood. They quoted Wasserman as the captain of the sinking ship. On December 5 all three daily papers reported that the Mayfair Casino was to be sold at auction. It would have to close, but only for a short time, Lew assured his newspaper buddies.

As acting manager, Wasserman was supposed to be earning $100 a week—a $40 raise over his salary as the nightclub's advertising manager. It was a tidy paycheck for a twenty-three-year-old newlywed in the middle of the Depression, but how much longer could it last?

The Mayfair was sold on December 15, 1936, to a shady character named Durnes "Duke" Crane. By that time Lew had already made his move.

"His forte was advertising," said Merle Jacobs. "He was very clever, knew how to present things. The way he impressed me was that he said MCA needed to be more progressive, and he prepared a big sort of one-foot-wide by two-feet-long presentation book. Each page was his idea of how to present Lombardo et cetera—all the leading orchestras of the time. I brought it to DeArv's attention, he showed it to Bill [Stein], and they sent Lew to Chicago to meet Jules Stein."

Jules liked the fast-talking string bean and offered him $60 a week to come to work for him. Wasserman liked Jules, too. Stein was short, dark, and compact, like Lew's father—but far more successful and a whole lot smarter. Stein's parents, like Lew's, were Orthodox Jews, but Stein wasn't. After his bar mitzvah he had all but abandoned his parents' religion. Likewise, Lew went through the ancient ritual to satisfy his parents and, as soon as it was over, promptly forgot about it.

Lew swiftly accepted the $40 a week pay cut. He told friends he would take over the agency; Stein was an "old man" and couldn't last much longer. At the time, Jules was forty years old.

The week after Christmas, the Mayfair was back in business. Newspaper reporters once again praised the stage revues. Harry Propper even underwent a miraculous recovery and returned as the club's glad-handing manager. Cleveland high society was invited back to ring in the New Year at the ritziest nitery in the Midwest. But Lew and Edie Wasserman were not among them. They were on a train to Chicago, where they stayed at the Eastgate Hotel until Lew got acquainted with his new job. "My wife and I ended up sharing a Murphy bed for six months," Lew remembered.

Before 1937 came to an end, the Mayfair Casino would close again, this time for good.

SEVEN

Chicago and New York

1937–1938

Though he liked to boast in later years that Jules Stein hired him as MCA's first national publicity director, Lew actually started the way everyone else started at MCA: in the mail room.

"He didn't stay in shipping very long, but that is where he started," said Dorothea Campbell, whose husband, George, took the youngster under his wing. "[Lew] was intelligent and very charming. He wanted George to fill him in about every agent in the office: what they liked, what they didn't like, how to get on their good side. Then he used that [information] to get where he wanted to go. And he never forgot that George was the first one who helped him. Never."

"Dad and Lew were very close," said George and Dorothea's son, Bruce Campbell. "He could say to Lew, 'You damn kike Jew bastard! I'm gonna fucking kill you!' When I told people that, they'd say, 'Nobody *ever* talked to Lew that way!' And I'd say, 'My father did.' Every time he did that, he'd get a raise. Lew loved my father."

George Campbell advised the young man not to waste time. Deals were made outside the office, and he had to dress the part in order to graduate from the mail room. When Lew reported to work on his first day, Jules Stein didn't even let him work in the mail room until he bought a decent set of clothes. "You look shabby, boy. Go get a suit and come back tomorrow morning," Stein told him.

The next day Lew showed up in a red-and-blue sport coat. "You look like a racetrack tout," Stein sneered. "Come back in a black or blue suit."

Lew did and eventually got his first out-of-the-office assignment: the 1937 Michigan State Fair. Billy Stein handed him a talent roster and put him on the next train to Detroit.

"Wasserman did a phenomenal job at promoting and putting on the show at the Michigan State Fair with our talent," Stein recalled nearly forty years later.

"Wasserman even came back with a contract for the following year, which he wasn't asked to do. He showed his talent and ability so fast that he jumped over everyone." Lew was learning. He returned from Michigan a conquering hero.

The Chicago of 1937 was Lew's kind of town. Gone were the speakeasies, booze wars, and flappers. The Jazz Age had given way to the swing era, with the likes of Lombardo, the Dorsey brothers, and Benny Goodman all rising to the top of the music world, and MCA right along with them.

"We used to call him the Praying Mantis," said Cleveland deejay Bill Randle. "Selling bands was like selling whores, and Lew'd sell his own mother. Get a good price for her, too. He sold me a band once, the night before New Year's Eve. Only four people showed up, but he didn't care. He already had his money. He was that good."

One struggling MCA orchestra still trying to find a foothold in the exploding big band business was led by a slow-talking, nearsighted jokester from North Carolina. James Kern Kyser was tall, thin, and undistinguished but desperately hungry for success, not unlike Lew Wasserman, and he became Lew's first assignment.

A mediocre musician whose six original orchestra members couldn't even read music, Kyser had initially been overshadowed by more talented MCA clients. But Kay Kyser was persistent, and what his orchestra lacked in natural aptitude it made up for in staying power. In 1933 MCA had sent them to San Francisco and Los Angeles. In California, at Santa Monica's Miramar Hotel, Kyser came up with a crowd-pleasing gimmick called Singing Song Titles: the orchestra played a bar or two, followed by a singer crooning the title; then, after another minute or two of instrumental introduction, the singer belted out the rest of the song. The gimmick was such a hit that Jules Stein brought Kyser home to Chicago where, in 1934, he booked him into the Blackhawk Restaurant, the launching pad for MCA's top acts. Kyser remained at the Blackhawk for nearly three years, breaking the restaurant's attendance records.

Kyser was the city's number one sensation when Lew and Edie arrived in Chicago, but his popularity did not extend much beyond Illinois because the Monday night broadcasts from the Blackhawk were not on a network. In the few years since Stein and Goodheart had first learned how to exploit radio, the networks, particularly NBC, had come to dominate the airwaves. Independent stations—even powerhouses like Chicago's WGN—couldn't hold a candle to the reach of CBS, Mutual, and NBC's powerful Red and Blue networks. The late night hours that early programmers were once so desperate to fill with any kind of music, comedy, or drama now went at a premium. The only way to get a radio show in 1937, particularly a network show, was to find a sponsor with money and clout.

Before MCA's new national publicity director took over the Kay Kyser account, the orchestra seemed doomed to play out its days in Chicago.

"Lew Wasserman took credit for coming up with the name, the Kollege of

Musical Knowledge," recalled George Duning, Kyser's arranger and the real musical leader of the orchestra, but it was Kyser's clarinetist and sometime vocalist, Sully Mason, who suggested they call an audience-participation segment of the show Kay's Klass.

Lew understood timing and exploitation better than his clients did. He refined Mason's "Kay's Klass" gimmick, and by early 1938 the orchestra had become the backdrop for "Kay Kyser's Kampus Klass." On Lew's advice, Kyser turned over the actual music-making to Duning so that Kyser could stake out the spotlight for himself as "the Old Perfesser," a stern-faced parody of an academician. Sallow-cheeked Kyser, whose face looked menacingly dour unless he grinned, took to wearing a cap and gown on stage. He led his orchestra with a conductor's baton and scribbled pictures and title clues on a blackboard to help his audience guess the title of a song. The rest of the time he played ringmaster to an orchestra that had become a circus, complete with a stand-up clown named Ish Kabibble and a torch singer, Ginny Simms.

Kyser's popularity soared, and Wasserman took over.

Stein discussed strategy over lunch with his protégé at Henrici's Restaurant or the Home Drug Store at Clark and Randolph, both of which were frequented by show-biz types as well as the surviving hoods of the Capone era. In their first successful joint effort, Jules Stein and Lew Wasserman took Kyser's show to George Washington Hill, head of the American Tobacco Company, who agreed to sponsor a weekly slot over Mutual Broadcasting, the smallest of the national networks and the one with which WGN was affiliated. Within weeks Mutual's *Kay Kyser and His Kollege of Musical Knowledge* made American Tobacco's Lucky Strikes the nation's leading cigarette brand. Kyser's record albums suddenly flew off record store shelves all over the country. His theme song, "Thinking of You," became an overnight radio sensation. Mutual and MCA printed thousands of *Kollege of Musical Knowledge* diplomas, had "Music Master" Kay Kyser sign them, and mailed them to fans.

Within a few months, Stein and Wasserman convinced American Tobacco that the company had been thinking too small. They wanted to sell the show to a larger network, for which MCA would take a larger fee in addition to the 10 percent they charged Kyser and each member of his troupe. Both Kyser and American Tobacco agreed. The national response to the *Kollege of Musical Knowledge* was so overwhelming that both Kyser and Lucky Strikes moved on from Mutual to NBC, where Kyser's Kollege owned Wednesday night for years. The orchestra leader's move won him over 20 million listeners each week.

And MCA's Lew Wasserman, who took credit for inventing the idea of the radio package, moved right along with him.

By the time Wasserman arrived in Chicago, Al Capone had been cooling his heels in Alcatraz for six years. Meanwhile, his successor, a natty little mobster named Frank "the Enforcer" Nitti, steered the Chicago Mob into the movie business. Nitti's Hollywood extortion scheme eventually cost the industry $2.5 million and continued to reverberate for years after the last gangster was caught, gunned down, or sent to prison. The great movie studio shakedown also cost Hollywood its innocence and, for decades afterward, spawned rumors of Mob influence in the movie capital. Chicago during this era made a fine introductory course to the agency business, but it was nursery school compared to New York.

"MCA's top client was Tommy Dorsey, and no one could get along with Dorsey but Lew Wasserman," recalled veteran Hollywood columnist Jim Bacon. Dorsey would "get drunk, had a terrible temper. For that reason, they brought Lew back to New York."

Lew got his first taste of the Big Apple just as MCA was hitting its stride in Manhattan. Goodheart's office was shorthanded at the time due to illness, firings, and defections to other agencies, which made Lew's arrival all the more propitious.

In the decade since MCA opened in New York, Goodheart had moved his growing crew of expensively tailored sharks from Tin Pan Alley's Paramount Building to a tonier address: the white granite tower at 745 Fifth Avenue. There, Midtown civility and old-money sophistication melded with savvy entrepreneurs and upscale wanna-bes. Because Goodheart's agents no longer sold only bands, the location was perfect. In 1938, MCA offered virtually anything that entertained, from tap dancers and the Folies-Bergère to slapstick and Shipstad and Johnson's Ice Follies. If an act made an audience laugh or cry or otherwise kept them in their seats for more than twenty minutes, MCA could be counted on to be lurking in the loges, waiting for the first chance to sign them up.

A glut of agencies worked Broadway in the 1930s, but MCA rose above the rest to a level where it seriously threatened the primacy of the venerable William Morris Agency. With its army of cigar-chomping old-school agents and its motto, "No act too big, no act too small," William Morris owned Manhattan in the twenties and throughout most of the thirties. Under the guidance of diminutive Abe Lastfogel, the agency built the most impressive client list of any talent organization on the East Coast. William Morris had been so successful at signing virtually every other kind of talent that it never really took band booking seriously. That was left to second-rate outfits like MCA. But Goodheart's incessant aggressiveness and inroads into vaudeville began to shift Lastfogel's blasé attitude.

"MCA had considerable economic leverage, didn't mind using its power, and could be cruel," recalled Stein contemporary Chuck Suber. "William Morris was almost the opposite in those days. It was kind of a paternalistic old-line firm."

For years Goodheart's troops nibbled away at the stage acts that were William

Morris's bread and butter. When Lew arrived, Stein and Goodheart even began underwriting Broadway musicals.

"Music Corporation of America is considering expanding its activities to include legit production on a permanent basis," reported *Variety* on August 10, 1938. "J. C. Stein and brother, W. H. Stein, have been mulling the idea for some time. They recently formed a legit casting department in the New York office for outside booking of legit talent."

Jules was also expanding far beyond Broadway and the Loop. MCA opened branches in Atlanta, Dallas, Detroit, and San Francisco during the thirties. Jules himself spent more and more time in Los Angeles, and Bill Stein, whose health was failing, ran the San Francisco branch.

"MCA figures opening half-dozen new branch offices through U.S. and Canada," *Variety* reported. "Outfit has been growing steadily, originally starting as band booking office. Then added acts, girl lines, etc. Hotels, expos and niteries with ice shows followed. Niteries are considered in expansion plan of future."

In short, Lew arrived just as MCA was poised to expand the William Morris war nationally — a war that would last for more than a quarter of a century. As far as vaudeville was concerned, William Morris still had the edge: the Marx Brothers, Eddie Cantor, Maurice Chevalier, Burns and Allen. But as the 1930s wound to a close, the two agencies began competing head-to-head in the two arenas that would ultimately decide who ran Broadway and, later, Hollywood: band booking and radio programs. It was no accident that Wasserman's first MCA triumph, *Kay Kyser's Kollege of Musical Knowledge*, involved both a band and a radio program.

But MCA began putting a lot more than just orchestras on the air. Stein delivered everything to the network: stars, writers, directors, producers, even sponsors. With invaluable assistance from his old pal James Petrillo, Stein got a waiver of the American Federation of Musicians rule that forbade agents to act in the dual capacity of talent bookers and program producers. MCA was the only major agency the union allowed to package radio shows with its own talent.

Perhaps MCA's greatest coup was creating a network radio star out of a ventriloquist. MCA had actually had a chance to sign Edgar Bergen years earlier, when he was a struggling young gag writer in New York. Bergen had paid Bill Stein a visit when he heard that comedian Ken Murray was looking for a writer. After reviewing Bergen's work, however, Stein handed it back to him. "This is crap," he said. "Get out of the business."

Fortunately, Bergen did not take his advice. He used his own material to develop a ventriloquist's act, and a few years later Jules Stein begged for a second chance. They became fast friends, on and off stage, and Bergen became one of Stein's earliest radio-star clients.

Nobody could actually *see* Bergen talking to Charlie McCarthy and his other puppets during *The Chase and Sanborn Hour*, but clever scripts and Bergen's vocal tricks made millions of listeners *believe* they were hearing a man conversing with a wooden dummy over the NBC radio network each week.

—*⁓*—

WILLIAM MORRIS BEGAN to strike back at MCA. Goodheart's top band agent, Willard Alexander, had grown increasingly angry over Jules Stein's edict that Count Basie and other black acts could not be booked into certain upscale nightclubs and dance halls in the South and Midwest. Alexander ultimately threatened to quit over the issue. Joe Glaser, Louis Armstrong's manager, had ended his own brief career as one of Stein's executives in the early 1930s for the same reason.

Goodheart himself was not happy with MCA's pandering to prejudice. He tolerated the two-tier booking policy because, as his son Billy put it, "seeing his friends work at a second-class club was better than their not working at all."

When Lastfogel heard about Alexander's unhappiness, the William Morris chief got word to the MCA agent that he planned to open his own band-booking division. Alexander would be the perfect choice to head it, he suggested.

Alexander made the switch. In addition to Basie and other black acts, he tried wooing Benny Goodman to leave with him—an act of treason that Stein would never forgive. Goodman was bound by contract and declined, though he did make the switch five years later. Meanwhile Stein promoted Manie Sacks, a Philadelphia bachelor, to take over MCA's band division.

Stein relied increasingly on lawyers. For years he had used outside counsel, and he continued to do so when MCA itself was threatened. But for contracts and other corporate chores, he decided it was time to hire an in-house lawyer. When he asked the Columbia Law School dean for recommendations, Stein got the name of a 1934 graduate with a shrill voice and a similar disposition. Appropriately, Morris Schrier's surname was Yiddish for "screamer."

Though hired to handle contracts, Schrier did not confine his duties to the office. He became a Broadway first-nighter, acting as an unofficial bird dog who reported back to Stein himself on promising actors and musicians before newspapers even reviewed their plays.

But the addition of a general counsel who moonlighted as a talent scout didn't stanch the hemorrhage of agents from the New York office. Billy Goodheart leaned more and more on nonstop dynamo Sonny Werblin, who turned out to be his best agent. By 1938 the former office boy was a vice president and second only to Goodheart in the hierarchy of the New York office.

Werblin warned newcomers that if they were not prepared to work twelve hours a day, six days a week, there was no point in their even showing up. Like Goodheart, Werblin was not above teaching through harsh example. He'd pat a subordinate on the back for landing a client and tell him to head on home as a reward for his hard work. Then he'd close the deal and take the credit. Confronted with this betrayal, Werblin would smile grimly at the stung agent and say, "Let that be a lesson to you: don't trust anybody."

Goodheart continued to be a taskmaster, abusing and shrieking at Sonny, but now Sonny shrieked back. Their civil war had settled into a kind of sport in the years since Werblin had more than proved his worth to the office. At one point, new agent Irving "Swifty" Lazar talked Werblin into leaving MCA so they could strike out together on their own. Lazar even marched into Goodheart's office after mustering the courage to tell him off. To his surprise, Swifty was rewarded with a raise for having the guts to challenge the boss, but that did not dissuade him. Lazar wanted no more of MCA's backbiting. After he slammed Goodheart's office door, he announced to Werblin that they were finally free. They could now start up that new agency.

"Well, Jesus, I'm not ready to quit," said Werblin. "You shouldn't have done that without talking to me first. I'm not ready."

Nor would he be ready for another thirty years. Sonny loved the agency business, but he especially loved the quiet power of MCA. By 1938, Werblin had become such a workaholic that Goodheart himself forced him to take a vacation. Werblin's hair had already thinned and gone gray, adding twenty years to his appearance. He drove himself so hard that, at the age of twenty-eight, Sonny Werblin suffered what doctors at the time diagnosed as a serious heart attack.

"I question that now," said Marguerite Madden, Goodheart's daughter. "It wasn't a nervous breakdown, but I don't think it was a heart attack, either. It was more just sheer exhaustion."

Werblin retired to a cottage near Greenwich, Connecticut, with his bride, big band singer Leah Ray Hubbard, and stayed there for nearly a year. While Sonny recuperated, Goodheart felt his absence sorely. Stein threw his new protégé into the breach, and once again Lew fit the role of indefatigable Broadway agent to a tee. Whether it was the quiet threat of a young comer threatening his position as Goodheart's favorite, or simply his own hunger to return to the job, Werblin champed at the bit to get back to Manhattan.

But he need not have worried about Wasserman replacing him as Goodheart's heir apparent in New York. Before 1938 came to an end, Jules Stein ordered Lew and Edie to California to launch MCA's full-fledged attack on Hollywood.

ACT II

CORPORATION

1938–1960

Corporations have neither bodies to be punished nor

souls to be condemned. They therefore do as they like.

EDWARD THURLOW

There's no business like show business.

IRVING BERLIN

EIGHT

Hollywood

1938—1939

T he Wassermans moved into a rented bungalow at the corner of Devon Avenue
and Wilshire Boulevard near the new Westwood campus of UCLA, just a
block west of the Gentiles-only Los Angeles Country Club. Edie adjusted
uneasily to a life of quasi-domesticity while Lew jumped headlong into the
eighteen-hour-a-day, seven-day-a-week work schedule of a young agent.

Stein had just opened his MCA world headquarters in the center of Beverly
Hills, a little over a mile east of the Wassermans' home. Lew could arrive each
morning on the West L.A. streetcar line and walk one block to an opulent office
that starkly contrasted with the modest quarters where the Wassermans lived. The
brand-new white pillared two-story Georgian colonial structure at the juncture of
Crescent Drive and Burton Way was as much Jules Stein's declaration of war on
Hollywood as it was a functional warehouse for his growing antique collection.[1]
Jules hired no less a decorator than Dorothy Hammerstein, the wife of lyricist
Oscar Hammerstein II, who had recently opened her own interior design shop in
Beverly Hills. Virtually everyone who saw the 25,000-square-foot MCA headquar-
ters for the first time drew one of two mistaken conclusions: that it was the shoot-
ing set for Tara in *Gone With the Wind* or that it was Beverly Hills City Hall, which
was actually located across the street.

Jules bought the site in 1937 and leased it back at 3 percent interest on March

---

[1] With the approach of war in Europe, Stein found yet another reason to expand his antique
collection. British pounds could not be taken out of England, but British furniture could. He
and Doris went on a buying spree, before and after World War II, stocking up on furniture that
they would be able to turn back into cash on the other side of the Atlantic.

1, 1938, to a wholly owned subsidiary he called the Movie Corporation of Amer-ica.[2] The building was designed by preeminent black architect Paul Revere Williams, whose colonial home designs were then all the rage, and everything about it bespoke money and power, from the twin sweeping circular staircases, the handcrafted eighteenth-century English furniture, the massive globe in the center of the lobby, and the glittering $50,000 crystal chandelier, to the private park and freestanding colonnade outside Stein's second-story office window. Stein bought the 30-foot-high Tuscan marble colonnade from silent era comedienne Marion Davies, who originally had it constructed to stand at the entrance to her 144-room mansion, Ocean House, on the beach at Santa Monica.

Stein rose to his office by private elevator each morning. Like the president's White House business office, Stein's office was oval, with a 13-foot ceiling, 6-inch-thick walls, pine wainscoting, hardwood floors, and an antique marble fireplace. It was patterned after an eighteenth-century drawing room that had been disassem-bled in England, shipped to California, and reassembled on the second floor of MCA headquarters. Executive offices, along with the motion picture and radio departments, were also located on the second floor. Agents who handled vaude-ville acts, bands, and one-night stands worked on the ground floor. In addition to thirty understated but expensively furnished office suites, the building housed a radio station, a screening room, a kitchen, and a hidden bar that swung into place in the dining room at the touch of a button.

It was an awe-inspiring place for Lew to arrive each day to take on a dozen major studios and the more than 150 other agencies that had been operating in Hollywood long before MCA arrived.

Mrs. Wasserman was not nearly so inspired. Within a year Edie was pregnant with their first and only child, Lynne Kay, born on October 18, 1940.[3] Edie, the princess from Cleveland Heights, was no more cut out to be a mother and haus-frau than was the imperious Doris Stein. She lobbied as hard as Doris to get men-tioned in the right columns, without a fraction of the success.

"Edie hired a publicist as soon as she got out here so she could get her name in the papers," said the daughter of one of MCA's earliest agents, "but what she didn't realize was that L.A. was just as anti-Semitic in its own way as any of the cities back east. All the country clubs—Lakeside, Wilshire, Los Angeles, Bel Air—excluded Jews. They just weren't mentioned on the society page."

Just as Jules became Lew's role model, Edie lusted after Doris's lifestyle, though her junior agent husband could ill afford the Steins' extravagance. In the

---

[2]   He also bought a building across the street, which he sold for a sizable profit to a developer in the 1950s. When the purchaser painted the building yellow, Jules bought the building back. He had it repainted beige, a color that was more to his taste.

[3]   Lew gave his daughter her middle name after his first major MCA client, Kay Kyser.

beginning, Edie was an agent's widow, watching helplessly as her absentee husband's boundless energy generated riches for the Steins, while the Wassermans got only a taste of affluence.

Doris, on the other hand, bit into the good life. She relegated child-rearing to a stern caricature of a German nanny named Maria Hirschberg and spent more time shopping, socializing, and globe-trotting than she did raising her daughters.

"I hate Hollywood orphan stories, but my parents were always traveling to Europe or New York, and I still remember writing pathetic little letters to them," recalled Jean Stein. "'Dear Mother and Dear Father, I hope you come home soon.'"

Jules once told his older daughter that, had she been born male, she would have "owned this town." But he and Doris were far too busy insinuating themselves into the Hollywood pecking order to bother much with girl children. Both Jean and her younger sister, Susan, had to look to each other for nurture while, in Lew Wasserman, Jules found the son he never had.

—◦◦◦—

YEARS BEFORE LEW and Edie arrived, the Steins had established part-time residence in L.A. Following his mother's death in 1935, Jules spent several months each year in California.

Recalled gossip columnist Hedda Hopper, "Soon after the Steins moved to California, the good doctor told me at a party: 'I'm going to be king of Hollywood one day.'"

Jules and Doris rented a Santa Monica beach house once owned by Douglas Fairbanks and Mary Pickford, and later leased the Beverly Hills home of director King Vidor, where they hobnobbed with a constant stream of film royalty, ranging from Edgar Bergen and Irene Dunne to Hal Roach, Raoul Walsh, William Randolph Hearst, and Marion Davies. Doris and Marion shopped together, attended opening day at Santa Anita and Hollywood Park, lunched at Chasen's and the Polo Lounge, and shared the fashionable hobby of cultivating rare orchids—the more exotic, the better. At forty, Marion retired from film after twenty years of Hearst trying to make her a star. She was a woman of leisure, which had great appeal to Doris.

The Steins dined often with Hearst and Marion in Sunset Strip glamour restaurants and frequently visited San Simeon. Hearst indulged Jules's passion for antiques by letting him prowl through the thousands of crates of Old World treasures stored in the San Simeon warehouses. The Steins even hired Charles Harris, the Hearst butler, when a bad heart forced Hearst to shut down his beloved castle following World War II and move back to Beverly Hills with Marion.

Jules learned firsthand from Hearst about manipulating the media. The newspaper tycoon's handpicked Hollywood crone, Louella Parsons, regularly mentioned Jules and Doris in her nationally syndicated column. Their social status soared.

Strictly from a business standpoint, it was the Ice Follies—a troupe of figure skaters led by entrepreneurs Roy Shipstad and Oscar Johnson—that really sparked Stein's interest in settling permanently in Hollywood. Until he gave it the MCA touch, the Shipstad and Johnson Ice Follies was essentially just another struggling vaudeville act.

The hottest ice-skating troupe in the mid-1930s was the Ice Capades, and Stein had sent Wasserman to Atlantic City during the young man's 1937 New York apprenticeship to see if he could persuade them to sign. No dice. It was one of the few failures Stein's young protégé suffered in his early years. If Lew couldn't sign them, no one could, Stein figured, so he decided that if he couldn't buy a successful ice show, he would create his own.

Stein simply used the same formula he had perfected with touring bands: exclusivity, hype, and limited engagements. With seventeen acts featuring several dozen young women skaters in ultra short skirts, advance publicity made the Ice Follies an instant hit. Because the show came to town for only a single three- or four-week engagement each year, patrons lined up to pay five times what they would normally pay for movie admissions just to get a peek. "Practically all ice rinks were in the red and in receivership until we came along with the traveling ice shows," said skater Everett McGowan.

In Hollywood, Stein's Ice Follies had an even bigger edge over rivals like the Ice Capades. The Steins urged MGM's Louis B. Mayer to order his stars to come out for an evening on the ice. After the show, everyone laced up and took to the rink for one enormous photo opportunity. Even those who had no interest in the fine art of figure skating found it hard to resist the possibility of seeing a real live celebrity slip on the ice.

Following the star-studded success of the Ice Follies, it made perfect sense that the show would become Stein's entrée into movies. Again it was Parsons who reported in her column of July 14, 1938, that "all the members of the Ice Follies troupe have been signed by MGM. The deal, so long pending between Metro and Jules Stein of the Music Corporation of America, was closed yesterday and the price is reported to be close to $150,000."

———⌇∿⌇———

UNIVERSAL STUDIOS FOUNDER Carl Laemmle created the star system back in 1915 when he discovered that audiences responded better to a Mary Pickford than to some anonymous Biograph Girl—Pickford's *nom de film* when she went by her real name, Gladys Mary Smith. Laemmle, a former pants salesman from Oshkosh, Wisconsin, found he could throw anything on the screen with Pickford in it and people would pay to see it. The unfortunate aspect of having stars to pull them in at the box office was that the stars were no longer satisfied to work for bus money and a sack lunch. They wanted star bucks and all the pampering that came to be known as star treatment. Within twenty years of Laemmle's discovery of Pickford, the actress was a retired multimillionaire, while Laemmle fell into bankruptcy, lost his studio, and died broke.

Nonetheless, the early movie moguls continued to rely more and more on their stars, keeping them in line a little better than Laemmle did through a rigid seven-year studio contract that cost performers much personal freedom but rewarded them with handsome salaries and perks such as Cadillacs, designer wardrobes, and personal valets. Throughout the twenties, thirties, and much of the forties, young actors and actresses flocked to Hollywood begging for these long-term deals, only to cry out in protest when they discovered later on that they had become contractual chattels who could defy their studio only at the risk of never working in movies again.

Irving Thalberg, Laemmle's production chief during the 1920s and later a legend in his own right at MGM, perfected the star system in the early 1930s. "He considered actors to be charming, vital, and beautiful children," wrote Thalberg biographer Bob Thomas. "Like children, they were to be enjoyed and admired for their ingenious qualities and to be tolerated when their behavior seemed abnormal. They were, after all, exceptionally emotional persons, since the very nature of their work required trafficking in human feelings. So they were to be forgiven tantrums and erratic behavior, as long as they caused no unreasonable interruption of the making of movies, which was Thalberg's consuming occupation. He also believed that actors, like children, should not be allowed to make major decisions about their own destinies."

Thalberg's philosophy became part of MCA's creed in its move into Hollywood. Another Thalberg utterance underscored Stein's own belief that the men who controlled the strings should never upstage their puppets: "If you are in a position to give credit, you don't need it."

Betty Grable first fell under the MCA yoke in 1933, when she joined the Ted Fiorito Orchestra. One of Stein's earliest discoveries, Fiorito was a degenerate gambler—the perfect prey for MCA. Whenever Fiorito dropped a month's salary at the racetrack, he'd turn to Stein for help, and he wound up signing himself deeper and deeper into MCA's debt. By the time Betty Grable began singing for him, MCA had come to own Fiorito, but Grable belonged to Frank and Victor Orsatti, college football stars who were among the first agents to represent stars of professional sports as well as Hollywood movies.[4] Besides Edward G. Robinson, Alice Faye, Judy Garland, and a host of directors, including Preston Sturges and Frank Capra, the Orsatti brothers signed blond Sonja Henie, the figure-skating star of the 1928, 1932, and 1936 Olympics, and created a traveling ice show around her that rivaled MCA's Ice Follies.

But Grable was not an instant success. At seventeen, she didn't act or sing very well. She did, however, have the breasts, buttocks, legs, and peekaboo smile to titillate audiences, and she could carry a tune. So Grable toured with Fiorito's orchestra for nearly a year before getting back into movies.

The Orsattis got her regular work, including a couple of supporting roles in Fred Astaire–Ginger Rogers musicals for RKO, and Grable's name crept higher and higher in the credits. She still worked from picture to picture with no offers of a long-term contract. Her real fame came from her offscreen love life.

On December 20, 1937, she married Jackie Coogan and spent the next year locked with her husband in a fearsome court battle with Coogan's estranged mother over the former child star's $4 million fortune. In the end, Coogan netted $35,000 after paying his lawyers. The marriage broke up shortly thereafter, on January 20, 1939. Newspaper columnists speculated that Betty dumped Jackie because he wasn't worth the millions she thought she had married, but that was only partially true. Practically from their honeymoon, Coogan made no secret of his own promiscuity, bringing girls home with him where Betty would catch them in bed.

But Betty was no angel. Like many young actresses of the era, she chose to abort troublesome pregnancies rather than jeopardize her career. She dated the reputedly well-endowed clarinetist Artie Shaw shortly after she left Coogan and even returned to former boyfriend George Raft's bedroom for a while, despite the fact that he was now married.

In 1938, Jules Stein bought Grable's contract from the Orsattis for $2,500 and proceeded to build her into a star.

Wasserman got involved in Betty's career shortly after her separation from Coogan, when MCA offered her as part of a radio package featuring bandleader Phil Harris and black comedian Eddie "Rochester" Anderson. MCA wanted $8,500 a week, but before any network made an offer, Harris bowed out and the package disintegrated. MCA rebounded and sent the gravelly voiced Rochester and lily-white Grable on tour together as a vaudeville act at $1,500 a week.

In July of 1939, MCA booked them both with Jack Haley, who played the Tin Man in *The Wizard of Oz*, in three shows daily at the Treasure Island Music Hall

---

[4] The Orsattis had an early advantage over MCA in signing talent, according to a March 22, 1962, Justice Department memo. "Frank Orsatti had a special in with MGM" because he supplied prostitutes to Louis B. Mayer.

in San Francisco. They were a hit. At Jules Stein's urging, New York theatrical scout Louis Shurr caught the act and recommended Grable for a starring role in the Cole Porter Broadway musical *DuBarry Was a Lady*.

That was all Stein's new Hollywood crew needed. Using the synergy of her Broadway contract plus the success of her road show with Rochester, MCA went to work. The same Darryl Zanuck who had dumped the Ritz Brothers was suddenly interested in the all-new Betty Grable. Betty signed with Twentieth Century Fox on November 14, 1939, at $750 a week, with the proviso that her seven-year contract was not to commence until thirty days after the end of her Broadway run. Her Fox movie career wouldn't begin until July 1, 1940, just in time for her to become the number one pinup girl of World War II.

But first she would have to clean up her tawdry image as a boy toy. With former press agent Lew Wasserman in her corner, she was well on her way to becoming America's sweetheart.

———∿∿∿———

BETTY GRABLE WAS an exception to the MCA formula. Jules Stein wasn't usually interested in building careers. He preferred to buy stars at their peak and exploit them for all they were worth as he had attempted to do with the Ritz Brothers.

Stein began shopping for whole agencies, as he had done with marked success back in Chicago. At the instigation of Stein's old friend James Petrillo and the American Federation of Musicians, the Federal Radio Commission — forerunner of the Federal Communications Commission — began holding antitrust hearings in 1939 on the legality of the networks both producing shows and representing their own talent. To keep Bill Paley's network out of hot water with the government, MCA gladly bought his Columbia Artists Bureau from CBS for a reported $500,000. Then Stein arranged to purchase twenty half-hour spots each week on the network to showcase his newfound treasure trove of talent.

"MCA was never part of old Hollywood," said former MCA executive Bob Hussong. "They had to work hard at getting into pictures when the MGM, Columbia, and Fox people were already there, and they did it through the agencies that they acquired."

Not every agency gave in to Stein so readily. To pull the bigger and more successful agents into its maw, MCA had to offer more than cash. Stein offered Johnny Beck Jr., head of Associated Artists, a vice presidency in exchange for a client list that included Errol Flynn and Phil Harris and, even more important, for getting him past the gates and into the offices of the studio brass, like Louis Mayer.

MCA offered an executive position plus a buyout fee to agent William Meiklejohn, who represented nearly a hundred actors and writers ranging from Oscar winner Hattie McDaniel to acerbic author Dorothy Parker. Meiklejohn joined

MCA in May of 1939 to set up the motion picture division, where he was later credited with signing Jackie Cooper, Judy Garland, and Jackie Coogan. But he did not remain an MCA vice president long. Within a year, Paramount named Meiklejohn executive in charge of casting and talent, a position he held for twenty-one years. During that time, MCA had a secure—some said "cozy" was a better word—relationship with Paramount, the studio in which the Stein Family Trust held a 10 percent shareholder stake.[5]

Part of Meiklejohn's legacy to MCA during his brief stay as vice president was a pair of star-crossed actors who wound up marrying shortly after Stein bought them. Sarah Jane Fulks, a.k.a. Jane Wyman, had signed with Meiklejohn in 1938 after knocking around Hollywood as a bit player for nearly a decade. Her future husband was a relative newcomer who had been with Meiklejohn since 1937, when he gave up his job as a sports announcer in Des Moines. Ronald Reagan earned $90 a week at radio station WHO before he came to Hollywood where Meiklejohn assigned him to agent George Ward. Ward negotiated Reagan's first twenty-six-week contract at Warner Brothers at $200 a week, and on June 1, 1937, Reagan officially switched careers.

Twenty-three-year-old Wyman was married at the time to a New Orleans dressmaker nearly twice her age, but that didn't stop her from flirting with Reagan. Reagan was himself engaged for a time to actress Ila Rhodes, but even before Wyman divorced her husband in December of 1938, Reagan had broken off his engagement and had begun dating Wyman.

By the time MCA bought the Meiklejohn Agency, Reagan and Wyman were a regular item in Louella Parsons's column. She even broke the exclusive news of their engagement. In late 1939, when Parsons sponsored a nationwide vaudeville tour featuring Hollywood actors, she happily reported Ronald Reagan and Jane Wyman had fallen in love.

With that kind of buildup, it made perfect sense that the Reagans would begin showing up on the social circuit as guests of Jules and Doris Stein. Their careers, however, had been handed off to Lew Wasserman.

—◦◦◦—

As WORLD WAR II approached, Hollywood's attitude toward Jews began to shift. In an August 4, 1937, memo to Colonel Jason Joy, head of Twentieth Century Fox

---

[5]   While Stein no longer held the 10 percent stake by 1961, antitrust prosecutors of the U.S. Justice Department revealed in an internal memorandum that they were investigating "a rumor in the industry to the effect that there is some sort of relationship between Paramount and MCA, and that MCA dictates the shows that will be produced at Paramount."

publicity in Europe, studio attorney Emilio C. de Lavigne gave him a rundown on Fox contract writers and directors who were Jewish.

Like other major studios, Fox did not see itself as anti-Semitic, just practical. As Hitler built his National Socialist Party into a killing machine, Germany continued to be a ravenous consumer of Hollywood films, and the studios, most of which were headed by Jewish East European immigrants, were content to take their share of the box office returns. But Nazi propagandists made it increasingly difficult for anything tainted by Jewish hands to find its way into German theaters. Thus, when tough-talking, cigar-chomping comic actor Ned Sparks caught the attention of German censors, they demanded to know his parentage. Fox attorneys complied: "Ned Sparks: Aryan mother, Scotch-English father. Canadian. Neither Jewish."

At MCA, also run chiefly by Jews, the impact was doubly vexing. The war not only shut down MCA's London office, but also dramatically cut the European tour commissions MCA earned from its bands and vaudeville acts.

There was also the specter of the draft. Reservists like James Stewart had been called up well ahead of Pearl Harbor, but the loss of leading men wasn't Hollywood's only worry. For Stein, there was also the prospect of losing his best agents. When they did go, he rewarded their patriotism. Harry Tatelman, the newly hired head of the MCA literary department, received a $100 check from MCA every month during his World War II service.

But most of the top echelon did not serve.

In New York a fully recovered Sonny Werblin took Goodheart's place at the MCA helm while former Columbia Artists Bureau chief Herb Rosenthal became Werblin's second-in-command. Neither was in danger of conscription. Werblin's heart attack rendered him 4F, and Rosenthal went from 1A to 4F to 3A, an exempt category for men with dependents.

In California, Taft Schreiber's weak eyes and constant sinusitis made him similarly exempt, but Wasserman was not quite so fortunate. With a wife and child as dependents, he was initially 3A, but his status changed seven times during the war. Twice he was classified 1A, but each time the draft board put his name in the pool of potential draftees, Wasserman quickly and mysteriously managed to get a deferment on grounds that his exemption from military service would aid the "national health, safety or interest."

From his deft handling of MCA's draftable stars, Lew knew how to dodge military service. When army reservist Ronald Reagan looked as though he'd get the call, for example, Wasserman kept his star client out of the impending war. Reagan had already won a deferment because Jane had just given birth to daughter Maureen, making Reagan responsible for two dependents, but the pre–Pearl Harbor military buildup once again put him in jeopardy.

"Attached is the type of letter which should go off immediately in connection with the Ronald Reagan matter," Lew wrote to the studio on September 3, 1941. "Again let me point out to you that we have been advised by high-ranking officials of the Reserve Corps that it is vitally important that Mr. J. L. Warner or Mr. Hal Wallis sign this letter."

Lew's form letter, addressed to the assistant secretary of war in Washington, D.C., pointed out on behalf of Warner Brothers Studio that Reagan "has been in our continuous employ as a motion picture actor since June 1st, 1937, and at present is under contract to our studio for the next three consecutive years.

"Lt. Reagan has been notified that he will be called to active duty with the army and subsequent to his receipt of this notice we requested and received from the War Department a deferment."

Wasserman advised Jack Warner to name some of the film projects the studio had purchased for Reagan and to point out that his absence would "represent serious financial loss to the studio and to him, especially as the studio does not have a backlog of pictures which has [sic] appeared and he would therefore be off the screen for a very long period of time.

"Therefore, in view of these facts we respectfully request that said Ronald Reagan be placed in the War Department reserve pool. In the event that this cannot be done, we also request that he be placed in a deferred class for so long a reasonable period of time as will be necessary to adjust our production schedules and rearrange our plans."

Lew's ploy did not keep Reagan out of the military for the whole war, but it did buy him enough time to make one more significant deal with Warner Brothers. In the summer of 1941, just before Reagan's active-duty dilemma, Wasserman hammered out a new seven-year contract with Warner Brothers, calling for three times the salary Reagan had been earning under his original contract. Now dubbed "the Errol Flynn of the B's," Reagan would earn a total of $758,000 over the life of the contract in exchange for forty weeks of movie work each year. Wasserman renegotiated Jane Wyman's contract at the same time, boosting her from $150 to $750 a week.

To underscore his own satisfaction with the new contracts, Jack Warner sent a $600 bonus check to the Reagans. What neither Wasserman nor the Reagans knew at the time was that Warner had seen an advance print of Reagan's latest movie, a melodrama called Kings Row, and was convinced the dark psychological tale of three friends growing up in small-town America was Reagan's breakthrough film. Indeed, Kings Row would become a 1942 Oscar nominee for Best Picture.

Reagan's performance in his role as a double amputee was universally praised. When Lew heard the strong positive reaction to Kings Row, and especially to Reagan, he returned to the bargaining table.

Kings Row — in which Reagan uttered the line "Where's the rest of me?"

which later became the title of his autobiography— is arguably his best film. Next to doomed quarterback George Gipp in *Knute Rockne, All American,* it is the role for which Reagan has been most remembered. And it is the role Wasserman used to coax Jack Warner back to the negotiating table while the ink was still wet on Reagan's new $758,000 contract.

The renegotiation, as it turned out, was designed to enhance Wasserman's reputation as much as to gain more money for his client. The new contract wouldn't go into effect until the war ended and Reagan was once more a civilian, but it was important that gossip about the new contract spread through the film colony immediately. As Reagan himself recalled,

In spite of the newness of my contract, Warner's contacted Lew about tearing that one up and starting all over. One thing about the new contract puzzled me. All contracts are for forty weeks a year; mine was for forty-three. This particular demand of Lew's puzzled Jack Warner too. When all the commas were in place, J.L. said to Lew, "Now will you tell me why I've given in to the only forty-three-week deal in the whole industry?"

Lew grinned like a kid with a hand in the cookie jar. "I knew you wouldn't go higher than $3,500," he said, "and I've never written a $1 million deal before—so three extra weeks for seven years makes this my first $1 million sale."

NINE

Bette, Betty, and the Big Time

1940–1941

With World War II about to begin, MCA still had no mega–movie stars in its stable — no actor with the same stature that Guy Lombardo had in the band business in 1929 when MCA broke into the big time in New York. As with Lombardo, Jules Stein understood that one hot celebrity would automatically draw other celebrities to his agency.

Buying client lists and seducing other successful agents to join MCA hadn't done the trick. MCA owned the Reagans and Betty Grable and had recently stolen a young New York stage actor named Jules Garfinkle from the Arthur Lyons Agency. The labor board forced Garfinkle to pay his former agents almost $25,000 in lost commissions, but he said it was worth it to have Lew Wasserman representing him. After moving to Hollywood and reinventing himself as John Garfield, he figured that only about one out of four roles that Lyons had gotten him had been any good. Lew would change all of that.

But Garfield and the other MCA clients were still a few years away from achieving bona fide superstar status, just as MCA was still a long way from conquering Hollywood.

In an ambitious three-part series titled "Hollywood's Ten Per Centers," published in the *Saturday Evening Post* in August 1942, journalist Alva Johnston devoted over 12,000 words to Hollywood's "flesh peddlers," naming every major player in town...except MCA.

To really play in the big leagues, MCA needed a magnet. Stein encouraged his troops to set their sights on the number one actress of the day: Bette Davis.

In some respects, Stein couldn't have picked a better target. Davis had been a star since 1934 when, at the age of twenty-six, she played opposite Leslie Howard in the melodrama *Of Human Bondage*. Since then she had made four pictures a year for Warner Brothers, won two Academy Awards — for *Dangerous* in 1935 and

Jezebel in 1938 — and was nominated for a third in *Dark Victory*. By 1941 she was earning $5,000 a week.

She was practical and regarded acting as a business, but she remained as quick-tempered and capricious as any star ever turned out by the studio system. Before MCA, she had at least half a dozen different agents, but found none who could deal with her tantrums and fight the studio for her at the same time. Those who catered to her often childish demands gave up on her hard-nosed attitude about the business side of making movies, and those who excelled at nuts-and-bolts contract issues couldn't handle her whining.

"She is a sensitive individual with immense talents, but she is moody," Stein explained to journalist Michael Pye thirty years later, in describing how he deftly handled the actress. "At least I could understand her problems. Go out to visit and not talk business, talk about everything else."

Schmoozing for the sake of schmoozing became a cornerstone of Lew Wasserman's agency education.

"Jules taught Lew the value of entertaining someone when you *don't* have a problem," recalled one of Wasserman's longtime lawyers. "The friendly lunch — that's the one the client will remember, because you did it just because they are a client, a *friend*, not because you can get them to sign a contract or make a deal at that particular moment."

Until Stein came along, Bette understood herself better than any of her agents.

"As a happy person, I can work like hell," she once observed. "As an unhappy one, I make myself and everyone around me unhappy. Also, I know in a business where you have a fickle public to depend on, the money should be made when you mean something, not when the public has had time to tell you to go to hell."

Stein got to Davis through Lester Linsk, an agent who roomed with Bette's ex-husband, bandleader Harmon Nelson. When Linsk came to Jules looking for a job and Stein discovered that Linsk and Nelson were pals, he put Linsk on the MCA payroll at $150 a week. He was not particularly interested in him as an agent; Stein hired Linsk for the express purpose of sweet-talking Nelson into pressuring his agency-hopping ex-wife to sign with MCA.

The gimmick worked. For a brief time Linsk acted as Bette Davis's personal agent at MCA. But by the end of 1940, Linsk was out of the picture.[1] He'd served his purpose, and Stein decided it was time to pass MCA's first superstar on to his newly appointed vice president for motion picture talent. From that point forward, Lew Wasserman handled Bette Davis's every need.

———

[1] Linsk remained attached to MCA through World War II, after which he started his own agency. He eventually became a producer at Twentieth Century Fox.

LEW LANDED HIS second star client on his own, and he found him on Broadway, not in Hollywood. Paul von Hernreid was an Austrian stage actor who had fled to the United State after the German invasion. He'd made a couple of films, but had gone unnoticed until he starred on Broadway in *Flight to the West,* a play about the German invasion.

"Suddenly Hollywood awakened to my existence and offers started pouring in," he recalled in his memoirs. Wasserman's was one of the first. He showed up at Hernreid's door in March 1941 dressed in the MCA uniform: dark suit, white shirt, black tie. Lew charmed him immediately. He seemed a bit too young to the thirty-four-year-old Hernreid, but there was no mistaking either his enthusiasm or his determination.

"You tell me what you want, and I'll get it," the tall, thin young man told Hernreid.

Hernreid made what he believed to be an impossible proposition. He demanded $2,000 for a two-week option. If MCA delivered a contract within that time, Hernreid would repay the $2,000 from his first studio paycheck. If MCA failed, Hernreid would keep the money and shop elsewhere for an agent.

"What else?" Lew asked without blinking an eyelash.

"I am, as you Americans say, hot now, so this is the best time to go after it," said Hernreid. "In this business I could be forgotten in another two weeks."

"Fair enough," Lew said. "And the contract?"

Hernreid wanted the standard seven-year studio contract at no less than $25,000 a picture, and he wanted to make only one film a year. He had to be cast as the male lead, and he was always to be the actor who wound up at the end with the girl. Furthermore, he would be available only from May 13 to September 1. The rest of the year he would spend on Broadway.

"I'll get it for you," Wasserman promised.

The following day Lew gave Hernreid a $2,000 check and shook his hand. Hernreid, who felt bad afterward for taking advantage of the young man's over-confidence, promised himself that he'd drop his $25,000 asking price if a studio met most of his other outrageous terms. Privately, Hernreid thought the dark-haired MCA man was crazy. But two days later Wasserman called.

"You're going to star opposite Ginger Rogers in a picture for RKO. I bettered your price. You'll get $32,000, and you're expected out on the coast by May 15."

Hernreid blanched and never questioned Lew's sanity again. He used his $2,000 advance to buy a Chrysler, which he and his wife, Lisl, drove from New York to Hollywood. When the Hernreids arrived in Beverly Hills, Wasserman told him RKO wanted to change his name to Paul Henreid. Then he stared off into space, avoiding eye contact with his new client or his wife. There was one other thing, he said: the studio demanded that Lisl disappear.

While Paul raged at this request, Lew patiently explained that a romantic male lead had to be single. Swooning ticket buyers didn't pay to see a married man ravishing women on the screen. Lisl Hernreid saw the point.

"I understand completely, and of course I'm all for Paul becoming a star," she said. "But since I'll be living without Paul, I'll need some money myself. After all, without Paul I'll have to pay different gentlemen to take me out, and I'll need a decent salary for that."

Wasserman sealed the bargain. The public didn't learn until much later that Bette Davis's frozen-faced heartthrob in *Now, Voyager*—whose simple act of lighting two cigarettes and handing her one of them became a widely imitated act of seduction—was actually married.

By 1941, Wasserman had carved out a place for himself in Hollywood. He hadn't been in California a year before the name Lew R. Wasserman began turning up regularly in *Billboard* and *Variety* as *the* consummate new dealmaker in town—wise beyond his twenty-eight years. He was clearly the dominant force in MCA's fast-rising motion picture department. His only real competitors within the company were vice presidents Taft Schreiber, head of the West Coast music department, and Sonny Werblin, chief of the New York office. Both were five years older than Lew, and both had been with the agency almost from its beginning. Schreiber and Werblin were Stein favorites. They were tough, exceptionally shrewd, and, when necessary, charming.

But neither possessed Wasserman's calculated mix of gracious tolerance and grim confidence. Lew could deal effectively with junior agents and studio titans. He pampered stars, but could just as easily dress them down and still not risk leaving them angry. He combined the cool magnetism of a courtier with the awful justice of an executioner. In another time and place he could have been a general, a prince, or a spy.

"He is the student who surpassed the teacher," Stein was fond of telling friends in later years. Lew did not share the same esteem for his mentor, even though he respected Stein's money and his power. He was a team player, but he had his heart set on sooner or later owning the team.

Stein lived like one of the European counts he and Doris so admired, but he hated to part with money. He eschewed the luxury cabins on the Superchief, preferring to travel in tourist class, and he drove himself if it wasn't too far. Once, on a trip back to Missouri to visit his in-laws, Stein's Rolls-Royce broke down outside of Albuquerque. He booked two seats on the next Greyhound bus to Kansas City and sat in the back of the coach with a black leather physician's valise between himself and his wife. Doris refused to go anywhere without her jewelry, but Jules was too cheap to insure and ship it. So he carried several thousand dollars' worth of pearls, diamonds, and rubies in his little black bag.

Stein delighted in telling how he snookered a movie pioneer out of one of the most exclusive hilltop estates in southern California. Location, location, location—at MCA and at home, Stein and Wasserman focused on getting a useful address.

It took four years of shopping to find Misty Mountain, a bargain mansion overlooking the entire vista of Los Angeles. Fred Niblo, the director of such silent movie classics as *Ben Hur* and *The Mark of Zorro* and the first chairman of the Academy of Motion Picture Arts and Sciences, built the semicircular Spanish-style estate in 1928 for $285,000. But sixty-six-year-old Niblo, who hadn't made a film since 1933, had fallen on hard times and the southern California real estate market was depressed. In the spring of 1940 he put his beloved 8,651-square-foot home up for sale at $60,000. Stein offered $50,000. Niblo refused.

In August, Niblo came across a piece of business property he wanted, made the down payment, and brokered his mansion through a realty firm in an effort to get his asking price. The broker offered the estate at $45,000. Weeks passed. No offers. Meanwhile, escrow was about to close on the land he'd bought. Niblo grew desperate and ordered the broker to sell to the highest bidder. In October he sold Misty Mountain to the Steins for $35,000.

The following year, Lew and Edie bought their first home, which they got for less than $10,000 from the writer Horace McCoy, whose novel would become the basis for the 1969 movie *They Shoot Horses, Don't They?* but it was a cracker box compared to Misty Mountain. Located in the déclassé flatlands, at the corner of Sierra Drive and Santa Monica Boulevard, the two-story stucco structure was a fine suburban family home, a veritable mansion by 1941 standards. But the neighborhood bordered on West Hollywood and the houses were among the least expensive in Beverly Hills. Most of the lots on the Wassermans' block remained undeveloped until several years later, and the vacant property grew thick with weeds. It was hardly the address of a major power broker in as ostentatious a business as motion pictures.

The home at 502 Sierra had none of the isolated baronial splendor of the Stein estate, which Doris had redecorated to resemble a smaller, more tasteful version of San Simeon. Though the Steins lived just ten minutes from downtown Beverly Hills, their hidden mansion remained pristine, almost primeval. Deer and coyote still roamed the nearby woods, and the nearest neighbors lived a half mile down the single winding road that ended at the Steins' guarded gate. Among its charms were a rose garden, a greenhouse where Doris cultivated cymbidiums, and two swimming pools. The pool for the adults was distinguished from the children's (complete with its own separate poolhouse) by a large planter that spelled out Doris's initials in carefully pruned foliage.

For water sports on a grander scale, the Steins bought another mountaintop estate three years later, on the shores of Lake Arrowhead next door to hotelier Conrad Hilton, and chauffeured an occasional star or two up the Crestline Highway to amuse their impressionable preteen daughters, Jean and Susan. When the girls went off to college in the 1950s, the Steins sold the Arrowhead retreat and lived in one of their apartments in New York, London, or Paris whenever they grew bored with Misty Mountain's splendid year-round weather.

The Wassermans had no such retreats and not even a single swimming pool. Nonetheless, to Lew and Edie their first Beverly Hills address had all the advantages. The Pacific Electric Railway ran down Santa Monica Boulevard right outside their door, and in the rare event that Lew was not on time to catch the train, MCA was only a ten-block walk from his front porch.

To the rear of the living room, through the entrance hall, was a separate family room with a bar, which Lew never used unless he had a prospective new agent over to the house. He'd sit back sipping a soft drink and wait to see just how liquored up the man would get. If he remained sober, Lew might take a chance on hiring him. Drunks who could not hold their liquor were rejected outright.

Lew had an upstairs study over the dining room where he could work late at night and make early morning phone calls to the East Coast without disturbing Edie or the baby. He had a second phone installed downstairs in the dining room so that he could take calls at the table even when he and Edie were entertaining. He left the decorating to his wife. From the dark walnut dining room table to the pale blue flower print fabric on the living room sofa, the furniture was tasteful but definitely of department store quality.

Edie's taste in art ran to Collagero paintings of large-eyed children, which she displayed in heavy baroque frames. In the stairwell and on the upstairs landing, Lew maintained a trophy gallery of framed charcoal sketches of some of his more famous clients.

After her pregnancy, Edie hired a Scottish nurse for Lynne, moved the woman into the vacant upstairs bedroom, and turned its tiny porch overlooking the backyard into the baby's room. Then Edie moved into the social mainstream, following Doris's lead like a baby duck imitating its mother. She worked for the proper charities, lunched with rising stars and studio wives, and accompanied her husband to all the industry functions. Edie understood completely the importance of correct appearances, especially when it came to helping her husband woo prospective clients and their mates. According to former MCA vice president Herb Rosenthal, Jules and Lew both used their wives to win over young actors. Edie was particularly effective when she worked with Temme Brenner, wife of MCA agent Herb Brenner. Between the two of them, they were able to wine and dine and lure as many as twenty actors to the agency, according to Rosenthal's estimate.

"One thing most people don't know is how important the wives were," said

Rosenthal, adding with a smile, "Remember what Polly Adler used to say: history is made at night."[2]

If either of the Wassermans was to be found at home, it was usually Edie. Lew was almost never there. When he wasn't at the office or away on business in Chicago or New York, he could be found at the Mocambo or the Trocadero with a client, gambling at the Clover Club, or sitting in on one of the regular high-stakes Beverly Hills poker games that drew the likes of David Selznick, Sam Goldwyn, Sid Grauman, Mervyn LeRoy, and a host of Hollywood's other high-stakes players, including at least one woman, actress Constance Bennett.

Lew usually won, but when he lost, he lost big. At least twice, according to family members, Lew literally lost the Wassermans' Sierra Drive home but won it back in subsequent games. According to one account, producer-agent Charles Feldman sent Wasserman a bill for $834 — the equivalent of about six months' worth of house payments. Lew paid with a single check. He got even, though. Before the year was out, Feldman owed him $3,483.

Jules played cards, too, but his game was nickel-a-point gin rummy. Unlike his young vice president, who had also developed a taste for shooting craps, Stein seldom gambled at cards. He preferred the stock market. The one time that he did play cards in Feldman's league, Stein walked away with $123.

———※———

THOUGH WASSERMAN FOUGHT the studios as effectively as Myron Selznick, he used none of Selznick's vitriol. He simply made it his business to know more details about his client's and the studio's needs than anyone else, and he negotiated accordingly. In some ways MCA operated more as an intelligence-gathering operation than an agency. Assigned to cover specific studios, agents brought back intelligence for round table sessions each Wednesday morning at the MCA citadel.

Lew worked with the studios as often as he worked against them. As a result, he was in a position to step in and advise studio publicists the moment he smelled disaster. He was among the first to know when one of his stars was in trouble and how best to protect the public persona from scandal.

After the 1940 release of the hugely popular *Down Argentine Way*, Betty Grable's career soared. She would become a wartime box office phenomenon if her agency and studio could keep her sex life out of the papers.

Wasserman's other superstar client at the dawn of World War II presented just as many public relations headaches. Bette Davis was as promiscuous as Grable, compounding her sins with adultery and several abortions. She and Harmon Nel-

---

2   Polly Adler, the Polish-born madam of New York's most famous bordello of the 1920s and 1930s, wrote the best-selling memoir *A House Is Not a Home* in 1953.

son were divorced in November of 1938 because he had caught her in bed with Howard Hughes, and her many affairs with stars, casual acquaintances, and servicemen continued through the 1940s and two more marriages.

When one of those marriages ended in 1943 with the death of her hard-drinking second husband, Arthur Farnsworth, a coroner's inquest looked into the possibility of homicide, with Davis as the central figure. Farnsworth died from a skull fracture suffered in a fall, but precisely when and how the fall occurred was never firmly established. Despite the inquest's finding of accidental death, for years afterward speculation ran rampant through the film colony that Davis had gotten away with murder. Jack Warner was cited as the man who pulled the right political strings to cover up the circumstances of Farnsworth's death, but MCA was just as interested in keeping its star client out of jail and out of the newspapers.

Davis's public image, like that of Grable, was treacly wholesome. The powerful Hays Office—the censorship arm of the Association of Motion Picture Producers that had come down so hard on Mae West—liked it that way. What stars did in the privacy of their own or anybody else's bedroom was fine as long as it didn't hit the gossip columns. Even amorous Errol Flynn, the very embodiment of Hollywood debauchery, remained untouched by the Hays Office until 1942, when two of his teenage paramours accused him of statutory rape. He beat the charges and continued to work, but his career never fully recovered from the negative publicity.

Hollywood's one inviolate axiom was never to allow private violence or depravity to become public scandal, and the example always held up to defiant stars was that of the unfortunate silent film comedian Roscoe "Fatty" Arbuckle, whose highly public criminal trials never resulted in a conviction but whose notoriety as an alleged murderous sex fiend utterly ruined him.

MCA was rarely out front in smoothing over scandal. That was the realm of lawyers, press agents, and studio executives. But the agency always stood by in an advisory capacity to protect its valuable assets. Lew's experience as a publicist and early spin doctor often paid off handsomely for the star, the studio, and MCA. Whether on the set, in Jack Warner's office, or in the courtroom, Bette Davis rarely made a career move without Wasserman at her side.

———

THOUGH JULES STEIN did his best to avoid the courtroom, MCA was sued regularly by bandleaders who believed they had been shafted and by performers who discovered that MCA kept more of their paychecks than they had bargained for.

In 1940 the owners of the Hollywood Palladium spent nearly $1 million to build a new ballroom only to have Tommy Dorsey's MCA agents double-cross them. Designed to accommodate five thousand dancers, the Palladium planned its grand opening on Halloween 1940, with Dorsey making his first and only L.A. appearance that year.

But the contract MCA drafted for the Palladium was not exclusive, and MCA decided to cash in. Wasserman wired Dorsey and asked him to appear at the Hollywood Paramount Theater a month before playing the Palladium. Dorsey balked. He was already committed to an exclusive grand opening, so MCA *ordered* him to play the Paramount. If he didn't, a guest shot by the Dorsey orchestra in an upcoming Paramount movie would be canceled.

The Palladium won a restraining order barring Dorsey's Paramount date, but the order didn't last a week. Wasserman and Stein filed affidavits claiming that the Palladium would gain, not lose, by the Paramount appearance and that Dorsey had every right to appear at other clubs. The judge reversed himself, tossing out the restraining order. Dorsey was as flabbergasted as the Palladium owners. He was forced to play the Paramount.

As it turned out, Stein and Wasserman were right. The Palladium charged an astronomical five dollars a head for Dorsey and filled the place night after night. One reason was Dorsey's soloist—a skinny kid from Hoboken, New Jersey, who was just beginning to leave pubescent females shrieking for more. In *Las Vegas Nights* (1941), the movie Paramount had promised Dorsey, Frank Sinatra made his film debut as the uncredited Dorsey crooner singing "I'll Never Smile Again."

TEN

Hollywood Canteen

1942–1944

According to legend, the Hollywood Canteen was born when John Garfield lunched with Bette Davis in the Green Room at Warner Brothers shortly after the bombing of Pearl Harbor. Garfield, a flag-waving socialist who may have loved his country nearly as much as he did women, desperately wanted to be a part of the action, but he had a weak heart. It would kill the original screen rebel ten years later, while Garfield was bedding down his umpteenth starlet, but during World War II, he claimed to be fit. Unlike many Hollywood denizens who rejoiced at their 4-F status, Garfield seethed.

Bette Davis listened politely and sympathetically, but it wasn't until her lunch partner came up with an idea to help the boys in uniform that her ears perked up. Back in New York, Garfield had performed at the Stage Door Canteen, a GI service organization made up of Broadway stars who entertained, fed, and cheered up the servicemen who were headed overseas. Why not do the same thing in Los Angeles? They could open a nightclub and offer free admission to any enlisted man in uniform. It would be in the heart of Hollywood, where big bands and film stars could show up to amuse the troops every night.

What better place to start than with Jules Stein? Garfield and Davis sought help from their MCA godfather, and within months the Hollywood Canteen was born.

"Jules Stein, up to this time, was seldom ever seen," Bette Davis recalled in her memoirs. "Few people even knew what he looked like. He preferred to live this way. It was a big decision when he said he would head the financial committee. He would have to alter his way of life. Without his hard work, advice, and investments of our funds, the Hollywood Canteen could not have been successful, to say nothing of the work of his wife, Doris, who I asked to be the head of the committee for the hostesses necessary for dancing partners for the servicemen."

95

For seed money, Stein twisted Harry Cohn's arm at Columbia. He got Cohn to donate part of the profits from Columbia's *Talk of the Town*, a lightweight comedy starring Cary Grant and Jean Arthur, in exchange for a plug associating Columbia with Stein's worthy cause. Next, MCA engineered a kickoff fund-raiser at Ciro's, a swanky nightclub. The event netted $6,500, and when the canteen opened on October 3, 1942, it was already in the black.

Two years later, when the club had become a phenomenal success, Lew Wasserman twisted arms at Warner Brothers and the Screen Actors Guild and got an all-star movie musical made about the Hollywood Canteen. It was great publicity, but it was also great money. Lew got a SAG waiver enabling stars to donate their salaries, and he struck a deal with Jack Warner guaranteeing the Hollywood Canteen Foundation $250,000 up front plus 40 percent of the film's net profits.

MCA would keep the Canteen Foundation in the black long after the war ended and the canteen itself was razed to make way for a five-story parking lot. On November 22, 1945, after Bob Hope, Jack Benny, and Jerry Colonna brought down the curtain for the last time, $500,000 still remained in the canteen account. As of 1995, after giving away millions to charity, the Hollywood Canteen Foundation was still worth $1.3 million. With Lew Wasserman as trustee, the foundation continues to make annual grants to California charities through Union Bank.

But when it first began, the canteen was strictly a wartime gimmick, as beneficial to MCA as it was to the military men who enjoyed it.[1] On opening night, MCA client Eddie Cantor was master of ceremonies, MCA's Kay Kyser Orchestra provided music, and MCA comics Bud Abbott and Lou Costello entertained.

Stein appreciated the lasting sheen of good publicity. Stars who could not be lured away from their agencies by promises of fame or money might be persuaded to switch if they witnessed MCA sponsor a good cause that won abundant praise in newspapers and on the radio.

Besides, Stein saw himself as a genuine patriot. He'd done his stint in the U.S. Army Medical Reserves, and he encouraged his agents, most of whom did not join the service, to do their part for the war effort. Thus Lew Wasserman, after working all day for MCA, served at night as a civilian defense volunteer.

Lew rarely had time to visit the canteen, but Edie did. "The war liberated Edie," recalled a close family friend. "She did all the scheduling and booking for the Hollywood Canteen, and she spent the entire war either at the canteen or on the road with one of the bond rallies."

---

[1] According to Jules Stein's FBI file, as early as August 1942 the FBI's Internal Security detail began regular scrutiny of the Hollywood Canteen and New York's Stage Door Canteen as possible Communist front organizations. When the war ended and the Hollywood Canteen shut down, one FBI report alleged that "Communist members of some of Hollywood labor unions" tried to share in the canteen's profits until Stein and Bette Davis created the Hollywood Canteen Foundation.

Doris Stein took credit for supervising the day-to-day arrangements at the canteen, even getting her name mentioned in director Delmer Daves's 1944 script for *Hollywood Canteen*, the Warner Brothers musical about the wildly popular nightclub.

But it was Edie Wasserman, forever in the shadow of the Grand Duchess of MCA, who actually scheduled entertainment and got actresses out to dance with the GIs. While Doris showed up for ribbon cuttings and photo opportunities, Edie seemed to be a canteen fixture. Sometimes she stayed all night, leaving the Wassermans' only child in the hands of her nanny, a separation of mother and daughter that contributed to lifelong friction between them.

But the Hollywood Canteen was irresistible. Located in an old barn on Cahuenga Boulevard that rented for $100 a month, it had a dance floor, a stage, and a snack bar that ran the length of the room. The boozeless club was decorated to look like a saloon, with western murals and chandeliers made of wagon wheels. And every night except Sunday it was filled with rugged young men in uniform.

According to MCA press releases, up to 2,000 servicemen showed up every night to gawk, talk, and dance with the stars. Two name bands performed nightly, and it took 300 volunteers just to check I.D.'s, clear the tables, and keep replenishing the free food.

The food and supplies were all donated by willing companies in exchange for a radio plug, an announcement from the stage, or a mention in a press release. It didn't take a Jules Stein to do the arithmetic. The Hollywood Canteen was a gold mine. Connecting a company's name with this proud, patriotic nightclub was great business, and MCA's name was connected more than any other.

Of course, beating just beneath the surface of the canteen's red-white-and-blue trappings was a lustful heart. Many, if not most, of the soldiers and sailors who packed the dance floor each night dreamed of holding a lot more than Lana Turner's waistline or Paulette Goddard's hand. Stein laid down strict rules for women, forbidding the smuggling of alcohol, fraternizing outside the club, and exchanging addresses with GIs. He demanded that the public image remain squeaky-clean. He also discouraged black, Filipino, and Hispanic servicemen from visiting the canteen. "Mixed dancing," he said, might spark a race riot.

All women were scrutinized to make certain no chippies got inside, and anyone caught pimping or plying a dance partner with liquor was handed over to the LAPD. The last thing Jules needed was his carefully orchestrated fount of apple-pie publicity revealed as some kind of celebrity bordello, with his own wife playing the role of madam.

Despite precautions, the inevitable happened. Hedy Lamarr found time to fool around with fellow canteen entertainer John Loder while her fiancée, actor George Montgomery, was off fighting the war. Susan Hayward dumped her overseas boyfriend, dallied with actor Jess Barker following a long night at the canteen, and married him three months into her pregnancy.

Even Bette Davis lived up to her whispered reputation as an off-screen siren. Just days after the mysterious death of her second husband, Arthur Farnsworth, she was performing her patriotic duty every night at the canteen by openly defying Stein's no-fraternization edict. Actor Jack Carson recalled bumping into one soldier who explained why Bette always seemed to be surrounded by GIs. "I hear she screws like a mink," he told Carson.

By 1943, Davis had sampled enough at the canteen to settle down to a long-term affair with an army corporal who was twelve years her junior. MCA and Warner Brothers made the best of it, playing up her romance with Corporal Lewis A. Riley as true love triumphing in the face of war. When Riley shipped overseas the next year, Davis returned to the trenches at the canteen.

"I'M THE KIND of girl truck drivers like," said Betty Grable.

Grable was a hussy with a heart. Throughout the war she toured the country for bond rallies, auctioning off her nylons and selling kisses for the cause. Her occasional traveling companion was Mrs. Edith Wasserman, who had an eye for the boys in uniform herself. She followed Grable's lead on and off the dance floor. For a while, Edie even wore her dark hair swept up in a topknot like Grable's blond locks.

Some fraternization on the road was to be expected, but as actor John Payne told his friends, getting caught alone with Edie Wasserman during a bond rally could be a risky proposition. Hotels where the actors and actresses stayed as they moved from town to town were "like an English country weekend," he said.

Edie's attraction to several of Hollywood's leading men grew with the years. Errol Flynn, who purportedly had his own flirtation with Mrs. Wasserman after dumping Myron Selznick and signing with MCA, gave Edie her nickname: "Legs."

She had a role model in Betty Grable. Grable was the woman of the hour—a heroine for every high school girl, housewife, and hubba-hubba wanna-be in America. In addition to being the top box office draw in the Western world, she was named America's Ideal Girl by Armed Forces Radio. In less than two years, MCA had turned a veteran of the casting couch into unsullied Betty Grable. MCA agents made deals for Betty Grable dolls, Betty Grable swimsuits, Betty Grable posters, and even a Betty Grable novel: *Betty Grable and the House with the Iron Shutters*, in which a pulp writer transformed her into a kind of peaches-and-cream Nancy Drew.

When she wasn't on the road or the soundstage, Grable was the principal attraction at the Hollywood Canteen. She held the record for jitterbugging, with three hundred cut-ins in a single hour. And when true love finally blossomed for her, it happened right there on the dance floor.

She had met trumpeter Harry James in 1940 during a public appearance in Chicago and once again a year later, during the filming of *Springtime in the Rockies,* but it wasn't until the summer of 1943 at the Hollywood Canteen that Betty and Harry fell in love.

"He went there every day to play for the boys and I went there on Mondays to dance with them," Betty explained to columnist Sheilah Graham.

In her interview with Graham, Betty Grable made no mention of her pregnancy, of Harry's hasty Mexican divorce, or of their hasty wedding in Las Vegas. What could have been a press agent's nightmare had somehow turned into the best-known love story since the king of England gave up his crown for the woman he loved.

For MCA, however, Betty's pregnancy created a problem. She might have been the most popular movie star on earth, but adoring matinee fans would not forgive an illegitimate birth. She had been pressured to abort before, with her handlers making up flimsy excuses for her hospital stays. In April of 1942, for example, the studio had explained that Betty was hospitalized so she could gain strength for an operation after strenuous dance routines had "aggravated her condition." Neither the condition nor the operation was ever named. But a year later, when she discovered she was carrying Harry James's baby, she refused to have an abortion. She now had the star status to make her refusal stick.

There was also the more immediate problem of naming the father. Privately, Harry James acknowledged the child as his and immediately arranged to dump his wife. His ex, however, was the loyal mother to his two toddler sons — a fact that newspaper reporters could ferret out rather quickly, once the news of the Grable-James liaison became public. It would not do to have America's Ideal Girl marry a heel.

In the meantime, the clock was ticking. Betty was already five weeks along — a predicament that called for masterful spin control. It helped that Lew Wasserman was spinning for Grable.

To begin with, the couple secretly eloped to Las Vegas on the Fourth of July, each taking a different train to throw off reporters and pesky photographers. Not photographer Frank Powolny, however. The studio camera wizard who shot the famous peekaboo bathing-suit pinup of Grable — the most famous cheesecake photo of World War II — got a tip from Fox publicity and caught the very same train that Grable did. Betty later breathlessly assured her moviegoing public that she was utterly astonished when she ran into Powolny on the train. She denied she was headed to Nevada to get hitched. Nevertheless, the photographer got some terrific shots of the happy couple the next day.

In Louella Parsons's column the following day, the gossip queen exclusively revealed that B-movie actress Betty Furness was one of only two official witnesses who actually saw and heard Grable and James exchange vows. The other witness was someone most Americans had never heard of—Mrs. Edie Wasserman, who just happened to be in town, escorted by Columbia Recording executive Manie Sacks, a former MCA agent. When she heard about Betty's wedding, she just had to offer to stand up for her friend.

Edie's husband, MCA hotshot Lew Wasserman, was not mentioned. If he was anywhere near Las Vegas, he kept his whereabouts secret, even from Louella.

"Edie and Lew seemed more like brother and sister than a married couple," said the wife of an MGM producer during the 1940s.

To anyone who knew the Wassermans, Edie showing up in Vegas on the arm of someone other than her husband would not have been all that extraordinary under most circumstances. But on the day Betty wed Harry, it did seem a little indiscreet. After all, July 5, 1943, was Lew and Edie's seventh wedding anniversary.

—◆—

"BILLY WAS A bachelor his whole life, but he was also quite a ladies' man," recalled Dorothy Barton. "He didn't really start to slow down until he lost his leg."

Billy Stein's lifelong battle with rheumatic heart disease brought on severe circulation problems, which began taking their toll at the outset of World War II. After more than fifteen years as MCA's chief talent scout, Jules's older brother lost a leg in 1941. Though he was fitted with a wooden leg, the amputation effectively ended his career. He still got around and occasionally discovered a new band or vaudeville act, but his energy steadily declined.

Billy Stein had none of Jules's somber intensity and still knew how to clown around, even as his health declined. He'd pull the false leg off at dinner to shock new girlfriends, and he delighted in telling and retelling the latest off-color jokes. He still traveled a good deal, exploring as much of the world as his condition permitted—Florida, Cuba, Mexico. But he knew his days were numbered. On May 14, 1943, Billy Stein's heart stopped in a Los Angeles hospital. He was forty-nine.

Jules got the news in Brazil, where he was attending the Pan-American Congress of Ophthalmology with his old mentor, Dr. Harry Gradle. Now recognized internationally as one of the world's leading eye specialists, Gradle remained Stein's friend. In many ways he was more of a paternal figure to Jules than his own father, who had died exactly thirteen months before Billy Stein.

Louis Stein was seventy when his heart gave out. The body of the Stein family patriarch was found next door to the dry goods store that he operated every day, except the Saturday Sabbath, until the day he died. His total estate was valued at $4,845.88.

Both Louis and Billy were buried in South Bend's Hebrew Orthodox Cemetery, next to the grave of Rosa Stein.

Though not unexpected, the two deaths had a profound effect on Jules. At forty-seven, he knew he would not live forever. His successful business maneuverings had created a fortune that supported all the Steins as well as Jules's in-laws and stepsons. Now he was also the nominal head of the family. Whatever lingering resentment and rivalry had existed between Jules and his father, and between Jules and Billy, now vanished. Jules was the undisputed head of the clan—and that included not only his own relatives but also his second family at MCA. He regarded Karl Kramer, Charlie Miller, Maurie Lipsey, and Mickey Rockford almost as brothers, elder statesmen in the agency, like Jules himself. Taft Schreiber, Lew Wasserman, and Sonny Werblin were as cutthroat competitive with each other as they were loyal to the old man. They represented the second generation of MCA brothers, always able to cease their internecine warfare and work as a team when the company was threatened.

Of all his loyalists, Jules liked Lew the best. He was tireless, charming, and ruthless. The two men began spending as much time with each other as they did with their wives. After office hours, Jules and Lew dined together, attended premieres and previews, and planned their next move in the never-ending agency wars. Together they could spot an opportunity the way a condor could spot carrion, and Lew was as adept at planning strategy as his boss.

In the five years after he bought out the William Meiklejohn Agency, Jules Stein systematically continued to absorb his rivals as the simplest way to build MCA.

"If you follow a loaded wagon, something is bound to fall off," Wasserman used to say when waxing philosophic about Stein's approach to gathering talent.

Stein's most notable purchase was the small but potent talent pool operated by Zeppo Marx. At the time MCA bought him out, the youngest of the five comic Marx Brothers had been selling talent since 1932 and had built a client list that included Joan Fontaine, Lucille Ball, Fred MacMurray, Barbara Stanwyck, Jon Hall, Dixie Lee Crosby, and Ray Milland. As he always did following a takeover, Stein kept the high-earning stars and banished less promising actors, with their smaller commissions, to other agencies.

"I was in New York, and Jules Stein used to have me to lunch in his beautifully paneled private dining room," recalled director Joseph Mankiewicz, whose older brother Herman had recently won an Academy Award for cowriting *Citizen Kane* (1941). "He also kept inviting me to parties and screenings. After three or four months of wooing, I ran into Lew Wasserman in Hollywood.

"Lew said, 'Why don't you level with me? I know that Jules has been talking to you in New York and trying to get you as a client. Now, why won't you come with us?'

"I said, 'Well, frankly, Lew, I don't think I should be represented by an agent who calls me Herman.'"

Stein's confusion was understandable. MCA's broad variety of acts now ranged from the baggy-pants burlesque of Joe E. Lewis to the classical conducting of Leopold Stokowski. Strippers, dancing horses, brass bands, juggling midgets, and Shakespearean troupes all worked for Jules Stein and his growing legion of arm twisters. MCA's influence dominated every entertainment venue in the country. Except one.

Barring a few actors such as Paul Henreid and John Garfield, the one place MCA didn't have much of a foothold, and where more venerable agencies like William Morris still dominated, was the Broadway stage. To Jules Stein and his socialite wife, MCA's meager influence among stage actors was more than a weakness in the agency. It was also a slap to their pride.

Doris's transformation from Kansas City divorcée to mink-and-champagne doyenne of New York café society was nearly complete, but it remained a facade. The Steins might be rich, but they had their cultural lapses. Forties film star Constance Moore recalls being greeted at the door of Misty Mountain by liveried servants, only to be served hors d'oeuvres of gherkins wrapped in bologna and pinned together with toothpicks. "That's what she served back home in Missouri, and that's what she served in Beverly Hills, because that's what she liked," said Moore.

For all their raw capitalistic prowess, Doris and Jules were still not in Broadway's innermost inner circle. They were interesting and powerful people from Hollywood who were usually among the first nighters at important new plays, but they did not always rate complimentary front row seats or invitations to private parties at Sardi's following a performance.

To the Steins, who now spent several months each year living in their riverfront home on Manhattan's East Side, the humiliation of being anything less than the most omnipotent couple on Broadway was unacceptable. For several years Jules had tried in vain to bridge the gap between his déclassé power base in Hollywood and the cosmopolitan sophistication of New York.

As World War II wound to a close, he finally found the chink in Broadway's armor, which he would use to make MCA's preeminence complete. Jules sent Lew to New York to meet with a bon vivant whose name was a legend on Broadway.

ELEVEN

Beverly Hills and Broadway

1945

Leland Hayward spent World War II training fighter pilots, worrying about whether clients Henry Fonda and James Stewart would make it back from Europe alive, and sneaking caviar past U.S. Customs so he could offer it at a discount to film moguls and Broadway investors.

A workaholic who rivaled the single-mindedness of Lew Wasserman, Hayward was no Jules Stein–trained penny-pincher; he traveled first class and found ingenious ways to make his clients foot the bill. Dashing and scheming, Hayward was the only son of a well-to-do U.S. attorney who gained fame during World War I as commander of a highly decorated regiment of black American soldiers. Colonel Hayward had raised Leland to be a responsible Connecticut aristocrat, but his son turned out to be even more restless, and colorful, than his father.

Leland entered Princeton in 1923 and dropped out the same year to become a New York newspaper reporter. After his father cut off his allowance in disgust, Leland found his patrician tastes could not be satisfied on $25 a week. He married and divorced the same well-heeled Texas society girl twice before he headed for Hollywood in the late 1920s.

There the unruly easterner scratched out an existence as a press agent, talent scout, and producer on a string of dreadful low-budget movies. He managed to get hired and fired from some twenty jobs before he found his true calling.

"All the agents I know started out in some other business," said Hayward. "Did you ever hear a little boy say, 'When I grow up, I want to be an agent'?"

Hollywood had spunk, moguls, money, and great weather, but limited talent. Leland returned to Broadway to recruit first-rate playwrights, actors, and directors for films.

In 1932 he opened the Leland Hayward Agency, his New York counterpart to Myron Selznick's Hollywood talent factory. During the next five years Hayward and Selznick developed a symbiotic relationship: Leland would sign Charles Laughton, Ben Hecht, Katharine Hepburn, Ernest Hemingway, and other gifted artists and send them west to Myron, who would seal their studio deals. But though Hayward earned commissions from dozens of stage stars, his real fortune came from selling literary properties. In a single year during the height of the Great Depression, he sold film rights worth $3 million to producers who wanted his clients' plays and novels as bases for their movies.

"He was a gentleman agent. A darling man," director George Cukor recalled some forty years later in an interview with Hayward's daughter, Brooke. "I loved him even though he was a buccaneer. By asking such outrageous salaries for his clients, I think he was responsible for jacking up the agency business into the conglomerate empire it is today."

In 1937, Leland and the increasingly inebriated Myron Selznick split up. To pick up the West Coast slack, Hayward moved his family to Beverly Hills. Though he found the film colony vulgar and its denizens common, he forced himself to live there during part of each year. In 1940 he asked agent Nat Deverich to handle his West Coast operations while he started his own airline, Southwest Airways. During the war, Leland—a civilian—opened a military air school just south of Phoenix, Arizona, at a place he called Sky Harbor. He divided his time between running the Hayward Deverich Agency and teaching soldiers to fly.

As the war wound down, Hayward began planning to move back permanently to New York, buy himself a farm, and split his time between Broadway and living the life of a country squire. It didn't take long for other agents to discover Leland's dream. Charles Feldman approached him in 1943 about merging with Famous Artists. While Hayward was interested, he rejected the proposal. He'd still be an agent and he'd still have to work on the West Coast but with twice as many clients to sell and service.

By the fall of 1944, Hayward had another dream. He commissioned playwright Paul Osborn to adapt John Hersey's acclaimed World War II novel A Bell for Adano for the stage, but Osborn agreed to do it only after Hayward promised to produce the play. Not only was the play a hit but Leland found a new passion for producing. Overnight his agency business became an albatross around his neck.

Hayward's plight did not escape the attention of Jules Stein, who saw the sudden shift in Leland's obsessions. Jules cared not a whit about producing plays, but he understood the passion: nurturing a project, bringing it to the stage, savoring the applause on opening night, and claiming the credit when the reviews spewed flattering praise among the literati.

"He was by far the outstanding man in the entire agency field in California, but he was never quite satisfied with himself," Stein recalled for Brooke Hayward. "He was always reaching for something further. I was perhaps perfectly happy to be the top agent in town, but he not only wanted to be an agent, he wanted to be a creator and he wanted to be a producer and he didn't want to stick to any one thing even though he was a success in it."

Jules also understood all too well the need to distance oneself from Hollywood and Broadway lowlife. If a gentleman like Leland couldn't afford to buy a secluded mountaintop, as the Steins had, the next best thing was a hideaway far from the grasping masses.

For Leland, that place was the rolling hills of Brookfield, at the western edge of Connecticut. He had his eye on Stone Ledges, a 95-acre Colonial estate, chiefly because his wife, actress Margaret Sullavan, demanded that they raise their three children away from urban madness. Leland accepted Stone Ledges as a compromise with his wife because he would still be able to commute each day to Manhattan. The question of how to pay for it remained.

Lew Wasserman was armed with this knowledge, and more, when Stein sent him to Hayward as MCA's emissary during the first weeks of 1945. Hayward's Madison Avenue offices rivaled those of Jules Stein himself: a roof garden, a private bath, a sun lamp salon, and a 22-foot-long dining board from an Italian monastery that had been converted into Hayward's desk. But punctual, pleasant, impeccably dressed Mr. Wasserman was not awed. He went straight to work.

Leland thought they were negotiating a merger much along the lines of the one that Charles Feldman had suggested a year earlier. But Lew had something different in mind. He knew how proud Leland was of the massive success of *A Bell for Adano*. Hayward might never be able to recapture that feeling, but wouldn't it be wonderful to have an opportunity to try?

Lew understood how trying Hayward's bicoastal existence had been, piloting his own plane back and forth between New York and Los Angeles as often as three times each month. Lew also understood how much more rewarding it would be for Hayward to raise his children in a healthy rural environment somewhere along the much more civilized eastern seaboard. And when the family did have to live in Los Angeles, why not have a more exclusive home high up in Beverly Hills rather than the place they now owned on Cherokee Lane, down near the flatlands of Hollywood?

What was more, MCA needed a seasoned pro like Hayward to act as a senior adviser. The company's hungry young go-getters lacked polish. Who better to bring them along than the smoothest agent ever to grace the profession?

If Hayward knew that he was being handled, he didn't let on. The merger talk had subtly shifted to a proposition for a dream buyout. It was almost as if he'd inadvertently rubbed Aladdin's lamp and now had to decide what his wishes would be.

Over the next few months Leland met with Stein, Sonny Werblin, Karl Kramer, Taft Schreiber, and the rest of the MCA hierarchy, but Wasserman remained the point man on the deal. While lawyers for both sides hammered out a final agreement, Schreiber sent Hayward a personal note apologizing for getting sick and failing to participate in the negotiations. Leland wrote back: "Everything has been fine so far and the marriage is still in the state of honeymoon. In fact I may marry Lew any day now."

By the end of April it was a done deal. The master agent had been masterfully handled by a silver-tongued spaghetti strand of a deal-maker eleven years his junior. When it was over, Leland paid Wasserman the highest compliment one flesh peddler can pay another: "He's the best agent I ever saw," said Hayward.

For giving up his agency, Hayward got MCA vice presidencies for himself and Nat Deverich, guaranteed by a ten-year employment contract calling for a base weekly salary of $500 plus half the commissions generated by every client the Hayward-Deverich Agency brought to MCA. Essentially Hayward and Deverich didn't have to do anything for the next ten years to earn a minimum of $100,000 annually.

In addition, MCA promised to help Hayward buy his Connecticut farm and a new home high up in the Coldwater Canyon section of Beverly Hills. MCA also helped Hayward sell his old home on Cherokee Avenue to MCA client Fred MacMurray.

Perhaps most important, MCA promised to help Hayward secure a theater in New York and to invest $7,500 in Leland's new project, *State of the Union*, in exchange for a percentage of any profits the play might earn. If it was another hit, Hayward could continue to produce and still carry the title of MCA vice president, or he could abandon Broadway and get back into the agency business that he knew so well.[1]

The Hayward-Deverich buyout put MCA into the stratosphere. One of Wasserman's first acts following the takeover was to fire Hayward-Deverich agents Barron Polan and John Maschio so he could take over their clients, according to Maschio. "I was the best agent in Hollywood, and that's all I ever wanted to be," asserted Maschio, who'd overseen such Hayward clients as Jean Harlow and Paulette Goddard. "But Lew had it in for me, for some reason, and I couldn't get a job anywhere after he let me go. The word was out against me. I finally gave up and went into real estate."

Lew wasted no time making the Hayward-Deverich roster his own. No other talent pool in the world was as rich or as diversified, including that of the venerable William Morris Agency. Hayward-Deverich actresses included Myrna Loy, Greta Garbo, Judy Garland, Gene Tierney,[2] Dorothy McGuire, Dame May Whitty, Ginger Rogers, Margaret Sullavan, and Gail Patrick. Actors included

---

[1]   In 1962, the Justice Department put the overall cost to MCA for purchasing the Hayward-Deverich Agency at $2 million.

[2]   "Oleg, can I just be bought and sold like that?" Tierney asked her husband, Oleg Cassini. Only Tierney and Van Johnson initially protested the MCA purchase. They were both brought into line.

Clifton Webb, Pat O'Brien, Andy Devine, Gregory Peck, Fredric March, Raymond Massey, James Stewart, Henry Fonda, Joseph Cotten, Van Johnson, Fred Astaire, Gene Kelly, Boris Karloff, Thomas Mitchell, Oscar Levant, David Niven, and Barry Sullivan; writers included Irwin Shaw, Dorothy Parker, Russel Crouse, Howard Lindsay, Edna Ferber, Lillian Hellman, Ben Hecht, Charles MacArthur, Dashiell Hammett, Walter Van Tilburg Clark, Arthur Koestler, and Walter de la Mare; producer-directors included Billy Wilder, Alfred Hitchcock, Arthur Hornblow, and Joshua Logan. Leland Hayward even represented Salvador Dali.

"His clients turned out to be our most important clients," Jules Stein told Brooke Hayward. "As a matter of fact, when I look back even today at the list of clients he represented, the lists we got at that time, it's bewildering. He overshadowed everybody in the business. Even our list was secondary to his. I was just flabbergasted to think that he had so many important people — not only performers but writers and directors — he had the best cross section of artists in the whole field."

MCA was no longer just boasting when it printed at the bottom of each sheet of stationery: "Producers of the world's greatest artists, entertainment and orchestras."

It was a fact.

It was also a fact that Leland Hayward was about to undergo some uncomfortable changes in his work habits.

One of the first things to go was his business attire. No more cardigan sweaters, short sleeves, and Italian loafers. MCA vice presidents were expected to set an example for lower-echelon employees by dressing in the fashion Stein and Wasserman adopted the moment they opened the Beverly Hills office: dark suit, white shirt, dark tie.

None of Hayward's office furniture fit in, either. Like every other senior MCA executive, Hayward was assigned an antique desk, a breakfront, chairs, and English fox-hunting prints for his walls. When he asked to bring in a big striped overstuffed couch from his old office, he was politely told no.[3] After a year of fighting, Hayward told a *Life* magazine reporter that he checked into a hospital and sent

---

[3] Bob Hope's agent-manager, Jimmy Saphier, also worked as an MCA agent until he too quarreled with Stein over the furniture. Hope had given Saphier an expensive new clock that clashed with Stein's antiques. Saphier couldn't just discard the clock, so they compromised: Saphier kept the offending clock out of sight. Stein had a special buzzer installed, which the receptionist was ordered to punch whenever Hope entered the building. The buzzer alerted Saphier who pulled the clock out of a drawer and displayed it prominently on his desk. When Hope left, it went back in the drawer. The arrangement lasted six months before Saphier quit.

word to Wasserman that he would lie there until he died if he didn't get his couch. MCA finally gave in.

Next came an end to his fits of unaccounted-for extravagance. Jules and, later on, Lew demanded to know where every penny went. Hayward's expenses were checked, just like everyone else's in the growing agency. Thus when Leland wanted to send a floral arrangement to a colleague's funeral or purchase a train ticket, he had to let the office know so that MCA could get the best possible deal.

One expense that was not limited was long-distance telephone bills. As before, Hayward conducted most of his business over the phone, from everywhere — restaurants, train depots, air terminals, bus stops. His bills ran into the hundreds every month, but then, so did those of every MCA man who was doing his job. In that respect, Hayward fit in.

One long-distance call Hayward made before the move from New York was to *Time* magazine's West Coast correspondent, Dwight Whitney. Unlike the dark-suited MCA regulars he was about to join, Hayward courted publicity. Despite warnings, he continued to do so discreetly.

Whitney, who'd had an early tip, wanted to know about the buyout. He particularly wanted to know about Jules Stein and "the Octopus." MCA's unflattering nickname had caught on in agency circles, but outsiders — including newspaper and magazine journalists — had rarely used it. The nickname's current popularity sprang from a widely reported lawsuit in San Diego, brought against MCA by an unhappy dance-hall operator and his wife who contended that the agency monopolized the band-booking business.

Did Hayward know about the lawsuit? Whitney asked.

Plaintiffs Larry and Miriam Finley alleged that "the Octopus" controlled every dance hall, auditorium, and nightspot in southern California — maybe across the entire nation. Except for Fred Waring, Glenn Miller, Duke Ellington, Jimmy Dorsey, and Paul Whiteman, there wasn't a name orchestra that MCA didn't have under contract.

The Finleys' headaches began January 3, 1945, when the city of San Diego awarded them a three-year lease on the Mission Beach Ballroom. But when the couple tried to book their grand opening, they found MCA had already given the pick of the agency's name bands to the Pacific Square Ballroom, their rival a few blocks away.

It seemed Pacific Square owner Wayne Daillard had been using MCA bands for years and got the agency's preferential treatment. This was standard MCA procedure, a quid pro quo known as an exclusive. If a dance-hall owner booked only MCA bands, he got first pick for as long as he wanted and his rivals got nothing unless they went to other agencies. The trouble was, other agencies had very few first-rate bands.

With MCA's help, Daillard packed his Pacific Square Ballroom every weekend while the Finleys hardly sold enough admissions to keep their doors open. They complained. They were ignored. When they threatened to sue, MCA offered them Jack Teagarden's orchestra[4] for a two-night stand. But at the outrageous price of $2,250, the Finleys declined. They also turned down a similar MCA offer for Ted Fiorito's band. They finally accepted the singing King Sisters for a two-night stand at the more attractive price of $1,500. But while they waited for MCA to send the contracts, Daillard used his exclusive and placed notices in the *San Diego Union* and *Tribune*, advertising that the King Sisters would be singing at Pacific Square, not Mission Beach.

That was the last straw. On February 6, 1945, the Finleys sued Jules Stein and his Octopus for $3.3 million—and not in the state courts, where MCA had never lost a case. The Finleys sued MCA in Los Angeles Federal Court, charging the company with conspiring to restrain free trade in the music entertainment business not only in California but throughout the country.

Time's Dwight Whitney wanted to know from Hayward how his new boss, Dr. Stein, was going to testify when the Finleys' attorney called him to the witness stand.

Whitney also wanted to know if it was true that MCA controlled the radio business. It was understood that any actor, singer, or musician who was not represented by MCA had little chance of ever performing on NBC, CBS, ABC, or Mutual, let alone getting his or her own show. MCA got 20 percent of every show it packaged, plus 10 percent of every salary on the show. Those who thought that was too steep didn't work on radio. Even Rudy Vallee, who had been an MCA holdout since he first went on radio in 1929, finally had to give in to MCA to keep his network radio spot.

Whitney also pointed out that Stein had some interesting friends. Why were he and Jimmy Petrillo of the musicians' union so cozy? How was he able to buy up so much airtime from CBS's Bill Paley and NBC's David Sarnoff?

Whitney also asked about Stein's rags-to-riches story. Where had the money come from to finance his fast climb to the pinnacle of show business? And what about his insistence on absolute secrecy in a profession that thrived on publicity? What *was* Jules Stein hiding?

Hayward had no answers. He suggested that Whitney ask Dr. Stein himself.

—*∿*—

THE *TIME* ARTICLE appeared in the April 23, 1945, edition under the title "The Octopus" and carried with it a close-up of the inscrutable Dr. Stein, with the cap-

---

[4] In 1941, Teagarden recorded a tune for Columbia that contained the line, "I woke up screamin'. I thought I was on the road for MCA."

tion: "He has reticence—and reach." Taking Hayward's advice, Whitney spoke directly to the reclusive tycoon, who told him that he never gave interviews because agents were not the stars.

He had no comment on the Hayward-Deverich buyout or the Finley suit. He'd met Finley only once, for "about half a minute" in the lobby of the Beverly Hills Hotel, when Finley stepped up and introduced himself.

Stein did offer Whitney an explanation for MCA's voracious appetite for radio airtime. He bought whole chunks of broadcast time "for the protection of artists," he explained. If MCA didn't buy the time from the networks and put MCA people to work in the choicest slots, advertisers would purchase the time, create their own programs, and hire outsiders who would put MCA talent out of work. He didn't discuss touchy issues, like MCA's packaging fees or the practice of blackballing other agencies' clients.

Stein's explanation for his wealth was as simple as his belief in the work ethic and the American dream: he'd toiled tirelessly, outguessed the competition, surrounded himself with able employees, behaved like a gentleman, and, on occasion, gotten lucky.

During the interview, Stein never raised his voice or forgot his manners. If he'd had enough influence with Henry Luce, Stein might have been able to get the story spiked. But he didn't. Stein braced himself for the worst and got it.

Whitney's story began, "Reputedly one of the richest men in the U.S., his name does not even appear in *Who's Who*." The reporter went on: "He keeps oak-paneled, antique-furnished offices in New York, Chicago, Hollywood, Cleveland, Dallas, San Francisco, London. As president of the Music Corp. of America, he is absolute monarch over the careers of scores of celebrated radio and cinema stars."

It continued in that vein, detailing Stein's career as an ophthalmologist-turned-agent and charting his move into every aspect of show business, including his fling as a bonded booze supplier in the 1930s. The portrait Whitney painted was that of a controlled and controlling autocrat, mild-mannered but steely, arrogant, ruthless. The article told how, dissatisfied with the Beverly Hills street sign outside his office, Stein ordered his own erected. It read "M.C.A. Square."

The article worried Stein, who feared a renewed government interest in MCA, monopoly, and the Sherman Antitrust Act. He ordered his troops to tread carefully in the coming months.

IN 1945, EDDIE Bracken was the hottest comic actor in America. The sad sack star of back-to-back Paramount hits—*The Miracle of Morgan's Creek* and *Hail the Conquering Hero*—Bracken was a favorite of legendary director Preston Sturges and the most popular funny man on the silver screen aside from Bob Hope. His career — carefully managed by Lew Wasserman, Taft Schreiber, and the rest of Stein's Hollywood storm troops — had nowhere to go but up.

Bracken was an early MCA client. He had been performing since he was ten years old, when he enrolled in New York's Children's School for Actors. He was already a seasoned stage and nightclub professional by the time MCA spotted him. When the nineteen-year-old vaudevillian known as Eddie Vincent married Connie Nickerson in 1939, MCA took note. Stein wanted him, but Vincent already had an agent. So MCA tracked down Monte Juro, the best man at Eddie's wedding as well as his agent, and offered him a job. In no time, Eddie Vincent switched agents, changed his name to Eddie Bracken, and began landing movie roles. Monte Juro's career at MCA, of course, went the same southerly direction as Lester Linsk's after he'd brought Bette Davis to MCA.

Not so Eddie Bracken. In 1942 the annual *Motion Picture Almanac* polled U.S. theater owners on their choices as the "Stars of Tomorrow," and Bracken came in second, ahead of Jane Wyman, Alan Ladd, Donna Reed, and Betty Hutton. After the success of Paramount's *The Miracle of Morgan's Creek* and *Hail the Conquering Hero* in 1944, Bracken was box office gold. His career was made.

But Bracken really wanted to get back to the Broadway stage. He was now a creature of Hollywood, however, the property of MCA. So he decided to take a fling at radio as next best thing to live theater. His MCA contract made no extra demands beyond the standard 10 percent commission on all his earnings, so he called on his agency to help get him on the air. MCA landed Standard Brands as sponsor for an NBC Sunday night program centering on the bumpkin with the heart of gold that Bracken had played in his two hit movies. The agency also steered Bracken toward ad representative Mann Holiner as a producer, and writer Robert Riley Crutcher to develop *The Eddie Bracken Show*. Both were also MCA clients, as was William Demarest, Bracken's costar in *The Miracle of Morgan's Creek* and *Hail the Conquering Hero*, who agreed to play his same gruff, hypercritical character on the radio series.

The Eddie Bracken Show looked like another Bracken triumph, clear up until the night it premiered on February 4, 1945. That night MCA handed Bracken NBC's final contract for the show. In it, MCA wasn't asking for 10 percent. The contract divided the show's profits 60 percent for Bracken, 20 percent for Holiner and 20 percent for MCA. At the same time, MCA handed Eddie a new agency contract which gave MCA 10 percent of the show's production costs in addition to 10 percent of Bracken's paycheck. Bracken refused to sign either contract. "It was a principle," said Bracken. "I was right and I did what was right, and it was as simple as that."

Eddie and MCA went to war. First, the agency found other jobs for Holiner and Crutcher. Bracken had to scramble for another production team to keep *The Eddie Bracken Show* on the air. Next, MCA claimed part ownership of the show and kept $7,000 out of the production budget. After four months, Standard Brands pulled the plug on *The Eddie Bracken Show*. Despite good reviews, the show's ratings had dwindled dramatically after Holiner and Crutcher left. At the end of its six-month run, NBC canceled the program.

In June of 1945, Eddie Bracken became the first major film star to fire MCA and sue them for a full accounting of his money. Individually, he accused Jules Stein, Lew Wasserman, Taft Schreiber, Karl Kramer, Hal Hackett, and Mickey Rockford of grossly violating their "fiduciary obligations," "lacking fidelity," and failing to represent Bracken's best interests.

After six months of legal jockeying, MCA settled, and Bracken dropped his case. He'd won. "It worked out in my behalf," he said. "I just wanted out of MCA. I wanted out of Paramount."

He signed with William Morris and packaged *The Eddie Bracken Show* himself, with a new producer, supporting cast, and sponsor. Bracken even cowrote the show, and Texaco put it back on the air over CBS in 1946. After less than a year, it was canceled again. Bracken finally admitted defeat and began looking around for a film job. But nobody was hiring.

"Fighting MCA cost me my career," Bracken recalled. "The thing is, I couldn't get a job in California. It was all over. I was completely blackballed. It took a long, long while to come back. My career was absolutely turned around. I was back on Broadway, and fortunately I got one show after another and kept on and on and on. It took many, many years before I could go back to Hollywood and get any role at all, but it was never anything that would do me any good."

In recent years, he has shown up in small roles on TV shows like *Murder, She Wrote* and in films like John Hughes's *Baby's Day Out*, but Bracken came to terms long ago with the fact that he'll never again come anywhere near the success he enjoyed before 1945. Nevertheless, if he had it to do over again, Bracken, now seventy-six, said he would do exactly the same thing.

"When all that happened, I didn't hold any bitter feelings toward anybody. What they did was what they did. If I'd gone along with them, I'd probably be a rich man today. I just couldn't go along with it. Who was my agent? Who was acting in *my* behalf?

"I still have friends there [at MCA]. I count [former agent] Arthur Park among my best friends. To this day I can shake hands with Lew Wasserman and smile and talk and have fun. It was the principle. I was in the right. It's really as simple as that.

"I have five kids and nine grandchildren and a great-grandchild and the happiest marriage anyone could possibly have. So what did I lose? I didn't care. Right is right," he said. "I came out of it happy, and they came out with all the money."

TWELVE

Octopus

1946

If the men of MCA had been the *only* ones who came out with all the money, their Hollywood success would never have metastasized.

As ruthless as MCA was in stifling dissent, Stein's growing army was equally generous in sharing its wealth and bestowing stardom upon those who played by the MCA rules. Some clients, like Jack Benny and Edgar Bergen, were even invited regularly to participate in lucrative ventures that Stein, Wasserman, and the rest of the MCA brain trust had developed in real estate and oil speculation.[1]

Kay Kyser, who willingly submitted to the MCA method in Lew Wasserman's first radio package, became wealthy enough by the end of the war to retire. Kyser turned over the *Kollege of Musical Knowledge* to bandleader Phil Harris in 1945 and returned to North Carolina to raise a family. As a favor to Wasserman, he emerged from retirement briefly in 1949 to launch his Kollege series over the new medium of television, but quit for good a year later following a cancer diagnosis.[2] Kyser converted to Christian Science, which frowns upon surgery and drug ther-

---

[1] Though MCA led the way in several postwar oil exploration ventures, the most ambitious was Calgush Oil Company, created in January 1951. The Hollywood roster of limited partners included Jack Benny; his brother-in-law and manager, Myrt Blum; Edgar Bergen; Gordon MacRae; Groucho Marx; Freeman Gosden; Clifton Webb; Kirk Douglas; Doris Day; her husband, Marty Melcher; her lawyer, Jerome B. Rosenthal; producer Sam *(The Joker Is Wild* and *Strategic Air Command)* Briskin; his wife, Sara Briskin; Metropolitan Theater chain owner Sherill Corwin; and department store magnate Wilbur May. The limited partners from MCA included Taft Schreiber, Larry Barnett, Sonny Werblin, Lew Wasserman, Jules and Doris Stein, Herb Miller, Harry Berman, Charles Miller, Leland Hayward, and the Management Corporation of America.

[2] MCA bought the rights to the name from Kyser and revived the *Kollege of Musical Knowledge* for a single season over NBC in 1954, using it to launch the career of the host, country singer Tennessee Ernie Ford.

apy, and his disease went into remission. He dedicated the rest of his life to his religion and lived comfortably for another thirty years on the nest egg Lew helped him build.

Joan Crawford, whose career ground to a halt in 1945, was another who benefited by submitting to MCA.

"It was all in a day's work when Joan Crawford was brought from the bottom," Taft Schreiber said. "The exhibitors were taking ads and saying she was box office poison. Some of our men went to Warner's and convinced them she was not box office poison. And she made a picture and she won the Academy Award."

Crawford credited Wasserman with her resurrection. Lew held out against Jack Warner's repeated attempts to put her into soap operas in order to cash in on her prewar popularity as a mannish shoulder-pad queen. Instead, he insisted on reinventing Crawford as Mildred Pierce, the self-sacrificing mother of a spoiled sociopath. The role was powerful, and her performance won her an Oscar nomination, but her competition was stiff: Greer Garson, Gene Tierney, Jennifer Jones, and Ingrid Bergman.

Lew and producer Jerry Wald put press agent Henry Rogers on the case. Before a rough cut was even available, gossips gushed about Crawford's incredible performance as the impassioned, long-suffering Mildred Pierce. Column plants and word-of-mouth campaign continued for months.

As icing on the cake, Crawford claimed to be too ill to attend the Oscar ceremonies. When she won, she was able to dramatically climb out of a sickbed, clad only in a negligee, and pose for photographers holding her statuette. She made front pages around the world. The publicity proved profitable. Lew renegotiated her contract, guaranteeing her $200,000 a picture.

Crawford's arch-rival, Bette Davis, also became independently wealthy, thanks to Jules and Lew. As B.D. Inc., a personal services and production company that Stein created for her in 1942, Davis now held a profit position in every film she made for Warner Brothers—as did Stein, who owned 10 percent of her company. Beginning with A Stolen Life in 1946, she still drew down a fat weekly paycheck of $7,000. But now, in addition to her salary, B.D. Inc. collected 35 percent of her films' profits. By 1948, the first of these films had already earned her $100,000 beyond her salary and promised to keep yielding for years to come.

Despite the financial coup, her contract still bound Bette to the whims of Jack Warner. She shrieked regularly to her MCA agents over the sappy melodramas and creaky romances Warner picked out for her, and Wasserman dutifully relayed her frustrations to Warner, but the studio chief paid no heed.

Bette's war became Lew's war. He warned Jack Warner that sooner or later his arrogance would blow up in his face.

Warner hadn't noticed the power shift in Hollywood. He saw no threat in an actress's tantrums, even if the actress was Bette Davis. He handled her the way he'd always handled stars: like a stern but affectionate parent.

So Davis began sabotaging the movies she didn't like. When she shot her next film after *A Stolen Life,* Warner secretly assigned a production executive to keep tabs on her. Sixteen different times, her maid or Lew called in sick for her. Once she had an injured finger. Another time she suffered uncontrollable crying fits. One day she walked off the set because she could do nothing with her hair. On another occasion her favorite cameraman called in sick and she refused to allow anyone else to capture her profile on celluloid.

Warner called such behavior capricious and irresponsible, but Wasserman tolerated his stars' whims and neuroses as part of the price of controlling them. At Bette's insistence, Lew kept the pressure on, backing her right to complain whenever she got a lousy script.

The final showdown came over King Vidor's campy murder melodrama *Beyond the Forest* in 1950, remembered today for Davis's oft-mimicked line, "What a dump!" While the picture was still in production, Davis complained to the press about the dialogue she was forced to spout on camera. Warner went through the roof once more. The last straw was an item in Erskine Johnson's column in the November 23, 1949, edition of the *New York World Telegram:* "Exclusively yours: Stars frequently become 'difficult' in order to win new contracts or bigger salaries. But Bette Davis is the first star I ever heard of willing to admit it. Bette now says she 'acted up' during filming of *Beyond the Forest* in order to break her WB contract. She says she never wanted to make the picture."

Warner went ballistic. He wired Wasserman: Couldn't MCA control its client?

Lew promptly and coolly declared that Miss Davis wouldn't seek interviews, but if asked direct questions, she would say exactly how she felt. That, he told Warner, was called freedom of speech. Warner was nearly as angry over Wasserman's condescension as he was over Bette Davis's outspoken trashing of her own movie. He was particularly furious over her admission to the *World Telegram* columnist that her behavior was designed to manipulate the studio.

When Bette Davis walked out of Warner Brothers and into the waiting arms of her MCA protectors, Lew didn't gloat. He simply went about business. The next picture he landed for her was *All About Eve* at Twentieth Century Fox.[3] She got $130,000 for twelve weeks' work as fading stage star Margo Channing and was nominated as Best Actress for the first time since 1944. Though she didn't win, the movie did. *All About Eve* took the 1950 Best Picture Oscar.

---

[3] Wasserman initially landed the part of Margo Channing for Barbara Stanwyck. Only after Stanwyck, Claudette Colbert, and Gertrude Lawrence passed did Davis get the role.

OTHER MCA CLIENTS followed the Davis pattern. They began by asking Lew or Jules Stein to turn them into corporations. High-earning stars, who were taxed at the 90 percent level on their personal income, could pay a fraction of that to the government in capital gains taxes if they incorporated. Before she began earning her B.D. Inc. income, for example, Bette Davis earned $328,000 from Warner Brothers in 1945 but kept only $90,000 after taxes.

But Jules didn't incorporate his clients just to be a nice guy. He saw a brand-new way to squeeze another 10 percent out of his clients. He didn't just collect a percentage of their salaries. He collected from their corporation profits, too. He and his agents encouraged the trend.

The studio chieftains began to see trouble. Negotiating with a corporation was a lot more difficult than negotiating with an actor. Echoing his fellow moguls, Warner railed at MCA for refusing to quell these star demands before they evolved into a full-blown revolution.

"We want to sign John Garfield exclusively and MCA should aid us in getting this done, rather than aid Garfield in getting a split contract with outside rights," Jack Warner groused when Wasserman demanded that Garfield have the right to make movies with studios other than Warner Brothers. No deal, said Lew. Despite Warner's bluster, Garfield got his way—and went on to win praise for his starring role in *Pride of the Marines* before starring opposite Lana Turner in the adaptation of James M. Cain's classic murder story *The Postman Always Rings Twice*.

The revolution was well under way. By 1946, the word "exclusive" was vanishing from star contracts. Before the decade was over, the standard seven-year contract would be as dead as silent movies. With MCA as their guide, movie stars progressed from handsomely paid wage slaves to independent contractors who chose their movies and decided how they would be written and cast, who would direct them, and what share of the profits the studio would keep.

Even venerable ne'er-do-well Errol Flynn, who loved being bound by contract for the sheer pleasure of writing off every binge and bimbo on his studio expense account, joined the corporate club. After signing with MCA, Flynn made *Cry Wolf* (1947) and became the second Warner client to collect twice: once as a salaried star and once from his own corporation.

While Jack Warner, Darryl Zanuck, Harry Cohn, Louis Mayer, and the rest of the moguls tried desperately to hold on to their power, they could see the advantage shifting to the new generation of agents and lawyers who represented stars. In the postwar years, box office receipts declined dramatically. Those stars who could still lure America back to the movies now enjoyed unprecedented bargaining power—a fact that Lew Wasserman exploited to the fullest, setting the tone for all of Hollywood.

In the final months of 1945, Wasserman's highly touted $1 million contract for Ronald Reagan finally went into effect at Warner Brothers. Thirty days after

Reagan's army discharge, he was earning $3,500 a week for making five pictures a year. But Reagan's lightweight reputation made him small potatoes compared with what Lew was able to bleed from the studios for top-flight stars like stage-trained Henry Fonda, whom MCA had acquired in the Hayward buyout. At the same time that Reagan was getting $3,500, Warner Brothers agreed to pay Fonda $6,000 a week, and the returning navy vet had to make only one picture a year.

Likewise, Lew tried putting U.S. Army Air Force pilot Jimmy Stewart back to work, but MCA's demand that MGM negotiate a new contract for the returning war hero fell on the deaf ears of Louis Mayer. Stewart, the 1940 Academy Award winner for *The Philadelphia Story*, hadn't made a movie since *Ziegfeld Girl* in 1941. Mayer didn't give a damn about his war record. Harking back to the language of Stewart's prewar contract, MGM demanded that Stewart make up the five years he'd spent as a bombardier in Europe before negotiating a new deal.

Not only did Wasserman raise hell with the Screen Actors Guild, he took the matter to Jules Stein, who knew exactly how to speak to the mightiest of Hollywood's moguls in the only language Mayer understood. Stein threatened to pull all MCA bands out of the East Coast theater chain owned by MGM's parent company, Loew's. Suddenly MGM's stance changed. Stewart's old MGM contract had indeed expired.

Stewart won the point, but lost the studio. He didn't work for a year. As a pawn in the growing war between MCA and the studios, Stewart was punished for defying Mayer. When Wasserman finally did land him a job, it was in a small independent production for director Frank Capra, quietly released through RKO. The film did poorly at the box office without the hype that MGM, Fox, or Warner Brothers could have given it. Nevertheless, *It's a Wonderful Life* went on to become a classic and the signature film of an astounding career. It also firmly reestablished James Stewart as a star.

—◦◦◦—

LEW WASSERMAN EMBRACED television in the 1940s the way Jules Stein had glommed on to the new medium of radio during the 1920s. Television programs were the wave of the future — an entertainment revolution about to sweep over the nation the way big band music and radio serials had swept over the previous generation. Lew liked to boast that he owned one of the first two TV sets sold in southern California. The other belonged to Don Lee, an L.A. Cadillac dealer who operated the West Coast division of the CBS radio network.

Since the early 1930s, television had been a pictures-through-the-air gimmick that its inventor, Philo T. Farnsworth, had first tried to sell to RCA's mighty David Sarnoff. Sarnoff just laughed. For years TV was the kind of sideshow novelty that brought oohs and ahhs from carnival crowds, but nobody seriously considered having it in their own home. Farnsworth was told that television would never replace radio, so he marketed TV sets himself, under his own brand name.

By 1938, the year Lew and Edie settled in Hollywood, Sarnoff had seen the error of his ways. RCA began competing in the fledgling home TV field, but sets were still little more than expensive toys. At $250 for a low-end model, when the average annual income was $1,223, only a handful of people could afford them, and what they got was a tiny video screen peering from a heavy piece of furniture that delivered scratchy, crude reception at best.

In 1946, Standard Brands, the sponsor of several MCA radio serials, including the ill-fated *Eddie Bracken Show*, sank $200,000 into a weekly TV variety show from New York called *Hour Glass*. It was a forerunner of Ed Sullivan's *Toast of the Town* and Milton Berle's *Texaco Star Theater* and remained the backbone of the new NBC-TV network for almost a year. Several MCA clients made appearances, including Edgar Bergen and Charlie McCarthy, who finally demonstrated to a viewing audience that Bergen was an honest-to-goodness ventriloquist.

That same year Bergen was elected the first president of the newly created National Academy of Television Arts and Sciences. Less than a half million households had TV. The following year NBC televised the World Series for the first time, and the medium exploded. Twelve years later, 51 million homes had TV sets.

For all of his visionary expertise in leading MCA into television, Lew remained cautious when committing time, resources, and money to the new medium. He was fond of reciting to subordinates in later years, "As a general rule of thumb, I think it is a good idea not to spend any more than you can get back." So TV would have to wait awhile.

Wasserman's personal investments remained conservative, too. He did not throw his MCA salary away on get-rich-quick schemes, hot stock tips, or anything so foolish as a movie or one of Leland Hayward's stage productions. Instead, he joined Karl Kramer, Taft Schreiber, and Stein's brother-in-law, Charlie Miller, in a real estate coalition that bought up property during the depressed early days of World War II. Among other land deals, the MCA group quietly purchased a whole city block along Pasadena's Colorado Boulevard, the route of the annual Tournament of Roses Parade. All but one building was vacant when they bought the property in 1941. Four years later their tenants included Woolworth's, Forester Jewelers, Reed's Millinery, Sontag Drugs, Burt's Shoes, and the Broadway department store.

Lew invested in other ventures with his MCA cronies, too, but never in the high-risk entertainment business. He put his money into Bernard's, a pair of ladies' ready-to-wear stores in the working-class communities of San Pedro and Huntington Park, and became a silent partner in the William Pitt jewelry company. By 1950, MCA's top echelon had investments in a shoe manufacturing company, an Italian marble quarry, railroad stocks, and an upscale confectionery company. In time, his fellow MCA executives persuaded Wasserman to speculate in gas and oil wells but not at first. For all the polish and surface self-confidence Lew had acquired since leaving Ohio, he still had painful memories of his impoverished childhood. If he needed any reminders, he had his family, who had followed him to California.

Minnie and Isaac Wasserman emigrated to the West Coast in 1943, and though there might have been enough room for them to squeeze into Lew and Edie's new two-story home on the eastern edge of Beverly Hills, the older couple moved into their own rented duplex in West Los Angeles. It was just as well. Lew's workaholic lifestyle would have been cramped by their presence, and Edie's trans-formation into a social butterfly would have been stunted. She had learned from years of expensive Bistro luncheons and swinging Sunset Strip nightlife that she looked best in little black dresses and black star sapphires, and she made the most of it, whether Lew accompanied her on her nocturnal jaunts or not.

Besides, working-class Minnie Wasserman had little in common with her well-bred daughter-in-law. Minnie might never have come to sunny southern California at all if doctors back in Cleveland hadn't diagnosed her with leukemia. Isaac, on the other hand, remained fairly healthy for a man in his early sixties. It seemed like a good time to go to California, where there was no winter to speak of, and where the Wassermans could live out their lives in relative comfort, close to their increas-ingly famous son, and to Lynne, the granddaughter whom they rarely got to visit.

Two years after Lew's parents arrived, Will and Dora Wasserman also moved to California. Minnie and Isaac had invited their older son and his family to come live with them.

Like his younger brother, William Wasserman had managed to stay out of the draft during World War II, but that didn't seem to give him much of an economic edge back in Cleveland. Unlike Lew, Will had finished four years of college, but that didn't help, either. He worked for Dora's father for a while, but prospects in the paint business were limited. Even Will came to accept that Lew had the head for business in the family and enjoyed all of the success. Perhaps Will thought that if he lived near Lew, some of the magic might rub off.

One thing was clear: Lew Wasserman was no Jules Stein when it came to rel-atives — he did not want them on his payroll in any capacity, ever. Lew wouldn't let his family starve, but neither would he use his business advantage to set them up the way Stein had taken care of both of his brothers. Bill Stein may have been a less than competent MCA talent scout while he was alive, and the youngest Stein brother, Herman David Stein, may have wound up as the nominal boss of MCA's Paris office following World War II,[4] but William Wasserman would never work for

---

[4]   "[MCA's office in] Paris was actually run by two very capable French ladies while David lived the bachelor life: traveled, had parties, played the piano, collected art," recalled MCA vice president Berle Adams. "He had a place in Spain and lived in a seven-room apartment where

MCA. Neither would any other Wasserman relative, including Lew's own daughter. Lew preached to all who ever worked for him that nepotism was an invitation to disaster. Unlike Stein, he practiced what he preached.

If Will was disappointed, he wasn't so discouraged that he planned to return to Ohio. He bought a shoe concession at a Hollywood department store, which did not last long. Then he tried his hand at being an entrepreneur.

Before he'd spent more than a year in L.A., Will met the owner of a gag and novelty manufacturing firm who promised him a gold mine. Martin Escovar, who operated the Hollywood Plastic Manufacturing Company, claimed to have a secret formula for producing a new kind of rubber mold. It could be used over and over to mass-produce top quality plaster figurines and novelties which sold like hotcakes at county fairs, gift shops, and carnivals. There was nothing like this secret rubber mold anywhere on the market. Escovar told Will that he was already raking in $10,000 a year in profits.

But he had a cash flow problem. He needed an infusion of $8,000. He'd cut Will Wasserman in for half, if he could just come up with the capital.

Will went to family and friends, borrowing and begging. There's no evidence Lew invested, but Will finally scraped the money together. Then he waited for the profits to roll in. He began dropping by the company's Sunset Boulevard headquarters, personally inspecting the fabulous rubber molds and trying to speed things along. Will even installed his own employee, hoping to spy on how Escovar managed the business. After six months, Escovar had spent the entire $8,000, but profits never materialized.

At about the same time, Minnie Wasserman died. Though she'd been ill for years, a single week of pneumonia finally killed her. The elder Wassermans still lived with Will and Dora at the time of Minnie's death, but it was Lew, not Will, who dispatched his personal Beverly Hills physician to Westwood to formally declare his mother dead. And it was Lew who made arrangements to have her buried in the Jewish quarter of Hollywood Memorial Park, near Rudolph Valentino, Douglas Fairbanks, and other Hollywood notables.

Isaac Wasserman lived four more years. He continued to stay with Will and Dora and their daughter, Natalie, in the kind of welcoming extended family home the Wassermans had always known back in Ohio: doors always open to neighbors and cousins and other long-lost relatives. It wasn't at all like the austere two-story house where Lew and Edie lived—and where, more often than not, nobody was home except Lynne and her nurse, Peggy Slater.

In 1947, Will and Dora salvaged enough from their Hollywood Plastics debacle to move out of the West L.A. rental. They bought their own tiny two-bedroom

_____

Doris and Jules stayed when they were in Paris. Lew couldn't fire him. He was Jules's brother. But he kept him as far away from Beverly Hills as possible."

home on Hayworth Avenue in the middle of L.A.'s borscht belt. By mentioning his brother's name, Will got a job selling film stock for United Artists, where those who came in contact with him over the years marveled at the difference between the two Wasserman brothers: Lew was outgoing and aggressive; Will was taciturn and a follower. Lew was tall and dapper; Will was short and drab. They had both invested their careers in the motion picture business, but at opposite ends of the industry.

When liver cancer attacked Isaac Wasserman, Lew once again stepped in. He sent his own physician to Will's house to fetch the old man, booked him into Cedars of Lebanon Hospital, and when death came, saw to it that he was buried next to Minnie in Hollywood Memorial Park.

Edie's father, Henry Beckerman, had died the previous October, and his passing was front-page news in the *Cleveland Plain Dealer*, the *Cleveland News*, and the *Cleveland Press*.[5]

Isaac Wasserman's death got a one-line notice in the back pages. He was laid to rest on July 5, 1950, Lew and Edie's fourteenth wedding anniversary.

—◦◦◦—

LEW'S ARM'S-LENGTH sense of responsibility for his family could be explained away easily enough. When his mother lay dying, Lew was at the brink of achieving his lifelong dream of becoming the biggest fish in the Hollywood pond, but that dream could be destroyed at any moment in as Machiavellian a barrel of barracudas as MCA. Taft Schreiber, Sonny Werblin, and the rest of the agency's ruling elite were as close to being friends as anyone becomes in the agency game, but an MCA pal could turn on a dime if there was enough at stake.

As Stein approached his fiftieth birthday, the rumors came thick and fast that he was finally planning to step aside as president of MCA and give a younger man a chance. Sonny Werblin was the odds-on favorite. He'd turned the New York office into an even bigger cash machine since Billy Goodheart left. He was now the toast of Broadway. He owned his own table in every nightclub from Sardi's to the Stork Club, and he controlled much of what America heard on the radio.

---

[5] Within the year, it was revealed that Henry Beckerman and his former business partner, Edwin P. Strong, had not been the only partners in Cleveland's Thistledown Race Track. Unlike Beckerman, who bequeathed everything to his wife, Strong left a tangled estate with investments in drive-in theaters, racetracks, and Florida real estate. Only after Strong's will was filed in probate did it become clear that Strong and Beckerman had been front men for four familiar Cleveland businessmen: Sam Tucker, Morris Kleinman, Lou Rothkopf, and Moe Dalitz, each of whom owned a 15 percent stake in Thistle Down. As a final familial touch, Edie's brother, Stanley Beckerman, was named co-trustee for Strong's $3 million estate. Working with co-trustee Samuel T. Haas, the former Mayfair Casino investor, Stanley oversaw the Strong estate's liquidation.

Quiet but shrewd Taft Schreiber, who had his fingers in every aspect of MCA's business—bands, movies, theater, radio, nightclubs, ice shows, county fairs, real estate—was also high on the list of candidates. Having fallen under Leland Hayward's patrician influence, Schreiber had taken to collecting Postimpressionist art, much to the delight of Jules and Doris. The Steins considered themselves connoisseurs of van Gogh and even some of the more recent painters—provided they were European and had been dead a generation or so. They admired Taft's newfound touch of class.

Leland Hayward himself, of course, had no interest in running another talent agency. His passion was his new play, *State of the Union*, which had taken Broadway by storm. He was available as an elder statesman, but succeeding Jules Stein was the last thing he wanted.

Of the rest of the ruling elite, Mickey Rockford declined, as did tactician and company treasurer Karl Kramer. Charlie Miller, Maurie Lipsey, Morris Schrier, Herb Rosenthal, and the rest lacked either the talent or inclination to succeed Dr. Stein. But Wasserman had both, and he was still a strong contender.

"None of them had the mind that Wasserman had," said Dorothea Campbell. "He could walk into a theater and tell you how many kernels of corn were in a bag of popcorn, how many bags were sold, and whether the house was being cheated or not. He had that kind of mind."

Stein regarded Wasserman's wizardry with numbers as a big plus. But in Hollywood, where appearance is everything, Lew had to have an extra edge. He couldn't afford to be seen at this particular moment in his career as anything less than a superman. He took credit for the Hayward-Deverich coup and his motion picture division was fast becoming as profitable to MCA as its band and radio divisions. His much-gossiped-about "$1 million contract" for Ronald Reagan had given Lew a strong psychological advantage in an industry fueled by rumors. His cool professionalism in the face of contemptuous studio heads had cinched his position at the peak of the pecking order. By acclamation, Lew Wasserman was now the most powerful agent in Hollywood.

In mid-February of 1946, Stein hosted the annual MCA board meeting in Palm Springs. He still owned the company, but he had begun sharing profits and policy-making decisions with his most trusted executives after Billy Goodheart left him. Wasserman, Werblin, Schreiber, Kramer, Charlie Miller, and Maurie Lipsey made up the board of directors of the privately held corporation.

At the Palm Springs meeting there was some discussion of Schreiber's recent postwar trip to England and Stein's plans to reopen the London office. With the war at an end, the company was looking to expand into continental Europe, starting with Paris and possibly Rome. But for the most part, the Palm Springs meeting was all rubber stamp and routine. Nothing unusual came up—until the directors got back to Beverly Hills.

There the news had already broken in *Variety*, *Billboard*, and the *Hollywood Reporter* as well as the daily newspapers: San Diego dance-hall owner Larry Finley had won a $55,000 judgment against the Octopus MCA.

The money was meaningless. MCA routinely took in $55,000 for half a day's work, and that was only from the band-booking side of the business. Stein used to carry that much cash in the glove compartment of his Rolls when he drove his kid brother and sister around the dirt streets of South Bend during the late 1920s.

What alarmed Jules was that a small-time promoter had spent a year labeling MCA a money-grubbing conglomerate. Now, an eleven-person jury agreed. Finley's allegations suddenly had the ring of official justice.

During the two-week trial, Stein himself had been called to the witness stand to defend his business practices. Finley's lawyers forced such trade secrets into the open as the fact that MCA earned $15 million a year just booking bands—a conservative estimate, to be sure. More importantly, they exposed MCA's cozy arrangement with the American Federation of Musicians.

MCA represented bandleaders, not band members, Stein had carefully explained on the stand. The agency collected tithes from leaders, not from AFM rank and file. MCA was not responsible for AFM members. Sometimes MCA didn't even book the bands; the orchestra leaders did the bookings themselves. Yet the agency still collected its 10 percent.

But everything was done with the blessing of James C. Petrillo, who ran the AFM. If exclusive booking practices were all right with him, why wouldn't they be all right with MCA?

After Stein stepped down from the witness stand, MCA agent Eames Bishop was sworn in. Against his lawyer's advice, Bishop detailed how MCA sewed up the West. Any dance hall that could accommodate 3,000 or more paying customers a night got an exclusive contract offer. The dance halls became dependent upon MCA. To switch agencies would be unthinkable because MCA controlled nearly all the name bands. Meanwhile, MCA had no overhead. It took its percentage directly from the gross. Each dance-hall owner, on the other hand, had to pay for rent, advertising, upkeep, security, payroll, and other expenses. In this way, Bishop explained, MCA controlled every major nightspot from Fresno to Spokane but bore none of the responsibility of owning or managing.

"They were angry with me, but I had to tell the truth," said Bishop, after MCA's lawyers told him to speak only of free enterprise and healthy business competition on the witness stand.

West Coast band division chief Larry Barnett, another rising MCA star, also appeared as a witness but added little to Dr. Stein's testimony. Shortly after the trial he was rewarded with an MCA vice presidency.

It was all very public, with the news media turning out in force to hear what the mysterious little titan from Chicago and his lieutenants had to say about the allegedly brutal methods that MCA used to deal with its enemies. Now, in the last week of February 1946, Stein's beloved MCA was officially declared guilty of conspiracy and monopoly. Could a government investigation be far behind?

Stein ordered everyone back to Palm Springs. In its March 5 issue, *Variety* announced that "Reports of a shakeup in the hierarchy of Music Corp. of America continue to circulate despite denials of top execs. With arrival here yesterday of Sonny Werblin, v-p and second to prexy Jules Stein, from the east, and M. B. Lipsey, Chicago chieftain of MCA, talk of changes has increased."

Two days later *Variety* reported even more alarming news. The *Saturday Evening Post*, the most widely read magazine in America, had dispatched a team of reporters to Hollywood as plans to publish a five-part exposé of MCA moved into high gear. One hundred twenty-one people had already been interviewed. The *Variety* article went on: "All this data will be assembled by one of mag's top writers and fashioned into complete case history of office. It's reported all MCA employees have been given strict instructions not to talk for publication."

On that same March morning that *Variety* revealed the *Saturday Evening Post*'s invasion of Hollywood, Herman Bennett, chief of the L.A. office of the Justice Department's antitrust division, added the finishing touches to an eight-page memorandum labeled "Request for FBI Investigation." He put the memo in the interoffice mail bound for Washington, D.C.

Larry Finley's wasn't the only voice protesting MCA's tactics, Bennett wrote. He detailed a dozen instances in which dance-hall owners from Seattle to San Bernardino had been forced to play by the MCA rules or not play at all. If this was happening up and down the West Coast, it must be happening all across the country, Bennett reasoned. He predicted that a half dozen FBI agents could slap together a solid case against Stein in less than a month.

"It is believed that an FBI investigation will disclose that other individuals, affiliates of MCA, and other corporations are implicated in the conspiracy and that such investigation will also disclose facts that will warrant a grand jury investigation," Bennett wrote.

But Bennett counseled caution. MCA was no ordinary trust and Jules Stein was no ordinary business baron. Bennett understood better than his D.C. bosses what they were up against. MCA's power had not evolved out of a vacuum, and its hierarchy wasn't composed of power-drunk buffoons who ignored public opinion. In fact, MCA existed because its leaders knew precisely how to *control* public opinion. Its low profile and shrewd emphasis on gathering all information before reacting was the key to its success.

Stein huddled with his troops in Palm Springs the following week. This time the meeting was neither routine nor leisurely. This time they rented a private home, locked themselves inside, and didn't leave until they had devised a plan to handle the crisis.

—⁓—

THE DECISION WAS made to stonewall the Justice Department. The only announcement to come out of the Palm Springs bivouac was Larry Barnett's appointment as an MCA vice president—via a conveniently timed defiant press release that said, in effect, "We don't care about the Finley decision; we're even promoting the man responsible for it."

Henceforth, all press inquiries were to be directed to Morris Schrier, the shrill company lawyer who answered nothing without advance approval.

With that, Stein left for New York. From there, he and Doris traveled on to England to reopen MCA's London office and to look into the possibility of starting up a new MCA office across the Channel in Paris. Unofficially, the Steins were also hoping to visit Palestine, but the State Department denied them visas to the increasingly troubled British protectorate. Too dangerous, they were told. In lieu of Palestine, the Steins opted to sail to Argentina and Brazil following their European sojourn. MCA might be opening offices in South America soon, too. MCA had its own manifest destiny, as anyone could see who entered its headquarters building or took a good look at the globe that graced its letterhead. MCA would someday interlink the world, as it had the United States. Someday soon.

Back in Beverly Hills, Stein's subordinates were left to carry out damage control on the Finley matter as well as the *Post* article. There the hard line toward press and publicity took a practical turn.

On April 11, 1946, MCA appealed Finley's $55,000 judgment but quietly began supplying the dance-hall owner with all the name bands he needed for his Mission Beach nightclub. On the *Saturday Evening Post* matter, MCA's no-publicity policy entered a new and subtle phase of cooperation. Unlike the long line of journals that had tried to crack MCA before, back doors seemed to be opening to the *Post*. When the long-anticipated series finally broke, the one universal response in the music business was how soft—even fawning—it turned out to be.

It seemed that, following his return from England, Stein had suddenly changed his attitude. It was almost as if someone with a background in media manipulation and a shrewd skill at finding the quid pro quo had sat the good doctor down, argued against the futility of warring with a national magazine, and told Stein how to defang the *Post*. To wrest control away from the magazine, Stein had to offer to cooperate, to do what MCA had always done best: make a deal.

Stein journeyed to the *Post's* headquarters in Philadelphia, where he promised to throw the doors open to David Wittels—on certain conditions. He would even let the *Post's* glamour photographer, Gene Lester, visit MCA headquarters for some "candid" shots of Stein and his boys cutting up like real human beings and consulting as a brain trust over serious matters. The photographer even gained entrée to Stein's Lake Arrowhead retreat, where he posed the screen's current heartthrob, Van Johnson, with Doris and the Steins' two bobby-soxers, fourteen-year-old Jean and twelve-year-old Susan.

And the *Post*'s editors were assured that the story would be an exclusive.

Stein's ploy worked. If Wittels had any hard evidence of Stein's long-rumored ties to the Capone mob, his global monopolistic aspirations, or MCA's extortionate business practices, it didn't show up in the *Saturday Evening Post*. In August of 1946 the *Saturday Evening Post* published "The Star-Spangled Octopus," a four-part series whose title would stick to MCA for the next twenty years.

Wittels's series might have seemed soft to show-business insiders, but it was all revelation to the rest of America. Dr. Stein made his national debut as the same type of Hollywood celebrity MCA created out of whole cloth for fan magazines. Wittels's version of Jules Stein was tough, brilliant, a bit threatening, but almost statesmanlike, even a little grandfatherly. From the first awed paragraph, Wittels portrayed Jules as powerful and enigmatic, but certainly not the embodiment of evil that MCA's victims would have liked to see unmasked: "Cursed, threatened and sometimes sued, he's the backstage Mr. Big of show business. Sinatra, Grable and Lombardo are among his clients, but he remains a mystery. His story has never before been told."

Under Wittels's less-than-critical eye, the cold, self-involved Doris Stein came off as "a famed hostess in the movie colony" and one of the ten best-dressed women in America. Dr. Stein, the ruthless robber baron who took no prisoners, became a Horatio Alger hero who sacrificed a brilliant career as an eye surgeon to bring big band music to all of America and who now spent his millions to support such charitable causes as a Hollywood medical center.

Stein's brain trust received scant attention in the series, save two MCA men whom Wittels described as "the greatest agents of all time": Sonny Werblin and Lew Wasserman.

Despite his adulation, Wittels described Werblin as one who had grown old before his time. Sonny was "in his middle thirties [with] well-grayed hair, and looks fifty. He suffered a serious heart attack when he was twenty-eight. When he was summoned for the draft the doctor rejected him swiftly."

Lew, on the other hand, was described as a human dynamo. What was more, he was a plucky up-from-the-ghetto hero to rival Jules Stein himself: "Handsome Lew Wasserman, currently Stein's right hand man, went in eight years from $100 a week as a press agent for a Cleveland nightclub to $100,000 a year as an MCA vice president."

Aside from Werblin and Wasserman, none of the MCA power elite who had convened in Palm Springs the previous spring made his way into the *Post* articles. There was no mention of Taft Schreiber. No Karl Kramer. No Mickey Rockford.

It was almost as if Wittels had taken on the task of narrowing the candidates for Stein's successor down to two front-runners — one worthy but in charge of yesterday's stars in New York and worn well beyond his thirty-eight years; the other, a fresh, good-looking man of thirty-three who firmly held the reins of power in Los Angeles, the city of movies, pop music, and the emerging technology of television. The city of the future.

—⁓—

WHILE THE KING brothers did not succeed in making a movie out of Jules Stein's biography, the *Saturday Evening Post* series did give rise the following year to a best-seller and a movie, both with unmistakable similarities to MCA and its double-dealing agents. Based on a thinly veiled anecdote lifted directly from David Wittels's article, "The Star-Spangled Octopus," Kansas author Frederic Wakeman wrote *The Hucksters*: a potboiling satire of the New York–Hollywood connection in the high-rolling world of radio advertising.

Federal prosecutor Herman Bennett noted the resemblance between fact and fiction and cited the novel as further proof that MCA was ripe for an antitrust probe. Though Bennett conducted his own year-long inquiry into MCA's monopolistic practices, he never got his FBI investigation. The movie version came and went with no reaction from Washington.

Tame by today's standards, *The Hucksters* raised a furor in 1947. Church leaders howled about the adulterous affair of the novel's hero, played on screen by Clark Gable. It might not have raised as many hackles if the novel's philanderers had met a tragic end, but Wakeman saw fit to stand Hollywood's moral vision on its head and have the sinners survive and get on with their lives, once they escaped the New York–Hollywood rat race. As a result of the controversy, script doctors made Deborah Kerr's character a war widow in the Hollywood version, so that she and Gable could live happily ever after.

But altering illicit sex scenes wasn't the only change forced on MGM when the studio brought *The Hucksters* to the screen. Most Americans would never know that the monolithic agency called Talent Ltd. in the movie was patterned after MCA, or that its founder, the fictional Dave Lash, was a smooth autocrat who looked far too much like Dr. Jules Stein to be a coincidence.

In Wakeman's novel, the newly respectable Dave Lash was a poor Jew who clawed his way to the top by playing footsie with the Mob, then made up for it by giving generously to charities that fought anti-Semitism. His chief lieutenant still got his hands dirty in the real world of deal-making the way Dave Lash once did, but Lash didn't want to know about it.

In the film version, there is no hint that Lash, played by grandfatherly character actor Edward Arnold, is Jewish or that his right-hand man is the conniving, deceitful agent of the novel. The MGM script transformed Lash's odious chief lieutenant into an eager Irish string bean named Freddie Callahan, who followed each step of his boss's clever but honorable deal-making like a graduate student.

Produced by MCA client Arthur Hornblow Jr., whose son was a playmate of the Wassermans' daughter, Lynne, the movie version of *The Hucksters* is oddly devoid of any direct similarities to MCA, nor does it invite any overt comparison of Lew Wasserman to the fictional Freddie Callahan. Most of the novel's vicious swipes at Jules Stein also disappear, including a particularly nasty scene in which the hero invokes a Shylock stereotype: "They're going to say a Jew did it. They're going to say that you, Dave Lash, a Jew, pulled this fast one. Yes, Dave, you know there are people who are going to say it just that way. And it'll help tear down what you've been trying to build up. What you've been spending money to counteract."

The same scene in the movie has a tough-talking Clark Gable threatening to expose Edward Arnold's past as a petty thief growing up in New York, but the movie gives no hint that Arnold's character is Jewish or that his early criminal conniving had anything to do with being Jewish. Dave Lash turns out to be an honorable man when forced to be, and Clark Gable's remorse for having descended to the level of a blackmailing talent agent is so profound that he quits the business, proposes to Deborah Kerr, and lives happily ever after.

One inside visual joke that did survive MGM's sanitizing of Wakeman's satire is a brief exterior shot of a gaudy white marble building, complete with Greek columns. It purports to be the Hollywood offices of Talent Ltd., but on the screen the Georgian mansion is unmistakable. For one uncensored moment the facade of the Beverly Hills headquarters of Music Corporation of America flashes across the screen, reminding those in the know that *The Hucksters* is only partly make-believe.

ON DECEMBER 20, Larry and Miriam Finley filed for their accrued damages in federal court and were turned down. With little media fanfare, the judge set aside the original $55,000 jury verdict and ordered MCA to pay only the Finleys' legal fees. The trust-busting case of 1946 became the old news of 1947. On June 17, 1947, a dismissal was filed. The *Saturday Evening Post*, which had made such an apocalyptic frenzy of the lawsuit the previous summer, failed to even mention it.

Larry Finley went on to play character roles in B westerns of the 1950s and to become co-owner of a Sunset Strip nightclub. He also worked as a disc jockey on Los Angeles radio station KFWB and as an executive at Dot Records, but he never again achieved the kind of fame he had enjoyed when he played David to Stein's Goliath. Big band music never again seemed so important, either. It was almost as if the Finley suit brought the curtain down on an era in American pop music.

"The high-water mark in big bands was the San Diego lawsuit between Pacific

Square and Mission Beach," said MCA's Eames Bishop. "After that, music and everything else began to change."

The Los Angeles office of the Justice Department was still interested in MCA, but Washington wasn't. After a friendly visit with MCA's Morris Schrier in New York, Justice Department attorney Elmo Flynt recommended that the investigation be dropped. Proving that MCA monopolized the band business would be just too hard, he argued.

MCA's agents breathed a collective sigh of relief. Stein's narrow escape from a full-blown antitrust probe was cause not only for celebration but also for an even more careful approach to the agency's ongoing efforts to take complete control of the entertainment industry.

On Christmas Eve of 1946, Louella Parsons made a modest announcement in her column. It concerned the leadership at Music Corporation of America.

Eames Bishop remembered the night it happened, when Jules Stein gathered his troops in the private dining room upstairs at Chasen's. With his loyal agents and their wives seated around the banquet table, Stein raised his glass in a toast to the coming era, when MCA would make its American show-biz success as global as its logo suggested.

Smiling broadly, Jules announced that he was moving up to a newly created position, as chairman of the board of directors at MCA. He would keep his hand in, of course, and continue to handle clients in whom he took a personal interest. But he and Doris hoped to travel more, as they had in 1946, and they wanted to devote more time to socializing and to their hobbies, including their passion for collecting rare English armoires and sideboards.

He was therefore turning over the day-to-day operation of his beloved MCA to the cabal of vice presidents who had effectively run the company for years. The names were familiar by now: Karl Kramer, Taft Schreiber, Larry Barnett, Mickey Rockford, Charlie Miller, Herb Rosenthal, Maurie Lipsey, Hal Hackett, David Werblin....

And to act as leader, the first among equals, Stein raised his glass to the impeccably dressed tiger sitting next to him. Ten years to the day after he walked out of the Mayfair Casino and into the offices of MCA, carrying his scrapbook of publicity gimmicks and press releases, Lew R. Wasserman became Stein's successor as president of the Music Corporation of America. All around the oak-paneled room, his peers and subordinates rose to applaud their new leader. Even Taft Schreiber, whom many thought Stein would select as his successor, stood and clapped.

The evening was pleasant, the food was terrific, and the weather was crisp, even bracing, Bishop recalled. Everyone was there. Almost. Glancing around the room, he noticed that one notable was missing. Sonny Werblin didn't show up for the passing of the baton.

THIRTEEN

Beverly Hills, Moscow, and Gangland, USA

1947–1950

No one told the receptionist at MCA's Manhattan headquarters about Lew, so when the new president flew to New York and showed up with a sheaf of papers and a stack of mail under one arm, she stopped him at the front door.

"I don't know how old he was at the time, but he looked like he was about twenty," recalled actor Charlton Heston, whose wife, Lydia, was waiting in the reception room that morning to speak with the Hestons' Broadway agent, Maynard Morris. "The receptionist stopped him cold. She told him that he couldn't just walk back into the executive offices. That was not how things were done at MCA. She said if he didn't know the proper way to distribute the mail, she would help him do it. She thought he was some new young kid from the mail room."

By naming the boyish Lew Wasserman as his chief executive, Stein hadn't ended MCA's East-West rivalry. Broadway agents like Maynard Morris were suspicious of the Hollywood contingent and vice versa. Lew's rise didn't repair the rift. It merely shifted the focus to the two tough cookies who didn't get the presidency.

Sonny Werblin became as silent as the Sphinx following the *Post* series. He never complained and he never explained. If he was bitter at being passed over when everyone in the agency knew that New York generated a dozen times more revenue than Beverly Hills did, he displayed no indignation. Outwardly he remained pleasant, philosophical, even jovial. When a reporter asked about Lew, he simply said nothing.

Taft Schreiber was equally silent. He usually ignored reporters' questions. During one rare interview, he explained his reluctance to talk as company policy.

"This is a seven-day-a-week job, but it's just a job," Schreiber insisted. "Naturally, we have an ethical reticence to talk to newspapers about our business because it's not really our business. It's our clients' business. But because we don't seek publicity, that doesn't mean we have anything to hide."

If there was something worth hiding, the bicoastal executives hid it from each other as often as they hid it from outsiders. MCA had become a unique nest of vipers in the late 1940s, where the profit motive had been distilled to a company creed. Agents lived or died by their year-end bonuses. During the year they earned subsistence wages, often as little as $100 a week. But they worked individually to build up the company's commissions, and those who could claim credit at the end of the year for signing a star, booking a nightclub act, or packaging a radio show took home a paycheck that could climb into five, even six figures.

"If you have the commission system, all the agent thinks about is his commission," preached Jules Stein. "He'll book an artist into a place just because it offers more, even though another place may be a better showcase for the artist. With the bonus system, he thinks of the artist first."

Unlike other agencies that worked as a team, MCA agents rarely referred to themselves as "we." Agents spoke in the first-person singular in describing their exploits. Stealing acts from each other became as routine as stealing clients from other agencies. As rival vice presidents, Schreiber and Werblin set the standard for undercutting each other's troops.

"Taft was facile and ahead of everyone else," said Berle Adams. "He never finished a sentence, and most agents didn't understand him. He was so smart that when he spoke, no one could keep up with him."

"He had what we'd call Blue Sky sessions," recalled Harry Tatelman. "He'd start by saying something like 'Okay, we're going to sign Dorothy Lamour for her next film with such-and-such a studio,' and then he'd just be off! He had every detail of what we were going to do with Dorothy Lamour all planned, down to the last detail, and we wouldn't even have her signed yet. It was complete fantasy, but he would be talking like it had already happened."

Werblin's meetings with his agents were more like locker room lectures from a losing football coach. Instead of indulging in fantasy, he held ass-kicking sessions.

"Sonny was like an All-Pro in sports," said Adams. "He could not tolerate or ease along anyone who wasn't as driven as him. He laughed when someone talked about taking the weekend off or having friends outside the business."

One former agent told journalist Bill Davidson,

Once, I was talking to an executive at MGM about a deal. Two minutes later I get a call from my superior at MCA, berating me about what I had said to the Metro man. He had the conversation almost verbatim. Later I learned that my colleague in the next office had flattened himself against the wall outside my door and had listened to every word of my conversation with the MGM executive. Then he had reported it to my boss.

I found that my most ruthless enemy was the man in the next office at MCA. I'd go to an advertising executive and sell him a TV show, and then a fellow MCA man would go to him and say, "Why do you want to buy that piece of junk? The show I represent would be much better for you." We were pitted against each other by the nature of the agency, and it was like living in a snarling, cannibalistic, primitive society where your survival depended on your brutality and your guile.

Those who couldn't cut it were asked to leave. Those who left on their own were never invited to return. Lew's two warring generals saw to it that only the strong survived.

"They were tough," said Adams.

Said Tatelman, "Both of them pissed ice water."

—

WITHIN THIS BELLICOSE atmosphere, MCA often created stars or crushed stars for the flimsiest of reasons. In the case of Tony Award–winning Broadway star Russell Nype, his screen career began and ended simply because of the petty jealousies ignited by MCA's ongoing civil war.

"Those shits," Nype said. "I should never, ever have trusted them."

His troubles began the night of his greatest triumph, when he opened on Broadway in Irving Berlin's *Call Me Madam*, one of the legendary composer's last musicals. Based on the life of European socialite and U.S. ambassador to Luxembourg Perle Mesta—a personal friend of Doris and Jules Stein—the show starred Ethel Merman as the ambassador and Nype as her assistant.

Stein invited Nype to MCA's Fifth Avenue offices, where he delivered an irresistible sales pitch. Nype recalled the speech "as if it were yesterday."

"Russell, I want to buy your contract," Stein told him. "I don't care who has it. I was in the audience last night, and you're the greatest talent who has walked across the stage since Jimmy Stewart and Henry Fonda. I think you will go on forever! Whoever's handling your contract, I want to buy it and personally supervise your career, because you're going to get the greatest deal that's ever been done in Hollywood."

Nype was stunned. He asked his agent, Gloria Safier, how she felt about releasing him from his contract. She resisted. Not only had she nurtured him through the lean years and helped him get his big break, but she also knew something about Jules Stein.

But Nype's friends and peers advised him to switch to MCA.

Safier reluctantly sold Nype's contract for $30,000 plus a percentage of his future earnings, and he was off to Hollywood. There, Nype was told, the movie offers did *not* come flooding in.

"What I didn't know was that Jules had gone to all of his people and said, 'You don't know *anything* about creating a star! I'm going to *show* you how it's done!'" Nype recalled. "That did me in, because no one wanted to help Stein prove that he was right."

After several discouraging years of splitting his time between New York, where he worked, and Hollywood, where he didn't, Nype finally gave up on the movies. He returned full-time to Broadway where he won another Tony, married, and raised a family. Unaware of what had gone on behind his back, Nype remained good friends with the Steins, dining with them at their Misty Mountain castle whenever he was in California. He even copied the Steins' taste in furniture, decorating his three-room East Side apartment in eighteenth-century English to match the quaint appearance of an MCA office suite.

Throughout their long friendship, Jules Stein never once let on to Nype that he had micromanaged Nype's film career into oblivion.

For the same capricious reasons that Russell Nype's rising star was shot out of the sky, MCA was equally capable of plucking a nobody from oblivion and turning him or her into a household name. Janet Leigh's career, for example, was the result of a dare over dinner one night at Romanoff's.

In the summer of 1946, Leigh and her bandleader husband, Stan Reames, lived in a cheap hotel near downtown Los Angeles. He worked nights in the clubs while Janet kept the books for the band. One day a letter arrived from MCA. She assumed that it must be about the band, but it was addressed only to her, and in her maiden name.

> **Dear Miss Morrison,**
> **We at MCA would very much like to meet with you to discuss possible representation. Please call at your earliest convenience.**
> **Sincerely, Levis Green**

At first she thought it was some kind of joke. But when she called the number on the letterhead and asked to speak with Mr. Green, the operator put her right through to the agent's secretary. Janet remained puzzled as to why MCA would have any interest in her, but went ahead and made an appointment to see Levis Green the following day. That night she borrowed a magenta crepe wraparound from a friend, and the next morning she dolled herself up with rouge and mascara and walked into MCA headquarters dressed to kill.

"What did you *do* to yourself?" hollered Green the moment he laid eyes on her. "No, no, no! You should look like this picture."

He held up her snapshot, taken the previous winter at a mountain ski resort where Janet's father worked as a desk clerk. Aha! At least now she understood how MCA had come up with her name. Her parents must have sent her picture to the agency.

In the photo she wore no makeup, her jacket was open, and her hair was blowing loose in the wind. She looked young, fresh, like the girl next door. And here she sat, dressed like a cut-rate Lana Turner.

"I'm taking you to MGM tomorrow, but not like *that*," Green told her. "Don't *ever* do that again."

True to his word, the MCA agent picked her up the next day in his Lincoln Continental. They drove through the gates of MGM and parked outside the offices of the studio's new talent division. There she was quizzed on her acting experience. That was easy enough: except for a college performance in *The Pirates of Penzance*, she had none.

Janet was ordered to wait in an outer office while Green and the MGM rep kibitzed. A few moments later Green walked out with a seven-year contract. She started immediately at $50 a week and spent the rest of the day working with a drama coach, still unclear as to how she'd wound up on the MGM payroll.

But Green knew, and could hardly wait to get back to his office to tell Lew Wasserman.

It seemed that during the previous winter Norma Shearer, Irving Thalberg's widow, had visited the ski lodge where Janet's parents worked. Shearer and her new husband, professional ski instructor Marty Arrouge, struck up a friendship with Janet's father, who spoke proudly of his little girl, now living in L.A., trying to help her husband break into the music business. Fred Morrison displayed snapshots of his daughter. Shearer was impressed enough to ask if she could take them with her back to Hollywood.

Shearer had the photos blown up to 8-by-10s, and the next time she and Marty had dinner at Romanoff's, they cornered Charlie Feldman of Famous Artists, who sat at a booth with two of MGM's top executives, Benny Thau and Eddie Mannix. She pulled out the photos and passed them around the table.

None of the three men could afford to be dismissive of Norma Shearer. Nevertheless, the photos went around the table as if they were red-hot cinders. There were weak smiles and appreciative nods, but no one wanted the task of turning Shearer's discovery into a star. No one could tell her to send the photos back to the ski lodge, either.

That was when Lew and Edie Wasserman dropped by the table to say hello.

"Ah! Here's the man to handle these pictures!" said Feldman. "A much better agency. Lew, we're sure you'll be happy to follow through on this."

Norma was placated, Feldman was off the hook, and the two MGM men would have plenty to laugh about around the water cooler the next day. Only

Wasserman was stuck with the envelope of pictures. He passed them on to Levis Green in MCA's new-talent department.

Thus, when Green told Wasserman that he'd located the young woman and signed her to a seven-year MGM contract, Wasserman grinned. It wasn't over the five-dollar-a-week commission that Green had secured for MCA. It was the fact that Green had turned Feldman's reject into a paying proposition—and at no less a studio than the one operated by Louis B. Mayer. Lew grabbed the phone and dialed MGM's Benny Thau.

"Benny, remember the night you unloaded some pictures on me? That girl Norma was pushing?" he said.

"Do I? Ha! Ha! You should have seen your face," Thau chortled.

"Well, guess what? We found her, and we just signed her to a seven-year studio contract," said Lew.

"Nooooo! Where?"

"At MGM."

Beaming, Lew hung up and gleefully went through the same exercise with Mannix and Feldman, savoring their annoyance at having passed up a paying client. Unlike that of the misdirected Russell Nype, Janet Leigh's movie career would last over thirty years and include such classics as *The Manchurian Candidate*, *Touch of Evil*, and *Psycho*.

"They were good to me," Leigh recalled. "I was this young, naive kid from Stockton who knew nothing, and MCA guided me through those early years. I owe them everything."

Janet Leigh's experience was rare. But just as rare is the fact that she learned up front the sobering fact that her entire fate could be decided by nothing more profound than an agent's dinner dare. Fortunately, she became close friends with Lew and Edie, and her career never faltered, even after her MGM contract expired in 1954. The Wassermans attended her wedding to her second husband—another Wasserman protégé, actor Tony Curtis. They even became godparents to the Curtises' second daughter, actress Jamie Lee Curtis.

———

IN HIS NEW role as president, Lew maintained a chain of command and ruled with iron discipline to rival that of any military organization, beginning with office attire.

"When I became a talent agent for MCA, the word 'agent' was synonymous with 'pimp,'" Wasserman explained in a newspaper interview some years later. "Talent agents wore green suits and hung around street corners with big cigars in their mouths. The badge of a talent agent was a Charvet tie. I wanted to change the image."

He did. According to several sources close to him, including his former son-in-law, Lew is color-blind. Thus, in his early days with the agency, he mismatched his ties and suits daily, until Edie began to homogenize his wardrobe. She refined Dr. Stein's Oxford look to a simple black suit, white shirt, and black tie, and lined Lew's closet with the impossible-to-mismatch uniform. With his basic black-and-white garb, Wasserman set a fashion standard for MCA that lasted close to a generation.

"The black suits and the black tie were almost like the uniform of a Chinese stagehand," said MCA publicist David Lipton. "A uniform so that they would blend into the background and not be obvious whenever they appeared."

Agents rarely wavered from Wasserman's black MCA business suit, which wags like veteran jazz critic Nat Hentoff compared to a Mafia outfit. "If you saw more than one of them sitting together at Sardi's, you figured they were planning a hit," said Hentoff.

Like a football coach, Wasserman reorganized his agents into a team. He wanted written daily reports, which were passed among the executives and discussed in weekly strategy sessions. Each studio was assigned a senior agent who watched over MCA interests on any given lot. For one of these key positions, Lew violated one of MCA's ironclad taboos by rehiring Irving "Swifty" Lazar, who had quit MCA in 1939 to become an independent—and very successful—agent. Upon rejoining MCA, Lazar was asked to cover Fox.

"I had no idea what 'covering' a studio meant," Swifty recalled. "This was, I soon discovered, one more way that MCA was different from other agencies."

During Lazar's first day at Fox, an MCA client flagged him down.

"Are you the new MCA guy?" he asked.

"Yes," answered Lazar.

The actor identified himself as Robert Sterling, a handsome leading man in several B movies during the forties, including *Bunco Squad* and *The Secret Heart*.

"I don't like the color of my dressing room," he told Lazar. "It's green. I want yellow."

"I don't handle dressing room colors," Lazar said.

"But you're my agent."

"I handle contract matters and any disputes you might have with the director or with your costars. But I don't handle paint," Swifty told him politely.

"If that's your attitude, I'm going to fire MCA," said Sterling.

"I don't care what the hell you do, but I'm not going to Darryl Zanuck and ask him to change the color of your dressing room."

When Lazar returned to his office, Lew was waiting. Why had he been so tough on Bob Sterling?

"Because he's a horse's ass," said Lazar. "He's carrying on about the color of his dressing room, and he's not even queer."

Wasserman was not pleased. He had rules, and he expected them to be followed. One of them was to keep the clients happy, even if it meant giving them pedicures, personally picking up their dry cleaning, or giving their dressing rooms a new coat of paint. It was a lecture that Lazar would hear more than once, but it was a policy he did not choose to follow. He believed agents made deals and handled business. Period.

"You have a Mafia-type routine here with all these guys reporting to you," Swifty finally told Wasserman. "I'm no robot. I do my own thing."

Within a year of Lew's ascendancy to the MCA presidency, Lazar quit. Edie later cornered him at a party and delivered the oldest cliché in Tinseltown: that he would never work in Hollywood again.

Lazar did not return to MCA a third time. For the rest of his life his relations with Wasserman remained cordial but cool.

Lew's team approach to covering the studios did work well with the proper team players — so well, in fact, that he didn't have to get personally involved in his stars' petty quibbles unless they mushroomed into a crisis. To prevent power plays and intercine warfare among his top agents, he named Herb Rosenthal president of MCA Artists.

"I got the job because three of the top MCA agents in California [Arthur Park, Herman Citron, and George Chasin] were fighting over it," said Rosenthal. "Lew decided to give it to me to avoid an earthquake in the company and maybe lose one or two of his best people. I got honored with the title, but I functioned in New York. So I was in charge, but I wasn't in charge. All the star talent was in California, and I rarely came to California. Lew was very smart about that."

Because Ronald Reagan and Jane Wyman had been among Wasserman's first clients when he came to Hollywood, they remained very special to him. Park treated the Reagans with kid gloves. When divorce came, Reagan took the breakup of their "perfect" Hollywood marriage far worse than Wyman did. Her Oscar win in 1948 for *Johnny Belinda* came as an added slap at Reagan's meager screen presence. Reagan still had his Warner Brothers deal, but the studio starred him in a pair of truly awful films, *Stallion Road* and *That Hagen Girl*, which merely emphasized the chasm between his own and Wyman's talent. He wanted out of his contract.

The end came in 1950 when Reagan broke his leg. While he convalesced, the Warner publicity department pestered him to hit the road to promote his next movie, *The Girl from Jones Beach*. From his hospital bed, Reagan bitterly told Associated Press reporter Bob Thomas that the heartless studio gave him such lousy roles that he could "phone in my lines."

Jack Warner usually forgave his stars for their public blatherings, but this time he and MCA were at war and Reagan was a suitable pawn. Stein and Wasserman had turned so many of Warner's best contract players into MCA freelancers that Jack personally barred Wasserman's agents from the lot — a futile tactic that lasted just a few months. But while the ban was in force, Wasserman gave all MCA clients the option of switching to William Morris. Reagan didn't want to switch. He instead tried to reason with Warner, whom he had come to regard over the years as a kind of father figure. "Dear Jack," he wrote, "I don't know anything about your difficulty with MCA nor do I care to know. Naturally it is none of my business. They have just notified me of my right to utilize the William Morris office — a right which I waived. Having been with MCA almost as many years as you and I have been together, I don't feel that strangers can suddenly take over and represent my best interests."

Unlike Humphrey Bogart and Errol Flynn, who constantly gave Warner headaches, Reagan pointed out that he had always "played ball." Now, with Lew Wasserman behind him, he planned to hang tough. He hoped Jack would understand. Reagan wanted some decent roles so that he could take his rightful place on the A-list of movie stars. Warner answered him bloodlessly, through the studio's chief legal counsel, Roy Obringer: "Maybe it would be a good idea to effect a mutual cancellation of your contract."

The troubled actor went to Wasserman. In his memoirs, Reagan recalled Lew's reaction:

> My contract had three years to go. Lew rewrote it to read one picture equal to half my yearly income, and full rights to do outside pictures. In other words, I was at last a free lance. My face was saved and the studio wasn't hurt because every studio in town was really trying to unload contracts as the result of the [Paramount Decree] antitrust decision. One week later Lew added a five-year, five-picture deal at Universal, and I bellied up to the bar like a conquering hero ordering drinks for the house. You could hardly see my wounded ego under all those $75,000 plasters.

The Universal scripts were actually worse than those Reagan had been given by Warner Brothers. Outside of MCA, one of the few things Reagan had going for him at the time of his divorce and his dimming star power was the Screen Actors Guild. The moment the army discharged him in 1945, Ronald Reagan leaped headlong into the dangerous waters of Hollywood politics. It took a Lew Wasserman to help steer him past the shoals.

On December 12, 1945, one of Hollywood's earliest antinuclear rallies advertised Reagan as a headliner. Also featured on the program were liberal Congresswoman Helen Gahagan Douglas, the wife of actor Melvyn Douglas, and equally liberal radio producer Norman Corwin. Flyers depicted a genie rising from an atomic cloud, with the caption "Atomic energy — slave or master?"

One of the flyers wound up on Jack Warner's desk and the right-thinking Republican studio chief objected loudly to Reagan's participation. Studio attorneys sent Reagan a telegram that read in part, "We feel that such performance on your part at such meeting would be in violation of the exclusive rights to your services as granted to us under your employment contract."

Like other left-leaning MCA clients, Reagan had to be convinced that his political convictions were irrelevant when it came to staying employed. Wasserman stepped in like a Dutch uncle, advising Reagan against going to the rally. Lew called the studio executives the same day and assured them that Reagan would not appear at the mass meeting. He didn't. Nor did Reagan show up at any other liberal functions over the next several years. His days as a New Deal liberal were winding down, particularly in the area of labor relations.

Though the full transformation would take nearly twenty years, he slowly molded himself to match more closely the politics of actors Edward Arnold, George Murphy, and other conservative SAG leaders. They encouraged Reagan to join the SAG board, where he built a power base that won him the union's presidency in March 1947. Reagan was no longer merely a B-movie actor. Now when he sat across the table from Jack Warner or Darryl Zanuck, it was as an industry power broker.

One month after Reagan's election to the SAG presidency, the FBI asked him to inform the government of any Communist activity in his union. With little coaxing, the newly conservative Reagan obliged—and went even further. When convinced that a conspiracy was afoot, he launched his own whispering campaign to stamp out the Red Menace that he thought might be festering in his own backyard.

In October of 1947, Reagan traveled to Washington, D.C., with Gary Cooper, Robert Montgomery, and George Murphy to excoriate Hollywood "fellow travelers" like Herbert Sorrel before the House Un-American Activities Committee. Reagan endorsed Murphy's conviction that the Communist Party was infiltrating unions in such a way that it could "reach a point where the screen may be used in a manner inimical to the best interests of our country."

At the same time, back at MCA headquarters in Beverly Hills, Hollywood's liberal establishment was mounting an ill-fated counteroffensive. Three writers were secretly allotted office space to draft a script for a full-blown stars-and-stripes revue called *Hollywood Fights Back!* The two-hour radio special went on the air over the new ABC network, featuring dozens of stars who sang, joked, and spoke out against the House Committee's witch-hunt. Many of them were subsequently blacklisted.

"MCA took a big risk, letting us use their offices," recalled actress Marsha Hunt, who learned years later that she was blacklisted for singing "My Country 'Tis of Thee" at the close of the *Hollywood Fights Back!* broadcast. "When my name showed up in *Red Channels* [an underground anti-communist roster], my agent told me the best thing I could do was get out of town. It was an awful time."

IN 1948, SIDNEY Korshak still lived in Chicago at Alex Louis Greenberg's Seneca Hotel. Part of each year he also rented several different homes in California—one in Beverly Hills, another in Encino. Since serving as counselor to both IATSE's Willie Bioff and the Capone Mob during the early 1940s, Korshak had joined the Army and married. He was thirty-six in 1943 and a corporal on leave from Camp Lee, Virginia, when he wed former dancer, skating star and model Beatrice Stewart at New York's Ambassador East Hotel. They had two sons and, despite his blatant, lifelong lust for leggy starlets and expensive hookers, Sidney never entertained the idea of divorcing his wife.

Following his two-year Army stint during World War II, Korshak returned home to Chicago where he shared a Gold Coast law office with two other attorneys who specialized in labor relations. As office secretary, the three lawyers hired Marie Accardo, the daughter of Chicago Mob boss Tony "Big Tuna" Accardo.

Korshak's first legitimate client was department store owner Joel Goldblatt who hired Sidney in 1946, after labor organizers threatened Goldblatt with extortion. According to the *New York Times*, Korshak resolved the merchant's labor difficulties, and Goldblatt didn't have to pay off the union. A year later, the Spiegel catalogue sales company, National Video and other Chicago retailers began hiring Korshak to assist them with union headaches too. The difference was that these clients simply wanted no unions at all. For a fat upfront fee, Korshak aimed to oblige.

Korshak never bothered taking the bar exam to practice in California, even though he would eventually conduct most of his business there. Instead, he often worked out deals from the back booths of trendy Wilshire Boulevard restaurants, in the lobby of a West Side hotel, or at the kitchen table in his own Beverly Hills home. For a time, he worked out of the offices of Associated Booking Corporation at 9477 Brighton Way, just three blocks from MCA headquarters.

Incorporated in 1940, Associated Booking was operated by former MCA man Joe Glaser. In addition to becoming one of Korshak's earliest and closest Hollywood chums, Glaser was also the agent for Duke Ellington, Louis Armstrong, and several other important black musicians during the thirties and forties.

Glaser's other close friend in Hollywood was his former boss, Jules Stein. Stein gave him the money to start his own agency, and for the first few years Glaser and Stein were equal partners. *Variety* reported that Glaser bought Stein out in 1946, though many in the band business doubted Associated Booking's independence the same way they doubted the independence of Tommy Rockwell and General Amusement Corporation.[1] Glaser's name might be the only one on the incorpora-

---

[1]   In 1946, Rockwell changed the name to General Artists Corporation, which remained the agency's name until it was bought out in the late 1960s.

tion paper, but MCA still seemed to be able to tell Glaser what to do. So did Sidney Korshak.[2]

While he was gaining a foothold in Hollywood, Korshak continued to practice law in the Chicago Loop. Among his closest associates was Alderman Jacob Arvey, a celebrated political fixer in his own right, as well as a pal of the Capone syndicate since the 1920s. Alex Louis Greenberg's longtime business partner in Lawndale Enterprises, Inc., Arvey was the most powerful figure in Chicago politics.[3] Korshak's younger brother, Marshall, also became an Arvey protégé and went on to become a state senator, and one of the primary conduits between the Chicago Mob and the Illinois Democratic political machine.

Besides the Korshak brothers, Arvey mentored several other future power brokers. Another Korshak pal who emigrated to the West Coast in the 1940s was Paul Ziffren, a junior partner in Arvey's Chicago law firm, and long rumored to be Arvey's illegitimate son.

"Arvey's protégé in Chicago was Paul Ziffren," said attorney David Leanse, who once worked for both Ziffren and Korshak. "He didn't have the contacts with labor that Korshak had, but Ziffren represented savings and loans and lenders, and that put him in touch with the entertainment business a lot."

When Ziffren first came to L.A. during World War II, he demonstrated just how well Arvey had taught him the lessons of political exploitation, by organizing a consortium of investors who bought property vacated by Japanese-Americans during their wartime internment. Ziffren worked closely with attorney David Bazelon, yet another Arvey protégé, who had been appointed by the Truman Administration to oversee "alien" land sales. Bazelon did such a good job that President Truman rewarded him with a federal judgeship.[4] Ziffren did such a good job that dozens of shady Chicago investors, including partner Alex Louis Greenberg, earned tidy profits from his real estate consortium.

Through Bazelon, Ziffren was able to purchase government-confiscated real estate in Los Angeles County at fire sale prices. Once released from their detention camps at the end of the war, the Japanese-Americans returned to find their for-

---

[2] By 1962, Glaser had ended all pretense of heading Associated Booking, formally signing over all "voting rights, dominion and control" to Korshak. Upon Glaser's death in 1969, Korshak officially took charge of the agency.

[3] Arvey's power lasted until 1955, when Eleventh Ward Committeeman Richard J. Daley upset Mayor Martin Kennelly, Arvey's handpicked candidate and puppet. Arvey remained a Democratic National Committee member, but he never regained the power that passed to Mayor Daley.

[4] Truman demonstrated his gratitude to Hollywood as well, personally granting a full pardon on Oct. 26, 1945, to Twentieth Century Fox chairman Joe Schenck for Schenck's conviction in the great movie studio shakedown scandal.

mer homes, stores, and farms turned into sites for restaurants, hotels, and places of amusement.

Arvey's influence on his young protégés also carried over into politics.

"When Ziffren got to California, before anybody knew him, he was a Democratic Party power, just on the strength that he was Colonel Jake Arvey's boy," said Leanse.

Ziffren hadn't lived in Los Angeles five years before he was elected California's Democratic National Committee delegate, a post he held onto for the next two decades. It was in this political capacity that Ziffren eventually became as close to Lew Wasserman as his other Chicago pal, Sidney Korshak.

"Ziffren was one of the nicest, most considerate, intelligent persons I ever met," said Leanse. "The fact that he was the Democratic National Committeeman, so well connected...Well, he didn't come off like that kind of guy. He was accessible, with not a bit of arrogance or pomposity. That was very attractive, I thought.

"Sid was the hotshot. He knew that he was important, and he would say so. He was kind of a dashing guy."

Korshak, Ziffren, and Wasserman all lived their lives in California as conservatively and as tax-free as Lew's Republican father-in-law had back in prewar Cleveland. But on the California voter registration roles, the three men appeared as lifelong Democrats. They cross-pollinated each other's Democratic party fundraisers for the next forty years. If the Wassermans threw a campaign bash for some congressional candidate, the Ziffrens and Korshaks would always appear on the guest list, and vice versa. Their apparent dedication to the Democrats' cause was deep and profound, especially in the area of purchasing favors from future elected officials.

But in 1950, the only important Democrat outside of Chicago that Korshak was concerned with was a good ol' boy from Tennessee — Senator Estes Kefauver, especially since Kefauver was about to hit the road on a nationwide exposé of organized crime and he let it be known that his number one target in Chicago would be Sidney Roy Korshak.

Korshak didn't appear before the Kefauver Committee, though. Following a forty-five-minute private session with the senator, Korshak was excused before ever being sworn in. Other witnesses, ranging from Charles "Cherry Nose" Gioe to Mob tax lawyer Eugene Bernstein, invoked Korshak's name during their own public grilling at the hands of the crime-busting senators, especially in connection with Willie Bioff and the great movie studio shakedown.

None of the lawmakers ever followed up on Korshak's Syndicate ties, though, and Korshak himself never testified. In *Crime in America*, Kefauver's own bestselling 1951 polemic about the menace of organized crime in America, the Tennessee senator and future vice presidential candidate never once mentioned Korshak's name.

According to a *New York Times* report published nearly thirty years later, Kefauver's sudden lack of interest in Korshak could be traced to a night he spent at Chicago's luxurious Drake Hotel. Somehow, Korshak had obtained infrared photos of the senator, wearing nothing but his Tennessee smile, delighting two young female employees of the Mob's Chez Paree nightclub. Once acquainted with those photographs, the senator lost interest in Sidney Korshak as a witness.

———

TAKING THE LEAD from HUAC's surprisingly popular 1947–1948 televised hearings into the influence of Communism in Hollywood and Washington, D.C., Kefauver invited network TV coverage of his investigations, and discovered what visionaries like Lew Wasserman already knew about the power of mass media. When Kefauver took his hearings on a fifteen-city tour in 1950, the crime fighters picked up an audience larger than any single motion picture ever made. Wearing his Davy Crockett–style coonskin cap and his crooked Nashville grin, Kefauver became a national icon, as popular as Gary Cooper or Mickey Mouse. As the show trekked across the nation, exposing mobsters and their mouthpieces over the riveting new medium of television, Kefauver and his fellows attracted over 20 million viewers.

The national crime syndicate had begun with Prohibition, TV viewers were told. It had started with the corrupting influence of weak-willed cops and greedy politicians who accepted graft to look the other way while booze, gambling, and prostitution infected the heartland. An ancient Sicilian organization called the Mafia oversaw much of the organized crime along the Atlantic seaboard in places like New York and Philadelphia. People with names like "Lucky" Luciano and Joe "Bananas" Bonanno ran the rackets there.

But another insidious influence entered the United States via the Great Lakes. Just as deadly as the Sicilians, this ethnic group did not wear flashy clothes or advertise itself with big cars, bimbos, and jewelry. With rare exceptions, these Eastern European mobsters, most of whom were Jews from Russia and Poland, maintained a low profile. Instead of spending their ransom, extortion, and blackmail cash on fast women and expensive entertainment, they paid token taxes to keep the government off their backs and reinvested the rest of their money. They usually remained married, put their children through the best schools, and commissioned murder only as the most extreme business measure. The Jewish Mob, as it came to be known, dominated places like Cleveland and Detroit and large Canadian cities like Toronto and Montreal.

The name of one Jewish-Canadian rum-running family came up repeatedly, but no member of the Bronfman family was ever called to testify. During the Senate committee's stop in New York, Kefauver himself was curious enough to quiz a former Bronfman partner, James "Niggy" Rutkin,[5] about the mysterious Canadian bootlegging clan that would eventually wind its way to Hollywood, just as Stein and Wasserman had:

> "Tell us about the Bronfmans. I have been very much interested in them."
> "Well, the Bronfmans are four brothers[6] from Montreal, Canada. They own little hotels up there. Now, if you want to find out more about the hotels, you can ask the Canadian Mounted Police, and they will tell you about the little hotels, and you can use your imagination."
> "Is it like certain types of tourist camps down South? Is that the kind of hotels they are?"
> "Well, I don't know how they are there. But only from what I read of hotels, the people sleep very fast. They rent them quite a few times a night."

Overseen by Sam, the youngest brother, the Bronfmans rose to power during the 1920s, when they switched from the by-the-hour hotel business to the manufacture, bottling and sale of distilled alcoholic beverages.

When Canada's Parliament restricted the sale of alcohol in 1919 by labeling it a drug, Harry Bronfman got a pharmacy license and renamed the family business the Canada Pure Drug Company. Though the Bronfmans denied any complicity in the transport of their wares across the U.S. border during Prohibition, notable gangsters like Abner "Longie" Zwillman and New York Mafia "Prime Minister" Frank Costello admitted to the Kefauver Committee that a steady stream of whisky flowed out of Bronfman distilleries and into millions of dry American mouths. It came across Lake Erie in speedboats. It came by rural country roads from Saskatchewan to Montana, smuggled in the gas tanks of Packards and Studebakers. It literally flowed by pipeline beneath the border at Emerson, Manitoba, into a vacant barn several thousand yards to the south in Pembina, North Dakota.

But the Kefauver Committee was powerless to do anything about the Canadian Bronfmans. When one of Kefauver's colleagues huffily labeled the brothers "notorious bootleggers," Zwillman deadpanned: "Well, they are pretty successful, if that is what they are. I was never that good."

Though part of the family had moved across the border and taken up resi-

---

[5] Rutkin sued his former partners in 1954, maintaining that the Bronfmans and their bootlegging partners—Abner "Longie" Zwillman, Joseph "Doc" Stacher, and Joe Reinfeld—had swindled Rutkin out of his share of the $1 billion Seagram fortune. Two years later, while he was being held on a separate matter in a New Jersey jail, Rutkin's throat was slashed. His death was ruled a suicide.
[6] Harry, Alan, Abe, and Samuel.

dence in New York by 1950, the Bronfmans on both sides of the border had all become quite respectable. Through a subsidiary called the Atlas Finance Company, they invested in real estate, commodities, stocks, and bonds. Their daughters were debutantes and their sons attended Ivy League institutions or studied in Europe. They supported the arts, attended synagogue, raised racehorses, and made generous contributions to charities, especially those that championed the emerging Jewish state of Israel. The Bronfmans' reach was global, not just North American. If Senator Kefauver had any hope of lassoing Canada's most notorious rum-running family into his coast-to-coast televised circus of crime, he was at least a quarter of a century too late.

As early as 1926, Sam and Harry Bronfman had engineered a business coup that would secure the family's place in the world of international commerce well into the twenty-first century. In a protracted transatlantic negotiation, the Bronfmans became the Canadian licensees and distributors for Distillers Company Limited of Edinburgh and London. The giant British whisky conglomerate, formed in 1877 by several tippling members of the House of Lords, sold all manner of bonded booze, including more than half the world's Scotch. DCL's board of directors—Lord Dewar, Field Marshal Earl Haig, Sir Alexander Walker, etc.— immortalized themselves in the brand names of their products. The Bronfmans were never so vain, and quietly took control of DCL without ever attaching the family name to any of their products.

The following year, the Bronfmans bought control of Canada's largest rye whiskey manufacturer: Joseph E. Seagram and Sons, Ltd. They adopted that name as their own for corporate purposes, and continued coming up with the millions in capital to buy out their competition.

By 1933, when Prohibition was repealed, the Bronfman brothers' Seagram Company was second only to Pennsylvania-based Schenley Industries as the largest distributor of distilled spirits in North America. When Cleveland's Mayfair Casino opened two years later, it was Bronfman whisky that the patrons were served.[7]

The Bronfmans had no interest in the entertainment industry in those early days. The most far-reaching contribution any of them made to the movies came from Sam's older brother, Harry Bronfman. Harry opened a theater in Yorkton, Saskatchewan, in the early 1920s to supplement the income from Seagram's smuggling operations. Besides introducing Pickford and Chaplin to farmers in the Canadian outback, Harry was credited with bringing popcorn to western Canada. The Bronfmans' enthusiasm for Hollywood, however, was at least two generations away.

By contrast, U.S. smugglers, conmen, and thieves couldn't seem to get enough

---

7   In 1935, the Canadian courts charged all four Bronfman brothers with bilking the government out of $5 million in unpaid duties on European liquor they allegedly smuggled into the country. They were not convicted.

of the movies and the stars during the first half of the century. Several all-American gangsters who appeared before the Kefauver Committee professed a keen interest in the entertainment business, and vice versa.

Johnny Rosselli, one of the original "Chicago Seven"[8] who went to jail over the Willie Bioff–George Browne shakedown scandal, was briefly married to actress June Lang in 1941 and actually went on the payroll at low-budget Eagle-Lion Films. After he was paroled from prison in 1947, Rosselli's title at Eagle-Lion for a little over a year was "associate producer"—the only legitimate salaried job he ever held.[9]

Longie Zwillman had a long history with Hollywood too. The boss of the Newark rackets counted Columbia Pictures' Harry Cohn among his closest pals. Besides helping Harry with his labor problems by bringing Rosselli's Chicago goons in to persuade striking workers to return to work, Zwillman invested in Cohn's struggling studio. A grateful Harry responded by introducing Zwillman to Jean Harlow, the star of Columbia's *Platinum Blonde*. Zwillman was well rewarded. For years after Harlow's death, he was still boasting nostalgically about the various ways he'd once banged the actress.

On the star side of the ledger, Hollywood loved gangsters as much as gangsters loved Hollywood. Before he took two steel-jacketed slugs in his handsome face, Benny "Bugsy" Siegel counted tough guy actor George Raft among his dearest friends. He and Raft had grown up together in New York's infamous Hell's Kitchen, along with Meyer Lansky, the financial mastermind behind the Jewish Mob.

Frank Sinatra gathered even more hoods unto his bosom. Capone's cousin Charlie Fischetti and Tony Accardo's top torpedo Sam Giancana played host to Sinatra whenever he came to Chicago. Jersey Mafia boss Willie Moretti showed the Hoboken kid a good time in New York. And Lansky rolled out the red carpet whenever Ol' Blue Eyes sang at one of his Cuban casinos.

Perhaps the ultimate marriage of Mob and movies was Kefauver witness Johnny Stompanato, bodyguard and errand boy to L.A. gambling czar Mickey Cohen. Stompanato became MCA star Lana Turner's live-in gigolo and the tryst might have resulted in an actual Mob and Movie Star wedding if Stompanato hadn't slapped the actress around once too often. After watching Stompanato beat

---

[8] Not to be confused with the seven antiwar activists who were tried for disrupting the 1968 Democratic National Convention in Chicago, the seven hoods who went to jail in 1945 for masterminding the great Hollywood shakedown were Paul "the Waiter" Ricca, Charlie "Cherry Nose" Gioe, Louis "Little New York" Campagna, Phil D'Andrea, Johnnie Rosselli, Frank Maritote, and Louis Kaufman.

[9] "He knew nothing about making movies," said then Eagle-Lion production chief Max Youngstein. "All Rosselli and [producer] Bryan Foy wanted was broads. They chartered a plane once to fly in eighteen actresses from Mexico City to audition for a part. They fucked every one of them, put them back on the plane, and sent them back to Mexico City. They never made the movie."

her mother on the evening of Good Friday 1958, Turner's sixteen-year-old daughter, Cheryl Crane, planted a butcher knife in his solar plexus.

"Johnny was running around with every broad in the movie industry," Cohen wrote in his memoirs. "I didn't really believe that he would fall as strongly in love with Lana Turner, because I had known Johnny when he was with Ava Gardner and Janet Leigh. Johnny was a funny guy with girls. He took them as they came, like they were nothing."

Cohen did not spend much time mourning Stompanato's death. He'd seen or participated in a number of violent exterminations during his Hollywood tenure. A former Cleveland boxer who was once managed by the Silent Syndicate's Lou Rothkopf, Cohen failed in the ring but succeeded as a thug. When Rothkopf and his partners—Moe Dalitz, Morris Kleinman, and Sam Tucker—wanted to open a West Coast office, Cohen got the job.

He wasted no time cozying up to Benjamin "Bugsy" Siegel, one of the Mob's first Hollywood emissaries. For more than a decade, Siegel had been organizing bookies, schmoozing with film stars and producers, and skimming from backroom casinos along the Sunset Strip, and Cohen became his chief assistant. When Siegel partnered with *Hollywood Reporter* founder Billy Wilkerson to open the biggest casino of all—the Las Vegas Flamingo Hotel—Cohen took over the Los Angeles rackets with the understanding that the position was temporary, until Siegel got the Flamingo out of the red.

But the Flamingo continued to lose money. Four months after its grand opening, Siegel made a trip back to L.A., where he visited George Raft and paid a visit to Cohen before stopping off at the Beverly Hills home of his mistress, Virginia Hill. There, in perhaps the best-known execution in Mob history, a gunman blew one of Bugsy's baby blue eyeballs out of his skull with a couple of .38 caliber slugs.

Following Siegel's death, Cohen stepped right into his shoes—both in the gambling business and in Hollywood. Among his own pals in the entertainment industry, Cohen counted Robert Mitchum, Sammy Davis Jr., Errol Flynn, and screenwriter Ben Hecht. When Sinatra's career took a nosedive in the early 1950s, Cohen threw a testimonial dinner for him at the Beverly Hills Hotel. He put up the money to bring unknown comics Dean Martin and Jerry Lewis to L.A. for the first time. He invested in nightclubs like Slapsie Maxie's, where stars worked when they were between pictures.

"There are a lot of people, some wholly legitimate and some not, that are attracted to my line of work and people in it," Cohen said. "See, a lot of non-racket people went out of their way to gain an invitation to my home. I hate to say this, 'cause it sounds egotistical, but it was like a status symbol at the time. Particularly when I was riding high and was, I guess, what you would call a celebrity."

On November 15, 1950, during the Kefauver Committee's booking in Los Angeles, chief counsel Rudolph Halley questioned Mickey Cohen about his Hollywood ties. Since Bugsy Siegel's gangland execution three years earlier in Beverly Hills, the natty little ex-boxer from Cleveland had assumed the mantle of southern California crime boss. Cohen spoke like a semiliterate and dressed like a pimp.

Nevertheless, colorful Mickey Cohen pleased TV audiences. He was an uncooperative witness, wisecracking while playing the stooge. But even Cohen must have been genuinely puzzled when counsel Halley began rattling off a string of names, demanding Cohen's connection to each of them. Some were well-known gamblers and bookmakers. Others were never explained and never appeared again anywhere in the official or unofficial record of the committee's seventeen-volume transcript. Among the roll call that Halley reeled off were: Louie Berman, Sammy Lewis, Eddie Borden, and Jules Stein.

"You never heard of him either?" repeated Halley.

Said Cohen, "No sir."

FOURTEEN

TV, Tantrums, and the Deal That Doomed the Moguls

1950

D r. Harry Gradle had retired in 1945 and moved to Sherman Oaks, California, just over the Sepulveda Pass from Beverly Hills. His most famous apprentice lived with his queenly wife and two teenage princesses at Misty Mountain, no more than a ten-minute drive away. Dr. Gradle could stand at his front door, peer upward, and almost see the regal mountaintop where his former pupil, Jules Stein, lived and flourished.

When he wasn't holding court on Misty Mountain or at MCA headquarters, Jules led the peripatetic life of a pseudo-retiree. He supported L.A.'s postwar cultural aspirations, lending his name to fund-raising efforts for the Pacific Art Museum and the Southern California Symphony Association. His interest in English antiques had grown to such a passion that he was obliged to warehouse his finds until he had somewhere to put them.

"And books...he bought books by the ton," recalled Berle Adams. "Leather-bound books. Everybody was getting rid of that crap in Europe, so he was buying it for nothing."

Every MCA office around the world was stocked with Stein's books and signature furniture, tagged with little brass identification markers so that each piece could be out on display where all who entered could marvel at Dr. Stein's good taste.

Jules continued to find time to chase stars. When Aly Khan married Rita Hayworth in 1950, Jules flew to the South of France to offer his heartfelt congratulations—and to wrest the actress away from William Morris. Khan saw how gracious and worldly the Steins could be, commenting learnedly about the Degas paintings and the Aubusson carpets, unlike many of the Hollywood churls who came to visit his new bride. Khan urged his new wife to dump Johnny Hyde, the Morris agent who had created her career and who was in the final stages of heart disease.[1] She was more practical. She asked Stein for a $125,000 loan so she could buy a house in Paris. Stein obliged, and Hayworth signed with MCA. She didn't make another movie until *Affair in Trinidad*, in 1952, after she'd divorced Aly Khan, but that didn't matter. Stein had stolen her away, like a prized piece in some cosmic chess game in which the one with the most stars wins.

Jules's "retirement" also took him to Britain. In the grand MCA tradition of buying talent instead of creating or nurturing it, he approved MCA's purchase of the late Myron Selznick's British offices. MCA not only inherited such formidable Selznick stars as Laurence Olivier and Vivien Leigh, it also landed David Niven-esque charmer Cecil Tennant, who continued to head Selznick's London operation long after the legendary agent had died. Arguably the best hands-on agent in all of Great Britain—he was known to temperamental Vivien Leigh as Uncle Cecil—Tennant organized a tweedy troop of talent sharks, as formidable on their own turf as Wasserman's organization was in Hollywood. He then began systematically snapping up every established name and promising newcomer on the West End, all on behalf of his new American bosses. Within ten years, MCA represented 341 of the finest actors and actresses in England,[2] as well as designers, composers, directors, writers, and such disparate show business powers as Hugh Carleton Greene, director general of the BBC.

But Stein didn't stop there. To ensure the same star stranglehold in England that the purchase of the Hayward Deverich Agency had given MCA on Broadway, he followed up the Selznick deal with the purchase of Linnitt and Dunfee, a talent agency that also produced many of London's biggest stage hits of the forties and fifties. In two tidy moves, the supposedly retired Dr. Jules Stein had added an unparalleled roster of English stars to his collection of English furniture, English art, and royal acquaintances.

Besides giving him access to the best British talent, his English acquisitions gave him an additional opportunity to exercise his favorite pastime: legally avoiding U.S. taxes. Congress was about to open an enormous loophole in the income tax code for citizens who were forced to live and work abroad. Under the new law, actors and directors who spent seventeen out of eighteen months in Europe paid no taxes during their time overseas. With the help of "Uncle Cecil" Tennant and

---

[1]   Hyde also managed the career of Marilyn Monroe, with whom he lived for a time.
[2]   Peter Ustinov, Michael Rennie, Michael Redgrave, Anthony Quayle, Rex Harrison, Christopher Lee, Patrick MacNee, John Mills, Robert Morley, Alec Guinness, John Gielgud, Peter Finch, Claire Bloom, Constance Cummings, Audrey Hepburn, and Genevieve Page, among others.

Linnitt and Dunfee, Stein and Wasserman stepped up the number of movie deals that severely taxed MCA clients were "forced" to film overseas.[3]

The MCA ploy worked so well that it launched a runaway production trend, leaving many Hollywood studios idle and teetering on bankruptcy throughout the 1950s. Wasserman later blamed those same studios for sending whole production companies to Europe to make films rather than shoot them on Hollywood back lots. Not only had Stein and his favorite protégé taken full advantage of U.S. tax laws but they were also able to deflect any criticism aimed at MCA. Once again they cast the studios as villains. It didn't matter that MCA negotiated the deals that sent productions overseas. It was the unpatriotic greed of the studio executives that was killing Hollywood.

For all his clever maneuvering, something was still missing in Jules Stein's life. Decades after Dr. Stein abandoned medicine for music, movies, and moguldom, he continued to brood over the course his life had taken. He topped his official MCA biography as well as his *Who's Who* entries with the singular fact that, back in 1924, he'd written and published an article titled "Telescopic Spectacles and Magnifiers as Aids to Poor Vision."

———

LEW WASSERMAN SUFFERED none of Stein's simmering angst. Wasserman's professional pride was invested solely in the care and feeding of his stars.

When forty-one-year-old bachelor Jimmy Stewart finally married divorcée Gloria Hatrick in 1949, Lew threw him a surprise bachelor's party to end all bachelor's parties at exclusive Chasen's. It included floodlights, a brass band, a 50-foot banner that read "James Stewart's Final Performance Tonight," and a fully liveried British butler who attended to Stewart's every whim.

"Lew had this man follow me everywhere," Stewart recalled to journalist Susan Deutsch. "Every time I took a drink, he wiped my mouth. If I reached for a canapé, he fed it to me. If I went to sit down, he wiped the seat with a lace handkerchief....

"But the best part was when we'd all sat down to dinner, and the main course was brought in. It was a huge silver tray with an enormous lid. The sort of thing they use for rack of lamb. Well, Lew said, 'Jim, it's your party, you'll have to do the honors.' I lifted the cover. Two midgets in diapers jumped out and peed on me."

Wasserman kept his stars supplied with cars. If Tony Curtis wanted a Rolls-

---

[3]　Around the same time, MCA began buying up New York literary agencies, including the Jay Sanford Agency and the Liebling-Wood Agency, which gave MCA control of the nation's three best-known playwrights: Tennessee Williams, William Inge, and Arthur Miller. Its growing roster of writers gave MCA first crack at best-sellers and hit plays, completing its ability to offer complete film packages to the studios.

Royce with his initials inscribed on the door, Lew arranged to have it custom-made and shipped directly from England. When Lee J. Cobb threatened to get sick on the first day of a major production if he didn't get a new Ferrari, Lew saw to it the car was delivered to his door. And when lovesick glamour girl Jane Russell wanted a car in which to elope to Las Vegas with football star Bob Waterfield, Lew lent them his.

Lew also tended to his stars' physical needs. If opera singer–actor Mario Lanza drank too much, Lew sent over a physician with the necessary injection to jump-start his star.[4] And when the reinvigorated Lanza threw a tantrum and demanded his paycheck *right now*, Lew delivered it personally by chauffeur-driven limo.

"Mario was one of those guys who wouldn't order a martini; he'd order a tray. He was that type of guy," recalled columnist Jim Bacon. "He needed a lot of care and handling. Lanza would get so fat they couldn't photograph him. He blew up so bad for *The Student Prince* (1954) that they went ahead and used his voice, but had to put someone else [Edmund Purdom] in his place."

Lew also handled the more unpleasant chores of his office with crisp, cold efficiency. When Shirley Temple, the most popular child star in history, grew up, married, became a mother, thickened a bit around the middle, and got divorced, all before her twenty-first birthday, her interest in moviemaking plummeted with about the same speed as the moviegoing public's interest in her.

As Temple recalled in her memoirs, Wasserman coldly told her that MCA would no longer represent her:

> "Wait a minute," she said. "Stars drop agents, not vice versa."
> "Maybe so," came his icy response. "But this time, we fire you."
> "Why?" I yelped.
> "Because you're through." His eyes were unwavering, inky black. "Washed up."
> I started to cry.
> "Here," he said, pushing a Kleenex box across the desktop. "Have one on me."

The MCA president still kept his hand in, whether it came to ending a career or making a groundbreaking deal, especially when the deal involved a pet — James Stewart, for example.

The deal Lew Wasserman struck for Stewart to make *Winchester '73* changed completely how Hollywood did business and hastened the funeral of the long-

---

[4]   Jack Warner refused to pay for the daily shots until Wasserman intervened. Lew later joked with the physician, Dr. Hans Schiff, that he was the first doctor he'd ever represented and he would, therefore, waive his usual 10 percent.

dying studio system. Long after the plot of the Jimmy Stewart western faded from memory, agents and actors alike still spoke of it reverently. *Winchester '73* was not the first ever gross profit deal, but it was the biggest.[5]

Winchester '73 became as much a part of the Lew legend as the $1 million contract he boasted of negotiating for Ronald Reagan at the beginning of World War II. But the *Winchester '73* deal was a double-edged sword for actors who had finally thrown off the yoke of the studio moguls and turned to their agents for help in the brave new world of freelancing. Many would eventually come to believe that they had merely traded one set of feudal lords for another.

The studios had been playing the net profit game since the days of the nickelodeon. Net profit was defined as any money left over once the studio met all expenses. The catch was that the studio came up with an endless and ingenious array of expenses. If expenses were not clearly defined, movies simply did not earn net profits, and any contract guaranteeing 5, 10, or 90 percent of the net essentially guaranteed nothing.

Gross profit, on the other hand, was real money.

Star percentage deals dotted the Hollywood landscape dating all the way back to 1919, when Charlie Chaplin, Mary Pickford, Douglas Fairbanks, and D. W. Griffith formed United Artists as their own unified answer to one-sided net profit contracts. Pickford alone earned $10,000 a week in salary plus half of the profits of all her pictures. In the early 1930s, Mae West and the Marx Brothers both had enough clout to demand a cut of the gross — every dollar that came in from the box office *before* the studio began deducting its substantial expenses. In 1943, Charles Feldman of Famous Artists negotiated a gross deal for Howard Hawks and Gary Cooper that forced RKO to guarantee the director and actor a minimum of $350,000 per picture plus 50 percent of any profits. Wasserman's *Winchester '73* deal, which was *not* a pure gross profit contract[6] — was also not unprecedented.

What made Jimmy Stewart's story particularly remarkable was that he had almost no clout following World War II. He was no longer the boyish hero of

---

[5]   Actually, *Winchester '73* was an adjusted gross deal, with a profit percentage guaranteed *after* the studio recouped its original investment. Rita Hayworth's contract for *Gilda*, negotiated by William Morris agent Johnny Hyde three years earlier, in 1946, similarly guaranteed the actress 25 percent of the gross after distribution and negative expenses.

[6]   According to the February 15, 1950, deal memo, Stewart was to receive 50 percent of the net profits. Net profit was defined as Universal's total box office take once the studio took out 25 percent for distribution, recouped its actual costs for producing *Winchester '73*, and deducted for general studio overhead — defined as 25 percent of the movie's actual production costs. As burdensome as these expenses might seem, they were minimal compared to most net profit definitions, before and after *Winchester '73*. Stewart eventually earned more than $600,000 from a movie it cost Universal $917,374 to make.

Mr. Smith Goes to Washington, but neither was he a John Wayne tough guy or a Cary Grant sophisticate. He floundered from film to film, trying to find his identity. There were minor hits, notably *Call Northside 777,* in which he portrayed a crusading Chicago reporter, but most of his films were lackluster. He was just another ex–MGM contract player on the skids. In 1947 he quit Hollywood for a while and returned to Broadway where he'd first started in the early 1930s. Back onstage where he had begun, Stewart replaced actor Frank Fay as an affable alcoholic named Elwood P. Dowd whose closest friend was an invisible six-foot rabbit.

Harvey utterly transformed Stewart's moribund career. Though the comedy had been on Broadway since 1944, it became such a huge hit with Stewart as the bumbling Dowd that studios lined up to claim film rights. Lew could have made a rich movie deal with any one of them, but he used Stewart's sudden acclaim to pressure a phenomenal deal out of the least likely studio in town: beleaguered, nearly bankrupt Universal International.

Harvey could change that standing. The prospect of having a real star and a real Broadway stage hit actually being filmed on one of the Universal soundstages turned studio head William Goetz to putty in Wasserman's nimble fingers. Now that he had Universal's undivided attention, Lew used the old tie-in gimmick that Jules Stein first perfected at the Muehlbach Hotel a quarter century earlier. Lew gambled that once *Harvey* hit the nation's screens, Stewart's box office drawing power would be back to the same level he'd enjoyed in 1941 after he'd won an Oscar for *The Philadelphia Story.*[7]

Lew told Goetz that Universal could have *Harvey* at a reasonable price — $150,000 for the rights to the Mary C. Chase play and $200,000 plus a share of the net for Stewart's services. But Goetz had to agree to make a second movie: a western, replete with clichés but with a nice twist at its end. The terms were to be quite different from the straight salary option in the *Harvey* deal. Stewart would forgo salary altogether, but he would get half the profits from *Winchester '73.*

A surefire Broadway hit for straight salary, and a forgettable western for half the profits? Goetz jumped at the chance.

But there was much more at stake in the deal than just money. There was ego, and there was control — the same kind of control that MCA clients like Bette Davis had been fighting over for years.

The contract Wasserman negotiated for Stewart to do *Winchester '73* required that no other cast member would have the same star billing as Stewart, and that Stewart's name was to be first on the screen, above the title of the movie. Stewart

---

[7]   Stewart never won again for Best Actor, though he was nominated for *Harvey* and others, but he did receive a special Oscar in 1984 for lifetime achievement.

also got director approval for both films as well as approval of his *Winchester '73* costars — Dan Duryea, Shelley Winters, and Steve McNally.[8]

As icing on the cake, Wasserman made the creative demands for Stewart's appearance in *Harvey* far less restrictive. It was understood that the story was at least as important as the star, so Stewart did not insist on the same name control. He did retain star billing and required that his own screen credit appear in type no smaller than half the size of the movie title, but he made no demands at all about who his supporting cast would be.

What might appear to have been petty quibbling over the size and placement of credits became serious business as stars grew in power. On *Bend in the River*, Stewart's next picture for Universal, the studio had to get written permission from Stewart before posters could be printed with a *B* in "Bend" and an *R* in "River" that were larger than the type used in Stewart's name. Whether Stewart really cared is doubtful; he never played the prima donna, on or off the set.

But Lew cared. What became apparent to studio executives all over Hollywood was that the *Winchester '73* deal marked an alarming increase in star approval of everything from director to cast. In effect, Wasserman was using MCA's stars to force package deals on studios without ever calling it packaging. The agency might not be able to make Jack Warner or Harry Cohn hire a particular director or an up-and-coming costar, but Jimmy Stewart could — and did.

When Louis Mayer heard about Goetz's *Harvey–Winchester '73* deal, he screamed that his lamebrained son-in-law had foolishly given away the store.[9] No star would ever again be satisfied with anything less than half of the gross, and the cost to all of the studios would be exorbitant. The greatest of Hollywood's moguls never did forgive his son-in-law for hastening the end of the studio system.[10]

As it turned out, *Harvey* flopped at the box office (although in years to come it would turn out to be one of Stewart's most famous roles) while *Winchester '73* hit big, earning Stewart more than three times his salary for *Harvey* and ultimately making him a millionaire.

---

[8] *Winchester '73* featured two newcomers in minor roles whom Wasserman would lure to MCA once they were stars: Tony Curtis, who earned $350 a week for three weeks before the cameras, and Rock Hudson, who was paid $5,500 for the entire shoot. Dan Duryea was paid $58,300 and McNally $17,000, while Shelley Winters earned a mere $8,000 for playing the female lead.

[9] Three years earlier Mayer had raged at his other son-in-law, producer David O. Selznick, when he hired MGM producer Dore Schary away from Mayer to head Selznick's new subsidiary, Vanguard Pictures. Schary's agent was Lew Wasserman.

[10] Mayer left nothing to Bill and Edie Goetz when he died seven years later. In his will, he remembered his other daughter, Irene Selznick, but much of his estate went to the Catholic church in deference to his close relationship with Francis Cardinal Spellman, an early champion of the church's censorship arm, the Legion of Decency.

Stewart's success launched a full-blown actors' revolt. Every star on and off the MCA client list now wanted Wasserman to swing the same kind of profit participation deal for him. Lew got an adjusted gross deal at Universal for Tyrone Power's Copa Productions in *Mississippi Gambler* (1953), and the actor earned more money than he had ever earned on a single movie in his twenty-year career as a leading man.

"I only started doing really well when I found Lew Wasserman in 1950," said Tony Curtis. "I was like a good soldier. Lew would say, 'Go here. Do this. Then go there. Do that.' And I would say, 'Yes, sir!' I always kept my trunk packed, like a guy who was ready to ship out. Lew was absolutely brilliant then, and at the height of his ability—an extraordinary man."

Similarly, Clark Gable swore by MCA agent George Chasin, a Wasserman favorite who made call after call and promise after promise to Gable until the megastar finally gave in and switched to MCA, once his contract had expired at MGM. As promised, MCA did what it had done with dozens of its other |stars: it made Gable a millionaire. During his twenty-three years at MGM, Gable earned no more than $300,000 a year. With MCA representing him as an independent, he earned twice as much on a single picture. In 1952, MCA sent Gable abroad to make three films—*Never Let Go*, *Mogambo*, and *Betrayed*. Under U.S. law, a citizen working overseas for eighteen months was exempted from the harsh graduated income taxes, so Gable was allowed to keep most of what he earned.[11]

"I never really made any big money until George took over the handling of my career," Gable said.[12]

When Lew negotiated Joan Crawford's contract for *Sudden Fear* (1952), he got her the right to accept either $200,000 in straight salary or 48 percent of the movie's profits. Producer Joseph Kaufman was to put the $200,000 in an escrow account until Crawford decided which way she wanted to go.

Wasserman took great delight in ringing up Kaufman after he and his client saw a rough cut of the finished film. "You can take the $200,000 and shove it up your ass," said Lew.

The romantic thriller not only earned Oscar nominations for both Crawford

---

[11] MCA repeatedly sent clients abroad for eighteen-month foreign residency until the United States closed the loophole in 1954. As a result, dozens of American movies were made in Europe instead of on Hollywood soundstages, further weakening studios that were already hurt by the advent of television and the federal government's 1948 order to sell off their theater chains.

[12] Gable was less enamored with Wasserman himself, according to Lew's former son-in-law, Jack Myers. At a cocktail party when he overheard Wasserman boast of the commissions MCA was pulling in, Gable challenged Lew to tell him whose picture appeared on a $10,000 bill. When Wasserman was unable to answer, Gable reached into his pocket, pulled out a $10,000 bill and said, "Samuel Chase."

and costar Jack Palance, it also earned back several times its $720,000 production budget.

The stars' good fortune signaled the moguls' ruin. Louis Mayer's prophecies of doom came true for him on August 31, 1951, when Nick Schenck forced an end to the original Hollywood mogul's twenty-seven-year reign as head of MGM.[13] Schenck replaced Mayer with his second-in-command, Dore Schary, a longtime MCA client whose career as a screenwriter had been reshaped into that of a producer, then studio executive, by his good friend Lew Wasserman. Schenck even offered the job to Wasserman before giving it to Schary, but Lew declined, explaining to his troops, "I run all the studios."

Under Schary, MGM continued to bleed talent. Fewer and fewer contracts were renewed. Hollywood was awash in unemployed actors. As Wasserman gathered more and more MGM refugees unto MCA's sheltering arms, the threats of suspension or blacklisting, which had once kept the remaining stars in line, simply disappeared. Actors were indeed being freed. Henceforth, stars would control their own destinies. Hollywood would never be the same. But the cost to the studios and to the producers was enormous, both economically and psychologically.

"This means that MCA has placed control of the motion picture industry in the hands of its least creative component: the actor," producer Jerry Wald observed in an off-the-record interview with journalist Bill Davidson.

It would take more than a decade for the studios to regain any sort of equilibrium. By then television, not movies, would rule Hollywood, and the tube's biggest programming supplier would be a studio that hadn't even existed when MGM, Universal, and all the rest of the motion picture factories dominated the entertainment industry—a studio simply called Revue.

———

MCA INCORPORATED REVUE Productions in 1943, but the studio didn't begin producing TV until seven years later. In the beginning, Revue wasn't supposed to produce TV at all.

"Years ago, when they were in the band business, they had a subsidiary called

---

[13] By contract, Mayer owned a 10 percent interest in the residual rights to every film MGM made from 1924 on. With the new medium of television drooling for programming, residual rights in old movies had shot up virtually overnight, and Mayer's stake in the MGM library soared accordingly. But with his resignation, Mayer had to sever all ties with his studio, and that meant selling off his 10 percent interest in thousands of MGM films.

Harry Cohn recognized the value of the films and put in a bid. So did David Selznick. And so did Lew Wasserman, whose agency was now deeply involved in creating TV shows through its Revue Productions. Ultimately, all the bids for Mayer's equity lost to First Bank of Boston. On behalf of MGM's parent company, Loew's Inc., the bank arranged to buy Mayer out for $2.75 million.

Revue Productions, which put on stage shows and revues," recalled MCA publicist David Lipton. "They went into production of television on a competitive basis because they saw a great future in it, and they were right. They did it tentatively and they needed a corporation name. So they called it Revue Productions."

The largest single producer of television shows in history actually began as a defunct MCA subsidiary. By the dawn of the 1950s, the big band era was over, and so was Revue. Its only assets were a corporate seal and reams of unused stationery. When MCA decided to break into TV, that was all that was needed. Frugal Karl Kramer appropriated the stationery, set up an office, and Revue was reborn.

The new company's first TV series was a video version of a Saturday morning radio show, *Stars Over Hollywood*, which had been an NBC staple since 1941. MCA packaged *Stars Over Hollywood* as a radio showcase for its own clients, but when the blue-chip Armour meatpacking firm signed on as the show's sponsor in 1949, Kramer and Taft Schreiber saw a chance to make Revue Productions a reality.

They persuaded the new sponsor to underwrite their TV experiment, even offering to change the name from *Stars Over Hollywood* to *Armour Playhouse*. Instead of doing the show live, as most television was done then, Kramer and Schreiber insisted that *Stars Over Hollywood*/*Armour Playhouse* be put on film at Eagle-Lion Film. It would be more expensive, but they were able to budget for the extra cost by paying MCA clients minimum scale: $500 per performance. Those same MCA clients, who included stars like Basil Rathbone, Phil Harris, Alan Ladd, and Merle Oberon, might have earned closer to $5,000 per performance if MCA were selling their talents to some other TV producer or studio. But Revue Productions *was* MCA, so it made no sense to pay top dollar to its own clients.

Although NBC aired Revue's first TV series for only a single year, the programs were preserved on film. Unlike most early TV fare, *Stars Over Hollywood* could be shown again and again — a Revue trademark that would make it a pioneer in syndication and foreign TV sales.

Stars Over Hollywood went on to find new life as *Armour Theater*. After the show ended its network run on August 29, 1951, Revue's salesmen began selling it off-network, station by station all across the United States. By cutting out the network and retaining Armour as its sponsor, MCA kept all syndication profits for itself.

"MCA insisted that its network shows be allowed to be sold into syndication at the end of a fixed year — like the end of the third year — even if it was a hit show," said Lou Friedland, an out-of-work English teacher who hired on as a syndication salesman and became one of Revue's leading executives in early TV. "That way, each station could be told that, on such-and-such date, 'You have this show for your station.' Instead of selling dead product at the end of its life, we were selling these shows at the height of their popularity. At that point, the price of everything went sky high, and MCA made major dollars."

Wasserman's own pioneering foray into TV was not that successful.

"Lew's big idea was to put the Pacific Coast Hockey League on TV," recalled Bruce Campbell, whose father, George, ran MCA's San Francisco office.

The hockey experiment was a classic demonstration of Wasserman's inge-nious—but occasionally disastrous—synthesis of existing MCA resources. Key ingredients in Lew's televised hockey scheme were San Francisco's Winterland Auditorium and the Pan Pacific Auditorium in Los Angeles, both longtime venues for traveling MCA shows. Beginning with the Shipstad and Johnson Ice Follies, which Stein first brought to California in 1936, Winterland and the Pan Pacific had always looked to MCA for bookings. By 1949, both the Ice Capades and a troupe called the Ice Cycles had joined the Follies as regular attractions. But even with MCA's hype, ice shows couldn't draw crowds year-round.

Ice hockey might, however. Thus the Los Angeles Monarchs, Fresno Falcons, San Diego Seahawks, and nine other teams of the Pacific Coast Hockey League were born. George Campbell sat on the board of directors, and even Shipstad and Johnson joined the experiment, buying the Portland, Oregon, franchise. If ice hockey seemed a little out of place in a section of the nation where it never snowed, none of its early supporters seemed concerned. According to Campbell, Wasserman struck a deal with fledgling Los Angeles television station KTLA to broadcast the L.A. Monarch home games.

Hockey, even today, is not the kind of televised sporting event that commands big TV ratings. In 1949 none but the terminally bored tuned in. By 1950, when Revue was reborn, Lew's grand experiment in sports television had died a quick and merciful death, along with the Pacific Coast Hockey League itself.[14]

MCA had much better luck with wrestling. MCA munchkin Mickey Rockford hatched a plan to turn snarling hulks like Gorgeous George, Lord Blears, Baron Leone, and Wild Red Berry into early television stars. With Maier Beer as their sponsor, the half-naked clowns crawled into the ring and bounced each other off the ropes several times a week, becoming southern California television's first bona fide number one program.[15]

Most of MCA's early TV triumphs weren't nearly so innovative. Like the *Stars Over Hollywood* experiment, MCA and its Revue subsidiary relied on radio for most of its inspiration. Top-rated radio quiz shows like Ralph Edwards's *Truth or*

---

[14] Lew, however, was not discouraged. He approved negotiation of TV rights to broadcast polo matches from the Beverly Hills Polo Club.

[15] Not so well remembered was MCA's short-lived twice-weekly broadcast of women's wrestling over KTLA and KECA.

Consequences and Groucho Marx's *You Bet Your Life* easily translated to TV. The same was true with the variety show formula, hence Lew's temporary resurrection of bandleader Kay Kyser's career as host of NBC's *Kollege of Musical Knowledge.* MCA stalwarts Wayne King and Horace Heidt also hosted their own variety hours.

But the new medium's real fire power was comedy. MCA's arsenal included comic Red Skelton, whose NBC radio show had consisted of skits and bits since it premiered in 1941. His real stage speciality—pantomime—made him a pioneer TV star. Jack Carter, Abbott and Costello, Phil Harris, and a host of other comic MCA clients brought both visual and spoken humor to early television as well. But the comedian who clearly established the agency as an 800-pound gorilla in the new medium was Benjamin Kubelsky, the son of a Lithuanian Jew, who grew up in Waukegan, Illinois.

He tried and failed to get Jules Stein to represent him when he was first breaking into radio in 1932, but by 1946, when he finally did sign with the agency, he was the biggest name in radio. He'd long since changed his name and was well established as the only kind of client that Stein and Wasserman ever really cared to represent: a driven, talented, moneymaking star. He was Jack Benny.

—◦◦◦—

"WHAT HAPPENED WHEN MCA began representing me? Well, I got into business," said Jack Benny. "They helped me set up a corporation, Amusement Enterprises, Inc., and they advised me to dissolve it by selling the shares and keeping most of the money as capital gains."

When Benny went into TV, MCA also advised him to create a new corporation, which he would call J & M Productions, and to use it as a means of beating income taxes while cashing in on television, the phenomenal new medium that Benny would dominate through most of the 1950s the way he had dominated radio in the 1940s. MCA also urged him to produce other TV series, such as *Checkmate* and *Ichabod and Me,* under his corporate banner, so that he could claim the deductions in the event that the series failed, or collect the profits should the series become a hit. MCA also put him into stocks, real estate, and oil exploration partnerships.

"They put me in a position where I could pay terrific taxes and still keep some money for myself," said Benny. "That was one of the attractions of MCA. They call it giving an actor an 'estate.' Believe me, I'm thirty-nine, and I have a wife, a daughter, and grandchildren. I would like to have an estate." One of Benny's running gags was that he was *always* thirty-nine years old, even when he was pushing seventy.

Benny's advisers were members of the MCA brain trust, all but unknown to anyone outside of the agency business. In addition to Wasserman, Werblin, and Schreiber, the financial counselors included old MCA hands like Mickey Rockford, Herb Rosenthal, and Karl Kramer, and young agents Berle Adams, Jay Kanter, and Jennings Lang. They were the real assets of MCA, the men whose finely honed skills at making and keeping dollars would have made them successful in any business but gave them a special edge in the free-spending world of entertainment.

Benny was a case in point. Contrary to the skinflint character that he portrayed, he was a poor money manager and a self-confessed spendthrift who was in and out of debt most of his life. Even after MCA came to his rescue, Benny lived beyond his substantial means. But Stein taught his agents well in the art of how to care for stars. MCA had turned all of its most compliant stars—from Guy Lombardo to Jimmy Stewart—into millionaires, and Jack Benny was no exception. All he had to do was follow orders.

But first, long before any of his good friends at MCA would make this financial magic happen, Jack Benny had to *become* a star. That was a task he achieved on his own, in spite of MCA.

In 1932, Benny had approached Jules Stein's brother Bill with a plan to parlay a modestly successful vaudeville career into his own radio spot. He wanted to pattern himself after Ben Bernie, an MCA bandleader whose own radio program evolved into a variety show with guest stars and skits built around Bernie's orchestra music and his opening refrain, "Yowsah, yowsah! Greetings and salutations, my friends!" Benny argued that his musicianship was at least equal to Bernie's. Like Jules Stein, Benny played a so-so violin, which would give him cachet as an orchestra leader. As for his stand-up routine, it was a hundred times funnier than "Yowsah, yowsah!"

Bill Stein didn't care how funny he was. He nixed the idea because Benny didn't have a stellar name. Even in 1932 MCA was doing business only with established stars.

Echoing his mentor's founding philosophy, Lew Wasserman would sum up Stein's advice during roundtable sessions with his troops in the decades that followed: "Let some other jerk build them. We'll buy them."

Undaunted, Benny turned to the little known Lyons Agency. He got Canada Dry ginger ale to sponsor a comedy half hour twice a week over NBC. In 1933, *The Jack Benny Show* switched to CBS once a week. Over the years sponsors changed (Chevrolet, General Tire, Jell-O), but Benny's radio presence did not. When NBC offered him a Sunday night slot, he returned to the nation's biggest network where he built a repertory group that set the standard for situation comedy to the end of the century: Eddie "Rochester" Anderson, Dennis Day, Phil Harris, Mel Blanc, Don Wilson, and Benny's wife, Mary Livingstone. His ratings soared through the late 1940s, and MCA finally decided he was big enough to steal from the Lyons Agency. After careful analysis, it was clear that one spot where the Lyons Agency was vulnerable was in getting Benny movie deals.

While Benny had become one of the most popular personalities on radio, he was a disaster in motion pictures.

"Jack walked into my office one day without solicitation from any of us," recalled Taft Schreiber. "We had just made a big deal for the *Amos 'n' Andy* program, selling it to CBS, and Jack seemed impressed with that. I told him we would love to handle him, but not if he had another agent. It was then that he paid off Arthur Lyons so we could sign him with MCA."

—◦◦◦—

THE *AMOS 'N' ANDY* deal did for radio what Wasserman's *Winchester '73* deal would do for motion pictures. It sent an electrified dollar-sign buzz through Hollywood. By combining good timing, shrewd planning, and all the right connections, MCA got big-money results where every other agency seemed to fail.

Lunching with CBS chairman Bill Paley one afternoon in Paley's private Midtown Manhattan dining room, Wasserman and Schreiber laid out the scheme. They proposed that the stars of NBC's *Amos 'n' Andy* (MCA clients Freeman Gosden and Charles Correll) incorporate. Then they would sell their company's assets to CBS. Their assets, Lew carefully explained, consisted of the characters they had made famous and the scripts from nineteen years worth of *Amos 'n' Andy* shows that were aired over NBC.

MCA's asking price was $2 million, plus a share in the profits of all future *Amos 'n' Andy* shows. It was a deal where everybody won. If the $2 million was simply paid directly to Gosden and Correll, they would have to pay the government's highest personal income rate: 77 percent of anything over $70,000. If Gosden and Correll took the money from their corporation, however, it would be considered a capital gain by the Internal Revenue Service, and the government would take 25 percent at most.

It was perfect. MCA's two clients would earn more than they ever could working strictly for salary, and CBS would own their show and characters, making it virtually impossible for the pair to take their talents elsewhere. The only ones who lost were NBC and the IRS. Such schemes quickly grew in popularity among high-earning show business types and became yet another reason for entertainers to sign on with MCA.

Like everyone else who read the trades, Benny knew about *Amos 'n' Andy*. He was ripe for the MCA plucking. With a generous loan from MCA, he bought out his Lyons Agency contract and signed on. Taft Schreiber immediately created Amusement Enterprises, and renegotiated the contract with the American

Tobacco Company so that Benny's sponsor paid his corporation $27,500 a week and sent Benny a separate paycheck for $10,000 a week. Expenses for his weekly NBC show now came out of the corporate account while Benny's salary was all his own.

Around the same time Schreiber was setting up Amusement Enterprises, Paley began eyeing Benny as he had *Amos 'n' Andy*. He asked Lew Wasserman what kind of deal he could make to buy Amusement Enterprises and got an asking price of $4 million.

This time NBC got wind of Wasserman's maneuver before he closed the deal, so Lew threw open the bidding. NBC balked. After all, Chairman David Sarnoff reasoned, what would his network gain? NBC was already airing *The Jack Benny Show*, which was tied to a five-year contract with the American Tobacco Company. Except for one summer replacement show and one forgettable movie, Benny's Amusement Enterprises hadn't produced anything other than *The Jack Benny Show*.[16] For $4 million, NBC would be getting nothing more than it already had.

Bill Paley saw things differently. He gladly bought Amusement Enterprises, and Benny promptly switched to CBS, taking the American Tobacco Company with him as his sponsor. In his first CBS broadcast, Benny played the NBC-CBS comedy raids for laughs by asking, "Do I get free parking at CBS?"

A steady stream of MCA comic acts followed Benny to CBS, including George Burns and Gracie Allen, Red Skelton, and Edgar Bergen. CBS became known as Paley's Comet. The joke was on David Sarnoff.

The Internal Revenue Service found none of this funny. The government challenged Wasserman's sale of Amusement Enterprises as a naked attempt to dodge Benny's personal income taxes. Once more MCA came to the rescue. It supported Benny's legal appeals all the way to the Supreme Court. The struggle lasted more than two years, but eventually Benny won. So did every other client that MCA helped incorporate as a tax hedge.

"When Jack decided to go into television, Wasserman asked me to negotiate his contract with CBS," recalled Berle Adams. "On the plane to New York I read Jack's radio contract and noted that there was no morals clause."

Adams recalled being both pleased and puzzled. The morals clause, which gave a network the right to fire anyone deemed guilty of an undefined immoral act, had long been the bane of entertainers. Wasserman had gotten it removed from Frank Sinatra's MGM contract in 1946, but that had been an uphill battle. Mayer granted the exception only because Sinatra was super hot at the time.

---

[16] The summer replacement show was a standard variety package, emceed by a young announcer named Jack Paar. Amusement Enterprises' sole attempt at motion picture production was *The Lucky Stiff*, a 1949 United Artists comedy flop.

Movie studios had used the clause for decades as an excuse to dump actors they couldn't get rid of any other way, and radio networks had taken to incorporating it into their contracts for much the same reason.

CBS demanded a morals clause for all on-air talent, including Jack Benny. Berle Adams soon discovered that the omission had been a CBS lawyer's error. In the TV contract, it was reinstated.

When Adams handed Benny his new TV contract, he began with an apology. "There's a morals clause in this contract," he said sheepishly.

"What's a morals clause?" Benny asked.

"Let me put it this way: if you are accused of having sex with a fourteen-year-old girl, and they can prove you're guilty, they can throw you off the air," Adams answered.

Shouted Benny, "*Halevei!* It should only happen! Give me the contract!"

Thus began a decade of *The Jack Benny Show* anchoring the CBS comedy lineup, and dominating Sunday night television.

———

AT MCA, SEX seemed as rigidly regulated as the dress code. There were affairs, to be sure, but there was also discretion of the highest order. Nowhere was it written that MCA agents *had* to be loyal to their spouses, but it was an absolute fact that none of Stein's senior executives ever divorced. That, of course, did not mean they didn't think about it.

"There were some bad times between the tenth and twentieth years," Edie Wasserman told author Dominick Dunne in her only public statement about the Wassermans' marital troubles. "He never stopped working, and I felt neglected, but we weathered it."

It was true that Lew worked late at the office, but that was not an excuse for an extramarital tryst, according to his colleagues. Wasserman really *did* work late at the office. And early. And every other time in between.

"When I'm in Hollywood, I'm in early because I have to talk to New York, and they're three hours ahead," he patiently explained to one interviewer. "When I'm in New York, I'm in the office until nine P.M. because it's still six o'clock on the Coast."

If his logic left something to be desired, his work performance did not. Jules Stein was more certain than ever that the sleepless man he'd picked to succeed him as MCA president was the right choice. Wasserman preferred wandering through the darkened MCA offices after midnight, inspecting his agents' desks for scraps of paper, to spending a quiet evening at home with his wife.

Edie, however, believed in having a good time, and her idea of a good time was not inspecting desks. Bandleader Johnny Singer, who had dated Edie back in

Cleveland, recalled being mildly shocked during one of his first visits to California in the late 1940s when Edie insisted that he take her out dancing. Singer obliged, though he felt a bit awkward that husband Lew was nowhere to be seen.

About the same time, the Frank Sinatra rumors began to circulate. There was no question that Edie and Sinatra had been great friends since the days of the Hollywood Canteen. But both within the agency and among its clients the suggestion now surfaced that the Frank-and-Edie friendship went much deeper.

"I heard…rumors about it, but I wasn't about to discuss it with anybody," recalled Tony Curtis, who was just starting his own career at MCA during that period. "It was a very powerful dilemma, [but] it was something I would not in any way expose myself to. There were other people besides Frank."

Bette Davis, no stranger herself to extramarital trysts, told her biographers that the Frank-and-Edie relationship was very close, off and on, for decades. As late as the 1960s, when Edie underwent surgery for breast cancer, Sinatra showed up at her bedside to offer comfort.

Whether the rumors had a basis or not, they definitely had repercussions. In an internal Justice Department memo from 1962, government prosecutor Leonard Posner puzzled over the Sinatra mystery, zeroing in on the inexplicable souring of his relations with MCA in the late 1940s when Lew Wasserman, usually the absolute master of star manipulation, lost control and fired Frank Sinatra.

According to Posner's memo, "Columbia Records [17] and MGM were protesting very hotly about the emotional instability of Sinatra.…Sinatra was kicked out [of MCA] around 1950, because Wasserman specifically said so. He said that Sinatra was a very difficult person to deal with. At that time, MCA gave Sinatra back his contract."

Wasserman and Sinatra clashed early. In 1945, when MGM was making *Anchors Aweigh*, Frank insisted on having his pal Sammy Cahn write the score, over Lew's objections. As Cahn recalled in his memoirs, "It came to such an impasse that Lew Wasserman, head of MCA, came to me to plead, 'Unless Frank gives in, he'll lose the picture. Won't you talk with him?' I of course went to Frank and said, 'Frank, you've already done enough for me. Why don't you pass on this one? There'll be others.' He looked at me—and this is where it will always be between us—and said: 'If you're not there Monday, I'm not there Monday.'

"I was there Monday. So was he."

Having caught on to the subtle way that Wasserman wielded power, Sinatra began regularly turning the tables on him. When the agency refused to pay him some $30,000 in living expenses, Sinatra and his lawyer protested to the American Federation of Television and Radio Artists and persuaded the emerging broadcast-

---

[17] In 1952, Sinatra switched to Capitol Records where he recorded many of his best-known bluesy love ballads.

ers' union to end MCA's status as an authorized talent agency. Wasserman screamed, but in less than twenty-four hours, Sinatra got his money.

Sinatra battled Wasserman over radio packaging too. Like Eddie Bracken, Sinatra had put his own show together and retained control, but MCA still demanded 10 percent of Sinatra's $15,000-a-week salary. Sinatra held out. Unlike Bracken, Sinatra had clout. He forced MCA to take the smaller commission. But Wasserman never forgave him. While relations between the two men went from bad to worse, Frank and Edie remained friends.

Sinatra's egomania finally got the best of him, however, and not just with Lew. Mickey Rockford began sending Sinatra's checks directly to his wife, Nancy, because Frank had been spending all of his money on himself. At that point Sinatra challenged Rockford to a fistfight. On a whim, Sinatra had two of his ever-present goons literally throw Sonny Werblin out of a New York rehearsal hall. When Jules Stein refused to grant him a personal loan, Sinatra completely lost control. He let every bartender from L.A. to Manhattan know exactly what he thought about the "Jew bastards" at MCA.

Wasserman had had enough. He accused Sinatra of welshing on $40,000 in back commissions. When Sinatra laughed at him, Wasserman took out ads in *Variety* and the *Hollywood Reporter*, stating that MCA no longer represented Frank Sinatra.

"How can you fire someone who earned $693,000 last year?" Sinatra said contemptuously. "Can you imagine being fired by an agency that never had to sell you?"

"Lew told me that he just didn't like the way Frank treated people," said Tony Curtis. "That's why he fired him."

Lew said nothing in reply to Sinatra's public taunts. He was content to sit back and watch the star snarl and sneer and make a fool of himself. When Frank abandoned Nancy to chase after Ava Gardner, Wasserman said nothing. He merely observed from a distance his former client's career plummeting straight to hell, without MCA there to help bail him out.

FIFTEEN

Laughs and Loose Women

1951–1952

One MCA agent who did not go home to his wife every night was Jennings Lang.

According to a 1962 Justice Department memo, Wasserman hired Lang away from the Sam Jaffe Agency in 1949 for the express purpose of using him to steal stars from other agencies. The tall, craggy Lang, with his dark, deep-set eyes, specialized in winning over female clients—a task he seemed to find as pleasing as it was effortless. Lang made no secret of the fact that he was well endowed and proficient at satisfying women, nor did he deny the frequency with which he did so, despite his ten-year marriage to the mousy but loyal mother of his two sons. If Pamela Lang ever complained about his philandering, she did not do so publicly.

Jennings Lang was as tough an agent as any who ever went on the MCA payroll. The son of a prosperous German merchant who had immigrated to New York at the turn of the century, Lang graduated from law school and started a practice before the talent business hooked him in the early 1940s. He was Jaffe's top agent when MCA snagged him. He brought his own clients over with him and signed even more within the first year, coaxing them into television during the difficult early days of the medium, when bona fide movie stars wouldn't consider appearing on the tube even as guests.

"I think Lew liked Jennings because he did what Lew would never dare to do. He drank. He horsed around with women," said Berle Adams. "Lew lived vicariously through Jennings."

But even a man of enormous appetites like Jennings Lang could not single-handedly satisfy the appetite of television. As the demand for TV programming increased, MCA needed more able agents than it could possibly steal from rivals like Jaffe.

"To us the most important thing is manpower because that's all we really have here," Wasserman said, waxing philosophical in a rare 1962 interview with the *New York Post*. "We have no inventory, and our assets, we put them under our hats at night and go home."

But able agents who were willing to work long hours for scant wages were rare, and MCA was expanding at such a furious rate that it could not afford to hire the wrong people. Thus the MCA mail room apprenticeship became an institution.

"Each senior executive picks a bright young man and trains him," said Lew. "That's our policy. There are no schools for agents. We have to train our own. You can only learn by watching the operation."

Jules Stein's policy had always been to hire the best and brightest and start them in the mail room. But the days when a Taft Schreiber or a Mickey Rockford or even a Lew Wasserman could start out as a delivery boy with nothing more than a high school diploma were long gone. By the 1950s, MCA policy had evolved to recruiting only college graduates, usually from UCLA and USC in Los Angeles and Columbia University in New York. Top grades were not particularly important. Ambition and quick thinking were. The first and most important requirement was the ability to survive, and then thrive, by one's wits.

"They paid spit," said one mail room graduate. "I didn't earn enough to keep my suit dry-cleaned. Lew used to tell us we ought to pay *him* for the privilege of working for MCA."

Mail room clerks learned by doing, and by being done. If they couldn't figure their own way out of the mail room, they were axed mercilessly so someone else could have a crack at scheming to outshine his peers while currying favor with the higher-ups.

"Karl Kramer used to subscribe to all kinds of magazines at the office and when he finished one, he'd ask one of the kids down in the mail room if he wanted to buy it from him," recalled Berle Adams. "How were they gonna refuse? One of them would buy a magazine and go tell all the others how he'd gotten on Mr. Kramer's good side. Pretty soon they're all buying the magazines! Karl had a pretty good little business going for a while."

Suckers didn't last long at MCA. College grads, some with law degrees, ran errands for less than fifty dollars a week. New recruits either shed their gullibility, quit, or were fired.

"MCA…made boot camp look sissified," recalled Herman Gollob, who went on to become a senior vice president at Doubleday books. Before quitting MCA, he advanced to the rank of literary agent, though MCA's idea of literary work still rang hollow with him nearly forty years later. "My crowning achievement was arranging for a sensitive young southern first-novelist to write a Tarzan movie," said Gollob.

Wasserman had no patience with liars, fools, or the perpetually naive. Those few who did move up from the mail room didn't fare much better as junior agents. But if they stayed long enough there were rewards.

Added up at the end of the year, MCA perks and bonuses could amount to ten times an agent's salary. Subsistence wages with a pot of gold at the end of the rainbow were basic to Stein's long-range game plan: find the right person, train him, and shackle him to the company with golden handcuffs. Such incentives inspired dozens of fired-up young men to wheedle their way out of the mail room and give their most productive years to MCA.

One of them was a UCLA business student who started in the mail room in 1949, the same year Lew stole Jennings Lang from the Jaffe Agency. Like most other entry-level MCA employees, Jay Kanter earned $30 a week—$24.30 after taxes. Kanter was smart, affable, and honest. He was also lucky.

When Kanter went to work in the mail room, Marlon Brando was hitting it big on Broadway in A Streetcar Named Desire. Naturally, MCA stole the brash young star from his New York agent with the same kinds of promises Stein had made to Russell Nype. In Brando's case, however, MCA kept its promises.

When Brando arrived in L.A. on the Twentieth Century Limited to begin work on his first movie, The Men, Kanter was assigned to pick him up at Union Station. For the next week, Kanter chauffeured the New York stage actor, who did not drive, all over Los Angeles. The eager young mail room clerk was punctual. He was compliant. He tried to anticipate Brando's every need. By the time Wasserman got around to calling a meeting to give the bright new star an opportunity to pick his own personal representative from among the agency's top agents, Brando had already made his selection. "I want the kid who's been driving me around," he said.

Wasserman tried to talk him out of it, but Brando was adamant. In one quick, clever, and lucky maneuver, Kanter graduated from mail room flunky to agent— but not without being subjected to one of Lew's patented sputtering, high-decibel lectures. If he screwed up, Kanter was told, he was through. Finished. He had one chance. If he blew it, he wouldn't even be able to get a job scraping gum off the floor at the local movie theater.[1]

Then Lew took the terrified neophyte under his wing and patiently showed him how to be an agent. Kanter demonstrated that his sudden promotion was no fluke. He was so good at handling Brando that he became MCA's specialist in pampering the agency's most neurotic clients. Within a short time he would add Grace Kelly and Marilyn Monroe to his list. And for years he was the only agent the quixotic Brando would deal with at all.

"He [Brando] refused to ever come in the building," another agent recalled.

---

[1]   A short-lived 1989 CBS sitcom about a talent agency, The Famous Teddy Z, starring Jon Cryer and Alex Rocco, was based on the Kanter-Brando story.

"Jay had to meet him out in front of MCA headquarters whenever he wanted to discuss any agency business."

Wasserman began to take such a shine to his newest mail room graduate that he set him up as MCA's chief emissary to Universal Studios.

"Lew was out to see the head of the studio," Kanter recalled in a 1985 interview with journalist Susan Deutsch. "They were talking about a deal for Jimmy Stewart, a two-picture deal—a western and some other picture. Lew said 'Okay,' and we left. On the drive back, I asked him why he hadn't closed the deal—it seemed to me it was all set and there shouldn't have been any more discussion. He said, 'Well, we'll close it. But it will be *you* who gets back to them, to tell them it's okay.' I said, 'Gee, thanks,' and Lew said, 'I want you to do it because from now on, you'll never have any trouble getting them on the phone or getting in to see them.' And that was the case. From that point on, I had instant entrée."

In a host of ways, Kanter was the precise opposite of Jennings Lang. He was well mannered, accommodating, and short of stature. Lang was coarse, opinionated, and as tall as Wasserman himself. But Kanter and Lang were both lifelong favorites of the MCA president, and their experience was a textbook example of how an older and more experienced agent mentors a younger MCA employee. Despite, or perhaps because of, their differences, Kanter and Lang became friends. It was a friendship that very nearly ended in murder shortly after it began, however, climaxing in MCA's best-known scandal and eventually inspiring a controversial Oscar-winning movie.

Kanter and Lang had no inkling they were headed for disaster in the fall of 1951. It began the way such disasters inevitably begin—with a beautiful woman.

A film star since the silent era, Joan Bennett remained a raven-haired beauty as she approached her forty-second birthday. For more than a decade she'd been married to the brilliant but fiery independent producer Walter Wanger. From *Stagecoach* (1939) to *Cleopatra* (1963), Wanger made an indelible mark on Hollywood. Though he left a legacy of sixty feature films, he starred his wife in only one of them: *Scarlet Street* (1945), in which Joan Bennett played opposite Edward G. Robinson, as a scheming, two-timing vixen. In real life, as it turned out, she played precisely the same role.

Not that Wanger was an angel. Like many movie executives of the era, Wanger liked his adultery one-sided. Joan was supposed to be a good mother and stay at home with their daughters while Wanger philandered late at the office or lingered on location in some exotic locale long after his movie had wrapped. So it had gone for years. When Bennett got around to doing the same thing—slipping away for weekends in New Orleans or the West Indies—he branded her a whore and hired a private detective to catch her in the act.

Bennett began driving to the parking lot across the street from the MCA building in Beverly Hills. There she met her agent, Jennings Lang, but not to discuss business. She got out of her Kelly-green Cadillac convertible, slid in beside him, and the two drove off together to a duplex apartment a few blocks away.

The landlady, Rowena Nate, later told reporters that Bennett and Lang showed up at the apartment often for an afternoon rendezvous, but in her own memoirs, Bennett maintained that she and Lang got together because she needed his support to raise her morale when her marriage was failing. She said that her accommodating agent listened patiently as she cried her eyes out over Wanger's increasing paranoia about his wife's adulterous behavior. She saw no irony in the fact that she confirmed her husband's worst fears every time she hopped into bed to weep on Lang's shoulder.

On one especially angst-ridden Thursday afternoon, twelve days before Christmas 1951, Lang drove his client-lover back to the MCA parking lot from the apartment. As she climbed into her own car and started the engine with Lang hovering over her open window, Wanger suddenly materialized.

"I couldn't hear what was being said, but I know it was arguing from the tone of their voices," said mechanic Rick Scott, who worked at a service station across the street. "All three of them were talking and arguing. The arguing went on for several minutes. Then suddenly I heard her say: 'Don't! Don't!'

"And then I heard the shots. When I got there, Wanger had gone. I don't know where he went. Lang said, 'Everything is all right. There's nothing wrong.'"

But the blood seeping down Lang's pant leg said otherwise. Something indeed was very wrong. One of two bullets from Wanger's .38 revolver had hit its mark, and Lang collapsed on the pavement in agony. Within hours the shooting became the number one news item on the Hollywood grapevine.

"Did you know that Walter got one of his balls?" Van Johnson wrote in a letter to Rosalind Russell a couple days later. "Yup. Right in the old cruller."

Lang hadn't even undergone surgery at nearby Midway Hospital before Lew Wasserman's brand of damage control got under way. Pamela Lang called Jules Stein in New York to ask what to do. He told her to sit tight and keep mum until she heard from San Francisco criminal attorney Jake Ehrlich. On Ehrlich's advice, Joan Bennett and Jennings Lang both declined to talk to the police or the district attorney. Neither would press charges, and the cover story they spoon-fed to reporters was that poor deranged Walter Wanger was distraught over financial reversals, bringing on delusions that his wife was having an affair.

Spinning the media further away from the adulterous theme of the story, a dour but deeply concerned Pamela Lang, whom Jennings had met when she was a singer for the Benny Goodman Orchestra, posed for photos at her husband's bedside the following day. Following Ehrlich's instructions, she held her philandering husband's hand as he lay in his hospital bed and spoke for him when she pledged her loving loyalty, ignoring questions about his alleged affair. MCA client Jane Wyman and Temme Brenner, wife of MCA agent Herb Brenner, stayed by Pamela

Lang's side as she ran the gauntlet of reporters to her car outside the hospital. They repeated the story that it had all been just a series of tragic mistakes.

Meanwhile, a tearful Joan Bennett went into seclusion at the Wanger family manse in Holmby Hills, surrounding herself with her children, who hoped Daddy would be home in time for Christmas. Bennett publicly pledged her support for her woefully misguided husband who sat in his lonely cell in the Lincoln Heights jail until the equally misguided district attorney's office would come to its senses, drop the charges, and set him free. To add a Hollywood touch to the masterfully manipulated story, restaurateur Mike Romanoff personally catered Wanger's jail-house meals.

But the scandal did not disappear. The media manipulation that had operated so well in the past, with MCA's cover up of Clark Gable's drunk-driving arrests, Betty Grable's shotgun wedding to Harry James, and Bette Davis's apparent participation in the manslaughter death of her second husband, did not work this time. The one thing Wasserman's troops had not counted on was the investigator Wanger had hired to stalk his wife. In a juicy five-page report, the investigator confirmed every salacious detail of the Lang-Bennett liaison. Among other things, the private detective let it leak that the apartment where he had witnessed Lang and Bennett spending afternoons together had been rented by a young man named Jay Kanter. Confronted with this fact, Kanter maintained that he had leased the duplex for Marlon Brando, but that Brando had been in New York for several months. How did Lang wind up with the key? How many others at MCA might also have had access to the apartment for their own afternoon liaisons? Speculation fueled the now out-of-control story.

Despite Lang's refusal to press charges, prosecutors rounded up enough witnesses to get Wanger indicted for assault with a deadly weapon. He faced fourteen years in prison. Hollywood rallied around him, with every mogul from Walt Disney to Sam Goldwyn contributing to his defense fund. Famed lawyer Jerry Geisler, whom Jules Stein had hired to defend Errol Flynn during his 1943 statutory rape trial, stood up for Wanger. In short order the district attorney became the bogeyman of the story while Lang, Bennett, and Wanger somehow metamorphosed into misunderstood and mistreated victims.

Wanger did make it home for Christmas, with Bennett's forgiving arms wrapped around his slumped shoulders and the children tugging at his pant legs. A few miles away, at the Lang home in Brentwood, Pamela nursed her man back to health, feeding him soup in bed as photographers snapped his pained expression.

Whether any of the pathos affected the sentence Geisler negotiated for Wanger four months later can't be measured. But there is little doubt that Wanger got off with amazingly light punishment: four months at a Los Angeles County Sheriff's honor farm. While he was serving time, an admirer sent him a sharpshooter's medal. Upon his release, he continued his career as a producer.

Aptly, his next picture was a low-budget prison film for Allied Artists: *Riot in Cell Block 11* (1954).

But Joan Bennett's career was over. As an adulteress, she was box office poison, especially given the prim roles she had taken in her last two films: the subdued mother in Vincente Minnelli's *Father of the Bride* and its sequel, *Father's Little Dividend*. A contract for a TV series that Lang had negotiated for her, shortly before the scandal erupted, was canceled. The only thing left for her was dinner theater. The same month that Wanger was sentenced to the honor farm, Bennett replaced Rosalind Russell in a road production of the Broadway hit play *Bell, Book and Candle*. She was booed at every stop. Except for minor roles in a few B movies, she didn't work again regularly in Hollywood until the late 1960s, when she starred in the popular ABC vampire soap opera, *Dark Shadows*.

Neither Kanter nor Lang suffered all that much. Wasserman did not summarily fire his two wayward agents, as many of their fellow MCA employees expected. They were lectured and given the rare second chance.

Like Wanger, Lang survived and thrived. Within a year, Wasserman promoted him to MCA vice president for television. With his left testicle intact, he went on to father more children. Moreover, his late nights at the Mocambo, the Trocadero, or the Cocoanut Grove continued once he had fully recovered.

Meanwhile, Kanter helped Wasserman forget his role in the unfortunate shooting episode by marrying into Hollywood's inner circle. Much to Wasserman's delight, Kanter took Paramount chief Barney Balaban's daughter Judy as his bride in early 1952. It became a wedding of MCA and Paramount interests that would prove to be pivotal in the coming years.

But like Mrs. Wanger, Mrs. Lang did not fare so well. Pamela began keeping much closer tabs on her unruly husband, attempting to travel with him wherever he went. Friends sympathized with her, openly commiserating about her husband's promiscuity. At home, she and Jennings slept in separate beds.

Meanwhile, she developed an overactive thyroid, according to her doctor. He prescribed sleeping pills. They didn't work. Ten months after the shooting incident in the parking lot of MCA, and just five days short of her forty-first birthday, Pamela Lang was found dead in her bathroom. A reportedly distraught Jennings Lang called the family physician, who pronounced her dead of a sudden heart attack before calling paramedics. Jennings left immediately for the home of MCA publicist Henry Rogers, who told the press that Lang was too upset to comment about his wife's death. The Los Angeles County Coroner's office accepted the family physician's conclusion that Pamela Lang had died from natural causes. No autopsy was performed.

Director Billy Wilder gave the entire episode a fitting postscript in his 1960 hit film *The Apartment*, with Jack Lemmon playing the Kanter-like role of a timorous junior executive currying favor with his bosses by letting them use his place for their afternoon quickies. Fred MacMurray[2] portrays a lecherous senior executive who sleeps with elevator operator Shirley MacLaine and leaves her to an attempted suicide. Wilder's dark sense of mischief didn't end with the plot similarities. Though Lemmon and Kanter bore only a passing resemblance to each another, MacMurray and Jennings Lang looked so much alike that they could easily have been mistaken for each other on the street—or in the MCA parking lot.

—◈—

DESPITE THEIR ANTICS, Kanter and Lang weren't MCA's greatest comedy team during the 1950s. That honor belonged to Dean Martin and Jerry Lewis.

The crooner and the stooge met in the spring of 1945. Within a year, they were performing together. Within two years, Martin and Lewis were drawing record crowds at New York's Paramount Theater. By the end of the decade, they'd struck gold with producer Hal Wallis's *My Friend Irma*, the first of seventeen hit Martin and Lewis films. They launched an NBC radio variety series that would propel them into TV, where Lew Wasserman finally laid claim to them in 1950.

But before they met Lew, and even before they became Martin and Lewis, they were Dino Crocetti, the devil-may-care barber's son from Steubenville, Ohio, and Joseph Levitch, the hammy offspring of two failed Jewish vaudevillians from New Jersey. Dean had had an undistinguished career as a boxer, a blackjack dealer, and, finally, a singer for the Sammy Watkins Orchestra in Cleveland. Jerry was equally undistinguished: a loud obnoxious juvenile with endless energy, tired jokes, and routine shtick that raised more hackles than it did laughs. Individually, they were mediocre; together, they were hilarious.

The man who saw the potential chemistry and brought the pair together was a fiercely independent Broadway agent named Abner J. Greshler who had made a career out of hating MCA.

From the 1920s on, Greshler grudgingly watched Jules Stein play the angles and cut the corners, putting MCA at the head of the pack. Like Jules Stein, Greshler had learned how to book bands while he was still a pasty-faced high school student. While his own father earned nickels a day as a laborer in order to pay the rent, he collected hundreds of dollars a week in commissions and stored the cash in a cigar box beneath his bed.

---

2   MacMurray, who had starred in Wilder's 1944 film noir classic *Double Indemnity*, was Raymond Chandler's first choice for the title role in *Philip Marlowe* on CBS. Chandler, who co-authored the *Double Indemnity* script, sent TV producers Mark Goodson and Bill Todman to talk to MacMurray's MCA agent, but they were turned down flat. MCA had other plans for MacMurray. *Philip Marlowe* never made it to CBS, but MCA steered MacMurray into *My Three Sons*, a Revue show that starred MCA clients, and ran on ABC and, later, on CBS for twelve years.

Unlike Jules Stein, Greshler was no organization man. He was fanatic about his independence. As early as 1929, Billy Goodheart sent agent Willard Alexander to Greshler with an offer to join MCA. He partnered with no one, Greshler explained, least of all MCA. While other agents forged raw talent into class acts, Stein stood by with a bankroll to buy the finished products. By Greshler's standards, Stein was a thief and a charlatan. Greshler certainly had no intention of becoming his employee.

Greshler loved show business and handled any raw talent who showed promise: jugglers, midgets, acrobats, mimics. He dreamed of spotting the next Milton Berle or Jack Benny among the dozens of young *tummlers* who warmed up audiences for borscht belt headliners. As it turned out, Greshler didn't have to go to the Catskills to find his ticket to success. He took the ferry to Staten Island one night in 1943 to see a gangly high school dropout perform pratfalls at the Ritz Theater and signed him on the spot. Greshler cleaned the boy up, dressed him in a suit, combed his hair into a well-oiled pompadour, shot some publicity glossies, and labeled them "Jerry Lewis, Satirical Impressions in Pantomimicry." Lewis was sixteen years old.

Over the next three years the "pantomimicry" slowly developed into a bona fide act. Though never worth top billing, Lewis could count on Greshler to find him work in one dive or another, either as a slapstick emcee or a stand-up specialty act.

During one such gig in a Baltimore burlesque house, a mutual pal introduced Lewis to Martin, who was crooning in a saloon just down the street. Instead of blowing off the pimply-faced teen with the whiny voice, the older and far more polished Martin took Lewis under his wing. There was instant symbiosis. Martin loved to boast about his boozing, betting, and babes, and Lewis, eight years his junior, sat and listened like a worshipful younger brother.

One show-biz horror story that Dean told was no exaggeration. It involved a company that bought and sold him like a piece of meat. Like dozens before and after, Martin tithed to MCA almost from the moment he took to the stage. His woeful tale began in 1943, the same year Greshler signed Jerry Lewis. MCA's Merle Jacobs, the same Cleveland agent who had discovered Lew Wasserman seven years earlier, told Martin that he could be the next Frank Sinatra. Jacobs advised Martin to quit the Sammy Watkins Orchestra, sign with MCA, and strike out on his own.

While he struggled to develop a solo style, MCA promoted him as a Sinatra knockoff. He wasn't; audiences booed, and bookings plummeted.

Meanwhile, Martin married, fathered two children, and got himself deeper and deeper into debt. When he turned to his agency for help, the advice he got was to work harder. He began holding back MCA's commissions, keeping his whole paycheck himself. MCA's hierarchy finally decided Martin had been a mistake. In 1944 the agency put him up for sale. The only taker was a bargain-basement Times Square agent named Lou Perry, who paid $200 for Martin's contract plus the $345 in unpaid commissions that MCA insisted the singer owed. Within a year, Martin declared bankruptcy—yet he did not curb his spending. He continued to play the ponies, borrow from loan sharks, and buy the last round at every bar he entered. Even second-rate Lou Perry was now convinced that MCA had been right. Dean Martin was a loser.

Then, during an Atlantic City engagement in the summer of 1946, Martin joined Lewis onstage, and Abbey Greshler's dream of beating Jules Stein at his own game was born. Mobster Skinny D'Amato, who owned the 500 Club, personally found Jerry Lewis grating and wanted to fire him after the first night. But when the singer he'd hired to perform on the same bill called in sick, D'Amato became desperate. Lewis suggested that he substitute Dean Martin, who was also in town.

Martin's music was lackluster, but when he began kibitzing with Lewis onstage, the audience loved it. It was an act that had never been executed in quite the same way before: the pairing of a geek with a gigolo, a putz with a playboy, schmaltz versus suave—a unique wedding of opposites.

Greshler caught their act when Perry refused to make the trip and remained in New York. Greshler knew what he had, but he had to move quickly. He advised Martin to quit Perry and let him book the two as a team: Martin and Lewis. Despite months of legal threats, Greshler finally persuaded Perry to sell him Martin's contract for $4,000. He now owned Martin and Lewis, and for the remainder of the 1940s, he built them into megastars. They were his boys, and that's how he treated them: like his own two favorite sons.

Over at MCA, they watched and waited. In June of 1950 they acted.

Freddie Fields, who had been with Greshler for nearly a decade, got a call one day from Sonny Werblin. How would he like to come to work for MCA? They would match the $100 a week that Greshler paid him, and he would no longer be just a gofer; he would be a genuine agent, with all the perks and opportunities that went with the job.

Fields was tempted but loyal. He asked Abbey what to do.

"You gotta take it," Greshler told him. "It's a good opportunity. I want you to have what's good for you."

When Freddie broke out in sobs, Greshler fought back his own tears. "You're my son," he croaked. "I want you to be happy and have—"

Abbey, too, choked up and cried. The two men hugged. Then Freddie called Werblin to let him know he'd take the job. The following morning, when he arrived at Greshler's office to clean out his desk, he found that the locks had been changed.

Greshler was no hypocrite. He meant every word he'd told his young assistant.

But he also knew what MCA was after, and it wasn't Freddie's remarkable agent-
ing skills.

Following Martin and Lewis's next New York engagement, Freddie Fields
went backstage after the show, armed with a well-rehearsed schmooze about the
power and plenty of MCA. He repeated one line over and over: "You guys have
gotta meet Wasserman!"

Dean, who had not forgotten his own shabby treatment at the hands of MCA,
was intrigued with the idea of giving the top guy a piece of his mind. He persuaded
Lewis to come along.

The next morning Lew held court in MCA's Manhattan headquarters. The
smooth executive with the steel-gray hair and the steely half-smile welcomed his
guests as if they were visiting royalty. Sitting behind his Queen Anne desk, comfortable but attentive, he seemed as dangerous as a Doberman. He offered no
bombast, no false promises, no subtle bribes or extortion, and no apologies for the
way MCA had once auctioned Dean Martin off like a lame stallion. He didn't
even mention Abner J. Greshler by name.

All Wasserman had to say was that Martin and Lewis were brilliant. His praise
was effusive, yet politely restrained. He seemed to know every detail of their rise to
national popularity and every nuance of their act. He painted a picture precisely
detailing how the two of them could build upon that popularity, turning their
moment in the spotlight into a lifetime of fame. Money, of course, was immater-
ial. Any agent could get top dollar for an act like Martin and Lewis. Not every
agent, however, was capable of creating a legend.

Wasserman never proposed that Martin and Lewis abandon Greshler and let
the MCA machine groom them for greatness. He merely pointed out that MCA
was the largest, most influential agency in the world, with branch offices in every
major city in the United States as well as in London, Toronto, West Berlin, Paris,
and Rome. Lew told them that he would be returning to Beverly Hills within a few
days and would love to pick up the conversation there. When they arrived in town,
he wouldn't make the mistake of sending a mail room clerk to meet them, as he
had done with Marlon Brando. No, he would have Herman Citron personally
greet them upon the arrival of the Super Chief and drive them wherever they
wanted to go.

By 1950, Citron had developed his own reputation as one of the half dozen
most powerful and persistent film agents in Hollywood. He assumed nothing and
took care of all details, no matter how minor. As a case in point, Lew delighted in
telling all new agents the story of Citron and Cecil B. DeMille. When Citron met
the legendary director on the Paramount lot one day, he presumptuously asked
who represented him. During his half century in Hollywood, DeMille said, he had
never had an agent.

"Why not?" Citron asked.

"No one ever asked," answered DeMille.

Citron signed DeMille to MCA on the spot.

This was the agent that Wasserman had offered to chauffeur Martin and Lewis. He would take nothing for granted and anticipate the pair's every need. After all, MCA was a full-service agency and Citron was a top-of-the-line full-service agent.

By the time the pair left Lew's office, the seduction was well under way. Dean had forgotten how he'd once been sold for $545 and Jerry had forgotten how Abbey Greshler plucked him from obscurity and patiently built him into a star. When Herman Citron delivered the pair to the front door of MCA Square a few days later, Wasserman greeted them with his deepest frown. He held up their NBC contract.

"How could you have signed this?" he asked.

Deadpanned Dean Martin, "With a pen."

But Lewis wanted to know what was wrong with the contract. After all, they were getting $25,000 for every show they did.

"You've been hoodwinked, boys," Wasserman said solemnly. "NBC's got you for peanuts."

Only then did Lew offer the bait: If they quit Greshler and signed with MCA, Wasserman would reopen negotiations with NBC and get them the money they deserved. To make it an even easier decision, MCA would give them a $40,000 signing bonus the moment they switched agencies.[3]

Dean and Jerry acted swiftly. MCA was in; Greshler was out. On the day they wrote Abbey his termination letter, they also notified Hal Wallis that all future film deals would be negotiated by MCA. Wallis panicked. He asked partner Joe Hazen to call Jules Stein, who assured Hazen that MCA wanted more money from NBC, not from Wallis. He had nothing to worry about.

Lew quickly made good on his promise to squeeze NBC. Within weeks of switching Martin and Lewis to MCA, he forced the network back to the table. There he quietly threatened to sabotage the network's *Colgate Comedy Hour* by withholding his clients' services if NBC didn't substantially up the ante. Despite shrieks from NBC's lawyers, programming chief Norman Blackburn told them to clam up and gave in to Wasserman's demands. Contract or no contract, Blackburn knew that with just one call from Wasserman, both Martin and Lewis would come down with a case of stomach flu an hour before airtime, and NBC wouldn't be able to do a thing about it. NBC's cost for Martin and Lewis jumped from $25,000

---

[3] According to a 1961 Justice Department memo, Martin and Lewis owed the government $75,000 in back taxes at the time, which MCA also offered to pay. Later on, the pair was told that the $75,000 had been a loan and that they were required to repay it. The money was then taken out of their paychecks.

to $150,000 per show—proof that Wasserman had been dead-on about Greshler's lack of clout with the network.

Greshler, however, was not about to go away. Just before Lew got hold of them, Martin and Lewis had signed a three-year agency renewal with Greshler. Wasserman knew that the hard-nosed New Yorker would not take MCA's larceny lying down. He urged the boys to take the offensive.

Before Greshler could formally complain to their union, Martin and Lewis accused Greshler and his wife of fraud and theft and put the whole matter before an arbitration panel of the Screen Actors Guild. According to the Martin and Lewis complaint, Greshler had been siphoning off twice as much commission as his contract allowed and chalking up the extra 10 percent to business management expenses. They claimed that Mrs. Greshler alone had pocketed $39,000.

Greshler countered with a $1 million lawsuit, naming Martin and Lewis along with MCA and a half dozen of its executives, including Lew and his wife, Edie, who had been in on the supposed seduction. They were guilty of "unlawful interference with contractual rights," according to the suit. What did that mean? Wasserman stole his clients, Greshler told reporters. That's what it meant. And Greshler intended to nail the Wassermans and their Star-Spangled Octopus once and for all.

"Several months ago [Martin and Lewis] were in debt to me for $40,000 in cash—not commissions or fees but in cash money put out in personal loans," Greshler told the press. And he wasn't the only one. They owed Hal Wallis nearly as much. They were also taking cash advances from the club owners where they were booked, then promptly losing the money at the racetrack or blowing it on sucker bets at the golf course. Neither star could handle his own money. They lost it the moment they got it.

On the wife-cheating front, they were world-class. Dean had an affair with June Allyson, who was then married to actor Dick Powell; Jerry carried on at the same time with actress Gloria DeHaven, wife of actor John Payne. In between, the pair slept with just about any attractive young thing while they were on the road. At home, their wives took care of the children and kept their mouths shut. When Betty Martin, mother of Dean's four children, could take it no more and started drinking heavily, Dean dumped her and married Jeanne Biegger, one of his many road conquests. Nearly fifty years later, Lewis confessed to biographer Shawn Levy that all the stories were resoundingly true.[4]

---

[4]   When Martin and Lewis dated gangsters' girls in Chicago, Greshler had to call upon Sidney Korshak to keep them from getting whacked. "[Korshak] is a very dear man, but some people say he's the mob's attorney," Greshler said. "I never asked him that. You learn not to ask."

Several years later, during the early 1960s, Lewis shared his affection for Stella Stevens with Korshak, who carried on a longtime affair with the actress. Stevens portrayed Stella Purdy in Lewis's comedy classic *The Nutty Professor* (1963).

Meanwhile, MCA's war with Greshler escalated.

In the end, Wasserman won, but Greshler exacted a price. MCA got the boys, but only after agreeing to pay Greshler his 10 percent commission for the next three years. Greshler maintained that he also got an undisclosed cash payoff, rumored to have been about $2 million, plus the deed to a Brentwood mansion.[5]

But Lew didn't simply fold his hand and declare Greshler the winner. MCA created separate corporations for Martin and for Lewis to act as repositories for their income. As in the case of Bette Davis, Jack Benny, Amos and Andy, and almost every other MCA star client, their corporations retained the bulk of the Martin and Lewis income while each of *them* drew a much smaller weekly pay-check—as little as $300—which they used as spending money. It was that money upon which the two comedians paid their income tax. In the settlement with Greshler, longtime MCA attorney N. Joseph Ross made certain that Greshler's commissions came out of the two stars' weekly paychecks, not their corporate income. Thus, Greshler's 10 percent was a pittance compared to the commissions he might have earned on the Martin and Lewis corporate cash.

A little over a year later, Wasserman worked the same kind of MCA magic on Hal Wallis, the versatile Warner Brothers producer who was responsible for such classics as *Little Caesar* and *Casablanca*. Jules Stein's assurances notwithstanding, the time had come for Wasserman to sweeten the Martin and Lewis movie deal. They were legally obligated to do two pictures a year for Hal Wallis and Joe Hazen, and that was what they delivered. Stein made his troops stick to that promise until March 24, 1952, the date production was to begin on Wallis's eighth Martin and Lewis movie, *Scared Stiff.*

A telegram showed up on the set that day instead of the two stars. They didn't like the script, according to their wire. Among other bitter accusations, Martin and Lewis attacked Wallis and Hazen for "subjugating our artistic and personal integrity to your greed."

Wallis flew into a rage. He gave the actors two days to show up on the set before he started legal action. Then he began looking behind the scenes. His own spies confirmed his suspicion that the entire mutiny was a Lew Wasserman pro-duction, with specific instructions to the boys to (a) get out of town, and (b) speak not a word to Wallis or any of his representatives. Martin hid out in Palm Springs; Lewis flew to Phoenix for a golf tournament. When Lew learned that Wallis was coincidentally going to be in Phoenix, he tore up the phone lines to contact Jerry before he bumped into the producer.

It was important that neither Dean nor Jerry show any weakness. It was equally important that they stick to the story that they didn't like the script. Under their

---

[5]   According to a 1959 FBI report, Greshler assigned MCA all rights to Martin and Lewis com-missions for $71,490.

contract, they maintained some degree of artistic control, but if either of them admitted that he was violating his agreement over money, Wallis and Hazen could sue them for breach of contract.

Now satisfied that it really was just about money, Wallis went through reams of old editions of *Variety* and the *Hollywood Reporter* in an effort to find stories that showed the MCA pattern: get the client to come up with an excuse to break a contract, then force a renegotiation. When Wallis found enough instances of MCA clients pulling the very same maneuver, he and Hazen took their findings to their attorney to see about filing suit. In the end, their lawyer argued against it. Wallis and Hazen might win the battle, but they'd lose Martin and Lewis.

Wallis finally agreed to sit down with Wasserman. To ratchet up the stakes, publicity-shy MCA sprang just enough leaks to make Hal Wallis the heavy in the gossip columns. Would hungry Martin and Lewis fans be robbed of their next film morsel by an avaricious producer? According to Louella, it was but a dim possibility, because surely Mr. Wallis would come to his senses and pay the boys what they really deserved.

In mid-May, Wasserman got what he wanted. A new Wallis-Hazen contract obligated Martin and Lewis to one picture annually for the next seven years at $1 million a year. The rest of the time the comedians were free to do whatever Wasserman wished. Once again, Lew had demonstrated who was really running Hollywood.

SIXTEEN

The Waiver

1952–1954

While he professed to have little in common with producers like Hal Wallis and studio executives like Zanuck and Mayer, Lew did share their politics. A decade later, that would change, and Wasserman would come to be identified as *the* top California Democrat, a kingmaker who would team up with attorney Paul Ziffren to decide who did and did not get Democratic Party gold in the Golden State.

But back in 1952, Lew was still Mr. Republican. Along with Sam Goldwyn, Jack Warner, and Darryl Zanuck, he was a member of the Independent Volunteer Committee of the Entertainment Industry Joint Committee for Eisenhower-Nixon. In the weeks leading up to the election, Wasserman personally contributed $1,000 to the Republican ticket — more than any other single committee member except Doris Stein, who gave $3,000. The week of the election, Wasserman gave an additional $500, as did MCA clients Fred Astaire, Cecil B. DeMille, Edgar Bergen, and Gene Autry.

But Lew's interest in politics was still secondary to his interest in Hollywood deal-making. He was very much a neophyte in the high-rolling game of greasing campaigns and handpicking candidates. In 1952 he was far more interested in the president of the Screen Actors Guild than he was in the president of the United States.

In the spring of 1952, while Ronald Reagan's career as a union politician reached its zenith, his acting career was in free fall. Lew Wasserman nurtured talent, but he didn't create it. A B actor was a B actor, and rarely climbed onto the A-list in Hollywood's artificial caste system. Thus, while Wasserman had been able to swing the fabulous *Winchester '73* deal for Jimmy Stewart, MCA's Arthur Park was able only to scrounge up projects like the dull Universal comedy *Louisa* (1950) for Reagan.[1]

MCA's script selections continued to come up sour, and Reagan's box office appeal descended accordingly. From 1948 through 1952 the SAG president appeared in a string of mediocre films. Except for *Bedtime for Bonzo*,[2] in which the future U.S. president co-starred with a chimpanzee, most have been mercifully forgotten.

On the domestic front, things were much better. To begin with, he had found Nancy Davis, or rather she had found him. Claiming she was being mistaken in casting calls for a Communist actress by the same name, the thirty-year-old Davis complained to director Mervyn LeRoy. He advised her to talk to the SAG president about the problem. After she asked Reagan to help keep her name off the studio blacklists, he went her one better. He asked the petite, attractive brunette to dinner. Reagan later described in his memoirs how they wound up at Ciro's watching Sophie Tucker perform until after midnight. It was just like the good old days, when Reagan first met Jane Wyman and the two of them lived it up at the Cocoanut Grove with other fun-loving couples, like Jules and Doris Stein.

On March 4, 1952, Reagan married Nancy Davis and moved with his bride into a three-bedroom, two-story home in Pacific Palisades. They began to live like real movie stars. Reagan even splurged on a 290-acre chunk of real estate in the Santa Monica Mountains which he called Yearling Row Ranch. All it had on it was a two-bedroom, two-bath house and a caretaker's shack, both built in 1918, but the price was a mere $65,000 and it seemed like a great site on which to build his dream ranch someday.

"The marriage to Nancy seemed to solidify him, because she was very supportive of his career," recalled actress Rhonda Fleming, his costar in *Hong Kong* (1952). "Suddenly, after a few years of being divorced, he had the solidity of a marriage, a woman who adored him, and he obviously adored her—plus he had the powerful position as leader of the actors' union. He was like a new person."

As he entered middle age, Reagan achieved balance in every aspect of his life except his career. His future was obviously not on any producer's A-list. To pay for his new marriage and his new mortgages, Reagan began taking anything MCA sent his way: magazine ads, personal appearances, testimonial dinners. He even

---

[1]   Reagan plays a straitlaced suburbanite whose widowed mother (Spring Byington) carries on comical affairs with both the grocer (Edmund Gwenn) and Reagan's boss (Charles Coburn).

[2]   *Bedtime for Bonzo* (1951) also marked the directorial debut of Fred de Cordova, who went on to produce television, notably *The Jack Benny Program* on CBS and *The Tonight Show Starring Johnny Carson* for NBC.

emceed a Las Vegas variety show.[3] The one thing Reagan resisted was TV. Television was déclassé.

Ronald Reagan had always been a movie actor, and he regarded television as strictly sideshow stuff. TV was beneath him. Besides, it was understood that movies were made in Hollywood while television belonged to Manhattan, and Reagan refused to move to New York.

The studios shared Reagan's scorn for the new medium. Even with the dethroning of Louis B. Mayer at MGM, old-school moguls like David Selznick, Jack Warner, and Darryl Zanuck refused to face the inevitable. Columbia's Harry Cohn went so far as to hire Beverly Hills furrier-to-the-stars, Al Teitelbaum, to cover his own TV set in skunk fur. Only after Cohn grudgingly gave his nephew Ralph $50,000 to start Columbia's Screen Gems TV division (the subsidiary turned out to be one of the studio's biggest moneymakers) that Cohn had the skunk skins removed.

It was in this poisonous atmosphere that Wasserman approached Reagan with a proposition to reconsider TV—not as an actor but as a union leader. The only way SAG members could make a steady living was to emigrate to New York where all three networks ravenously consumed live programming seven days a week. But New York was no place to produce television, Wasserman argued. Everything broadcast from CBS headquarters on West Fifty-seventh Street or from NBC at Rockefeller Center had a distinctly claustrophobic air about it. Six months out of each year, bad weather forced the networks to shoot everything from cop shows to Westerns indoors. Desperate for pseudo exteriors, CBS once even commissioned a western in a jury-rigged soundstage at Grand Central Station. In a desperate attempt to duplicate the Old West in Midtown Manhattan, the producers hauled a herd of horses through rush hour commuter crowds every week so actors could ride around on a Dodge City set in the upper reaches of the train station. Television was not purely auditory, as radio had been. The sound of hooves simply wouldn't do. Horses had to be seen as well as heard.

"Lew Wasserman and Jules Stein came to us and said, 'Do you know what's happening?'" recalled SAG Executive Director Jack Dales. "'It's all going to New York. Your membership is going to be a New York membership. Your guys here are not going to get a whiff of it.'"

As a group, Hollywood's moguls had already demonstrated that they would make no effort to bring television back to Los Angeles where it belonged. They

---

[3] On February 15, 1954, MCA booked Reagan for the first and last time as a Las Vegas headliner in a show at the Chicago Outfit's Last Frontier Hotel. Also on the bill were vaudeville duos, a singing quartet called the Continentals, and several bosomy Vegas showgirls. Reagan maintained that he took the gig only to pay back taxes. Despite good reviews, he declined an invitation to go on the road with the Continentals. At the end of two weeks, he left Vegas, never to return as a performer.

even refused to rent their movie libraries to the networks. The embargo wasn't broken until CBS and NBC complained to the Justice Department and the federal government sued the studios in 1952 for acting as a cartel.

Even after grudgingly agreeing to parcel out old movies for broadcast over the networks, the executives of Fox, Paramount, Warner Brothers, and MGM adamantly refused to turn over their vacant soundstages to TV producers. The Hollywood hierarchy continued to view television as competition, and they believed that putting something as ephemeral as a television show on film stock was just too costly. Unlike movies, TV shows were worth seeing only once. Nobody in his right mind would want to watch them over and over again.

Stein, Wasserman, and Schreiber believed otherwise. With SAG's help, they argued, MCA could create a brand-new studio with the expansion of Revue, the agency's production subsidiary. *Armour Theater* had already proved that shows could be shot cheaply on film.

"Lew knew from the word go to get it on film because film was an asset," said pioneer TV producer Henry Denker. "A kinescope degraded almost immediately, and the quality was no good to begin with, whereas if you put the show on good film stock, you had something that was good for twenty-five or thirty years."

What was more, a filmed show didn't have to be broadcast live, it could be aired any time. Shows could be sold station-by-station across the country, completely bypassing the mighty networks if they turned their noses up at Revue's programs. With SAG's help, MCA could break the stranglehold that New York had on the TV industry.

"We would like to do it," Wasserman told Dales. "We'd like to go into it, and we'll guarantee to make lots of filmed television *if* you can work it out with us as an agent."

But that would have meant bending the rules. Ever since its birth in the 1930s, the Screen Actors Guild had forbidden its members to work with any agent who also produced films. The conflict of interest was obvious: if an agent attempted to get top dollar for his client, how could that same agent also act as the client's producer? Producers had to keep costs down so the film would turn a bigger profit. An agent-producer could not work in the best interests of his client and his movie at the same time. One or the other would get shortchanged.

On rare occasions the Guild waived the rule—notably for Charles Feldman, who continued to preside over his Famous Artists Agency at the same time he was producing such movies as *Follow the Boys* (1944), *The Glass Menagerie* (1950), and *A Streetcar Named Desire* (1951). But with each movie, Feldman had to go back to SAG for permission.

Wasserman and Stein sought a much broader kind of waiver. In many ways, it was a carbon copy of the sweetheart deal that Stein had gotten from Jimmy Petrillo during the band-booking days of the twenties and early thirties when the American

Federation of Musicians allowed MCA to hire MCA orchestras for nightclub shows and radio programs that MCA also produced. Wasserman asked Reagan to consider an agreement between SAG and MCA that would allow Revue to produce television shows for the rest of the decade without interference from the Guild.

Even though he could see Wasserman's logic, Reagan balked.

"Reagan found it awkward to make the decision on Lew's request without looking as if he was favoring MCA," recalled Berle Adams.

There had to be a quid pro quo: the Guild had to get something in return for surrendering such sweeping powers to a talent agency's production company. With Jules Stein's blessing, Wasserman assigned the problem to Larry Beilenson, an old World War II chum of Leland Hayward's who had helped found both the Writers Guild of America and the Screen Actors Guild in the 1930s and who wrote SAG's original constitution and bylaws.[4]

"Beilenson studied the situation and a few weeks later came back with a plan," recalled Adams. "He suggested that MCA be asked to pay the actors and actresses residual fees for their performances. Until that time, talent was paid once for their work, regardless of how many times the films they appeared in were repeated. As an agent, Lew agreed to the idea of residuals immediately. After all, it meant that we would continue to receive 10 percent commission on the residual payments from our clients."

In Hollywood, "residual" was as dirty a word as "television." When Beilenson approached SAG's board of directors with his proposition, the board was actually pondering whether or not to call a strike over the issue. Meanwhile, the newly formed Alliance of Television Film Producers and the old-line studio chieftains were screaming "Extortion!"

"Both sets of producers were absolutely adamant that this is...practically un-American," recalled Dales. After all, actors were well paid the first time they went before the cameras. Why should producers have to keep on paying?

"One studio head said, '[Movies are] mine to throw off the end of the dock if I want,'" Reagan recalled, adding his own self-deprecating comment: "I made some that I wish he had."

At one negotiation session with the producers, Reagan and *Our Gang* comedy producer Hal Roach nearly came to blows over the issue of residuals.

"Now, Hal," began Reagan, "this is not an offer, but let me ask you: You

---

[4]   With the announcement that MCA had purchased the Hayward Deverich Agency in 1945, Lieutenant Colonel Beilenson wrote to Hayward from his post in China: "I am pleased that you and Jules Stein joined forces. As you know, I like and admire you both, and the merger should be mutually advantageous. Good luck." According to Beilenson associate Gunther Schiff, the lawyer came to Hayward's rescue when the ex-agent was called before the House Un-American Activities Committee. Beilenson arranged for Hayward to testify in private, avoiding the criticism he would have received for publicly naming suspected Communists.

wouldn't give an actor $1,000 for a repeat. You wouldn't give him $100. Would you give him that pipe you're smoking? Would you give him a pencil? Would you concede the principle at all?"

"Absolutely not!" Roach roared.

But Lew Wasserman was ready to make the concession. All he wanted was a waiver, allowing MCA to represent actors while Revue made TV programs.

The Screen Actors Guild remained wary. The SAG board demanded more conditions. In exchange for such a sweeping waiver, MCA would be forbidden to charge its own clients commissions if they acted in a Revue production. Furthermore, if MCA wanted to hire its own clients, Revue had to match the actor's highest previous TV salary.

"It [the MCA waiver] was just loaded with that kind of thing," said Dales.

On July 14, 1952, the SAG board of directors approved the blanket waiver for MCA. Though Reagan voted with the majority, it was vice president Walter Pidgeon who put the motion before the twenty board members.

"Walter Pidgeon talked about how everything was going to New York," recalled Chet Migden, the attorney who replaced Beilenson as SAG legal counsel. "It was Pidgeon who convinced the board to give MCA the waiver. It wasn't Ronnie."

Nevertheless, from that day forward, Reagan's floundering career made one of the most remarkable comebacks in U.S. history. At the same time, the fortunes of Revue Productions soared, and Lew Wasserman solidified his position as the most powerful man in Hollywood.

The simple, far-reaching document would shift forever the balance of power in the entertainment industry, yet the waiver didn't even rate a paragraph in the trade newspapers. What was important at the time was that Revue had agreed to pay residuals to actors. The waiver itself was regarded as an insignificant bit of union business that no one outside the guild hierarchy knew or cared about. The SAG-MCA waiver read, in part, "At the present time you are engaged in the motion picture and television film agency business, and the television film production business; you expect to continue in both. You have explained to us your reasons for so doing. We agree that for a period commencing with the date hereof and expiring October 31, 1959, if any contract, rule or regulation made by us prevents your engaging in both businesses, we hereby give you a waiver thereof for such period."

With the SAG waiver in hand, Wasserman and Beilenson next took their same dire warning to the Writers Guild of America: "Allow us to produce TV programs or the studios will shut down, everything will move to New York, and your members will move there too. And you will have no union." A few weeks later, the Writers Guild granted MCA permission to represent screenwriters as their agents at the same time that Revue produced their scripts for television. In exchange, MCA agreed to pay residuals to the writers.

Even with these sweeping new powers, however, Revue didn't exactly flood the market with great television. In 1953 Hollywood's newest studio set up shop next door to MCA headquarters, at 7324 Santa Monica Boulevard, and began assembly-line production of early television's version of B movies. The fledgling studio's first major effort was a series of dreadful half-hour melodramas aired as the *Gruen Guild Playhouse* over DuMont, an ill-fated fourth TV network that went out of business in September of 1955. The half hours, which gave dozens of young actors their first television exposure, were passed on to ABC and aired over and over again under eighteen different program titles.[5]

Revue's other early efforts included the syndicated western series *Adventures of Kit Carson,* another syndicated recycling effort called *Chevron Theater,* and two CBS series: *Revlon Mirror Theater* and *Biff Baker, U.S.A.,* which starred Alan Hale Jr., the future Skipper of the *Minnow* on *Gilligan's Island.* As Biff Baker, Hale played a globe-trotting import salesman who led a double life as a secret agent and invariably wound up duking it out with Communist spies.[6]

But Ronald Reagan would have none of this. In his eyes, television remained a mishmash of quiz shows, burlesque, and bad drama. His Vegas experience had reinforced his stubborn refusal to become a baggy-pants song-and-dance man backed by a gaggle of scantily clad women. That was all right for Milton Berle or Red Skelton, but Ronald Reagan had his pride.

Thus far, Revue had produced nothing to alter his opinion. The only genuinely classy TV production that MCA had helped to mount was the all-star *Ford Fiftieth Anniversary Show,* which CBS and NBC simulcast on June 15, 1953. It featured MCA clients Ethel Merman, Amos and Andy, Mary Martin, Marian Anderson, and Oscar Hammerstein II, but credit for producing the lavish musical spectacle went to Leland Hayward, not to Revue. Revue's cookie-cutter approach to programming was all right for young actors who needed a break and for older SAG members whose careers had hit the skids, but not for Ronald Reagan. He per-

---

[5] Dr. Allen B. DuMont founded DuMont Laboratories in New Jersey, which marketed the first 14-inch TV set in 1938. In 1944 he began the DuMont Television Network in New York to supply programs for his TV sets. After beginning with flagship station WNEW Channel 5, DuMont expanded to include several dozen affiliates by the early 1950s, but the network was never able to compete with the resources of NBC, CBS, and ABC. Actors introduced to TV via *Gruen* included Cliff Arquette, Buddy Ebsen, Helen Parrish, Cesar Romero, Vincent Price, Hans Conried, Raymond Burr, and Anita Louise, and the *Gruen Guild Playhouse*'s other names included *Twentieth Century Tales, Film Festival, Dark Adventure, Gruen Guild Theater, Playhouse Number 7, Straw Hat Theater, Return Engagement,* and others.

[6] In 1954, Taft Schreiber proposed a similar series called *The FBI Story,* but ran into opposition from FBI Director J. Edgar Hoover's chief lieutenant and roommate, Clyde Tolson. Tolson objected to the melodramatic scripts, Schreiber's "high pressure tactics," and MCA's proposed sponsor, a cigarette company. Despite endorsements from Washington power-broker attorneys Ed Weisl Sr. and Hyman Raskin, MCA's FBI series never got off the ground.

sisted in wanting to chart his own career as a movie star — until Jules Stein and Lew Wasserman suggested something completely different.

Producer Henry Denker remembered Reagan's TV debut as a guest star on *Medallion Theatre*, a Saturday night anthology series independently produced with no help from Revue and broadcast from the CBS studios in New York. "He's a bad actor now, and he was a bad actor then," Denker recalled forty years later.

Medallion Theatre was not designed with bad acting in mind. What set it apart from other dramatic anthologies of early television was its top-quality writing and casting. Because the teleplays were first-rate and usually adapted from literary classics, New York stage actors who had regularly shunned television finally agreed to give it a try. The result was spectacular live TV of a quality that has never been seen again. The very first *Medallion* offering on July 11, 1953, starred MCA client Henry Fonda and was adapted from Nobel Prize–winning author Sinclair Lewis's novel *Arrowsmith*. Other MCA clients who made their first TV appearances on *Medallion Theatre* included Claude Rains, Janet Gaynor, Jack Lemmon, Robert Preston, and Charlton Heston.

Medallion Theatre drew critical raves but poor ratings. In April 1954, CBS canceled the series, but not before Ronald Reagan appeared in one of its final presentations. According to Denker, Reagan walked through his role. But his performance following the broadcast remained fixed forever in Denker's memory.

"His agents came into the studio before the crew broke down and had Reagan go through several takes for the camera. What he was doing was an audition film, introducing *General Electric Theater*," Denker recalled.

Making an audition reel on another sponsor's dime might have been unethical, but MCA acted so audaciously that nobody on the set lifted a finger in protest, said Denker. Reagan and his MCA representatives walked out of the studio with the bootleg reel they would use to convince General Electric that the company needed Reagan.

Revue's *General Electric Theater* had premiered on February 1, 1953, and aired for a year before Reagan and MCA approached the sponsor. During its inaugural year, the show was broadcast every other Sunday on CBS, with *The Fred Waring Show* appearing on alternate Sundays. By early 1954, CBS had phased out *The Fred Waring Show*, just as it had canceled *Medallion Theatre*. The network wanted to expand *General Electric Theater* into a weekly show, but it needed a gimmick to keep deep-pocketed sponsor General Electric interested.

MCA had the answer. In his bootleg audition reel, Ronald Reagan fit the bill perfectly as a sincere, easygoing host who could ease the viewing audience into a weekly dose of melodrama. General Electric's executives were delighted. As long as Ronald Reagan got the job as host, the company was willing to stay on board for another season, and Revue retained the job of producing *General Electric Theater*.

To sweeten the deal, MCA ordered up several of its top-rung stars to appear in the first season's episodes — among them Joan Crawford, Tyrone Power, Henry Fonda, Joseph Cotten, Jane Wyman, and Fred Astaire.

MCA negotiated a starting salary of $120,000 a year for Reagan. In addition, Reagan agreed to star in an occasional *General Electric Theater* presentation and also carried the title program supervisor. He even took screen credit for producing at least one episode of the series: "Seeds of Hate," starring Charlton Heston. This despite a strict SAG taboo against its members engaging in production.[7]

By June of 1954, Reagan was firmly entrenched as the amiable host of *General Electric Theater.* It didn't matter that half of the dramas were produced in New York. Reagan could shoot his introduction and closing in Hollywood, where he continued to make movies, and never have to leave Pacific Palisades. In Hollywood, he was also able to continue in his role as a SAG board member and take part in an extension of MCA's blanket waiver.

On June 7, 1954, attorney Larry Beilenson once again appealed to the SAG board on behalf of MCA. By now Revue's assembly-line approach to TV programming had finally begun to pay off, with syndicated fare like *Studio 57* and *City Detective,* starring Rod Cameron as a metropolitan crime fighter, selling briskly in regional markets. Revue had also cracked all three networks with series like ABC's *Pepsi-Cola Playhouse,* NBC's *Fireside Theatre,* hosted by Reagan's ex-wife, Jane Wyman, and CBS's *Meet Mr. McNutley,* a sitcom starring Ray Milland as an eccentric English professor at a women's college.

Realizing that Revue's network foothold could be exploited only if MCA had more time to perfect its assembly line, Beilenson asked the SAG board to extend Revue's blanket waiver by one year, from 1959 to 1960. With no fanfare, SAG went into closed session and approved the extension.

Meanwhile, several other talent agencies sought waivers through their trade organization, the Artists Management Guild. Ignorant of the blanket waiver that had been granted to MCA, they proposed doing away altogether with the SAG prohibition on agents acting as producers. But SAG turned them down. The 66-page amended SAG Rule 16(e), which forbade agents to act as producers, went into effect on June 30, 1954. The only agency allowed to continue producing television unimpeded by Screen Actors Guild rules for the remainder of the decade was MCA-Revue, and during that time Reagan would move from host and "program

---

[7]   On March 10, 1947, seven top officers of the Screen Actors Guild, including Franchot Tone, Dick Powell, John Garfield, and SAG President George Montgomery, resigned en masse because they owned percentage interests in their own films. They announced to the trade papers that owning a percentage technically made them producers, which ethically disqualified them from continuing as SAG board members. Reagan stepped into the vacuum to assume the SAG presidency that same year, but when he became a producer for *General Electric Theater,* he did not resign.

supervisor" of *General Electric Theater* to actually producing and claiming a stake in the show itself.

Reagan later maintained that, in 1959, when his five-year contract for *General Electric Theater* was coming up for renewal, he played the same game of hardball with MCA that he'd seen them play with the networks, sponsors, and unions. He began by placing a call to Wasserman.

"Lew, it's now apparent to me, as it must be to you, that I represent a certain measure of the success of the show," Reagan recalled telling the MCA chief. "In other words, I am now in a bargaining position that I wasn't in when the show started. We are approaching negotiations, so I have a question. I have known you many years. I want to know one thing: In the show for General Electric, what are my services worth to go on with General Electric?"

If Wasserman was worried that his star host was going to mutiny now that *General Electric Theater* had become a mainstay on CBS Sunday nights, he didn't show it. Answered Wasserman, "That's a very good question and it deserves a very good answer. I'm going to [Palm] Springs and I'll let you know when I get back."

A few days later Wasserman called Reagan and offered to cut him in on a percentage deal. In addition to his salary for hosting *General Electric Theater* and whatever fees he received as a bonus for being a segment producer on the show, Reagan was to get 25 percent ownership in the show itself. Thus Ronald Reagan formally became a partner of MCA-Revue.

"Reagan saw no conflict in this arrangement, though others did," wrote Reagan biographer Lou Cannon. "He also saw no conflict in giving MCA, represented by his former agent Lew Wasserman, a blanket and secret waiver that violated the long-standing practice of allowing actors to retain agents who were also movie producers — in effect serving as spokesman for both sides."

With MCA's help, Reagan went on to become General Electric's official spokesman when he wasn't hosting the TV program. He traveled to GE facilities throughout the nation to offer inspirational speeches to plant employees. He appeared to have given up the Hollywood movie rat race altogether in favor of becoming a new kind of celebrity: a face as identifiable with a product as its advertising slogan or trademark logo. When America thought about Ronald Reagan, it thought about General Electric, the company that brought good things to life. Wasserman's role in charting this new career course for his client remained out of the public view.

"Though dark hints were made about the nature of Reagan's relationship with MCA, nothing was ever proven against him," said Cannon.

According to Garry Wills, another of the future president's biographers, Reagan simply "was always prepared to think the best of his own bosses."

"He displayed an attitude conducive to success," Cannon concluded.

SEVENTEEN

Equity

1953–1954

When Lew got angry, his eyes went flat and his thin lips pursed. "He used to get white around the eyes, like Hitler," recalled one assistant.

In anger the MCA president rose to his full height, preferring to stare down at his prey. The icy silence that always served as his ominous overture might have been for the gathering of his thoughts, but witnesses and survivors alike maintain that it was for effect. In that cold moment before he attacked, Lew Wasserman became feline, his jaws already lubricating with saliva. His shoulders tensed, and his long, thin arms trembled like the tail of a cat, twitching in anticipation.

It was always the same. The volume started low, then climbed steadily from harsh whisper to accusing snarl to molar-aching scream, until invective and spittle exploded in a single acid stream. The whole event could build in seconds or take the longest minute ever recorded to unfold. Regardless of how many spectators saw or heard, a Wasserman rage was always startling.

"People walked out of his office and threw up," recalled Bruce Campbell. "I sat outside of his office once when he was bawling out [agent] Pat Kelly. You could hear him through all the carpeting, through the walls, all the way up through the chandeliers. I walked out of the office, down the hall, and out of the building. You could still hear him screaming out on the street."

"I made a deal once to pay an experienced guy $800 to direct an episode of *M Squad* at a time when scale for a half-hour TV show was $720," recalled Jerry Adler, an early Revue executive. "Now, you would think that a deal like that would be so far below Lew Wasserman's perspective as to be a joke. Well, he caught me outside a screening room about a month later, comes over, and reams my ass. He took me like a tidal wave. It was so startling and so devastating. Man, I tell you: you have not been chewed until Lew Wasserman chews you.

"So three hours pass. I'm in my office. The phone rings. It's Lew apologizing—*not* for chewing me out but for not chewing out my boss who, in turn, should have chewed me out. He was telling me that he should have gone through channels and reamed me properly."

"If you were called in, it was for a drubbing-down," recalled George Chasin, who handled Clark Gable and Marilyn Monroe. "But he never let a man leave his office unhappy. After he'd scold somebody, he'd put his arms around their shoulders, assure them it was strictly professional, then offer them a drink or dinner."

One former MCA executive's first brush with Lew took place shortly after he dropped out of UCLA to go to work in the MCA mail room in 1954. As a mail clerk and general gofer, he ran into Fred Astaire in the MCA hallways from time to time. They became friendly, and he found that the aging hoofer had always harbored a secret dream of doing his own album, so he signed Astaire to a record deal.

When Wasserman summoned the youngster to his office, Astaire's MCA agent, Harry Friedman, was already there, glowering. Friedman gave him the smug sneer of one who is about to see an enemy vanquished. Lew demanded to know by what authority the young pup had brazenly signed an MCA client to a recording deal. The novice shrugged, speechless. He thought that the MCA tattoo he'd been hearing since his first day on the job—"Keep the clients working and paying commissions"—was the agency's only real rule. He didn't realize he had to get permission.

What followed was a fearsome exercise in high-decibel butt-kicking. He sat and took it as Wasserman railed about procedure, protocol, and pecking order. There was a *reason* for guiding a client's career and making him do what MCA wanted him to do *when* MCA wanted him to do it! Music Corporation of America was a team, with a game plan, a defensive line, a backfield, and a head coach—and this young dipshit was *none of the above!* He wasn't even a junior agent. He was *abso-fucking-lutely less than nothing at all!*

The young man was still gasping for air when he left the room. He wandered through the outer office like a mugging victim, not even making eye contact with Lew's secretary. He was about to return to the mail room, uncertain whether he had been fired or not, when the secretary took pity on him. She put a finger to her lips and pushed the interoffice intercom button so that they could eavesdrop on Wasserman and Friedman.

First he heard only the ominous tapping of a swordlike letter opener clicking on the immaculate surface of Lew's antique desk. The young man could not see what was going on, but he imagined Friedman, about five feet tall, sitting on the edge of the chair with his feet barely touching the floor. However vitriolic the young man had believed the boss to be when Lew tore into him, his manner had been peaches and cream cheese compared to the sheer volume and vile language that Wasserman now spewed on Harry Friedman.

How could Friedman call himself an agent? Lew demanded. How could he call himself anything other than a complete and total fool? While Friedman was sitting in his office, enjoying the balmy weather, this kid from the mail room had signed Fred Astaire to a recording deal. What the hell was Friedman doing? Sitting on his tiny little ass with his tiny little thumb jammed up his rectum?

The storm the young man endured had been a summer squall compared to Harry Friedman's hurricane. The young man left before it was over, but the shrieks and venom could still be heard echoing through the walls all along the second-floor corridor. Not until he reached the basement mail room, at the opposite end of the building, did the sound of Lew's wrath subside.

Within a week, the young man was promoted out of the mail room. As for the hapless Harry Friedman, he continued to be one of Lew's favorite targets for abuse for many years thereafter. During one especially vicious session, Friedman actually fainted while Wasserman spewed venom at him in the presence of several other agents. Wasserman didn't pause. He kept right on howling at the prostrate little man. After he'd finished, Lew ordered Friedman hauled to a hospital, where he sent over his own personal physician to make certain that Harry was all right. It didn't seem to matter whether Harry was right or wrong, so long as he was convenient.

Clark Gable once got drunk and ran his Duesenberg into a tree that happened to be located on Friedman's property, off Sunset Boulevard. Harry thought fast enough to call MGM publicity chief Howard Strickling. Strickling concocted a story about Gable swerving to avoid a reckless driver and made the actor remain in Cedars of Lebanon Hospital for a week to evoke public sympathy. But Lew was not sympathetic. Far from getting the credit for keeping Gable's idiocy out of the papers, Friedman was accorded the blame. Couldn't he control his own clients?

Similarly, when actor Robert Mitchum was arrested in 1948 for possession of marijuana, Lew had to go to downtown Los Angeles to bail him out of jail. The next day Friedman caught hell. He had committed an unforgivable sin by going out to dinner with his wife that night. Somehow that translated into failure to keep a close enough eye on his client. Mitchum subsequently had to serve a two-month jail term, which destroyed Lew's long-range plan to turn Mitchum into a teeny-bopper matinee idol à la Tony Curtis.

While Wasserman seemed to take the most pleasure in skewering Friedman, no one was immune from his wrath. He fired one executive during a staff meeting because he did not know the meaning of the word "fiduciary." At the close of the meeting, every man present raced back to his office to look the word up. So perverse was Lew's logic that he supposedly fired one agent for being too popular. The young man was smart, amiable, and a team player. Everywhere Wasserman went, he heard the agent's praises, from studio executives and producers to other MCA agents and clients. Lew finally called the man in and told him to clean out his desk. No agent who was so well liked could possibly be doing his job, he reasoned.

———⁓⁓⁓———

LEW MAY HAVE solidified his position as the most feared man in Hollywood, but he was still just a hired gun. The massive MCA commissions that were now pouring in from TV, movies, nightclub bookings, and concerts throughout the United States and most of Western Europe continued to funnel into bank accounts controlled by another man.

Jules Stein was no Fagin. He was extremely generous with his top executives and spared no expense to induce the very best manpower to defect to MCA. Those who remained loyal to him were well rewarded. When they needed medical treatment, he got them the best. When they traveled, he put them up at the finest hotels. He paid to straighten their teeth, dry them out when they hit the bottle too hard, supplement their income when they had to serve in the military, and set up trust funds for their wives and children.

Yet he held tight to the company purse strings, relinquishing control in only the tiniest of increments. When Wasserman, Werblin, or Schreiber brought up the touchy matter of company ownership, Stein changed the subject.

While his own lifestyle could be lavish, even extravagant, Stein remained a penny-pincher. He instructed his closest family members always to call him collect if it was a long-distance connection. That way he could identify who was calling, refuse to accept the charges, and then return the call over a low-cost WATS (Wide-Area Telecommunications Service) line. He and Doris even declined to pay the extra fare to fly first class; they always went tourist.

Until Leland Hayward eased his fear of flying in the late 1940s, Stein forbade his employees to fly at all. Since 1934, when the crash of an American Airlines plane in upstate New York killed Harry Pinsley, a rising young MCA executive, Stein had declared that all MCA personnel could travel only by bus, train, ship, or car. After World War II, Hayward finally convinced Stein that the rule had to be abandoned for competitive reasons. By then air travel had made ocean liners and railways obsolete. An agent who arrived by ship or train could almost certainly count on someone from William Morris getting there first and closing the deal.

Stein resurrected his flying paranoia for a time in the mid-1950s after another rising MCA star, band division vice president Hal Howard, died in a snowstorm when his private plane crashed during a trip between Las Vegas and Reno. Stein could no longer forbid his agents to fly, but he did prohibit the use of private planes and of any airliner that had not flown safely for at least a year. Airlines that used Lockheed's ill-fated Elektra prop jet, for example, were off-limits to MCA employees. Stein also advised his executives to follow his own example and heavily insure themselves. At Jules's insistence, Lew took out a $5 million life insurance policy in the mid-1950s, when the average policy in the United States was written for less than $50,000.

When Stein finally did begin flying to Europe instead of taking an ocean cruise, he learned that intercontinental flight rules allowed him to carry twice the baggage that he was normally allowed to take on domestic flights between Los Angeles and New York. To avoid paying for extra baggage, he began scheduling all of his eastbound flights from Los Angeles to London with a stopover in New York. When the plane sat down at La Guardia, he and Doris got off, retrieved their extra baggage, and took a waiting limo into Manhattan. On the return trip to Los Angeles, they would book the same way: two seats to Honolulu or Tokyo, with a stopover in L.A. Though they never flew the last leg of the trip, Doris and Jules were able to carry all of their latest buys home for free.

In New York, Stein needed no automobile. He had moved MCA headquarters to a skyscraper at 598 Madison Avenue, within walking distance of his Sutton Place apartment. He put up his executives, including Wasserman, in permanent MCA suites at the stuffy but exclusive Sherry Netherland Hotel, three blocks from the new offices. Edie made certain that the Wassermans' eighteenth-floor suite was above those of all other MCA personnel.

Stein purchased his new office building through a holding company he called the 57th Madison Corporation. For installation over the building's entrance, he commissioned a sculpture of the Western Hemisphere, depicting the far reaches of his MCA empire, from North America to the Middle East. Inside the lobby, the mahogany and brass interiors of the elevator cars reflected the plush decor of the upper reaches of the building, where Stein had a banquet room and a full-time chef. The trademark MCA decor on the eighteenth and nineteenth floors was as richly appointed with Stein's British antiques as his Beverly Hills headquarters.

On his desk, Stein kept a small ceramic figurine of a turbaned Turk whose head bobbed up and down on a spring when touched. When his executives delivered blather or excuses, he flicked the Turk with his forefinger and said, "That's the only yes-man I want or need. Now, give me some answers!"

Stein's antique collecting had moved far beyond a hobby. It was now an insatiable lust. He didn't want to be just a connoisseur of fine furniture, he had to be the world's foremost collector. In their New York apartment, the Steins kept a roped-off area in the living room where they set up handcrafted pre–Revolutionary War furniture in a quasi-museum setting for visitors to admire but not touch.[1] Just one block east of the New York offices on Fifty-seventh Street, Stein even

---

[1]   Most of Stein's vast collection was not museum-quality because Jules carried his bargain-hunting ways into auction houses and estate sales, refusing to pay premium prices that truly

opened his own furniture boutique: the New York branch of Stair & Company, a staid old London antique dealership, which he purchased as a retail conduit for his ever-growing collection of Queen Anne and King George tables, sideboards, and chairs. Within a few years he opened a second store in Midtown, which he named for his obsession: the Incurable Collector.

In London he moved his MCA headquarters to an elegant old building at 139 Piccadilly Circus, which the agency leased from the duke of Marlborough.

"Jules and Lew got loaded one night at Les Ambassadeurs with the English director Sir Carol Reed, and, when they took a taxi back to Claridge's, they saw this To Let sign on a building owned by the British Crown," recalled Berle Adams. "They ended up signing a ninety-year lease. Later on, I made a deal for the house next door, which belonged to Lady Hamilton. We got permission to break out a wall between the two, and that was our offices. It was terrific."

At the rear of the building was a covered carriage entrance that led to the servants' quarters, known in eighteenth-century British parlance as a mews, or courtyard apartment. When Doris beheld the ramshackle mews apartment, she adopted it as her own personal project. She commissioned interior decorators to turn it into a first-class dwelling, complete with full-time British butler.[2]

Among Doris Stein's closest friends in London was the notorious duchess of Argyle whose promiscuity landed her regularly in the Fleet Street tabloids. Like Doris, the duchess liked her alcohol and loved to party well into the night with the Steins. Though she was married to the lackluster duke, the duchess caused an international scandal when a photo of her posing with an unidentified naked male circulated through polite London society and found its way onto the pages of the morning newspapers. Though the gentleman's genitalia and face were discreetly disguised, he was clearly not the duke of Argyle. The guessing game as to the man's identity became a Hyde Park parlor game for years.

"Doris ordered us to fly all the newspapers to her every morning so she could gossip about it the next day back in Beverly Hills," recalled Berle Adams, who had taken up residence in the MCA mews apartment for a few weeks during the period when the duchess of Argyle story broke.

The Steins adored all things British, including stage talent. While Jules wasn't interested in investing much time or money in his own stars, he admired the way English agents nurtured actors. When Jack Dunfee introduced Jules to a young brunette who had knocked out the West End critics in the title role of *Gigi*, Stein

---

exquisite antiques command. He stored much of his collection in East Coast warehouses and incorporated the Burton Crescent Company to act as a holding company.

[2]   The MCA mews butler, nicknamed "Ziggy," was actually a Polish expatriate who fled to England during World War II and learned to speak the King's English as well as or better than most Brits. He came from the part of Poland from which Stein's parents had fled during the pogroms of the late 1800s.

gave her the same enthusiastic I'm-going-to-make-you-a-star speech he'd given Russell Nype. He assigned Wasserman to find some way around an onerous contract she'd signed with a B-picture mill called the Associated British Pictures Corporation. When she took *Gigi* to Broadway in 1951, the young woman, Audrey Hepburn, got $500 a week and had to pay her own expenses.

MCA got Hepburn $12,500 a week for *Roman Holiday* (1953), a fairy tale about a princess who falls for a commoner. In her first American film, she shared top billing with Gregory Peck and won an Oscar. Stein officially welcomed her to Hollywood with a gala party, during which Billy Wilder spoke to her about starring in his next project: a romantic fantasy about a young girl's blossoming love affair with an older man, based on an off-Broadway play called *Sabrina Fair*. Columnists relished writing about Hepburn, whether it was listing the number of celebrities who dropped by the set to meet her or commenting on what a dedicated actress she was. A young *Variety* columnist named Army Archerd wrote, "Audrey Hepburn underwent minor surgery Tuesday and reported back to *Sabrina* yesterday without telling anyone." She was just the kind of dedicated show horse that Stein loved to add to his stable.

Despite his public protestations that he'd long ago turned MCA over to younger men, Stein was still very much in the agency business. While he might have fooled the antitrust investigators in Washington, his semiretirement ruse had become a standing joke in Hollywood. He'd signed more star clients since relinquishing the presidency to Wasserman than he'd ever signed before. Stein became such a demigod in Hollywood that he never had to go looking for talent. It came to him. One Sunday in early 1954, Rosalind Russell called Doris Stein to discuss a costume ball they were both planning to attend, and the conversation turned to Russell's career.

"I've handled everything myself for quite a while, but I'm thinking about doing a musical version of *My Sister Eileen* in New York, and I suppose I should have an agent," Russell said matter-of-factly. "Is Jules home?"

Rosalind Russell was the exceptional MCA client. Unlike most of Stein's stars, she needed him less than he needed her. Besides being married to Broadway producer Fred Brisson, an old friend of Leland Hayward as well as the Steins, Russell had the special cachet of a grown-up East Coast debutante. That subtle difference alone gave her immediate entrée to Jules.

Jules and Doris guided their own daughters into eastern society with mixed results. Jean graduated from the exclusive Katharine Branson School near San Francisco before making her social debut in New York in 1951. Susan followed two years later.

"Doris and Jules Stein's girls were all about dollars and cents," recalled Peggy Madden, Billy Goodheart's daughter. "They didn't just buy a dress. They bought a dress *for fifty dollars!*"

Both young women studied and traveled extensively in Europe, and both were as strong-willed as their parents, though the consensus among Jules's peers was that Jean became something of a dilettante, like her mother, while Susan took after her father: tough, shrewd, and bloodless when it came to business, but compassionate with friends and family.

"Susan was one child with whom I tried extra hard to seem confident, although inside I wasn't at all," recalled Judy Lewis, the daughter of Loretta Young and Clark Gable who grew up with the Stein girls. "Something about her frightened me. I felt Susan could sense the lame duck in a crowd—in this case, me—and that could be dangerous. I felt far more comfortable around her older sister, Jean."

"I'm like my mother but afraid of being like her," Jean Stein admitted in a 1991 interview. "Father was a man who needed to control. He would send me memos at the Katharine Branson School, instructing me on my behavior, and when I wrote back I was always sure to make my y's and g's with strong vertical strokes. That showed you were stubborn and determined. You were a pushover if you made a loop."

Jules had the same God complex when it came to his clients, according to Jean. "He treated artists as if they were patients," she said.

By the mid-1950s, Stein's other family—his stable of MCA stars—had taken on its own social ecology, complete with A-, B-, and C-list celebrities. Brits, quasi-royalty, and East Coast prep schoolers generally made the Steins' A-list, while rising film stars like Burt Lancaster and old cronies like Jimmy Stewart and the Reagans topped the Wassermans' B-list. The A- and B-lists mixed socially as rarely as did their sponsors. Jules and Lew understood their roles as MCA emperor and chief mandarin, and behaved accordingly. Their wives never did.

Just as her husband had clearly demonstrated that he was the logical successor to Jules, Edie Wasserman had taken her rightful place as heir apparent to Doris Stein. While Edie once tried to mimic Doris, the two women could now barely tolerate each other. Edie's power as a social doyenne was clearly on the rise. Her picture began popping up in the society pages of the Los Angeles *Examiner, Times, Herald-Express,* and *Daily News* nearly as often as her arch-rival's. When she wasn't attending a tea or a charity ball, she was prattling on about social responsibility.

"Edie is charming socially, but ruthless in her own way," said one of her contemporaries. "She quietly ran the house and her charities, and scared the shit out of people who got in her way. When someone died at MCA, Edie would literally go in and take over, making all the arrangements and seeing to it that the family was taken care of."

Like Doris, Edie had her nose tipped by a plastic surgeon and further side-stepped her Semitic heritage at every opportunity. According to one former MCA agent, she complained loudly and in public when she believed that the agency's film projects had become "too Jewish," as in two 1947 films dealing with anti-Semitism: *Crossfire* and the Oscar-winning *Gentleman's Agreement.* Neither Lew nor Edie attended synagogue unless someone was getting married, bar mitzvahed, or buried. But Lew chaired the amusement industry division executive committee of the United Jewish Welfare Fund. Through Wasserman's efforts at pulling strings among stars and studio executives, Universal's Bill Goetz was able to produce *The Key,* the official UJWF documentary of 1953.

The Wassermans had become quite civic-minded by the early fifties. Lew organized a drive to underwrite a new polio hospital, and Edie contributed time and money to Mount Sinai Hospital, helping arrange the annual Bal de Rose, an invitation-only fund-raiser, at the newly opened Beverly Hilton Hotel. At home, however, Edie continued to be unhappy—to the extent that she almost left Lew at one point.

"Edie had a big affair with the director Nicholas Ray right around that time," said her former son-in-law, Jack Myers. "It was during and just after he did *Rebel Without a Cause* (1955). She almost left Lew for Ray."

The flamboyant Ray, whose first film in 1949 was titled A *Woman's Secret,* lived an offscreen life as wild as any of his on-screen characters. His third and last wife, ballerina and network TV censor Betty Schwab, described Ray as a private nudist who shed his clothes after coming home from work the way some people kick off their shoes.[3]

Like Lew, Ray was addicted to poker. He moved quickly from one directing job to another throughout the early 1950s, not so much out of choice but as to pay off his gambling debts. He fought incessantly with his producers at Republic Studios and tried to walk off the quirky low-budget *Johnny Guitar* (1954), but couldn't afford to quit. Starring Joan Crawford and Mercedes McCambridge as a pair of warring lesbians straight out of the Old West, *Johnny Guitar* turned out to be one of Ray's enduring classics.

While sorely tempted, Edie chose not to abandon her marriage, but she continued to be an absentee parent. Lynne was growing up with many of the same advantages as the two Stein girls, but in reality she was an insecure only child passing through puberty in a well-heeled vacuum. In the most fashion-conscious enclave in southern California, she always seemed to be overweight, with unkempt hair and out-of-style clothes. One contemporary described her voice as a monotone that seemed to lack any inflection, and she behaved like a spoiled waif: tentatively superior and withdrawn at the same time. Although the Stein girls attended private schools, Lew and Edie insisted that Lynne go to public schools just as they

---

[3]   After Ray's death in 1979, Schwab remarried and became executive coordinator of Elysian Fields, an exclusive Los Angeles nudist colony.

had done back in Ohio.[4] Public school in Beverly Hills, however, was quite different from public school in Cleveland.

Lew and Edie's answer to their daughter's peer-pressure dilemma in high school was to fire her governess, take out a second trust deed on their house, add another bedroom, and build a swimming pool so that Lynne could have friends over. When she was old enough to drive, she got the car of her choice. "She was always so snotty, driving around in her T-Bird. So *very* superior," recalled the daughter of one of Lew's executives.

Advantages aside, Lynne remained average. Unlike the Stein girls, she didn't even have a sister to cajole or to confide in. Her rising star was obliterated by a workaholic absentee father and a spotlight-hungry mother with an instinct for the jugular. "They made quite a terrifying pair," said Bruce Campbell, son of MCA's San Francisco chief, George Campbell. "It's a miracle that Lynne lived through it."

The more powerful Lew became, the more dismissive was Edie's attitude toward the wives of his underlings. Only one thing could put her in her place. When Doris entered a room, Edie's brass and flash shut down. The Steins held the power whenever there was a grand convocation of MCA stars, and Doris never let Edie or any other MCA wife forget it.

On opening night of the Ice Follies each autumn, the A-, B-, and C-list gradations became very apparent. Well into the 1950s, MCA stars were still required to put in an appearance at the Pan Pacific Auditorium, and Stein presided over everything.

"The invitations for dinner before the show were handed out in a fixed, almost religious order," recalled comedian Phil Silvers in his memoirs. "The lowest level, for peasants, was Chasen's. The next level was Romanoff's, for bishops and the lower angels. The summit, Mount Olympus, was dinner at the home of Jules Stein."

Silvers, a vaudevillian who would eventually earn a small fortune for MCA starring as TV's Sergeant Bilko, never graduated beyond the Wassermans' B-list. Like most MCA clients, he was just an employee. Only the crème de la crème of Hollywood ever got an invitation to Misty Mountain, and even they were subject to rules. When Cary Grant showed up to dinner without the proper jacket, he was turned away at the door.

"No dinner jacket, no dinner," said Stein.

While Stein doted on his movie stars, the world he had created by wresting power from the studio moguls was already rapidly disappearing. He might refuse to share ownership of his empire with his subordinates, but those very subordinates

---

4   "The one year she attended the Westlake Girls School in Bel Air, it is my understanding that her parents found out that the school had a Jewish quota and they removed her," said one of Lynne's classmates.

had now taken control. As Wasserman was clearly proving every day, MCA's real future lay in television, not movies.

———⟋⟍⟋⟍⟍———

AT THE END of 1954 the gross income from MCA Artists Ltd., which represented the agency side of the business, was $6 million.[5] At the same time, fledgling Revue Productions had earned $9 million. Unlike their boss, who continued to live with one foot in the band-booking Broadway past, Wasserman, Werblin, and Schreiber understood that the growing mass audience for television demanded pure, unadorned escapism. There was no better example of the new style in mass entertainment than that of game show producer Ralph Edwards.

In 1948, Edwards's saccharine biographical celebration of Hollywood, *This Is Your Life,* ran for a single season on NBC radio. Unlike his hugely popular game show, *Truth or Consequences,* which had been on the air since 1941, *This Is Your Life* never found its radio audience. Edwards was unable to persuade CBS to try the show on TV, either, even though the network eagerly took on *Truth or Consequences.* With sight gags and audience participation, Edwards's game show became an instant hit, but *This Is Your Life* was as hard a sell on TV as it had been on radio.

Still, MCA saw merit in it. Through the sustained efforts of Karl Kramer in Hollywood and Sonny Werblin in New York, Edwards finally got a pilot sponsored by Hazel Bishop lipstick. NBC refused to take the full risk of producing, but it did give Edwards a shot at prime time: the death slot on Wednesday evening, opposite ABC's high-rated weekly boxing matches from Madison Square Garden. For production, NBC rented him its facilities. The rest was up to Edwards and MCA.

MCA reached into its talent roster and drew upon the same parade of stars that Stein commanded to appear each autumn when he opened the Ice Follies. Edwards came up with stars whose heart-tugging Horatio Alger stories unfolded amid hankies and happy tears each week. Through the miracle of MCA, his Ralph Edwards Productions also furnished the writers, producers, and union crews to put the show on the air.

When *This Is Your Life* became an unexpected hit shortly after its 1952 pre-

---

[5]   According to a confidential Dun and Bradstreet report issued May 21, 1957, MCA Artists had a tangible net worth of $1,387,291 as of December 31, 1948. While all the MCA companies, including the talent agency, had satisfactory credit ratings, the scant financial data available about the privately held MCA empire "indicates a large debt," concluded the D&B analyst. He added, "No outside financing reported."

miere, Edwards — not NBC — owned the show. Combined with the continued success of *Truth or Consequences*, Ralph Edwards Productions — and MCA — went on to become masters of the early TV game show (*Place the Face, It Could Be You,* and others). Nearly forty years later, decades after Edwards hosted his last show, *Forbes* named him one of the richest men in show business.

Another early MCA television triumph was *Jukebox Jury*, carried over ABC during the 1953–1954 season before switching to syndication. *Jukebox Jury* featured celebrity panelists who decided whether a new record release would be a hit or a miss. Though the program is now barely a footnote in TV history, *Jukebox Jury* illustrated just how remunerative the new medium had become. Berle Adams, the MCA agent who represented *Jukebox Jury* host Peter Potter, recalled agent George Chasin storming into his office with a year-end commission tally sheet in his hand and threatening to take Adams upstairs to Wasserman's office for an ass-chewing. "He was pointing at the numbers and saying, 'This has got to be a mistake!'" recalled Adams. Chasin demanded that the two of them go to Wasserman and straighten out the error.

It seemed that Chasin, who represented Gregory Peck, was going down the alphabetical listings and found that the next name on the list, Peter Potter, showed twice the commissions of Chasin's star client. No mistake, explained Adams. He sat Chasin down and explained the video facts of life to him.

"Peck earned $500,000 a picture and made two pictures a year," said Adams. "Our commission from him was $100,000 a year."

Peter Potter, on the other hand, represented a TV package. Not only did Potter pay his 10 percent commission every time the show aired, but MCA also took an additional 10 percent from the network budget for bringing all the elements of the show together: writers, producers, director, and panelists. The panelists were any MCA clients who might be between movies and in need of something to keep them busy. Even Cary Grant and Fred Astaire, who almost never did TV, occasionally sat in on *Jukebox Jury*.

Peter Potter himself was about as dynamic as the toothpaste that sponsored his show, but that didn't matter. Millions more watched his weekly TV program than ever paid to see a Gregory Peck movie. The bottom line was that, in the new era of MCA television, the Gregory Pecks might be movie stars, but it was the Peter Potters who paid the bills.

The eminently forgettable Peter Potter was no fluke. MCA's power to create a TV star out of whole cloth was probably nowhere better illustrated than in the case of George Gobel.

A minor club comic who'd knocked around West Coast cafés and hotels for eight years, Gobel signed with MCA in 1953 and put his dormant career in the agency's hands. He appeared once on a summer replacement show, got a lukewarm response from the nation's TV critics (one called his performance as a likable doofus "promising"), but that was enough for Sonny Werblin to get on the phone to Gobel's manager, David O'Malley. He told him to catch the next plane to New York.

When Werblin met him at the airport, O'Malley had no idea what was up. During the short cab ride from MCA's Manhattan headquarters to Rockefeller Center, Werblin explained he was about to sell Gobel as host of his own TV series. O'Malley started to chuckle, but noticed that Werblin wasn't smiling. "Sure," O'Malley said. "You bet."

Werblin ignored his skepticism and continued chattering, as if the deal had already been made. NBC programming chief Sylvester "Pat" Weaver would want to know where to send the checks, he said. They had to come up with a corporate name. O'Malley played along. He thought for a minute and offered up Gomalco, a composite of his own and Gobel's surnames. If he'd known what would happen next, he said later, he might have come up with a better name.

Over the next five hours O'Malley watched Werblin drive a magical bargain, hammering out a range of details and demands that would make both O'Malley and his client independently wealthy for the rest of their lives. When the negotiation ended, Gomalco had a five-year contract, starting at $1 million the first year and climbing by 25 percent with each succeeding year. O'Malley was speechless. The network had signed a virtual unknown—a burr-headed squirt with a handful of homegrown nonsense phrases—"Well, I'll be a dirty bird" and "You don't hardly get those no more"—and a folksy delivery. According to O'Malley, it came down to Weaver trusting Werblin's instincts. The NBC chief knew MCA would not serve him a turkey, and he was not disappointed.

"George started from nowhere," said O'Malley. "Within six months he became the number one show in the country. He was the comedian of the year, the man of the year, the best TV performer, the best TV comedian."

But MCA's services didn't end there. Werblin and Karl Kramer urged Gobel and O'Malley to build upon their TV windfall by diversifying. When the Ramada Inn franchises in El Paso, Phoenix, and Los Angeles came up for bid, Gomalco grabbed them. The company further broadened its investment base by underwriting a pair of producers who had come to Revue with a pilot script for a sitcom. It was about an upper-middle-class suburban family, and it centered around an eight-year-old boy nicknamed "the Beaver." Five years later, when Gomalco sold its 50 percent interest in *Leave It to Beaver*, MCA's Revue Productions paid $1 million for the hugely successful series and called it a bargain.

George Gobel came and went after seven television seasons and was rarely seen on TV after 1960. The catchphrases that had made "Lonesome George" so popular in Eisenhower's America disappeared along with him. But Gobel turned out to be anything but a dirty bird. He and O'Malley were set for life, thanks to MCA.

———∿∿———

DESPITE HIS ENTHUSIASM for TV, Wasserman continued to drive the hardest movie bargains in town. His deals had moved up from mere profit-sharing to out-and-out ownership. At star-hungry studios like Paramount and Universal, he was able to taunt them with the likes of Alfred Hitchcock, Lana Turner, and Gregory Peck.

"No matter what people say now, it was a good deal for us back then," maintained Ed Muhl, Universal's production chief during the 1950s. "Television was killing us. If you could get a star at any price, it was worth it."

When MCA struck a deal for Cary Grant in which the star took three-quarters of the profits and, in addition, acquired sole ownership of *Operation Petticoat* after eight years, Universal called it a good enough deal to repeat four years later, when Grant was starred in *Father Goose* under the same terms. Desperate for stars who could pull Americans away from their TV sets and pack them back into theaters, executives traded away by increasing degrees the very product they produced: their movies.

And it wasn't just actors that Wasserman's agents parlayed into star equity. Star directors had begun to come into their own. With *Rear Window*, Wasserman got Hitchcock a nine-picture deal with Paramount that returned ownership of five of his films to him eight years after their release. *Rear Window* was the third most profitable film of 1954, taking in $9.8 million at a time when a matinee ticket cost 25 cents. Within two years, the movie had earned five times its cost, and it would remain a valuable commodity for generations to come.

Even lesser lights began feeding at the desperate moguls' troughs. Tony Curtis, who credited Wasserman with systematically building him into a matinee idol in the early 1950s, was a big enough name to begin sharing in the gross profits by 1958 with *The Defiant Ones*.

"I know that on *Some Like It Hot* I got 5 percent of the gross," said Curtis nearly forty years later. "On movies like *Taras Bulba* and *The Vikings*, 7 percent. I still retain those rights, so I'm always generating some income on them."

Curtis echoed the sentiments of a generation of MCA star clients when he praised Wasserman's deal-making wizardry. Though Lew was just twelve years older than Curtis, the actor spoke of him as if he were his father. "In my case, Lew Wasserman was great—the greatest," he said. "I trusted him and every piece of advice he ever gave me implicitly."

For his own part, Lew listened to Edie. He might not always have agreed with her, but he never ignored her advice. Lew's clients as well as his employees began privately referring to Edie as "the general." The Wassermans became mater- and paterfamilias to a generation of rising stars.

A recurrent theme of Edie's mini-lectures to her husband was that Jules owned everything and Lew owned nothing. The homage now being paid to her worka-holic husband made his stewardship all the more vexing. More than once Lew had been offered better, more powerful, higher-paying positions, and more than once he had turned them down. Edie grated under Stein's insensitivity. Lew counseled patience.

On Lew's forty-first birthday, March 15, 1954, after years of quiet but sustained pressure from his top agents and executives, Jules Stein finally gave in. He agreed to divvy up the three main components of his personal empire: MCA Artists, Man-agement Corporation of America, and MCA itself. In an elaborate ceremony wor-thy of the division of a medieval kingdom, Stein turned over 57 percent of the voting stock to five profit-sharing trusts and nine trusted executives, most of whom had been with MCA since its Randolph Street inception during the Roaring Twenties.[6] The anointed nine were Taft Schreiber, Maurie Lipsey, Mickey Rock-ford, Karl Kramer, Charles Miller, Sonny Werblin, Herb Rosenthal, Larry Barnett, and Lew Wasserman.

"He wouldn't tell us what it was all about, but Dr. Stein himself ordered all the men and their wives to fly to Los Angeles," recalled Lillian Lipsey. "They flew in from all over the country. It was all very mysterious and very wonderful. We were driven to the Beverly Hills Hotel, given our rooms, and told to dress for dinner."

In the private dining room in the lower level of MCA's Beverly Hills head-quarters that evening, Jules Stein offered a toast to the future of the company and to the men who made it happen. His management cabal and their loyal spouses were the reason that MCA was an acronym now known and feared in show busi-ness the way MGM had once been, Stein said.

Stein handed out nine leather-bound and numbered copies of a twenty-seven-page book, printed on fine parchment and published expressly for his valued exec-utives. The MCA global insignia gleamed in gold leaf from each cover. Inside was Stein's rags-to-riches biography, plus the story of the company that he and his small army of agents had built into a show business institution. While the history was rife with MCA's triumphs in band booking, radio, motion pictures, and television, it also hinted at some shady ethics and the occasional pact that Stein had made in the early days with unsavory characters. For that reason Stein admonished all pre-sent never to let their copies fall into the wrong hands. Neither the government nor

---

[6]   Each man received 1,200 shares of MCA, valued at $16.50 each; 1,200 shares of MCA Artists, valued at 50 cents each; and 1,200 shares of Management Corporation of America val-ued at $7.50 each.

the media had any need to know MCA's origins. What was important was that the men, and their wives, who built the company from nothing, never forget the sacrifices that had gone into its creation and the good fortune that followed.

As they all glanced self-consciously around the banquet table, there were absences noted. The Nine Old Men, as the original shareholders came to call themselves, did not include such loyal MCA pioneers as George Campbell, Arthur Park, George Chasin, Herman Citron, DeArv Barton, and Morris Schrier. For years afterward several of the MCA executives, particularly Schrier, remained quite bitter about not being asked to join the first pool of MCA shareholders.

But Stein's standard for deciding who was selected and who was not remained as hard and heavy as a bar of gold. As in all MCA decisions, it ultimately came down to money.

"Mr. Stein expected an agent to earn seven times his salary in commissions," explained Herb Rosenthal. "Someone like Morrie Schrier simply couldn't compete with us when it came to commissions. He didn't sign talent. He didn't create revenue. I signed Jackie Gleason, for instance, and by 1954, Gleason was worth $6,000 a week in commissions. That's the kind of money that television was bringing into the agency then."

Newcomer Berle Adams, who had joined the agency in 1950, was already generating thousands in commissions. He too was cut in as an early stockholder along with the Nine Old Men, though Stein singled him out with the news that he was to be included some time after the ceremony; politically, Jules knew better than to invite so new a face to a convocation of MCA agents who had been with the company most of their lives. Even Rosenthal, the most junior MCA man among the original nine shareholders, had been with the agency since 1939.

Jennings Lang was another newcomer who produced big commissions, but he was not invited to share in the wealth even after the ceremony—a circumstance that Herb Rosenthal traced directly to the Walter Wanger–Joan Bennett affair. Even after Pam Lang's death, Jennings proved that he'd learned nothing about decorum. He immediately resumed squiring starlets, oil heiresses, and his own clients' ex-wives to high-profile places like Ciro's and the Mocambo. Stein wanted no negative publicity stemming from his gift, but he still wanted to acknowledge Lang's contribution to the MCA coffers. Most of all, Wasserman did not want to lose Lang to William Morris or some other agency. So he crafted a way to reward him.

"Jennings was paid out of expense-account cash that he got whenever he stayed at the Sherry Netherland in New York," explained Rosenthal. "It was a way of paying him under the table. He paid no taxes on the money, and the company benefited at the same time because it was written off as a corporate expense."

It might not have been as terrific as owning stock in the company—which

Lang and most of the other executives, including Schrier, would eventually receive anyway—but under-the-table payments did demonstrate that Lang was a valued team member.[7] In the long run, that meant more than anything else, even being an MCA star. Stars came and went at a fickle public's whim. The bigger the star, the harder the fall. But a good agent could go on making deals forever.

---

[7] On June 6, 1958, Stein made a second distribution, giving each of his top executives 1,200 shares of MCA-TV and 1,200 shares of Revue Productions. The following January, when he prepared to take the company public as MCA, Inc., Stein awarded each executive an additional 1,200 shares of the new corporation.

EIGHTEEN

Blondes and Big Spenders

1955–1956

On December 13, 1949, Betty Grable fired MCA. When asked why, she flippantly answered that her new agent owned racehorses, just as she did. "It gives us more in common," she said.

Grable and Harry James had become addicted to the ponies, losing regularly at Santa Anita and Hollywood Park. The Jameses hobnobbed with other racing addicts, like Fred and Phyllis Astaire, Bill and Edie Goetz, and Mervyn and Kitty LeRoy. They even began raising their own thoroughbreds on a spread near Ronald Reagan's Yearling Row Ranch. On their sixth anniversary, they exchanged colts as gifts.

But horses weren't their real reason for switching agencies. In 1949 Grable turned thirty-three. After giving birth twice, she found that the weight did not come off as easily. She began detecting creeping cellulite in her million-dollar legs and feared her career was sliding toward the dumper. She and Harry spent like there was no tomorrow and blamed all their problems on Lew Wasserman.

"It was around that time, when she and Harry James were among the highest paid performers in the world, that Wasserman drove out to their estate to try to reason with her," recalled Bruce Campbell. "Grable and James had a huge spread near Calabasas where they raised racehorses. When Wasserman pulled up to the gate with his driver, they sent a butler out to tell Lew he'd have to drive around to the servants' entrance."

Grable's popularity and that of her husband had peaked during the war. By the end of the 1940s, the blond bombshell and her horn-blowing spouse were elder statesmen in the public imagination. Like Bette Davis and Ronald Reagan, they needed a radical image adjustment to keep their feckless audience from straying. Wasserman understood that, but Grable was blinded by her fan mail. Her movies began bleeding red ink as early as 1947. Though Fox lost $1.1 million on *The*

Shocking Miss Pilgrim, Darryl Zanuck gave the green light for her next project, *Mother Wore Tights*, which returned a modest profit of $344,000. The film that followed, however, *That Lady in Ermine*, was one of the biggest bombs of 1948. The movie lost nearly $1.5 million. The Grable magic was fading. Her reaction was to fire MCA.

MCA didn't stay fired long. Wasserman might suffer private indignities in stoic silence, but he would never allow even his highest-profile stars to publicly humiliate his agency or, more important, to walk away with MCA's commissions. MCA sought a SAG arbitration; when Grable refused to cooperate, MCA sued. Meanwhile, MCA had her money tied up. The agency disputed both the commissions she owed and loans that MCA had made to keep the Jameses' lavish racetrack lifestyle afloat. On December 15, 1950, Grable caved in. Just one year after her brave act of defiance, she dutifully returned to MCA.

But she did not give up her servants, her first-class lifestyle, or her ponies. She told Wasserman she wanted to work less and spend more. Since she and James now had two children, she pled domesticity: she needed to stay at home with her family, even though the bulk of her maternal duties were relegated to maids and nannies. "I'm tired and need a rest," she grumbled to the gossip columnists.

In fact, Grable wanted to retire, but she found that the high cost of star maintenance plus an ever-worsening gambling habit made that impossible. Zanuck shrieked at her for putting in more time at Hollywood Park than on Hollywood movie sets. In 1951 he suspended her for refusing to appear in *The Girl Next Door*, one of several intended Grable movies that never got made. She also refused to appear in director Sam Fuller's *Blaze of Glory*, a film that was never made.

MCA tried to intercede on her behalf, relaying a message to Zanuck that Miss Grable would no longer accept any of Fox's scripts unless they were musicals. Like other studio heads, Zanuck sorely resented being manipulated by agents, and he was as fed up with Grable as Jack Warner had been with Bette Davis a few years earlier. MCA drove too hard a bargain. Zanuck didn't need an aging sex symbol that badly. There were other blondes on the horizon.

In Norma Jean Baker, Fox found the perfect revenge: a hot new star who openly patterned her walk and talk after Grable and who was *not* represented by MCA. The creation, and the lover, of William Morris agent Johnny Hyde, Marilyn Monroe had been making movies since 1948, when she first became a Fox contract starlet in exchange for willingly kneeling before the unzipped presence of seventy-one-year-old Twentieth Century Fox production chief Joe Schenck.

"Marilyn was banging every casting director, but she was banging [Schenck] the most because he gave her little bit parts," said her first agent, Johnny Maschio.

A lifelong bachelor, Schenck had lost none of his zeal for women during the year he'd spent in prison for his role in the great movie studio shakedown. Monroe later told friends that the aging mogul had trouble maintaining an erection, but he loved playing with her breasts.

But satisfying the boss didn't automatically guarantee stardom. It wasn't until five years and eighteen films later that Fox began positioning Marilyn as the logical successor to Betty Grable.

Zanuck saw Monroe as just another bit-part bimbo, but after Schenck zipped up his career at Fox in 1953 and she began sleeping with his successor, Fox chairman Spyros Skouras, Marilyn began getting her way. She had talent, both on and off screen, and one of her skills was maneuvering her way into the right role. When she heard that MCA was trying to secure the part of Lorelei Lee in *Gentlemen Prefer Blondes* for Betty Grable's comeback, Marilyn sweet-talked Skouras into giving it to her.

"A lot of people think I'm jealous of Marilyn, but that's not true," Grable protested to Hedda Hopper. "I was told *Gentlemen Prefer Blondes* was bought for me, and naturally I wanted to make the picture. Who wouldn't? Marilyn got it. That's her good fortune."

Grable could afford to be magnanimous. Marilyn still earned a mere $1,500 a week and rated only an extra's dressing room, compared to Grable's $150,000 per picture, with all the perks the studio could supply.

But Skouras knew as well as Zanuck did that Grable's days as a superstar were over. When Fox finally did give Betty another shot, it was as a costar to Marilyn and Lauren Bacall in *How to Marry a Millionaire*, a follow-up comedy to Marilyn's triumphant appearance in *Gentlemen Prefer Blondes*.

After Skouras called all three actresses into his office to tell them that they would be working together, Marilyn was the first to leave. She bent over Skouras's desk on her way out. "These two old bags are washed up," she whispered.

At that time, "old bag" Bacall was all of two years older than twenty-seven-year-old Monroe. "Stems and mountains don't make actresses," Bacall muttered after Monroe had filed out and shut the door behind her.

Grable was the last to leave. Skouras praised her for her professionalism, but Grable knew the routine. She might be getting top billing over Monroe and Bacall, but she knew who the real star was going to be. At the door, she turned to Skouras and announced in a pained voice, "This will be my last picture."[1]

How to Marry a Millionaire grossed $7.5 million, was the fourth most profitable film of 1953, and boosted Monroe into the stratosphere. If she understood that she was replacing Grable, Marilyn never gloated. In fact, she became utterly worshipful. On the first day of shooting for *How to Marry a Millionaire*, Grable

---

[1]   Despite her melodramatic exit line, *How to Marry a Millionaire* was not Grable's last picture. She made three more, each one a bigger bomb than its predecessor: *The Farmer Takes a Wife* (1953), *Three for the Show* (1955), and *How to Be Very, Very Popular* (1955).

cornered Skouras to say: "Marilyn insists on calling me Miss Grable, even after I told her to call me Betty."

"Of course," Skouras said shrewdly, playing one blonde against the other. "She thinks you're a goddess."

Despite the bonhomie on the set, Grable's relations with Fox steadily disintegrated.

"When Judy Garland bowed out of *Annie Get Your Gun*, I was dying to take over, but Twentieth wouldn't lend me," Grable grumbled to Hedda Hopper.

Zanuck got the message and loaned Grable out to Columbia to make a comedy called *The Pleasure Is All Mine*. On MCA's advice she refused, and again Zanuck suspended her. It was the last straw. After spending most of her career with Fox, Grable made a public spectacle of tearing up her contract.

Wasserman couldn't have been more pleased. He was now in a position to do for Grable what he had done for Jimmy Stewart, Bette Davis, Tyrone Power, and a host of other contract stars whom the studios had fired or otherwise forced off their payrolls. He could resurrect her career and make her bigger than ever.

Until the right film project came along, however, MCA's chief task was to keep her working. In the fall of 1954, Grable hosted her first TV show: a live CBS special featuring Harry James and Mario Lanza, called *Shower of Stars*. That same year, MCA began booking the couple into lucrative one-night and week-long stints as casino headliners in Las Vegas. Before the year was over, she and Harry decided to quit Hollywood altogether and move to a new home on Las Vegas's Desert Inn golf course. Living in Nevada put the pair closer to the gambling tables, where they lost nearly as often as they had at southern California's racetracks. Nevertheless, they continued to live like high-rolling stars.

Meanwhile, Wasserman campaigned for Grable's comeback: the role of Miss Adelaide in Sam Goldwyn's film version of the 1950 Broadway hit *Guys and Dolls*. The MCA brain trust even came up with a dynamite star package for Goldwyn: Betty Grable, Clark Gable, Bob Hope, and Jane Russell. "There isn't a banker in the world that wouldn't back this setup!" rhapsodized one columnist.

Unfortunately, Clark Gable was out of the country filming *Mogambo* and *Betrayed*, Jane Russell signed a multi-year $1 million contract with quixotic Howard Hughes,[2] and Bob Hope was represented by the independent agent Louis Shurr, who found plenty of offers to keep his client busy. Nevertheless, Grable remained chief contender for the role of Miss Adelaide. But even mighty MCA could not always countermand the destructive whims of its clients.

---

[2]   Hughes followed Jane Russell's triumph for Fox in *Gentlemen Prefer Blondes* with a profitable rip-off for his own RKO Studios called *The French Line* (1954). Russell's most memorable scene involved dancing in gloves, high heels, and a then-scandalous bikini.

Grable concluded one successful meeting in July of 1955, behaving like her old charming self in the presence of Sam Goldwyn, the first and most successful of Hollywood's independent film producers. But she could not suppress her deadly star attitude long enough to sign a contract. On the day she was to meet with Goldwyn to seal the deal, one of her servants called to cancel the appointment. Grable had to take one of her dogs to the vet. Goldwyn went into a rage. He would not be stood up for a dog. Grable had blown her last chance.[3]

In the meantime, the Jameses' profligacy caught up with them. The IRS slapped a lien against their MCA monies for failure to pay $46,579.66 in 1955 income taxes. Instead of retiring, Grable now had to work harder than ever just to keep even. She spent more and more time working the Vegas casinos for quick cash, and less time in Hollywood, where she made the occasional guest appearance on *The Dinah Shore Show* or a Bob Hope special.

On December 18, 1956, Betty Grable celebrated her fortieth birthday. Instead of being on easy street, she and Harry James were nearly broke. Both of them had slipped into the beginnings of alcoholism. They worked clubs and did TV guest spots, but Betty was finished as a movie star. MCA kept her working, but made no heroic effort to resurrect her career.

Lew was less upset about Grable's spiral into oblivion than he was philosophical about the fickle nature of show business. To Wasserman it was always equal parts "business" and "show." He'd already moved on to the next blonde.

—◆—

ALTHOUGH HE NO longer worked for MCA, Irving Lazar continued to do business with the agency's clients. He made his reputation buying and selling movie rights to novels, plays, and short stories, often swiftly cinching six-figure deals during the time that it took to fly from New York to Hollywood. Hence, Humphrey Bogart's permanent nickname for the nattily dressed "Swifty" Lazar.

In February of 1953, Lazar did it again: he sold the Broadway hit *The Seven Year Itch* to agent-producer Charles Feldman. Feldman, in turn, lassoed Lew Wasserman and his client Billy Wilder into the deal.

As a producer, Feldman already had four films under his belt, including the

---

[3]   The role of Miss Adelaide went to Vivian Blaine, who had portrayed the ditzy doll on Broadway. The remainder of *Guys and Dolls*, which did not get made until 1955, was horribly miscast. At one point, Wasserman campaigned on behalf of MGM's Gene Kelly for one of the roles, but chairman Nick Schenck rejected him out of spite because of long-standing bitterness toward Sam Goldwyn. Non-singing MCA client Marlon Brando finally won the lead singing role of Sky Masterson, while singing non-MCA client Frank Sinatra took the secondary role of Nathan Detroit.

much-honored 1951 film version of A *Streetcar Named Desire* by Tennessee Williams.[4] Feldman figured that *The Seven Year Itch* could be bigger than any of them—especially if it starred his brightest and newest client, Miss Marilyn Monroe.

Marilyn became a Famous Artists client in the usual way: through a combination of mismanagement by her former agent and patient seduction by her new one. The blond bombshell's history with agents had been very nearly as star-crossed as her history with men in general. After her original mentor, fifty-five-year-old Johnny Hyde, suffered a fatal heart attack in December of 1950, she stayed on with the William Morris Agency for another two years. Hyde had poised Marilyn on the brink of stardom by landing her a small but widely noticed role as a vacuous, ambitious starlet in *All About Eve* (1950).

Following Hyde's death, however, she was shuffled from one William Morris agent to another, each of whom was more interested in his own clients than in the late Johnny Hyde's bimbo. Her career floundered through a dozen second-rate Fox pictures until Feldman moved in and took over.

Feldman's Famous Artists Agency skillfully steered Monroe through the minefield at Twentieth Century Fox. Only when Feldman simultaneously became both Monroe's agent and her producer on *The Seven Year Itch* (1955) did their relationship begin to get a little rocky, and Lew Wasserman was there to catch his falling star.

On February 3, 1954, following a public lambasting that Monroe gave to the press about Twentieth Century Fox, Zanuck ripped a clipping from the *Los Angeles Times*, circled her comments in red pencil, and fired it off to Feldman. The clipping detailed one of the many habits that Monroe had picked up from Betty Grable: refusing a role and getting herself suspended.[5]

"I'm now under suspension," she told reporters. "I read the script of the new movie, and I didn't care for it. That doesn't mean I don't like musicals—I like *good* musicals."

"You had better advise your client to take it very easy," Zanuck warned Feldman. "I am, of course, assuming that she is still your client."

She was, but not for long. Serving as Marilyn's agent was difficult at best. Acting as producer of her next movie to boot was turning into an even harder task for Feldman. With MCA trolling for Monroe, it was utterly impossible.

MCA started wooing Monroe before *How to Marry a Millionaire* was in the

---

[4] Feldman also produced *Pittsburgh* (1942), *Follow the Boys* (1944), and *The Glass Menagerie* (1950).
[5] Ironically, the script Monroe refused was *How to Be Very, Very Popular*, which became Grable's last movie.

can, but she remained loyal to Feldman. Wasserman understood better than anyone else, however, that there was more than one way to seduce a star. He began by nibbling away at control of *The Seven Year Itch* before Feldman had even officially cast Marilyn.

As Billy Wilder's agent, Lew told Feldman that the director was quitting "over artistic control" just before the movie was to go into production. It was the opening gambit of a now familiar MCA game: pull out a key player at the brink of production and extort more from the studio—more money, more perks, more control. Two of MCA's agents spread the rumor that Wilder had already left the Fox lot to accept another directing assignment across town at Allied Artists. Feldman called Lew's bluff. He had his New York office wire a veiled threat to Wasserman, daring him to pull Wilder off at the risk of losing his chance to regain the choice project.

The crucial bit of intelligence that Lew had on Feldman had come to MCA through its studio spies: more than anything else, they had learned, Marilyn Monroe wanted to work with Billy Wilder. At the time, he was the hottest director in Hollywood and Monroe let it be known that she would even be willing to accept a second-rate role in the cliché-ridden *There's No Business Like Show Business* (1954) if she could just follow it up with a Billy Wilder picture. Feldman's problem was clear: no Billy Wilder, no Marilyn Monroe...and no *Seven Year Itch*.[6]

The inevitable meetings between MCA and Feldman began. As it turned out, Wasserman's definition of "artistic control" meant that Billy Wilder got to make every decision, from casting to distribution. As producer, Feldman would meet the payroll and stay out of Wilder's way. Feldman railed, but in the end he knew he was whipped. Marilyn would not do the film without Wilder. Ultimately, the credits for *The Seven Year Itch* opened with a line reading "A Charles K. Feldman Production," but in reality it was a film by Billy Wilder, engineered by Lew Wasserman.

While Wilder was directing her in *The Seven Year Itch*, Monroe's nine-month marriage to baseball great Joe DiMaggio broke up. The actress normally wore no underwear (a habit she shared with Edie Wasserman, according to her son-in-law Jack Myers), but for the famous scene where blasts from a New York subway blow

---

[6]   Of the ten films he had directed since 1942, Wilder had been nominated five times for the Best Director Oscar and won it once, for *The Lost Weekend* in 1945. After he got his fifth nomination in 1954 for the comedy *Sabrina*, Marilyn became obsessed with working for him after *There's No Business Like Show Business*, which was meant to cash in on the breathy singing voice that Monroe had delivered in *Gentlemen Prefer Blondes* and *How to Marry a Millionaire*. Her sexy rendition of "Heat Wave," which she deplored for perpetuating her dumb blonde image, turned out to be almost the only memorable scene in the otherwise lackluster Fox musical.

Marilyn's skirt above her waist, she wore two pairs of panties. It didn't matter. The underwear was sheer, and the crowds that gathered in midtown Manhattan at 2:00 A.M. to watch the filming still caught glimpses of Marilyn's pubic triangle.

Infuriated, DiMaggio reportedly beat her so badly that she couldn't appear before the cameras for several days thereafter. Marilyn filed for divorce, and after *The Seven Year Itch* went into postproduction, she remained in New York instead of returning to Los Angeles. She planned to take a year off from the screen and belatedly study her craft, she announced. Marilyn enrolled in Lee Strasberg's famous Actors Studio to study the Method in an effort to shed her sex-symbol image and become accepted as a serious actress.

While in New York, Marilyn became reacquainted with Milton Greene, a well-respected fashion magazine photographer with whom she'd reportedly had a fling during the late forties. Now married, Greene nonetheless still had a Svengali effect on Marilyn. He understood her angst and insecurities. She had been victimized over her entire career, Greene told her. Learning how to really act with Strasberg would solve only half of the problem. If she wanted to make something more of herself, she would have to take charge of her own life.

Greene persuaded her to incorporate, name him her personal manager, and put her career in his hands. Marilyn Monroe Productions was born, with Marilyn as president and majority owner (50.4 shares) and Milton Herman Greene in the minority position (49.6 shares).

Greene found her a new attorney and a new publicist. He got her into psychotherapy. Then he turned to the biggest problem of all: her agent. For all of Charles Feldman's efforts in building her career, Greene explained, Marilyn was still just another contract actress working for peanuts. What was more, Feldman had a blatant conflict of interest. He was her producer at the same time that Famous Artists had been acting as her agent. He might have the necessary SAG waiver to act in both capacities, but Marilyn was the real loser. Why would Feldman want to get her more money on one of the pictures he produced when that would have meant cutting into his own profits?

There was only one place to go, Greene counseled: MCA.

Sound as this advice might have been, it was ultimately suicide for Milton Greene. No sooner did Marilyn formally discharge Feldman than Lew Wasserman personally took over her career. Even before she signed with MCA, Lew was already positioning Marilyn for a new studio contract.

Marilyn formally signed with MCA on July 6. It took threats, logic, heart-to-heart talks, schmoozing, and every other maneuver in MCA's bottomless bag of tricks, but six months later, on December 31, 1955, Marilyn Monroe had her new contract with Fox. It was the richest that any studio had awarded an actress up to that time: $100,000 a picture, unlimited expenses, $500 a week for incidentals, a studio maid, her choice of dress designer, director, and script. In addition, she was awarded a house that was paid for by producer Jerry Wald with the stipulation that she could pay him back "when financially able."[7]

During a press conference announcing the Fox deal, when asked what the new contract meant to her, Marilyn gave one of her most poignant but least-reported public comments: "It means I'll never have to suck another cock again!"

The comment did not make the newspapers.

In its well-known tradition, MCA acted as a full-service agency for its top stars, and Marilyn was *the* top star. Jay Kanter and Mort Viner indulged Marilyn's every whim while she was in New York; Lew took care of her needs in L.A. When she wanted to fire her longtime drama coach and lover, Natasha Lytess, it was Lew who stood at Marilyn's front doorway to prevent Lytess from entering. The desperate woman pleaded with him to let her see her student. Lytess explained that she had just been diagnosed with cancer and desperately needed Marilyn's help to retain her job at Twentieth Century Fox.

As he stood in the doorway, Lew's icy expression did not change. "Your engagement with the studio is none of Miss Monroe's concern," he said.

As Wasserman stared blankly at her, Lytess looked upward. From a second-story window, Marilyn watched this scene play out on her front porch. She accepted her agent's advice and let him handle everything. Lytess had become a clinging liability to Monroe's rising star and had to be shut out. With Lew still barring the doorway, the woman who had coached Marilyn since her first screen test in 1948 walked away and never saw her most famous student again.

Word got out quickly that MCA had secured it all for Marilyn: money, perks, choice of scripts.... She even landed an MCA playwright for a husband. On June 29, 1956, she and Pulitzer Prize winner Arthur Miller were married, and less than a month later Marilyn was off to London — again, courtesy of MCA — to star opposite MCA client Sir Laurence Olivier in *The Prince and the Showgirl*.

In April of 1957, when it came time to fire Milton Greene, Wasserman remained practical. Arthur Miller wanted control of his wife's production company and disparaged Greene at every opportunity. The conflict with Greene was inevitable.

"The truth is that suddenly Milton was left out in the cold," recalled MCA's Jay Kanter.

Even though the facts of her career — her money, her films, and her personal security — all argued in Greene's favor, Marilyn privately began raging about his continuing role as her manager. She reviled both her publicist and Kanter as "shitty friends of that shitty Mr. Greene, who got me a psychiatrist who tried to work against me and for Mr. Greene!"

---

7   Despite his generosity, Wald — who produced *Clash by Night* (1952), with Marilyn in a supporting role — did not get another chance to make one of her films until *Let's Make Love* (1960).

Despite her abuse, Kanter and the rest of her MCA handlers remained Marilyn's agents long after she ordered her lawyers to buy out Milton Greene's shares of Marilyn Monroe Productions. For two years of work, Greene was paid $85,000. When Marilyn discharged him from her life, MCA dropped him from its own roster. Greene's career as a fashion photographer continued for several more years before going into a tailspin. In the late 1970s, he died following years of drug abuse.

Despite the ongoing troubles that would lead to her own prescription drug addiction and eventually hound her to death, Marilyn's life had never looked brighter than it did at the beginning of 1957. She was the biggest female star on the planet, and MCA's ruthless efficiency deserved much of the credit. Her triumph was just as much Lew Wasserman's triumph. The synergy from her well-publicized success brought blond clones by the truckload knocking at MCA's door.

Shortly after signing her first $1,350-a-week contract with Fox, bosomy Monroe imitator Jayne Mansfield informed her agent, Bill Shiffrin, "I feel I just *need* MCA. I know I could make more money freelancing. MCA says they could get me $300,000 a picture."

In addition, she told Shiffrin, MCA's scouts had promised her a $50,000 bonus just for signing with them. How could Shiffrin compete? It was a refrain independent agents were hearing all over town in the wake of Marilyn Monroe's success.

"They're trying to steal [Jayne Mansfield]," raged Shiffrin at the time in an interview with the *Los Angeles Mirror-News*. "That's the way MCA operates. As soon as you build somebody up, then they want to take her."

Another Shiffrin client, starlet Jill St. John, also got the MCA romance. But shrewd St. John didn't leap at the opportunity to become just another filly in the most powerful star stable in show business.

"They never offered anything substantial," she told the *Mirror-News*. "They're as subtle as you can get. They'd say 'Why weren't you interviewed for this or that part?' It's a very good agency, but I'm not big enough to rate attention. They have so many."

St. John remained with Shiffrin and never got top billing, but she did have a steady film and TV career as a second-banana ingenue.

Jayne Mansfield, on the other hand, did get her shot at top billing. MCA paired her with Cary Grant in *Kiss Them for Me* (1957), but the movie bombed. After just one film, MCA gave the boot to the remarkably well endowed star, who had first busted into the public imagination with *The Girl Can't Help It* (1956).

Within two years Mansfield and her bodybuilder husband Mickey Hargitay were starring in an unintentional Italian farce called *The Loves of Hercules* (1960). For the remainder of her career she continued making third-rate movies like *Las Vegas Hillbillies* (1966), *The Fat Spy* (1966), and *Panic Button* (1964).

At the end, she was relegated to playing nightclubs. On June 27, 1967, she died in an auto accident. She was thirty-five.

———∿∿∿———

ONE THING MCA could not talk Marilyn Monroe into doing was television. The closest her new handlers ever got was a high-brow NBC loss leader called *Producers' Showcase*, but she backed out at the last minute and appeared instead in the Fox filmed version of William Inge's *Bus Stop*.

Monroe's absence from television was hardly catastrophic to MCA. By 1955 the agency had insinuated itself into every niche of the new medium. Revue Productions had grown so rapidly that it had to move its TV assembly line from rented office space near MCA's Beverly Hills mansion to new quarters at Republic Studios in the San Fernando Valley. Home to the fast-fading singing cowboys Roy Rogers and Gene Autry, Republic's square footage was generous, and its sound-stages were cheap and available. Revue signed a five-year lease on May 1, 1954. Instantly the languishing lot became a beehive.

MCA eventually bought Jack Webb's Mark VII Productions and the rights to his landmark cop show, *Dragnet*, which Webb had begun as an NBC radio program in 1949 and moved over to TV in December of 1951. Webb got a residence, complete with butler, and an office building on the Republic lot as part of the deal, and Revue rented office space from him.

"MCA built the building there for Jack Webb, and Jack had the only air-conditioned office on the lot for a while," recalled MCA vice president Al Dorskind.

In October of 1955, Revue launched *The Crusader* starring Brian Keith[8] and *Alfred Hitchcock Presents* on CBS; the anthology programs *Star Stage* and *Jane Wyman Presents the Fireside Theatre* on NBC; and a syndicated adventure series called *Soldiers of Fortune*.

Though Wasserman blandly admitted that Revue charged the networks more for production than any other lot in town, he had a cost-effective reason for the premium payments: "We are far more efficient and can do a job in two days which requires other lots three days," he said.

Nevertheless, through a combination of high-pressure production schedules and ingenious accounting methods, Revue maximized its return on every show. Besides hiring its own MCA talent at bargain-basement prices, Revue pioneered techniques that future independent producers would come to depend upon in their own efforts to make a profit.

---

[8]   In 1956, Keith quit the role and Revue after fifty-two episodes because he could not get MCA to boost his salary above the $650 a week for which he originally contracted to do the series. He did not appear again in a regular series until 1960, when he starred in NBC's *The Westerner*.

Even Lew Wasserman, long a champion of television, must have been stunned by the cash flow. Everything else MCA sold, from movie stars to radio packages, didn't add up to one-tenth of the revenue generated by Revue and the agency's other TV commissions. Band booking, the very trade that had brought MCA into existence just a generation earlier, was virtually dead. Only a handful of nightclubs in big cities like New York, Los Angeles, and that cash register in the desert, Las Vegas, kept the division alive at all.

———

LAS VEGAS WAS a boom town in the 1950s, and the Wassermans visited often.

"Lew is a big gambler," recalled Berle Adams. "He gambled in Vegas. He gambled with the company. He is a good risk-taker."

Edie went to Vegas as much for the company she could keep as for the thrill of gaming.

"She'd go by herself, without Lew, for days at a time," said Leonora Hornblow, widow of MGM producer Arthur Hornblow. "She wasn't the only one who did, but she was so indiscreet."

Las Vegas was the libido capital of the United States in the fifties, but there was little to do there but gamble and go to bed. That was the idea: no distractions. Yet it soon became apparent to casino operators that even the habitués who stayed at the tables until they lost house, wife, and children needed more than roulette and a craps table. They came to gamble *and* be entertained. MCA, which was now incorporated in Nevada as well as Delaware, New York, California, and Florida, aimed to oblige. Sheep waiting to be fleeced at the casinos needed a floor show or a lounge act to see them through to the loss of their last nickel, and anything would do. If performers hit the skids elsewhere, stalling in the movie career, taking a nosedive on TV, or dropping off the record charts, they could still count on being loved in Vegas.

Big bands had been replaced on television, radio, and the big screen by rock and rollers, but MCA could still find them work along the Strip. When Mario Lanza blew up like an early-day Pavarotti and became such an obnoxious drunk that even TV wouldn't have him, he could still get Vegas bookings. And every washed-up Catskills comedian from George Jessel to Joe E. Lewis had a home away from home at the Sands, the Flamingo, or the Tropicana.[9] MCA established its Vegas beachhead early and not until the mid-1960s did William Morris, GAC, or any other talent agency bother to challenge its virtual monopoly.

---

[9] "God help them if they pissed off the casino manager, though," said a former MCA agent. "I booked a comic named Will Jordan at the Sands and the manager didn't like him, so he literally made him play out his four-week contract in the men's room."

In many ways the agency had much in common with the casinos. The founding fathers of both came from Chicago and Cleveland. In the early fifties Capone heir Tony Accardo dispatched Sam Giancana to Nevada to watch over Chicago's investments, and Cleveland's Silent Syndicate had long ago left Ohio behind.[10] Of the four charter members, Moe Dalitz turned out to be the biggest risk-taker. From humble beginnings in the 1920s as heir to his father's Ann Arbor laundry business, Dalitz parlayed his long working relationship with Detroit's Purple Gang and the ruling bosses of the International Brotherhood of Teamsters into a network of midwestern nightclubs and bookie operations worth millions.[11]

When Dalitz and his three partners moved to Nevada in 1950 to lay claim to their fair share of the gambling profits, they made the most successful investment in their long careers. According to Virgil Peterson, the former FBI agent who headed the Chicago Crime Commission during the 1950s, "The Cleveland Syndicate got a foothold in Las Vegas in 1950 when it began operating the Desert Inn. Before long it gained control of other casinos, and for many years dominated the Las Vegas gambling industry."

Dalitz demonstrated that he'd learned a thing or two about showmanship from his days as a Cleveland nightclub owner. When the new casino was ready for the Los Angeles lemmings, Dalitz instructed Desert Inn manager Wilbur Clark to stage a grand opening on the same day that the U.S. Army was scheduled to detonate an atomic bomb in the desert north of Las Vegas. The place was packed with thrill seekers who wanted to lose their money in the shade of a mushroom cloud. When A-bombs were not going off, Moe Dalitz used MCA talent to pull in the suckers.

Among Dalitz's frequent guests at the Desert Inn were Lew and Edie Wasserman, along with Edie's widowed mother, Tillie Beckerman.[12] When Lynne Wasserman was growing up, Dalitz used to bounce her on his knee.

"Lynne used to call him Uncle Moe," said Lew's former son-in-law Jack Myers.

---

[10] According to *Eliot Ness: The Real Story* by Paul W. Heimel, "On April 26, 1939, grand jury members returned indictments against almost twenty-five gangland figures....Several Mayfield Road Mob members, Moe Dalitz among them, fled Cleveland, further evidence that the organization's stranglehold had been loosened."

[11] Maurice Maschke Jr., the son of Henry Beckerman's former law partner, was chief executive for Dalitz's Pioneer Dry Cleaning and Linen Supply in Cleveland. Beckerman and his son, Robert—Edie Wasserman's brother—also went into the dry-cleaning business in 1947, as secretary and treasurer of the Miller Brothers Lakewood French Dry Cleaning Company. Prior to that, Robert managed Prudential Finance Company, owned by Morris Kleinman's nephew Edward C. Kleinman. According to Hank Messick's *The Silent Syndicate*, Prudential was created "to hold money for later investment and to 'loan' it out in such a way as to avoid identification of the syndicate with a legitimate business."

[12] After Henry Beckerman died, Tillie moved into an apartment on Maple Drive in Beverly Hills to be near her only daughter. In her little red Mercedes sports car with personalized plates reading "Edie 1," Mrs. Beckerman's dutiful daughter regularly drove the six blocks from the

After opening the Desert Inn, Dalitz and his partners formed the Paradise Development Company, which went on to build what seemed like half of Las Vegas, chiefly with Teamsters' Central States Pension Fund loans. The Sunrise Hospital, the Boulevard Mall, the Desert Inn Country Club, the Landmark Hotel, the city's convention center, several residential tracts, and a number of buildings at the University of Nevada–Las Vegas were all constructed by the Silent Syndicate.

They also took over the Riviera Hotel, naming an old Jules Stein acquaintance from his Chicago days—John "Jake the Barber" Factor—as the hotel's general manager. They had another silent partner, representing Chicago's interests: a lawyer named Sidney Korshak.[13] Whenever he was in town, Factor saw to it that Korshak stayed in the Riviera's Presidential Suite, even if it meant evicting visiting dignitaries like Teamsters President James R. Hoffa.

Since moving to the West Coast, Korshak hadn't been idle. In 1952 he put together an odd assortment of Chicago con men, gamblers, and Hollywood lawyers to buy RKO Studios from Howard Hughes. Though the $7 million deal fell apart shortly after the *Wall Street Journal* published an exposé, it illustrated the unique expertise that Korshak brought to bear in Hollywood. Like fellow Chicagoan Paul Ziffren, Korshak found creative methods of investing Mob capital in California business. And like Lew Wasserman, he loved the organic joy of making a deal.

In the case of RKO, Korshak introduced Greg Bautzer's law partner, Del Mar Turf Club president Arnold Grant, to a pair of Chicago con artists who ran a bingo-type lottery operation known as "punchboards." Completing the investment group were Metropolitan Theater chairman Sherill Corwin and a notorious high-stakes gambler and Texas oil wildcatter named Ray Ryan.[14] As dealmaker, Korshak would have walked away with a fat finder's fee plus a share of the studio. Following the *Wall Street Journal* article, Hughes got cold feet and backed out. It was not the first time, nor would it be the last, that a newspaper article had ruffled Sidney Korshak. Like his good friend Lew Wasserman, Korshak had a lifelong love-hate relationship with the press: he loved cooperative journalists, like *Chicago Sun-*

Wassermans' estate to visit. Despite chronic heart disease, Mrs. Beckerman lived another thirty years, and loved to visit Vegas. She died in 1984 at the age of 101.

[13] According to a 1963 FBI report, Sidney Korshak also began watching over the Flamingo Hotel interests of John Guzik, son of Capone Mob treasurer Jake "Greasy Thumb" Guzik, in 1955.

[14] Ryan, a sometimes business partner of Frank Costello and other hoods, popped up in several Hollywood deals over the years, beginning with the Martin and Lewis comedy *At War with the Army*. Ryan's Screen Associates sued the two comedians for ownership of the 1951 movie, based on a contract Abbey Greshler negotiated before MCA took over their management. "Legally, the Screen Associates contract was no good and probably wouldn't hold up in court," recalled MCA agent Herman Citron, "but I figured the only clean way I could get them out of it was for them to give up their interest in *At War with the Army* and walk away."

Times columnist Irv Kupcinet, who printed only his praises, but he loathed any reporter who asked too many questions or invoked the ghosts from his shady past.

When the RKO deal fell through, Korshak, having lost his chance to become a bona fide studio mogul, moved back into the shadows of Hollywood and hovered on the fringe, where organized labor, organized crime, and movie-making all come together. Meanwhile, he watched peers like Lew Wasserman forge ahead, finally getting their piece of the Hollywood pie. If Sidney was envious, he never expressed himself publicly. The key to his power lay in silence. He wielded influence without fanfare.

As other survivors of the great movie studio shakedown learned, curbing one's tongue was the best insurance against premature death.

NINETEEN

Octopus II

1957–1958

In 1939, *Hollywood Reporter* founder William R. "Billy" Wilkerson opened Ciro's, but he sold out to Broadway burlesque producer Herman Hover five years later. Hover, one of the greatest spendthrifts ever spawned in the capital of extravagance, knew how to run a nightclub. For the next twenty years, Ciro's, at 8433 Sunset, flourished as L.A.'s answer to Manhattan's Stork Club and Copacabana.

From outside, Ciro's looked like all the other lath-and-plaster boxes along the north side of the Sunset Strip. Inside, it resembled a baroque brothel: red ceilings, red silk sofas, and pale green ribbed silk draped over everything that didn't move.

Louella Parsons and Hedda Hopper staked out front booths and equipped them with private phone lines so they could call in brawls, benders, and adulterous affairs to the city desk as they were actually happening. Frank Sinatra gave the place brief notoriety by punching Hearst columnist Lee Mortimer one evening after he overheard him refer to Italians as "wops."

Despite his many show-biz connections, Hover never got involved directly in the movie business. His flamboyant lifestyle was totally dependent on packing the 650 tables at Ciro's every night. That, in turn, made him dependent on MCA.

As early as 1950, Hover was publicly squabbling with MCA vice president Larry Barnett over so-called block booking practices. Barnett told Hover that Ciro's had to take small-time acts along with top draws like Lena Horne. If Hover refused, Ciro's would get no MCA acts at all. Hover called it blackmail. Barnett called it business.

The squabbling continued, with Barnett twisting the knife every time Hover squawked to the media. If he complained about having to pay $6,000 a week for Dinah Shore, MCA would book the singer across town at the Cocoanut Grove instead. When Hover pointed out that Liberace was costing him three times what another nightclub owner paid, Barnett left him two choices: pay up or find another pianist.

By May of 1955, Herman Hover had had enough. He went to court and charged that MCA handled 70 percent of the name acts in show business but refused to book them at Ciro's. From 1952 through 1955, he contended that MCA's tactics had cost him $562,500. Hover demanded treble damages ($1,687,500) and named Stein, Wasserman, and Barnett as defendants. All three should be forced to resign, he told the court.

Fred Weller, Hover's attorney, declared that Stein, Barnett, and Wasserman "by plan and design, have pursued the purpose and policy of eliminating competitors in the business of booking name acts, name bands, and other attractions in the entertainment industry, thus forcing independent operators to book entertainment through MCA in a market devoid of competition. No branch of the entertainment industry is free of the coercive force which can be wielded by MCA."

The same legal notes that had been struck in the Finley case ten years earlier resonated throughout Hover's accusations. Before addressing Hover's charges, the judge tackled a key question that was not satisfactorily answered when Larry Finley sued: Was block booking a local or a federal matter? After all, Ciro's was a California nightclub, but most MCA acts played every state in the Union. For the first time in MCA's long and successful history of avoiding that key question, Weller succeeded in getting a federal judge to find that booking entertainment qualified as interstate commerce.

MCA saw trouble ahead and so did Herman Hover. His former friends were deserting him and he had trouble booking any talent, not just MCA acts. Daring to publicly embarrass Jules Stein and Lew Wasserman carried with it a heavy price.

Weller wound up settling the case out of court for an undisclosed sum, and the suit was dismissed in August of 1956.

But it was too late for Herman Hover. Whether because of MCA's vindictiveness or Hover's own mismanagement, within a year he had sold Ciro's.[1] Hover's last day of business was New Year's Eve 1957.[2] The following year the Mocambo, down the street from Ciro's, also closed. It marked the end of an era, when the unincorporated Sunset Strip between Beverly Hills and Hollywood served as a mini-Vegas to Hollywood's stars, hoods, and wanna-bes.

---

[1] Under new management, Ciro's hung on well into the 1960s, when it featured rock acts like the Byrds and Buffalo Springfield. In 1976 comedian Sammy Shore and his wife-manager, Mitzi, reinvented the aging nightclub as the Comedy Store.

[2] MCA's final insult came four months later, when Hover's twenty-seven-year-old wife, Yvonne, divorced him. She kept her maiden name and custody of their two children, along with Hover's Beverly Hills mansion. She also collected $385 a month in alimony, even though she had recently been hired as a hostess on MCA's long-running daytime game show, *Queen for a Day*.

Hover lived the rest of his life broke and in relative obscurity, but he unwittingly had the last laugh on MCA. While his lawsuit was pending, the U.S. attorney's office in Los Angeles had taken an interest and asked his lawyer for more information. Attorney Weller was happy to oblige. One document that federal antitrust investigators found most intriguing was the judge's opinion that MCA's talent booking constituted interstate commerce. That meant federal, not state, jurisdiction.

While Hover settled out of court with MCA, the Justice Department had no such intentions. The month following the dismissal of *Hover vs. MCA*, federal prosecutors quietly reopened their long-dormant investigation into MCA's monopoly of the talent business.

—◈—

EVEN AFTER THE passage of nearly forty years, many who lived through the war between MCA and the Justice Department insist that political revenge and a beautiful woman brought down the talent agency that Jules Stein and Lew Wasserman built. If Lew had not treated Marilyn Monroe so shabbily, and if Bobby Kennedy had not been so taken with Marilyn, MCA would have continued to dominate Hollywood to the present day.

In her 1995 memoirs, Shirley MacLaine spoke for some of her peers when she maintained that "Marilyn Monroe was unhappy with her agency, MCA, during the time of her relationship with Bobby Kennedy. She went to Kennedy and complained. He commenced proceedings that culminated in the breakup of the most powerful talent agency in town."

But the events that broke up MCA actually began a lot earlier than Marilyn's anger at being exploited by Lew Wasserman, and before her affairs with Jack and Bobby Kennedy. The election that put John F. Kennedy in the White House and Robert Kennedy in charge of the U.S. Justice Department was still nearly three years away when the reinvigorated MCA antitrust investigation first got under way. Though there is little doubt that the Kennedy brothers' keen interest in Hollywood eventually kicked the antitrust prosecution into high gear, the most ambitious investigation ever mounted against the entertainment industry actually began as the vision of a single man: a heavyset government trustbuster who chain-smoked cigars, never married, wore off-the-rack suits and loud ties, and had both a face and a personality like a bulldog.

"Leonard Posner was one of the most respectable men I have ever met in my lifetime," said Eddie Clayton, one of twenty-three men and women who sat on a federal grand jury for nine months in 1962, listening to the case that Posner had carefully constructed against MCA.

"He was a heck of a nice guy," said Walter Kuencer, the deputy foreman of the grand jury. "He used to tell us he got a flat salary of $5,000 a year, while the MCA attorneys got $100,000 a year, but he kept on doing what he did because it was the right thing to do. We all felt sorry for him."

"He was a nasty little man," insisted MCA's Arthur Park. "He was a nasty guy. He was insulting and intimidated you. Posner's got a big mouth and is the rudest man I've ever met. He's really an ill-bred bastard."

Actually, Leonard Posner was all those things: a tough, well-educated New England attorney given to rich foods and a single-minded approach to antitrust enforcement. During most of his career with the Justice Department, he had chiefly prosecuted theater chains for block booking—the practice of forcing a theater operator to take bad movies along with the good. With MCA, the similarities leaped out at him. From the moment the briefs from the Ciro's lawsuit first crossed his desk, Posner knew he was facing off against a wily and particularly sinister force in MCA. A cursory check of Justice Department files told him that eight times before, dating all the way back to 1941, the antitrust division had started, then stopped, legal action against the talent agency. Bits and pieces of those investigations were strung out over fifteen to twenty files scattered throughout the division.

When he began poking through those files, Posner kept coming across the word "packaging." While many agencies practiced packaging, and most simply called it good business, Posner saw the word in a much darker light. Like block booking or tie-in sales, in which the customer is given no choice and must take an inferior product in order to get the one he really wants, movie and TV packaging seemed perilously close to extortion. Posner compared it to the old Prohibition-era tactic of forcing a speakeasy to buy mediocre booze along with the bonded stuff: "If you want the Scotch, you have to buy the rum."

One of the first witnesses Posner interviewed corroborated his suspicions. Former NBC president Sylvester "Pat" Weaver described a typical MCA package that had arisen out of Weaver's suggestion that NBC develop a new series starring MCA client Phil Silvers.

"We had production facilities; top scripts, writers, and directors; our own production facilities in Burbank," said Weaver. "All we wanted was a star. MCA agreed to furnish us Phil Silvers, but only if it took a package commission: 10 percent from every producer, director, writer…everyone who worked on the show. If we protested that we wanted our own writers because the best ones were not MCA clients, MCA would simply say, 'That's the deal. That's the way it's got to be.'"

The practice worked very well for Lew Wasserman. He dealt with the sticky topic of possible illegality by simply denying that MCA ever did any packaging at all.

"One did not mention this [packaging] directly to Wasserman, as though he was not supposed to know about it," one of Posner's earliest informants told him.

"Wasserman...was careful never to refer to it specifically but only obliquely, although he left the inference that he knew it was being done."

To underscore his purported ignorance of the practice of packaging, Wasserman lied in the same way a U.S. president lies: boldly. Questioned about MCA's packaging practices by Murray Schumach of the *New York Times*, Wasserman said, "We have never made a package deal. The truth is that presidents of movie companies have asked me if I have a package. I laugh at them. They want us to do their job. I know that many of these executives and producers look upon themselves as creative people and upon us as flesh-peddlers. The truth is that one of the reasons agents are needed so badly is because clients cannot trust movie executives. I look upon our agency as a business and a profession."

Yet Lew personally oversaw the packaging of dozens of films and TV shows, usually with remarkably lucrative results. When a longtime MCA client, the producer-playwright Norman Krasna, wrote a turkey called *Who Was That Lady I Saw You With?* it mattered very little that the play closed on Broadway almost as quickly as it opened. In March of 1958, Lew offered Columbia's Harry Cohn a cast consisting of Dean Martin, Tony Curtis, and Janet Leigh, and suddenly film rights to Krasna's second-rate play were worth $350,000.[3]

Through his sources, Posner learned that Wasserman routinely told his executives that MCA was all-powerful and that he meant to keep it that way. As Posner saw it,

> The agents were told to remember that they were MCA and that all doors were to open to them. They were also told that if anyone tried to stop an MCA agent from entering a door, to get his name and to refer it to Wasserman. Because of this power, MCA was able to get scripts from studios when nobody else could get them. These scripts were valuable to MCA because knowledge of the script gave some idea as to what talent would be needed for each part, and MCA would be able to get prior jump in suggesting talent to the studio. If a studio producer or director refused to give a script, MCA's agents would not only report him but would finally get the script anyway from the secretary.

Studio stenographers were treated kindly by MCA, especially on their birthdays and at Christmas. That way, during the rest of the year MCA agents could always count on the working women of the studio typing pool. More often than any other agents in town, the MCA men heard those welcome words: "Be sure to get this script back by tomorrow morning before they miss it!"

---

[3]   Two years later, Ansark (Krasna spelled backwards) Productions produced *Who Was That Lady?* directed by George Sidney and starring Martin, Curtis, and Leigh. It did respectable business as a wacky comedy with a strained second act but a zany payoff at the end.

But MCA didn't always have to be devious. As producer Sy Bartlett (*Cape Fear, Pork Chop Hill*) put it to Posner, "I think they're unjustly accused of being an octopus. Their great crime is they're much better than anyone else in the business."

Including the venerable William Morris Agency. Said one studio executive to Posner, "The William Morris Agency operates in the same manner as MCA, but does not give the same quality service and is generally less satisfactory. When I phone a complaint to MCA, it's handled immediately and the problem is out of my hands. MCA handles it. They tell me when the problem will be taken care of and in what manner. I can forget about it."

In the beginning Posner set out to investigate both agencies. Besides being the target of a constant stream of complaints from smaller agents, both MCA and William Morris were still competitive with each other as talent agencies in 1957. According to California state labor commission records, MCA grossed $49.8 million in salaries and other fees for its clients that year, and collected $4.7 million in commissions, while William Morris grossed $41.3 million and collected $3.7 million in commissions. In the touchy area of packaging, Abe Lastfogel's agents were as active as Lew Wasserman's. Danny Thomas, Steve McQueen, and Sammy Davis Jr. were among the William Morris clients who could be — and were — used to force a package on a network or a studio.

But on the whole, Posner found William Morris transgressions were not reputed to be as pervasive nor as rapacious as MCA's. When it came to television, there was no contest. With its blanket waiver, MCA's Revue Productions raked in ten times the revenue that MCA Artists earned in commissions, making MCA's overall operation many times more powerful than William Morris. Even the William Morris hierarchy grudgingly understood this fact of life.

One New York advertising executive told Posner that the perfect show business job belonged to a young MCA Artists agent named Jerry Zeitman, who sold MCA clients to MCA producers for use in Revue TV shows.

"Somehow Zeitman doesn't have a very difficult job," the executive observed dryly.

In 1958, according to Justice Department documents, Morris senior partner Bert Allenberg planned to level the playing field. He actually met face to face with Werblin and Wasserman and told them that he knew about the SAG waiver and that the time had come for William Morris to get the same deal.

"Now look, boys," he said, "this is it."

It was one thing for MCA to have gotten the jump on things back in 1952 by wangling the waiver out of SAG and the Writers Guild. Allenberg gave MCA its due. Stein's boys had been smart where the rest of the agencies, including William Morris, had been either naive or just plain stupid. But the blatant unfairness of a blanket waiver for a single agency was now an open scandal among Hollywood's ruling elite, and Allenberg planned to end it. He was particularly interested in get-

ting a Revue-type waiver for Four Star Productions, which was Dick Powell's production company but which, by default, had become a William Morris outpost
because none of its principals were represented by MCA.[4] Just as Revue used MCA
clients in 90 percent of its productions, Four Star used William Morris clients in
most of its shows. If William Morris could hire its own talent, the agency could
absorb Four Star and use it the same way MCA used Revue.

But Allenberg's plans were cut short. Before he could apply for the waiver, he
suffered a brain hemorrhage and died at the age of fifty-nine. No one at William
Morris or Four Star picked up where Allenberg had left off. Once again MCA
went unchallenged as the only producer-agency in town.

By 1960 MCA would utterly dominate television, controlling more airtime
than any other single entity, including studios, networks, and independent producers. About 45 percent of prime time alone would belong to MCA.[5]

Yet even Revue's furious production pace couldn't keep up with America's
growing TV habit. ABC chairman Leonard Goldenson started the trend toward
running movies on TV as an effective counterprogramming measure. Movies
became a real rating threat to the powerhouse prime time lineups of NBC
and CBS.

By the end of 1955, MGM, Fox, RKO, and Columbia had all sold or leased
their pre-1948 film libraries to television. Warner Brothers joined the club in 1956,
selling off 850 movies and 1,500 cartoons and short subjects for $21 million. By
the end of 1957, only Paramount Pictures among Hollywood's venerable studios
held on to its library.

When an aggressive new TV syndication company called National Telefilm
Associates was formed in 1956, Paramount became one of its first targets. A distributor of such early syndicated fare as *China Smith*, starring Dan Duryea, *Com-*

---

[4]　Incorporated in 1955, Four Star was actually founded by only three stars: Powell, David
Niven, and Charles Boyer.
[5]　As of 1961, MCA had either produced through Revue or otherwise owned an interest in *The
Jack Benny Show*, *Bachelor Father*, *The Polly Bergen Show*, *Shotgun Slade*, *The Burns and Allen
Show*, *Riverboat*, *The Tennessee Ernie Ford Show*, *Bringing Up Buddy*, *Hy Gardner Calling*, *It
Could Be You*, *KTLA Wrestling*, *The Lux Show Starring Rosemary Clooney*, *Wagon Train*, *Ford
Startime Theater*, *The Gisele MacKenzie Show*, *The Dean Martin Show*, *Club 60*, *Queen for a
Day*, *Truth or Consequences*, *The Investigators*, *The Overland Trail*, *Checkmate*, *The Spike Jones
Show*, *Make Up Your Mind*, *An Evening With Fred Astaire*, *The George Burns Show*, *Coronado
9*, *Chance for Romance*, *On Trial*, *Liberace*, *Ted Mack's Original Amateur Hour*, *This Is Your
Life*, *The Tall Man*, *The Victor Borge Show*, *The Deputy*, *The Jackie Gleason Show*, *Johnny Mid-
night*, *The Jerry Lewis Show*, *General Electric Theater*, *Thriller*, *Arthur Murray's Dance Party*,
Who Do You Trust? Alfred Hitchcock Presents, *The Bob Cummings Show*, *Markham*, *A Date with
the Angels*, *Johnny Staccato*, *The Millionaire*, *Suspicion*, *Leave It to Beaver*, *Lux Playhouse*, *Tales
of Wells Fargo*, *The Adventures of Ozzie and Harriet*, *The George Gobel Show*, *M Squad*, *The
Eddie Fisher Show*, *Twenty-One*, *Do-Re-Mi*, *Laramie*, *Tic Tac Dough*, *Concentration*, *The Phil
Silvers Show*, and *The Ed Sullivan Show*.

bat Sergeant, and *The James Mason Show*, the New York–based syndicator made a successful bid for Paramount's pre-1948 library, according to NTA executive vice president Oliver Unger. An FBI memo on the NTA episode read, "At that time, MCA was not even in the business of distributing pictures to television stations.[6] Suddenly, while the National Telefilm offer was still pending, NTA was advised that MCA had purchased the pre-1948 films for which National Telefilm had been negotiating."

Indeed, before the NTA deal closed, the Paramount board of directors chose instead to sell its 764 pre-1948 Paramount films — including such classics as *The Lost Weekend, Double Indemnity, Five Graves to Cairo, The Ox-Bow Incident*, and *Sullivan's Travels* — to MCA.

Posner speculated that Jules Stein's company might have gotten the nod because Stein was still a major stockholder in the studio,[7] or because rising MCA executive Jay Kanter had become Paramount President Barney Balaban's son-in-law. But the deal may have been more politically charged than that. The key player in the transaction turned out to be New York attorney Edwin L. Weisl Sr., a senior partner at Simpson, Thacher & Bartlett.

In addition to having sat on Paramount's board since 1938, Weisl had the unique distinction of having graduated from the University of Chicago with Jules Stein. Weisl also had something in common with Lew Wasserman, a lapsed Democrat who had renewed his party allegiance near the end of the Eisenhower administration. Just as Wasserman's close friend and ally Paul Ziffren quietly controlled the California delegation of the Democratic National Committee for many years, so Weisl ran the New York delegation of the party,[8] particularly during the 1960s when all three men would become confidants of President Lyndon Johnson.

But the Paramount sale was no giveaway. When Weisl took MCA's offer to his board in February of 1958, Paramount's directors dictated terms that included a down payment of $10 million in cash and an additional $25 million to be paid in installments. On top of that, the studio wanted an additional $15 million to be paid out of any future grosses the films might generate. Regardless of Posner's speculation as to exactly how MCA swung the deal, the terms were by far the richest that any studio had yet been able to get from a TV syndicator.

"You must remember that, at the time, everybody thought that old movies were junk," recalled Lou Friedland, one of the MCA agents whom Wasserman

---

[6] In fact, MCA had already purchased and was distributing fifty-six Gene Autry films and sixty-seven Roy Rogers movies (tailor-made for TV because none of them were more than sixty minutes long) that had been produced as early as 1936 at Republic Studios.

[7] The previous year, Stein had arranged for Paramount to buy Dot Records, which then topped all other pop record companies in the nation with annual sales of more than $6 million.

[8] Weisl replaced Tammany Hall leader Carmine DeSapio as New York's Democratic National Committeeman in August 1964.

tapped to distribute his newly acquired trove to TV. "Nobody thought they were worth anything."

With the close of the Paramount sale, MCA controlled a film library second only to that of MGM. For Lew Wasserman, it was cause for both elation and anxiety. When word got out that MCA would put the films up to competitive bids, calls poured in from TV stations across the United States, demanding the films at virtually any price. Wasserman answered by setting up a separate corporation, EMKA, with its own sales force to handle the rental of Paramount films through three regional divisions.

At the same time, he sniffed trouble from Washington. Just two months after the Paramount deal closed, the Justice Department sued Screen Gems for buying the Universal Pictures library to show on TV. Because Screen Gems was a subsidiary of Columbia Pictures, whose film library was also being shown on television, the Justice Department's antitrust division reasoned that Screen Gems was trying to corner the market on old movies, calling the Universal purchase "an illegal combination and conspiracy to fix prices and eliminate competition."

Lew knew that MCA's growing success as a television producer had already aroused minor Justice Department interest in its long-dormant antitrust investigation. He now feared that the Paramount coup might trigger a full reawakening.

During a luncheon interview with one of his informants, Posner heard MCA described as "scared to death." Posner was told that "Wasserman has been shuttling back and forth to Washington like a yo-yo."

Lew clearly understood that buying the Paramount library dangerously skirted federal antitrust prohibitions. For weeks following the sale, he and his top echelon repeatedly developed and then disposed of sales plans that would keep the government from taking a harder look at MCA. They finally came up with a printed price list for 700 of the 764 films in the library,[9] simultaneously releasing the list to every TV station that requested it to ensure a fair and equitable auction.

On April 2, 1958, Wasserman and three MCA lawyers—Cyrus Vance, Ed Weisl Sr., and Ed Weisl Jr.—flew to Washington, D.C., to meet with government attorneys who wanted to know MCA plans. Lew explained the regional division setup and promised that EMKA would distribute strictly on a station-by-station basis—no network sales, no block booking, no tie-in sales—nothing that the Justice Department might construe as exclusive or monopolistic marketing practices.

Now under a Justice Department microscope, Wasserman forbade his agents to do anything that smacked of unfair competition. When Sonny Werblin sat down with CBS officials at New York's Pierre Hotel to discuss a $27 million sale of the Paramount films for airing over all seven of the network's owned-and-operated stations, Wasserman interrupted with a panicky call from California. Stop the meet-

---

[9]   Sixty-four of the films were judged to be "dogs" and weren't offered for sale.

ing, he insisted. The library could be sold only on a station-by-station basis. If there was any network involvement, MCA could get in hot water.

As a red-faced Werblin apologized and asked the executives to leave, CBS President Merle Jones asked sarcastically, "Is it all right if we stay for a cocktail?"

Despite Wasserman's public relations campaign with the government, Leonard Posner remained suspicious. In October the skeptical Connecticut lawyer visited New York to begin interviewing prospective witnesses in his own campaign to see how deep MCA's tentacles extended into broadcasting and movies. He was stunned by what he found.

"Posner got the impression...that MCA had contributed to the demise of RKO," wrote one of his assistants in a Justice Department summary of Posner's New York trip.

In the summer of 1955, General Tire Company had purchased RKO Radio Pictures from Howard Hughes for $25 million. Despite a much publicized collaboration with David O. Selznick, the studio was never the same. Selznick protégé Daniel O'Shea was named president and set out to lure bona fide stars to the studio with promises of big paychecks. Before the year was out, General Tire sold off the studio's entire library of 740 features to television for $15.2 million to capitalize O'Shea's plan.

That dream never materialized. The following year, RKO made fifteen undistinguished pictures, but none of the nation's top box office stars appeared in any of them.[10] The most memorable and profitable RKO production of the year was the musical comedy *Bundle of Joy*, featuring Eddie Fisher and Debbie Reynolds.[11] By 1957, RKO's filmmaking fortunes had dipped so low that the studio produced exactly one movie during the entire year—*I Married a Woman*, starring TV star George Gobel and released the following year through Universal. In 1958, General Tire sold the RKO Studios to Desi Arnaz and Lucille Ball, whose Desilu Productions came closer than any other company to competing with Revue for the lion's share of network TV airtime.[12] RKO was out of the movie business forever.

"MCA had put the heat on O'Shea," one of Posner's New York informants told him.

When Posner pressed him as to how MCA could hurt RKO, the informant said, "By withholding talent and other similar means." A Harvard-educated lawyer

---

[10] In 1956, RKO did release the last film that Howard Hughes produced—the dreadful $6 million biopic *The Conqueror*, starring John Wayne as Genghis Khan in what many critics characterize as colossal miscasting in one of the worst films ever made.

[11] Their real-life bundle of joy, born October 21, 1955, helped boost ticket sales. Fisher and Reynolds named their daughter Carrie Fisher—the actress-novelist who starred as Princess Leia Organa in the *Star Wars* Trilogy.

[12] Besides *I Love Lucy*, Desilu produced such early TV classics as *Our Miss Brooks*, *December Bride*, *The Lineup*, and *Wyatt Earp*.

who had a long history of dealing with Jules Stein, Dan O'Shea understood MCA's methods. But he had made the mistake of having "money dealings personally with MCA," according to the informant. When MCA demanded that O'Shea play ball, he refused.

"O'Shea tried to keep RKO alive, but MCA helped destroy that company by refusing to deal with RKO as to talent," Posner concluded in his own report about the demise of RKO Radio Pictures.

By the end of October, Posner knew he had a tiger by the tail. One lawyer who had dealt with the agency for years described MCA glowingly, as a brilliant organization that was good to its employees, set up trust funds for them, and offered the best star representation money could buy. If they occasionally used questionable methods to achieve their noble ends, the agents of MCA were very careful to cover their tracks. "You will not be able to prove your case against MCA, because they are brilliant," he told Posner. "Moreover, MCA has been extremely careful not to do anything overtly which could be construed as illegal."

Another one of Posner's New York sources put things far more bluntly. "If you go after them too hard, watch out for the concrete shoes," he said.

—◦◦◦—

ON JUNE 18, 1956, Martin and Lewis announced that they were splitting up. Wasserman didn't take them too seriously. He'd heard the bickering a hundred times before.

The previous year Lew had ordered the pair to MCA's offices for a reconciliation. He and attorney Joe Ross laid out their commitments: Wallis-Hazen Productions, NBC, numerous product endorsements, and nightclub engagements from Ciro's to Chez Paree. There was no way they could break up the act. There was just too much money riding on it. They would have to find a way to work together.

But when Jerry returned from a vacation in the Catskills six months later, he went directly to Wasserman's office and laid out his demands. He would no longer play the bumpkin to Martin's sophisticate.

"What about Dean?" Lew asked.

"We don't talk to each other," answered Jerry. "Just get me out of my commitments and I'll be happy."

Others remembered Martin precipitating the split by refusing to work with Lewis. Regardless of who made the first move, the comedy team of Martin and Lewis separated into actor-singer Dean Martin and comedian-director Jerry Lewis.

The following year MCA landed NBC comedy specials for each of them, but neither program was particularly successful. Together Martin and Lewis could have had a regular TV series, but NBC showed little interest in making either a regular host of his own variety show. At the moment, their future as solo acts seemed to be in the movies.

The first two films that Jerry Lewis made without Martin — *The Delicate Delinquent* (1957) and *The Sad Sack* (1957) — were unqualified hits. For the next three years, until his directorial debut with *The Bellboy* (1960), Lewis made hit after hit, taking producer credit on more than half of them. Meanwhile, Dean Martin's film career bombed.

"I used to hang out at MCA, concerned about my own career moves, and I'd hear the agents talking," recalled Shirley MacLaine in her 1995 memoir, *My Lucky Stars*. "Lew Wasserman, as head of MCA, was determined that Dean would succeed on his own. Maybe Lew's true genius has always been to turn an impossible situation into a triumph. In any case, he put Dean in a picture at Metro with Anna Maria Alberghetti called *Ten Thousand Bedrooms* (1957). I guess he figured that the title would match Dean's smoldering sexuality. Or maybe he liked the idea of two Italians working together.

"*Ten Thousand Bedrooms* was a disaster. Reviewers said Dean was an uninspired, empty straight man, and certainly no actor. It looked like the end of the beginning of Dean's movie career as a single leading man. He couldn't get a hit record, either, and no one wanted him in nightclubs. The agents at MCA scratched their heads."

The scratching paid off at one of Lew's Wednesday morning brainstorming sessions — so-called Fagin meetings, at which casting information was correlated. After a careful review of all the scripts that MCA's spies had pirated from upcoming productions, the agents who assembled around Wasserman's conference table agreed that the most promising appeared to be Twentieth Century Fox's film version of Irwin Shaw's best-selling novel of World War II, *The Young Lions* (1958). Like his pal Frank Sinatra, who had salvaged his own career with an Oscar-winning portrayal of the doomed Private Angelo Maggio in *From Here to Eternity* (1953), Dean Martin immediately grasped the importance of MCA's recommendation. If he could land the role of the playboy in *The Young Lions*, he could follow in Sinatra's footsteps.

Sinatra never forgave Wasserman for firing him and never returned to the MCA fold, but he did learn the great lesson that Lew taught all of his stars. The former bobby-soxer idol even preached his own version of it. "People often remark that I'm pretty lucky," he told *New York Times* reporter Tom Pryor. "I don't think luck as such has much to do with it. You've got to have something more substantial. The competition is too fierce."

Within four years Sinatra had parlayed his Oscar into a serious acting career that made even Wasserman sit up and take notice. The minuscule $8,000 salary Sinatra accepted for *From Here to Eternity* had risen to $120,000 plus 25 percent of the profits of *The Joker Is Wild* (1957) and Sinatra's Kent Productions negotiated an even larger take on his next film: $150,000 plus 30 percent ownership of *Pal Joey* (1957).

The synergy from Sinatra's movies spilled over into his nightclub appearances, concerts, and recording business, where he earned an estimated $250,000 a year. ABC-TV signed him to host his own weekly variety show for $3 million. He owned three music publishing companies, four prizefighters, and a piece of the Sands Hotel in Las Vegas. He even underwrote his own talent agency.

Dean Martin saw the same future for himself if he could shake a public perception of him as Jerry Lewis's talent-free straight man. Unfortunately, the meaty role of a playboy-turned-soldier in *The Young Lions* had already been given to Tony Randall.

Lew knew there would be no reasoning with Randall and little chance of buying him off with promises of future plum movie roles or guest shots on Revue TV shows. The young stage actor who had wowed critics in a 1955 Broadway production of *Inherit the Wind* already had an agent—an agent who knew all about MCA and Dean Martin. An agent whose distaste for Jules Stein and Lew Wasserman dated back more than two decades.

"I don't mind fighting if you fight in the open, but not the way they fight," said an older, wiser Abner Greshler in the wake of the *Young Lions* affair. "They took over Martin and Lewis from me to begin with, and I sued them. They hired Freddie Fields, my best agent. They recruit my help and my talent. And now this. Randall did all right without *Young Lions*, but he could have been badly hurt."

In Hollywood, Randall, like Dean Martin, had developed a reputation as a light comedy actor, but he showed dramatic flair as a bitter alcoholic used-car dealer in director Martin Ritt's seamy examination of suburban America, *No Down Payment* (1957).[13] On the strength of that performance, Greshler secured the playboy role in *The Young Lions* for his client, and by the time MCA began putting the squeeze on, Randall had already begun memorizing his lines.

MCA simply blackmailed the studio: either replace Randall with Martin or every other MCA client involved with *The Young Lions* will walk, beginning with the two other stars, Marlon Brando and Montgomery Clift.

"Tony had already been fitted for lifts in his shoes, [a] uniform, and so forth," said Greshler. "He and his wife had already taken their shots to go overseas where part of the movie was going to be filmed. Then they [Fox] called us in and said, 'Brando and Clift and the director, Edward Dmytryk, don't think Tony's right for the part.' I said, 'I don't want to be rude, but I don't think you're telling the whole truth.' But it was no use: Randall was out and Martin was in.

"[The role] was crucial to Tony at that stage in his career. We spent the rest of

---

[13]　Randall's first two films as a Fox contract player were *Will Success Spoil Rock Hunter?* (1957) and *Oh, Men! Oh, Women!* (1957).

the afternoon trying to phone Dmytryk somewhere, and we finally caught up with him in Paris and he said, 'Kid, there wasn't a thing I could do about it.' Tony and I went into a bar next door to Fox and drank ourselves blind until midnight, and our families didn't know where the hell we were. That's how bad we felt."

Despite public pronouncements to the contrary by director Dmytryk and screenwriter Edward Anhalt, the last-minute casting switch was universally acknowledged to be a glaring example of MCA's ability to use its packaging muscle to play hardball with the studios.[14] In an off-the-record remark to journalist Bill Davidson about *The Young Lions* affair, Twentieth Century Fox production executive Buddy Adler said, "The movie industry has come to a sad state when a flesh peddler has reached a level of power where he can dictate the casting of pictures to one of the largest studios in Hollywood."

Forty years after the fact, Randall recalled Adler telling him the same thing. Randall credited his own God-given "easy disposition" for getting him through *The Young Lions* affair, and also for giving him the last laugh. "I never saw the movie," he quipped. "How was Dean?"

As it turned out, Martin was good enough to follow up with critically applauded roles and fat paychecks for a dramatic role in *Some Came Running* (1959) and for Howard Hawks's western, *Rio Bravo* (1959).[15] Meanwhile, Randall was back to second-banana fluff as costar to Rock Hudson and Doris Day in *Pillow Talk* (1960).

———&—

BILLY GOODHEART GREW bored with retirement after a few years. Eager to get back in the game, he left the farm and returned to New York, but MCA wouldn't have him. He had committed the unpardonable sin of quitting. Though he moved to Sutton Place and briefly became Jules Stein's neighbor,[16] Goodheart would never be allowed to return to the company he'd helped create.

In 1950, Billy became president of Official Films, a New York distributor of such early TV staples as *The Adventures of Robin Hood*, *The Buccaneers*, *My Little Margie*, and *Terry and the Pirates*. His love of big bands aside, he recognized that their time had passed and that TV represented the future. He resigned in 1955, turning over the presidency of Official Films to another former MCA agent, Hal Hackett, so that he could accept a post as vice president for network sales at NBC.

---

[14] In his memoirs, Dmytryk maintained that he alone made the decision to switch Martin for Randall. He said he testified to that effect before a grand jury and risked prosecution for perjury.
[15] Martin earned $35,000 for eleven weeks' work on *The Young Lions*. Five years later he was earning $50,000 a week plus profit participation.
[16] By the early 1960s, Jules and Doris had moved to a duplex at 2 East Seventieth Street, overlooking Central Park.

Goodheart didn't stay away from talent long, though. In 1956 he developed a daytime variety show hosted by Bert Parks, called simply *Bandstand*. It combined his love of big bands with the new medium, but TV audiences weren't buying old fogey music. Goodheart's *Bandstand* was eclipsed the following year by a rival *Bandstand* program that aired over ABC. It featured young rock 'n' roll singers and was hosted by a rising young Philadelphia disc jockey named Dick Clark.

With NBC's cancellation of the Bert Parks *Bandstand*, Goodheart retired from show business again. This time he moved to Phoenix, Arizona, where he took up real estate development with his old friend and fellow former agent Russ Lyons. Two years later, at the age of fifty-eight, Billy Goodheart died suddenly from a heart attack. If Jules Stein sent a sympathy card, neither of Goodheart's children remember seeing it.

Had he lived, Goodheart could never have competed with his old partner. Stein's machine now owned key executives in every corner of the business. Goodheart's best student, Sonny Werblin, had broadened his role as a talent agent by representing broadcast and studio executives in addition to stars—a kind of early day executive headhunter. Once he'd found a job for an executive, MCA would often waive its customary 10 percent commission. Instead, the understanding was that the agency would receive valuable favors when the time came.

"They had friends in positions of power throughout TV," said producer Julian Blaustein. "They had gotten them their jobs, loaned them money, and controlled them by giving them MCA's big-name stars or withholding them as they pleased. The MCA attitude was, 'Hit 'em hard and the hell with what they think about us. What are they going to do? We have the talent, and if they want it they've *got* to deal with us.'"

Among those who owed their jobs to MCA during this period were Paramount production chief Don Hartman (1951–1956); his successor, Martin Rackin; Fox production chief Buddy Adler; MGM production chief Dore Schary; and Universal production head Rufus La Mare.

A 1961 Justice Department memo noted, "There was gentle wailing at MCA when La Mare died, because it was thought that it lessened MCA's hold on Universal."

NBC president Robert Kintner also owed his job to MCA. "Kintner is sort of a Quasimodo," said one of his contemporaries. "He is a big ugly man with a tremendous penchant for drinking and getting sloppy drunk because he feels nobody loves him. Kintner has few social graces and not too many really close friends."

Nonetheless, the heavyset network executive was a powerhouse in the broadcasting business. He started his career as a New York newspaper reporter during the 1930s, then went into radio as a public relations man following World War II. By 1949 he had risen to the presidency of ABC, the also-ran network in the ongoing battle between David Sarnoff's mighty NBC and William Paley's only slightly less formidable CBS. Relying on westerns, crime shows, and a pact with Warner Brothers that gave the third-rated network access to the Warner library of vintage movies, Kintner steadily raised his network's ratings. Then, following a 1953 merger with Paramount Theaters, the theater chain's chief executive, Leonard Goldenson, moved into the presidency at ABC and there was friction between the two men immediately. In 1956, Kintner handed in his resignation.[17]

Through NBC vice president Manie Sacks, who also owed his job to MCA, Sonny Werblin was able to convince Sarnoff that he could not live without Kintner.[18] Sarnoff's son Robert had run NBC since Sylvester "Pat" Weaver quit, and the network was a ratings shambles. As Weaver put it, "Bobby Sarnoff is highly inexperienced and not excessively bright."

Werblin seized the opportunity and tracked Kintner down to the Caribbean, where he was vacationing, brought him back to New York, and successfully brokered the job. Kintner emigrated to NBC and quickly rose to the presidency.

"Shortly after his succession to the throne at NBC, Kintner went out to Hollywood and was told by Lew Wasserman that he was invited to a birthday party that [Wasserman's] wife was giving for Wasserman," a Kintner associate told the FBI. "On the night appointed, Kintner came in his best bib and tucker, and there he found every big star on MCA's roster.

"Kintner is somewhat of a hero worshiper and somewhat starstruck. He adores the idea of going back to New York and saying to some of his friends, 'As I was saying to Gregory Peck...' In the midst of this glittering assemblage, Wasserman stood up and announced to the multitude 'This is not a birthday party for Lew Wasserman. This happens to be a surprise party for my good and true friend Robert Kintner to celebrate his having taken over the throne at NBC.'"

A workaholic, Kintner kept the same ungodly hours that an MCA agent was expected to keep, rising at 5:00 A.M. and often remaining at the office until after midnight. He refused to delegate authority, overseeing sales, programming, and all five of NBC–owned and operated stations himself. He hired three secretaries to work in shifts, cranking out as many as seventy memos a day. Robert Kintner was the uncrowned king of NBC, and he owed it all to Sonny Werblin and MCA.

---

[17] Even after Kintner's departure, ABC remained dependent upon Warner, Disney, and independent producers like Lou Edelman (Make Room for Daddy), but never MCA.

[18] According to Justice Department documents, after Sacks had been let go from Capitol Records, "Werblin was at dinner with General [David] Sarnoff of NBC. Sarnoff turned to Werblin and said that they needed a man for their programming department. Werblin told Sarnoff: 'I know just the man for you, but you will never be able to get him. He is all locked up.' This aroused Sarnoff's interest, and Sarnoff determined to get Sacks, who was recommended by Werblin. This resulted in Sacks getting the job at NBC at a very handsome salary." Sacks died at fifty-six of leukemia in 1958.

So when Kintner met with his programming staff in the spring of 1957, in the presence of NBC Chairman Robert Sarnoff, no one was surprised when Werblin walked in with a pencil and a programming grid for the fall season.

"Here's how I think NBC's evening prime time should be programmed," he allegedly said, handing over the grid with fourteen spots bearing the names of MCA shows and one spot with a show packaged by the William Morris Agency.

"How did you let William Morris get one show?" one of Sarnoff's aides asked dryly.

"Kintner was MCA's guy," an NBC executive told the FBI. "He was put into NBC as a patsy. Most of the MCA shows are utter shit. Everybody in the industry knows it, and nevertheless NBC swallows these programs by the dozen."

When the story was later repeated in *Fortune* magazine, Kintner indignantly denied that the incident ever happened. Kintner, not MCA, was the master of NBC programming, he proclaimed.

Werblin wasn't bothered much by any of the outcry that followed. Though most of the 1957 fall schedule bombed, Kintner kept his job, which meant MCA could go back to him again the following year with more Revue product.

And most important of all, Werblin's total sales figures for MCA shows he'd placed on NBC that year totaled more than $50 million.

Jules Stein (upper right) and brother Bill, founders of Music Corporation of America, circa 1913, the year of Lew Wasserman's birth. *(Photo courtesy of Shirley Stein)*

One of MCA's silent partners in its early years was the Chicago Syndicate, organized under the control of Al Capone. *(Photo courtesy of Archive Photos)*

Dr. Jules Stein abandoned ophthalmology for the agency business in 1924. *(Bison Archives)*

Wasserman (rear row, center) began
his show business career ushering in
Cleveland movie theaters.
(Photo courtesy of Maurice Englander)

A natty Lew Wasserman moved from
ushering to publicity in the mid-1930s.
(Photo courtesy of Phil and Sylvia Bartok)

OPPOSITE, TOP: Sketch published in the *Cleveland Press* of opening night at the Mayfair Casino. *(Photo courtesy of Western Reserve Historical Society)*

Paul Henried and Bette Davis, co-starring in *Now, Voyager* (1942), were among MCA's first Hollywood clients. *(Springer/Corbis-Bettman)*

OPPOSITE, BOTTOM: Band leader Kay Kyser's Kollege of Musical Knowledge was Wasserman's first big coup for MCA. *(Corbis-Bettman)*

One of Wasserman's earliest clients—sportscaster-turned-actor Ronald Reagan—eventually had loftier goals than a film career. *(Irv Letofsky collection)*

Band leader Harry James wed MCA's Betty Grable in a Las Vegas ceremony publicized across the U.S. *(UPI/Corbis-Bettman)*

Hollywood Canteen hostesses Anne Shirley, Deanna Durbin, and Edie Wasserman. *(Photo courtesy of Julie Payne)*

Wasserman favorite Jimmy Stewart (center) starred in the hit western *Winchester '73* (1950). *(Irv Letofsky collection)*

Lynne Wasserman (age 14, left)
and father, Lew, with friends
during an Eisenhower Era
soirée. *(Photo courtesy of
Julie Payne)*

Lew and Edie,
New Year's Eve, 1954.
(Photo courtesy of Julie Payne)

Jerry Lewis and Dean Martin, pictured here with Wasserman discovery Janet Leigh in *Living It Up* (1954), were two of MCA's biggest clients during the '50s.
(Irv Letofsky collection)

Tony Curtis and Marilyn Monroe, together in *Some Like It Hot* (1959); both fell from Lew's favor.
(Irv Letofsky collection)

Frank Sinatra and ex-MCA executive Mannie Sacks were both cast in the role of escort for Edie Wasserman when Lew was too busy with MCA. *(UPI/Corbis-Bettman)*

Edie almost left Lew for director Nicholas Ray, according to the Wasserman's former son-in-law. *(Globe Photos)*

Sidney Korshak during a rare public appearance before the Senate Labor Rackets Committee in 1957. *(UPI/Corbis-Bettman)*

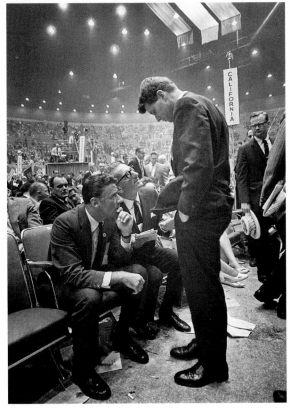

During the 1960 Democratic National Convention, Robert F. Kennedy confers with Wasserman confidant Paul Ziffren (center) and actor Peter Lawford. *(UPI/Corbis-Bettman)*

Lew Wasserman addresses master filmmaker Alfred Hitchcock during a 1962 industry dinner. *(UPI/Corbis-Bettman)*

By 1972, Lew consolidated his power, stepping up to the chairmanship of MCA while Jules Stein (center) retired and Sidney Sheinberg (right) was named MCA president and Lew's heir apparent. *(Bison Archives)*

Pictured here outside a burning set of a plantation mansion on the Universal Tour, Lew and Sid Sheinberg ran MCA with an iron hand throughout the '80s. *(Bison Archives)*

OPPOSITE, BOTTOM: MCA's Black Tower, circa 1964. *(Bison Archives)*

With *Jurassic Park* (1994), MCA scored big both at the box office and with its theme park ride, pictured above. *(Globe Photos)*

As Wasserman and Sheinberg began to lose their grip on MCA to the Japanese, Sheinberg's best student—Steven Spielberg—formed his own studio with pals Jeffrey Katzenberg (left) and David Geffen (right). They called their new company Dreamworks SKG. *(Archive Photos)*

LEFT: Creative Artists chief Michael Ovitz engineered the 1990 sale of MCA/Universal to Matsushita Electrical Co. of Japan. *(James M. Kelly-Globe Photos)*
RIGHT: Edgar Bronfman Sr. and Jr. bought MCA/Universal in 1995 for $5.7 billion. *(Globe Photos)*

Lew and Edie groomed grandson Casey (pictured with friend Danielle Mendez) for a job in show business, but he has thus far failed to step up to the challenge. *(Lisa Rose/ Globe Photos)*

Lew Wasserman at a 1996 United Jewish Appeal dinner honoring Edgar Bronfman Jr., the new master of Universal. *(Marina Garnier)*

TWENTY

Universal

1958-1959

S ad to report that today *The Perfect Furlough* starring Janet Leigh and Tony
Curtis is the last picture to be made at Universal International for a long time,"
wrote Louella Parsons in her January 8, 1958, column.

Parsons soft-pedaled the news, but the cold facts leaked through her fawning
prose: the studio that had given the world Frankenstein, Deanna Durbin, and
Francis the Talking Mule had overproduced itself almost out of existence. During
the previous year, Universal had spent almost $40 million to make thirty-two films
that sat on a shelf, waiting for release dates. If every soundstage on the Universal
lot stood idle for an entire year, one source told Louella, the studio would still have
a film backlog.

Meanwhile, payroll, taxes, and overhead had to be met and the films that did
go into release were laying egg after egg: *Girls on the Loose, The Thing That
Couldn't Die,* and *Monster on the Campus* were among Universal's universal disappointments. The oldest studio in Hollywood was headed for a record annual loss
of $2 million, and its president, Milton Rackmil, could only promise angry stock-
holders that things would somehow get better.

Among Hollywood's old guard, the Universal chief had always been a joke.
Jack Warner called Rackmil "a fucking bookkeeper," and Darryl Zanuck wouldn't
even speak to him. A CPA when he began his show business career at the height
of the Roaring Twenties, Rackmil openly acknowledged that keeping the books
was what he did best. He never aspired to great art, and he lived in New York, leaving the studio's operation in California to his production chief, Ed Muhl. "Let others make pictures for prestige and glory," said Rackmil. "I make them for money."

But he wasn't going to make pictures at all without an infusion of capital. By
1958 Universal's cash flow had slowed to a trickle. Decca Records, the studio's par-

ent company since 1952,[1] was loath to dump any more money into the sprawling complex in the Hollywood Hills known since 1915 as Universal City. In less than six years, Rackmil had run the studio into the ground.

When Decca's bean-counting former comptroller first assumed the studio presidency in 1952, he spoke with characteristic pomp and sweep about Universal's future. After years of balancing Decca's books, Rackmil boasted that he would do the same for Universal. He said he had developed "a diagnostic sense to detect the exact spot in a financial operation that spelled the difference between success and failure."

One of the first spots where Rackmil's keen diagnostic sense told him to invest Universal's resources was in television. Unfortunately, he sold off more than six hundred pre-1948 Universal movies, which could have aired on TV, to Columbia's Screen Gems and invested instead in United World Films, whose contribution to early TV included such unmemorable documentary series as *Animal Fun and Mischief, Stranger Than Fiction,* and *Great Moments on the Gridiron.* While Screen Gems, Revue, and Four Star Productions were all raking in money, Universal's television track record was actually worse than the movies it produced. Ironically, the studio that had practically invented the comedy series (Ma and Pa Kettle, Abbott and Costello, and Francis the talking mule, among others) never made a single television sitcom.

As the disastrous year of 1958 wore on, finances grew worse. Except for the occasional lease to independent producers, Universal's back lot and most of its sixteen soundstages stood idle. Rackmil laid off most of the employees and reported a $450,000 loss for the first quarter. Production chief Muhl thought he'd struck a home run when he persuaded Orson Welles to direct and act in his first two U.S. films in eight years. Welles appeared in *Man in the Shadow* (1957) so that he could direct the quirky, dark murder mystery *Touch of Evil* (1958). That movie eventually became a cult classic, but it barely earned back its $900,000 production budget during its first release.

In the spring, Rackmil got another hopeful sign. Kirk Douglas talked about bringing his production company, Bryna, to Universal, to make a western costarring Rock Hudson. As it turned out, Douglas really wanted to produce a Roman spectacle that would rival every other gladiator saga of the era, from *The Robe* to *Ben-Hur.* It would be based on novelist Howard Fast's best-selling yarn about a Roman slave uprising led by a rebellious gladiator. It would require a wide screen, Technicolor, a cast of thousands, and a great deal of capital — capital that Univer-

---

[1] In a hostile takeover, Decca bought control of the studio from British film magnate J. Arthur Rank, leading to the ouster of Bill Goetz as production chief in September of 1953. Goetz moved on to Columbia, where he was a producer for the remainder of his career.

sal didn't have. While Universal's brass dickered with Douglas over *Spartacus*, the studio descended deeper and deeper into the red.

Meanwhile, MCA was swimming in cash. The Paramount film library that the agency bought for $50 million in February had already yielded $60 million in rentals by the early summer of 1958. What was more, Revue had so many television series in production that it outgrew its adopted home at Republic Studios, where its five-year lease was almost up. MCA had already taken advantage of Universal's plight by shifting several of its Revue shows from cramped quarters on the Republic lot, a few miles up Ventura Boulevard, to Universal's vacant soundstages in the Cahuenga Pass, where rent was cheap and Rackmil paid the overhead.

Universal International wasn't the only company in trouble. The old-line studios were also on the ropes. In ten years, average weekly box office attendance had dropped from 90 million to 40 million. Twentieth Century Fox sold off most of its back lot, turning it into a new development called Century City, and Desilu moved into the old RKO Studios. Ed Muhl took the credit—or the blame—for coming up with the idea of selling Universal's excess real estate to keep from sinking into bankruptcy. "I've taken a lot of criticism for it since, but at the time it was about the only thing we could do," said Muhl.

Wasserman seriously began to consider the possibility of taking over Universal. In his dealings on behalf of Jimmy Stewart, Janet Leigh, Cary Grant, and other MCA clients who'd made pictures on the lot, Wasserman had already learned enough about Rackmil and his hierarchy to understand that buying Universal outright was out of the question. Rackmil might be shallow and vain, but he wasn't stupid. He was not about to surrender the studio itself. If that had been an option, even Rackmil would have had enough common sense to sell it off long before Universal began to teeter on the edge of insolvency. Universal survived because of Rackmil's stubborn pride and the sycophantic support of his executives.

"Unlike Lew and Jules, who didn't want their portraits displayed anywhere, Rackmil hung his picture in every Universal office around the globe," recalled Berle Adams. "On Mondays he always went to the mid-Manhattan steam baths and then to Danny's Hideaway for dinner, usually with a pack of young Universal executives who thought that dinner with the boss would lead to a promotion. Rackmil never noticed his power slipping away, and none of his lackeys bothered to tell him. Neither did Lew."

Before making his offer, Wasserman drove Jules Stein, Berle Adams, and Taft Schreiber to Universal one Saturday afternoon to secretly appraise the studio. The MCA men walked through replicas of the streets of New York and Paris, stood atop a medieval English castle, and tested the wood plank sidewalks of Dodge City. In all, Universal City had 196 buildings containing over 500 offices in addition to the sets and facades where a thousand movies had been shot. It was a self-contained community, with its own post office, hospital, commissary, fire department, sheriff's office, lumber mill, tram service, and three lakes.

But there were problems. The foundations of several soundstages had begun to be washed away in the winter rains. Inside the soundstages, things weren't much better.

"They didn't invest any money in them," recalled MCA attorney Al Dorskind, whom Wasserman would later tap as studio chief. "With a little money you could change some of the lighting and wiring, but there was no backup power, no synchronized generators. They just didn't invest that kind of money. Even their accounting department still used an old punch card system from the forties."

Calculating the cost of refurbishing it all, Wasserman pointed to a shabby African village here and a rusty railroad depot there. As the MCA men neared the end of their tour, Schreiber counted heads and noticed that somewhere along the way they had lost Dr. Stein. Retracing their steps, the three executives found their board chairman playing with Old West paraphernalia, papier-mâché boulders, intergalactic space hardware, and other movie props stored in one of the Universal warehouses. Stein pointed out stacks of period furniture in one corner of the building and ordered Lew to make a mental note: the furniture had to be of a better quality when they took over. Jules knew furniture, and this stuff all looked fake.

Wasserman proposed to Rackmil and Muhl that MCA buy everything but the studio — the land, the soundstages, the sets, the warehouses, the vaults, and the offices. Then, for a fee of $1 million a year, Universal would lease back any production facilities it might need to make its films. Revue would vacate Republic Studios and move in as a new tenant, but MCA would not interfere in Universal's business in any way.

The way Wasserman spelled it out, MCA would actually be doing Rackmil an enormous service. The studio would have the capital to concentrate on production, wouldn't have to vacate its home of nearly half a century, and would no longer have the headaches of being a landlord. Lew would handle everything.

On December 18, 1958, MCA bought Universal International's 367-acre lot for $11.25 million. At a press conference, Milt Rackmil carefully explained that Universal was not quitting show business. In fact, he said, his studio was "in business to stay." Rumors that Universal or its parent company, Decca Records, might be sold off were totally false. It simply made more sense to put the studio's real estate equity to work making movies. MCA and Universal would have more of a partnership than a landlord-tenant relationship, Rackmil explained. He couldn't have been more pleased, he told the gathered members of the press.

Wasserman, who was sitting next to Rackmil, smiled and said nothing.

—◆◆◆—

MCA's PURCHASE OF Universal kicked the pace of the Justice Department's inquiry up a notch. Leonard Posner brought in John Fricano, another career Justice Department lawyer, to help him expand the inquiry to Los Angeles. On July 1, 1959, they began subpoenaing records from MCA, but FBI Agent Carter Billings, who had the job of going through the documents, generally came up disappointed.

From July through December of 1959 an average of three FBI agents a day continuously examined files, but MCA controlled the entire process, beginning by persuading investigators not to visit any of MCA's regional or foreign offices. When Agent Billings demanded files from the regional offices, the files in question were sent to New York. In fact, everything was to be examined in New York in two separate offices that had been rented by MCA inside MCA headquarters. The FBI's accommodating hosts produced nothing from MCA's foreign offices or from Wasserman's or Stein's personal files. Asked why not, MCA general counsel Morris Schrier replied that such files simply did not exist.

"One of the legends of Lew is that he put very little in writing," recalled Tom Schatz, a film scholar and author of *The Genius of the System*, which chronicles the final years of the studio system. Lew was the polar opposite of David Selznick, who put everything in writing, according to Schatz.[2]

"Selznick was one of these guys who were keenly aware of their place in history," said Schatz. "Wasserman is very different. I don't know if it's because of the legalities or what."

The records search yielded some leads but no hard evidence. Potential witnesses told Posner and Fricano that they would be far better off talking to MCA rivals whom Wasserman or one of his minions had stabbed in the back.

The attorneys heard over and over that stars were the key to MCA's monopoly. A star, one source told Posner, was "like a famous painting, such as *Blue Boy*: You can't get another painting and say that it is a substitute....There is just no substitute. A Greta Garbo is a Greta Garbo, and that's all there is to it."

If Posner could pinpoint how Wasserman's agents got the stars, used them, and held on to them, he would understand exactly how the Octopus worked. The way MCA acquired Rock Hudson was a perfect example.

After *Magnificent Obsession* (1954) turned Hudson into a bona fide star, MCA offered to build him a house if he'd dump Henry Willson, the agent who created a string of hunky stars in the 1950s, including Rock Hudson.[3] Hudson refused.

---

[2] Jack Warner also had a penchant for memos, and ordered the following message printed at the bottom of all Warner Brothers internal stationery: "Verbal messages cause misunderstandings. *Please put them in writing.*"

[3] Besides Hudson (real name, Roy Scherer), Willson invented Tab Hunter (Andrew Arthur Gelen), Troy Donahue (Merle Johnson), John Saxon (Carmen Orrico), Rory Calhoun (Francis Timothy Durgin), and Guy Madison (Robert Moseley).

"An agent often becomes a sort of father after discovering and grooming a personality," Willson said during a 1985 interview, recalling the circuitous way in which he lost Rock Hudson to MCA. "I've paid to get teeth fixed, ears pinned back, and contact lenses fitted. I've shown which fork to use and which wines to order and taught all the amenities. After educating them in every way possible, and eventually wrangling a long-term deal at one of the major studios, then when it appears that the box office years are in the making, another agent comes along and takes over."

Seeing that Hudson couldn't be bought in the usual way, Wasserman made Willson an offer he couldn't refuse. If Lew could better Hudson's contract at Universal, MCA would take 10 percent of the raise in salary and Willson would continue to get the same 10 percent he'd already been receiving. That way, Lew argued, everyone would win—MCA, Willson, and Rock Hudson. Willson pondered Wasserman's altruism carefully. He knew that MCA never acted out of generosity.

"If the first agent is protected by a contract, the commission checks keep flowing in," said Willson. "The [Screen Actors] Guild has a rule that if an agent gets a client fifteen days' work out of ninety, [the client] can't up and leave. Sometimes, though, you're left with egg on your face while the other agent gets the bacon."

Wasserman made good on his promise. He did boost Hudson's salary—so high, in fact, that Willson and MCA both earned higher commissions. Inevitably, self-interest prevailed over old loyalties, and when Hudson's contract came up for renewal, he left Willson for MCA.

"This sort of maneuvering very often happened in those days, and I suppose it still does," Willson recalled. But, he added, such maneuvering also took its toll on all concerned.

"I hadn't seen Lew in some time, and he looked weary and wrinkled," Willson said, after bumping into Wasserman several years after Rock Hudson left for MCA. "The fast-paced life of an agent can age one faster than any other profession—outside of wrestling. There is no time for a private life. Even heads of studios like Jack Warner, Louis B. Mayer, and Sam Goldwyn had an easier time of it, because they were kingpins of a group of contract players and technicians and, having huge working plants, knew how to delegate authority.

"A Lew Wasserman has to be in there pitching every moment, setting deals, knowing what star's contract is up with what agent and when to step in with a better offer, keeping track of pictures in production, holding hands with stars who are having professional or private problems and supervising subagents. It can be killing. I know from experience."

The moment an agent believed his own legend and stopped pitching, holding his clients' hands, or setting the right deals for them, he stood to lose the game. To illustrate the point, several informants told Posner how Danny Kaye became an MCA client.

As far back as World War II, Abe Lastfogel—the grand old man of the William Morris Agency—patiently explained to new clients like Danny Kaye that stars come and go. Lastfogel was more interested in building careers than in creating stars. After he persuaded Sam Goldwyn to pair Kaye with Dinah Shore in *Up in Arms* (1944), Lastfogel gave his new client the speech. Patience, he said. Leave your career in the agency's hands. For more than a decade, Kaye's career coasted from one comedy to the next, never soaring but never souring, either.

When Kaye brought up the touchy subject of his big break—when would he take that stellar leap from workaday actor to genuine fame?—Lastfogel again counseled patience. The William Morris Agency followed a blueprint, a formula for success, which called for a balanced number of comedies and serious plays each year. Kaye bit his tongue and followed Lastfogel's advice like a dutiful son. And why not? Abe treated him like a son. When Kaye first emigrated west to Beverly Hills, Lastfogel let him move into his hotel suite until he got his feet wet. They ate at the same restaurants, patronized the same tailor.

Danny Kaye was the quintessential William Morris client: loyal, obedient, patient. Never mind that he seemed to be outliving many of Lastfogel's best agents. When agent Johnny Hyde suffered a fatal heart attack in 1950, Kaye delivered the eulogy. Eight years later Bert Allenberg died while having dinner with Danny and his wife, Sylvia. But short, stocky Lastfogel showed no sign of giving up the ghost. He remained a dynamo, guiding his clients and giving Jules Stein's MCA a run for its money. Clients like Danny Kaye who owed their careers to William Morris stayed right by Lastfogel's side, no matter how tempting it might have been to leave. In short, Danny Kaye was such a well-known Lastfogel protégé that Lew Wasserman didn't even bother to resort to seduction.

Be patient, said Lastfogel.

So when no less a director than MCA's Billy Wilder gave William Morris a script for Danny Kaye, Lastfogel considered it from every angle. Would it really be right for his client? Would it advance his career or merely put a few more shekels in his bank account? Lastfogel finally told Danny Kaye to forget it. He shouldn't waste his time on this "junky little script." There were far better projects to showcase Kaye's musical talents. Kaye listened and went on to star in the lighthearted *Merry Andrew* (1958) and *The Five Pennies* (1959), which told the life story of jazz great Red Nichols. Neither was a hands-down hit, but neither was a box office flop, either.

About a year later Lastfogel and Kaye attended a sneak preview together. Afterward Lastfogel continued laughing so hard his eyes watered. "That's one of the greatest things I ever saw," he giggled as he climbed out of Kaye's car. "It was one of the funniest vehicles that ever was put out. It was simply great."

"You think that the vehicle was really good?" asked Kaye.

"It was absolutely magnificent," said Lastfogel.

"You think anybody could have been good in the Jack Lemmon part?"

"Sure. Anybody could have been hot with a great story like that."

"You think I could have been good in that, Abe?"

"Why, with your great talent, Danny, you would have knocked them dead and made fifty million in a picture like that."

"You miserable little fuck," Kaye snarled. "You're fired."

With that, Danny Kaye drove the half dozen blocks from William Morris to MCA and told Lew Wasserman's secretary he was ready to sign up. Until that moment, Lastfogel had completely forgotten that the "junky little script" he'd returned to Billy Wilder without comment the previous year was *Some Like It Hot.*

—◦∾◦—

Whether Danny Kaye ever really stood a chance is doubtful, because *Some Like It Hot,* the classic Billy Wilder comedy about Jazz Age cross-dressing, had always been an MCA package. Lew Wasserman decided who would get the role, and certainly no one represented by the William Morris Agency would get serious consideration.

"I think Lew Wasserman had a great deal to do with getting me in *Some Like It Hot,*" said Tony Curtis. "He knew that the idea of Tony Curtis and Jack Lemmon in drag, with Marilyn Monroe singing and Billy Wilder directing—this one was going to go down in the history books."

Curtis, Lemmon, and Billy Wilder were all MCA clients. Against her better judgment, Marilyn Monroe completed the MCA package by accepting the dumb blonde role of ukelele-strumming Sugar Kane. Wasserman and Jay Kanter persuaded her to cash in on her sexy image—something she had refused to do in her previous two films, *Bus Stop* and *The Prince and the Showgirl.* Two years of effort to counter her dim-bulb image and be taken seriously as an actress vanished in an MCA moment.

Everyone made money on *Some Like It Hot,* including a sixty-three-year-old ophthalmologist whose name came up but whose face never appeared in the movie. In a scene in which saxophonist Tony Curtis and bass player Jack Lemmon make the agency rounds looking for work, Curtis popped his head in one office and asked, "Anything today?"

"Nothing," answered a receptionist.

"Thank you," Curtis said, slamming the door. Only as it shut did the lettering on the window come clearly into focus: "Music Corporation of America, Jules Stein."

Director Billy Wilder, who regularly trounced Lew Wasserman at gin rummy and aimed his irreverence at everyone, loved skewering MCA. A year after *Some Like It Hot*, his next film, *The Apartment*, became a somber tribute to the Jennings Lang testicle affair—as much an MCA legend as Jules Stein during the Roaring Twenties.

Billy Wilder was not the only Hollywood insider to find humor in the Octopus. Posner discovered during his interviews that MCA's power was too pervasive to fight, so Hollywood's creative community did the next best thing: they laughed at it. References to Stein and his henchmen got to be such an inside joke that recognizing the references took on the trappings of a parlor game among those in the know.

On television, George Burns and Gracie Allen resided at 123 South Camden, for example. Anyone who checked the actual Beverly Hills address would have found that MCA agent Mickey Rockford lived there. When the scriptwriters for *The Jack Benny Show* or one of the Bing Crosby–Bob Hope Road pictures needed a name for some offscreen character, the name would inevitably turn out to be Mr. Kramer, Mr. Schreiber, Mr. Rockford, or Mr. Stein.

For the most part, the public remained ignorant of MCA and its far-reaching tentacles, but within show business circles, the agency had become a frequent target for satire. Lew Wasserman was Ali Baba, and his agents, the Forty Thieves. One joke involved an actor running from the police. "Where can I hide?" he breathlessly asks another actor.

"Join MCA. Nobody'll hear from you or see you again."

Actors scratching to get to the top of the Hollywood food chain wanted MCA to sign them, but once they got on board, they often found that they couldn't even get their agent to return a phone call if they weren't superstars. With unintended irony, singer and MCA client Mel Tormé once told an interviewer, "It's such a gigantic organization [that] personal attention is difficult to get, unless you're a Danny Kaye."

MCA performed particularly badly with rising teen heartthrobs. Ozzie Nelson held Wasserman personally responsible for mishandling David Nelson's movie career and Rick Nelson's recording opportunities. Robert Wagner and Tommy Sands both fired MCA. In his letter terminating his agent, Sands noted: "None of the alluring plans talked about...materialized in even one motion picture commitment."

"They're large and unless you have a personal contact inside the agency you don't get much attention," said comic Mort Sahl, who quit MCA after a year and a half. "But go out and talk to thirty-two MCA clients and all thirty-two will say, 'I have a personal contact.'"

Another ex-MCA comic, rising young "sick" comedian Lenny Bruce, used his own experiences with the agency in a stand-up routine.[4] He offered up the novel explanation that Adolf Hitler's ascent to power was nothing more than bad casting on the part of two MCA agents: "We take you to Bremerhaven, 1927, the largest theatrical office in Germany: MCA—Mein Campf Arises. And we listen to the two German agents, and the agents are in peril. The kaiser, it seems, sort of flipped."

The agents are given two days to find a new dictator, says Lenny Bruce. They call Central Casting, but they're all out of dictator types. As the agents are about to give up, they notice a goof in overalls painting the wall outside their office.

> **Agent #1:** (To the painter): Sonny, put down the paint. You do that later. Come here. That's right. (To his partner) Look at this face. Is this an album cover? (To the painter) What's your name, my friend?
> **Painter:** Adolf Schickelgruber.
> **Agent #1:** You're putting us on.

After changing his name ("We should have something that's really going to hit the beat. Hit...Hit-ler. Adolf Hitler! I like that") and his clothes ("Get the designers up here. Get him something, not too hip. Two button, but a natural shoulder there"), the MCA agents stand back and admire their star transformation: "We're going to make a lot of money with you, sweetie."

Despite warnings from friends and peers that he was hitting too close to home and that most audiences would not get the joke, Bruce kept the routine in his act. General audiences didn't get it, but Bruce found that the bit was especially effective among show business Jews like him.

—⁓—

As soon as MCA took over Universal City, the studio's profits began to climb. The film slate for 1959 was half what it had been for the previous year—a mere eighteen features. But among them were three of the biggest moneymakers of the decade: *Operation Petticoat* ($18.6 million), *Imitation of Life* ($13 million), and *Pillow Talk* ($15 million). All were MCA packages, and all bore the indelible mark of Lew Wasserman.

He paired Tony Curtis with Cary Grant in *Operation Petticoat*, the World War II comedy about life aboard a pink submarine with an all-female crew. According to an early edition of the *Guinness Book of World Records*, the profit-participation

---

[4]   When a young agent invited Taft Schreiber and another senior MCA executive to catch Bruce's act on the Sunset Strip, Lenny came out on stage wearing nothing but a pair of white gloves. Schreiber was not amused. He walked out, and Bruce was not signed to MCA.

deal that Wasserman negotiated for Cary Grant's production company, Granarte, made Grant the highest paid actor in history.

Similarly, Wasserman put Lana Turner back to work shortly after the Johnny Stompanato murder, gambling on the thematic similarities between her real-life tragedy and producer Ross Hunter's remake of a 1934 "weepie," *Imitation of Life.* Like Turner herself, the character she portrayed was an actress who put her career ahead of the well-being of her teenage daughter. Turner either did not recognize or, more likely, did not care about the irony, either of the story or of the title. It was at least as important to her that she jump-start her own career before she faded into the pathetic mists of middle age, like Bette Davis and Betty Grable.

In deference to Universal's fiscal troubles, Lana took Lew's advice and agreed to accept a minimal salary up front with a promise of half the profits plus interest, à la *Winchester '73*. It proved a good career move. *Imitation of Life* grossed more than $50 million worldwide over the next decade. Fifteen years after its release, Turner was still receiving $2,000 weekly paychecks for her twelve weeks of work.

Wasserman guided another fading blonde away from the fiscal precipice of middle age when he packaged thirty-five-year-old Doris Day as a virginal interior decorator opposite playboy Rock Hudson in *Pillow Talk*. It was a formula that worked again and again for Doris Day and Universal through the 1960s, in *Lover Come Back* (1961), *That Touch of Mink* (1962), and *The Thrill of It All* (1963). It was also the second time that MCA had resurrected Doris Day's career.

In 1948, big band singer Doris von Kappelhoff was washed up. At twenty-four she was a single mother, twice divorced and living in the Midway Trailer Park west of Hollywood. She married her agent, Marty Melcher, just as Melcher and his partners in Century Artists Agency were selling out to MCA. It was in Wasserman's capable hands, not Melcher's, that Doris Day became a star.

Melcher became Doris's full-time manager and producer—a position he used to promote his own career rather than to help his wife. Nicknamed "Farty Belcher" by his detractors, Melcher could be abrasive, loud, and profligate.[5] From 1952 on, he collected his $150,000 producer's fee on Doris's pictures whether he showed up on the set or not. In fact, Day's career seemed to falter only when Melcher insisted on overriding the advice of her agents at MCA.

"Marty berated them for not doing a good enough job for Doris," recalled publicist Warren Cowan. "He got angry, yelled at them, said they were lousy agents,

---

[5]   When Melcher died in 1968, he left his widow nearly half a million dollars in debt. His business partner, Chicago lawyer Jerry Rosenthal, mismanaged Day's assets—estimated at $20 million—down to nothing. As a result, Day had to return to work. She starred in her own CBS sitcom from 1968 to 1973, before retiring from show business. In *The Doris Day Show*, she portrayed a widow who had to go back to work.

just out for the buck, banged the table, threw his weight around something awful. Lew Wasserman just sat there, watching Marty's performance, not showing any emotion. When Marty had gotten everything off his chest, Wasserman rose, announced that the meeting was adjourned, and walked out. Marty admired that kind of executive cool but, pathetically, didn't have the makeup for it."

In his first two producing efforts, Melcher made two of the few Doris Day duds: *Julie* (1956) and *Tunnel of Love* (1958). With *Pillow Talk*, Wasserman was back firmly in control. Despite Melcher's meddling, Lew put the actress together with Universal producer Ross Hunter, who established a Doris Day–Rock Hudson franchise that kept her film career alive for another ten years.

But 1959 wasn't just a big year for Universal at the box office. MCA's facility with star packaging also brought Universal its biggest, most prestigious film since *All Quiet on the Western Front*. Through innovative foreign financing and profit-participation deals with MCA clients Laurence Olivier, Charles Laughton,[6] and Peter Ustinov, Kirk Douglas was able to begin production of his sword and sandal spectacle, *Spartacus*. The three-and-one-half-hour saga of a Roman slave uprising would take close to two years to finish.

Before the ordeal was over, Douglas himself, long an MCA holdout, finally caved in and became a Wasserman client. "They have most of the top stars, and now I won't have to go through a big hassle every time I want one of them for a picture," Douglas explained at the time to journalist Bill Davidson.

Within a year, Wasserman talked Academy Award–winning producer Stanley Kramer into relocating to Universal. He also persuaded Alfred Hitchcock, the most highly praised producer-director of his generation, to move to Universal City for the remainder of his career. Of the many assets Wasserman brought to Universal, none would be more valuable than Hitchcock.

A frequent dinner guest of both the Steins and the Wassermans, the pear-shaped British director had been a major MCA asset since the early 1950s, when Wasserman moved him, at a substantial raise in pay, from Warner Brothers to Para-mount. In 1955, despite some initial grumbling, Hitchcock agreed to host a Revue anthology show for Wasserman called *Alfred Hitchcock Presents*. Though Hitch-cock considered television beneath him and had little to do with the program except to introduce each week's story, the weekly exposure planted his jowly image firmly in the national imagination.

"Our sales pitch to other clients was 'If Hitchcock can do it, why can't you?'" recalled Berle Adams.

Along with *General Electric Theater*, the Hitchcock series became Revue's first

---

6   When Wasserman offered Laughton the role of Senator Gracchus, the actor kvetched that Peter Ustinov had a better part. That was because Ustinov rewrote his part, said Lew, suggesting that Laughton ask Ustinov to rewrite Laughton's part, too. He did, and both actors signed.

bona fide mega-hit. As part of MCA's merchandising, the TV show spawned best-selling short-story collections, board games, and a mystery magazine, which publishes to the present day.

Most important of all, Hitchcock's instant folk hero status gave him license to move freely from studio to studio, dependent on none, and loyal solely to Lew Wasserman. Besides negotiating top dollar for his contracts and packaging the best MCA clients for his films, Wasserman brought together—and kept together—the production team that made Hitchcock the first universally acknowledged star director in post-mogul Hollywood. The writers, cinematographer, editor, composer, costumer, and line producer, as well as the actors who collaborated with Hitchcock again and again, were all part of the Wasserman package. According to film historian Tom Schatz, Lew Wasserman was Hitchcock's "virtual production manager."

In 1959, at the top of his game and the height of his popularity, Hitchcock made *North by Northwest* for MGM for $250,000 plus 10 percent of the gross. The spy thriller starring Cary Grant and Eva Marie Saint was a runaway hit. Even though he ran $1.2 million over its $3.1 million budget and the film came in twenty days late, Hitchcock could have gone on making stylish Technicolor thrillers at MGM for the remainder of his career. Instead, he wanted to film a sympathetic tale about a misunderstood young man who cares for his mother and runs the Bates Motel.

Against all advice, Hitchcock ordered MCA to make a deal with Paramount to shoot *Psycho* on a budget of $800,000.

Pundits predicted such a total loser that Wasserman was able to persuade Paramount to let Hitchcock finance part of *Psycho* himself in exchange for 60 percent of the profits.[7] Unlike his stuffier peers in the Directors Guild, Hitchcock had come to admire the speed with which TV crews whipped together an hour of film. *Psycho* was shot in black-and-white, using technical support from Hitchcock's TV show rather than Paramount's higher paid movie crews, and most of the filming was relegated to rented quarters on the Universal lot, where Hitchcock's MCA agents indulged his every whim. He completed *Psycho* in half the time it had taken to finish *North by Northwest*.

When it was released the following year, *Psycho* was such a resounding success that it became the prototype for every slice-and-dice thriller that came afterward. While critics panned its perverse depiction of mother love and sleazy look, *Psycho*

---

[7] On August 31, 1964, MCA acquired all outstanding stock in Hitchcock's Shamley Productions and acquired assets that included *Psycho* as well as Hitchcock's half-hour and hour-long TV productions. In exchange, Shamley's four principals—Hitchcock; his wife, Alma; his attorney; and his longtime partner, Joan Harrison—shared in 90,000 shares of MCA Inc. Because the exchange constituted a "reorganization," no one paid any tax and Alfred and Alma Hitchcock became MCA's third-largest shareholders, behind Stein and Wasserman.

took in $8.5 million at the U.S. box office alone and made Hitchcock the wealthiest director in Hollywood. *Psycho* also made "Hitch" a permanent Universal fixture, where the Bates Mansion still stands as a monument to Hitchcock's dark imagination and Lew Wasserman's faith.

Under MCA's stewardship, Universal City made a remarkable comeback. By the end of 1959, Milton Rackmil announced that his studio was back in the black. He was also able to report a $4.7 million profit—the highest annual profit in Universal's history. Instead of reinvesting in the company, Rackmil gave the stockholders a huge dividend.

Albert Dorskind, MCA's own corporate treasurer at the time, was among the happy stockholders. "Right after MCA bought Universal City, I went out and bought Decca stock," recalled Dorskind. "Lew asked me how I knew it'd go up, and I told him 'Rackmil's a bookkeeper. Everything goes to the bottom line.'"

The year-end news was even better for MCA, though Wasserman did not funnel everything to the bottom line. Jules Stein had other plans for his suddenly cash-rich company.

MCA reorganized on September 1, 1959, combining all of its subsidiaries, including Revue Productions, into MCA, Inc. Within three months MCA was formally listed for the first time on the New York Stock Exchange.

Wall Street underwriters greeted MCA's initial public offering with a written warning to potential investors: MCA had gone public chiefly for the "tax convenience" of the Stein family. Jules himself owned 1.43 million of MCA's 4 million shares. Lew had another 715,000 shares, and each of the other Nine Old Men whom Jules had singled out to own a piece of the company in 1954 held 170,400 shares.[8] By listing his company on the New York Stock Exchange and establishing a market in as little as 400,000 shares of common stock, Stein automatically lowered his estate tax liability.

In its first annual report to shareholders, MCA reported its gross annual income as $57.8 million and its before-tax earnings as $10.6 million. Instead of paying out generous dividends, like Rackmil, Chairman Stein and his board elected to build the company's treasure chest. There would be a time to judiciously spend the agency's windfall profits soon enough.

Everything was booming for MCA: domestic television production, foreign

---

[8]   Under the tax-free reorganization plan, each executive exchanged five shares of his stock in the old MCA corporations (MCA Talent, Management Corporation of America, Revue Productions, MCA-TV, and MCA) for 142 shares in the new MCA, Inc. For the original Nine Old Men, who owned 1,200 shares each in the old corporations, their stake in the new company came to 170,400 shares apiece. While the new stock's par value was 17 cents a share, the moment MCA stock went on the market, it began trading at $17.50 a share, making each of the Nine Old Men an instant millionaire. Within a year, MCA stock was being traded for as much as $38 a share.

distribution, talent commissions, studio rentals. The only cautionary note in an otherwise glowing tribute to Wasserman's management team was listed at the back of that first annual report to shareholders under a footnote regarding contingent liabilities: "An investigation of the company's activities by the U.S. Department of Justice with respect to alleged violations of the federal antitrust laws by talent agencies was begun in 1959. In the opinion of the company and its counsel, no such violations have existed or do exist."

TWENTY-ONE

Monopoly

1960

On February 23, 1960, Cyrus Vance and Ed Weisl Sr. showed up at the Justice Department, looking to draw and quarter Leonard Posner. Assistant Attorney General Charles Whittinghill listened politely as the two lawyers described how the cigar-chomping prosecutor had broadened the MCA investigation far beyond the purchase of the Paramount film library. MCA management was livid. Posner was out of control. Couldn't Whittinghill put his bloodhound on a short leash so the agency didn't have to waste so much time delivering documents?

Put it in writing, Whittinghill advised. After they left, he buzzed Posner. The antitrust investigation was starting to make waves, Whittinghill warned. Posner thanked him for the head's-up. As he put down the receiver, he chuckled and lit up another stogie.

"That's the way Leonard was; he was a fighter," recalled Malcolm MacArthur, Posner's junior co-counsel on the MCA case. "No neutrality whatsoever."

Posner knew he must be getting close if a pair of Park Avenue lawyers the caliber of Vance and Weisl were trying to stop him. During the early days of his investigation, when Eisenhower's attorney general, William P. Rogers, had given Posner free rein to pursue MCA wherever it took him, Posner methodically cataloged his interviews and built his case file in relative anonymity. He'd heard the Octopus rumors for years. Now he had license to find out if they were true...and the rumors were leading into some surprising places.

By the time MCA first began trying to stop him, he'd already heard half a dozen versions of *The Young Lions* story. But no matter how different the details, the story always ended with MCA ordering Twentieth Century Fox to dump Tony Randall and replace him with Dean Martin. Likewise, the NBC board room incident in which Sonny Werblin dictated the fall TV schedule to Robert Kintner came up in interview after interview.

Posner also heard the recurring tale of an outraged Blake Edwards, who angrily demanded his release from MCA after Revue's Jennings Lang cloned his NBC hit, *Peter Gunn*, and put it on the air as *Johnny Staccato*.[1] Both TV shows featured off-beat private detectives who hung out in New York jazz bars, but Edwards's series had run for two seasons before NBC's Kintner obliged his close pal Sonny Werblin and gave *Johnny Staccato* a prime time slot.[2] The series starring John Cassavetes was universally panned as a bad *Peter Gunn* rip-off, but it remained on the air until the spring of 1960. NBC had been forced to buy twenty-seven episodes.

Sam Northcross, an advertising executive for *Johnny Staccato*'s sponsor, Reynolds Aluminum, told Posner that he wanted to ax the show after the first couple of airings but stayed with it out of fear of MCA. His agency finally had to take another MCA show just to get out of its *Johnny Staccato* commitment—a typical MCA take-it-or-leave-it tactic.

Producer David Susskind, whose own shows had been bumped to make way for Revue series, told Posner he didn't like MCA's cloning and bait-and-switch tactics either, and he knew whereof he spoke. He had been both an MCA victim and an MCA predator. Susskind started in show biz in the mail room of Marty Melcher's Century Artists following World War II, but went to work in 1949 for MCA, where he peddled talent as a junior agent. When he refused to blackmail a client, Werblin called him on the carpet.

"Over and over again I said, 'If I do that, the customer won't talk to me. They'll be furious,'" said Susskind. "The answer was, 'Look, they've got to do business with us. They may be mad for a week or a month, but they're going to want Jack Benny, they're going to want Marlon Brando, they're going to want Cary Grant, and they've *got* to come back to us....They have to come back knockin' at the door when they want Benny or George Burns and Gracie Allen. They gotta do business with us.'"

But blackmail and the old bait-and-switch were the least of it. The fact was that Posner's FBI agents kept coming across more remarkable and often shocking stories about MCA's rise to power, including claims that the agency prostituted its growing corps of starlets in order to win favors from ad or network executives.

---

[1] An actor turned writer who directed four successful comedies at Universal including *The Perfect Furlough* (1958) and *Operation Petticoat* (1959), Edwards discharged MCA on December 15, 1959, but apparently made peace a few years later. He went on to direct such Wasserman star packages as *Breakfast at Tiffany's* (1961) and *Days of Wine and Roses* (1962) before teaming with actor Peter Sellers for his string of Pink Panther movies in the late 1960s.
[2] *Peter Gunn*, starring Craig Stevens, premiered over NBC in September 1958. It moved to ABC in October 1960, the same month that NBC premiered *Johnny Staccato*, starring John Cassavetes. Following its NBC cancellation, ABC reran all the episodes, which the network renamed simply *Staccato*, during the following season.

NBC's Robert Sarnoff was literally seduced by MCA, according to FBI informants. And there was more.

"It is not beyond reason for MCA to try to insert someone into the Justice Department in order to get an information pipeline," one source warned Posner. He scoffed at that conspiracy theory, but he also began to exercise a greater degree of caution. Posner knew that if it was merely a matter of buying someone's favor, his adversary wouldn't think twice. He'd already discovered that MCA acquired most of its rising talent through its checkbook. If a Wasserman lieutenant saw someone he wanted, he simply promised the actor the moon and bought him a signing bonus, a car, or a no-interest loan. Any rival agent foolish enough to protest could sue and be damned. In one of his weekly summaries, Posner wrote: "A specific case in point is Harry Belafonte.[3] Belafonte began in a bistro in Greenwich Village, and became an overnight sensation. This as the result of several years of grooming by an independent talent agent (Jack Rollins) who had been working Belafonte up the ladder. Rollins got Belafonte to drop the type of singing that he had been doing and to begin the calypso format. As soon as Belafonte achieved some success, MCA jumped on him, put him under contract, and told Belafonte to break his contract with his old manager and that MCA would take care of the litigation for him."

Lillian Smith, the widow of another independent talent agent, faced financial ruin following her husband's death but continued to represent actress Inger Stevens. She told Posner how Inger moved into her house, where Lillian fed and clothed the young blond beauty while she struggled to gain a foothold in Hollywood. The Smith agency was about to go under when Inger got her break, but shortly thereafter, Inger told Lillian that MCA had made her a better offer. Within two years, Stevens had her own ABC sitcom, called *The Farmer's Daughter*, but Lillian Smith never saw a dime in commissions.

Posner's investigators learned that MCA didn't just steal and bribe. It was equally ruthless about destroying neophyte careers. Carolyn Jones had been knocking around Hollywood since 1952, but MCA hadn't done much with her. She was too quirky—not mainstream enough for the MCA talent mill. After she played a minor role in *The Seven Year Itch*, her future was put to a vote. Should the invisible cabal that silently ran Hollywood under Wasserman's stewardship give the actress another chance, or should they dismiss her? The MCA brass voted 11 to 2 to dump Jones. She got her revenge soon after they gave her her pink slip. She went to William Morris and landed a supporting role in *The Bachelor Party* (1957), which won her an Oscar nomination. MCA suddenly reconsidered and wanted

---

[3] Belafonte also became a personal favorite of Mrs. Wasserman, according to United Artists executive Max Youngstein. Edie's relationship with the singer-actor was rumored to have been as close at one time as her relationship with Frank Sinatra.

her back, but it was too late. Best remembered today as Morticia Addams on the 1960s TV series *The Addams Family,* Carolyn Jones never again worked for MCA.

But Jones was the exception. Most unfortunate actors and actresses who did not make the star grade at MCA simply vanished without a trace once Wasserman's team put them on waivers.

"The MCA executives I dealt with were efficient, hard, and completely lacking in compassion," recalled producer Josh Logan, who asked journalist Bill Davidson not to quote him by name in a 1962 *Show* magazine interview. "Their stock-in-trade was creative, gifted human beings, but they handled their clients' lives as if they were so many inanimate objects, like bales of cotton or crates of furniture. A movie star or playwright was to them 'a piece of talent,' and I heard that cold expression so often that after a while it nauseated me."

The kid gloves with which MCA first handled talent turned to brass knuckles once they were signed. The mandate became "Work them at the highest price as often and as long as possible." Like a prize steer, an actor had only so many good years before he or she lost cash-register charisma. Posner began to hear stories about physicians on the TV or movie set who injected stars with "vitamins" to keep them performing. Though he was unable to directly link legal studio drug pushers like Dr. Lee Siegel and Dr. Max Jacobson to MCA, it became clear after a while that agents did not interfere with the addictions that were killing Alan Ladd, Montgomery Clift, and Judy Garland. In fact, MCA's Freddie Fields would eventually be accused of working Garland to death.

Lew didn't mind playing the role of bogeyman.

"I back into elevators, and I've hired a taster," he used to joke at the regular Wednesday morning strategy sessions.

"He is the most reviled and most revered man to come out of that whole era," said producer Bruce Campbell, son of MCA pioneer George Campbell. "He left more than an indelible mark. Lew had this liberal heart, and at the same time, he was as cold as steel. My father said that if you were at MCA and you were drowning, they would throw you an anchor."

But stars were no longer the spoiled "children" of the Irving Thalberg era. They knew they'd made Faustian deals, yet were so obsessed or narcissistic that they could not, or would not, walk away. The best they were able to do was occasionally tweak the devil's nose.

When producer Stanley Kramer cast *Judgment at Nuremberg* (1961), he asked Montgomery Clift to emerge from his alcoholism long enough to play a small part, only twelve minutes in the film. Kramer offered him $50,000 for five days' work, but MCA came back with a firm refusal. Either pay Clift $200,000, his standard fee, or no deal. Kramer had begun looking around for someone else to play the role, when Clift himself phoned.

"I want to play that part, and I'll do it for nothing," he told Kramer. "You only have to pay my travel and hotel expenses."

Clift's role as a castration victim was edited to only seven minutes of film time in the final cut of *Judgment at Nuremberg*. Despite his tremors and a memory so damaged by alcohol and drug abuse that he could hardly remember his lines, he won an Oscar nomination for his performance. One of Clift's friends later told Posner that the actor took the part just to stiff Lew Wasserman. In his notes, Posner quoted Clift as saying that he'd worked for nothing "so that when the picture is over, I can take a big empty paper bag, tie a blue ribbon around it, and send it to MCA with a note saying, 'Your commission is inside.'"

Only actors who understood the power of their own charisma and could match MCA's ruthless concentration on the bottom line, dollar sign for dollar sign, stood a chance. In Posner's growing collection of files, Cary Grant was one of the few who could pass the test.

Grant had once been a business partner of his original Hollywood agent, Frank Vincent. After Vincent's death in 1946, Grant dissolved the agency and Jules Stein approached him about coming with MCA. He accepted Stein's offer to let MCA negotiate deals on his behalf, beginning with *The Bishop's Wife* (1947), but he signed no contract. After his years with Vincent, he was too wise. Stein oozed charm and promises, pointing up the many fabulous investment schemes he had at his disposal that would make Grant rich. Jules and Doris even had him up to Misty Mountain as a frequent dinner guest — an honor the Steins rarely accorded Hollywood riffraff who worked for MCA. Cary Grant knew better than to be taken in by promises and flattery. Through his long association with the Steins, he remained nonexclusive. Under his handshake agreement, MCA could negotiate film deals, but the agency did not own him and had to split commissions with Grant's attorney, Stanley Fox.

The arrangement worked well for ten years, until Cary read the script for *Bell, Book and Candle*. He loved the play about a New Yorker who unwittingly falls in love with a beautiful witch, and he recognized that the leading role was tailor-made for him. He told MCA he wanted it, only to hear the lame excuse that Columbia Studios couldn't wait; they'd already given the part to Wasserman's favorite client, James Stewart. The final outrage came a year later when Grant was summoned to appear at Wasserman's Beverly Hills office for a career discussion. There, several executives told Grant he ought to follow his triumphant appearance in *North by Northwest* by doing his own TV series.

"Grant immediately became hostile," an informant told the FBI. "He asked again whether they really believed that he should appear in television and MCA replied, 'yes.'"

Grant asked who would produce the show and was told it would be MCA, of course. He stood up, scanned the roomful of Wasserman clones, all clad in dark suits, white shirts, and black ties, and said, "Our contract is over as of now." He walked out and never returned.

But for every Cary Grant, who learned to keep his own counsel, Posner's investigators were discovering a dozen Paul Newmans.

As one of the last studio contract stars, Newman signed on with Warner Brothers at age twenty-nine, debuting in *The Silver Chalice* (1954)—a film so bad that the young actor apologized for making it in a *Variety* ad. He worked his way through seven more features until he gave his Oscar-nominated performance opposite Elizabeth Taylor in *Cat on a Hot Tin Roof* (1958). As in the old days, the studio could, and did, loan Newman out to MGM and Fox for as much as $150,000 while continuing to pay the actor a salary of as little as $1,000 a week. Warner pocketed the difference.

Newman was no fool. After *Cat on a Hot Tin Roof*, he knew his stock had climbed sufficiently to allow him to begin making a few demands. His contract had three years to run when he confronted Jack Warner. Warner told him he'd let him quit for $500,000. Newman's next stop was MCA, where Wasserman advised the young star to accept Warner's offer and walk. MCA could get him $250,000 a picture as a freelance. Newman would pay off his contract in no time.

But Lew was an agent, and agents are ultimately loyal only to the deal. When Otto Preminger was casting the lead in *Exodus*, the movie based on Leon Uris's best-selling novel about the creation of Israel, Wasserman told Newman to take the part, even if MCA could get him only $200,000. Newman agreed. When Wasserman met with Preminger, however, he couldn't get the producer to budge a penny over $100,000. Wasserman returned to his client and told him he still ought to take the deal. After two lackluster films in a row—*The Young Philadelphians* and *From the Terrace*—Newman's star appeal had dulled. But *Exodus* would pay off in the end.

Exodus, which cost $4 million—a staggering sum at that time—reestablished Newman's box office drawing power and his ability to command plum roles. Two years later he firmly gripped the national imagination as Fast Eddie Felson, the original 1960s antihero, in *The Hustler*.

LEW'S INSTINCTS PROVED equally effective in transforming the career of a different sort of hustler in the spring of 1960. The previous fall, *General Electric Theater* had begun its seventh season on CBS with Ronald Reagan as host. Though Reagan himself initially spurned the TV show as beneath his movie-star status, he ultimately acknowledged that it changed his life.

In his 1990 memoir, *An American Life*, Reagan waxed fondly about GE, the company that had brought good things to his and Nancy's life: "My income from

General Electric had enabled us to build a dream home overlooking the Pacific Ocean that GE stuffed with every imaginable electric gadget. We also bought a 350-acre ranch in the Santa Monica Mountains north of Los Angeles that we loved. And, although GE kept me on the road a lot, there were long stretches of my life during that period when my daily routine focused entirely on my family, our ranch, and a horse."

But Reagan's cowboy fantasy had its price. Shortly after Wasserman cut Reagan in as a 25 percent owner of *General Electric Theater* in the spring of 1959, the studios opened contract talks with the Screen Actors Guild. The exploding power of television had brought a new kind of militancy to the union, especially over TV residuals. While studios grew richer every day collecting TV fees for syndicating old movies, actors still got nothing, and a growing faction within SAG as well as the Writers Guild began talking seriously about shutting Hollywood down.

The old-line studios weren't about to budge. They owned their films and could do what they liked with them. Wasserman foresaw trouble in taking that kind of hard line. Now that MCA owned the Paramount film library, Lew had an even bigger stake in the SAG negotiations. With that in mind, he asked his client—and new business partner—to step into the breach.

Though Reagan was now officially a producer as well as an actor, he continued to vote on SAG policy. He retained SAG membership in much the same way that Jules Stein remained a lifelong member of the American Federation of Musicians long after he'd given up playing the fiddle. Reagan had surrendered the presidency to Walter Pidgeon in 1952, following the blanket waiver that he helped engineer for MCA, but Reagan never quit the SAG executive board.

Thus when SAG President Howard Keel tendered his resignation on September 16, 1959, SAG's executive director, Jack Dales, advised his board to support a "draft Reagan" movement. Dales called Reagan and asked him to guide the union in its upcoming negotiations.

"Give me a few days to think about it," Reagan told the executive director.

With that, Reagan went to Lew. To his surprise, he later recalled, Wasserman told him to take the position. Reagan never revealed Lew's reasons, but he did accept the SAG draft. Six months later, on March 7, 1960, the Guild struck for the first time in its sixty-year history.

SAG did not strike MCA or Universal, however. Lew had already made preemptive moves. Along with several small production companies, MCA agreed to abide by whatever contract SAG finally negotiated with the major studios, just as long as SAG members could continue working at Revue during the strike. In addition, MCA's newest tenant, Universal Studios, became the first major studio to cave in to SAG demands. Before SAG could picket, Universal's president, Milt Rackmil, secretly met with Reagan and promised to break ranks with the other studios. Universal guaranteed SAG up to 7 percent of its take on all movies rented to

TV, the money to go into a pension and welfare trust for actors. If it came to a strike, nobody would stop working at Universal.

Wasserman was now ready for a strike, and just to make certain that all of MCA's bases were covered, he imported Dr. Stein's secret weapon from Chicago. Though his name never appeared on any contract or in the minutes of any negotiating session, the fine fixing hand of Sidney R. Korshak made certain that MCA finished first in the SAG sweepstakes. Whenever he might be in doubt, SAG President Ronald Reagan now had both Lew Wasserman and Sid Korshak to turn to.

At the beginning of the strike, the International Alliance of Theatrical Stage Employees looked as if it might cause trouble. Its president, Richard Walsh, encouraged his members to go ahead and cross SAG picket lines. After all, their union wasn't on strike. Reagan accused Walsh of being "a lousy damn strikebreaker," apparently forgetting that Reagan himself had once crossed other unions' picket lines — and carried a loaded pistol in his pocket while doing so. In order to force the stage employees to honor the SAG pickets, Reagan complained first to AFL-CIO President George Meany about Walsh. When that didn't work, he complained to someone far more powerful than Meany.

As Walsh bitterly revealed to author Dan Moldea some twenty-five years later, "Korshak's involved in that whole proposition you're talking about there, and it would tie back into Reagan.... Reagan was a friend of, talked to, Sidney Korshak, and it would all tie back together."

By 1960, Korshak's influence surged beneath the surface of Hollywood like an underground river. The tall, tailored lawyer with the permanent half-smile and Bugsy Siegel's sleepy eyes, had come to feel just as much at ease dining and schmoozing with Dinah Shore and Frank Sinatra as he was with Jake "the Barber" Factor, Murray "the Camel" Humphreys, and Capone enforcer Gussie Alex. Behind every word Korshak uttered was a veiled threat. He had Meyer Lansky's stamp of approval as organized crime's chief consigliere in Las Vegas and Hollywood.

In addition to selling labor peace, Korshak specialized in circumventing probate. When Hollywood movers and shakers died, Korshak got there faster than the undertaker. After Abner "Longie" Zwillman allegedly hanged himself rather than face a prison sentence for tax evasion, Korshak compassionately helped Zwillman's widow dispose of the bootlegger's Vegas casino holdings, including a stake in the Sands Hotel.[4] Mary Zwillman paid minimal inheritance tax, Korshak collected a hefty fee, and most of Zwillman's assets simply disappeared into thin air. Similarly,

---

[4] Jean Harlow's favorite hood was found hanging from a pipe in the basement of his New Jersey home on February 27, 1959. Zwillman's death was declared a suicide in spite of the fact that his hands had been tied, he had been garroted with wire, and his body was bruised from head to heel. Justice Department sources later disclosed that Zwillman had made the fatal decision to testify against the Mob in exchange for a lighter prison sentence.

Columbia's Harry Cohn died unexpectedly in 1958, leaving his estate an easy government target. Korshak quickly arranged a marriage between Cohn's widow, Joan, and Korshak's pal, shoe manufacturer Harry Karl. After three weeks, they were divorced. It was not enough time to form much of a relationship, but plenty of time to shift Cohn's assets away from the prying eyes of inheritance tax examiners. If Cohn had been on the Capone payroll since the early 1930s, as many investigators suspected, those facts never came out in probate court.

But Sidney's star shone brightest when he was called upon to get organized labor to agree with management. From the Teamsters to the International Restaurant and Culinary Workers Union, Sidney had developed a reputation for starting or stopping a strike with a single phone call. When the Pari-Mutuel Clerks Union walked out of Hollywood Park racetrack, twenty-eight lawyers could not settle the labor dispute. The twenty-ninth lawyer, however, was Korshak, who was called in by Hollywood Park Racing Association president and filmmaker Mervyn LeRoy. Within forty-eight hours, Korshak persuaded the clerks to accept a sweetheart contract with the racetrack owners and return to work.

"Everybody *thought* he had power, so he had power," said Martin Bacow, a longtime Teamster labor negotiator who crossed paths with Korshak.

Despite the best efforts of Korshak, Reagan, and Wasserman, SAG's strike did drag on for six weeks. On April 18 the union finally accepted a compromise: for a onetime payment of $2.65 million, SAG surrendered its members' rights to any TV residuals from movies made before 1960. The $2.65 million became seed money for SAG's pension and welfare fund. After 1960 the studios agreed to pay 6 percent of gross TV sales, minus distribution costs, to the Screen Actors Guild.

Reagan and SAG Executive Director Dales told the rank and file that it was the best deal that they were going to get. The question of whether they were being candid is still debated among older SAG members. More than a generation later, many actors still vilify Reagan for his role in what came to be known as "the great giveaway." On the eve of her stint as grand marshal of the 1997 Tournament of Roses, actress June Lockhart—known for her role as the mother on the long-running hit TV series *Lassie*—told ABC Radio talk show host Michael Jackson that she did not collect residuals on anything she made prior to 1960 because Reagan and MCA "sold us out." Even Bob Hope, who later became one of Reagan's staunchest political supporters, viewed the 1960 SAG contract as a rip-off.

"I made something like sixty pictures, and my pictures are running on TV all over the world," said Hope. "Who's getting the money for that? The studios. Why aren't *we* getting some money?"

Mickey Rooney also blamed Reagan, whom he called a pawn. "The crime of showing our pictures on TV without paying us residuals is perpetuated every day and every night and every minute throughout the United States and the world,"

Rooney said. "The studios have a reservoir of over five thousand pre-1960 pictures that they don't have to pay residuals on. The studios own your blood, your body, and can show your pictures on the moon, and you've lost all your rights. They own you, and they own the photoplay. We're not human beings, we're just a piece of meat."[5]

But Ronald Reagan was no longer just a piece of meat. Like Lew Wasserman, he was an owner, an equity player, and had been since the spring of 1959. On June 7, 1960, less than two months after negotiating "the great giveaway," the SAG president suddenly remembered that he was a producer. In his letter of resignation, he conveniently forgot that he'd been a 25 percent owner of *General Electric Theater* for more than a year. That letter said, in part, "Up to now I have been a salaried employee with no interest in profits. Now I plan to change that status by becoming a producer with an interest in profits. Therefore, with deep regret, I tender my resignation as president and member of the board of directors of the Guild."

———

ACCORDING TO THE July 1960 issue of *Fortune* magazine, Paul Newman and Cary Grant were not under contract to Wasserman, but virtually everyone else in Hollywood was.

In the most sweeping exposé since the *Saturday Evening Post*'s three-part examination of "The Star Spangled Octopus" in the autumn of 1946, *Fortune* published an eleven-page article detailing the rise of the MCA monopoly from band booking to Beverly Hills to television and the whole mix of music, movies, and pop culture that had come to be known as "the industry." The article, titled "There's No Show Business like MCA's Business," could have been a blueprint for the antitrust case that Leonard Posner was developing against MCA.

At sixty-four, Jules Stein finally understood that he was going to die...someday. Four years earlier he had secretly undergone abdominal surgery to have an intestinal cancer removed. While the operation was a success, it led to complications. Adhesions formed, necessitating further surgery for an intestinal blockage in 1959, and although that operation was also a success, going under the knife roused Stein to an awareness of his own mortality. With the future of MCA now safely in the hands of Wasserman, Jules began to turn his attention to the legacy that he would eventually leave.

---

[5] In 1981, Mickey Rooney sued MCA-Universal and seven other studios in a class action on behalf of SAG members who had been cheated out of their pre-1960 film residuals from movies rerun on television. He did not win.

Stein wanted to reclaim his *own* fame but didn't want to go down in history as the shrewd band broker who'd struck platinum with the heirs of Al Capone and taken over all of show biz. Even the slightly more palatable image of world traveler, social lion, and English antique aficionado did not fully satisfy his hunger for immortality. It was Doris who showed him the way.

She had joined other Upper East Side society matrons during the late 1950s in raising funds for the Lighthouse, an organization that benefited blind New Yorkers. When Jules visited its headquarters, all he saw was another do-gooder outfit that taught braille and provided Seeing Eye dogs. The Lighthouse catered to the handicapped instead of actually attempting to prevent vision loss or to restore eyesight. When he pointed this out to Doris, she crossed her arms and dared him to put his money where his mouth was. He'd be serving mankind and his own ego at the same time. At the nagging behest of his image-conscious wife, Jules decided to reclaim his title to the medical degree that he had earned at the University of Chicago nearly half a century earlier. He wanted to be remembered as Dr. Jules Stein, ophthalmologist and humanitarian.

Thus Dr. Jules Stein set out to create and publicize his own blindness-prevention foundation, to be subsidized with MCA capital and staffed by the best medical talent that money could buy. Research to Prevent Blindness, Inc., opened in New York just a block away from MCA headquarters during the same summer the *Fortune* article appeared. The foundation's mandate was stated in its title. Research to Prevent Blindness marked the beginning of a revision of Stein's career that would continue for the rest of his life. Once known to strangers and peers alike as Doc Stein, or simply J. C. Stein, the band booker, he would now bristle when introduced or addressed as anything other than Dr. Jules Stein.

As had been his policy ever since the drubbing he took at the hands of David Wittels and the *Saturday Evening Post*, Dr. Stein refused *Fortune*'s request for an interview. Wasserman, however, did agree to speak to Edward Thompson.

Lew's sentences were clipped and his answers terse, but he seemed clearly to understand what Jules did not: that the media were there to be used, not feared.

As much as he enjoyed playing such games with journalists, Wasserman was ever conscious of the damage that too high a profile could cause. So when the Federal Communications Commission came to Los Angeles that autumn to investigate the sorry state of television broadcasting and to demand that an MCA representative appear at its hearings, Lew weighed the pros and cons. He would not be in total control of the situation, as he had been during his *Fortune* interview. The stakes were too high and the odds too chancy—like filling a flush or drawing to an inside straight. He might get lucky, but that wasn't likely.

Ultimately, it was not Lew Wasserman who attended that public spectacle. He turned the task over to the designated president of Revue Productions: Taft Schreiber got the subpoena.

—⁓—

SCHREIBER HAD NOTHING but contempt for the East Coast yahoos who rolled into Los Angeles in October, acting as if they owned his town and demanding to know how so much sex, violence, and just plain garbage seemed to be getting on the airwaves. The FCC itself hadn't even come to L.A. Instead, the commissioners sent a stuffed shirt named James D. Cunningham, who proclaimed himself the FCC's chief hearing examiner and presiding officer. Taft viewed the hearings the same way Stein and Wasserman saw them: as a dog and pony show à la the HUAC hearings, with witness after witness standing before the microphone, humbly and often apologetically describing the state of television programming while the commissioners' appointees asked pointed questions and preened for the media. More than either Stein or Wasserman, Schreiber envisioned himself a sophisticate—a self-made man who had no time for pomp and cross-examination from a bunch of Washington lawyers.

Wasserman's second-in-command had developed vast cultural pretensions since Leland Hayward first introduced him to art. He would much rather have discussed the fine points of postmodernism than the number of pistol shots fired during an episode of *Mike Hammer* or *The M Squad*. Schreiber spent very nearly as much time appreciating fine painting as he did squeezing commissions from the shows that he and Sonny Werblin had managed to plant in the NBC, CBS, and ABC fall lineups. But he had no time at all for hand-wringing over the tripe America watched each night on the boob tube.

Politics appealed to Schreiber in many of the same ways as fine art: to truly appreciate both, one had to rise above the masses and join the ruling class. Although Schreiber's politics were as adaptable as spandex, as his keen interest in Richard Nixon would indicate later in the decade, he was more interested in art in 1960—especially if it was expensive art, bought cheaply and held to maturity, like a tax-free municipal bond.

When he learned that MCA client Charles Laughton knew the intricacies of the art world, Schreiber made a rare exception to his rule about fraternizing with actors. Their friendship ripened as quickly as Taft saw the depth of Laughton's cultural knowledge. Laughton saw no harm in buying promising art for Schreiber. Unlike Laughton, however, the FCC's James D. Cunningham had no appreciation at all for Taft Schreiber's newly acquired sophistication. When Cunningham had Taft served with a subpoena, all he wanted was answers about MCA's stranglehold on prime-time television. What he got was Schreiber's contempt.

Schreiber showed up as ordered on October 21, 1960, with MCA's legal counsel Larry Beilenson in tow. He followed William Morris's Abe Lastfogel, who had been a compliant toady of a witness. But when Cunningham ordered Taft to produce documents about Revue's remarkable rise to power in the broadcast industry,

Schreiber turned over some, but not all. Schreiber explained that the FCC could have all of the requested documents only if Cunningham agreed to keep them confidential.

"I certainly wasn't comfortable, because I'm a law-abiding citizen," Schreiber later told the press. "But they wanted information we considered to be not only confidential but detrimental to our business."

No deal, said Cunningham. He wanted everything immediately. Beilenson took over. The FCC asked too much, he argued. He was advising his client not to comply. Cunningham ordered Beilenson to shut up and sit down. The face-off escalated into a shouting match. When Beilenson snarled that he had a right to "make a record in this matter," Cunningham shot back, "You have a right to make a record through your client. This is not an adjudicatory proceeding. It is investigatory. I will not hear argument or objections from counsel. The witness is at liberty to refuse for any reason you advise to answer any questions propounded here. I shall not hear you."

Schreiber then read a statement into the record, maintaining that he would no longer be a witness because Cunningham denied him the right of counsel. While a red-faced Cunningham banged his gavel and ordered Schreiber back to the witness stand, Schreiber and Beilenson calmly packed their papers and dramatically walked out of the hearing.

"Thus the witness acted in complete defiance of commission authority," Cunningham sputtered when giving the FCC his official version of events. Schreiber also set a precedent. The following week, two more witnesses defied Cunningham. Attorneys for Promotions Unlimited and Dick Fishell and Associates both challenged his authority. After that, the hearings fell apart. An indignant Cunningham returned to Washington and asked the FCC to force Schreiber to testify. Failing that, he asked the full commission to haul MCA into federal court.

"I've never seen anything like this in my life," muttered Frederick W. Ford, the FCC commissioner. "It seems as if you can't even go to the bathroom in Hollywood without asking MCA's permission. What upsets me most is the way people tell me that MCA says, 'Nobody in Washington can touch us.'"

—◦◦◦—

ONE FALL AFTERNOON in 1960, Lew Wasserman and his driver, a twenty-seven-year-old MCA trainee named Fred Specktor, listened on the car radio to the final moments of Ted Williams's major league career. As they made their way through the streets of West Los Angeles, the unmistakable crack of a bat came over the radio, followed by a roar from the crowd. The announcer shouted that the veteran Boston Red Sox star, who had been playing the game since 1939, had knocked the ball clean out of the park.

Three decades later Specktor recalled his awe: "What a fantastic thing for an old man to hit a home run like that!"

And he also remembered Lew's response from the back seat of the car: "At forty-four, Ted Williams is an old man for baseball," said Wasserman. "And at forty, I'm an old man for the agency business."

Lew was forty-seven. Whether or not he meant to lop seven years off his age to test his impressionable trainee, Wasserman still made his point. Being an agent was a young man's profession. Lew was getting too long in the tooth to hustle clients. It was time to move on.

ACT III

AMERICA

1960–1995

And so, my fellow Americans, ask not what your country can do for you;

ask what you can do for your country.

JOHN F. KENNEDY

Look out, kid, They keep it all hid.

BOB DYLAN

TWENTY-TWO

Kennedy Justice

1960–1961

When the Glenville High School Class of 1930 held its thirtieth reunion, its most illustrious graduate was a no-show. Nevertheless, Wilbur and Mollie Marshall sent classmate Lew Wasserman a program from the celebration that he'd missed, along with their congratulations on his success. They planned a California vacation, they said, and hoped to drop by for a visit.

"He wrote us back a nice note on Universal stationery saying that unfortunately he wouldn't be in town at that time," recalled Mollie, "but he said if we presented the letter at the gate, we could come in and look around at a real movie studio."

When the Marshalls arrived, it turned out Lew hadn't left town after all. Mr. Wasserman was on the lot, and a studio guard told the Cleveland couple how to get to his office.

"Lew had his own bungalow. Wilbur and I walked right in," said Mollie. "Lew just stared at us for the longest time. Then he said, 'I don't remember you. I never saw you people in my life.'

"Lew wasn't rude," Mollie said. "He wasn't abrupt or discourteous or anything like that. But he absolutely didn't remember us. He just looked right through us. He didn't know who we were at all."

Nor was he being cynical or disingenuous. At forty-seven, Lew Wasserman was utterly and absolutely a stranger to his Cleveland roots. He was now a creature of Beverly Hills, recast in his own imagination as completely as any movie star. He had even manufactured a biography that fit his self-image: a Horatio Alger myth that demonstrated that hard work, pluck, and good old Yankee ingenuity spelled success in America, even if you were the fanciful son of Russian Jews, had a ruthless streak when it came to business, and owed at least some of that success to a lifelong touch-and-go relationship with gangsters.

Lew boiled his sanitized biography down to a single paragraph: "I was born in Cleveland in 1913," he told an interviewer for the *New York Post*. "The date was March 15. I have one brother, five years older. His name is William and he sells film for United Artists. My father was retired. We did not live in a rich section. I ushered in theaters, did publicity work, and finally joined MCA. It's all in *Who's Who*."

But *Who's Who* doesn't check the information in biographies provided.

Lew's salary in 1960, excluding bonuses, was $175,000—more than that of Jules Stein ($150,000), more than Taft Schreiber ($125,000), and more than Sonny Werblin ($100,000). Jules was still chairman and chief stockholder, and MCA would have been hard put to do without the services of either Schreiber or Werblin. But it was Lew Wasserman who was indisputably in control, the master of his own fate and that of half the men and women in Hollywood. For most of his adult life he and Edie had lived well but in cautious moderation. With the burgeoning triumph of MCA, they were finally prepared to splurge a little.

On June 23, 1960, the Wassermans bought a second home at 295 Hermosa Place in the resort town of Palm Springs, a two-hour Bentley ride southeast of Beverly Hills. The sleepy community tucked behind Mount San Jacinto at the edge of the Mojave Desert was a nexus for all things political, powerful, and Hollywood in the 1960s. Palm Springs was also a weekend getaway for plastic surgeons, trial lawyers, studio executives, and mafiosi.

With its understated landscaping and secluded pool area, it was a perfect location for entertaining prospective clients, presidential aides, and priapic business associates. When Universal's Milt Rackmil fell for the gift shop clerk at the Racquet Club, Lew and Edie turned over to him the keys to their new house. Eventually, Rackmil married the shop clerk, Gladys Strycker, and Lew stood up for them as a witness at their wedding. When he was away from the studio, Lew changed dramatically.

"Sundays were reserved for their inner core of friends," said Janet Leigh. "Everyone gathered for cocktails, swimming, and barbecue. This was a completely different Lew Wasserman: fun-lover, prankster, joker, throw-in-the-pooler. The brilliant executive disappeared. The shrewd, hard-bargaining wielder of power was absent; instead you knew an affable, regular guy. Edie was an invaluable partner for him. She established a rule—and God help those who broke it and faced her wrath—*no* business discussions; *no* pulling Lew aside and talking deals or getting advice. His haven was not to be disrupted."

The Wassermans were moving up, in Beverly Hills as well as in Palm Springs. In November of 1960, Lew and Edie sold their home on Sierra Drive and moved twelve blocks northwest to a new five-room home off of Sunset Boulevard. At $450,000, the floor-to-ceiling glass-and-plaster shrine at 911 North Foothill Drive was billed at the time as the most expensive single-bedroom home in Beverly Hills.[1]

"That was the only house my wife wanted, and that was [the price] the owner wanted," Wasserman explained in an interview several years later. Indeed, the previous owners who built the house had lived in it for only two years before the Wassermans made them an offer they couldn't refuse.

Five months later, to ensure their privacy, Lew and Edie bought the vacant lot next door to Billy Wilder. The house, pool, and koi pond were set back so that, out front, Edie was able to indulge her fondness for tropical plants: ferns, palms, succulents, and jungle flowers. She became such an orchid fanatic that Malibu botanist George Vasquez named a new *Phalaenopsis* hybrid for her: a cream-white bloom with a deep red throat—the Edie Wasserman orchid.

As she strove to keep up with the Schreibers, Edie's taste in art progressed from big-eyed baby portraiture to fine art, including a Vuillard self-portrait, a gouache by Degas, and Soutine's *Valet de Chambre*. A T'ang dynasty bronze horse stood next to the fireplace, a Henry Moore sculpture occupied the center of the circular driveway, and an exaggerated oil portrait of somber Lew Wasserman himself—a gift from Alfred Hitchcock—hung in the foyer.

"Lew looked like some stern-faced personification of evil in the painting," said a senior MCA executive during the sixties. "I once asked Hitch, 'Doesn't he get it?' and he just blinked at me, as if he didn't quite understand what I meant. But I'm sure he did."

Lew scanned his daily delivery of newspapers, and Edie religiously worked the *Times* crossword puzzle every morning, but the Wassermans rarely took time to read anything much deeper. Still, the wall shelves throughout the house were lined with hundreds of decorative books. Lew moved his TV sets from Sierra Drive and installed them side by side in the living room so he could continue to monitor all three networks at once. His obsession with media took him one step further when he commissioned the home's original architect, Harold Levitt, to build a bungalow across the driveway to serve as a private projection room. From his master's console at the rear of his new mini-auditorium, Lew could regulate everything from the sliding aluminum roof to the lighting to the temperature, all with the push of a button. He screened new movies for friends and family virtually every night of the week, ordering the maid always to keep bowls filled with peanuts and

---

[1] Five years earlier, Lew's brother Bill also moved up, though on a far smaller scale. He and Dora sold their one-bedroom pink stucco at 1857 South Hayworth in the Fairfax district and bought a slightly larger two-bedroom tract home at 2735 South Oakhurst Avenue, two miles west, near Culver City. The Hayworth residence was worth $15,000 at the time; the Oakhurst property was valued slightly higher, according to assessors' records.

M&M's for his guests. It was just like escaping to the movies in Cleveland, only this time Lew was in absolute control.

As had been the arrangement back on Sierra Drive, Edie got the bedroom while Lew still slept in the study. He got by on five hours' sleep and often just stayed up, talking through the night over the phone. There was no extra bedroom for Lynne, but then, the Wassermans' only daughter hadn't needed one since she graduated from high school. In 1958, Lynne had left for college in New York.

Unlike the Stein girls, Lynne had no great love for Manhattan. New York City winters confirmed for her that she was very much a California girl. She told childhood pal Maureen "Merm" Reagan that each time she bundled up to venture outside her apartment, she remembered sand and surf and summers at Santa Monica beach. But if she missed Beverly Hills, she didn't miss quarreling with her domineering mother.

"Lynne was no beauty and I think her mother thought that was a crime," said Leonora Hornblow, who had known the Wassermans since they first set foot in Beverly Hills. "The poor child was starved for affection."

While their relationship could never be described as warm, Lynne got on better with her father than she did with her mother. When he wasn't preoccupied with MCA, Lew could be attentive, even protective.

Lynne met young MCA agent Ronnie Leif after she quit school in New York and returned to Los Angeles to finish her undergraduate work at the University of Southern California. While her romance with Ronnie appeared to be a success, USC was not. She became engaged and dropped out of school again before taking her degree. "Lynne was very bright, but she never seemed to apply herself," said high school classmate Irwin Warsaw.

On July 5, 1962—her parents' twenty-sixth anniversary—amid much fanfare created by her socially conscious, socially correct mother, Lynne married the twenty-nine-year-old Leif at her parents' new Palm Springs retreat. She subsequently told her more intimate friends that it was an "arranged marriage," designed to satisfy Edie, not Lynne.

"She felt like she had to please Daddy and Mommy," said a former fiancé.

If Leif believed that marrying the boss's daughter would be some kind of coup, he was soon disappointed. In the same breath with which he congratulated his new son-in-law, Lew told him he could no longer work for MCA. It was a company rule, he explained.

"I've always said 'No relatives,'" said Jules Stein, giving his own official position on nepotism at MCA. "For every good relative you have, you get ten bums. So when Lew Wasserman's daughter, Lynne, married Ronnie Leif, he had to quit."

Leif might have pointed to Stein's brothers and sisters as glaring examples of the chairman's breathtaking hypocrisy, but instead he quietly accepted his father-in-law's help in starting his own talent agency. Contemporary Artists Management went on to serve dozens of MCA refugees over the ensuing decades, long after Bobby Kennedy had forced Lew and Jules to abandon the agency business.

—◈—

WITH THE PRESIDENTIAL election of 1960, federal antitrust prosecutor Leonard Posner had a new boss and a new problem in prosecuting MCA. The fate of Posner's two-year investigation depended upon how badly Bobby Kennedy wanted to nail Taft Schreiber, Jules Stein, and Lew Wasserman. At first blush, the new attorney general appeared to have far too many conflicts of interest to want to take on the giant talent agency…and if Kennedy's own conflicts didn't get in the way, his family's probably would.

The Kennedys of Massachusetts had a long history in Hollywood. As early as 1926, father Joe Kennedy invested part of his bootlegging fortune[2] in the Film Booking Office of America, and went on to take over Pathé-DeMille Productions and the Keith-Albee-Orpheum theater chain. At the time, Kennedy scoffed, "Look at that bunch of pants pressers in Hollywood making themselves millionaires. I could take the whole business away from them."

And he nearly did. Besides producing fifty low-budget, high-profit movies each year, Kennedy forged lifelong friendships with filmland denizens like William Randolph Hearst and movie morality czar Will Hays. At the same time, he rented a Rodeo Drive love nest for himself and Gloria Swanson, the biggest film star of her day. It mattered little to Joe that 3,000 miles away, the stoic Mrs. Rose Kennedy raised his brood and tended the mansion.

When Joe did journey east to check up on his family, he usually had a few cans of film under his arm. In the basement of their estate, Jack, Bobby, and the rest of the Kennedy clan regularly previewed father Joe's movies. The children were fascinated. Action heroes and femmes fatales hooked all the Kennedys into Hollywood's fantasyland when they were barely able to walk.

By the time the stock market crashed in 1929, Kennedy had dumped Swanson and retreated to Massachusetts. But during his Hollywood fling, he made movie history by merging three companies to form Radio-Keith-Orpheum. He sold the company to RCA's David Sarnoff for a cool $5 million, and RKO went on to

---

[2]   Mafia boss Frank Costello maintained that he and rumrunner Joe Reinfeld were Kennedy's partners in his bootlegging operation, smuggling liquor into New York and New England. With the repeal of Prohibition, Kennedy legitimized his operations as Somerset Importers and became the exclusive U.S. distributor of Haig & Haig Scotch, Gordon's Gin, Ron Rico Rum and Dewar's Scotch. During World War II, the Roosevelt administration allowed Kennedy to import Scotch whisky duty free aboard U.S. Navy ships, labeling the booze as ballast. Costello created Alliance Distributors and became exclusive distributor of House of Lords and King's Ransom Scotch. Both were in direct competition with Seagram's, Sam Bronfman's company.

become one of Hollywood's biggest production mills. While Joe never dabbled in moviemaking again, the patriarch of the Kennedy clan did retain his Hollywood contacts, visited Beverly Hills often, and encouraged his children to do the same.[3]

Thus, when John F. Kennedy was old enough, the film capital became his playground, and movie stars were his playmates. During World War II he dated Sonja Henie, June Allyson, and Gene Tierney, among others. One of his earliest and most legendary affairs involved Danish-born Inga Arvad, a Washington *Times-Herald* correspondent who migrated west to briefly substitute for gossip columnist Sheilah Graham before accepting a screenwriting job at MGM.

By the time the future president entered Congress for the first time in 1946, JFK was already a Hollywood habitué, numbering actor Walter Huston, producer Sam Spiegel, and agent-producer Charles Feldman among his West Coast pals. Whenever he needed R&R, he headed to Hollywood.

John Kennedy visited sunny California often. In the early 1950s, while she was sleeping with every Hollywood veteran from Gary Cooper to Bing Crosby, Grace Kelly found time for a tryst with the boyish JFK.[4] He also met Marilyn Monroe for the first time at one of Feldman's parties. In Hollywood, discretion never seemed as important as it did in Boston and Washington.[5] If he was feeling particularly randy, Kennedy could usually count on spending himself in southern California. The young politician's legendary appetite for big-screen bedroom conquests per-

---

[3] Joe Kennedy never completely quit Hollywood. In 1936, when Sarnoff asked him to save RKO from bankruptcy, Kennedy completely reorganized the corporation, slashed hundreds of jobs, and charged Sarnoff $150,000 for his advice. When Adolph Zukor asked him to do the same for Paramount Pictures, Kennedy charged only $50,000, but it cost William Randolph Hearst $10,000 a week to get Kennedy to overhaul his newspaper and newsreel empire.

[4] Kelly, who abdicated stardom in April of 1956 to marry Prince Rainier of Monaco, had a distinguished history of Hollywood promiscuity. MCA's Jay Kanter landed *Dial M for Murder* (1954) for her, during the filming of which she had an affair with costar Ray Milland. Though warned by Hedda Hopper that the twenty-four-year-old actress was a nymphomaniac, Bing Crosby starred opposite Grace later that same year in *The Country Girl*. During production, she slept with both male leads, William Holden, age thirty-six, and the fifty-three-year-old Crosby, just as her character did in the movie. Kelly won the 1954 Oscar for Best Actress for her portrayal of the wife of an alcoholic in *The Country Girl*.

[5] Indeed, California's Democratic National Committeeman Paul Ziffren had developed a reputation with the LAPD as a ready supplier of accommodating women for businessmen or politicians. According to one confidential police summary, "Ziffren was observed delivering two known call girls to a Tahoe gambler named Mandrel Agron in the bar of the Beverly Wilshire Hotel. Agron, a dealer at the North Shore Club at Lake Tahoe, was observed escorting the first to the room section of the hotel, and later leaving the hotel with one of the girls. It is a matter of general police knowledge that Ziffren's name appears in many of the call girl trick books which are confiscated by police when these individuals are arrested. These include the trick books taken from Carol Brandi, arrested in 1955, Paula M. McNeil, arrested 12/8/55, and Marilyn Anderson, arrested 12/8/56. Under Ziffren's phone number in each case, the word 'French' is printed. All readily admit to being in the Ziffren service department."

sisted long after he'd married, fathered a child, and won the presidential election. Brother Bobby's lust was more subdued.

"A very important and conscious part of the male Kennedy mystique is a pride in womanizing," wrote historian Garry Wills. "Only Robert broke free of this — he had other demons."

Unlike his brother, the youngest attorney general in U.S. history obeyed his head more often than his groin. Like countless movie cowboys, getting the bad guys was more important to him than getting the girl. Bobby Kennedy behaved like a man with a mission — a Puritan who had little tolerance for incompetence and venality. When he first entered the Justice Department, he had no courtroom experience, no antitrust experience, and a big score to settle with an implacable foe.

The grudge match between Bobby Kennedy and James R. Hoffa, the steel-willed president of the International Brotherhood of Teamsters, was already well known on Capitol Hill. As chief counsel in 1957–1958 for Senator John McClellan's Select Committee on Improper Activities in the Labor or Management Field, Bobby Kennedy had already carved out an image as an incorruptible Mob-buster. Though Senator McClellan offered to assign an FBI agent to him, Kennedy refused a bodyguard. Bobby saw himself as Senator Estes Kefauver's self-appointed successor and Hoffa's sworn nemesis. If he knew about long-standing links between the Mob and Hollywood, he either didn't care about them or chose to ignore them.

Meanwhile his popularity soared. *The Enemy Within*, Kennedy's 1960 account of his crusade against organized crime in organized labor, became a best-seller, and his father was able to sell the film rights to Fox chairman Spyros Skouras for $50,000.[6] In a memo dated February 13, 1961, Joe Kennedy promised Twentieth Century Fox producer Jerry Wald that Bobby would use "his good offices" at the Justice Department to help screenwriter Budd Schulberg research and develop the screenplay. Fox assigned Lester Linsk — the former MCA agent who had helped Jules Stein land Bette Davis as a client back in 1939 — to oversee script development.

Problems developed immediately. Jerry Wald reported receiving "several veiled threats and many wild telephone calls, using all kinds of language to condemn the present attorney general of the United States for his action against the Teamsters Union." The producer of *The Enemy Within* wasn't the only one to feel the heat. Fox officials began turning over their hate mail to W. Matthew Byrne in

---

[6]   Kennedy grilled Sidney Korshak at length during the McClellan hearings about Korshak's ability to negotiate sweetheart labor contracts and about his friendship with Jake "the Barber" Factor in heading off a strike at the Max Factor cosmetic plant in Hollywood. Despite the well-documented ties both men had to the Chicago Mob, Bobby did not mention Korshak or Factor in *The Enemy Within*.

the FBI's Los Angeles office. In a February 15, 1961, memo, Fox lawyer Ed
Colyer wrote:

> Yesterday I received a phone call from Ralph Clare, Business Agent of Local
> 399, Studio Transportation Drivers. Clare informed me that he had read an arti-
> cle in the *Los Angeles Herald-Express* on Monday which reported that we had
> acquired a property called *The Enemy Within* which I understand, was written by
> Robert Kennedy and deals with crooked labor unions, testimony before the
> McClellan Committee, etc., etc. Mr. Clare said that his call to me was a "cour-
> tesy call...."
>
> Clare said that he wanted to go on record that a picture of this type would cause
> unfavorable reaction within many of the labor organizations in Hollywood and
> that it would disparage labor unions in general. Clare also informed me that Bar-
> ney Balaban had personally told him that this property had been offered to Para-
> mount and that he, Balaban, had rejected it because Paramount did not wish to
> get into a controversial situation.
>
> I made no comment to Clare other than that I would bring his conversation to
> the attention of Management.
>
> Clare informs me that the only person he has talked to concerning this situa-
> tion is Jimmy Hoffa, and that Mr. Hoffa has instructed his attorney, Bennett
> Williams, to file a multimillion dollar suit if this picture is going to be made, and
> also to file an injunction to prevent its being made. He further agrees that he will
> not discuss this with anyone else including the Film Council pending hearing
> from us as to what action we are taking.
>
> I would like to alert you to the fact that not only is Ralph Clare Business Agent
> for the Teamsters but he is also the spokesman and leader for the so-called Basic
> Craft Unions which embrace Local 40, IBEW Electricians; Local 724, Laborers;
> Local 755, Plasterers; and also the Culinary Workers.

Clare had two other salient associations that Colyer failed to list in his memo.
The veteran Hollywood labor leader lunched regularly with Sidney Korshak,[7] and
at the invitation of Dr. Jules Stein, he became a founding trustee of the Hollywood
Canteen Foundation. Indeed, as the founding president of Studio Transportation
Drivers Local 399 of the Teamsters, the oldest (1930) and most powerful Teamsters
organization in Hollywood, Clare was in a position to shut down every studio in
Hollywood if he was so inclined.

If Bobby Kennedy saw potential conflict in any of this, he did not mention it
to any of his subordinates, including Leonard Posner. Neither did he see conflict

---

[7]   Korshak handled Hoffa's reservations whenever the Teamsters president stayed at the Beverly
Hills Hotel.

in hiring a bright young New York lawyer named William J. vanden Heuvel as special counsel to the Justice Department. After all, vanden Heuvel had an impeccable track record as an Ivy League lawyer and Democratic blue blood. It did not appear to matter all that much that the thirty-year-old vanden Heuvel was also Jules Stein's son-in-law.

Years earlier, in 1954, during one of their worldwide jaunts, Jules and Doris met vanden Heuvel in Bangkok, where he was an air force captain serving as an aide to retired U.S. Army General William "Wild Bill" Donovan, then ambassador to Thailand. When vanden Heuvel returned to New York, the Steins introduced him to their elder daughter, Jean, a twenty-one-year-old bohemian with a spotty but expensive European education who liked to boast that money meant little to her. When she met her future husband, she was dabbling in high-brow journalism (*Paris Review, Esquire*) and was winding up a four-year affair with Mississippi literary lion and Nobel laureate William Faulkner. By December of 1958, that affair was over and Jean was ready to settle down.

She dutifully married the cigar-smoking, Cornell-educated Roman Catholic, whose career in law and government seemed preordained. When Jules proudly gave his daughter away in an elaborate Fifth Avenue ceremony at Saint Patrick's Cathedral, vanden Heuvel had just finished a stint as special counsel to New York Governor W. Averell Harriman. Two years later, Senator Jacob Javits made vanden Heuvel a partner in his own high-powered firm, Javits, Moore and Trubin.

And then there was the issue of vanden Heuvel's politics. Jean had just made Jules and Doris grandparents for the first time when her husband became Tammany Hall's choice to run against Republican John V. Lindsay for the Seventeenth District congressional seat in midtown Manhattan. In the same 1960 election that propelled JFK into the White House, vanden Heuvel lost by a slim margin to Lindsay. Nonetheless, he had shown sufficient party loyalty to get a job offer from Bobby Kennedy.

Knowing little if any of this background, Leonard Posner prepared to take the case against MCA to his new boss. Less than three weeks after President John F. Kennedy proclaimed in his inauguration speech that the torch had been passed to a new generation, Posner's "Memorandum Regarding Alleged Antitrust Violations of MCA in the Entertainment Business" landed on Attorney General Robert Kennedy's desk. It was twenty-seven pages long, complete with a two-page table of contents, and outlined a litany of business practices, both sophisticated and sleazy, that had turned MCA into the most powerful force in show business.

"MCA uses espionage," wrote Posner. "It plants girls in typing pools to pick up information...

"To effect sales of TV shows or to get talent to sign with it, MCA has used underhanded methods involving the use of lavish gifts, whisky, girls, bribes, and lavish entertainment....

"MCA will get a buyer to sign a contract on a verbal promise to deliver Jack Benny or Harry Belafonte 'or talent of a similar calibre.' Then MCA will deliver minor talent such as Henny Youngman."

But perhaps there was no better illustration of MCA's exploitation of talent for the sake of its own greed than *Ford Startime*, Posner wrote in his memo to Bobby Kennedy. The high-brow anthology series was on and off NBC in less than a season, but during its brief life, *Ford Startime* delivered some of the most spectacular televised drama (as well as some of the worst, including Jerry Lewis at his hammiest in a wretched remake of *The Jazz Singer*) ever seen in the United States. The series featured Ingrid Bergman in her first dramatic TV role, in *The Turn of the Screw* by Henry James; Rex Harrison in a rare TV appearance; and Alec Guinness in his American TV debut. One of the first series broadcast entirely in color, *Ford Startime* used stars who would not ordinarily have agreed to appear on television. But they appeared when MCA told them to appear.

"The reason for this reduces to a simple matter of MCA's economic interests, rather than the stars'," Posner concluded.

While Ingrid Bergman could have earned $750,000 for a motion picture, her salary for *Ford Startime* topped out at $100,000. The difference in commission for MCA might seem substantial — $75,000 versus $10,000 — but its package fee for delivering stars like Bergman far outweighed any losses the agency might suffer in commissions. NBC's budget for *Startime* was $160,000 per show, and the contract called for 39 shows (12 dramas and 27 variety shows) totaling a season budget of $7.24 million. MCA's 10 percent cut as the *Ford Startime* packager was $724,000. "In such a case," Posner concluded, "MCA will blithely sacrifice Bergman's interest for its own interest."

Similarly, MCA blithely wielded a star against the networks like a blunt instrument, with or without the star's permission. If the star's interests coincided with MCA's, as they did in the case of Jack Benny, so much the better.

When Benny's CBS contract expired in 1959 and both the network and his sponsor, Lever Brothers, wanted the comedian back for another season, Sonny Werblin told them Benny would quit unless CBS and Lever Brothers launched a new detective drama called *Checkmate*. With Benny as a wedge, Werblin forced the network to take show after show from J&M Productions (for Jack and Mary, his wife), the new company MCA had created for the comedian.

Benny didn't mind being used. In an interview, he recalled, "So MCA would find these shows and we would invest J&M money in them and help get them started: *Checkmate, Ichabod and Me, The Marge and Gower Champion Show, The Gisele MacKenzie Show...*"

None of the shows had much to do with Jack Benny, but once they were lodged in the CBS schedule, Benny exchanged his J&M Productions for $2.5 million in MCA stock. Benny's own tax liability was minimized, his Sunday night show was assured of a spot on CBS through 1963, and MCA assumed responsibility for everything.

If Benny played any active role in blackmailing the network, MCA gave him no logical reason to confess it to Leonard Posner. Posner's theory that star leverage amounted to monopoly blackmail was easy to observe but difficult to prove. Some even shared the official MCA view that using star power wasn't blackmail at all.[8]

Following his defiant appearance before the Federal Communications Commission, for example, the usually silent Taft Schreiber came out swinging. In an interview in the *New York Post*, he delivered his own theory of star leverage. Everyone did it, he claimed; it was just good business.

"You talk about Jack Benny selling other shows from his company?" asked Schreiber. "Look at Warner Brothers and ABC. Never before has one company sold eight programs to one network."

If Jack Warner could do it, why not Jack Benny? Besides, all Benny and MCA were doing was allocating shows, he explained. It was no different from selling cars.

"When Ford sells cars, they *allocate*," said Schreiber. "You have to sell so many trucks with your cars or you don't become a dealer."

Posner didn't buy Schreiber's tortured analogy. Selling a TV show was not the same thing as selling a car. What Schreiber shrugged off as "allocation," Posner called extortion. He hoped that Bobby Kennedy would see it the same way.

Less than a month after submitting his twenty-seven page memo, Posner got good news. Newly appointed FCC Chairman Newton Minow had also been to see Bobby Kennedy. Minow formally asked the Justice Department to charge Schreiber with criminal contempt.

Posner smiled. Perhaps the sanctimonious Schreiber would eat his own words when Posner offered him immunity in exchange for his testimony.

And another branch of government was suddenly taking an interest in the shows that MCA "allocated" to TV too. A Senate subcommittee investigating juvenile delinquency informed Posner that it was using an MCA show, *Whispering Smith*, a short-lived western starring Audie Murphy, as a case study on TV violence. In addition, the Senate Interstate and Foreign Commerce Committee wanted to open its own investigation of MCA's monopolistic practices. While greatly encouraged by this burst of interest in the case, Posner begged the Senate committee to hold off until he'd completed his own inquiry.

On May 9, 1961, Minow delivered his famous "vast wasteland" speech to the

---

[8] The practice persists to the present day. To keep a star happy, a network will buy a show produced by the star's production company—hence NBC bought specials and series from Carson Productions to satisfy the longtime host of *The Tonight Show* and, more recently, CBS aired *The Bonnie Hunt Show* in the 1995–1996 season in large part because it was produced by David Letterman's Worldwide Pants Company.

National Association of Broadcasters, deploring rigged game shows, formula comedies, and violent westerns. Broadcasters denied Minow's allegations, but the FCC
was flooded with encouraging letters and telegrams.

Hank Brennan, a vice president of the McCann-Erickson advertising agency,
wrote confidentially to JFK's newly appointed press secretary, Pierre Salinger,
advising him that Minow didn't have to look any further than MCA for the source
of the vast wasteland. The agency's enormous power "is the basic source of much
of the mediocrity on America's TV screens," wrote Brennan. Salinger, who had
begun his Washington career as one of Bobby Kennedy's investigators, passed
Brennan's note on to his old boss at the Justice Department.

Posner took his investigation to L.A.

In one of his earliest interviews there, with a timid talent agent who had gone
head to head with Wasserman more than once, Posner felt his own spirits rise as
the agent abandoned his fear and finally opened up. There would be many more
such moments for Posner, but his bulldog face always blossomed into a grin when
he recalled what the formerly reluctant agent told him: "At least MCA hasn't been
able to get to Bobby Kennedy."

—⁓—

WHILE MAINSTREAM AMERICA paid scant attention to the MCA investigation, the
trade papers followed every degree of escalation in the war. But instead of revil-
ing the Octopus, *Daily Variety* and the *Hollywood Reporter* systematically built
the strategically silent Lew Wasserman into a potential Moses whom government
investigators impeded from leading the children of Hollywood into their
Promised Land.

"It is known the guy [Wasserman] walks around with blueprints in his head,"
wrote a business columnist for *Hollywood Close-Up* magazine. "An acute student
of facts, figures and trends and percentages, Wasserman reduces moviemaking to
the science of the slide rule."

"Lew Wasserman...the most potent single figure in show business today, is
mightily admired for his imaginative approach to taxes," wrote another in *Show
Business Illustrated*. "'Without formal legal training,' says one top theatrical lawyer,
'he knows more about taxes than any of us.' Show business contracts have jumped
from two to a hundred pages since the war, partly to accommodate the deals
devised by Mr. Wasserman."

The legend of Lew had turned Wasserman into a messiah at a time when the
original movie moguls were literally dropping dead[9] and every major studio

---

[9]   Louis B. Mayer died in 1957; Harry Cohn, 1958; Buddy Adler, 1960; Joe Schenck, 1961;
David O. Selznick, 1965.

seemed to be desperate to produce the next blockbuster. In 1961, Twentieth Century Fox had embarked on the $40 million boondoggle *Cleopatra*, and MGM followed its successful $12.5 million gamble on *Ben-Hur* with the $30 million Marlon Brando debacle, *Mutiny on the Bounty*.[10]

By contrast, Universal's *Spartacus* appeared to have saved the studio from financial ruin. *Spartacus* cost $12 million to make — $750,000 more than MCA had paid to buy the entire studio two years earlier — but the movie eventually took in more than twice that at the box office.

The company's image and its luck were both changing, but not because of Milton Rackmil. One of Lew's great strengths was that he never felt compelled to take the credit — all he demanded was the money. While Rackmil gave interviews and held press conferences to announce Universal's new efficiency, Wasserman remained where he always had been, in the background, like kindly old Frank Morgan pulling the levers from behind the curtain in *The Wizard of Oz*.

Spartacus won four Academy Awards and reestablished Universal in the public imagination as a home to much more than quickie B movies. The saga of the Roman slave turned freedom fighter also impressed the new president of the United States. The night that John F. Kennedy attended a screening in Washington, D.C., he arrived ten minutes late. To deliver the full effect of the sweeping spectacle, the theater manager made the projectionist start the three-and-a-half-hour film over again. Bobby Kennedy's brother sat through every minute and applauded at the end.

In August, Jules Stein approached Jacqueline Kennedy with an offer to lend some of his priceless antique furniture to the White House as part of her campaign to spruce up the 150-year-old presidential mansion. The offer seemed harmless enough, and the First Lady gave a tentative yes to the offer. But after a couple of Republican congressmen got wind of Stein's offer and went to the Justice Department, Lee Loevinger sensed trouble.

"I will never forget the day I called up Tish Baldridge, Jackie's friend, secretary, and chief of staff, and told her that this Stein was the head of a company we were about to sue and they shouldn't accept the furniture from him," said Loevinger.[11] "Believe me, that was something for a guy like me from the Midwest.

---

[10] On the day of President Kennedy's inauguration, Fox had already invested $6 million in *Cleopatra* and had only eleven minutes of usable film. *Ben-Hur*, the 1959 Roman spectacular starring Charlton Heston, won a record eleven Oscars and brought in more than $40 million at the box office. Brando alone took in $6 million on MGM's remake of *Mutiny on the Bounty*, the 1935 Charles Laughton–Clark Gable classic tale of a nineteenth-century mutiny in the South Seas, but the studio wound up taking in only $9.8 million at the box office.

[11] When Jackie redecorated the White House, she did choose the same wallpaper that graced Stein's basement conference room at MCA Square, however. Created in France from hundreds of hand-cut wood blocks, the wallpaper depicted important battles in American history.

The Kennedys were hard-charging and partisan people and Bobby was a tough player, but, by God, it was straight and honest."

In an August 31 memo, Loevinger asked J. Edgar Hoover to open a full-blown FBI inquiry into MCA. Nevertheless, a pall of paranoia began to hang over the MCA investigation, even as it kicked into high gear. Loevinger cautioned the FBI chief to exercise discretion: "Please do not go to NBC-TV or MCA or to any sources known to be friendly to either organization for information."

Meanwhile, from his own roster of prospective witnesses, Posner began picking up a rumor that Frank Sinatra and his Rat Pack pals—including Peter Lawford, a brother-in-law of the president and the attorney general— had already killed the MCA probe. Posner had to convince both the witnesses and his own investigators that the rumor was unfounded.

During the intensified investigation, Posner learned that MCA attempted to intimidate at least one witness. Actor Joseph Cotten was warned to watch what he said because MCA officials would receive a copy of his prospective testimony. Most witness intimidation was a complex combination of threats and promises that was far more subtle than in the Cotten case.

When an FBI agent showed up at Betty Grable's Las Vegas home on September 29, for example, the jaded blond bombshell listened politely to his request. Could she supply any information on MCA and the way the agency might have mishandled her career?

Grable thought for a moment, then lied without blinking. "I've been with them for over twenty years and never had any difficulties with MCA."

Never mind that she was currently trying to break her eight-year contract with the agency because MCA had all but abandoned her. The best she'd been able to exact from the agency that had once bowed and scraped to her was a few East Coast bookings and a standing date at the Flamingo Hotel in Las Vegas. Her motion picture career had ended years earlier, and she couldn't even get any TV exposure. Her husband, Harry James, was having the same difficulties, though MCA still got him enough one-night stands to help pay the rent.

Nevertheless, Grable told the FBI that all of her current problems were routine. She harbored no ill feelings toward MCA. She had no letters or documents relating to MCA, nor did she see much point in discussing it further. She delivered her million-dollar smile before thanking the agent for dropping by. After shutting the door, she phoned MCA, reported the FBI visit, and pointed out that she hadn't had much work lately. Four months later she made a guest appearance on MCA's *Andy Williams Show*.[12]

---

[12] Though Andy Williams himself was represented by General Amusement Corporation, his personal services company, the Barnaby Corporation, was represented by MCA. Named for Williams's dog, the Barnaby Corporation produced his TV show.

THE WEEK OF September 15, 1961, *Variety* speculated that MCA would preempt the Justice Department's investigation by spinning off Revue Productions. On the street, the rumors went even further: Revue would merge with Paramount, and Wasserman would take over Barney Balaban's job. In the media guessing game, MCA's impending date with Posner's Raiders more closely resembled a grand opportunity than a grand jury crisis.

But the speculation did not match the facts. Across the nation, Newton Minow's "vast wasteland" tattoo had taken on a life of its own. MCA's Taft Schreiber became the nation's top broadcasting bogeyman. When the MCA executive continued to resist FCC demands for MCA documents, the U.S. attorney's office sued: Schreiber would either produce the records or face a contempt fine of $1,000 and a year in jail.[13]

At the same time, the clock began ticking on the blanket waiver granted to MCA by the Screen Actors Guild and the Writers Guild. Though not officially a secret, the waiver had been effectively soft-pedaled for a decade, but in the summer of 1961, Posner's investigation made it big news. Other agencies finally realized just what kind of strategic advantage MCA had. With newly discovered indignation, they demanded equal treatment. First to call for its own waiver was General Amusement Corporation, the late Tommy Rockwell's former band agency. Next, Charles Feldman wanted one. Finally, the William Morris Agency asked to produce television and movies and be allowed to represent talent at the same time.

By October, SAG and the Writers Guild could see the trend. MCA had grown fat on its waiver. But if every agency had the same deal, why even bother to have a rule separating producers and agents? The trend had to be stopped or both guilds would effectively be surrendering to the agencies. On October 10, the guilds granted waivers to General Amusement and Feldman's Famous Artists Agency, but announced at the same time that all waivers, including MCA's, would expire as of December 1, 1961. Because Revue had been operating under its waiver for close to a decade, the Screen Actors Guild gave MCA until September 30, 1962, to choose between the talent business and television film production. In a letter to his boss, Famous Artists vice president Harry Sokolov guessed what would happen next: "It is logical to suppose that there will be a spin-off of the MCA agency business in some form or another that will legally satisfy SAG and, as well, the antitrust

---

[13] On May 24, 1965, the U.S. Supreme Court reversed the lower court's decision and found in the FCC's favor. While Chief Justice Earl Warren chided the lower court for blocking the FCC hearings, the effect of the long-delayed ruling was moot. Schreiber never testified. Belatedly the FCC won its point but lost the war.

authorities; that there will be a complete separation either in ownership or control of the MCA spin-off agency business and the remaining MCA production company — undoubtedly Revue."

As to the spin-off agency, Sokolov predicted that Wasserman would simply turn it over to loyalists like Chasin, Park, and the rest of "the boys." MCA and Revue would be separated in name only, and business would continue as usual.

It all seemed quite convenient, predictable, and orderly, but Bobby Kennedy's trustbusters had something else in mind. On November 2, Kennedy gave Loevinger permission to impanel a grand jury in Los Angeles. Two weeks later Posner called his first witness. The headline in the Tuesday, November 21, edition of the *Los Angeles Herald Examiner* read, "Talent Agency Quiz: Call 20 Stars to Testify."

Before it was over, far more than 20 stars would testify. In all, more than 150 Hollywood witnesses would be summoned, and their testimony would affect the entertainment industry as well as presidential politics for the remainder of the twentieth century.

"The government better be careful," quipped Bob Hope after the news broke. "MCA might declare war, and then they won't get any more movies or television in Washington."

Hope's producer, Jimmy Saphier, was just as flippant, though in later years his observation would seem more sober than sarcastic. "The government can't prosecute those guys," he said. "The best they can do is have the State Department make a treaty with them, like a foreign government."

TWENTY-THREE

USA v. MCA

1962

Several weeks after he began calling witnesses, Leonard Posner met at a restaurant with a nervous informant who warned him to watch his back. Wasserman and Schreiber had found leaks in the grand jury.

"You mean from witnesses who have appeared?" Posner asked, shifting his bulky frame in his chair and sizing up the intense little man who sat across from him.

"No. MCA has a means of obtaining information from the grand jury itself," the informant told him. "MCA has a reputation for penetrating other organizations. They do things like hiring cleanup personnel, and they also have a reputation for sometimes getting information from papers left in wastebaskets."

Posner found it hard to believe that an agency with MCA's clout would stoop to hiring trash pickers.

A week later, however, when Posner was about to write off the witness as paranoid, another former MCA employee reported similar skulduggery. This man refused to talk at all in a public place. He kept looking over his shoulder, even as he sat in Posner's office. He had others to think about besides himself, he explained in a low voice. Worried he might be recognized coming out of Posner's office, he wondered: Could Posner's secretary *really* be trusted?

"Don't misunderstand me," began the ex–MCA employee. "I hate MCA, and I would like to see Wasserman and Schreiber six feet under. But I'm terribly vulnerable."

In his summary of that interview, Posner wrote, "He is exceedingly scared, as he frankly admits, and he also was concerned lest eventually he might have to give evidence in an open trial. He continually begged me to remember his wife and children. He said that he can be tough and he is not afraid of being hurt himself, but he is terribly concerned about them. He was terribly concerned lest we start a suit which we might lose."

One of the MCA chief's critics told Posner that Lew's real power lay chiefly in his ability to con others into believing he was a genius. "If a particular horse won a race and paid a big price, word would get around that Wasserman had bet on that horse," Posner was told. "In fact, Wasserman probably bet on every horse in the race in order to spread the rumor that he was a genius. In the same manner, if a particular stock went up, word would immediately go around that Wasserman owned a number of shares of the stock."

———

FROM THANKSGIVING THROUGH Memorial Day, Leonard Posner spoke each morning to a captive audience of twenty-three men and women, sequestered in a room on the tenth floor of the federal building in downtown Los Angeles. The grand jury consisted of an engineer, salesmen, aerospace workers, a janitor, an heiress, housewives, and others unconnected with the movie business. All were admonished on the first day, and on every day thereafter, not to speak with anyone about the proceedings — especially not the press or anyone from MCA.

According to jury foreman John W. Hamer, a Long Beach aerospace engineer, Posner began by giving the jurors a brief history of how Stein had started his agency in Chicago, booking bands into hotels and speakeasies and gathering around him the men who would transform the talent business into a million-dollar multinational entertainment enterprise.

"He told us how Stein took Lew Wasserman like his son and developed him into a superman," juror Eddie Clayton recalled thirty-five years later. "About everybody said the man was brilliant, but he could be vicious too. People who loved him, loved him dearly, and people who were affected by his maneuvering hated him. The man was good-looking, very suave, very charismatic, but also a very vicious businessman. He hired people with charisma. I never saw one on his staff who wasn't good-looking. And they would woo people without them even knowing."

Wasserman was slick enough to seduce even an old Hollywood hand like Jack Warner, who was one of the first witnesses Posner called upon to testify. Warner detailed for the jury how his studio suffered almost from the day MCA hit town in 1938. "He told how they stole Bette Davis away from him," said Clayton.

Instead of pointing the finger at the courts for abolishing the standard seven-year contract in the 1944 de Havilland case, or for splitting up the studios and their theater chains with the 1948 Paramount Decree, Warner blamed MCA. The agency took advantage of the end of the studio system, Warner declared, and exploited stars at the expense of the studios. Despite his kvetching, Warner admitted that he remained friendly with Stein, Wasserman, and the rest of the MCA hierarchy. He had to in order to survive, he explained. That translated into hypocrisy in the eyes and ears of the grand jury. Living as he did in the lap of luxury, Jack Warner was not the government's most credible witness.

Several witnesses who followed, including former NBC president Sylvester "Pat" Weaver and CBS entertainment chief James Aubrey, parroted Warner. MCA, they said, had turned the industry on its head, with agents dictating when, where, and how a studio or a network produced its programming. MCA owned the biggest stars.

"Some of the agents used to think they were God," recalled singer Gisele MacKenzie, who briefly had her own CBS show, courtesy of MCA. "If you were having a drink or laughing with them, they used to say, 'We can make or break anybody.' They knew they could pull the strings and create a lot of careers, but also put the kibosh on a lot of careers."

"MCA controlled the sponsor, the show, the guest stars, and me," said singer Eddie Fisher, who also had his own show. When his MCA contract came up for renewal and he tried to leave, four agents cornered him in a suite at the Beverly Hills Hotel and told him, "If you leave MCA, we'll see to it that you never work again."

"The consensus was the same," said juror Eddie Clayton. "You could not play in the game if you were an artist, unless you were in bed with MCA."

Nonetheless, neither the networks nor the stars seemed to be suffering too badly from MCA's controlling methods.

Posner's witness list during the first few weeks included names better known to the public than Aubrey or Weaver but not as celebrated as the movie stars who were yet to come—names like producer David Susskind, agent Swifty Lazar, and director Alfred Hitchcock. Agent-producer Sid Luft testified on behalf of his wife, Judy Garland, who had just finished a difficult engagement at the Palace Theater in New York. Despite her triumphant reception, Garland came out with nothing, Luft grumbled. Medical bills and the high cost of living in Manhattan had left the couple broke—a fact that Luft thought Wasserman ought to have remedied by coming up with more money. The grand jury concluded that, instead of admitting that he and his wife were profligate, Luft had decided to accuse MCA of penny-pinching. This was a recurring theme throughout the closed-door hearings.

The real celebrity parade in the grand jury chambers began with Lucille Ball and Desi Arnaz. As two of the toughest producers in the business, the original ditzy redhead and her English-mangling husband were often dependent upon MCA's beneficence. While neither was prepared to accuse MCA of conspiracy, they did confirm for Posner that their Desilu Productions worked against a big handicap in having to negotiate with an agency that also happened to compete with them for prime-time slots. The unfair advantage MCA had in its cozy waiver with Screen

Actors and Writers guilds was a sour note that rang through several weeks of similar testimony from representatives of William Morris, rival producers from MCA competitors like Four Star and Danny Thomas Productions, and several other television executives.

Grand jury foreman John Hamer and deputy foreman Walter Kuencer both remembered their fellow jurors being impressed with the appearance of the two stars of *I Love Lucy*—a fact that did not escape the attention of Posner and his chief aide, John Fricano. They warned the jurors not to let their judgment be clouded by the celebrities who testified. They were just people, after all, not gods and goddesses.

"Paul Newman testified truthfully that he was the actor in the family and that his wife was always the businesswoman," said juror Clayton. "He didn't get involved with any of the MCA deals because he relied on Joanne Woodward, who I guess was in Mensa, she was so smart. It didn't matter what Newman said one way or the other, though. All the women [on the grand jury] could seem to talk about during the break was how blue his eyes were."

The grand jury got to see stars at their best—and their worst. Rosalind Russell and Audrey Hepburn shone from the witness stand, as poised and winsome as they had ever been on-screen, but a bleary-eyed Carroll Baker showed up at eight o'clock one morning, hair mussed and makeup smeared, still clad in the same black velvet dress she'd apparently worn the evening before. The jurors guessed she'd been up all night and probably remembered at the last minute that she had an appointment for a command performance at the federal building.

"Tennessee Ernie Ford really acted like a dummy, and that was surprising," said Clayton. "It was at a time when he had his own show and yet he claimed he didn't know *anything* about how the show was put together. He acted like the character he played on TV, and we all thought he was phony because you don't get to his stature without knowing how you got there."

The parade of stars continued. Most of them praised or at least seemed sympathetic with MCA and its agents. Jack Benny, Rita Hayworth, Rock Hudson, Bob Cummings, Cary Grant, and Danny Kaye all testified, soberly recounting relationships with the giant talent emporium that generally benefited them and saying nothing that could put them in a bad light, should their secret testimony wind up in the hands of Lew Wasserman.

"Tony Curtis was a pro-Wasserman man," said Clayton. "Lew loved him like he was his son, and Curtis was always very protective and loving toward him."[1]

---

[1]   As a gag, Curtis once carried business cards at the height of his stardom that said simply, "I can't make a deal." The cards listed Wasserman's name and telephone number for those who still insisted on trying to hire him.

Despite the dazzling smiles and smooth speeches of the dozens of stars who passed before their eyes, the grand jury members felt that MCA had an unholy lock on the men and women who appeared on the nation's motion picture screens and television sets. The portrait the stars painted of Lew Wasserman was a hybrid of the Pied Piper and Santa Claus: much too good to be true. He emerged as too shrewd to be a saint and too saintly to be a human. And always there was a hint of fear in the stars' praise.

Of all those who testified to Lew's purity, the MCA grand jurors remember one above all others. "Oh, yes, I remember Ronald Reagan," said foreman John Hamer. "I ran into him on the elevator, and he asked me something, and I said, 'I can't talk to you. I'm on the jury.' He looked very nervous."

On the afternoon of February 5, 1962, Ronald Reagan swore to tell the truth and took his place on the dais facing John Fricano and the twenty-three anonymous faces in the grand jury room.

"State your name and residence address," said Fricano.

"Ronald Reagan, 1669 San Onofre Drive."

"What is your profession, Mr. Reagan?"

"Actor, I think."

Reagan tried to keep the interrogation light and entertaining for the next several hours, but Fricano's questioning grew increasingly pointed. Clearly he was after a lot more than Reagan's acting credits. He wanted to know about Lew Wasserman and Taft Schreiber—Reagan's relationships that dated back a generation—and he wanted to know whether those relationships evolved into a felony in the summer of 1952. When Fricano zeroed in on the blanket waiver that Reagan helped engineer for MCA as president of the Screen Actors Guild, the actor's memory failed.

"I think I have already told you I don't recall that," said Reagan. "I don't recall."

Similarly, his memory lapsed when Fricano asked him about the 1960 actors' strike and Reagan's role in getting SAG to surrender all pre-1960 movie residuals to film library owners—including MCA. Reagan's folksy, conversational answers became convoluted, indecipherable, and finally, gibberish.

Asked why SAG extended MCA's blanket waiver in 1954, Reagan said, "All I can say, usually these negotiations and things of that kind seemed to fall in the even years, so I would have to say probably 1954, yes, this would be. To tell you of my own memory, in my mind I can tell you whether we did or not, no, I can't. Serving with Screen Actors Guild, long years of negotiation on meetings for a long time, just retaining things that happened, the lawyers' reports and then so forth, and then you find yourself in a battle like we had with the Communists or with the strikes—"

"Excuse me, sir," said Fricano. "I don't mean to interrupt you, but we would like to focus on this one question. Is your answer—I don't quite understand it, quite frankly—but is it your answer at this time you do not remember whether or not you were aware of the 1954 negotiations between SAG and MCA?"

"That's right," answered Reagan.

The grand jury soon lost count of the number of times Reagan used the words "I don't recall." Jack Warner's backbiting hypocrisy and Tony Curtis's obsequiousness began to seem almost sincere in comparison to Reagan's memory void.

"We were suspicious," Fricano told *Variety*'s Dave Robb twenty years later. "We thought that somebody had been paid off. It seemed unusual that they [MCA] were the only ones to get a waiver."

The grand jury shared Fricano's gut instinct.

"The only thing he [Reagan] knew was his name, so we didn't get too much out of him," said juror Ruth Ragle. "I just know that the whole thing smelled, but there was nothing definite you could put your finger on."

"One of the things we believed was that there was collusion with SAG," said Eddie Clayton.

"During the time Reagan was [SAG] president, he was saying how MCA convinced SAG to let them have the talent and production agency at the same time," recalled juror Bernard Jasinski. "He had all these excuses."

"Runaway" production was the culprit, not MCA, Reagan testified. If the studios hadn't increased their overseas production and if the networks hadn't concentrated production in New York, why, the Screen Actors Guild would never have granted MCA its waiver. MCA was no grasping octopus. MCA was the savior of Hollywood.

"Ronald Reagan said [the waiver] was experimental," recalled Clayton. "The actors didn't really care because they were interested in working. But then he said it was exclusive, and once MCA got in, the actors couldn't get out of it. The consensus of the jury was that Lew Wasserman paid Ronald Reagan to help him maneuver this deal."

The likely payoff was Reagan's hosting and later serving as producer of *General Electric Theater*. And perhaps there was some other form of inducement that the grand jury had not yet heard about.

The week after Reagan testified, Fricano asked the IRS for Ronald and Nancy Reagan's 1952–1955 tax returns.

———

As HE CALLED his witnesses, Posner's work came under constant review in Washington. By April 3, Lee Loevinger of the Justice Department was already convinced that the government had a strong enough case to haul MCA into court. It was just a matter of how hard to hit them.

"Wasserman flew to Washington and had a face-to-face meeting with Bobby around that time," recalled Malcolm MacArthur, one of three co-counsels assigned by Loevinger to file the antitrust suit against MCA.

During the meeting, Wasserman repeated the same argument Reagan had made behind closed doors: Hollywood was dying on the vine because of runaway production. MCA was only trying to stanch the flow of jobs to Europe and New York, and wound up getting punished for its altruism. He even held up a newspaper photo of a sign outside a Los Angeles restaurant which named MCA "loser of the month." The same newspaper carried an article about an out-of-work actor who had committed suicide. Wasserman seemed to suggest that the government, by attacking MCA, was somehow guilty of driving people to take their own lives.

Robert Kennedy scoffed at Lew's logic, according to MacArthur. The attorney general remained adamant: he would follow the recommendations of his staff and the grand jury.

Behaving like a man who sensed disaster, Lew Wasserman next delivered a preemptive strike. In an interview with Murray Schumach of the *New York Times*, Lew dazzled the reporter, leaving him, and later his readers, with the impression that he had been accorded a remarkable and rare opportunity: being ushered into the presence of a show business genius.[2] In the April 22 edition of the *Times*, Schumach painted an awe-inspired, almost worshipful portrait of the MCA president: "The name 'Lew R. Wasserman' on a movie marquee would mean nothing to moviegoers. But in Hollywood—and in the nation's entertainment industry—he is regarded with a mixture of admiration, fear and animosity that suggests Richelieu during the reign of King Louis XIII."

The Wasserman whom Schumach introduced to his readers was a sly but dead serious wizard "who chooses words as carefully as if he were on the witness stand," and who rigidly held his emotions in check, even though they obviously roiled beneath his impeccably conservative exterior. He was proud of his profession and resented the Justice Department's implication that being an agent was sleazy or deceitful.

Wasserman spoke deliberately to Schumach. "The greatest art in Hollywood," he said with cold contempt, "is just talk. I have never made a deal at a party. I can't tell you how many times clients have called me in the morning and said, 'I promised so-and-so at a party last night to do a movie for him. Please get me out of it.' When I do it, I am accused by the studio of all sorts of things. That I am favor-

---

Upon hearing of the Wasserman interview, director Billy Wilder reportedly said, "All you have to do to get a story in the *New York Times* is to take Murray Schumach to dinner at Chasen's and reach into your pocket and hand him the copy, which you have prepared in advance, and that is just about the way it appears in print."

ing another studio. That I talked the client out of doing a part he wanted to do. That I enjoy being ruthless."

In an interview he gave the *New York Post* on the heels of his session with Schumach, Lew was even more defensive about the noble calling of the agent:

> We feel that we have a fiduciary relationship with our client and it's not ethical for us to talk about his business. When you accept the basic philosophy that it's all right to function with ethics, such as a doctor or a certified public accountant or an attorney, then why condemn MCA for functioning with the same ethics?
>
> Even when it may prove embarrassing to us to remain silent, our first responsibility is to our client.
>
> They keep talking about how we "control" these stars. You can't "control" a star. Have you ever met Marlon Brando or some of these people? You can't control people like that.
>
> If there is any "control," they control us. We're not their boss, they're our boss. *They* hire us. They can fire us on one day's notice. And yet Guy Lombardo has had a contract with us for thirty years. He renewed his contract year after year. Now, why did he do it? We didn't force him. Do you think maybe he liked us? Do you think maybe we were good for him?
>
> MCA's secret formula for success is that you work hard....With all this talk about power, isn't it possible we've built a better mousetrap?

There was more than fear of the grand jury at work in Wasserman's unusual decision to grant newspaper interviews about his professional pride. That same month, Jules Stein sent a proxy statement to MCA shareholders, proclaiming his board's intent to buy Decca Records, the holding company of Universal Studios. After collecting rent from Universal for three years, MCA was about to make the inevitable move and take over Milt Rackmil's entire operation.

Even though so bold a move would make MCA a bona fide studio, with a record label and motion picture distribution arm as well as the Revue television series assembly line, Stein still hadn't decided whether to spin off the agency. "MCA has no agreement, arrangement, plan, or understanding and is conducting no discussion with respect to the disposition of its agency business," he said.

The proposed Decca takeover infused Posner's investigation with a new urgency. On June 13, Posner hurriedly finished with the grand jury, thanked the jurors for their service, and put together his final report. His staff summary of the evidence came to over 150 pages. Loevinger promised Bobby Kennedy that Posner would have a rough draft of an indictment within a week. On June 18, in their boldest repudiation of the grand jury, Stein and Wasserman thumbed their noses at the Kennedy Justice Department and bought an 80 percent controlling interest in Decca Records.[3] In one carefully orchestrated move, the world's most powerful agency and biggest television producer had become the world's largest entertainment conglomerate. The scene was set for a showdown.

—⌇∿⌇—

TEN DAYS LATER, on the afternoon of June 28, 1962, lawyers for both sides convened in Washington. Speaking on behalf of MCA, yet another high-powered Washington attorney, Whitney North Seymour, delivered a preemptive strike: There would be no need for an order from the Justice Department. MCA had decided to voluntarily spin off Dr. Stein's beloved talent agency by July 15. Though staffed by former MCA employees, the new agency would be completely separate from MCA and Revue.

Posner had gotten wind of the MCA plan weeks earlier. George Chasin, Herman Citron, Larry Barnett, Mike Levee Jr., and Jay Kanter were to inherit MCA Artists. They would have to buy it from MCA, but the price—approximately $2 million—would be loaned to them by none other than Jules Stein. From where the Justice Department sat, the "new" agency appeared as though it would be separate from MCA in name only.

"Frankly, we don't trust MCA," Loevinger told Seymour. "The conflict of interest which has long existed between MCA and Revue is outrageous and operated to the prejudice of MCA talent."

Allen Susman, Larry Beilenson's junior partner, had a ready answer. Holding to the argument that MCA was Hollywood's savior, he conceded that the agency's means might not always have been kosher, but the end result benefited all.

"MCA merely went into television production to fill a void," Susman explained. "While the conflicts were perceived, even at the time that the waiver was obtained, they did not operate to the detriment of the talent, but rather to their benefit."

Seymour crossed his arms, as if to say, "So what's the problem?"

"I can't see any evidence of criminal intent, or anything else that would lend substance to criminal charges," he said.

"MCA has engaged in block booking, tie-ins, and has held a dual role that has lent itself to conflict of interest," Loevinger shot back testily. "All these practices are a result of the power of MCA. This power is the root of the trouble."

---

[3] Having bounced back after selling off Universal City, Decca had become a very attractive stock on Wall Street by 1962, and most analysts viewed the proposed merger with bewilderment. "Decca stockholders are gaining little and giving up much under terms of the proposed exchange," reported the research department of Schweickart and Company. "Having recommended Decca stock for its earning power and potential value last October, we would advise those who made commitments on our recommendation to vote *against* the exchange."

"I've read the magazine articles that accuse MCA of tie-ins, but I haven't seen any evidence of it," said Seymour, shrugging his shoulders. "And even if it were true, how could it be considered criminal action?"

"At the very least, it's unethical," replied Loevinger.

"Well, it's wrong to use antitrust criminal laws to punish merely unethical practices," said Seymour.

"I said that they were *at the very least* unethical," said Loevinger. "These and other practices are not only unethical but illegal and may be considered in deciding whether or not we file criminal charges. It will involve a very fine and delicate matter of judgment which we're only going to be able to resolve after we confer with the attorney general, who is not going to be back to Washington until late July."

There was no point in discussing details, Loevinger added, because he had no intention of revealing Posner's grand jury findings until Bobby Kennedy had a chance to review the evidence.

"We ask this," said Seymour. "After you've made your recommendation, if you should decide to go criminally, we would want another conference. We would also want to appear before the attorney general, with the staff present, of course. It would be a tragedy to bring criminal charges without our at least having a chance to discuss it."

"How do we know you won't try to claim that we abused our grand jury investigation?" asked Loevinger.

"There will be no claim of abuse of the grand jury," Seymour promised.

The question of criminal charges would have to wait, Loevinger insisted. What about the proposed merger of MCA and Decca-Universal?

Susman grew vague. He wasn't sure whether it would be an actual merger or whether MCA would simply gobble up the studio and recording company. Whichever it was, MCA was guilty of nothing more than sound, aggressive business practices.

"A number of other motion picture companies have more assets than the combined MCA and Decca-Universal company will have," he protested. "Many of the motion picture companies now in existence have far superior assets. The new combined company, MCA-Universal, will rank low in assets and sales. Besides, the whole industry is depressed."

When asked what MCA planned to do with Universal's film library, Susman again played down its significance. Lots of other companies had far larger libraries, he said. United Artists alone controlled its own library plus that of Warner Brothers and RKO. Even with its seven hundred Paramount films, MCA-Universal would be a relatively minor player. There wasn't even that much demand for the Paramount films anymore because they'd been shown so many times that TV audiences were tired of them.

The meeting broke up stiffly, with Loevinger refusing to back off a single step from the threat of a criminal indictment and Seymour virtually begging for a meeting with Bobby Kennedy before the July 15 deadline. "Once the divestiture has been made," he promised, "MCA won't be able to tell the new talent agency what to do."

—∿∿—

SEYMOUR NEVER GOT his meeting with Kennedy, but the worst aspects of the government's case disappeared anyway. For reasons Posner never understood, Loevinger told him the decision had been made to drop the criminal indictment. They were to stick solely to forcing MCA to give up its talent agency—a decision MCA had already opted for on its own.

On July 3, Wasserman sent a three-paragraph notice to the Screen Actors Guild, surrendering MCA's agency franchise effective July 18. But the Justice Department was not satisfied. Posner's antitrust team met in a rushed session to decide how to prevent the agency from continuing to deal with itself by "giving up" representing star talent when, in reality, it was giving up nothing at all. The government lawyers decided to go ahead and sue before the agency lost its franchise.

A week later, Loevinger sent Posner's proposed complaint to Bobby Kennedy for his signature. MCA would not face criminal charges, but four of its subsidiaries—MCA Artists, MCA-TV, EMKA, and J & M Productions—were all to be named along with MCA as co-conspirators in a grand plan to monopolize the talent agency business and prime-time television. The Screen Actors and Writers guilds were also named as defendants.

In addition, Loevinger wanted MCA charged with restraint of trade for its acquisition of Decca-Universal. MCA would be barred from quitting the agency business at the same time that the Justice Department blocked them from buying Decca. Kennedy signed the complaint, along with a small squad of his antitrust attorneys.

In all, the government cited six reasons for canceling the Decca deal and keeping Wasserman's alleged co-conspirators from inheriting the agency. According to Posner, MCA had been in violation of the Sherman Act since 1938.

"Long after the investigation herein commenced, and shortly before grand jury proceedings were instituted, the government wanted MCA's agreements with SAG declared illegal," Posner said.

"Selling" the agency to its own agents was the final straw. The divestiture Wasserman proposed was a sham, argued Posner. While the new MCA Artists would supposedly be separate from MCA-Universal, it would be headed by George Chasin and Larry Barnett—two of Lew Wasserman's staunchest allies. In reality, MCA would still be negotiating for talent with itself, only now instead of just controlling television, the Octopus would own a movie studio and a recording company to boot. The Justice Department charged MCA with ongoing conspiracies and abuses of U.S. antitrust law, which could be resolved only by a true separation of its talent agency and production businesses.

On Friday the thirteenth, Posner filed suit and mailed the complaint to Wasserman, Schreiber, and Jules Stein at their home addresses. Wasserman hotly responded that the government's charges were "unjustified, unsupported and untrue."

"There's not one iota of truth to the contention MCA is not acting in complete good faith in its effort to preserve jobs for its employees," he told the ever-receptive Hollywood press corps.

Over three hundred loyal MCA employees would be out of work as a result of Posner's action, MCA's lawyers charged. "A lot of damage has been done that cannot be undone," Larry Beilenson said in trembling tones. At one point during the hearing on the matter, Beilenson's impassioned plea for a quick decision in MCA's favor produced a memorable Freudian slip. "Everybody has this wrong! It's the agent who employs the actor," he said, catching himself and correcting, "Excuse me, it's the *actor* who employs the *agent*."

Posner told the judge that Beilenson had gotten it right the first time: MCA's agents rode herd on their actors like cowpunchers on a cattle drive. He urged the judge to look deeper. Would MCA *really* turn over its agency business to its employees with absolutely no strings attached, especially in light of the fact that MCA Artists had raked in $8.4 million in commissions the previous year?

"Don't decide until you know the facts," Posner cautioned. "There is no need for a decision now as to what should be done ultimately."

By July 23, MCA and the government had reached a compromise. Both stipulated that they would make nothing public except in court. MCA had agreed in principle to everything the government demanded: no talent agency, no more packaging, no more coercive business practices.

It was clear that the only thing Wasserman wanted was a public statement that MCA had committed no criminal act or any kind of wrongdoing. An acknowledged twenty years' worth of antitrust violations were wrapped up in ten days. MCA could go ahead and buy Decca as planned, but it had twenty-four hours to quit the agency business, notify its clients, and issue a press release. MCA, the talent agency, was history. The telegram that former MCA vice president and now producer Leland Hayward received on July 23, 1962, was the same stiffly worded notification that went to more than 1,400 MCA clients, all over the world:

Dear Mr. Hayward:

Effective immediately, MCA Inc. and all of its domestic subsidiaries have surrendered or will surrender all of their guild, labor union and other franchises and licenses with respect to their talent agency functions.

MCA therefore is no longer engaged in the representation of talent in the entertainment industry and you may seek representation by anyone you desire.

MCA deeply regrets that circumstances beyond its control precluded the Company from having the opportunity to arrange this transition in a more orderly manner....

Sincerely,

Lew R. Wasserman, President

The trade paper reporters dubbed July 24 "Black Tuesday" in Hollywood. Hundreds of former MCA clients suddenly had no agent. They'd grown so dependent upon their representatives that some actors scurried to their doctors for sedatives to get them through the crisis. Their agents were even more self-absorbed.

"We all went out and had a drink," recalled Gisele MacKenzie. "And I remember some of the agents crying in their beer, saying, 'Oh, God!' and carrying on like babies."

New agencies quickly filled the void, notably Artists Agency Corporation, also known as Chasin-Park-Citron, which did exactly what Posner had predicted Chasin and Barnett would do with a spun-off MCA Artists. George Chasin, Arthur Park, and Herman Citron retained the cream of the MCA crop and continued to deal regularly, if not exclusively, with their former compatriots, now housed in the administrative headquarters of Universal Studios.[4]

With the end of the agency, several senior executives faded into retirement. Karl Kramer, George Campbell, Charles Miller, and Mickey Rockford began slowly relinquishing control to younger men, while Larry Barnett left for a top position with Chris-Craft television and Herb Rosenthal moved on to an executive position at NBC.

Others—like Chasin, Park, and Citron—remained players in the talent business. Herb Brenner teamed up with fellow MCA refugee Howard Rubin to form International Management Associates. Freddie Fields joined David Begelman to

---

[4]   The client list of the Chasin-Park-Citron Agency as of September 15, 1965, included Marlon Brando, Glenn Ford, Charlton Heston, Gene Kelly, Jack Lord, Fred MacMurray, Dean Martin, Raymond Massey, John Mills, George Peppard, Anthony Perkins, Frank Sinatra, Frank Sinatra Jr., James Stewart, Julie Andrews, Elizabeth Ashley, Anne Baxter, Jocelyn Brando, Sandra Dee, Laura Devon, Celia Kaye, Janet Leigh, Shirley MacLaine, Hayley Mills, Kathleen Nolan, Nancy Olson, Suzanne Pleshette, Donna Reed, Rosalind Russell, Eva Marie Saint, Jean Seberg, Elke Sommer, Camilla Sparv, Inger Stevens, and Stella Stevens.

create Creative Management Associates. Jerry Zeitman started a company he called simply The Agency. Harry Friedman led several former MCA agents to Ashley Steiner Famous Players. The Agency for the Performing Arts took up the slack in several MCA locations, including Miami where former MCA vice president William Beutel simply pulled down the MCA logo and replaced it with an APA sign.

"The attack on MCA is a blow that will set Hollywood back five years," whined Jaik Rosenstein in a dramatic front-page *Hollywood Close-Up* editorial. He chided the stars "who ran like rats" and did not "champion the one organization that marks the symbol of progress in the motion picture industry today....This has all the marks of a deliberate vendetta against MCA, and the Justice Department is moving into an area of which it hasn't the remotest concept, exactly as it did in block-booking, and in effect what it has done is to imperil the one organization that has the chance of preserving and maintaining film production in Hollywood in the traditional sense, instead of relinquishing complete dominance of the industry to Rome and London and Paris....The blow has been sudden and mean, and the havoc has been tremendous."

The rest of Tinseltown echoed Rosenstein's gloomy sentiments.

"I think MCA is getting a bum rap," said Warren Beatty.

"It all happened so quickly, I haven't really made any plans," said Janet Leigh.

It took Billy Wilder to see the silver lining: "Oh, isn't that marvelous! I'm going to be ten percent richer every week!"

—◦◦◦—

ONE ACTRESS WHO had been operating off and on without MCA for some time was Marilyn Monroe. Like that of Sinatra, with whom she'd had a brief fling two years earlier, Marilyn's pampered lifestyle mismatched the militant efficiency of MCA. As early as *Some Like It Hot*, shot in the autumn of 1958, MCA's platinum superstar had begun squaring off with Lew Wasserman in much the same way Betty Grable had done a decade earlier.

"I remember near the end of the movie, Lew Wasserman came to the set," said costar Tony Curtis. "And Marilyn came walking by, and Lew said, 'Hi, Marilyn. How are you doing?' And she said, 'Lousy,' and never stopped, never acknowledged him or anything else. I knew then that was the kiss of death....I knew then that she would not be with the agency long."

Marilyn remained for two more MCA packages: *Let's Make Love* (1960),[5]

---

[5]   Originally titled *The Billionaire*, the Twentieth Century Fox film was originally to have co-starred Gregory Peck. MCA's Herb Brenner and George Chasin sold a package that would have guaranteed Marilyn $200,000 plus a percentage of the gross receipts in excess of $2.5 million.

costarring French singer Yves Montand, who was represented by MCA's Paris office, and her final film, *The Misfits* (1960), which appropriately costarred three of MCA's biggest misfits—the fading fifty-nine-year-old Clark Gable, the vodka-guzzling Montgomery Clift, and the increasingly drug-dependent Marilyn Monroe. Despite the richest contract that MCA ever negotiated for her—$750,000 against 15 percent of the gross—Monroe showed up late or not at all during *The Misfits* filming, driving Clark Gable crazy. When the movie finally wrapped, Gable groused: "Christ, she didn't show up until after lunch some days. I'm glad this picture's finished. She damn near gave me a heart attack."

The following day, November 16, 1960, he did suffer a fatal heart attack.

Marilyn spent the next year in and out of mental hospitals coping with the guilt, along with the detritus of three failed marriages, two miscarriages, and the inevitability of her fading celebrity as a sex symbol.

By the spring of 1962, Marilyn Monroe was only slightly improved. But at the urging of MCA, she finally got back to work. Several months before she quarreled for the last time with Wasserman and her other MCA handlers, Twentieth Century Fox hired her to costar with Dean Martin in *Something's Got to Give*. The film was never completed and its director, George Cukor, later told author Peter Harry Brown, "She should have been in an institution instead of on a soundstage."

At the same time production got under way, her occasional "dating" of John Kennedy, which had begun at a Charlie Feldman party in 1954, blossomed into a full-blown affair. During the second year of his administration, JFK and Marilyn trysted regularly in Palm Springs, in New York, and at the Malibu beach house of actor Peter Lawford, who routinely pandered to his brother-in-law's insatiable lust.[6] One FBI report quoted an unnamed informant who said Marilyn, Lawford, the president, and the attorney general regularly participated in "sex parties which took place at the Hotel Carlisle [*sic*] in NYC."

But by far the most notorious and public display of Marilyn's affections for the president occurred during her now legendary appearance at Madison Square Garden during Kennedy's forty-fifth birthday celebration. On May 19, 1962, Marilyn sang a breathy rendition of "Happy Birthday, Mr. President." The videotaped performance, rerun thousands of times since, raised so many eyebrows that Monroe instantly became a political liability to Kennedy.

John Kennedy finally listened to his head instead of his loins. After one final coupling that evening in the Carlyle Hotel, the president cut Marilyn off cold. Just

---

After many delays, it was retitled *Let's Make Love*, and Montand became both her leading man and the latest in a long line of lovers.

[6] Angie Dickinson, another MCA starlet and an unofficial member of the Sinatra Rat Pack, has been frequently cited as yet another of the president's many Hollywood conquests, along with Sinatra ex Judith Campbell—the notorious courtesan who slept with JFK at the same time she carried on an affair with Chicago mobster Sam Giancana.

as Joe Kennedy had chosen Rose over Gloria Swanson a generation earlier, JFK stopped seeing Marilyn or even taking her calls.

But another Kennedy waited in the wings, ready to pick up where his brother had left off. According to Monroe's hairdresser, Mickey Song, on the very evening the actress sang her farewell "Happy Birthday" to JFK, Bobby Kennedy moved in backstage before the show. Song told author James Spada: "The door was open and Bobby Kennedy was pacing back and forth outside, watching us. Finally, he came into the dressing room and said to me, 'Would you step out for a minute?' When I did, he closed the door behind him, and he stayed in there for about fifteen minutes. Then he left, and I went back in. Marilyn was disheveled. She giggled and said, 'Could you help me get myself back together?'"

Later that evening, at a post-celebration invitation-only Democratic fundraiser hosted by United Artists chief Arthur Krim at his Park Avenue apartment, no less a Kennedy insider than Harvard historian Arthur Schlesinger noticed the electricity between Marilyn and the attorney general: "Bobby and I engaged in mock competition for her. She was most agreeable to him and pleasant to me — but then she receded into her own glittering mist. There was something at once magical and desperate about her. Robert Kennedy, with his curiosity, his sympathy, his absolute directness of response to distress, in some way got through the glittering mist as few did."

Over the next six weeks, Bobby frequently got through Marilyn's glittering mist — and through her bedroom door. According to dozens of accounts by housekeepers and hairdressers, journalists and FBI agents, Bobby and Marilyn carried on so torrid an affair that she forgot about JFK. Marilyn even confided to friends that Bobby planned to divorce Ethel and marry her.

Bobby seemed to spend as much time in Los Angeles as he did in Washington during the spring of 1962. The attorney general had a built-in excuse for spending so much time in L.A.: the Justice Department was wrapping up its case against MCA. Kennedy was also actively pushing Twentieth Century Fox to begin production on *The Enemy Within*. For nearly two years, novelist Budd Schulberg (*What Makes Sammy Run?*) had been developing a script, but the result was a melodrama pitting the Kennedy brothers, in white hats, against the odious Jimmy Hoffa, in a black hat — a screenplay that one critic called "a tedious, mawkish nothing." The movie was never made.

Regardless of its quality, *The Enemy Within* resonated with irony in light of Kennedy's own life and political ambitions. The planned motion picture reflected Bobby's hard-nosed opposition to organized crime at the very moment in history when his older brother was making deals with Chicago mobsters Sam Giancana and Johnny Rosselli in a top-secret CIA plot to assassinate Fidel Castro. Known as Operation Mongoose, the far-out plan to slip poisoned cigars to the Cuban dictator was only one link between the Kennedy White House and the Chicago Outfit. John Kennedy's affair with Judith Campbell was another. Marilyn Monroe was a third.

In addition to having dated Rosselli, Marilyn knew Giancana through his association with Sinatra. Marilyn frequently played footsie with mobsters as well as moguls throughout her well-documented life.[7]

Her dalliances caught up with her on June 13, when Fox fired Marilyn from *Something's Got to Give* because of her chronic absences from the set. MCA offered no support.

The romance between Bobby Kennedy and Marilyn Monroe may have burned bright, but it was short-lived. By the second week in July he had cut her off as cold as had his older brother. Phone records from both private lines in Marilyn's Brentwood home show that she attempted to get through to Kennedy at the Justice Department in Washington on at least eight different occasions during the last three weeks of her life. At one point she threatened to call a press conference to announce details of their affair if Bobby continued to refuse to talk to her.

Marilyn Monroe's last romance wound down to a tragic close. After midnight on August 5, 1962, the thirty-six-year-old actress died in what Los Angeles police called an "accidental suicide." To this day, various conspiracy theories abound.

Amid the millions of words that have been written about the mysterious final days of Marilyn Monroe, no one has dwelled on her soured relationship with Lew Wasserman and MCA. Regardless of how she died—whether by her own hand or that of another—the death of Marilyn Monroe coincided with a quick and tidy end to the MCA monopoly probe.

—⁂—

THE SAME WEEK Monroe died, orders filtered down from Bobby Kennedy's office that Leonard Posner was to wrap things up quickly. If MCA gave up its talent agency, Stein and Wasserman could proceed with the acquisition of Universal Studios.

Still, MCA quibbled over the wording of the settlement. Infuriated, Posner accused the agency of filibustering. He delivered his own ultimatum: sign the compromise or return to court. MCA begged for thirty more days to finish up agency business. After thinking about it overnight, Posner told his superiors it might be advantageous to give MCA more time. "If the judge hears all the ugly facts about MCA's practices and becomes well acquainted with the beast, and further learns of the large number of MCA acquisitions, he might well resolve any doubts…in our favor," Posner reasoned.

Regardless of what the judge might hear, the public was unlikely to learn any

---

[7]   More than two hundred books have been written about the life and death of Marilyn.

further facts about MCA. In the space of a few months, with Murray Schumach of the *New York Times* leading the pack, the nation's newspapers rehabilitated the MCA image from octopus to underdog.

The AFL Film Council, representing more than 24,000 Hollywood employees, appealed to the president and the attorney general for "sympathetic consideration" of MCA. Echoing a now familiar argument, Film Council president George Flaherty cited a "severe economic crisis confronting Hollywood labor due to runaway production." He said, "In view of these circumstances, the Hollywood AFL Film Council views with dismay and alarm the current efforts by the Antitrust Division of the Department of Justice to prohibit MCA from carrying out its plans for developing Universal Studios as a modernized and improved center of both TV and theatrical film production."

Bobby Kennedy granted MCA thirty days to finish up agency business. At the end of thirty days, he granted Wasserman's request for another thirty days. On September 18, Kennedy finally issued a two-page press release, announcing an end to the antitrust suit. MCA's sole concession was surrendering control of 215 of the 229 films in Universal's film library.[8] Under the consent agreement, MCA-Universal could acquire no new TV, movie, or recording company for seven years without Justice Department approval.

"Today's action brings about a prompt and successful conclusion to this case without the necessity for extended litigation," proclaimed Kennedy. "The result is in the best interest of the public and the industry."

Two days later MCA announced that it would raze the old Universal Studio administration building to make way for a new fifteen-story MCA world headquarters. Stein was forced to put his beloved Beverly Hills headquarters on the auction block, eventually trading it for stock in Litton Industries, a defense contractor.[9]

George Chasin told Bruce Campbell that when the Justice Department nailed MCA, Stein fought desperately to keep the agency. Had it been his choice, MCA would have jettisoned Revue in favor of representing talent. But in the end, Lew Wasserman retained control. Jules Stein's day had finally passed. "Chasin

---

[8] MCA leased 215 of the films in the Universal library to Seven Arts for ten years in a deal that MCA syndication chief Lou Friedland predicted would yield MCA between $21 million and $24 million.

[9] Four years later, Litton brought architect Paul Williams out of retirement to build a second office building in the same style as the original. Located due south of the original MCA headquarters, the new structure was three stories high with six times as much floor space. Inside, Litton overmatched Stein's ostentation, with custom-made brass chadeliers, Italian marble floors, oak-paneled walls, and hand-stitched Greek wall tapestries. The corridors and offices were dotted with over three hundred works of art from twenty-eight countries. In the courtyard, Litton constructed a public park with a two-tiered fountain featuring a bronze Italian statue of Neptune flanked by four satyrs fighting off a sea serpent and four mermaids riding horses. In 1967, Litton Chairman Charles B. "Tex" Thornton was elected to the board of MCA.

said, 'I carried him out of the office in his chair and he [Stein] was crying,'" recalled Campbell.[10]

In Chicago a savings and loan association bought the MCA building at 430 North Michigan Avenue, which Stein had acquired in the mid-1930s. It was razed to make way for a new building.[11] MCA's New York building at the northwest corner of Fifty-seventh Street and Madison Avenue remained a part of Jules Stein's personal empire, but the new MCA-Universal headquarters overseen by Lew Wasserman moved a block away, to the corner of Fifty-sixth and Park.

To friends as well as to inquisitive reporters, Leonard Posner insisted that "there was absolutely no politics involved in the termination of these [investigations]."

At the end of September, when it was all over, Lew Wasserman personally invited Posner and co-counsel Malcolm MacArthur to tour Universal Studios. Lew welcomed the two government lawyers, had them shown around the soundstages and movie sets, and took them to lunch at the commissary.

"Wasserman himself was very cordial," recalled MacArthur. "I had never met the man. He had been represented as this monumental ogre, and he certainly wasn't. I had no evidence of that. He was charming and pleasant to us."

But for all his charm, Lew made it abundantly clear to those closest to him that Posner's investigation was a bitter episode that he would never forgive or forget. Twenty years after the fact, he remained resentful. "When the government sued us for being a monopoly, it was the major surprise of my life," he said in a 1982 interview. "It was a useless, unwarranted act."

As for MCA's sworn enemy at the Justice Department, two years in Hollywood infected even as hard-bitten a government prosecutor as Leonard Posner. A month after closing out the MCA case, Posner retired from twelve years of government service and joined the Beverly Hills law firm of Zagon, Aaron and Schiff.

Posner's new career as a Hollywood lawyer ended abruptly before it began. He died on the evening of January 5, 1963. Los Angeles County Coroner Thomas Noguchi, who had performed Marilyn Monroe's autopsy just five months earlier, was suspicious enough about the circumstances surrounding his death to stamp "investigation" on his case file and turn it over to the Hall of Justice. But there was no autopsy. According to the attending physician, the attorney dropped dead at forty-seven of heart disease. The combination of a blocked artery and high blood pressure had killed him.

In one of the last official memoranda Posner wrote before leaving the Justice

---

[10] Until Lew talked him out of it, Jules planned to cut the old MCA building into twelve pieces and transport it over the Cahuenga Pass to Universal City, where it would be reconstructed opposite the Black Tower.

[11] Today the squarish building that occupies MCA's old address houses the National Association of Realtors.

Department, he left a one-paragraph warning for trustbusters who came after him: "If Wasserman gets the idea that he is another Irving Thalberg, all will be not well for MCA and Wasserman. But MCA is not accustomed to gambling. It bets on sure things and Wasserman is not interested in creative aspects; he is interested in money."

TWENTY-FOUR

Blind Ambition

1963–1964

hortly after MCA took over, Universal publicity chief David Lipton wrote a press release for his new boss. It stated simply that MCA now owned the studio. "He read it and approved it," Lipton said, "and looked at me and said, 'Do you know that this is the first press release issued at MCA?'"

Unlike the other movie moguls Lipton had dealt with, Lew Wasserman abhorred publicity. Lipton, a public relations expert with thirty years' experience in the fine art of planting stories in newspapers and magazines, spent more time on the phone trying to keep his boss's name *out* of the paper than he did getting it in. Lew didn't even want the public to know what he looked like.

"In 1959, when I first came to L.A. for Time-Life, the bureau chief told me they needed a photo of Wasserman, but none could be found," recalled former *Los Angeles Times* film critic Charles Champlin. "Reporters who got in to see him were instructed to steal one off his piano if necessary."

Indeed, there were no official pictures of Wasserman. "He wouldn't have one taken," Lipton recalled in a 1969 interview. "I had an enormous row with the head of the [Associated Press], who said, 'It's impossible. There is no corporation on the New York Stock Exchange, or a corporation of your size, that has a president who doesn't have a picture of himself.' And I had to fight that battle for a long time. To this day, those pictures of Lew Wasserman that exist are in his desk drawer, and if I want one, I have to go up to him and tell him why I want it and who wants it and what it's for. It's that sort of anonymity."

Lipton learned soon enough that his new boss cooperated with reporters only if he felt he had something to gain. And how often did that happen?

Time, which had never been able to get Wasserman to sit for an interview, was so desperate to speak with the MCA president after the Decca merger that a *Time* editor begged Screen Actors Guild president Dana Andrews to intercede on the magazine's behalf. To everyone's surprise, the actor got Lew to agree to a meeting.

"I was there with a woman reporter from *Time* and with Wasserman and his wife," Dana Andrews recalled some years later. "We sat down and had a drink, exchanged some chitchat, and after five minutes Wasserman said to the reporter, 'Well, let me tell you right off the bat that I know what this is all about. You're going to ask me a lot of questions and try to get me in a corner, and then you're going to write a big article about what kind of son of a bitch I am, and how I'm going to take over Hollywood.'

"There was a pause," said Andrews, "and then he said, 'I don't feel inclined to answer any of your questions.' The *Time* reporter never got a question out at all. Wasserman just stopped it right off the bat. He really blasted that woman, and he wanted to scare the shit out of her so that she wouldn't go through with it, which she didn't. The article never came out."

A little over a year later, however, *Time* got its revenge. The magazine that had labeled MCA "the Octopus" thirty years earlier, when it profiled Jules Stein, once again skewered MCA, but this time, writer John McPhee targeted the new master of MCA:

> [Wasserman] is a new kind of cinema king. He doesn't wear smoked glasses, carry a bull whip and snap orders over his manicurist's shoulder like the major bosses of old. And of course he is not one of the modern independents who incubate their eggs in other people's nests. Wasserman is a corporate president in show business, a modified First National City banker who has wandered through an unusual door, and he has shaped MCA into a trimly efficient manufacturing corporation, ample in size, and self-sufficient, whose net earnings have risen without setback from $7.2 million in 1959 to $13.6 million in 1963 — and 1964 is well ahead of last year.

True to his promise, Wasserman had continued to refuse to speak to *Time*, but McPhee found other sources of information, including Tony Curtis. "As long as I've known Lew, everybody's been frightened of him," Curtis told him, but he went on to say, "He has a genius for what people like. He wouldn't make a boring picture, like what I call *Breakfast at Nuremberg*."

For the most part, those McPhee spoke with about Lew were complimentary. Yet despite a two-page spread that most would have described as glowing, Wasserman was furious. Not only did *Time* rehash MCA's long-running war with the Justice Department, but it also revealed a closely guarded secret: "Mrs. Wasserman sleeps in the bedroom," McPhee wrote. "Wasserman sleeps on a couch in the study where he gets up at five each morning and starts making phone calls to breakfasting subordinates in New York." Those two sentences became the talk of

Hollywood. Now the whole world knew what only a handful of Wasserman's closest associates had been privy to — that Lew and Edie did not sleep together.

The Wassermans ended their friendship with Curtis, though Tony always assumed that the falling-out was a result of his 1962 divorce from Janet Leigh,[1] who remains an intimate of the Wassermans to the present day. Nevertheless, long after the Wassermans froze him out Curtis continued to sing Lew's praises.

"Losing my friendship with Lew has always been one of my great regrets," Curtis said thirty-five years later. "I see him out at restaurants or industry functions, and he's perfectly cordial. I gave him a beautiful painting of mine once and I got a nice note back from him, but I never get invited to the house. That's all right, though. Life is like that. You can't make an omelette without breaking an egg."

HIS TUSSLES WITH *Time* aside, Lew felt congenial enough at the beginning of 1963 to grant several interviews to handpicked newspapers. Wasserman had all of the reporters screened to make sure they were not planning a hatchet job or working on a hidden agenda. Only then did he issue invitations. Lew, the former press agent from Playhouse Square, had his own publicity agenda: to reintroduce the new MCA-Universal-Decca conglomerate as the logical savior of show business.

Wasserman invariably began by putting interviewers at ease. A reporter from the *New York Post* started out by asking how much MCA was worth, and Lew glanced at his copy of the *Wall Street Journal*, then answered whimsically, "I don't know. I haven't read the paper yet."

Likewise, Lew started his interview with Associated Press reporter Bob Thomas by announcing how unimportant he really was in the grand scheme of things. "I'm a paper pusher," Wasserman began.

Then why, Thomas asked, was his desk spotless at nine o'clock in the morning?

"Oh, I've already pushed all the papers."

Wasserman admitted that his associates believed he didn't spend enough time in the office, while his wife groused that he spent too much. Lew didn't deny that Hollywood *was* his life. He breathed, ate, and drank movies. Even at home and at his weekend retreat in Palm Springs, Lew couldn't relax without watching the latest feature.

"You can never see all the film you need to in this business," he told Thomas, before launching into a speech about the state of the industry. He spoke thought-

---

[1] Curtis left Leigh after becoming involved with seventeen-year-old actress Christine Kaufmann during the filming of the costume epic *Taras Bulba* (1962). Though a repentant Curtis flew home from Europe to patch things up with Leigh, their marriage ultimately failed and Kaufmann became the second Mrs. Tony Curtis.

fully, as if he'd delivered this lecture many times before. During the interview, Universal's new leader behaved more like a conquering hero than an ex-agent who had just had his wrist slapped by the Justice Department. Striking a professorial pose, he pontificated,

> History has shown that entertainment mediums go through tough periods when a new medium is introduced. When the movies became popular, many people said it was the end of live entertainment. But it has survived.
>
> Radio was supposed to have killed the record business, but it is doing better than ever. Television looked like the death of radio. But the radio stations have gone through a change of operation, and I saw recently that two local stations sold for more than $10 million each.
>
> The movie business has been adjusting to the changes that were brought by the challenge of television. We have had to change our methods of production and of exhibition.

The answer to all this media mayhem, Wasserman suggested, would be MCA's modern, slick, and efficient Universal City.

Universal instituted a 20 percent overhead fee on all independent productions shot on the lot—10 percent higher than that charged by any other studio. But independents like Stanley Kramer gladly paid the premium because the studio's well-tuned efficiency more than made up the extra cost. In less than half the time it took for principal photography at other studios, filmmakers were in and out of one of Wasserman's thirteen new soundstages. Lew promised to bring that kind of efficiency to the entire entertainment industry.

Universal would meld all media into a single driving force, he prophesied. It would end the scourge of foreign film production by bringing the movies back to Hollywood where they belonged. Wasserman's troops would work smarter, more effectively, and more energetically than their rivals overseas: "Foreign competition in movies is no different from that faced by any other American industry. The auto industry wasn't worried when foreign cars came into the American market; it went on making the same kind of car. Obviously the automakers misjudged the market. They realized it and started making compacts. The result is that there is only one important foreign car in this country—Volkswagen, which fills a certain need."

The analogy ended there. If Wasserman's master plan involved Universal cranking out the feature-film equivalent of the Volkswagen, he didn't volunteer the information or the irony. He did say that Universal would make its movies in California, not Europe or New York. And MCA would see to it that those movies were made on schedule, profitably, and within a tightly controlled budget.

On the other hand, movies cost a lot to make. At Universal, he vowed, logic would prevail.

The new Universal Studios *definitely* did not run on emotion, though some would have argued that the pressure was very much intact—particularly when it came to money. Under Wasserman, studio accountants could undercut almost any director's authority. A soundman could cut a scene that went on too long and wasted valuable film stock. Spies were everywhere. The studio might shave a little here and fudge a little there, but nobody cheated the studio.

"We're guilty," Lew said defiantly. "If we're accused of running our company as a business should be run, we're guilty. We think it is a business."

It was the frills and fringes that were killing Hollywood, argued Lew, not big-budget features and high-priced actors. The fabulous salaries commanded by an Elizabeth Taylor or a John Wayne would not be paid if the studios didn't earn the money back, plus profit, at the box office.

As for developing new stars, Wasserman planned a giant step backward. By opening a New Talent division that would bring along young actors at low contract salaries, MCA reinstituted the very studio system that Lew had helped topple in the 1940s while he was still an agent. Even the old seven-year slave contract that Wasserman had helped destroy was reinvented. "We have more than one hundred players under contract. That's more than all the other studios put together," he said. "Universal has had success in developing talent like Rock Hudson, Tony Curtis, Sandra Dee, and Ross Hunter. We'll continue that policy. We'll not merely run a school for new actors; we'll put them to work in our television shows, so they can gain real experience."

Almost limitless acting experience could be gained in TV. Clint Eastwood, Burt Reynolds, James Brolin, James Caan, Carrie Snodgress, and Katharine Ross all began their careers as Universal contract players, appearing on TV as often as film.

Even more than its higher-profile movie division, Universal Television represented assembly-line efficiency. In its annual report, MCA boasted, "If your family watched television fifteen hours a day for one full year, they still would not see all the 5,840 hours of filmed programming distributed annually by MCA-TV Ltd."

But assembly-line entertainment resembled just that: formula drama and cookie-cutter comedy. Looking back on the 1960s, television historian Robert J. Thompson would observe, "The assembly line nature of television production, which leads so many people to ignore the medium as a potential locus of serious artistic achievement, was epitomized by Universal."

The one exception was *Bob Hope Presents the Chrysler Theater*.[2] Like *Ford Startime*, the hour-long NBC dramatic anthology, which ran from 1963 through

---

[2]   The series brought such classics to TV as Aleksandr Solzhenitzyn's *One Day in the Life of Ivan Denisovich*; *The Seven Little Foys*, starring Mickey Rooney and the Osmond Brothers; and *Double Jeopardy*, with a rare television appearance by Lauren Bacall.

1967, was designed "to move the quality level perception of the company forward," according to MCA-TV executive Jerry Adler. As such, cost was to be no object… but with Lew involved, cost was always important.

"He promised NBC the moon," said Adler. "Then, every month when production cost reports came out, Lew used to call me and ream me out. It was a very expensive series, and we *always* went over budget. And I would listen to him and think, You son of a bitch. You *knew* you couldn't do it cheap. And now you're chewing *me* out for a deal *you* made?"

Jennings Lang was Wasserman's wonder boy — a perfect executive for the new Universal. He found ways to use the same set over and over again in different movies or TV shows, and he developed a reputation for turning the worst disasters into gold.

When Academy Award winner Ernest Borgnine made a pilot about a naval commander in the South Seas during World War II, based on a script from an *Alcoa Premiere* drama, the acting was so wretched that the MCA men who first screened it laughed out loud. What was supposed to be a serious study of the conflicts sailors face at sea came out as a farce in the hands of producer Eddie Montagne, who also produced *The Phil Silvers Show (Sergeant Bilko)*. Instead of shelving the film, Lang's TV division repackaged it and sold it as a sitcom. "McHale's Men" became *McHale's Navy*, one of the most popular series of the 1960s.[3]

"In his own way, Jennings Lang was a genius," said Jerry Adler, a rising 1960s MCA executive who helped shepherd *McHale's Navy* and dozens of other series to prime time. As MCA stepped up its television assembly line, Lew Wasserman publicly defended Lang and Universal TV's every move.

As for the creative raw material for MCA's new TV-movie-record production line, Wasserman planned to raid Broadway. To help feed MCA's assembly line in Hollywood, MCA would begin underwriting New York plays, Wasserman declared, just as the agency once had done for Leland Hayward with *State of the Union, Mister Roberts*, and his other productions. "We are not interested in financing plays just to make money out of their Broadway runs," Wasserman said. "Of course, if the plays make money, we won't object. But what we are primarily interested in when we finance shows is the ultimate acquisition of basic rights for motion pictures, television, and records."

Reaction from Broadway was swift and sour. MCA represented only the latest in a long line of jackals who had no imagination of their own, so they had to feed

---

[3]   *McHale's Navy* was also one of the cheapest, shot entirely on location in a shallow lagoon on the Universal backlot. Rather than pay for footage of the open sea, *McHale's* producers reused footage from *Operation Petticoat*. Cary Grant noticed, demanded a usage fee, and forced Universal to pay him a percentage every time *McHale's Navy* aired.

off those who did. Snarled David Merrick, the venerable producer of *Look Back in Anger*, *The World of Suzie Wong*, *Gypsy*, and dozens of other Broadway shows, "Lew Wasserman, the head of MCA, continues to be a monopolist at heart. If by some miracle such a plan [as MCA's] is fully carried through, it would result in the same set of conditions for which the Justice Department forced MCA into a consent decree. That Hollywood bunch think they can use Broadway as a laboratory for their films, or they think they can buy their way into the theater."

Wasserman didn't trust his own judgment, said Merrick. Thornton Wilder's play *The Matchmaker* was on the market for seventeen years and could have been snapped up by Hollywood "for practically nothing," but the film rights finally sold for $250,000 after it proved a hit on Broadway.[4] Wasserman was just another Hollywood thief, trying a new ploy to buy hit stories cheap and exploit them. It would not work, predicted Merrick.

"Hollywood could have bought *Irma la Douce* for as little as $25,000 after it opened in Paris. But they paid me around $300,000 for the film rights after I produced it for the stage," he said. "Ultimately, it's the material that counts and not the financing."

ON JULY 9, 1963, Jules Stein donned a hard hat, pushed a shovel into the dirt, and broke ground for a new Universal City Plaza adjacent to a massive fourteen-story MCA Tower, which would become the world headquarters for MCA Inc. Master of Ceremonies Jack Benny mugged to the crowd, "I have a feeling this whole thing will turn out as a pilot for a new series for Revue."

Speaking publicly for the first time in his career about the new era dawning in show business, Stein called the event "the golden rivet ceremony." Following brief remarks by other senior MCA executives, polite applause, and photos, the sixty-seven-year-old chairman of the board of MCA Inc. turned his shovel over to his silent protégé. MCA President Lew Wasserman then signaled the construction crews to begin bulldozing.

"There are now about one million people living in the [San Fernando] Valley," Wasserman told *Forbes* magazine. "It's the seventh-largest 'city' in the U.S. Yet it doesn't have a single hotel or a high-rise office building."

MCA was about to change all of that. In the saddle of the Cahuenga Pass, straddling the hills between Hollywood and Studio City, Universal City underwent a renaissance that was at least as much about cashing in on the booming California real estate market as it was about making movies.

---

[4]   *The Matchmaker* was resurrected as a musical in 1964 and renamed *Hello, Dolly!*, one of the biggest hit musicals of all time.

While other studios were selling off their property, Universal was buying. Universal was "my Erector set," said Wasserman. "We now have 450 acres, having acquired a driving range from Bob Hope on the other side of the studio. We intend to develop 200 acres. That will still leave us with the biggest studio in the world."

If Wasserman did sell any part of his growing empire, it was only at a premium price, which he could reinvest at a profit. When neighboring Forest Lawn mortuary desperately needed 40 acres on the Universal back lot to expand its cemetery, MCA obliged and used the equity to buy even more land along the Cahuenga corridor as a buffer against residential development butting up against the bustling Universal City. At 410 acres, Universal was still 40 acres larger than the principality of Monaco.

Bolstered by two $25 million lines of credit—one from First National Bank of Chicago and the other from Bank of America—MCA was at the beginning of a five-year building spree that would utterly alter the face of Universal City.[5] To make way for eight new soundstages, Wasserman persuaded the state of California to use taxpayers' bulldozers to level a small mountain. Then the California Highway Department bought 650,000 cubic yards of the dirt from MCA as fill for its extension of the Hollywood Freeway across the San Fernando Valley. MCA got an off-ramp leading directly to Universal City and a new parking lot to boot.[6]

At Stein's urging, MCA also began diversifying. In 1962, over Lew's objections, Stein bought Columbia Savings, a small ($62 million) savings and loan association in Denver. Stein persuaded Jack Benny to open a new branch and to star in a series of regional TV commercials to coax prudent Coloradans to do as Jack did: keep their nest eggs in Columbia.

The diversification trend would continue through the rest of the decade, with MCA's purchase of Danelectro Corporation, a New Jersey electric guitar company, in 1966; Gauss Electrophysics and Saki Magnetics,[7] makers of high-speed tape recorder components, in 1967; and Spencer Gifts, a nationwide mail-order and hotel gift shop operation specializing in novelty items, in 1968.

At Universal City, MCA's bullish outlook could be measured by the number of its new soundstages, bringing Universal's total to thirty-six. Lew kept them all busy, approving budgets for fourteen new Universal films in 1963—more than any

---

[5] The credit lines were unsecured until 1971, when Federal Reserve officials pointed out that a federally insured bank had to secure such a huge loan. According to FNBC's Weston Whiteman, MCA solved the problem by using its library of old Revue TV shows as collateral. One of the first directors Stein and Wasserman named to MCA's new board of directors was FNBC director Walter M. Heymann, an old friend from Stein's band-booking days.

[6] In one of his final acts before leaving office in 1982, California Governor Jerry Brown approved a $4 million Hollywood Freeway overpass leading directly to the western entrance of Universal Studios.

[7] Gauss and Saki were consolidated and became MCA Technology in 1970.

other studio. The following year, the slate jumped to twenty-five. In addition to soundstages, MCA got new wardrobe buildings, color labs, cutting rooms, a power station, and a 250-seat commissary.

The old Universal commissary, overseen by Bill Goetz's personal chef, had long been acclaimed for serving the best food on any studio lot in Hollywood. Some even quipped that the commissary's apple cake was the best thing that the venerable old studio ever produced. But that commissary was also losing $100,000 a year. MCA executive Al Dorskind wanted to replace it with a cafeteria, but Milt Rackmil told Wasserman that movie stars wouldn't eat lunch in a cafeteria. While no longer the power at Universal, Rackmil still held the title of MCA vice chairman, so he technically outranked Wasserman in the executive pecking order. His comments could not be ignored. No cafeteria, Dorskind was told.

One Saturday, Dorskind stopped at the Farmers Market, where he saw tourists filing out of a Gray Line tour bus to get lunch after a hard morning of strolling down Hollywood Boulevard and trying to fit their hands into the star prints at Grauman's Chinese Theater. It hit Dorskind: why not bring the tour buses through the Universal lot and have them stop at the commissary for lunch? Universal could boost prices 20 percent, keep the commissary busy throughout the day, and charge the bus company a dollar a head in the bargain. He called Gray Line Tours, Universal became a stop on its Hollywood excursion, and the commissary turned into yet another MCA moneymaker.

Wasserman's only proviso was that Dorskind fit half the commissary with 150 quick-service seats so that Universal's three thousand employees could get in and out in a hurry. Mornings were for working, he said, not coffee breaks.

—◦◦◦—

JUMPING THROUGH HOOPS to get the Kennedys' attention during the antitrust investigation had left Lew determined never to be without pull in Washington again. Within a year of the agency bust-up, Wasserman had established himself as one of the Democratic Party's chief contributors. He also sought the counsel of attorney Ed Weisl, who arranged MCA's purchase of the Paramount library and ran interference for Wasserman in Washington during the antitrust investigation. A ranking adviser to the Democratic National Committee, Weisl suggested that Wasserman throw a fund-raiser for West Coast high rollers to gather support for John F. Kennedy's 1964 reelection campaign.

On June 7, 1963, Lew and National General Theaters owner Gene Klein cohosted a $1,000-a-plate dinner for President Kennedy at the Beverly Hilton Hotel, inviting southern California businessmen and industrialists whose access to the president had been limited at best. Lew was credited with using his gift for star exploitation to invent a gimmick called the eleventh chair: the president moved from table to table throughout the dinner, eating a different course at each table. Thus each person present was given a chance to dine with the commander in chief.

Aided by Arthur Krim, chairman of United Artists, and attorney Paul Ziffren, whom the media had referred to as the Democrats' "man of mystery" during the 1960 presidential campaign, Lew came up with an additional gimmick called the President's Club, which gave businessmen increased access to the president in exchange for sustained contributions to his campaign coffers. A $1,000 contribution guaranteed each club member a gold-engraved membership card, invitations to cabinet briefings and to the annual dinner, and — most important of all — cachet. Auto salesmen, aerospace entrepreneurs, and Hollywood agents were now able to talk about the night they dined with Kennedy. At a time when JFK was still mopping up the deficit from his 1960 campaign, the instant success of the President's Club made Wasserman a hero to the Kennedy administration.

Lew also came up with a plan for Kennedy to help raise money for a new National Cultural Center in Washington D.C.[8] One Monday evening each year, every theater, movie house, nightclub, and concert venue in America was to contribute its gross for that evening to the center. Cultural Center Night helped cement Lew's position as the Kennedys' point man on the West Coast and provided some seed money for the center.

If Bobby Kennedy felt any vestige of animosity toward MCA, it was erased with his older brother's assassination in November of 1963. Though he stayed on another year as LBJ's attorney general, he did nothing further to hold MCA in check.

Bobby Kennedy and the Justice Department's Antitrust Division were no longer a consideration in the MCA master plan. Following JFK's assassination, Wasserman immediately switched his allegiance to LBJ, who had an entirely different attitude toward big business.

Ed Weisl, who was far closer to LBJ than he ever was to the Kennedys, had an autographed photo of President Johnson sent to Lew with a note from LBJ reading: "We are grateful for your help now as we were in 1960." Jack Valenti, a Dallas PR man who ingratiated himself with Johnson and landed the post of Special Assistant in the new administration, called Weisl "probably the closest confidant of Lyndon Johnson," with ties dating back to the 1930s, when FDR's secretary of commerce, Harry Hopkins, introduced Weisl to newly elected Representative Lyndon Johnson.

"Weisl took the young congressman in hand, and from that day forward no one held a more intimate grip on the president's affections and needs," said Valenti.

Except for Larry Beilenson and Sidney Korshak, no lawyer held a tighter grip

---

[8]   It was renamed the Kennedy Center for the Performing Arts after JFK's assassination. Lew became a founding director as well as a trustee of the John F. Kennedy Library in Boston.

on Wasserman's loyalty and affections, either. Lew had come to rely on Weisl for much of his political string-pulling. He also depended on Cyrus Vance, another bright young attorney in Weisl's firm who first impressed Wasserman when he joined Weisl in defending MCA against the government's antitrust threats. As everyone from Ronald Reagan to Tony Curtis could testify, Lew was not easily impressed, and he never forgot.

Through Weisl, LBJ asked Lew to continue the annual Democratic Party fund-raising ritual at the Beverly Hilton. The President's Club Dinner established Lew and Arthur Krim as Hollywood's two premier political fund-raisers. Gaunt, stringbean Lew Wasserman and squat, round Arthur Krim made one of the oddest of Hollywood's many odd couples, but nobody laughed at them when they showed up together at Democratic functions.

"Wasserman was one of the first to realize that Hollywood could have clout in government," remarked Sam Goldwyn Jr. "He said, 'We can be an influence — but don't kid yourself, it means patronage.'"

While he was always gracious to the MCA chairman of the board, LBJ's closest and most enduring bond was with the company president. With Lyndon and Lady Bird, Lew and Edie first experienced the emotional surge of presidential preference. They traveled by helicopter from the White House to Camp David, visited the president and first lady often at their ranch east of Austin in the Texas hill country, and could get through the gauntlet to the Oval Office, either by phone or in person, in seconds.

A free exchange of jobs developed between the White House and MCA. When Assistant Secretary of State Fred Dutton wanted to quit government and get into the movie industry, White House press aide Bill Moyers recommended him to Lew Wasserman. Lew could ring up Moyers or Valenti and tell him that Milt Rackmil's wife and children were on their way to Washington and needed a VIP tour of the White House, Congress, and the FBI.

"Hollywood and Washington are like Troy," observed one bicoastal lobbyist, familiar with the pecking order in both cities. "You can't get in without a horse."

Valenti was an even greater pal of Lew and Edie than the president was. He frequently accepted their invitation to use the Wassermans' Palm Springs home as a getaway when he came to California.

"Wasserman had that quickness of thought and that curious anticipatory instinct that is the baggage of the great political and industrial captains," Valenti effused in his memoirs. "He spoke quietly and seldom, but when he did speak, everyone in the movie world listened. I was impressed by him, by both his intellect and by his exposition of what lay ahead in the international film marketplace."

In his first memo to the newly reelected president, dated November 10, 1964, Valenti recommended nine men for the new cabinet, including "Lew Wasserman: President of Music Corporation of America. Independently wealthy. Ed Weisl called him 'the best business brain I have ever known.' Brilliant organizer and administrator. Tough, smart, full of common sense. Goes to heart of problems — practitioner of the art of the possible. A 'can-do' man who could work miracles, if anyone could, as Secretary in a Department like HEW."

Lew turned down Johnson's invitation to join the cabinet and instead persuaded Valenti to become president of the Motion Picture Association of America. In the spring of 1966 Valenti quit the administration to lead the Washington lobby of the movie industry, which had been without a president for two years. Valenti landed *the* plum career post: a Hollywood executive's job in Washington, D.C., with an additional office in New York.[9]

"Wasserman had convinced me that the presidency of the MPAA would give me spacious opportunity to continue my interest in global politics and international affairs," said Valenti. He joined the MPAA on April 25, 1966. Upon Valenti's departure from the White House, LBJ wrote to him: "I thank you and love you and am very proud of you."

---

[9]   Trial attorney Louis Nizer acted as MPAA co-president for a short time, but he resigned within a few months.

TWENTY-FIVE

Universal Studios Tour

1965–1966

arl Laemmle abandoned the original Universal Studios tour in the early 1920s. His dime-a-head bus rides past Universal movie sets had become so popular that guiding, feeding, and policing hordes of tourists cost more than what Laemmle figured he could charge for admission.

Like Lew Wasserman, Laemmle was penny-wise. As one of many ingenious ways of subsidizing his studio operation, the original owner of the Universal Studios and chicken ranch sold eggs to his stagehands. Thrifty Laemmle also housed a herd of horses at Universal for his stampede scenes. When one of them came up lame, he'd have it shot, then fed to the mangy pack of lions that he kept caged next to his jungle serial set.

In 1964 the Universal back lot still contained dozens of those original movie sets. There were the spooky castles where *Dracula* (1931) and *Frankenstein* (1931) first roamed; the lake where the vessel from *Show Boat* (1929) now occupied a berth near the ships used in *McHale's Navy*; the stage where the original *Phantom of the Opera* (1925) sent a massive chandelier crashing into the audience; and the battlefield where the Germans lost World War I but won Universal its first Best Picture Academy Award for *All Quiet on the Western Front* (1930).

Studio manager Al Dorskind suggested that tours of these movie sets and others could be profitable as well as great public relations. "If they come to see our studio, they're more likely to watch the shows we produce here," he told Wasserman at the time. "Also, it helps the studio commissary. The tourists eat there, and it increases the turnover."

On July 4, 1964, MCA officially inaugurated its Universal Studios Tour. For $3.50 a head, visitors got to explore the same prop rooms that had fascinated Jules Stein in 1958 when he was trying to decide whether to buy the studio. In addition to fake boulders, the pyrotechnics of western shoot-'em-ups, and the feats of stunt-

321

men, Universal visitors got to see such marvelous MCA inventions as rubber grass that could be rolled over a parking lot to create an instant meadow; rubber dirt over paved streets to give them an Old West look; and rubber bricks that would bounce off actors' heads like rectangular Nerf balls.

The stars were the biggest attraction, however, and MCA executives encouraged their actors to show up smiling for the fans as often as possible. Cary Grant used to hide behind his bungalow until the trams passed before sneaking into the commissary, but wise tram drivers began doubling back whenever some sharp-eyed tourist caught a glimpse of the elusive actor. He was mobbed every time.

By far the most popular early attraction on the tour was the brainchild of MCA's Herb Steinberg, a former Paramount press agent who came to be a favorite of Edie Wasserman. Steinberg suggested that Hollywood makeup artist Perc Westmore—a veteran who had rouged and pancaked actors in over one hundred movies since 1930—give tourists an inside look at how actors became mutants, monsters, and magnificent beauties.

As Perc's younger brother Frank recalled, "On July 15, 1964, in the basement of the newly opened Universal commissary, Perc, resplendent in his trademark clothes of white jacket, white pants, and white shoes, began his twice-a-day lectures and makeup demonstrations."

"It was like plasma," recalled Frank Westmore. "He loved the exposure, the adulation of the crowd, the joy of being 'on.' He was an instant success."

And so was the Universal Studios Tour. One of the first to take the tour was an eighteen-year-old senior from Saratoga High in northern California. Steven Spielberg liked what he saw so much that he wheedled his way onto the Universal lot during summer vacations beginning in 1964 and apprenticed himself to Universal Television librarian Chuck Silvers and purchasing agent Julie Raymond. Years later Spielberg began reconstructing his own myth in much the same way Louis Wasserman re-created himself. While Spielberg did not change his name, he did change his birth date by a year—from December 18, 1946, to December 18, 1947[1]—and he spun the story that he got past Universal security by wearing the MCA uniform of suit and tie, carrying a briefcase, and setting up his own office in a vacant bungalow. He even claimed to have spelled out his name in plastic letters on the building's directory. "That's a bunch of horseshit," Julie Raymond told Spielberg biographer Joseph McBride.

In reality, Spielberg took the tour like everybody else, but found a way to stay behind, by fetching coffee, filing purchase orders, and running errands for free. It

---

[1] According to a former business partner who sued Spielberg over film profits, the director changed his birth date to invalidate a contract that he had signed. Spielberg's attorney maintained that the contract was no good because Spielberg had signed it before he turned twenty-one and could legally do so.

took him five years, two student films, and countless errands to land his first direct-ing assignment—a segment in the 1969 pilot film for the Universal-TV sci-fi hor-ror series *Night Gallery*.

While Spielberg paid his dues on the dull side of the studio routine, the tours continued to thrill those who wanted to visit Lew Wasserman's empire for only a few hours. Herb Steinberg put out the word in the spring of 1965 that the new attraction had grown so quickly that Universal would hire ten new tour guides: five young men and five young women. The jobs were nonunion. The pay was only $250 for the entire summer and the guides were expected to work six days a week, sometimes up to fourteen hours a day. Nonetheless, a studio tour guide's position promised to be high-profile entrée into show biz. Steinberg's office was swamped with applications.

One of the kids, a high school senior who had played Little League with Steinberg's son in Van Nuys years earlier, was among the applicants, and he sought special consideration. He was going to the University of California at Santa Bar-bara the following autumn and could have used a better paying job, but he was not dissuaded. He really wanted to work at Universal. It was the same kind of low-pay, high-energy dedication that Lew had once demanded of his mail room trainees back at MCA Artists.

On June 21, 1965, the nineteen-year-old landed one of the ten coveted spots. Michael Steven Ovitz, eldest son of a former Chicago sales rep for Seagram's Liquor, was officially a Universal Studios Tour guide.

———

LEW MIGHT HAVE had a public image as a visionary movie mystic, but in the upper reaches of the Black Tower, his subordinates began to have their doubts. In addi-tion to his initial reluctance to green-light the studio tours, he seemed to know nothing about MCA's very namesake: music. One of the great ironies of MCA is that the company that virtually created Big Bands and ushered in the modern pop music era completely missed the birth of rock 'n' roll—from Elvis Presley and early Motown in the 1950s through the British invasion launched in the early 1960s by the Beatles and the Rolling Stones.

Once a pioneer in recording Broadway shows, by the time Decca became part of MCA it had come to be known as Decadent Records. A powerhouse of treacly dance music during the 1950s, Decca's catalog hadn't been updated in years. Decca releases seldom earned money, and the artists on Decca's subsidiary labels, Coral and Brunswick,[2] were very nearly as ancient. But because Decca was run by

---

[2]   Home to such widely varied artists as the Mills Brothers and Buddy Holly and the Crickets, Brunswick was also the first label for which Frank Sinatra cut a record, on July 13, 1939. By the

Milt Rackmil's son-in-law, Marty Salkind, Wasserman issued a hands-off decree to his executives. With little else on its roster besides the British rock group the Who, Decadent Records soon became known as the Music Cemetery of America.

In 1966, Wasserman authorized a $750,000 stake to start a new record label without the geriatric Decca taint. Rising MCA executive Ned Tanen moved into rented quarters at A&M Records several miles from the Black Tower, produced a *Flower Power* album, and followed that with a novelty rock act called the Strawberry Alarm Clock. But Tanen's UNI Records really took off after his A&R (artist and repertoire) man, Russ Regan, signed Neil Diamond, Hugh Masekela, and a pair of Johns—Olivia Newton and Elton. UNI became MCA's answer to the pop music money machine that the Beatles had plugged in, turned on, and tuned up in the early 1960s. Brian Brolly, president of the United Kingdom office of UNI Records, signed the British composing team of Tim Rice and Andrew Lloyd Webber, whose first joint effort was a concept album called *Jesus Christ Superstar*, which other British record companies had rejected.

To revive Decca's roster, Berle Adams bought Kapp Records from Decca's cofounder Dave Kapp. Artists included crooner Jack Jones and composer-arrangers Burt Bacharach and Roger Williams, and among its records were Louis Armstrong's rendition of "Hello, Dolly!" and the cast album of *Man of La Mancha*.

When a deal arose that would add venerable Mills Music to the MCA fold, Berle Adams leaped at the opportunity. As publisher of standards like Hoagy Carmichael's "Stardust" and virtually everything Duke Ellington ever wrote, Mills Music owned a catalog that could be used in Revue TV series, Universal pictures, and MCA record albums for generations to come. And owners Jack and Irving Mills were asking only $4 million!

After Adams sealed the deal, he sent MCA music department executive Harry Garfield to New York with a check, then left for a week-long business trip to Australia. He returned to the appalling news that the Mills deal was off. It seemed that Wasserman himself had flown to New York, met with the Mills brothers, and instead of handing over the $4 million, offered them a check for $3.5 million. Jack Mills shrieked at Lew's last-minute chiseling, ran out of his office, and let his brother Irving tell Lew the deal was off. Later they sold Mills Music to a Palm Springs real estate speculator for $5 million. The Mills catalog, which has since changed hands several times, continues to generate big income.[3]

Adams was determined to buy a standards catalog with music that could be

_____

time MCA took over, however, Brunswick had fallen on hard times, with hit makers like Little Richard moving on to other labels. In the late 1960s, just before MCA cut the label loose, a future actor named Joe Pesci recorded an album under the name Joe Ritchie for Brunswick: *Little Joe Sure Can Sing*.

[3]   Similarly, Ned Tanen arranged for MCA to purchase A&M Records from co-owners Jerry Moss and Herb Alpert in 1969 for $7 million, but Jules Stein intervened and nixed the deal at

used over and over in MCA's TV shows, and he found the opportunity in 1964, when chronic gambling caught up with Leeds Music founder Lou Levy. Adams bought the Leeds label for $4 million, and this time he personally carried the contract and check to Levy's attorney. With that purchase MCA picked up a catalog that included "I'll Never Smile Again," "La Vie en Rose," "The Girl from Ipanema," "Hawaiian Wedding Song," "Heartaches," "C'est Si Bon," and "Is You Is or Is You Ain't My Baby?" Like the Universal Studios tour, Leeds Music became a perennial source of income for MCA, as did Duchess and Pickwick Music, two other Leeds divisions that MCA swallowed in the mid-1960s.

Adams recognized the promise of a similar steady cash flow when New York Titans owner Harry Wisner approached MCA in the spring of 1965, offering to sell his AFL franchise for $300,000. Adams literally ran to Lew's office. "This is the hottest deal we've made!" he said. "We're *stealing* a franchise! I can put the thing together in five minutes. I'll get the coach. I'll get the manager. I'll do everything, and we'll have the heart of entertainment."

"Let me think about it overnight," said Lew.

The following day Wasserman said no. If MCA bought the franchise, he explained, Adams would be in the football business instead of TV, records, and movies. His other MCA duties would slide. Berle left Lew's office disappointed, but not as disappointed as Sonny Werblin, as he soon discovered. On his next trip to New York, all Adams heard during dinner, over cocktails, or even while he and Werblin sat in the stands together at Yankee Stadium, watching a baseball game, was how Sonny had grown to hate the new MCA.

"Everything's disappeared," Werblin complained. "Everything's lousy now. It's no longer a personal business."

Ever since MCA abandoned its agency business, Werblin had found himself schlepping cans of film from one advertising agency to another instead of personally handling talent. The work left him cold. The new MCA was as cold and impersonal as Wasserman. It just wasn't the same.

Berle casually asked Werblin if he had ever thought about buying his own football team. When Sonny scoffed at Berle's bad attempt at humor, Adams brought up the New York franchise: he could get it for him in a New York minute if Sonny had the money.

Sonny didn't wait that long. "Okay," he said. Werblin instantly found four partners who came up with $300,000 to buy the team and another $2 million to put in the bank as a guarantee against losses.[4] Then he made Adams call Stein

---

the last minute. A&M went on to become the biggest independent record label success story of the 1970s.

[4] Partners in the Gotham Football Club, which owned the Jets, included garment manufacturer Phil Iselin, investment broker Townsend Martin, Bowie Racetrack president Don Lillis, and Hess Oil president Leon Hess.

and Wasserman with the bad news. Stein was saddened, but Lew was pragmatic to a fault. Werblin's departure, after more than thirty years as MCA's Manhattan agent-in-chief, was disturbingly simple. Once Lew's chief rival for the MCA presidency, Sonny left without rancor or reprisal and launched a new career at the age of fifty-seven as 23 percent co-owner and president of the New York Titans.

—◈—

SIDNEY KORSHAK NEVER stopped being a happy man.

"The few times I worked with Sidney Korshak, I knew what he was doing, I knew who he was doing it with, but somehow he carried it off with a kind of grace," said United Artists executive Max Youngstein. "He could never do anything in a straight line, but he could always handle the curves. He was like some fat guy who turns out to be the best dancer in the world."

Like Lew Wasserman, Sidney Korshak hit his stride in the mid-1960s. While Bobby Kennedy's Justice Department had been investigating MCA, at least four different state and federal law enforcement agencies were investigating Korshak. But again like MCA, Sidney Korshak beat the odds. The FBI, IRS, LAPD, and Chicago Police Department all knew about his long-standing links to Las Vegas, Meyer Lansky, and the Chicago Mob, but they could pin nothing on him.

Korshak moved with ease between New York, Paris, Chicago, and L.A. As his pal *Chicago Sun-Times* columnist Irv Kupcinet put it, Korshak did not stay in one place long enough to wrinkle his suit. One confidential FBI informant described the Sidney Korshak of 1965 as "one of the biggest guys in the country today who has a pipeline right to the government in Washington." In addition to political kingmakers like former Democratic National Committeemen Paul Ziffren and Jake Arvey, Sidney hobnobbed with the likes of Secretary of Labor Arthur Goldberg and former Truman Vice President Alben Barkley. He also socialized with Kirk Douglas, Dinah Shore, Tony Martin, Cyd Charisse, Vincente Minnelli, Debbie Reynolds,[5] George Raft, and a host of other Hollywood notables.

And there was a third class of celebrity whom Korshak called friends. When FBI agents interviewed him in both Chicago and Los Angeles, Sidney admitted that he counted among his associates Jake "the Barber" Factor, Johnny Rosselli, Moe Dalitz, Murray "the Camel" Humphreys, Jake "Greasy Thumb" Guzik, and

---

[5] Sidney introduced Debbie Reynolds to her future husband, shoe magnate Harry Karl, and when she was ready to make her Las Vegas debut in January of 1963, Korshak booked her into his Riviera Hotel.

Gus Alex.[6] "I won't back away from anyone or repudiate anybody," Korshak told the agents.

In addition to politicians, hoodlums, and Hollywood stars, Korshak trafficked with board members of Fortune 500 companies like Minnesota Mining and Manufacturing, Hyatt Hotels, General Dynamics, Schenley Distributors, Seeburg Corporation, Hilton Hotels, and, of course, Max Factor Cosmetics. He represented the International Brotherhood of Teamsters and several other unions at the same time that he represented management, but that apparent conflict of interest never seemed to raise eyebrows. Sidney Korshak specialized in solving labor disputes, often before they began.

Outside his law practice, Korshak also found time and opportunity to invest in all manner of cash-and-carry businesses. In addition to his Las Vegas casino interests—none of which the Nevada Gaming Control Commission ever seemed able to detect[7]—Korshak shared his brother Marshall's ownership of Windy City Liquor Distributors, Duncan Parking Meters, and Affiliated Parking.[8]

Korshak handled all of his legal work out of his Chicago office. Sidney never took the bar exam in California and never officially practiced law in his adopted state. On a 1961 application for a $300,000 insurance policy on his Bel Air home, he gave his occupation as "semiretired." If he had urgent legal business that could not be handled in Chicago, he simply turned it over to his unofficial California law partner, Greg Bautzer.

While Korshak kept a high profile at the Beverly Hills Bistro Restaurant and made no secret of his eclectic friendships, he played down his actual commercial dealings with Hollywood, the Teamsters, and the Mob. Although he and Lew Wasserman or Jules Stein could be seen chatting at receptions and parties or lunching on occasion at the restaurant, there was no outward hint that they were

---

[6]   On an apartment application, Alex listed his Chicago employer as Sidney's brother, State Senator Marshall Korshak. At that time, Alex was Sam Giancana's chief enforcer.

[7]   This was an amazing oversight on the part of the gaming commission, given the following item published in the January 27, 1963, edition of the Sunday newspaper supplement *Parade Magazine*:

Q. I would like to know if a Chicago mouthpiece named Sidney Korshak represents both Jimmy Hoffa and the Chicago Syndicate in Las Vegas—F. L., Chicago.
A. Attorney Sidney Korshak reportedly represents the Cleveland interests in the Desert Inn and Stardust Hotels in Las Vegas. He is also reportedly the attorney for the Riviera Hotel in Las Vegas. Korshak is also a friend of such theatrical personalities as Dinah Shore and Debbie Reynolds. His exact relationship with Hoffa is not known.

[8]   Using Teamster muscle, Korshak persuaded Los Angeles Dodgers owner Walter O'Malley to give the parking concession to Affiliated Parking. When Dodger Stadium opened in 1962, O'Malley initially granted the concession to another contractor, but he was forced to pay premium wages to Teamsters Local 399 for his parking attendants. Korshak hired attendants from a different Teamsters local at a fraction of the cost and substantially underbid his competition.

conducting business. As more and more government agencies investigated him, Sidney increased his discretion. He made it a point to shy away from known Mob hangouts, like St. Huberts Old English Grille in Chicago. If a wise guy needed to speak with him, he went through the proper channels. There was no need to invite more curiosity about his activities than absolutely necessary.

Thus it came as a rude wake-up call to Los Angeles County district attorney's investigator Frank Hronek when he heard about a meeting in Stein's office in 1965—a meeting which, if the story was true, seemed to confirm thousands of suspicions that had grown over the years about Korshak and the legend of MCA.

"Frank Hronek had an informant—a secretary to Jules Stein," recalled a Chicago political operative who, along with *Sports Illustrated* investigative reporter Jack Tobin and a third investigator for the U.S. Department of Labor, confirmed the story that Hronek repeated to his closest associates before he died in February 1980.

"Frank had been a Czechoslovakian freedom fighter during World War II," the political operative said. "Stein's secretary was Czechoslovakian, too. She was the one who told Hronek and me about Sidney Korshak having a meeting, a very secret meeting in Stein's office. What she was so impressed with was the fact that, when Korshak came into the office, Jules got up from behind his desk and walked over and said, 'Sidney, you sit there. That's your chair, not mine. You sit there. That is *your* chair behind the desk.'

"The woman was flabbergasted! Here's the man who created MCA and he is saying to Sidney, 'That's *your* chair!' And of course Sidney didn't say 'Oh, no.' He went over and sat down."

But the astonishing events did not end there. A short time after Korshak made himself comfortable in Stein's chair, according to the secretary, another visitor entered the room.

"MCA was a great place to meet in the mid-sixties because they had their own internal police force," said the political operative. "You just give a phony name to the front security and you're in and you're upstairs. No one knows nothing.

"So this little guy comes in and sits. The secretary serves coffee and liqueurs, and then she and Stein leave the room. He shuts the door behind them, and Sidney's in there talking privately with the little guy for maybe twenty minutes. When the meeting's over, the little guy leaves. A car is waiting for him at the front door downstairs, and he's gone. Then Sidney calls Stein back in, shuts the door, and they talk for a while. Finally Korshak leaves, and it's as if the whole thing never happened. If Stein's secretary hadn't seen it and told Hronek about it, no one would have ever known a thing."

After the secretary told him the story, Hronek asked her to look through some photos to see if she could identify the man who had joined Korshak in the tempo-rary takeover of Jules Stein's office. In no time she pointed to an FBI mug shot and nodded vigorously. Without a doubt, she told Hronek, this was the same little guy she'd seen meeting with Korshak.

The man in the photograph was Meyer Lansky.[9]

—⁓—

IN JUNE OF 1965 racial tensions rose across the nation, accompanied by a clamor-ing for equality in Hollywood. The NAACP formally declared its intent to end black caricatures perpetuated by the film and TV industry. No more *Amos and Andy*. No more Stepin Fetchit. No more Aunt Jemima. Characteristically, Lew Wasserman wanted more information before he acted on behalf of Universal or spoke on behalf of the industry in general. When the *New York Times* asked him for a comment, he declined until he had "read carefully what has been said by the NAACP."

His fence-sitting didn't last long. Two months later, on August 11, 1965, the south central Los Angeles ghetto of Watts detonated in the worst race riot of mod-ern times. For six days the chant "Burn, baby, burn!" ruled the streets. Fire destroyed nearly 200 buildings, and the war between residents and police killed 34 and injured another 1,032. The National Guard patrolled the streets for looters while the LAPD made over 3,000 arrests. Property damage totaled nearly $200 million.

In the midst of this chaos, according to one newspaper account, Mayor Sam Yorty called on Lew Wasserman—an early champion of the Civil Rights move-ment—to drive an unmarked car through the neighborhood that had come to be known as Charcoal Alley. Whether the story is true or an exaggerated bit of PR, Lew was certainly well equipped to make such a trek. As a workaholic, he'd already had a two-way short wave installed in his car so that he could stay in touch with his office at all times.

His presence did little to quell the riots, nor did any lasting impression of the Watts wreckage translate into executive action at MCA. Throughout the 1960s, MCA remained as white as Disney, both in front of and behind the cameras. With the exception of actor Don Mitchell who portrayed a reformed delinquent on NBC's *Ironside*, none of MCA's TV series had recurring roles for blacks, and Oscar winner Sidney Poitier was the only black actor with enough cachet to land a lead-

---

[9]   The only other report of Lansky meeting face-to-face with Korshak was in a series of high-level organized crime sessions conducted in 1969 and 1970 at the lavish Acapulco Towers Hotel, a resort hideaway partly owned by Korshak, Lansky, and National General Corporation chairman Gene Klein. Among others who joined Korshak and Lansky at the meeting in the Mexican coastal resort were Sam Giancana and several Vegas emissaries, including Moe Dalitz.

ing role in a Universal picture.[10] Another eleven years would pass before Lew authorized the creation of MCA New Ventures, a short-lived MCA subsidiary devoted to minority projects. No black, Hispanic, Native American, or Asian would ever sit on the MCA board of directors.[11]

Nonetheless, both the media and career politicians perceived Lew as a beacon of Democratic enlightenment in Neanderthal Hollywood. The same week the riots exploded, President Johnson appointed Wasserman to the President's Committee on the Bicentennial of American Independence. A month later, on September 15, 1965, LBJ named Lew to the National Advisory Committee of the Peace Corps. The following year he became a member of the Radio Free Europe Committee.

Wasserman's President's Club of Southern California also began to attract higher-powered board members, including aircraft pioneer Donald W. Douglas Jr. and Home Savings and Loan chairman Howard F. Ahmanson.[12] The annual $1,000-a-plate fund-raising dinners were still held in June, but Lew made himself available when LBJ needed to raise a few bucks in a pinch. The *Hollywood Reporter* gossiped in its August 23, 1965, edition, "Lew Wasserman assigned a crew of sixteen, all of them twelfth-floor Universal Citizens, to blueprint that $500-a-plate party for President Johnson in October....All guests will be screened by the FBI."

During the few years he had occupied the White House, the president's personal affection for Lew had grown. When Wasserman asked him for a picture, Johnson changed his standard autograph from "To a good and loyal American, LBJ" to "To a good and great friend, LBJ." Neither man slept much, so they often held transcontinental phone chats between midnight and dawn.

Lew endeared himself to Lady Bird Johnson too. He took her home movies with him from the LBJ Ranch to Hollywood, where he had Universal editors, dubbers, and sound mixers transform them into a mini-documentary called *Trails Through Texas*.

But neither of the Johnsons could persuade their new friend to quit MCA and move to Washington. Unbeknownst to Lew, the White House had authorized an FBI name-check investigation of Wasserman. Not only was he being appointed to presidential advisory committees, but Johnson also considered him for the cabinet post of Secretary of Commerce. According to LBJ adviser Harry McPherson, the White House never formally offered him the job, fearing that confirmation hearings would turn up embarrassing details about Lew's ties to the shady side of

---

[10] In *The Lost Man* (1969), Poitier is a black militant who steals to provide money for families of jailed civil rights demonstrators.

[11] In March 1976, MCA added its first woman to the board of directors: Mary Gardiner Jones, a former member of the Federal Trade Commission.

[12] In 1967, Ahmanson was also elected an MCA director, but he died after serving less than a year on the board.

Hollywood. Lew preferred Hollywood anyway, where he could rule an empire of his own.

On July 27, 1966, the board of the Association of Motion Picture and Television Producers elected Lew chairman. He was to succeed Paramount's Y. Frank Freeman who had guided the studios' chief management bargaining unit for eighteen years. If ever a baton was passed between generations in the movie business, it happened when the seventy-six-year-old Freeman handed AMPTP control to fifty-three-year-old Wasserman. The significance was not lost on LBJ, who instructed his special assistant, former NBC President Robert Kintner, to send a commendation: "I wanted to congratulate you and tell you that this is a well-deserved recognition of an outstanding career, if not *the* outstanding career, in what, for want of a better word, I shall call 'Hollywood.'"

As much as he enjoyed the fringes of presidential politics, Lew flexed even more muscle at home. In 1966 he campaigned for Democratic Governor Edmund G. "Pat" Brown, who was running for a third term.

Ironically, the Republican challenger was Lew's first star client in Hollywood—Ronald Reagan. Stranger still were Reagan's choices for campaign manager and chief personal fund-raiser—Taft Schreiber and Jules Stein. But according to producer-turned-author Henry Denker, who would fictionalize Stein's role as Reagan's patron in a 1972 roman à clef called *The Kingmaker*, it wasn't strange at all.

"That was Stein's idea," said Denker. "Taft was the Republican and Lew was the Democrat. That way, they had both camps covered and they gave equally to both sides, and everybody knew that."

During the campaign, a brash young MCA-TV executive wrote Lew a memo about ways to make Brown appeal to younger voters—an appraisal Wasserman regarded as brilliant. Hired away from UCLA six years earlier to work in the MCA legal division, thirty-one-year-old ex–law professor Sidney Sheinberg had already made an indelible impression on the boss as one of the very few junior executives who would not put up with Wasserman's outbursts.

"Lew took note of Sid because he was one of the very few people who would stand up to him," said Jerry Adler. "I remember Lew reaming me once, and after he started in on me, Sid pipes up and says, 'I can't listen to this.' And he leaves. Lew was stunned. I am absolutely convinced that that was the moment Sid started his ascent in the company."

Despite the impression he may have made on Lew, Sheinberg's fresh new ideas didn't help Governor Brown's campaign. Brown sealed his own doom with a remarkably tasteless TV commercial in which he told an integrated class of schoolchildren: "I'm running against an actor, and you know who shot Lincoln, don'tcha?"

Governor Ronald Reagan's successful march to Sacramento had actually started two years earlier, after his final big-screen appearance in Universal's *The Killers*.[13] During the 1964 Republican National Convention that nominated Arizona Senator Barry Goldwater to run against LBJ, Reagan delivered the rousing keynote address, stirring the delegates in ways Goldwater never could. Referred to as "the Speech" by pundits and political scientists, Reagan's address became the enduring theme of his political career—damning all intellectuals who promoted the welfare state while exalting the working man who paid his taxes and supported all things American, especially American business. Without consulting a single opinion poll, California's Republican power brokers sensed immediately that Reagan had touched a nerve.

Reagan had delivered "the Speech" for the first time some months earlier, during an international convention of General Electric executives in Schenectady, New York, according to one of Taft Schreiber's protégés. When a politician who had been scheduled to deliver the keynote address failed to show up, a panicky GE executive called MCA and asked Schreiber if he thought the host of *General Electric Theater* would mind standing in. Schreiber blandly said, "He'll do as he's told."

As Schreiber later explained to Berle Adams, Asa V. Call first tapped Reagan to run against Governor Pat Brown in 1966. The owner of Pacific Mutual Life Insurance and longtime president of the Automobile Club of Southern California, Call had been a primary force behind Richard M. Nixon's rise in the 1950s. After Nixon self-destructed in his run for California governor in 1962, Call began looking for another likely candidate. He found one in Reagan.

Call put together a group of conservative Reagan advisers who later became known as the Kitchen Cabinet: Leonard K. Firestone, president of Firestone Tire and Rubber Company; engineer Henry Salvatori, president of Western Geophysical Company; department store heir Alfred Bloomingdale, founder of the Diners Club; Holmes Tuttle, millionaire Ford dealer; Justin Dart, president of Rexall Drugs and, later, Dart Industries; Earle M. Jorgenson, founder of Jorgenson Steel; and William French Smith, senior partner in Gibson, Dunne and Crutcher, L.A.'s largest, richest, and most powerful law firm. Despite this formidable lineup, Call sensed that something was missing.

"He realized that they had no one in the group representing L.A.'s substantial Jewish community," said Adams. "That's when Firestone recommended Taft Schreiber: 'He's Jewish, a member of the Hillcrest Country Club, and his company was Reagan's agency.'"

---

[13] This MCA picture, originally produced for NBC, is the only one of Reagan's fifty-five films in which he plays the villain, a crime czar. He reluctantly played the heavy after Wasserman talked him into it, but it was a decision that Reagan the politician came to regret. Nixed by network censors as too violent, *The Killers* was released in theaters to critical raves but poor box office. Costarring Lee Marvin and Angie Dickinson, *The Killers* is a tale of corruption and contract murder loosely based on an Ernest Hemingway short story.

Asa Call's candidate now had all it took for a full-press statewide political campaign except one thing: an income for the candidate. No longer host of a TV series like *GE Theater* or *Death Valley Days*, Reagan still had a wife, two young children, and a household to support.

In order to facilitate his former client's new career, Schreiber asked Jules Stein to set up a Reagan trust. Jules named himself as trustee, and in the month following Reagan's election as governor of California, the Reagan trust sold 236 acres of Reagan's 290-acre Yearling Row Ranch, located in rural Malibu Canyon 30 miles north of Los Angeles.

"I could not have run for office unless I sold the ranch," Reagan later told biographer Lou Cannon.

The buyer was Twentieth Century Fox Studios. Twelve years earlier Reagan had paid $225 an acre. Fox now paid a whopping $8,178 an acre. Through the miracle of real estate appreciation, the rocky Reagan ranch land had increased in value by a phenomenal 3,635 percent. Fox, which owned the 2,500 acres surrounding the undeveloped Reagan property, enriched the Reagan trust by $1.93 million. The sale not only helped defray Reagan's personal expenses, it also made the new governor an instant millionaire.

Two years later the Los Angeles County Tax Assessor's office raised questions about the inflated price that Twentieth Century Fox had paid. At a 1968 property tax hearing, Fox's own appraiser agreed that the fair market value was less than half what the studio had paid. Reagan's profits from the sale had financed his run for governor, but that was not the reason the studio paid the premium price. According to the studio officials who bought the land, Fox paid the hefty price because someday they planned to relocate there.[14]

Meanwhile, Taft Schreiber, who was personally acquainted with Philip E. Watson, the county assessor, interceded on Reagan's behalf. The assessor's office lost interest after Fox agreed to a higher assessment. The sale to Twentieth Century Fox stood unchallenged, and Reagan's trust continued to increase in value under Jules Stein's careful supervision.

—⁓—

ON NOVEMBER 3, 1966, five days before Ronald Reagan was elected governor, UCLA opened the Jules Stein Eye Institute. Jules had first proposed the monument to himself and to the science of sight five years earlier. The deal was vintage

---

[14] The bill of sale was signed by Fox president Richard D. Zanuck, who found a home as an independent producer at Universal after his 1970 ouster from Fox. Fox never did build on the land. In 1974, just as Governor Reagan was leaving office, the studio sold all of its Malibu Canyon property to the state of California for $1,800 an acre. The land has since become Malibu Canyon State Park.

Stein: if the university regents would give Dr. Jules C. Stein a free hand, Jules the agent would put in the seed money and twist arms to secure the funds necessary to erect a state-of-the-art clinical institute and research facility.

Jules didn't simply want his name engraved on a plaque. His institute was to be a reflection of himself. Thus his plans called for closely packed Portasanta marble chips for nonslip flooring, a peach brick exterior with matching mortar, concrete pilasters painted to match the pink Roman travertine walls, floors, and columns.[15] A $25,000 bronze bust of Dr. Stein sculpted by artist Jacques Lipchitz, would be prominently displayed in the foyer of the institute, along with a Salvador Dalí painting titled *Emotions on the Recovery from Blindness*.

To finance this unusually opulent medical facility, Jules and Doris mounted a personal crusade. Dozens of Sunday afternoon receptions and Friday evening cocktail parties kept the Steins' Misty Mountain retreat filled with L.A.'s high rollers.[16] Stein demonstrated that he knew exactly how to put the arm on his wealthy friends. Even the usually tightfisted Alfred Hitchcock ponied up a $175,000 pledge.[17] According to UCLA Chancellor Franklin Murphy, Stein's fund-raising efforts "exceeded any previous private philanthropy in both the history of ophthalmology and the history of the University of California."

When the Jules Stein Eye Institute opened, Jules and Doris had contributed only $1.35 million toward the original $6 million cost of the neoclassic structure.[18]

"I am happy that we have been able to build this institute, and I am proud that it bears my name," said Stein. "But far more important than the bricks and mortar, however beautiful, is the work that will be done here."

---

[15] Jules had to fight the university administration to keep the columns at the front of the building, which was the only marble structure on campus.

[16] The donors who gave $25,000 or more were members of the Hollywood establishment (Mr. and Mrs. Mervyn LeRoy; the law firm of Beilenson, Meyer, Rosenfeld and Susman; Mr. and Mrs. Jack Benny; Chasin-Park-Citron Agency; Hollywood Canteen Foundation; the Disney Foundation; Cary Grant; Mr. and Mrs. Alfred Hitchcock; Mr. and Mrs. Bob Hope; Mr. and Mrs. James Stewart; Mr. and Mrs. Jack Warner; and Mr. and Mrs. Gregory Peck), MCA (Mr. and Mrs. David A. Werblin, Mr. and Mrs. Lew Wasserman; Mr. and Mrs. Taft Schreiber, Mr. and Mrs. Toby Schreiber, Mr. and Mrs. Bernard A. [Leonore Schreiber] Greenberg, Mr. and Mrs. Milton R. Rackmil, and Mr. and Mrs. Karl Kramer), and the Stein family (Mr. and Mrs. Charles [Adelaide Stein] Miller, Mr. and Mrs. Gerald Oppenheimer, Dr. and Mrs. James R. [Ruth Stein] Cogan, Colonel and Mrs. Harold L. Oppenheimer, Mr. H. David Stein, Miss Susan R. Stein, and Mr. and Mrs. William [Jean Stein] vanden Heuvel). Almost no contributions came from oil companies, real estate developers, aerospace executives, establishment attorneys, or entrenched power brokers like the Chandler family, which ran the *Los Angeles Times*.

[17] The Alfred Hitchcock Science Theater was to have been constructed in his honor, but it went unnamed.

[18] Stein's charitable efforts during this period weren't confined solely to eyesight. In March 1966 he succeeded Bette Davis as president of the Hollywood Canteen Foundation, and in April he gave $100,000 each to USC and the Motion Picture Relief Fund.

TWENTY-SIX

The Black Tower

1967–1968

The new MCA World Headquarters was as angular and prosaic as the man who ordered it built: a monolith of smoked glass and anodized aluminum, as tall, austere, and forbidding as Lew Wasserman himself.

"It's what I call toilet architecture," scoffed United Artists executive Max Youngstein.

To its many critics, the Black Tower represented bland L.A. high-rise architecture at its worst. Designed by Skidmore, Owings and Merrill, architects of the postwar glass box, the rectangular black nerve center of the new MCA empire seemed oddly out of place overlooking the squat subdivisions and vanishing chaparral of the San Fernando Valley.

"Universal went off in all different directions after they built that Black Tower," said Tony Curtis. "All of a sudden what used to be kind of a home-grown, funny, countrylike little studio that I started at in 1948 had nothing to do with MCA or IBM or up your ass. It had nothing to do with anything. It was just about 'getting in the movies,' you know?"

Off the parking garage, just beneath the ground floor, Wasserman installed a $500,000 state-of-the-art Honeywell 400 computer capable of handling 100,000 bits of information per minute. It occupied 6,000 square feet and symbolized the new streamlined MCA in much the same way the Black Tower itself did. Many considered the Honeywell "just a stand-in for Lew Wasserman," according to journalist Joe Hyams.

"Lew always, always knew the numbers," recalled MCA film executive Bob Hussong. "He knew the budget of the motion picture. Say the budget was $600,000, which was a considerable amount of money then. He'd come up and say, 'Well, how do you stand today?' You'd answer, 'We're under budget' or 'We're on schedule. We've spent $530,000.' He'd say, 'No. You're a tiny bit over budget. You've spent $562,000.'"

Lew was a numbers man, and Jules Stein valued that quality in him above all others. With his big band mementos, British hunting prints, and agency souvenirs, Stein transformed his own Black Tower office into a time capsule. But he did not stand in the way of Wasserman's version of progress.

"Jules was a classicist," said Berle Adams. "He just hated the new building. When you entered his top-floor office, the clock turned back to Jules's era."

Stein reluctantly acceded to his protégé's wishes. Lew might have no eye for architecture and no ear for music, but he did have his finger on the financial pulse of show business. Despite their many differences, Jules still regarded Lew as his greatest discovery—the brilliant son he'd never had.

Yet for all his visionary moneymaking skill, Lew had no one to take his place if and when he retired. From where Jules sat at the pinnacle of the Black Tower, that seemed like a big mistake. Wasserman showed no interest in relinquishing MCA's daily operation to a younger man. Stein reminded him often that as soon as he turned fifty, he had asked Wasserman to step up to the MCA presidency. Lew was fifty-four. It was time for him to pick someone to do the same.

Instead of naming a successor, Wasserman created an executive vice presidential triumvirate: MCA studio executive Al Dorskind to head up land development, labor negotiations, and the back lot; Dan Ritchie, who had been hired away from Lehman Brothers to run Columbia Savings as well as MCA's financial affairs; and Berle Adams, chief of corporate affairs. They occupied the floor directly beneath Lew and Jules, and each had some measure of autonomy. Adams and Dorskind even wore pastel dress shirts, brown suits, and an occasional paisley tie while Ritchie audaciously wore suspenders.

The rest of the Black Tower continued to be run Wasserman's way—efficiently, profitably, and in an orderly manner. One junior executive who never dared detour from the black suit, white shirt, black tie uniform, kept a motto posted on his wall that read, "To err is human, to forgive is against company policy."

The Tower became the very symbol of Hollywood oppression. During the first season of CBS's *Mannix* (1967–1975), the character played by series star Mike Connors worked for a computerized high-rise detective agency called Intertect, which was overrun by automatonlike employees. Everything at Intertect operated from the penthouse office of a starchy push-button tyrant named Lou Wickersham[1] who seemed always to be at odds with Joe Mannix's relaxed, shoot-from-the-hip style. From his peevishness to his black horn-rims, Lou Wickersham's similarities to Lew Wasserman were too obvious. Even though Paramount TV produced *Mannix*, by the second season, all traces of Lew and his high-rise were gone.

---

[1]   According to actor Joseph Campanella who portrayed Wickersham, the name was a composite of Wasserman and Lankershim, the San Fernando Valley boulevard where the MCA Black Tower is located.

During the next seven seasons, Joe Mannix was an independent, working out of his own West L.A. office.

Out of earshot and away from the Black Tower, Wasserman came to be known as "Lew-baby," and Universal was simply "the Factory." Inside the tower, Lew was always Mr. Wasserman. Jennings Lang was his factory foreman, running a tight assembly line that tolerated no interruptions.

"Universal didn't pay a lot of attention to what actors wanted," recalled Jay Bernstein. "It was simply 'Do it!'"

Most actors were happy to get work. After being diagnosed with cancer, a financially strapped Ann Sheridan gratefully showed up on time every day on the set of the 1967 CBS comedy *Pistols 'n' Petticoats* until she collapsed. She died a few weeks into the series.

According to one executive, when *Run for Your Life* lead Ben Gazzara began making demands for star treatment, MCA suggested that the lawyer Gazzara portrayed in the NBC series survive a serious accident in one episode. When the bandages came off at the beginning of the next episode, Gazzara would look just like Cesar Romero.

MCA appeased only that rare actor—the star of the moment. Thus, an inebriated Patty Duke could ring up the Black Tower from her bungalow while she was starring in *The Patty Duke Show* and order an executive to pilot her through the studio on her own private Universal Studios Tour. At the height of his popularity as the *Six Million Dollar Man*, Lee Majors had MCA catering to his every whim. "They would paint his dressing room if he was upset or give him twenty-four-hour limo service or give him one of the first phones in a briefcase. Anything to keep him working," said Bernstein.

That was Lang's standing order from the Black Tower: keep them working. By 1967, Universal had added yet another soundstage, bringing the total to thirty-three. Lang kept them all busy all of the time with his pecuniary programming innovations. Lang's long-format shows might have been designed more to save money than to produce quality TV, but they utterly changed broadcasting—occasionally, for the better.

One type of long-format series was the so-called umbrella. Beginning with *The Name of the Game* (1968–1971), an ABC series spun off from an NBC Movie of the Week about the magazine business, Universal packaged several related dramas that rotated under a single name, often using the same sets and airing in the same time slot each week.[2] *The Name of the Game* was followed by *The Bold Ones* (1969–1973); *Four-in-One* (1970–1971), which delivered *The Psychiatrist, Night*

---

[2]   Lang had first tried this umbrella concept in 1964 with *90 Bristol Court*, three NBC sitcoms set in a southern California apartment complex. Despite the fact that the initials of the series matched those of the network, NBC canceled the low-rated series after two months.

Gallery, San Francisco International Airport, and *McCloud,*[3] starring Dennis Weaver as a cowboy cop; and the most successful rotating omnibus series of all, *The NBC Mystery Movie* (1971–1977), which gave Rock Hudson a second career as a police commissioner in *McMillan and Wife,* and launched the phenomenal double-decade run of actor Peter Falk as the seemingly absentminded homicide detective, Lieutenant Columbo.

A second long-format series was the made-for-TV movie, or movie of the week. Launched as the *NBC World Premiere* in 1966, Universal's first two movies of the week became pilots for series — *Fame Is the Name of the Game* and *Dragnet 1966.* Once a TV movie had aired, Universal could syndicate it, air it internationally, or sell it overseas as a theatrical motion picture. Universal could also pack the casts with young hopefuls and grizzled veterans.[4]

The miniseries was the third long-format product. *Vanished,* a four-hour Richard Widmark spy thriller, initiated the format over two nights in 1971. Universal later pushed the miniseries to its limits with twenty-six hours of James Michener's *Centennial* during two weeks in 1976.

It was in the spirit of MCA efficiency that producer Harry Tatelman wandered through Universal's back lot, looking for likely sets to use in a movie of the week called *Slow Fade to Black.* Originally credited to Rod Serling as a 1964 hour-long drama for NBC's *Bob Hope Presents the Chrysler Theater, Slow Fade to Black* was Tatelman's paean to old Hollywood, featuring Rod Steiger as an aging mogul and Robert Culp as the young company man who would replace him.

"Any similarities to Jules and Lew were purely accidental," said Tatelman with a wry half smile some thirty years later.

Two years after the NBC airing, Tatelman hired a young writer named Steven Bochco to write additional scenes so that *Slow Fade to Black* could be expanded to ninety minutes. Then he began scrounging around the Universal lot for likely places to shoot. Tatelman found the set he wanted on Stage 12: a ship being used in *The King's Pirate,* a theatrical vehicle for *The Virginian's* Doug McClure. One of Edie Wasserman's personal favorites, the blond, muscular McClure was a hunk with easygoing charm but scant talent. Wasserman kept trying to make him a star because Edie told him to — a fact that irked anyone who cared about acting. Tatel-

---

[3]   A weekly version of the Clint Eastwood film *Coogan's Bluff* (1968), *McCloud* was the first in a long line of Universal TV series that were "inspired" by hit movies — usually with poor results. In 1971, *McCloud* switched from *Four-in-One* to *The NBC Mystery Movie,* rotating with *Columbo* and *McMillan and Wife* for most of the remainder of the decade.

[4]   Lang's first attempt at a movie of the week was *Project 120* in 1964, but after just three NBC movies — *The Hanged Man, See How They Run,* and *The Killers,* which was deemed too violent for TV and never even aired — *Project 120* was abandoned. When Lang revived the concept two years later, he named Wasserman favorite Sid Sheinberg to head the new *World Premiere* production unit. *World Premiere* was eventually responsible for producing 116 TV movies, 31 of which went on to become series.

man knew none of this when he wrote McClure's pirate ship into his own script as one of the sets in his TV movie-within-a-movie. He was simply trying to save the studio a pile of cash.

"*The King's Pirate* was a silly costume drama," recalled Tatelman. "The crew was about to strike the set, but I ordered them to hold up until we had a chance to shoot a few scenes for *Slow Fade to Black*."

When *King's Pirate* director Don Weis and producer Robert Arthur heard about it, they raised hell with Universal production chief Ed Muhl. How would it look if the set for their picture showed up in some movie of the week? Muhl, a lame duck from the fading Rackmil regime, exercised his waning power and over-rode Tatelman. He ordered the set struck.

That same day, Wasserman ordered Tatelman to his office. "What are you trying to do?" Lew demanded. "You can't use that set. It's in the McClure movie!"

Had someone else been in the office, Tatelman might have let Lew slap his wrist and let it go at that. But they were alone, so he reminded Wasserman that it was more efficient to get two pictures out of a single set. "Besides, nobody's going to pay to watch Doug McClure run around in tights," he said.

Wasserman frowned, then grinned, then broke up at the thought of Edie's current favorite leaping from sprit to bow in leotards.

"If you got Lew alone and you could make him laugh, you had him," said Tatelman.

Tatelman shot his TV movie on Stage 12, and it fared far better than *The King's Pirate*, which sank at the box office. The expanded version of *Slow Fade to Black* became *The Movie Maker*, which garnered both critical praise and one of the highest TV movie ratings of 1967.

—◦◦◦—

ON A CLEAR day the view from the top floor of MCA headquarters could be heady. MCA's horizons seemed endless. By 1965, MCA was telecasting 19,039 hours of programming in eighty-one countries.[5] Lee Marvin growled in German for

---

[5]   According to their own advertisement in the March 14, 1965, edition of the *Los Angeles Herald Examiner*, MCA-Universal seemed to have offices in more cities around the world than the CIA: Adelaide, Albany, Alexandria, Algiers, Amsterdam, Ancona, Athens, Atlanta, Auckland, Bahía Blanca, Baltimore, Bangkok, Barcelona, Bari, Belo Horizonte, Berlin, Bogotá, Bologna, Bombay, Bordeaux, Boston, Bromfield, Brussels, Buenos Aires, Buffalo, Butte, Cagliari, Camden, Caracas, Casablanca, Catania, Charlotte, Chicago, Cincinnati, Cleveland, Copenhagen, Córdoba, Dacca (Dhaka), Dallas, Denver, Des Moines, Detroit, Djakarta, Düsseldorf, Florence, Frankfurt, Fukuoka, Genoa, Georgetown, Guadalajara, Guayaquil, The Hague, Hamburg, Havana, Helsinki, Hong Kong, Honolulu, Indianapolis, Jacksonville, Johannesburg, Kansas City, Kingston, Lahore, Lille, Lima, Lisbon, London, Los Angeles, Luxembourg, Lyon, Manila, Marseilles, Melbourne, Memphis, Mendoza, Meridian, Mexico City, Miami, Milan, Milwau-

Munich fans of *M Squad*; a Spanish version of *Wagon Train* aired in Mexico City; and *Mister Ed* drawled in high-pitched Japanese for Tokyo audiences. Indeed, MCA's corporate reach now stretched quite literally around the world, and with that global reach came global predicaments.

After Berle Adams set up an international film and television distribution system, one of the first calls he received was from the United State Information Agency, urging him—and finally badgering him—to place a U.S. operative in MCA's Rome office. The government feared that Italy might be leaning toward communism, it was explained, and needed a cover for a U.S. agent.

It was the beginning of a series of favors that agency[6] asked of MCA, including the filing of reports with the agency whenever an MCA executive made an extended visit to a foreign country. Adams was met by a U.S. agent at each stop on a South American trip, for instance, and was asked to file a report upon his return. Though he wearied of the intrusion, he was obliged to cooperate. He'd long been aware of an unspoken agreement between MCA and the U.S. government. Jules regularly had employees bring watches, jewelry, and other contraband through customs as part of their luggage so that he didn't have to pay duty. LBJ was Lew's pal, after all. As far as he knew, however, MCA rarely asked for help abroad. Years of selling shows to Australians, Eskimos, Hottentots, and Tartars around the world had instilled in him a shrewd self-sufficiency.

Said Berle Adams, "Once, Universal had money frozen in Egypt. They wouldn't let us exchange Egyptian money for U.S. dollars."

The solution turned out to be sesame seeds.

"I met a dealer at a party in New York so desperate for sesame seeds that he offered to pay in dollars for a shipment," Adams said. "I asked MCA's Egyptian rep to purchase the seeds with our frozen funds and ship them to New York. We exchanged the shipment for $400,000, and a month later the sesame-seed guy and I met for coffee. I asked, 'How'd you do with the shipment?' He said, 'Are you kidding? We got rid of the seeds immediately. Everyone thinks sesame seeds are for

---

kee, Minneapolis, Monterrey, Montevideo, Montreal, Munich, Nagoya, Naples, Nashville, New Haven, New Orleans, New York, Oklahoma City, Omaha, Osaka, Oslo, Padua, Panama City, Paris, Perth, Petaling Jaya, Philadelphia, Pittsburgh, Portland, Pôrto Alegre, Port-of-Spain, Pyrton, Quezon City, Ramat-Gan, Recife, Rio de Janeiro, Rome, Rosario, Saigon, Saint Louis, Salt Lake City, San Francisco, San Juan, Santa Fe, Santiago, Santo Domingo, São Paulo, Sapporo, Seattle, Singapore, Solna, South Brisbane, Stockholm, Strasbourg, Sydney, Taipei, Tel Aviv, Tokyo, Toronto, Trieste, Tucumán, Tunis, Universal City, Vienna, Washington, D.C., Wellington, West Allis, Woodside, and Zurich.

[6] While USIA officials maintained that the agency had no record of any involvement with MCA, the Central Intelligence Agency responded to the author's three-year-old Freedom of Information Act request in June 1998, acknowledging that seventeen separate computer searches revealed MCA did work with the CIA. The CIA refused to release any of its MCA documents on grounds that it might endanger national security.

bagels. You'd be surprised what you can use them for. When can I get another shipment?'"

MCA's sesame-seed shuffle taught Adams an important lesson in international economics. Poland froze its currency, as Egypt had done, but that didn't prevent Adams from accepting Polish zlotys as payment for TV shows. He arranged to subsidize the U.S. embassy in Warsaw with MCA's zlotys, then received reimbursement from the State Department in U.S. dollars. Thus zlotys never left the country, the Poles got to watch Astaire dance across their TV screens, and MCA still extracted its money.

Buenos Aires also forbade the export of U.S. dollars in the 1960s. With the Argentine peso inflating at a rate of 103 percent a year, MCA had no interest in waiting for a lift on the export ban. Instead, MCA struck the same sort of deal with the Vatican that it had made with the U.S. embassy in Poland: the church would use MCA's Argentine pesos for its Buenos Aires operations while repaying MCA in U.S. dollars through its offices in New York City.

But Adams saved his most ingenious MCA diplomacy for Japan. At the beginning of the decade, MCA exported *Alfred Hitchcock Presents* for broadcast over NTV, Japan's first television network. By the mid-1960s, with offices in Osaka, Sapporo, Fukuoka, and Tokyo, MCA's foothold had grown to a solid presence. Japanese TV audiences could not get enough westerns, sitcoms, and detective shows. It was then that MCA's original Japanese partners came up with a remarkable offer: why not build a duplicate of the Universal Studios tour facilities in the shadow of Mount Fuji?

Because yen were as hard to get out of Japan as zlotys were in Poland or pesos in Argentina, Adams negotiated a deal that would allow NTV access to MCA's pre-1948 Paramount film library in exchange for financing the MCA theme park. It would be constructed adjacent to a golf course in a rural area located halfway between Osaka and Tokyo, Japan's two biggest cities. There was already a nearby stop on the main railway, guaranteeing a regular flow of tourists.

"I returned home and outlined the deal for Lew Wasserman," Adams wrote in his memoirs. "He thought it was a great idea. Three months later, Lew decided to go to Japan with his wife, Edie."

Adams began to get very excited, but he might have saved himself the letdown. Lew and Edie did not like Japan. Their first night there, the Wassermans were invited to a reception at the home of Edwin Reischauer, the U.S. ambassador to Japan. As one of President Johnson's confidants, Lew expected royal treatment, but Reischauer kept mistakenly referring to him as Mr. Green. The Wassermans were mortified.

The next day things got worse. With "Mr. Green" still in a foul mood, the clouds opened. In the downpour, Lew and Edie made the long train ride to the golf course to meet with the publisher of the *Yomiuri Press*, chief financier for the proposed theme park. As soon as they got off the train, the Wassermans passed three Japanese laborers urinating in public. Lew complained. His interpreter smiled, nodded, and ignored him.

Lew's frustration escalated with the arrival of Nobutu Shoriki, the *Yomiuri Press* publisher. In the samurai tradition that accorded the highest respect to business "warriors," Shoriki was treated like royalty. The same workers who peed in the Wassermans' presence now threw rope carpets down for Shoriki to walk across so that he would not muddy his shoes. When they entered the golf clubhouse, the workers ignored the Wassermans while spreading a rug for Shoriki. He never opened a door, lit a cigarette, reached for food, or did anything for himself. When Lew discovered Shoriki had little interest in motion pictures, he'd heard and seen enough. As soon as he arrived back in Tokyo, his interpreter put in a cautionary phone call to Berle Adams.

"You're going to have trouble," he warned. "All the way back to the city after the meeting Lew bitched about the [theme park] idea."

Lew argued that the golf course was in the middle of nowhere. There were no roads, no bus service, no city, nor would there ever be. He didn't like it.

Adams pleaded with Lew to reconsider. MCA didn't have to invest a cent and would hold a sixty-year lease on the golf course.

"I'm against it. Get out of the deal," said Lew.

Now, thirty years later, the city of Kawasaki with a population of 500,000 stands on the site. The bullet train between Tokyo and Osaka stops at the golf course and the adjoining Yomiuri Zen Park.

"The MCA theme park would have been easily accessible to more than 14 million Japanese who have enthusiastically embraced our Western culture," said Adams. "Disney built a theme park much farther out, at Yokohama, and is doing very well. We gave up on a sure thing."

BACK HOME IN Beverly Hills, Lew finally began getting the respect he deserved — but not because he was samurai. When Mrs. Dorothy Buffum Chandler wanted to build a new $18 million Music Center in the middle of southern California's cultural wasteland, she discovered well into the project that she was going to need Hollywood's help in pulling it off.

Buffy Chandler didn't know many show business types. In the sheltered department store heiress's world, "Hollywood" was a euphemism for "Jew." The WASPs of San Marino and Hancock Park rarely mingled with the Jews of Brentwood and Beverly Hills. WASP business clubs (Jonathan, California, and others) and country clubs (Los Angeles, Bel Air, Lakeside, and so on) traditionally excluded Jews, leaving few places for the two most affluent forces in southern California to share common ground.

But Lew Wasserman and his fellow Democratic mover and shaker Paul Ziffren did manage to meet and mingle enough to impress Mrs. Chandler.[7] As a first step toward detente, she asked her husband, former *Los Angeles Times* publisher Norman Chandler, to get Lew elected to the Caltech board of trustees. While flattered, Wasserman pointed out the obvious: he was a liberal Jewish Democrat. Not to worry, Chandler assured him. The board had already voted unanimously to accept him.

With that beginning, the parochial community that ran L.A.'s institutions began to break down. For the first time, a cosmopolitan meld of old-money Protestants and new-money Jews banded together to erect a square city block of culture in downtown Los Angeles. The Los Angeles Music Center would be the citadel of this evolved affluence, and Buffy Chandler and Lew Wasserman, the new standard-bearers.

"He was the only one who could cross the line from the West Side to downtown L.A.," said one of MCA's most prominent senior executives. "He had the Chandlers, and he had those people from the California and the Jonathan Clubs. He could bridge the class differences in L.A. even more so than any other Jew."

When he was named honorary chairman of the Music Center Theater Group in November of 1967, Wasserman wrote his own essay in *Performing Arts* magazine, comparing his fellow Music Center directors to the Medicis, the court of Louis XIV, and the Thessalian oligarchy of ancient Greece. Like Buffy and Lew, they had all seen the need to bring art, poetry, and theater to the masses. That, after all, was what democracy was all about.

Taft Schreiber had also fully embraced culture by the late 1960s, though not quite so selflessly as Lew. Schreiber's art collection had grown into one of the most impressive in Los Angeles. His epicurean pretense topped that of Jerry Wald, Bill Goetz, Jean Negulesco, Alfred Hitchcock, Billy Wilder, Jack Warner, and other Hollywood collectors who had learned to channel their nouveaux richesse into cultural refinement.

Alone among Jules Stein's charter employees, the art-loving Schreiber maintained his power base throughout the transformation of MCA from agency to conglomerate. After Maurice Lipsey retired in 1967, only four of the original Nine Old Men remained: Lew Wasserman, Mickey Rockford, Charles Miller, and Schreiber. Although he carried the title of president, Universal Television Divi-

---

[7] Ziffren resigned his Democratic National Committee position in the late 1960s amid revelations of his Chicago underworld connections, but he remained an active party leader, chairing Senator Edmund Muskie's doomed bid for the presidency in 1972.

sion, Taft turned over most of those responsibilities to Jennings Lang and his triumvirate of junior executives: production boss Jerry Adler, talent liaison Gerry
Hinshaw, and fast-rising business affairs chief Sidney Sheinberg. Officially, Taft
was also an MCA vice president. He had no specific duties, but he was much more
than a midlevel executive.

As Stein's oldest and most trusted employee, Schreiber had a special dispensation. He was not the leader Wasserman was, but Taft had been invited to sit on
the board of directors. A Stein favorite, Taft did not answer to Lew. He was a plan-
ner, a schemer, and a liaison between the Black Tower and the powers that be.
Schreiber was to the Republican Party what Lew had become to the Democrats —
a silent power whom party leaders could count on to conjure up cash with a
phone call.

Schreiber's success as a member of Ronald Reagan's Kitchen Cabinet brought
him to the attention of Richard Nixon's advisers during the 1968 campaign. At
Stein's urging, Taft signed on with attorney Maurice Stans as a Nixon fund-raiser,
accepted the challenge, and turned his MCA office into Republican Finance
Central.

Schreiber was so successful that most of the cash he and Stans solicited didn't
even have to be used during the campaign. Instead, it became a slush fund. In January of 1969, as Washington prepared to inaugurate President Richard Nixon,
Stans was turning the excess campaign money over to Nixon aide Herbert Kalmbach. Kalmbach later testified during the Watergate hearings that Schreiber and
Stans gave him $1,098,000 in hundred-dollar bills. The money was then salted
away in safe-deposit boxes until Nixon's 1972 reelection campaign.

But Stein and Schreiber represented only half of MCA's political fund-raising
efforts in 1968. Lew represented the other half. His party loyalties were as obvious
as the faded photograph that hung on his office wall. When President Johnson
heard that Lew had had his picture up so long that it had turned yellow at the
edges, he sent him a new one, signed, "To Lew Wasserman, from his friend, LBJ."

By March 31, 1968, Johnson's thunder was gone.

The Vietnam War had taken its toll. He'd lost important primaries to both
Senator Eugene McCarthy and Senator Robert Kennedy, and despite his whole-
hearted approval of Lew and oil tycoon Ed Pauley to head up his reelection campaign in California, it appeared he would lose there too. With Johnson's stunning
withdrawal from the race, the primary and the nomination were suddenly up for
grabs. In the chaotic days following LBJ's announcement, Lew and Edie offered
the Johnsons their Palm Springs home as sanctuary. Though LBJ politely
declined, he never forgot the gesture.

On the weekend before the California primary, Lew and Edie set out by private plane with Gregory and Ann Peck for a nostalgic celebration at the LBJ ranch.
After a drive around the ranch, Lyndon and Lady Bird escorted their guests to the

house where Lyndon was born, followed by a trip to Johnson City to see the home — now a museum — where Lyndon had grown up. The capper was a helicopter ride to Austin and the future site of the LBJ Presidential Library.

Robert Kennedy won the California primary that year, but ultimately lost to an assassin's bullet. By the end of a tumultuous political year that also saw the assassination of Martin Luther King and a televised civil war on the streets of Chicago, Wasserman's party was on the ropes. Contributions dried up and Vice President Hubert Humphrey's near-bankrupt campaign went down in flames against the prosperous bid of Taft Schreiber's well-heeled Republican candidate.

—◆—

LEW'S PARTY LOYALTY and friendship with LBJ paid off in more than gratitude and 8-by-10 glossies. As Wasserman correctly guessed, there were big profits to be made in Washington, and all it took was a nod from the president.[8]

Despite charges of unfair competition,[9] LBJ's Interior Department granted MCA's wholly owned subsidiary, Landmark Services, a ten-year exclusive license to operate guided tours of the nation's capital. Landmark vowed to do for Washington, D.C., what the Universal Studios Tour had done for Universal City. During its first year of operation, 320,000 paying customers took the Landmark tour of the White House, the Washington Monument, the Lincoln Memorial, the Capitol Building, and Arlington National Cemetery.[10] That number doubled the following year. The combined demand for tour bus fleets in Washington and Universal City increased so rapidly that MCA bought Minibus, Inc., just to keep itself supplied with vehicles.

LBJ could do nothing to help Lew pick his movies, though.

Feature films from the Black Tower consistently bombed.

"Wasserman was always invoking the ghost of Irving Thalberg," recalled one of his film executives. "The fact is, he didn't have a clue. You look at his list of pictures and you say, 'My God, who would keep *making* them?' It's one thing if you make them and it doesn't work. Okay, you get the joke. But he'd keep making them! He'd keep making these ridiculous westerns with Alain Delon or Andy Williams or romantic comedies with Ross Hunter. And you would sit there and

---

[8]   It only took a nod from LBJ to establish a National Eye Institute, too. After languishing in Congress for almost three years, the bill that would make real Jules Stein's dream of a national center for ophthalmological research was signed into law on August 16, 1968...but only after Jules flew to Texas and personally lobbied to make the institute one of Johnson's last presidential acts before leaving office.

[9]   A lawsuit went all the way to the Supreme Court before MCA got its way.

[10]   In 1972, MCA added Mount Vernon — and an additional 1 million customers a year — to its Landmark tours.

say, 'What the fuck are these assholes doing?' The bad movies were *always* Universal. They didn't even have to advertise it. Everybody knew it."

Though statistics showed that people under twenty-five constituted half the moviegoing audience, most studios in the 1960s were still run by and for older executives. MCA tried to be different, hiring younger men in every department from publicity to production. To Lew, teens were aliens. "They're completely different from us," he said. "They have different tastes in everything from clothes to music. They speak a different language. They can't understand us, and we can't understand them."

But junior executives only had the power to turn a project down. MCA vice president Edd Henry, Lew's right-hand man in the sixties, earned the nickname "Mr. No" because "that's what he told nearly every agent who came to him with a project," said one of his contemporaries.

Only Wasserman or those who constantly consulted with him were empowered to say yes. Even though Lew knew he could no longer see the world through the eyes of a teenager, he continued to insist on control.

"Wasserman had the ultimate say about everything in motion pictures. He was very hands on," said Bob Hussong.

He did not seem to learn from mistakes, or perhaps he didn't care. Lew reasoned that a theatrical bomb made up its losses when it aired on TV. Berle Adams recalled Lew green-lighting two pictures that illustrated his cavalier attitude: *A Lovely Way to Die* (1968) with Kirk Douglas and *Blindfold* (1966), a spy film starring Rock Hudson and Claudia Cardinale. "Both had the same sex scene with the protagonists smoking afterward," said Adams. "Lew had a 'So what?' attitude because movies would always make their money back on TV."

Even though Wasserman's open-checkbook policy lured the best and the brightest to Universal, the studio came to be known as the place "where the best people did their worst work," said Harry Tatelman. Alfred Hitchcock, who hadn't made a hit since *The Birds* (1963), was the classic example.

Both Lew and Hitchcock had urged legendary costumer Edith Head to move to Universal, but she remained loyal to Paramount until *Torn Curtain* (1966), when her failing health and a changing regime at Paramount[11] finally tipped the scales in Universal's favor. The ingredients for another Hitchcock masterpiece seemed to be in place. But Lew insisted that Hitchcock's next film be a hackneyed spy drama called *Torn Curtain*. Lew also demanded stars, so Hitchcock obliged, casting Julie Andrews to play opposite Paul Newman.

Putting Mary Poppins opposite the Hustler in a spy thriller was a bad idea to

---

[11] Barney Balaban, who had been Paramount president since 1936, was replaced by George Weltner, who left two years later with the takeover of Charles Bluhdorn's Gulf and Western conglomerate. At the behest of Sidney Korshak, he was replaced by Robert Evans.

begin with, but audiences who booed at the prerelease screenings underscored Hitchcock's shame at having caved in to Lew's commercial casting demands.[12] Each film he made for Universal thereafter grew progressively worse, both in the eyes of the critics and at the box office. Under Wasserman, Hitchcock became a grotesque caricature of his former glory—a circumstance he seemed to accept with the same good grace and humor that Charles Laughton once had.

While a generation of new auteurs like Martin Scorsese, Francis Ford Coppola, Arthur Penn, and Robert Altman waited in the wings, Lew still played by the old rules that had been established a generation earlier by Louis B. Mayer, Harry Cohn, Adolph Zukor, and Darryl Zanuck. When Stanley Kubrick brought *2001: A Space Odyssey* (1968) to Universal, Lew told the director of *Paths of Glory* (1958), *Spartacus* (1960), *Lolita* (1962), and *Dr. Stangelove* (1963) that his budget was too high. Science fiction movies had always been made on the cheap and anything over $1 million was simply out of the question. Besides, it had no stars.

No one was exempt from Wasserman's vainglory. Even Stein's old friend Mervyn LeRoy,[13] who had made *The Wizard of Oz* and *I Am a Fugitive from a Chain Gang*, produced the so-so thriller *Moment to Moment* (1966). As a follow-up, Ed Muhl handed him a book called *The History of Los Angeles*.

"You want me to make a movie out of this?" LeRoy asked. "Has it got a story?"

"Did that picture about San Francisco with Spencer Tracy and Clark Gable have a story?" asked Muhl.

"You bet it had a story," answered LeRoy. "That was about real people with a real love story and a great drama.[14] Remember, that was set against the background of the San Francisco earthquake and fire. What's this about?"

Muhl mumbled something about Los Angeles historic sites. LeRoy went to see Wasserman. If Lew wanted an L.A. travelogue, he'd have to find somebody else to direct it. Instead of getting sympathy from Lew, he found Muhl's co-conspirator. Lew wanted him to make the movie. LeRoy stormed from the office.

"I won't say good-bye, Mervyn, because I know you'll be back," Wasserman called after him. Lew was wrong. LeRoy never made another movie.

During the late sixties the only MCA executive whose movie judgment proved consistently worse than that of Lew and Edd Henry was Jay Kanter, whom Wasserman named in 1965 to head MCA's European production. A month after arriving

---

[12] Hitchcock made three more films, each one slicker and more expensive—and each one worse—than its predecessor: *Topaz* (1969), *Frenzy* (1972), and *Family Plot* (1976).

[13] LeRoy had been close to the Steins since Jules and Doris first came to Hollywood in 1936. In 1943, Doris played matchmaker and introduced Mervyn to his second wife, Kitty.

[14] In the *Cinebooks Motion Picture Guide* 1995 edition, *San Francisco* (1936) starring Tracy, Gable, and Jeanette MacDonald, is described as a film that "left no doubt that MGM was the most omnipotent studio in Hollywood. Star power, a great, rowdy story, and one of the most awesome special effects sequences in the history of film made *San Francisco* a masterpiece."

in London, Kanter announced four major film deals, including Charlie Chaplin's *The Countess from Hong Kong* with Marlon Brando and Sophia Loren, Francois Truffaut's production of *Fahrenheit 451* with Julie Christie and Oskar Werner, Albert Finney's *Charlie Bubbles*, and Noel Coward's *Pretty Polly*.

Kanter supervised such disasters as *The Brothers of the Gun, Three Into Two Won't Go*, and director Joseph Losey's *Boom!*, starring hot twosome Elizabeth Taylor and Richard Burton in one of their least memorable films.[15] He also authorized two red-ink lemons by director Michael Winner: *The Jokers* and *I'll Never Forget What's 'is Name*. Ironically, Winner then turned around and directed Charles Bronson in three hugely profitable *Death Wish* movies—all for another studio.

Universal's first big wake-up call should have been the costly *A Countess from Hong Kong*, an eternal triangle comedy ploddingly filmed with minimal laughs. Even a cast topped by Marlon Brando and Sophia Loren could not save screen legend Charles Chaplin's directorial swan song from oblivion. Film critic Robert Windeler summed it up as "an unfunny, mindless mess."

But the Universal carnage did not end. In its 1967 annual report, MCA boasted that the Julie Andrews vehicle, *Thoroughly Modern Millie*, at a cost of $6 million, "will be the most successful in our history." In the following year's annual report, the boast was toned down: "While the film did not generate the revenue anticipated in general release in 1968, *Thoroughly Modern Millie* is nevertheless the most successful film in the Company's history."

Later in the same report, management projected the $8 million *Sweet Charity* to be Universal's 1969 blockbuster: "Based on its early engagements, management is of the opinion that gross revenues from this film may exceed those of *Thoroughly Modern Millie*."[16]

---

[15] *Boom!*, the film adaptation of Tennessee Williams' *The Milk Train Doesn't Stop Here Anymore*, cost Universal $4.6 million to produce and took in only $514,725 at the U.S. box office. During a screening for Kanter, Wasserman, and other MCA brass, producer John Heyman fell asleep. Afterward one executive effused: "We've got *Virginia Woolf* in color!"

Before *Boom!* was released, Universal committed $3.1 million to the next Losey bomb, *Secret Ceremony* (1968) costarring Elizabeth Taylor, Robert Mitchum, and Mia Farrow. Losey had more than doubled his fee from $100,000 to $225,000 and cut himself in for a profit percentage. There were no profits, however. *Secret Ceremony* only took in $2.7 million at the domestic box office. It was the last movie Losey ever made at Universal.

[16] In management's judgment, the other big releases of 1969 would include *Winning*, a race car film starring Paul Newman; *Angel in My Pocket* with Andy Griffith; *Hellfighters* starring John Wayne; *The Lost Man* with Sidney Poitier; *Secret Ceremony* with Elizabeth Taylor and Mia Farrow; Alfred Hitchcock's *Topaz*; *In Search of Gregory* starring Julie Christie; *Three Into Two Won't Go* with Rod Steiger and Claire Bloom; *Tell Them Willie Boy Is Here* starring Robert Redford; *The Love God* starring Don Knotts; *Can Hieronymus Merkin Ever Forget Mercy Humppe and Find True Happiness?*; and *The Loves of Isadora* starring Vanessa Redgrave.

At the bottom of the list management also mentioned a release planned for late in the year called *Airport*, starring Dean Martin and Burt Lancaster.

TWENTY-SEVEN

Palace Coup

1969

MCA could make money. What it could not make was movies. Despite the brave rhetoric of MCA's annual reports, Universal Pictures bled over $30 million in red ink during 1968. The upcoming year looked even gloomier. There was little question about who was to blame. Lew decided not only which movies got made but also how, by whom, and under what circumstances — and he decided wrong most of the time.

"He could count the box office in every hamlet in the world and knew exactly how many people took the tour, but he could not make a movie worth crap," recalled a then-ranking member of the MCA hierarchy.

Producer Saul David (*Our Man Flint, Logan's Run*) offered a scathing study of Lew's insidious exercise of absolute power in his 1981 Hollywood memoir, *The Industry*. A chapter ironically titled "Complete Artistic Control!" detailed David's own cautionary experience in trying to make *Skullduggery* (1970), a campy jungle story about the discovery of the missing link in a New Guinea rain forest. After he had signed a contract with Universal guaranteeing no studio interference, David was summoned to the Black Tower. The scene in Lew's office was vintage Wasserman: plush but simple decor and a desk so clean there wasn't a sheet of paper in sight. What struck the producer upon their first meeting was that Wasserman had,

> ...an apparently limitless grasp of the worldwide structure and detail of film distribution. Currency rates, booking policies, governmental restrictions, competitive practices, favorable and unfavorable seasons, and so on. He was not showing off for a visitor; he was discussing what he thought important.... Those dreary numbers and percentages and schedules were passion and reality to him, and while he spoke (and I made proper responses), I was genuinely impressed. I'm familiar enough with the language of business to know that a lot of corporate tal-

ent is bluff and the manipulation of personality plus knowing how to use lawyers and accountants. This man seemed to be without an act at all — an atmosphere thin as the moon's, every detail visible in that airless clarity.

What followed, David recalled as "calm ferocity": Lew's firm but unemotional evisceration of the man Saul David had selected to direct *Skullduggery*. He was "an undependable hysteric," Wasserman announced. The man lied. He stole. He'd been thrown off his last two assignments. Lew knew precisely where and when the director had screwed up and how much money he'd lost.

Despite his "complete artistic control," David got the message. He chose a director who was more acceptable to Lew. But when Wasserman demanded he change the star of *Skullduggery*, David refused to back down. He'd cast Burt Reynolds, who'd tangled with MCA years earlier. Reynolds had costarred in Revue's short-lived NBC adventure series, *Riverboat* (1959–1961), and in a fit of anger one day Reynolds had literally thrown an MCA official off the riverboat. Reynolds was fired and hadn't set foot inside the Universal lot since. Lew made no secret of his hatred for the actor.

"I'm not going to make a $4 million picture with Burt Reynolds," he declared.

"Mr. Wasserman, according to my deal here, I can decide these things myself," said David.

"I know your deal, but I'm sorry," Lew repeated. "I'm not going to make this picture with Burt Reynolds."

"I'm sorry, too," said David. "But I don't know what to do now."

Lew smiled. "You just go back and think about it. I'll come up with some other names and send them over to you."

Saul David stuck to his guns. He demanded the artistic control that his contract guaranteed. To his surprise, and that of everyone else involved in the movie, he did get to keep Reynolds. Cherubic Berle Adams delivered the happy news, and it was seconded by a young production executive named Ned Tanen. David did not question how they had been able to override the iron-willed Mr. Wasserman. Instead, in their honor, he created a composite bit character in *Skullduggery* named "Berle Tanen" and played the role himself.

What David would not know until nearly a year later, after *Skullduggery* had failed miserably at the box office, was that both he and his movie had been pawns in the opening gambit of a deadly game of corporate control. Along with Jay Kanter, another pawn, Saul David and *Skullduggery* would both become casualties of that game, and none of them would even know who the real players were until years after Lew Wasserman confidently announced "Checkmate!"

Kanter had been and always would be a Wasserman favorite. Lew might have found it grating, even impossible, to keep Universal's contractual promises of creative control with its producers, directors, writers, and stars, but he willingly turned over absolute autonomy to Kanter, whose wretched film judgment was rivaled only by that of Lew himself.

But Kanter's second chances ran out with *Isadora*, an extravagant biopic featuring Vanessa Redgrave as the seductive, freethinking turn-of-the-century dancer Isadora Duncan. So confident was Wasserman that Kanter had finally picked a winner that he approved the booking of L.A.'s Paramount Theater for its premiere, selling advance tickets on a reserved-seat basis.

But British director Karel Reisz (*This Sporting Life, Saturday Night and Sunday Morning*) turned in a three-hour version of *Isadora*, so plodding and dense that the premiere had to be canceled and an hour trimmed from the film. MCA tried to salvage the result with a premiere at the 1968 Cannes Film Festival. Redgrave won a festival prize, and went on to be nominated for a Best Actress Oscar, but the movie was stillborn at U.S. box offices. *Isadora* became Kanter's last stand.

"The picture division was a catastrophe," said a former MCA vice president. "There was a constant flow of money going out and nothing coming back. The company was fairly close to going under."

With *Isadora*, Universal's losses crept above the $40 million mark. Finally, even Jules could no longer be mollified. "Everybody tells me our European pictures are terrible," he told Lew following one of his trips to Britain. "I'm sick and tired of hearing it. We've got to do something about it."

Still, Lew did not act. At the first board meeting of the year, there was a showdown. Behind closed doors, Stein chastised Wasserman.

"That's the only time I ever heard Jules criticize Lew," said Berle Adams, who witnessed the browbeating. "He said, 'I want that [the British production operation] closed. I want out of London and the production company.' Lew said, 'All right, I'll go there and take care of it.' Jules made the mistake of making me the heavy by saying, 'Lew, you stay here. I'd rather have Berle close it and get out of all of our contracts.'"

At that same meeting, Stein expanded the MCA board from six to ten members. Taft Schreiber and Lew's three executive vice presidents—Adams, Albert Dorskind, and Daniel Ritchie—formally became part of the corporate leadership. Adams saw the expansion as a first step toward restructuring MCA into a dynamic oligarchy instead of a semi-benevolent autocracy. He would step up to a new position as MCA's chief operating officer while Lew remained president and CEO. They would work as a team and dominate the entire entertainment industry, including motion pictures. Eventually, Jules would retire, Lew would be named chairman, and Berle would become president of MCA. It never occurred to Adams that some deeper treachery might be in the wind and that he too could be just another pawn in the game. But it occurred to Lew.

He saw the board expansion as a subtle power grab by one of his earliest MCA allies. In Wasserman's corner were directors Walter Heymann of First National Bank of Chicago, Charles Thornton of Litton Industries, Stein's brother-in-law Charles Miller, and possibly Dorskind and Ritchie. Lew felt he still had an edge with the board.

But he could sense his nemesis moving like a ghost behind the scenes. With Sonny Werblin gone, the only other man Jules Stein ever seriously considered for the MCA presidency was finally within striking distance.

"Taft Schreiber was just like Lew in that he could see ahead. He could see what was going to happen next," remembered Tony Curtis. "Both of them had their eye on the sparrow. It was the same damn sparrow. They were just two different men going after it in two different directions."

Schreiber gave Berle Adams his full support. Adams never thought for a moment that he might simply be Schreiber's stalking horse. Lew understood, though. For over thirty years he'd witnessed Schreiber practice deceit as if it were an art form. His opponents never even knew they had been castrated until Schreiber mailed them their testicles. Wasserman understood exactly what he was up against, and it wasn't the capable, cheerful, and fatally ambitious Berle Adams.

At the end of February, Wasserman saw yet another sign of his crumbling future when his handpicked protégé Jay Kanter handed in his resignation. Kanter then formed a new independent production company with Alan Ladd Jr., Elliot Kastner, and ex–MCA executive Jerry Gershwin. Lew was left to defend the 1969 Universal feature film lineup by himself.

Meanwhile, Saul David claimed that an unnamed MCA board member had met privately with him on location in Jamaica, where *Skullduggery* was nearing completion. Changes were afoot, David was told. At an upcoming board meeting in June, Wasserman would be stepping down. Adams would be taking his place. The board member wanted David to consider taking over as Universal's new motion picture production chief.

"There was intrigue. There was side-taking. There were different rumors as to what Jules Stein was thinking," Sid Sheinberg, Universal TV president at the time, said more than a decade later.

Jules Stein remained Sphinx-like through it all. As he approached his seventy-third birthday, he thought more than ever about his legacy: the show business empire he'd crafted through a combination of wile, loyalty, intense effort, and innumerable deals with the devil. He wanted to leave it in Lew's hands, but did he dare?

—⌇⌇⌇—

DESPITE A STRING of box office stinkers and a declining share of the domestic television market,[1] MCA Inc. continued to shine on the New York Stock Exchange. Though Wasserman had made his share of blunders since the Decca-Universal takeover, the stock-buying public hadn't seen them. In the five years since it quit the agency business, MCA had diversified and doubled its annual gross income. What Lew lost in bad movies, the rest of MCA more than made up in domestic and international TV syndication, music publishing royalties, Universal Studios Tour admissions, pop record sales, and Columbia Savings and Loan profits.

On paper, MCA looked like a plum that was ripe for the picking. In the summer of 1968, Pittsburgh-based Westinghouse Electric took notice. With over 8,000 consumer products ranging from lightbulbs to nuclear reactors, Westinghouse's total sales for 1967 — $2.9 billion — dwarfed the revenues of all the Hollywood studios combined. Westinghouse annual profits were ten times those of MCA.

Through MCA executive vice president Dan Ritchie, Westinghouse tendered its offer. With scant hesitation, Jules Stein opted to sell. In Westinghouse he saw a rare chance to meld MCA with an old-line blue-chip industrial, permanently etch the name of Jules Stein in the history of American commerce, and gracefully cash out of show business with minimal tax consequences.

In MCA, Westinghouse saw a nearly perfect example of vertical integration — an opportunity to own the movies, pop records, and television programs that Americans played over Westinghouse stereos, radios, and TV sets. Furthermore, as a Westinghouse division, MCA would have rock-solid security and virtually unlimited capital. The manufacturing giant had already promised Stein that it would help MCA develop condos and subdivide some of Universal City's vacant property, once the merger went through.

In special session on October 7, 1968, at Chicago's Blackstone Hotel, a majority of MCA stockholders approved the merger.

"I've always had great respect for Westinghouse since the days I attended school [at the University of West Virginia] just south of Pittsburgh," said Stein. "It's a delightful marriage."

But before the wedding could be consummated, a familiar sour note sounded from Washington, D.C. Both the Justice Department and the Federal Communications Commission noted that Westinghouse owned and operated seven radio stations and five TV stations, each of which might be programmed with MCA movies, records, and television series. Within weeks of Richard M. Nixon's 1968 election as the nation's thirty-seventh president, the old antitrust question arose

---

[1]   Down from more than half the prime-time programming in 1961 to a still very healthy 30 percent of prime time in 1969.

once more: was the Octopus alive and well and planning to live again in the belly of Westinghouse?

Until the Justice Department and FCC resolved the issue, the Westinghouse-MCA marriage was put on hold.

———◊◊◊———

ON MARCH 17, 1969, Lew Wasserman planned a two-week convocation of MCA sales personnel from around the world. It was to be the biggest, most comprehensive gathering of MCA executives in the company's history.

The sales convention was to be a prelude to the grand opening of the $15 million, 21-story, 500-room Sheraton Universal Hotel on March 26, followed by four days of parties hosted by Dr. and Mrs. Stein and highlighted by the March 28 premiere of Universal's biggest release of the year, the musical *Sweet Charity*, directed by Bob Fosse and starring Shirley MacLaine.

Doris and Jules Stein spent months planning the opening of their hotel, with Doris herself designing the 1,100-seat grand ballroom and personally attending to the motifs in each guest room, right down to the wall hangings, color schemes, and white tulip floral arrangements.[2] The Steins invited Ron and Nancy Reagan to act as honorary chairpersons at the hotel's inaugural, lining the hallway to the Governor's Suite with framed photos of the governors of all fifty states.

Through trade-out charter deals that Jules swung with Continental Airlines and Germany's Lufthansa, the Steins would fly in 75 counts, dukes, and various deposed European royalty, and an assortment of 165 tuxedoed freeloaders, Park Avenue swells, and East Coast gossip columnists — all to bear witness to the biggest high-society bash Hollywood had ever seen. It was to be MCA's crowning triumph.

Universal City Plaza was now a reality. The Steins meant to celebrate.

But on the morning of March 15, two days before the sales conference was to begin, Universal publicity chief David Lipton called Berle Adams in a panic. Edie Wasserman had phoned with news that Lew had suffered heart trouble. Mrs. Wasserman wanted it immediately announced in a press release that Lew Wasserman, who had given his whole life to Jules Stein's MCA, had suffered a heart attack on his fifty-sixth birthday.

Lipton wanted to know what to do.

"Which hospital is Lew at?" asked Berle.

No hospital, said Lipton. Lew was at home.

---

[2]   Jules had lusted after owning his own hotel since passing up a chance to buy the Beverly Hills Hotel in the late 1930s. According to Century City developer Hernando Courtright, who raised the $1.5 million to buy the old boardinghouse and turn it into the city's most famous hotel, Stein planned to turn it over to Wasserman and let him run it for him. Ultimately, Stein nixed the purchase as a bad investment.

"The president of the company has a heart attack and *he's at home?*" Adams asked incredulously. "David, don't do anything."

Wasserman seemed a most unlikely candidate for heart trouble. He ate like a bird, did not smoke, rarely drank, and had never taken a day of sick time in his entire career. As a precaution against germs, he even assigned an office boy to clean his telephone with alcohol once a week. In the twenty years that Adams had been with the company, he could remember Lew taking exactly one brief vacation, and even then Wasserman had called in several times a day to make sure things were running smoothly. The home heart attack sounded suspect.

Adams called Stein, who told him to find Schreiber and report to Misty Mountain pronto. Berle tracked Schreiber down at the Hillcrest Country Club, where he was playing golf with Stein's personal physician, Dr. Eliot Corday.

By the time he arrived at Misty Mountain, Schreiber already had a partial explanation for Lew's sudden sickness. He told Stein and Adams that the golf foursome playing directly behind Schreiber and Dr. Corday at Hillcrest had included Dr. Rex Kennamer, Lew's personal physician. Lew hadn't suffered a heart attack, Kennamer told Corday. Wasserman simply had a "blood disorder."

The next step was to confront the Wassermans. While Stein and Adams listened in, Schreiber phoned Edie. "Edie, I understand that you want to release the story that Lew has had a heart attack," he said. "We just spoke to Rex Kennamer, and we know what the problem is, and it isn't heart."

Schreiber talked her out of releasing the story, but she never explained why she'd wanted to exaggerate Lew's illness.

After Schreiber hung up, Stein briefly pondered the situation in silence, then nodded to himself as if he had just made up his mind. "I've decided to become chairman emeritus," he announced. "I want Lew to become chairman of the board and managing director, and I want Berle to become president of the company."

It was a possibility that Adams recalled Stein discussing with him earlier, but Lew's ailment seemed to accelerate Stein's decision. Until Lew recuperated, Jules said, Adams would be acting president. They would announce the new executive lineup in two weeks, after the opening of the Sheraton and the premiere of *Sweet Charity*.

Schreiber interrupted. He had always wanted Lew's title, he confessed. It wasn't the power or the responsibility so much. Just the right to call himself MCA president. Would it be too much to ask if he might step up to the presidency for a year with Adams continuing in his role as executive vice president? Berle would be the *real* CEO. Schreiber's title would be purely ceremonial.

"If it's all right with you, Berle, it's okay with me," said Stein.

Schreiber and Adams agreed to find an experienced producer to become executive vice president for film production. Between them, Schreiber and Adams would retain control of the purse strings, but they would defer to the new production chief on all creative questions, including the green-lighting of Universal's movies. Stein agreed.

"Jules felt that Wall Street would be comfortable with the knowledge that two experienced executives would control the film budgets," said Adams.

The following Monday, David Lipton released the news that Lew was at home recuperating from a virus—a minor illness that Berle Adams brushed off as "a cold."

For the next ten days, Adams was provisional president of MCA, Inc. During one session, Adams produced his own slide show. It began with a screen reading "The winds of change are blowing." Wasserman's name was rarely mentioned. By the end of the sales conference, rumors were thick.

"I remember a buffet at the Sheraton," said Hussong. "I sat down with Berle and Lucy Adams. I cheerfully said, 'Oh, my God, what's this vicious rumor I hear that Lew's not going to be here and that *you're* going to be president? I can't believe that would happen.' And there was dead silence. I was given a very sharp look— not by Berle, who can hide his feelings, but by Lucy. And then I knew. I whispered, 'Oh, my God, it must be true!'"

On Wednesday, March 26, Stein's European and East Coast guests began arriving. The lobby of the Sheraton swarmed with overdressed barons, sabled marquesses, and oddball aristocrats. One bejeweled Palm Beach heiress snarled at the concierge when told that her bichon frise could not have a separate suite. Another insisted on satin pillowcases in her room so that her coiffure would not be mussed.

In all, 750 guests packed the hotel for the festivities. Another fifty or so got invitations to stay at least one night at Misty Mountain, where the Steins wined and dined the crème de la crème. During the day they took the Universal Studios Tour, made the trek south to Anaheim to visit Disneyland, accompanied Jules to his new Eye Institute at UCLA, or played the ponies at Santa Anita. At night they dressed in black tie and peacock couture in a fashion far better suited to London or midtown Manhattan than to the San Fernando Valley.

No one heard from the ailing MCA president during the first days of the celebration. The Wasserman rumors began to include the possibility that he might be marshaling his forces while he "recuperated." Privately, Doris heaved a sigh of relief. Without Lew, there could be no Edie, and by now Doris Stein made no secret of her loathing of Mrs. Wasserman. It did seem a shame that the Wassermans would not be present for the premiere of *Sweet Charity*, though. It was very much Lew's picture.

With its hype, high energy, and mixed message, *Sweet Charity* paralleled MCA's own troubles at the close of the turbulent 1960s. Like the confused bimbette Shirley MacLaine portrayed in the movie, MCA also seemed to be desperately searching for a knight in shining armor, whether it be Westinghouse or a new president, or both. At the end of *Sweet Charity*, MacLaine winds up dumped, diddled, and back on her own, apparently no wiser, but eternally optimistic. Film critic Rex Reed called the musical about a New York taxi dancer looking for love in all the wrong places "the kind of platinum clinker designed to send audiences flying toward the safety of their television sets."

But the Steins and their guests smiled politely and declared *Sweet Charity* yet another MCA triumph. Jules had no interest in compounding his problems by brooding over this latest Universal boondoggle. If he saw any ironic parallels with his own MCA, Stein kept his observations to himself. There was no room for irony at the Sheraton Universal after *Los Angeles Herald Examiner* columnist James Bacon broke the news that afternoon about the future of MCA President Lew Wasserman: "[G]ratitude is an unknown commodity in the business and entertainment world. You're only as good as your last financial statement, which for MCA was somewhat disappointing.... Doris Stein is much too social to let her husband spoil her parties with nasty business details like firing the guy who built the company."

"I wrote a column at the same time that Stein was gonna fire him," recalled Bacon. "Doris Stein had a big party with dukes and earls and everybody else there. I wrote [that] Jules Stein will never fire Lew Wasserman with Doris Stein having this big party coming up 'cause she wouldn't stand for it."

Stein was mortified. Berle Adams was stunned. Schreiber was silent. Bacon's column could not have been more effective if it had been a dagger in the hand of Jack the Ripper. At first, Adams guessed the veteran Hollywood reporter was simply peeved that he hadn't been invited to any of Stein's parties and wanted to stir things up a little among the elite at the Sheraton. Bacon himself boasted years later that it was a perfect way to end a thirty-five-year-old personal beef with Stein. It seems that while Bacon was an undergraduate at Notre Dame and Jules was a band booker, Stein had refused to let Benny Goodman play at Bacon's college prom. A generation later, Bacon evened the score.

But neither explanation took into account the timing or placement of Bacon's diatribe. His words were arrows aimed straight at Stein's heart. More than a dozen key executives, including Lou Friedland, Edd Henry, Sid Sheinberg, and Jennings Lang, hastily petitioned Stein to retain Wasserman as CEO. If Wasserman went, they vowed, so would they.

"I told them to put my name down," recalled Al Dorskind. "I liked Jules, but I was naive about all the politics. Next thing I knew, I was reading that Lew was out and Berle Adams was trying to be president. I didn't give a damn about who was what title, but I did give a damn about Lew. If Lew wasn't going to be president, that was a different matter."

"Berle would give you family talks, fatherly talks, but he wouldn't give you a fifteen-dollar raise," said one executive, explaining why he turned on Adams. "He was very family oriented. His wife, Lucy, was a great strength, but she and Edie clashed head-on, and that was fatal."

"You must remember that the nearer you got to the top of the pyramid, the worse it got," said Bob Hussong. "There wasn't just the battle among the guys for the corner office. It was the battle at home among the ladies for the prestige of being Mrs. Corner Office."

But how did Bacon know that Lew and Edie might be losing their own corner office status?

"He was tipped by Gene Klein, the National General chairman who helped Lew found the President's Club and went on to buy the San Diego Chargers," said Adams.[3]

It seemed that Bacon's wife, Doris, was Klein's niece. Klein, of course, had been a close friend of the Wassermans for years. Klein visited Lew while he was convalescing and discussed Stein's anger over the Kanter affair. Berle chose to believe that Klein took it upon himself to plant the story of Lew's impending doom in his nephew-in-law's newspaper column.

"It certainly was not Lew's style to do so," he said. "Jules was hurt and shocked that he would be accused of dumping Lew Wasserman. With all of the excitement surrounding the arrival of his overseas guests and the opening of the hotel, his planned meeting with Lew never took place. If they had met, I believe that Lew would happily have accepted the promotion to chairman of the board and managing director. There would have been a smooth transition to Schreiber as president. The rumors would have been put to bed, and the James Bacon article would never have been written."

But the best laid plans of Berle and Schreiber had gone out the window by the following Monday. At an emergency meeting, the MCA board unanimously extended Lew Wasserman's authority as president and offered him a new fifteen-month contract. All talk of elevating Adams to chief operating officer vanished, and no one ever knew about the proposed ceremonial handoff of the MCA presidency to Taft Schreiber.

Three weeks later Westinghouse abandoned its merger plans, blaming the FCC and the Justice Department for holding things up far too long.

Reflecting upon the failed merger fifteen years later, Lew told the *Los Angeles*

---

[3] When Klein bought the Chargers, critics pointed out that he had once been partners with Meyer Lansky and Sidney Korshak in the Acapulco Towers. Klein, who also retained Korshak as the Chargers' attorney, maintained that he was unaware that Lansky and Korshak were among his partners. NFL Commissioner Pete Rozelle rose to Klein's defense, telling the media: "A lot of times you invest in something and you have no idea who the other investors are."

Times, "I went along with it, but I felt that it was too early in our corporate career. The government prevented the merger, and I turned out to be right."

A second shot at a merger materialized in July, when Firestone Tire and Rubber offered $325 million for MCA's 8 million shares, but by September that marriage, too, was dead. Privately, MCA executives called it a mismatch. The bloated salaries and expense accounts that Wasserman awarded his stars and top executives appalled Firestone's board. How would a Firestone vice president react when he learned that his MCA counterpart earned two or three times his salary?[4] A company that produced good, competitively priced tires simply could not coexist with a company that produced high-priced fantasy and paid outrageous wages.

By year's end Lew had dissolved the three executive vice presidencies. Adams, Dorskind, and Ritchie[5] were downgraded to mere vice presidential status and removed from the board of directors. Schreiber remained on the board, however.

On the same day Lew was reelected president, Saul David was told to forget about becoming Universal's production chief. Lew seemed to take special glee in summoning David to his office after his private screening of the final print of *Skullduggery*. The man David faced did not appear to be suffering from heart warnings, viral infections, or even a lingering cold, and he certainly hadn't called David in to congratulate him on his movie.

"He loathed the picture, he had no intention of putting any money or effort into its distribution, he would teach me a lesson," recalled David. "He was another man. The cords stood out on his neck as he spoke—it was [the murderous movie mogul played by] Rod Steiger in *The Big Knife*, but colder, more controlled."

—◦∾◦—

LEW'S VERSION OF the events that led to his reaffirmation as MCA president didn't surface until seven years later, in a lengthy story about the aborted coup in the inaugural issue of *New West* magazine. Business writer Andrew Tobias interviewed Stein, Wasserman, and virtually every other principal, and still came away with an incomplete account.

For his part, Stein all but refused to talk. Jules tried to steer the interview toward the Eye Institute and his many charities, but failing that, all he would tell Tobias was that he had never considered dumping Lew Wasserman.

Wasserman went into considerably more detail, however. To begin with, he

---

[4] Excluding stock options and pension fund, Wasserman earned $250,000 a year; Adams earned $185,000; and several other MCA executives earned six-figure salaries. No comparable Firestone executive earned above five figures.

[5] Stripped of his role as MCA's Wall Street liaison, Ritchie quit at the beginning of 1970. He eventually went to work for Westinghouse.

took Tobias back to March 13, 1969, the day before his "heart warning." His two-and-a-half-year-old granddaughter, Carol Ann, had been to the house, and Wasserman had "knocked himself out showing her a good time," he told Tobias.

The following day, he and three other white community leaders had met with 150 angry black leaders in South Central L.A., trying to nip another Watts riot in the bud. The day was hot, tempers were high, and Lew suffered chest pains. By the time he'd driven back to Beverly Hills, Edie had Dr. Kennamer waiting. He prescribed two weeks of complete bed rest—no phone, no newspapers, no business. There was no more mystery to it than that. Everything else—Bacon's column, Stein's chagrin, his supporters' petition—simply happened while Lew followed doctor's orders. No mystery, he said. Things just happened to turn out in his favor. That was all.

"What really happened was Lew threatened to sue Stein's ass off," said Wasserman's former son-in-law, Jack Myers.

There was also much more to Lew's "heart warning" and his granddaughter's visit than Wasserman chose to reveal to Tobias, according to Myers. At the time, Lynne Wasserman was in the final throes of a divorce from Ronnie Leif.[6]

"I thought they were very happy together," said an MCA vice president. "I don't know what happened. It was none of my business, but I thought they were quite happy."

What went wrong, according to friends, was that history was repeating itself. Like her mother before her, Lynne married an agent who was driven by deal-making and obsessed with success. Unlike her mother, Lynne had neither the temperament nor the social skills to find intimacy outside the marriage. The result was war.

Their only child, Carol Ann, had become an unfortunate pawn in her parents' court battle. Lew and Edie, who had remained married for thirty-three years despite obvious reasons for calling it quits, did not approve of the divorce. They sided with Leif.

Lynne retaliated by withholding Carol Ann from her grandparents. On those rare occasions when Lew and Edie did get to visit, they tended to overdo things by taking the little girl to the most expensive, elaborate, and high-energy places in town.

But an even darker secret was at the root of an estrangement between Lynne and her father that would last for much of the next twenty years.

According to Myers, Lynne had stumbled upon the true source of her workaholic father's remarkable ability to get by on little or no sleep at night, and it had

---

[6]   Charging Leif with mental cruelty, Lynne formally separated from him on March 28, 1968. The divorce became final on May 20, 1969.

nothing to do with his sleepless childhood in Cleveland or his restless love of rising early to get the worldwide box office results.

"He took Seconal[7] to get to sleep at night," said Myers. "Lynne found out about it and tried to get him to stop. They got into huge fights about it, and Lew just stopped talking to her for years."

Though Dr. Kennamer would never elaborate on his patient's sudden "blood disorder" or his miraculous recovery, Myers maintained that Lynne knew exactly what had temporarily felled her father. The "heart warning" was just that: a warning that if he did not stop the Seconal, he would wind up like Marilyn Monroe, Dorothy Dandridge, and a dozen of Lew's other permanently silenced clients.[8]

"[Lew] told Lynne to mind her own business, and the two of them stopped speaking to each other," said Myers.

Lew's recovery did seem nearly miraculous — almost like that of an alcoholic who stops drinking or a diabetic who gives up sweets. Progressing from "heart warning" to reinvigorated president in two weeks, Wasserman was back in charge at the top of the Black Tower, his challengers vanquished and the pretender to the throne shunned by his fellow mutineers. All signs of ill health vanished, and he was back to his old office routine: in before dawn, home after sunset, and no vacations.

---

[7] A barbituate seldom prescribed today because of its addictive effects, Seconal was widely used in the 1950s and 1960s as a sleep aid.

[8] On June 22, 1969, just three months after Lew's "heart warning," Judy Garland died of a prescription drug overdose while sitting on the toilet in a London hotel. She was forty-seven.

TWENTY-EIGHT

The Heir Apparent

1970–1973

In the early months of 1970, Jules Stein prepared to die.

At seventy-four he had already lived longer than either of his parents and had been regularly cheating death since he was diagnosed with an intestinal malignancy in 1956. Following that first abdominal operation, his surgeons had pronounced him cancer free, but periodically he reentered the hospital under the guise of some other malady to have new growths removed from his intestinal tract. For example, when he entered the Harkness Pavilion at Columbia Presbyterian Hospital, his cover story was that he suffered from a serious case of hepatitis.

In the months following the palace coup, Stein underwent exploratory surgery at UCLA Medical Center. For press release purposes, his doctors diagnosed ventriculitis, an inflammation of the digestive tract. Privately they agreed that his cancer had resurged and that it appeared terminal. After consulting with a team of physicians, Stein's old friend Dr. Eliot Corday resorted to the use of gentamicin, which was an experimental drug at the time. The powerful antibiotic did seem to halt Stein's abdominal problem, but brought with it a lethal side effect: kidney failure. While his bowels healed, Stein's overall condition worsened. He suffered dementia, his mind wandering like that of an Alzheimer's patient. For two months he slipped in and out of a coma.

Finally Dr. Corday called Stein's daughters, stepsons, brother, and sisters to his bedside to prepare for the worst. Doris asked the UCLA chancellor, Dr. Franklin Murphy, to write a eulogy. In his will, Stein had already named Doris as heir to his controlling shares of MCA. And as Jules wavered between life and death, the ailing corporation he had created nearly half a century earlier seemed headed for an extraordinary recovery.

Overall profits were up. A $10 million Universal melodrama, about a crippled airliner in a blizzard, had hit the box office jackpot. Universal producer Ross

Hunter had paid $400,000 for the rights to Arthur Hailey's best-selling novel, hired an all-star cast headed by Dean Martin and Burt Lancaster, and watched the finished product take in over $45 million in domestic ticket sales alone.[1] Nominated for ten Academy Awards, *Airport* won Helen Hayes an Oscar as Best Supporting Actress and became the largest-grossing film in Universal's history.

Lew had learned from the Kanter affair that neither he nor any of his most trusted mandarins understood how to make movies. *Variety*'s A. D. Murphy observed that once the 1969 palace coup was aborted, MCA "virtually gave up all pretenses to a viable in-house feature film organization and began relying on affiliated independents like Hal Wallis, Robert Wise, Mark Robson, Fred Zinnemann, Norman Jewison, and Zanuck-Brown."

George Roy Hill, William Friedkin, Billy Wilder, the Filmmakers Group, and the Mirisch Corporation migrated to Universal. Lew built a separate Producers Building behind the Black Tower to accommodate them all, and in a 180-degree about-face, Universal quickly became known as a hands-off studio: if an independent producer brought in his movie on time and under budget, the men in the Black Tower kept their distance. Although Universal still made occasional clinkers like *I Love My Wife* (1970) and *Cockeyed Cowboys of Calico County* (1970), most of its releases were now coproduced by tried-and-true independents.

Universal also had the number one TV show of 1970: *Marcus Welby, M.D.,* which revived the career of Robert Young, who starred as the kindhearted physician. Two more of its series—the cop series *Ironside,* starring Raymond Burr, and *Adam-12,* starring Martin Milner and Kent McCord—finished among the top twelve Nielsen-rated shows.[2] Thanks to Sid Sheinberg, eight and a half hours of prime time each week belonged to MCA, jumping up to thirteen and a half hours the following year. Despite its success with series television, Universal's assembly line switched increasingly to TV movies of the week: seventeen in 1970 and twenty each in 1971 and 1972.

MCA Records had top-selling albums from Elton John, Loretta Lynn, Bill Cosby, the Who, Neil Diamond, and the cast of *Jesus Christ Superstar.* MCA tours, both in Washington, D.C., and at Universal Studios, had grown at a steady pace of 25 percent a year, and Atlantic City–based Spencer's Gifts expanded beyond

---

[1]   Lancaster called the script "a piece of junk," and Martin didn't want to play a serious role that would clash with his laid-back TV persona. They were both persuaded with contracts that called for $1 million each up front plus 5 percent of profits once the film hit the $50 million mark. *Airport* earned more money for both actors than any film either of them had ever done. Ross Hunter was not so fortunate. He gave up his own percentage in exchange for having MCA pay off his mortgage in the Trousdale Estates section of Beverly Hills.

[2]   "One thing they could not make was a hit TV comedy," said an executive of that era. "They didn't have a clue." Even after poaching comedy talent like producer-actor Sheldon Leonard from Desilu, MCA was unable to produce anything but dramas and movies of the week.

catalog sales, adding thirty-five new retail stores in malls along the eastern seaboard.

One day in October, Lew summoned Berle Adams to his office. When he entered, Adams noted that Charlie Miller, Jules's brother-in-law and a member of the board of directors, sat silently next to Lew.[3] They were both frowning. Berle thought they'd heard bad news about Jules. Wasserman's irritatingly unruffled lisp pierced Adams to the quick. It didn't dawn on him until afterward that Lew had asked Miller, a Stein family member, to sit in as a witness while he gave Adams the boot.

"Berle," Wasserman began, "I don't think there's room for you at MCA. The time has come for you to go out on your own."

"Are you telling me I'm fired?" Adams asked.

"You're not being fired," said Wasserman. "Call it a voluntary retirement. But I think it would be wise for you to function in your present role until the first of the year. That will give you time to turn your responsibilities over to others and will qualify you to receive this year's pension contribution and the growth in the pension fund. We'll work together in preparing the press release announcing your decision to leave the company. The announcement will be slanted in your favor."

Adams left the office in a numbed haze. He walked around like a robot for several days, letting it all sink in. Then he returned to Lew's office, and this time he demanded an explanation. He did not deserve this. For twenty years, he'd been a good soldier. He'd been a team player.

Yes, but as Wasserman explained, Berle was also too old to become president. Jules Stein was dying. The time had come for Lew to find his own successor, and Berle was only four years Lew's junior. Wasserman had to find someone substantially younger, and that someone could not work in Berle's shadow. Adams would automatically undermine the younger man's authority. The only solution was for Berle to leave.

Lew's cold logic was cold comfort. Adams suspected there was more to it than picking his successor. He confronted Schreiber. When Lew first reported his "heart attack," Taft had urged Berle on. Was it possible that Schreiber had double-crossed him?

"I think it was the publicity that did you in," Schreiber said without answering Berle's direct question.

Merely the perception that Adams might be waiting in the wings was enough for Wasserman to act. But it was the dying Dr. Stein who sealed Berle's doom, Schreiber pointed out. While he lived, Taft held Jules's stock proxy. Once he was gone, Doris would take control. Lew had to get rid of Berle before that happened,

---

[3] With Dan Ritchie's resignation earlier in the year, Miller took over as MCA's liaison with Wall Street.

Schreiber explained. Doris tolerated Lew, but she openly loathed Edie. The Steins had always depended on Lew to run MCA, but they rarely invited the Wassermans to Misty Mountain. Doris was the wild card, and Lew could not be absolutely certain what she might do once Jules died. Given the opportunity, she might move Lew out if she thought Berle was standing by. Lew couldn't take that chance.

"Leaving MCA was an emotional jolt," Adams recalled. "I was second-in-command and very fond of the company. I loved my work. Lew and I had worked together in great harmony for twenty years. All of a sudden it changed."

As a hedge against a potential Adams mutiny, Lew dispatched Berle to Europe for a few weeks to tidy up his affairs. While he was gone, Wasserman called in all key personnel with any loyalty to Adams, gave them raises, and signed them to contracts that bound them to MCA.

"Until my dismissal, no executive had a contract with MCA," said Adams. "I had insisted that we give contracts to our important manpower, but Lew said that was not MCA's way. Not, that is, until he decided to move me out of the company."

As Berle prepared to leave, Jules Stein unexpectedly emerged from his coma. Dr. Corday had convened eleven of the finest physicians in the country to help him work a miracle, and after months of monitoring, testing, discussion, and study, one of Stein's specialists finally determined that the essential element that had leached from Stein's system during his antibiotic ordeal was magnesium. The doctors added the trace mineral to his intravenous drip and worked out a protocol that would balance Stein's body chemistry, giving him one more chance.

Within a week he was sitting up, drinking milk shakes that Doris sneaked past his nurses, and catching up on the stock market. One of his first phone calls was to Berle Adams. He apologized and offered his personal regrets over Lew's decision to force Berle out of the company. Alas, he told him, it was too late for Stein to do anything about it. Stein might own the largest block of MCA stock, but Lew had mustered the support of enough other large shareholders—including the duplicitous Taft Schreiber—to guarantee his control of the corporation.

—◦◦◦—

THE SAME MCA board of directors that had endorsed Lew as president named five new vice presidents, including Ned Tanen as executive producer of the theatrical films division and Sidney J. Sheinberg to head up Universal Television. Adams and Dan Ritchie were both gone. Al Dorskind was stripped of his real estate development responsibilities and demoted to vice president in charge of studio operations.

"I never wanted Lew's job," said Dorskind, who remained with the company for two more decades. "I had a nice family, and I like my golf game. I did it my way."

Of those who had fomented revolution, Taft Schreiber alone remained and made his peace with Wasserman.

"Lew knew when to stop," said one insider.

While the Justice Department barred movie studios from banding together to distribute their films in the United States, there were no antitrust restrictions overseas. Thus, in 1970, MCA invited Warner Brothers to join Universal in a new European venture called Cinema International Corporation. The corporation would pool costs, own theaters overseas, hound foreign box office deadbeats, and find the best currency conversion rates while shrinking taxes. Everyone would win.

But Wasserman nixed the deal. He told one confidant that he didn't think Steve Ross, Warner Brothers' new owner, was serious enough about the motion picture business. A New York entrepreneur who had spun his father-in-law's funeral parlor, Riverside Memorial Chapel, into the Kinney parking lot empire, Ross rolled through the 1960s like a snowball, gathering businesses along the way until finally he took over the venerable Warner Brothers/Seven Arts studio in March of 1969, renaming it Warner Communications.

Ross was young and connected—a hustler rumored to have ties to more than one of New York's five Mafia families. In Lew's eyes, Mob ties were not necessarily bad *per se*, but Ross didn't go to great lengths to hide them. By contrast, Wasserman and Stein had struggled mightily over four decades to camouflage their own shady beginnings, and now that MCA was publicly traded on the New York Stock Exchange, they wanted no hint of the company's ties to disreputable characters.[4] It also didn't help Ross's case that he'd aced out Lew's old pal Gene Klein, whose National General Corporation had also bid for Warner Brothers.

Lew regarded Steve Ross as a high roller with neither discretion nor the proper commitment to the entertainment industry. With Lew's own metamorphosis from agent to mogul complete, he now looked upon show business as his personal fiefdom. He was no longer a predator; he was a proprietor. As such, he wanted a return to the power structure that had run Hollywood before the advent of TV—a kind of gentlemen's club that operated on a polite code of honesty among thieves.

In the coming decade Lew's attitude would nearly cost Universal one of its most valuable assets: Steven Spielberg. For the moment, Wasserman spurned Ross and offered CIC instead to another high roller—an Austrian immigrant named Charles Bluhdorn.

During the early years of the go-go sixties Bluhdorn had begun selling auto

---

[4]   In 1969, when it became apparent to the newly respectable MCA that a mobbed-up New Jersey hood named Nat "the Rat" Tarnopol was operating its Brunswick record label, Milt Rackmil was ordered to cut Tarnopol and the label loose. Tarnopol had risen to prominence by managing and virtually owning R&B star Jackie Wilson. Though his conviction was overturned, federal prosecutors indicted Tarnopol twice in the mid-1970s for using payola, drugola, and strong-arm goons to get radio airplay for Brunswick recording artists.

bumpers out of a chain of retail outlets in Michigan and eventually wound up chairing Gulf and Western Industries. With interests in zinc, apparel, cigars, rice, financial services, sugar, and real estate, Gulf and Western went on even more of a buying spree than Ross's Kinney Service Corporation. Ed Weisl, the Wall Street lawyer whose fingerprints could be found on MCA, Paramount, and Democratic politics dating back more than a decade, became one of Gulf and Western's chief advisers, although another attorney—one Sidney Korshak—acted as Bluhdorn's personal attorney.

Bluhdorn acquired the controlling interest in moribund Paramount Studios in 1966, at the same time that Gulf and Western was buying up more than 100,000 acres of the Dominican Republic.[5] He landed the studio in much the same way Ross had swallowed Warner Brothers: by offering more than he could afford for less than what the studio was worth.[6]

In Sid Korshak and Ed Weisl, Bluhdorn had a double edge over his competition. Korshak counted Bluhdorn a buddy as well as a client, and made the proper introductions to Weisl who brokered the deal.[7] It was inevitable that Bluhdorn would soon be lunching regularly at Sid's Bistro table along with another of Sid and Ed's best friends, Lew Wasserman. Lew gave Bluhdorn the neighborly mogul advice that Ross didn't want or seek, while Korshak helped Bluhdorn actually rebuild Paramount, beginning with a new chief for its beleagured motion picture division.

At its nadir, Paramount had been punching out as few as seven features a year, with such forgettable titles as *Arrivederci, Baby!*, *The Night of the Grizzly*, and *The Last of the Secret Agents?* At Korshak's urging, Bluhdorn installed a former actor named Robert Evans as production chief in 1967. Within two years, Paramount was once again making hits like *The Odd Couple*, *Rosemary's Baby*, and *True Grit*.

Sons of a New York dentist, Bob Evans and his brother Charles were exposed early to mobsters. In his autobiography, Evans boasts of his fascination with Meyer Lansky, Frank Costello, and the "guys who ran the action" in Havana following World War II.

By 1950 the brothers had partnered with tailor Joe Picone to form the Evan Picone clothing label and began dealing regularly with goons in the garment trade along Manhattan's Seventh Avenue. In a business dominated at the time by

---

[5]   President Johnson sent Weisl's former protégé Cyrus Vance to oversee the installation of the Dominican Republic's provisional government in 1966 at the same time that Gulf and Western launched its buying spree in the country.

[6]   Another large Paramount shareholder at the time of the Gulf and Western takeover was Edgar Bronfman Sr., heir to the Seagram fortune. He switched his allegiance from Paramount to MGM after Bluhdorn made his move.

[7]   In 1970, Gulf and Western bought the Acapulco Towers Hotel for $1 million from the ten partners of Sidney Korshak's Meymo investment group.

mobbed-up unions, Evan Picone flourished using nonunion labor. With the daring introduction of Evan Picone pantsuits in 1956, the Evans brothers became millionaires.

But Bob Evans sold out his share of the business while still in his twenties and moved to Hollywood. Like Janet Leigh, he was "discovered" by Norma Shearer, who then foisted him off on MCA. The darkly handsome Evans walked blandly through several features, including the role of Ava Gardner's matador lover in Ernest Hemingway's *The Sun Also Rises* (1957), but after bombing in the title role of the horror western *The Fiend Who Walked the West* (1958), Evans recognized his limits as an actor.[8] He quit, returned to New York, began paying publishers to slip him the galleys of promising new novels, and sold the film rights. Without a single production credit to his name, he began calling himself a producer, and landed a deal to make *The Detective* (1968) with Frank Sinatra at Twentieth Century Fox.

It helped that Evans knew people like Lew Wasserman and Sidney Korshak. Since they first met at the Palms Springs Racquet Club in the late 1950s, Korshak had been Evans's consigliere. Though Sidney chided Evans for his high-stakes gambling, he admired his chutzpah. Like Sidney, Evans steamrollered resistance and took what he liked. He regarded Korshak with awe: Sidney didn't make movies, but he owned people who did. With Evans in charge of production, Sidney increased his behind-the-scenes grip on Paramount to a degree that rivaled his influence on Universal.

"He was known as the Myth, from the [Palm Springs] Racquet Club to the '21' Club in New York," Evans wrote worshipfully in his 1994 memoirs, *The Kid Stays in the Picture*.[9] "Many said they knew [Korshak]; few actually did. One thing was for sure, he was one powerful motherfucker."

Sidney "the Myth" was powerful enough to take credit for creating Cinema International Corporation, even though the idea wasn't his and his hand in its creation was all but nonexistent. Berle Adams had actually laid the groundwork for CIC years earlier when he began consolidating Milt Rackmil's expensive overseas distribution system. He shut down dozens of Universal's foreign offices and made the initial deal with Ross, and later with Bluhdorn, with no help from Korshak. Nevertheless, Korshak took a $50,000 fee for putting Bluhdorn and Wasserman together to create the Cinema International Corporation.

Three years later, in October of 1973, Sidney would take MGM's Kirk Kerkorian to the Bistro for lunch, sign him up as a third partner, and charge Cinema International another $250,000—again taking credit and cash for the work of oth-

---

[8]   Wasserman and MCA's George Chasin created Barrington Productions as Evans's personal services corporation for *The Fiend*.
[9]   The title comes from Darryl Zanuck's answer to director Henry King when King tried to fire the wooden Evans from *The Sun Also Rises*: "The kid stays in the picture," declared Zanuck.

ers.[10] By contributing MGM's overseas theaters to the CIC kitty, Kerkorian walked away from the deal with enough cash to finish building his MGM Grand Hotel.

———

By 1972, MCA's recovery was as complete as Dr. Stein's.

Tour guides at Universal Studios began parting the Red Sea more than a hundred times a day. A new generation of super trams had a fourth car added as a caboose, increasing the tourist payload by 25 percent per tour. Over 1.5 million visitors a year paid to stand in the eye of a hurricane, watch a mansion burn, pass safely through a flash flood, and survive a torpedo attack.

With the grand opening of the Universal Amphitheatre, another cash spigot opened into the MCA trough. By the end of 1973, Wall Street analysts fixed the company's value at $160 million. MCA had enough cash the following year to pay $14 million for its own publishing house: the venerable G. P. Putnam's Sons.

And Wasserman's new management team won yet another monopoly with MCA's purchase of the Yosemite Park and Curry Company. As it had done for the Landmark tours of Mount Vernon, Washington, D.C., and Arlington National Cemetery, the U.S. Department of the Interior granted MCA exclusive control of tours, lodging, concessions, and hotels in Yosemite National Park, one of the most revered scenic wonders in the world. MCA's contract allowed it to return only three-fourths of 1 percent of its revenues to the park.

When Lew and Edie made their first trek to MCA's newest domain, the Yosemite Park and Curry Company rolled out the red carpet. MCA liaison Ed Hardy even bought a color TV for the library of their exclusive fifth-floor suite in Yosemite's elegantly rustic Ahwahnee Hotel, only to find that TV signals didn't reach into the Yosemite Valley. Fearing Lew's wrath, Hardy had a microwave repeater station built on a mountainside and a cable snaked down to the hotel, at a cost of several thousand dollars.

When Lew walked in and saw the TV, he said, "TV? Here in God's country? Jesus, who would watch it?" Nonetheless, shortly after he returned from Yosemite, Lew signed off on a pilot for a weekly network drama called *Sierra*. MCA also launched a marketing campaign to encourage more conventions in "God's country." While environmentalists raised questions about the close connection between the Nixon administration and MCA's Taft Schreiber, the outcry was too little too late. Vacationing Americans on two coasts now had nowhere to go but MCA if they wanted to visit national treasures like Yosemite Falls or the home of George Washington.

---

[10] In 1981, Kerkorian added United Artists to the CIC stable. Its name would be changed to United International Pictures.

But most important of all, Universal was back in the movie business in a big-dollar way. In its 1973 annual report, MCA proudly boasted, "Four of the Company's films have received seventeen nominations for this year's Academy Awards. This is the highest number of nominations in any one year for the Company's product."

That year the "product" included *American Graffiti* and *The Sting*, both of which were nominated for Best Picture, with the Oscar going to *The Sting*. A tale about a pair of likable con artists (Paul Newman and Robert Redford) who cheat at poker and horse racing in order to rip off a cold-blooded gangster (Robert Shaw), *The Sting* is set in Chicago in 1936, the same year that Lew went to work for MCA. *The Sting's* sound track is pure Scott Joplin, premier composer of the turn-of-the-century ragtime era, when Jules Stein began working his way through school playing in bands. The *Sting's* producers could not have invented a better nostalgia package to sell to the aging president and chairman of MCA.

"Wasserman never asked to read scripts except for *The Sting*," recalled coexecutive producer David Brown. "That subject interested him personally."

Lew won a special Oscar that year too: the Jean Hersholt Humanitarian Award. Lauded for his good works, particularly in the area of civil rights, Wasserman graciously accepted with a minimum of words, quickly getting out of the spotlight and back into the shadows, where he felt more comfortable.

"What you had in Lew Wasserman was a consummate observer, not a conversational kind of guy," Max Youngstein said nearly twenty-five years later. "He uses less adjectives in a sentence than most of us do. He thinks wasted words are like wasted time. His mind works like a cash register."

The Sting put $68.5 million into Universal's cash register that year. The other Universal cash cow in 1973 began as a teen exploitation film that Lew and his cabal of middle-aged executives nearly refused to release at all. "He hated *American Graffiti*," said an executive who worked on the movie. "He thought it was about blacks who wrote graffiti on walls somewhere in the ghetto. But it was absolutely perfect for its time. *American Graffiti* turned out to be the first film where the sound track *was* the script."

Following his directorial debut two years earlier, twenty-six-year-old George Lucas had left Warner Brothers under a cloud. Warner production chief Ted Ashley hated his quirky sci-fi drama *THX 1138* (1971), as did movie audiences. While *THX 1138* cost less than $1 million to make, it also took in less than $1 million at the box office.

Word of Ashley's distaste for Lucas and his movie got around to other studio executives, and the only one willing to take a chance on him a second time was Ned Tanen, a Universal vice president. Following the surprise success of *Easy Rider* (1969), MCA scrambled to create its own "youth" movies division, turning

to the architect of hugely successful UNI Records to lead Universal into this
uncharted territory.

"I was the guy at MCA with the sideburns," recalled Ned Tanen. "I was the
guy with the beard and the tan suit sitting next to Wasserman while all these other
guys are looking at me like 'What the fuck is that asshole kid doing up there?'"

Tanen carved out a niche for himself with minor hits like the drag-racing
drama *Two-Lane Blacktop* (1971), starring folk balladeer James Taylor and Warren
Oates, and *Diary of a Mad Housewife* (1970), harbinger of the women's move-
ment, starring Carrie Snodgress in an Oscar-nominated performance. But getting
Lew to hire Lucas was an uphill battle. Wasserman hated the young director's ideas
and was particularly lukewarm about Lucas's proposal for a period comedy about
coming of age in small-town America in the early sixties. Wasserman saw the no-
star ensemble story as a cheap TV movie at best.

Against Lew's better judgment, Tanen bought *American Graffiti*,[11] but he had
to limit the young director to a budget several thousand dollars *less* than Lucas
was given to make *THX 1138*.[12] Tanen begged for more money, but got the standard Black Tower answer. Lucas and executive producer Francis Ford Coppola
had to find creative ways to shoot on a shoestring. By coming up with cost-cutting
gimmicks such as recruiting car clubs with vintage automobiles to voluntarily
converge on the northern California town of Petaluma where *American Graffiti*

---

[11] At the same time, Tanen also optioned a two-page outline for another Lucas idea—an intergalactic epic called *Star Wars*. Tanen tried three times to get Wasserman to give Lucas $25,000
in development money, and three times Wasserman said no. Lucas eventually took the outline
to Alan Ladd Jr. and Jay Kanter, now ensconced at Twentieth Century Fox. On their recommendation, Fox invested $11.5 million in a film that launched a billion-dollar franchise and
changed forever Hollywood's attitude toward sci-fi and special effects. *Star Wars* (1977) was so
successful that a bonus clause in Ladd's contract calling for 1.5 percent of Fox's net profits
boosted Ladd's 1978 salary from $278,000 to $1,944,384.92. As his second-in-command, Kanter
also earned over $1 million.

[12] By contrast, Universal gave director Dennis Hopper $1 million to make *The Last Movie*
(1971). MCA indulged the cocaine-addicted Hopper at least as much because he once dated
Susan Stein and had been married to Leland Hayward's daughter as because of the unexpected
box office success of his landmark *Easy Rider* (1967), one of Columbia's surprise hits of the late
1960s.

"*The Last Movie* was crap, but [Hopper] had the credentials because he married Brooke Hayward," said Universal vice president Ned Tanen. As a result, Jules Stein flatly told his executives:
"Give the kid whatever he wants."

A melodrama about a movie stuntman who goes native after shooting a western on location
in Peru, *The Last Movie* began as forty hours of film. After a year of editing, Hopper winnowed
it down to six hours. In an interview some years later, Wasserman himself described a press preview in which the first and last reels of the film had been reversed: "The end of the film was
shown at the end, but the film was so confusing anyway that the audience didn't know the difference." Critics called the final cut unreleaseable, but Hopper maintained for years that it was
his masterpiece.

was being filmed, Lucas and Coppola were able to shoot everything in twenty-eight days.

When the movie previewed at San Francisco's 800-seat Northpoint Theater, Tanen was not buoyed by the enthusiastic audience reaction. He believed Lucas had loaded the theater with cheering friends and reportedly predicted that *American Graffiti* would be a disaster. Lucas and Coppola cut four and a half minutes from the film before it had to pass muster with Lew and a graying MCA hierarchy headed by sixty-one-year-old Edd Henry. Tanen feared he would be fired, so he stacked the deck for the next preview.

"I only got it released because I ran a screening at the old Directors Guild and got [popular disc jockey] Wolfman Jack to give me about 1,200 nutty kids who started tearing the walls down," said Tanen. "Lew and all of the penguins who were sitting there all of a sudden thought it might be the next *Graduate*."

But no one thought *American Graffiti* would be the biggest hit of the year, grossing over $55 million at the box office. Only then were Lucas, Coppola, and Tanen grudgingly declared heroes. For the remainder of the decade, Tanen served as Universal's production chief, shepherding more than a dozen directors through their earliest films, including Robert Zemeckis, John Cassavetes, Joel Schumacher, and Milos Forman.[13]

While *The Sting* and *American Graffiti* were catching MCA by surprise, Universal's old guard continued to concentrate on disaster. When *Airport* aired over NBC, its Nielsen ratings were higher than those of any other motion picture ever broadcast over television. Veteran director Robert Wise—*The Day the Earth Stood Still* (1951), *The Sound of Music* (1965), *West Side Story* (1961)—was putting the finishing touches on *The Hindenburg* (1974). And Jennings Lang, MCA's original idea man, was about to introduce the world to the thrill of the Richter scale.

During the Sylmar earthquake in the spring of 1971, the Black Tower rocked and rolled with minimal damage, but three years later it was utterly destroyed on the screen in *Earthquake*—all because Jennings Lang took his wife to the movies during an aftershock. It hit him: why not scare the bejesus out of an entire nation by giving them the illusion of sitting through the Big One?

Lang's intuition won him a special Oscar for Sensurround, a patented Universal system of low-frequency stereo sound that cost MCA less than $1 million to develop. It was supposed to enhance the illusion of a rumble, building to an 8-point Richter reading, signifying death and destruction—disaster just the way

---

[13] In gratitude to Tanen for giving him his first break in the American cinema with Universal's *Taking Off* (1971), Czech-born Milos Forman brought Tanen his second American film. Tanen screened the movie for Wasserman and his "penguins," who turned it down. Executives at United Artists proved more savvy. The following year, *One Flew Over the Cuckoo's Nest* (1975) dominated the Oscars, winning five major awards, including best picture.

Lew Wasserman liked it: lots of predictable screams, loads of artificial thrills, but no real surprises.

"Lew used to tell all of us, every day: 'I can handle bad news. I love good news. But I hate surprises,'" recalled one of Wasserman's young disciples.

Earthquake shook film audiences loose of $66.4 million, but it had no more staying power than the Pet Rock or the Hula Hoop. Within five years, Sensurround was history.[14]

WHEN I CAME back for *Earthquake* in 1973, the studio was definitely set up the way Wasserman wanted," said Charlton Heston, who hadn't been on the lot since he made *The War Lord* for Universal in 1964.

Universal belonged to Lew in 1973. By this time, all who had ever posed a threat to Wasserman or stood in his way had been eliminated or banished, from Milt Rackmil to Ed Muhl to Sonny Werblin, Dan Ritchie, and Berle Adams. Taft Schreiber was the only exception, and now even Taft was under control. All Lew really lacked was the successor that Jules Stein demanded.

"Lew wanted to clone himself, or Jules," said his then son-in-law, Jack Myers. "But Jules had a real fun-loving side to him. He liked to act up, at least when he was younger. He drank and chased women and drove too fast in his [Mercedes] 300 SL. Jules had some *joie de vivre*. He was not a steel robot who had shut off his emotions the way Lew had."

At one time Jay Kanter had been heir apparent. Then Jerry Gershwin, who shared Lew's bungalow office at Universal before the Black Tower was built. Gershwin was so close to Lew at one time that he wasn't able "to tell who I was, myself or a part of Lew Wasserman," Gershwin once told an interviewer. When Gershwin quit MCA in 1969 to join Kanter in his independent production company, Lew never forgave him. Like Tony Curtis and other Wasserman intimates who had the temerity to walk away, Gershwin simply became a nonperson.[15]

Until the palace coup, Berle Adams had been odds-on favorite. Afterward Lew played his cards exceedingly close to the vest. Ned Tanen moved into the office right next to Lew's, and for a time, some guessed that he might be the anointed one. His track record was spectacular and, still in his thirties, he was certainly young enough. The only thing anyone knew for sure was that the successor would

---

[14] Sensurround, which cost about $2,000 to install in a theater, went the way of 3-D glasses and Smell-o-Vision after just four Universal productions, each one less successful than its predecessor: *Earthquake* (1974), *Midway* (1976), *Rollercoaster* (1978), and *Battlestar: Galactica* (1979).

[15] In a 1979 interview, Lew dismissed the very idea that he had ever considered Gershwin his heir. All he would say about the man he once regarded as a son was that "Jerry made the wrong decision."

be someone from the younger ranks. When Wasserman finally did make his selection, reaction was mixed.

"Lew once described in a management meeting the three most important things that happened at MCA under his reign," said one twenty-five-year MCA-Universal veteran. "One was the purchase of the Paramount pre-1948 film library. The second was the purchase of the studio property and converting it over. And the third was, of course, picking a successor. I wholeheartedly concur with two of the three."

On June 5, 1973, at the age of seventy-seven, Jules Stein retired. Lew R. Wasserman, age sixty, was elected chairman of the board and CEO of MCA Inc., and the board appointed the thirty-eight-year-old Universal Television chief, Sidney Sheinberg, as MCA's new president. "[Sheinberg] really wanted to stay nearer to the creative end," Wasserman recalled ten years later to one interviewer. "I had to negotiate with him to take [the presidency]."

In many ways Lew and Sid were alike. Both were lean six-footers, though Sheinberg was always a good twenty pounds heavier than his boss, and both were sons of Russian Jews who had fled Eastern Europe's anti-Semitism and settled in middle America—Lew's family in Ohio, Sid's in Texas. Sheinberg liked to boast that he had grown up "the only Jew in Corpus Christi," though his relatives point out that the Gulf port city had a substantial Jewish population.

Like Lew, Sid dabbled in show business early. As a teenager he worked as a disc jockey at a local radio station, where he developed a loud, commanding voice that matched his hair-trigger temper—another trait he shared with Wasserman. Both were workaholics, though Sid did make some time for his two sons. Both married young and remained married to the same woman for the rest of their lives.[16]

Those values and idiosyncracies that made Sid and Lew quite different began with their education. Unlike Wasserman, whose lifelong regret was that he could not afford to continue on to college and law school, Sheinberg made a brilliant academic career for himself after high school.

He transferred to Columbia University from Del Mar junior college in Corpus Christi in his sophomore year. The only Texan in the class of 1955, he went to law school at the University of Texas at Austin, but returned to Columbia to get his law degree following a dispute with Texas administrators over their treatment of black students. After graduating third in his class in 1958, he accepted an associate professorship at the UCLA School of Law and moved to California. While Sheinberg was awaiting the results of his California bar exam, Al Dorskind asked

---

[16] Sid married his college sweetheart, Lorraine Gottfried, on August 19, 1956. His father-in-law, Beverly Hills business manager Harry Grossman, introduced Sheinberg to MCA executives — Grossman's clients — and helped him land his first job with MCA.

him to join the MCA legal department. In less than ten years, he moved quickly from legal to business affairs to production to a position as Jennings Lang's assistant at Universal TV. When Jennings bowed out of TV in 1968 to begin easing himself into Ed Muhl's job as Universal feature production chief, Sheinberg quickly stepped up to the top spot at Universal Television.

Sheinberg remained sloppy and coarse much of the time. All who knew the impeccable Wasserman and the disheveled Sheinberg agreed that if there was one overriding quality that distinguished one from the other, it was finesse. Wasserman was equally at ease chatting with congressmen or construction crews. Sheinberg dealt with all people like a battering ram: do it his way or get out of the way.

As in his marriage to Edie Beckerman, however, Lew stuck to a deal once he had made it. Whatever their differences, Lew and Sid were bound together, for better or worse, unto the very end of MCA.

TWENTY-NINE

The Heir Unapparent

1974—1976

In September of 1974, after eight years as chairman of the Association of Motion
Picture and Television Producers, the labor-relations arm of the Motion Picture
Association of America, Lew Wasserman stepped down. He had never wanted
the job, according to MPAA president Jack Valenti. With characteristic hyperbole,
the short but voluble Valenti blustered that it was only his pleading that had persuaded Lew to take the job in the first place back in 1966. "You're the fellow they'll
agree on," Valenti had told Wasserman.

And he was. During Lew's chairmanship, guilds hammered out better contracts, and Hollywood in general seemed to enjoy a longer labor peace than it had
during the previous eighteen years under Paramount's Y. Frank Freeman.

But other studio heads tended to regard Wasserman as dangerously liberal,
chiefly because Jules Stein had taught his protégé early in his career that unions
were a fact of life. As a constant reminder of the importance of organized labor in
MCA's rise to power, Stein—and later Wasserman—prominently displayed
MCA's number one charter membership in the American Federation of Musicians
on the office wall. If Western Conference of Teamsters chief Andy Anderson and
Chet Migden of the Screen Actors Guild phoned, Stein and Wasserman treated
the calls with equal deference.

The question, Stein always preached to Lew, was how to view labor: as friend
or enemy? If the labor unions were the enemy, then MCA had to gear up for war
and not just oppose them but utterly destroy them. If they were friends, the nuance
of possibility was far greater. The nice thing about deciding they were friends was
that when friends helped friends, friends usually reciprocated.

"One of Lew's great strengths," recalled Ned Tanen, "was his ability at the last
moment to stop a strike, to get the union and the companies together and bang
heads."

But by 1973, Lew had wearied of head banging. He wanted to step down. As the great peacemaker, however, he couldn't. Taft Schreiber's good friend Richard Nixon had seen to that.

During the summer of 1971 in a purported effort to check inflation, President Nixon had imposed a national freeze on wages and prices. Studio executives gloated that, with the help of the White House, they had the unions over a barrel. Actors, technicians, and writers could holler about shrinking paychecks all they wanted. It made not a whit of difference. By 1973, with one contract after another expiring, studios faced strike threats from virtually every union that had been forced to give up wage increases two years earlier. Wasserman alone among studio heads searched for ways to accommodate the guilds without giving away the store, and he usually succeeded by pointing the finger of blame at someone else.

During Stage Employees union negotiations, for example, Lew demonstrated his unique sly wisdom by pointing out that the only way to deliver a better contract was to limit overtime, and the only way to cut overtime was to get the TV networks to stop their annual one-upmanship ritual. All year long, CBS, NBC, and ABC jealously guarded the secret of their fall prime-time lineup. Then, each spring, all three networks announced their schedules and rushed like mad to prepare their series for airing. Result: overtime. Gobs of overtime.

"It is not labor and its demands that are killing us on television," Wasserman told his fellow studio heads. "It is the overtime."

To the labor unions, he preached that the networks — not the studios — were the problem. Waiting until the last minute to announce their fall lineup inevitably led to costly production budgets for several months of each year, Lew argued. As a result, budgets for the rest of the year shrank to zero. Enriching a few skilled technicians each summer wounded the golden goose for the union majority, and the damned networks were to blame.

MCA, on the other hand, remained the unions' best friend. Wasserman kept their trust by knowing what they wanted, occasionally before they knew themselves.

"He had a way of manipulating," said a veteran Wasserman aide. "Nothing was going to happen unless he wanted it to."

During one heated battle, union employees objected to two and three people having to share hotel rooms while filming on location. Despite the additional cost, Wasserman overrode his own advisers and agreed to pay for separate hotel rooms. The unions couldn't believe their good fortune, and Lew's fellow executives couldn't figure out why the tough old hard-liner had caved in on such a cream puff issue. But Lew knew what he was doing.

"Lew loved one-upmanship," said another aide. "If you gave him something that put him one step ahead of everyone else, he'd eat right out of your hand."

He had learned what no other studio executive had bothered to find out: that many rank-and-file Teamsters and Stage Employees didn't care whether they had to share a room. What many of the redneck blue-collar workers *really* objected to was having to share a room with a black union member. Separate rooms might not have been politically correct, but they were utterly practical. Wasserman figured it was cheaper to underwrite de facto segregation than to risk a strike.

Despite such ponderous issues as pay hikes, per diem, and overtime, Wasserman strove to keep things light at the negotiating table, where weary representatives of as many as thirty unions could be squawking over arcane provisions in thirty different contracts for up to twenty-four hours a day. As he did in his screening room at home, Lew ordered a steady supply of M&M's, candy bars, and other sugary snacks[1] and sent out often for Chinese food, and he rarely left a session early, especially when a compromise looked as if it might be right around the corner.

According to Jack Valenti, "When Lew speaks at that table, while the guilds and unions may disagree, they may argue and they may oppose, I think it is fair to say that they believe that Lew's word, to coin a phrase, is his bond." Keeping his word, no matter how trivial or petty the demand, became Wasserman's hallmark, and earned him unprecedented respect at the bargaining table.

During the 1973 SAG negotiations, actors complained that television audiences had to squint to make out their screen credits at the end of a show. The letters were so small as to violate a contract provision requiring readable credits. When Wasserman asked his chief negotiator about the complaint, he said, "I don't know, Lew. I'd like to tell you, 'Who cares?'"

"This is business," Wasserman snapped. "It isn't about caring, and, goddammit, *are...they...readable?*"

The negotiator ordered a reel containing every opening and closing credit on TV, then sat through several torturous hours in a Universal projection room. All credits were plainly readable. As he prepared to tell the actors where they could stick their complaint about unreadable credits, Wasserman ordered a second look. "We can read this stuff on a 30-foot screen," he said. "What about on television?"

The negotiator converted the film to video, ran it again on a regular television set, and finally had to concede that, on the small screen, many of the credits were, in fact, unreadable.

"We agreed by contract that credits would be readily readable," Wasserman said sternly, as if he were lecturing an undergraduate who had failed the final. "And they *will* be readily readable! I don't want to see white credits on white backgrounds. No blue letters on blue sky. None of that sort of thing."

Most Universal credits began showing up yellow, a color that stood out against any background. While the problem seemed finally solved, Wasserman followed

---

[1] Hectored by Edie, Lew himself began laying off the junk food. Following his 1969 "heart warning," he continued to live the life of a junk-food addict vicariously, however, by chewing on popcorn, which he spit out instead of swallowing.

up on his edict just to make sure. Several weeks after his tirade, he called his chief negotiator back into his office. "Remember the readily readable provision we just negotiated?" he hollered. "Well, I looked at some on TV last night. They are *still* not readable."

"Lew, this is August. Those are reruns," his negotiator said with a patronizing sigh. "What you saw last night were shows from earlier in the season, before we signed the new contract."

Wasserman stared at him for a second before swatting him down. "I looked at our *new* episodes in the projection room at the house," Wasserman snarled, lowering his voice to a menacing hiss. "I don't want to see this happen again!"

When the negotiator reviewed the offending show, he swallowed hard. Lew was right. One of the credits at the end of one of the shows could not be read. He had it fixed and never let an unreadable credit get past final editing again.

The negotiator knew he had gotten off easy. Blameworthy executives rarely got a second chance with Wasserman, especially in labor matters. "He would just probe and probe until he found all the information," said the negotiator. "Then he'd make the decision he thought was appropriate and cremate some poor bastard he'd caught withholding information."

An MCA corporate psychologist who once sat in on a firing of an unfortunate executive recalled watching in amazement as Lew berated and publicly humiliated the victim in front of his peers. While Wasserman stripped the man of his dignity, security guards stripped his office of all personal effects and loaded them in his car. By the time the man had been dismissed, the locks were already changed on his office door and the guards escorted him from the building like some petty thief who had been caught picking pockets.

Employees weren't fired. They were expunged. One former Universal writer told *Los Angeles Times* film critic Charles Champlin that when his own dismissal came, his name had been painted over on his parking spot before he even left the Black Tower.

"With Lew it was always very personal," recalled another executive. "It was never about 'You are idiots.' It was, '*You* are the idiot! This is why *you're* fucking lowlife!' I cannot think of a time when he didn't go through Defcon position 1, 2, 3, 4, and 5. When the shoes were off, the jacket was off, the collar was open, and he'd be spitting…that was Defcon 1."

Age had done little to mellow Lew Wasserman. He rewarded loyalty, effort, and candor, but he punished deceit, foolishness, and passing the buck, often hideously and always without mercy. Sometimes he seemed to whip himself into a frenzy over nothing at all.

"He would start to talk louder, and people would cough louder, and the sound of his own voice made him think people were arguing," recalled one of his peers. "He ended up shrieking while everyone just sat there. And no one had said anything. No one had even asked a question. Finally some brave soul would bite the bullet and say, 'No one's arguing with you.'"

His wrath occasionally seemed capricious, even whimsical. Once, at a meeting of MCA department heads, the marketing chief made a routine plea for a bigger budget.

"Every time we have a meeting, you ask for more money. I have a solution. We won't have any more meetings!" Wasserman said with a matter-of-fact sneer, and left the room.

Borrowing an old trick from Billy Goodheart, Lew would throw pencils at an offending employee while howling at his idiocy. Everyone knew the signs.

"He had a letter opener that looked like a sword from *Spartacus*," said a former vice president. "When he started pounding that letter opener, you knew you were in trouble. When he started fiddling with his Rolex, you knew you were in big trouble. If he took it off his arm and threw it at you, you were fired."

David Brown, the executive producer of *The Sting*, described Lew's smile as "dazzling but dangerous," but his anger remained utterly terrifying—a fury so total that it could leave a grown man in a $1,500 suit nauseous and hugging the toilet in fear.

"He had this paternalistic thing about him: the strong father figure, almost abusive," said one trusted survivor of Lew's wrath. "He could be gracious and a perfect gentleman and then turn on a dime. He would be very kind, very courteous; then he would kick the shit out of these guys. They would fall off the sofa and crawl out of his office."

His fury worked within the MCA autocracy, and a slightly muted version of it served to keep most union negotiations running smoothly, but Wasserman's tantrums did not play well among his fellow studio heads. Peers like Twentieth Century Fox president Dennis Stanfill and Frank Wells of Warner Brothers were suspicious of Wasserman's close union ties in the first place. Thus, when Sam Arkoff of American International Pictures joined Wells and Stanfill in criticizing Lew's hot-and-cold tactics with the International Alliance of Theatrical Stage Employees, the Teamsters, and the basic crafts unions during the summer of 1975, Wasserman took personal offense. He stood up and walked out. He did not return.

On September 3, 1975, Universal formally withdrew from the Association of Motion Picture and Television Producers. Paramount joined Universal, and, over time, MGM, United Artists, and Disney also pulled out. The association, which had turned fifty just one year earlier, was in ruins.

Meanwhile, Wasserman ran Universal's negotiations with the Stage Employees his way. Twenty-four hours after MCA and Paramount met with the unions at the Hollywood Roosevelt Hotel, they had an agreement. The new three-and-a-half-year contract called for the most generous pay hikes in a generation: 15 percent the first year, followed by 12 percent the succeeding two years and 6 percent the final six months of the contract. Frank Wells and Sam Arkoff called the agreement lunacy. Even Lew's own people thought their boss had gone nuts. Months later it became apparent that Wasserman had deftly worded the contract so that most of the additional labor expense would be passed on to the three television networks.

While the remaining members of the producers association scrambled to catch up, the old fox from the Black Tower hardly paused to gloat. He was still Hollywood's emperor of one-upmanship, and that was all that mattered to him.

—◦∾◦—

AS HE APPROACHED his eightieth birthday, Jules Stein prepared to take his place in history.

There were the honors, of course: the Albert Lasker Public Service Award, an honorary doctor of science degree from the Medical College of Wisconsin, and the Academy's Jean Hersholt Humanitarian Award, presented during the 1976 Oscar ceremony.

In his own new role as co-chairman of President Gerald Ford's election committee, Taft Schreiber also pushed to have Stein recognized with the Presidential Medal of Freedom. Ford's assistant director for Health, Social Security and Welfare, Sarah Massengale, listed Stein's dollar and time contributions to ophthalmology research as reasons for awarding him the nation's highest civilian honor. Stein's negatives included the fact that he had a heart condition and was "a strong Democrat."

No one apparently pointed out that Stein was, in fact, a Republican, and he did not win the Medal of Freedom. He did win another honor, however, that meant even more to him. For the first time in its eighty-one-year history, the stuffy *American Journal of Ophthalmology* altered its practice of listing only its table of contents on its cover. The April 1976 issue displayed the grandfatherly visage of Jules Stein, M.D., wearing a stylish but oddly offbeat white-and-pastel polka-dot tie. Inside, a two-page biography barely mentioned MCA. Instead, the article gushed over Stein's crowning achievement, the Jules C. Stein Eye Institute at UCLA, and his efforts to pour millions into eye research at Johns Hopkins, Columbia, the University of Louisville, Baylor, Wisconsin, and his alma mater, the University of Chicago.

A philanthropist and scientific visionary. That was how Jules wanted to be remembered. Thus he turned to *New York Times* reporter Murray Schumach to write his memoirs.

"Jules and Lew were both remarkable, but of the two, Lew was easily the more interesting," said Schumach. "One of the smartest men I've ever met."

Stein's was a story well worth telling, but Schumach remained hesitant until *New York Times* editor Clifton Daniels personally urged him to take a leave from the paper. Schumach moved into an office next to Jules's at Fifty-seventh and Madison. Murray's editor at the *Times* didn't have an office half so plush.

But Schumach's first real shock was Stein's utter lack of pretension. The richest man in show business dressed in a simple business suit, answered his own phone, and ate lunch every day at the Bun and Burger at Sixtieth and Madison. Jules's one affectation was his title.

"Everything was 'Doctor,'" recalled Bob Hussong. "God help anyone who'd call him 'Mister.'"

If Jules was remembered in coming generations, it certainly wouldn't be as founder of a family dynasty. On the occasion of MCA's fiftieth anniversary, Jules inscribed his daughter's MCA annual report with a revealing line: "To my daughter, Jean, with whom I disagree politically, socially, financially, economically, and otherwise, but still love very much. Devotedly, Father."

Following her divorce from Bill vanden Heuvel in 1970, Jean nearly got herself disinherited by carrying on an affair with author and professor Roger Wilkins, the nephew of civil rights leader Roy Wilkins.

Her sister, Susan, was quite a different story. A Vassar drama major who later studied Chinese at Columbia, Susan showed a business flair that was utterly foreign to Jean. Despite her drama degree and her father's Broadway connections, Susan's sole stage credit had been a minor role in the comedy *Take Her, She's Mine*. Though she was no actress, Susan joined the board of directors and gave generously to keep producer Joseph Papp's New York Shakespeare Festival alive throughout the 1970s.[2] Like her father her real talent lay in business. Jules's younger daughter eventually pooled resources with four friends and set up Ports of Call, a luxury travel agency that operated out of Saks Fifth Avenue.

On April 6, 1965, after she suffered a near fatal motorcycle accident in the Bermudas, Jules called in extraordinary favors from the same medical community that had saved his own life. Susan had a skull fracture and was in a coma for five days. Her father flew in Yale University's Dr. William Scoville to perform brain surgery that saved her life.

But while Jules held Susan in higher regard than Jean, he confided in neither daughter. "Don't ask my daughters about me," he told Schumach. "They know *nothing* about me."

As the years advanced, Stein resigned himself to the fact that he had no male heir and would never have one. Though he helped both of Doris's sons start and develop their own businesses, he regarded neither Oppenheimer as bright or sophisticated enough to invite into MCA.

Jules's heir, by default, would be Lew Wasserman. He couldn't even bring himself to pass the throne to Susan. Women were for marrying, having children,

---

[2] In 1984 one of the six stages of the Joseph Papp Public Theater was named for Susan.

attending cocktail parties, Stein maintained. Women weren't men—all they could do was find a good one and marry him.

When Susan married, on December 2, 1968, her father's worst fears about his daughters' capriciousness were confirmed. Even sensible Susan had let him down. He wound up giving her away to a native-born Israeli who struck Jules as a fop rather than a Sabra. Guedaliahou "Gil" Shiva's given occupation was that of manager for Merce Cunningham and other Manhattan dance groups, but he showed up just as frequently in gossip columns as "escort," "playboy," or simply "man about town."

Writer Anita Loos introduced Shiva to Susan at an African art exhibit, and eight months later, Rabbi Edgar Magnin married the couple at Misty Mountain in a private ceremony that left several guests puzzled. According to Jewish tradition, a daughter could not be married by a rabbi if her mother was a Gentile, and everyone knew that Doris's maiden name was Jones.

Not so, said Magnin. Doris *passed* as Gentile, telling her social circle that she had only married a Jew. On occasion, she even made a point of attending mass with her girlfriends at Saint Basil's on Wilshire, right next door to Rabbi Magnin's Wilshire Synagogue. In reality, she was as Jewish as Jules. In fact, the only time Murray Schumach ever saw Stein truly enraged was following a social function during which Doris publicly denied her own Jewish heritage. "You and your goddamned anti-Semitic friends!" shrieked Jules, ordering his imperious wife out of his sight.

Lew and Edie had no such identity problems. They were Jews who simply didn't practice Judaism on any conscious level. Lew maintained that he had abandoned his parents' Orthodox views the moment he finished his bar mitzvah. When MCA produced *Jesus Christ Superstar*, among the loudest protests came from the American Jewish Committee, which claimed the movie once again laid the blame for Christ's death on the Jews. Lew ignored them.

"I must tell you in all candor, in my judgment, under oath, Pentothol—whatever you like—I would testify with my last breath that I don't know of a Jewish community, if you're talking about a structured community," Wasserman told Robert Scheer of the *Los Angeles Times*. "It is nonexistent.

"Are there many Jews who share the same concerns? Yes. There are also many Irish…and this bugaboo about the American Jewish Committee speaking for all Jews in America, well, I know one Jew they don't speak for—they don't speak for Lew Wasserman."

One Orthodox tradition Lew did observe was marriage. He frowned on divorce. He discouraged it among his clients and his executives, and he went absolutely berserk when it involved his own family. Lynne's divorce left him cold. It didn't help that Lynne was utterly dependent upon her parents. She had no profession and no income outside the meager dividends from the MCA stock Lew had given her. Though Lew and Edie helped Lynne buy a five-bedroom home a block away from their own Foothill Drive estate, the gesture seemed aimed more at ensuring that their grandchild, Carol, would have a decent place to live than at fulfilling their parental obligation to aid their only daughter. "I was unfortunate not to have a son, only a daughter," Lew said cruelly in a 1979 interview published for all of Lynne's friends to read in *Los Angeles Magazine.*

Lynne was not always the victim. She had been raised with a silver spoon in her mouth and could be something of a bully when she thought she could get away with it. When she went into partnership with childhood friend Julie Payne in a Beverly Hills needlepoint shop, Lynne hired a lawyer in a power play to wrest the business away from Payne. During the skirmish, Lew and Edie actually wound up siding against their own daughter. Indeed, Edie stopped calling Lynne her daughter at all for several years, cruelly reserving that title for Ronnie Leif's new wife, Juanita.

Similarly, when Lynne became engaged to a stockbroker following her divorce from Leif, the Wassermans did not approve. In their eyes, Jack Meyrowitz was a fortune hunter, far beneath Lynne's station.

Meyrowitz saw his instant friction with his prospective in-laws in a slightly different light. He learned first from Lynne, and later from dozens of other Wasserman friends and associates, that Edie's promiscuity was one of Hollywood's worst-kept secrets. He was further appalled when Lynne told him that Edie had insisted on enlisting her own daughter as a confessor for her trysts.

These experiences with her mother left Lynne traumatized and much more sympathetic toward the workaholic she had once endearingly called Poppy, according to Meyrowitz.

Meyrowitz was not nearly so beguiled by Lew. "Lew's power didn't impress me," he said. "He was a fucking bluffer. Pure bluff. And people were afraid to call his bluff. I wasn't."

Unlike the formal ceremony and reception that Lew and Edie gave the Leifs when they were married, Lynne got no second wedding. She and Jack Meyrowitz eloped and were married in Las Vegas on September 5, 1970. Six months later, the couple went to court and formally changed their name from Meyrowitz to Myers.

Several more years passed before the freeze between the Myerses and the Wassermans began to thaw. Everything changed on June 28, 1974, with the birth of Casey Wasserman Myers. Unto Lew Wasserman a grandson was born — not a direct successor, perhaps, but an heir nonetheless.

Lynne and Jack were once more welcome at the Wasserman home. Once, while Lew and Edie were away, Lynne suggested they sneak into Lew's closet, where he kept his personal safe and see just what they stood to inherit. It stood to reason, after all, that the safe would be the logical place for Lew to keep his personal will.

Lynne remembered the combination from her childhood, and while Jack scoffed that Lew would surely have changed it during the ensuing years, Lynne pointed out that her parents never changed anything. They had had the same telephone number since she was a kid back on Sierra Drive.

Sure enough. Jack peered over his wife's shoulder as she turned the tumblers: 25 right, 50 left, 25 right. It produced a click, and the door to the safe swung open. But they found no will inside.

"All there was," said Jack Myers, "was an unloaded revolver and a textbook on epilepsy."

—◈—

As FAR AS talent agents were concerned, no one had emerged since MCA's exit from the talent field in 1962 to match the lofty position once held by Lew Wasserman.

William Morris became the monarch among agencies, but its personnel were even more anonymous than the men of the old MCA. In sheer volume of business, no one could dispute that the Morris Agency dominated entertainment throughout the 1960s and 1970s, but except for ancient Abe Lastfogel, the colorless agency had no recognizable personality. Two MCA spinoffs — the Citron-Park-Chasin Agency and Creative Management Associates[3] — held on to many former MCA clients and Creative Management's Freddie Fields showed some flair as a hotshot, brokering some of Hollywood's biggest deals, but he did not approach the lofty stature Wasserman had once achieved.

As a talent factory, Hollywood seemed to have settled down to cookie-cutter tedium. So when five young renegades broke away from William Morris in January of 1975 to start their own talent agency, hardly anyone outside of the business even noticed. Their new company, Creative Artists Agency, was known as "Ca-Ca" around William Morris. They were undercapitalized, overambitious, and outgunned.

One of the founders of Creative Artists had begun his show business career a decade earlier, pointing out Beaver Cleaver's house and *Psycho*'s Bates Motel to paying customers of the Universal Tours. A brash twenty-eight-year-old UCLA graduate who enrolled in and quit law school twice before resigning himself to his true calling as a William Morris talent broker, Michael Ovitz studied and patterned himself after the young Lew Wasserman. But there were subtle differences. Creative Artists had no deep-pockets mentor like Jules Stein, for example, and the

---

[3] In 1973, International Famous Agency bought Chasin-Park-Citron. Two years later International Famous Agency merged with Creative Management Associates to form International Creative Management.

street-fighter instincts Wasserman brought to the job were more formalized and fine-tuned by Ovitz, who steeped himself and his four partners in Oriental philosophy. While Lew may have believed he invented one-upsmanship and playing-for-keeps during the 1940s, Ovitz found that Sun Tzu had first put the practice down on paper 4,500 years earlier in *The Art of War*. The Chinese warrior-philosopher equated commerce, politics, and virtually every human interaction with the life-and-death struggle of a soldier, and advised pragmatism, deceit, betrayal, and even murder in the pursuit of cold-blooded victory.

In most respects, though, the band of brothers who launched Creative Artists were very much like the five-man crew Jules Stein had dispatched to Beverly Hills back in 1939. Lew Wasserman, Taft Schreiber, Karl Kramer, Mickey Rockford, and Larry Barnett had formed the MCA vanguard in its mission to conquer the movies. Michael Ovitz, Ron Meyer, Rowland Perkins, Bill Haber, and Michael Rosenfeld employed exactly the same star power, packaging pressure, and publicity techniques that MCA had pioneered close to half a century earlier.

"If you wanted a star, they pressured you to take other elements, like a costar," said former United Artists production chief Max Youngstein, who dealt with both Creative Artists and MCA during his fifty-year movie career. "As they raised the costar's stature, they also raised his salary. The only thing that's changed in fifty years is the names. In those days it was Burt Lancaster or Ava Gardner. Today, it's Arnold Schwarzenegger or Sharon Stone."

But getting those stars took sacrifice. For two years the partners took no salary and pretended to be far more prosperous than they actually were.

They hustled. And they poached, clamoring after other agencies' clients, letting them know how very much they admired their work, how they had a plan to turn them into the next Cary Grant or Elizabeth Taylor, and how they would love to take them out to dinner — just to get acquainted, of course.

Sean Connery, who got his start in American film courtesy of MCA in the 1950s, was one of Creative Artists' first major catches, followed by Paul Newman, another MCA alumnus. Sons and daughters of some of the original MCA clients also became the property of Creative Artists: Jane Fonda, Michael Douglas, Jamie Lee Curtis, and others.

But most of the original MCA clients of the early 1940s had either died, faded into obscurity, or retired from acting altogether by the time Ovitz and Company oozed onto the Hollywood scene. Betty Grable, who had divorced Harry James in 1965, died nearly broke in 1973, her famous pinup photo having been sold to Geritol to be used in magazine ads.[4] John Garfield and Errol Flynn were both dead. Ronald Reagan loved screening his old movies, but did not intend to return to Hol-

---

[4] Without MCA to underwrite her, Betty had to keep working even after she was diagnosed with cancer. At one road performance of *Hello, Dolly!* she overheard a blue-haired lady in the

lywood. He had different plans for continuing his acting career after his second term as California governor ended in 1974. Encouraged by his Kitchen Cabinet, Reagan began to seriously eye the White House.

—◈—

AFTER STARRING IN a string of horror movies launched by *What Ever Happened to Baby Jane?* (1962), fifty-eight-year-old Bette Davis contacted one of her former MCA agents and proposed a Las Vegas lounge act in which she would appear topless in her Queen Elizabeth I costume.

"I still have great tits, don't you think?" she asked the agent.

While he agreed, he could not sell any of the Vegas hotels on the concept, so Davis consigned what remained of her career to MCA television. In the 1970s, dozens of other aging movies stars followed her example. Joan Crawford, Davis's *Baby Jane* costar and decades-old nemesis, also finished out her career on TV, courtesy of MCA. One of Crawford's final roles was that of a blind woman who briefly regains her eyesight during a blackout in an ironic 1969 segment of *Night Gallery*. Her director was Universal vice president Sid Sheinberg's twenty-two-year-old protégé, Steven Spielberg.

Initially, the sixty-three-year-old Crawford was dismissive, even insulting about the young pup assigned to direct her, but Spielberg was humble, almost obsequious, behaving at times more like a fawning talent agent than a director. With his show of the proper awe in her presence, Spielberg soon had Crawford eating out of his hand.

Spielberg's real breakthrough, however, came with TV's highly rated and critically praised *Duel* (1971), which starred Dennis Weaver as a traveling salesman pursued by a faceless diesel truck driver in a deadly cat-and-mouse road game. Two years later, Sheinberg turned Spielberg over to Richard Zanuck and David Brown, who gave him his first theatrical film assignment. *The Sugarland Express* (1973) was another cat-and-mouse road game featuring Goldie Hawn as a renegade mom who breaks her husband out of prison to help wrest her baby from adoption authorities. When the husband is shot to death, a film that began as farce ends in tragedy—a dose of harsh reality that angered escapist movie audiences who went to laugh at the wacky blonde from *Laugh-In*, but came away with the non-Hollywood lesson that the good guys do not always win in the end. *The Sugarland Express* was box office poison.

Nevertheless, Zanuck and Brown still had enough confidence in the young director to offer him *Jaws* when their first two choices for director didn't work out.

---

front row remark how she didn't look the way she had twenty years earlier. Planting her hands on her hips, Grable zeroed in on the woman and hollered, "Madam, who the fuck does?"

Wasserman wasn't so sure. Sheinberg backed Spielberg, but Lew continued to function as de facto production chief.

"Wouldn't you be better off with one of the sure-handed guys who's done this kind of picture before?" he asked Zanuck and Brown.

The producers fought for "the kid." They didn't want a remake of *Moby Dick* with teeth, which they believed was just what they would get with someone more experienced. After they finally convinced Wasserman that Spielberg's fresh vision could bring an exciting edge to the project that no older director could deliver, Lew approved the deal and stuck by it despite the problems that followed.

A glut of tourists, unpredictable weather, and interminable glitches with three mechanical sharks stretched two months of location shooting on Martha's Vineyard into more than five months. Budgeted at $4.5 million, *Jaws* cost twice as much. The repair bill alone for Bruce, the sinking mechanical shark, topped $100,000.

In Hollywood studio circles, memories were still fresh of experiences like Marlon Brando's version of *Mutiny on the Bounty*, which had come to symbolize the long, cruel decline of MGM, and *Cleopatra*, which nearly sank Twentieth Century Fox. Wasserman in particular was keenly aware of the danger of cost overruns, following his own near extinction in 1969. As summer turned to autumn on Martha's Vineyard, with cost overruns and production delays straining the *Jaws* budget to the breaking point, a Universal executive went to Wasserman with a plea to pull the plug and order Spielberg back to L.A.

"Do we know how to make it better than they do?" snapped Wasserman.

"No," said the executive.

"Then let them keep going," he said.

One frequent visitor to the set was Sid Sheinberg, there as much to visit with his wife as he was to keep tabs on Spielberg. Using the stage name of Lorraine Gary, Mrs. Sheinberg was making her big screen debut as the police chief's wife in *Jaws*.

"My husband and I have always been close to Steve," she told one interviewer. "There's almost a father-son or an older brother-younger brother relationship between Sidney and Steve. It's something spiritual. They both have the same number of letters in their names, for example."

While Gary did not directly intervene on Spielberg's behalf when the film's budget began climbing toward the moon, she sang the young director's praises to her husband, giving Spielberg far more leeway than he might otherwise have received.

The results of putting Spielberg on a long leash were nothing short of spectacular, launching the tradition of the summer blockbuster. Until *Jaws*, most major movies were distributed just the way they had been when Lew first began ushering in the 1920s. They opened first in New York or Los Angeles, then moved to other urban areas, and finally reached the heartland. Studios depended on press publicity and word of mouth from both coasts to sell a movie. With the selling of *Jaws*, MCA changed everything.

Universal blitzed prime-time TV with ominous ads the same week that the movie opened in nearly a thousand theaters nationwide. Even as late as 1975 when television no longer posed the imagined threat that it had in the 1950s, most studio heads continued to view TV as the enemy. Paying networks to advertise a movie seemed nothing less than heresy, but none was prepared to argue with the results.

On the June weekend that *Jaws* opened in 1975, Robert Evans recalled sitting next to Lew on an early morning flight from New York to L.A. Lew had a calculator and the city-by-city box office results. When they landed, Lew predicted the movie's gross and said he'd be right within 5 percent. He was.

Jaws grossed $192 million for Universal in 1976. By comparison, the studio's total gross revenues from all filmed entertainment that year was $597 million. *Jaws* was the biggest moneymaker in cinema history until it was dethroned two years later by *Star Wars*.

ALTHOUGH JULES STEIN'S medical philanthropy did not win him the Presidential Medal of Freedom, President Gerald Ford did recognize Stein's Republican protégé Taft Schreiber with a seat on the National Heart and Lung Advisory Council. It was an apt appointment, given Schreiber's lifelong battle with asthma, which had become so awful that he'd grown dependent on steroids to keep his bronchia and sinuses clear.

On the whole, however, Schreiber was the picture of health for a man of sixty-eight. His only real complaint was typical of older men: an enlarged prostate that kept him up half the night, making frequent trips to the bathroom. During an April office visit in 1976 his urologist, Dr. Joseph Kaufman, recommended prostate removal—a simple operation that could be performed in little over an hour. Schreiber would be in and out of the hospital in a couple of days.

On the morning of June 4, Dr. Kaufman wheeled Schreiber into the operating room at UCLA Medical Center. As promised, the routine surgery was over by 9:30 A.M. Just before noon, Schreiber took Demerol for pain, an antihistamine for his sinuses, and an antiemetic to ease post-op nausea. Then things began to go haywire.

His heart raced, then stalled, then raced again. Attending nurses couldn't fathom what was going wrong. He'd lost some blood during the operation, but not enough to induce irregular heartbeat. At 5:30 P.M. Dr. Kaufman's assistant, second-year resident Stephen Johnson, prescribed a drug to control arrhythmia. At 9:00 P.M. Dr. Johnson added a diuretic and an antibiotic. Nothing helped. Nurses changed Schreiber's dressings and, at three minutes past midnight, gave him a transfusion to make up for the blood he'd lost.

By the following morning, Schreiber's heart irregularity had worsened and his kidneys had begun to fail. When he heard about Schreiber's turn for the worse, Dr. Eliot Corday, the same world-renowned heart specialist who had helped save Jules Stein's life six years earlier, abandoned his Saturday morning golf game and rushed to Taft's bedside. There he discovered a blunder that had gone undetected by a small army of physicians, nurses, and technicians for more than twenty-four hours. Though Schreiber's blood type was O positive, his transfusions since the previous morning had all been type B.

While Corday had arrived at the hospital in time to stop any further transfusions, he did not discover the mistake before Schreiber got a second pint of B blood. Corday ordered dialysis and added a muscle relaxant and antacid to Schreiber's I.V.

The following day, Schreiber returned to the operating room for exploratory surgery, to remove any type B blood clots that might have coagulated and remained in or around his prostate wound. He finally began to regain some color, and his heartbeat stabilized. For the remainder of the week, it looked as if he might recuperate.

As he convalesced, his doctors traced the mixup to a scheduled surgery for another patient, who was to have had surgery the same morning Schreiber had his prostate removed. The second man had canceled his surgery, but the blood ordered for his transfusions remained in the operating room: type B positive. For twenty-four deadly hours, until the near-tragic error was corrected, Taft Schreiber got the wrong blood.

Even with the right blood, Schreiber's kidneys never recovered. Clotting from the type B blood brought on anemia, red corpuscle breakdown, and irreversible organ damage. On June 14, ten days following his simple prostatectomy, Taft Schreiber died.

Jules eulogized him as "one of the most brilliant men that has ever been with our company," a boy who started at the bottom and ended as a man "very close to the top." Only Stein himself had been with MCA longer. Lew—the one who had kept Schreiber from capturing the top spot for himself—also eulogized his lifelong rival, but unlike Stein, Wasserman didn't even hint that Taft had finished the MCA race in second place.

"His contributions to the success of MCA were many," Lew said. "His brilliant mind, sage counsel, and dedicated service were important factors in establishing the initial solid foundations of the company and directing its course to its present eminent position. Taft Schreiber will indeed be greatly missed."

At the Black Tower, routine efficiency was set aside for a few hours—a sure sign that the corporate equivalent of a head of state had passed away. At 1:00 P.M. on Wednesday, June 16, MCA closed its offices. Schreiber was buried an hour later at Hillside Memorial Park. From 2:00 to 2:30 P.M., all production stopped at Universal in memory of the fallen agent.

No cause of death was immediately given, but a little over a month later, Los Angeles County Coroner Thomas Noguchi announced the findings of forensic specialist Dr. Peter Dykstra. After "extensive studies," Dykstra had concluded that "death was due to complications of a transfusion reaction due to incompatible blood after prostate surgery." Taft Schreiber suffered "hemolytic transmission reaction."

His kidneys shut down, and he died.

Six months later, Rita Schreiber and her two grown children sued the Regents of the University of California for $5 million, charging wrongful death and medical malpractice. UCLA's lawyers blamed the lab technicians who switched Taft's blood sample with that of the other patient, but the Schreibers were not appeased. They settled out of court, and though the dollar amount was not revealed, it was enough for the Schreibers to establish a blood bank in Taft's memory at Cedars-Sinai Hospital, UCLA Medical Center's chief West Side rival.

—◈—

As THE SCHREIBERS pointed out in their lawsuit, one of their biggest forfeitures was "loss of gain in the value of MCA stock." Indeed, during the year following Taft's untimely death MCA stock split two for one and paid an additional 3 percent stock dividend at the end of 1976. Following the bite *Jaws* took out of the box office, MCA soared on the New York Stock Exchange.

And yet MCA stock paid almost no cash dividends. The federal government taxed dividend income at a whopping 70 percent, and Jules Stein, who still held 1.6 million shares of MCA, would have slit his wrists before he ever paid such a premium in taxes. MCA's founders and top executives still controlled 32 percent of MCA's outstanding stock, with Lew's share now posted at 900,000 shares. MCA had become "one of a number of family-run public concerns whose dividends appear to reflect tax consideration more than ability to pay," according to Prescott, Ball and Turben's leisure-time stock analyst William D. Schwartz.

Beyond *Jaws*, Universal's movie output offered little, even in the way of modest hits. Big-budget disappointments included *The Hindenburg* (1975), Robert Wise's all-star movie; *Family Plot*[5] (1976), Alfred Hitchcock's swan song; *MacArthur* (1977), starring Gregory Peck; and *Sorcerer*[6] (1977), wunderkind Billy

---

[5] While not nearly as highly praised as most of Hitchcock's earlier films, *Family Plot* did double its $3.5 million cost in box office returns.

[6] To Lew's mortification, the Chicago-born Friedkin used his working class South Side roots to endear himself to Jules Stein, who made a three-picture deal with Friedkin without consulting Wasserman. As in the case of Dennis Hopper, Friedkin's special relationship with Stein gave

Friedkin's follow-up to *The Exorcist* (1973) and his Oscar-winning *French Connection* (1971).

As with *American Graffiti*, Universal's real strength continued to be the quirky smaller films that Ned Tanen shepherded past Lew Wasserman's patrician objections, including *Slap Shot* (1977), *Car Wash* (1976), and a cross-country car chase movie called *Smokey and the Bandit* (1977). All objections ended when Lew began adding up the weekend box office.

"Ned Tanen was smart enough to immediately take the project," said Ray Stark, whose Rastar Productions distributed *Smokey and the Bandit* through Universal. "It cost $3 million and grossed over $120 million, which was great for Burt Reynolds, who probably made $12 million for eighteen days' work. Only God and Lew Wasserman know how much Universal made with *Smokey* and the two sequels and a rip-off TV show."[7]

The various MCA subsidiaries were also punching the cash register. In addition to recording perennials Elton John, Olivia Newton-John, the Who, and Loretta Lynn, MCA Records signed Neil Sedaka, Lynyrd Skynyrd, and Conway Twitty and made killings on sound track albums for *The Sting* and *American Graffiti*. Along with *Kojak* lollipops, *Emergency* lunch boxes, and the shark from *Jaws*,[8] the Six Million Dollar Man and the Bionic Woman became the first in a long line of product licensing triumphs for the MCA merchandising division, and Spencer's Gifts now had nearly three hundred stores operating in thirty-six states. Up in the High Sierra, the Yosemite Park and Curry Company raked in more than the venerable Universal Studios Tour and the Universal Amphitheatre combined.[9]

"The company that brought us *Jaws* has no meaningful debt and does have more than $80 million in short-term investments and cash," said Prescott, Ball and Turben analyst Schwartz.

Wasserman offered $35 million for San Diego's Sea World and, a couple years later, bid for the Cedar Point amusement park in Ohio. Both attempts failed.

---

him leverage that few other Universal filmmakers had. For example, Friedkin discovered that Universal executives, acting against his orders, secretly reviewed his *Sorcerer* dailies as he sent them back to Hollywood from his location in the Dominican Republic. He trained a Spanish-speaking set laborer to speak enough English to announce into the camera before each day's shooting: "Mr. Wasserman, you a jerk-off." *Sorcerer* (1977), which cost $22 million, brought in only $5.9 million at the domestic box office.

[7]   *Smokey and the Bandit II* (1980) — originally titled *Smokey Is the Bandit* — and *Smokey and the Bandit 3* (1983), and NBC's *B.J. and the Bear* (1979–1981). At one point, MCA planned yet another sequel titled *Smokey and the Bandit Have a Baby*.

[8]   In 1980, MCA successfully sued Montgomery Ward in federal court, barring the company from marketing garbage disposals as Jaws One, Jaws Two, and Jaws Power.

[9]   In 1975, the tour and amphitheatre earned $19.3 million; Yosemite Park and Curry earned $24.5 million.

"They really low-ball," remarked Sea World president David DeMotte, who sold out to publishing house Harcourt Brace Jovanovich instead of MCA.

In 1977, Wasserman phoned the chairman of the L.A. Coca-Cola Bottling Company and brusquely informed him that he planned to buy his operation for $410 million. The chairman, Arthur D. MacDonald, was so galled by Lew's condescending manner that he fought MCA off with newspaper ads and threatened to haul Wasserman into court. Again, MCA lost out.[10]

MCA did buy a sprightly new weekly newsmagazine called *New Times* and launched a magazine about marathoning called *The Runner*. But *New Times* went out of business within a year and MCA abandoned the magazine business altogether when it sold *The Runner*.[11]

Despite its seemingly random acquisitions, MCA itself was ripe for the plucking according to Wall Street. Some speculated that Philips, the Dutch electronics giant with whom MCA was jointly developing DiscoVision, could have its eye on the company. Others heard that Charles Bluhdorn's Gulf and Western Industries might be angling for a possible takeover. Indeed, Paramount's new chairman, Barry Diller,[12] and president, Michael Eisner, joined Sheinberg and Wasserman in a secret meeting during which key executives from both camps discussed a Paramount-Universal merger.

"The plan was for Paramount to sell off its lot [on Melrose Avenue in Hollywood] and move to Universal, where they were going to build a second Black Tower on Lankershim, across the street from the original, as headquarters for the Gulf and Western empire," said one of those who attended the secret merger meeting.

The merger fell through, but others were interested in taking over MCA. In a 1976 article written for *New West*, journalist Dan Dorfman bluntly asked Seagram's chairman Edgar Bronfman Sr. if MCA was an attractive target. Answered Bronfman, "You know, I'd like to go to bed with Brigitte Bardot, but I'm not thinking of any campaign to seduce her."

---

[10] Particularly grating to MCA executives was the fact that Twentieth Century Fox was able to invest $27.5 million of its *Star Wars* (1977) windfall to purchase Coca-Cola's midwestern franchise and watch its investment double in no time at all.

[11] MCA also passed on an opportunity to purchase a small Long Island toy company called Fisher-Price.

[12] Though Gulf and Western chairman Charles Bluhdorn had a deep personal affection for Paramount production chief Robert Evans, Evans's worsening cocaine habit prompted Bluhdorn to replace him. In 1974, Bluhdorn recruited thirty-two-year-old ABC programming executive Barry Diller, a former Beverly Hills High classmate of Lynne Wasserman, to chair Paramount Pictures. Korshak again came to Evans's aid, negotiating an eight-year, twenty-four-picture deal for Evans, who remains tied to Paramount in his housekeeping production deal down to the present day.

Ten years earlier, Edgar Bronfman had developed a taste for Hollywood, first with a modest block of Paramount stock, which he sold in 1967 when Seagram's paid $40 million for a 15 percent stake in faltering MGM.[13] In the spring of 1969, Bronfman was even chairman of the board for a few months until wildcat financier Kirk Kerkorian paid $100 million for a 25 percent stake in the studio.[14] After a bitter boardroom struggle, Kerkorian installed former CBS president James Aubrey as MGM president and systematically began a decade of dismantling the studio, selling off its film library, real estate, and other assets until virtually nothing was left but the name MGM.

Meanwhile, Bronfman kept his stake in moviemaking with a production company he called Sagittarius. Beginning with New York stage productions like *1776* and *The Me Nobody Knows*, Sagittarius moved to Hollywood and produced half a dozen films during the early 1970s, including *Jane Eyre* (1971), *Joe Hill* (1971), and several of British producer David Puttnam's earliest efforts, including *Melody* (1971) and *The Pied Piper* (1972). Bronfman's son, Edgar Junior, also took an early shine to Hollywood, apprenticing himself to Puttnam, eventually assuming control of Sagittarius, and co-producing two movies of his own: *The Blockhouse* (1973) and *The Border* (1982),[15] which he made for Universal.[16]

For all the speculative talk, however, neither the Bronfmans nor any other prospective predators made a move on MCA. Jules Stein understood full well the salivation his company had set off among takeover buccaneers and took steps to protect MCA by amending the original incorporation charter to include a phrase requiring a 75 percent shareholder approval of any proposed merger. Because Stein and Wasserman still controlled 29 percent of the stock, the charter change effectively checked any hostile takeover...at least for the time being.

—◦◦◦—

---

[13] While Edgar had a wife and five children and had been married for over twenty years, he didn't let it keep him from dating starlets like Sue Lloyd and Samantha Eggar and jetting off mogul-style in his private Gulf Stream to San Francisco, Los Angeles, or Acapulco, where he owned a villa.

Family patriarch Samuel Bronfman purportedly asked his son: "Tell me, Edgar, are we buying all this stock in MGM just so you can get laid?" Edgar answered, "Oh, no, Pop, it doesn't cost $40 million to get laid."

[14] Comedian Don Rickles saw Bronfman enter a Hollywood nightclub shortly after his ouster and hollered: "Hey! There's Edgar Bronfman! He was chairman of MGM for five whole minutes!"

[15] One of Jack Nicholson's few flops during the 1980s, *The Border* took in $6 million at the domestic box office.

[16] Bronfman wanted to paint his office, but discovered that "Universal white" was the only color permitted. When he complained to Ned Tanen, the production chief responded in an exasperated tone, "I hate this job."

THE SUMMER OF 1975 began a nervous year for Sidney Korshak. On July 30 his friend and occasional client Jimmy Hoffa climbed into a car in the parking lot of the Machus Red Fox restaurant on the outskirts of Detroit and disappeared forever.

While Hoffa's apparent assassination became the best-known vanishing act of the decade, it was by no means the only one associated with organized crime. Just a month earlier, Sam Giancana, another Korshak associate, had been gunned down in the basement of his Chicago home. A week before his death, Giancana had been subpoenaed to testify before the Senate Select Committee on Intelligence chaired by Senator Frank Church. Johnny Rosselli, Korshak's friend and client since the Bioff-Browne shakedown in the 1930s, did testify before the Church Committee on June 24, 1975. A year later, Rosselli's corpse was found stuffed inside an oil drum floating in Florida's Biscayne Bay. The three murders were never solved.

"Korshak started traveling with a bodyguard after Hoffa disappeared," said a Labor Department investigator who had followed the Chicago lawyer's serpentine career for nearly twenty years. "Lew Wasserman beefed up security at his home around the same time."

There was more trouble brewing for the two men beyond the threat of abduction or assassination. In June of 1976, Lew Wasserman's cozy longtime relationship with Sid Korshak hit the front page of the *New York Times*.

A scathing four-part series reported by Seymour Hersh, the investigator who won a Pulitzer Prize for uncovering the My Lai massacre,[17] exposed Korshak's half century of shady dealings, beginning with the seventy-year-old Hollywood labor fixer's ties to Capone, Nitti, Bioff, and Browne. Hersh detailed Korshak's migration to Beverly Hills, where he continued to counsel thugs like Tony Accardo, Rosselli, and Giancana while at the same time cultivating star friendships with Debbie Reynolds, Kirk Douglas, Frank Sinatra, and David Janssen. Hersh also tied Korshak directly to Jimmy Hoffa's Teamsters and offered example after example of the sweetheart deals Korshak had "negotiated" between corporations and unions.

The *Times* series linked Sidney to studio titans as well—names like Paramount's Charles Bluhdorn and Robert Evans, MGM's Kirk Kerkorian, and Universal's Lew Wasserman, who quickly came to Korshak's defense. According to Lew, Sidney was, in fact,

> [A] "very good personal friend" and one of the forty or fifty people in Hollywood with influence. "He's a very well-respected lawyer," Mr. Wasserman said in an interview. "He's a man of his word and good company."

---

[17] In 1997, Hersh would score another hit with *The Dark Side of Camelot*, his best-selling chronicle of the sleazy side of the Kennedy dynasty.

Told of some of Mr. Korshak's connections with organized crime, Mr. Wasserman said: "I don't believe them. I've never seen him with so-called syndicate members or organization members."

But Hersh and his assistant, Jeff Gerth, found otherwise. After six months of investigating, the two reporters were able to show, in "The Double Life of Sidney Korshak," a lifetime of straddling both sides of the law. The Korshak they profiled had perfected his own distinction between veiled threats and illegal influence-peddling.

Though widely read and often cited as a classic example of investigative journalism, the series of articles did not win Hersh a second Pulitzer. And on the surface, it appeared to have little effect on Sidney Korshak. An ongoing federal investigation of Korshak, which the *Times* reporters had predicted in the fourth and final part of their series, petered out and never produced a single indictment.

Korshak's usual defenders, like *Chicago Sun-Times* columnist Irv Kupcinet and *Los Angeles Times* gossip columnist Joyce Haber, shrilly attacked Hersh as the worst kind of character assassin. According to Haber, the Korshaks and the Wassermans were two-thirds of the crème de la crème of West Side society, and not even the *New York Times* could alter that reality. Haber, who came up with A-list, B-list, and C-list social demarcations that separated L.A.'s truly powerful from the merely famous, regarded Lew and Edie Wasserman, Paul and Micki Ziffren, and Sid and Bea Korshak as "the Big Six" of "the Super-A's." If any one of them accepted an invitation, the social event was an instant success.[18]

The *Los Angeles Times* didn't even acknowledge the Hersh series. Seven years earlier, during the Parvin-Dohrmann stock scandal, *Los Angeles Times* staff writer and, later, *Wall Street Journal* editor Paul Steiger published his own soft-edged Korshak exposé, pointing out many of the same underworld links that Hersh had found, but in a far less accusatory manner. In Steiger's profile, Sidney Korshak was "[the] Man Who Makes Things Happen."

Despite Steiger's generally laudatory tenor, Korshak let the reporter know he did not appreciate reading his name in the paper. Several months later, when *Times* publisher Otis Chandler's mother, Dorothy "Buffy" Chandler, asked Korshak for a contribution to the Los Angeles Music Center, Sidney brought up the sore subject again.

"She approached Sidney at the Bistro one day when he was lunching there with [Teamsters president] Frank Fitzsimmons," said a close companion who accompanied Mrs. Chandler on her arm-twisting expedition. "He took out his

---

[18] The A, B, and C lists were the centerpiece of *The Users*, a gossipy best-selling 1977 novel about Hollywood, allegedly authored by Haber, but actually ghost written by producer-turned-novelist Dominick Dunne.

checkbook and told her he'd give her $25,000 on the spot on one condition: his name would never appear in the *Los Angeles Times*. Buff agreed, and he handed over the check."[19]

In an extraordinary four-page critique in the August 2, 1976, edition of *New West* magazine, executive editor Frank Lalli concluded that Hersh and Gerth had set off "firecrackers, not dynamite" with their investigation. Their report certainly hadn't damaged Korshak's relationship with Wasserman. Three days after the *New York Times* published the final installment of the Hersh series, the Wassermans invited Sidney to a weekend bash celebrating their fortieth wedding anniversary. When Korshak left the exclusive gathering at the Wassermans' home later that evening, Lew gave Sidney a bear hug.

A month later they both laughed it up at the reception following Frank Sinatra's wedding to longtime girlfriend Barbara Marx. In a private ceremony behind the high-security fence of Walter Annenberg's Palm Springs estate, Bea Korshak acted as Barbara's maid of honor. And two months after the *New York Times* series was published, during a Democratic fund-raiser at the Wassermans', Lew personally introduced Sidney to Jimmy Carter, Wasserman's candidate for president. Sidney even switched doctors, making Lew and Edie's doctor, Rex Kennamer, his own personal physician. If the *New York Times* reporters had meant to ostracize the Korshaks from the Beverly Hills version of polite society, they failed completely.

The exposé didn't seem to hurt Korshak's business relationship with Wasserman, either. Thanks to Sidney, the King Kong attraction wound up becoming one of the biggest draws on the Universal Tour.

The making of the movie that inspired the attraction also generated attention. In the spring of 1975, MCA sued Italian producer Dino De Laurentiis over the right to remake the 1933 RKO classic, *King Kong*. Chief target of the suit was RKO, accused of selling Universal the rights to *The Legend of King Kong* after granting those very same rights to De Laurentiis for a Paramount production titled simply *King Kong*. But RKO—by now a shell division of General Tire—wouldn't suffer from dueling Kongs; De Laurentiis and Wasserman would. As a close personal pal of Paramount's Charlie Bluhdorn as well as Wasserman, Korshak was called upon to mediate. He invited Dino and Lew over to the house.

---

[19] Korshak's name did appear subsequently in the *Los Angeles Times*, but rarely in a derogatory or critical manner. In one widely publicized incident during the second week of July 1979, *Times* editors censored "Doonesbury" because the comic strip implied that California Governor Jerry Brown hobnobbed with Korshak at Lew Wasserman's parties, accepted a $1,000 campaign contribution from Sidney, and wanted to cover it up because of the lawyer's Mob ties. A few other West Coast newspapers followed the *Times's* lead, citing the excuse that Sid might sue for libel. Most major U.S. newspapers that carried "Doonesbury"—including Korshak's hometown paper, the *Chicago Tribune*—printed the comic strip without incident.

In Korshak's kitchen, Lew and Dino agreed to a compromise: Wasserman would drop *The Legend of King Kong* and share distribution expenses with Paramount for *King Kong*. De Laurentiis, in turn, would cut Universal in on Paramount's *King Kong* profits. As a result, Wasserman dropped Dino as a defendant in the RKO suit, and began planning MCA's thrill ride version of the giant ape as the newest fright stop on the Universal Tour. De Laurentiis' *King Kong* (1976), which introduced moviegoers to actress Jessica Lange, went on to gross over $80 million and turn a profit of $46 million.

And for getting the boys to schmooze around his kitchen table for a couple hours, Korshak earned $30,000.

Lew would not deny his friendship with Korshak when contacted by NBC's reporter Brian Ross, but neither would he comment on it. For his part, Korshak stiffly walked away from Ross when the correspondent tried to corner him for an interview on the streets of Beverly Hills.

"Quit pestering me," Korshak said. "You're not going to ask me any questions. Now, good-bye."

Korshak found newspaper reporting far more to his liking than broadcast journalism. As he had done with his 1969 *Los Angeles Times* profile, Korshak took to boasting that the Hersh series was free advertising. Indeed, *Playboy* magazine founder Hugh Hefner admitted to investigators that the *New York Times* stories inspired him to give Korshak a $50,000 retainer to help Hefner avoid going to court against MCA.

It seemed that Hefner's private film collection contained a number of bootleg Universal features—a clear case of copyright infringement at best and receiving stolen property at worst. The *Playboy* publisher so feared the public humiliation such a lawsuit might carry with it that he paid Korshak to smooth things over with his good friend Lew Wasserman. He never did get to meet with Wasserman, and the story of the pilfered films came out anyway. A chagrined Hefner returned them to MCA without comment. Hefner later told investigators that while Korshak was "remarkably unsuccessful" in helping him avoid negative publicity, the lawyer did keep every penny of the $50,000 Hefner paid him.

Sidney also continued his labor-fixing business unfazed. It was Korshak who aided, then betrayed, legendary labor leader Cesar Chávez in his quest to organize California's immigrant farmworkers. In what many labor scholars have cited as a cynical abuse of Chávez's trust, Korshak engineered a groundbreaking pact between Chávez's United Farm Workers and Schenley Industries, a holdover client from Korshak's Chicago days. Chávez signed the pact on the same kitchen table where Wasserman and De Laurentiis had worked out their differences over *King Kong*. With the leverage given him by Schenley, one of the nation's largest grape producers and processors, Chávez was able to force smaller grape growers to recognize and negotiate with the farmworkers union. What he did not count upon was a Korshak double cross.

Once the United Farm Workers became the recognized union, Teamster organizers systematically lured members away, using a combination of threats and perks. In the mid-1970s, the Teamsters and Farm Workers openly warred for the hearts and minds of migrant workers in the fields of California's Central and Coachella Valleys. The Teamster organizers sent to break the United Farm Workers took the nickname "Anderson's Raiders" after Western Conference of Teamsters chief Andy Anderson. Belatedly, Chávez realized he and his union had been set up as a stalking horse for the Teamsters: each time the Farm Workers struck a bargain with a grower, Anderson's Raiders would appear as if by magic and take away members and contracts. Behind Anderson stood Sidney Korshak, the grand manipulator who profited from all sides—growers, Teamsters, and Farm Workers.

But Korshak didn't just double-cross venal millionaires like Hefner and folk heroes like Chávez. He was an equal-opportunity swindler who was just as happy preying on other swindlers.

When Mob assassin and shakedown artist Jimmy "the Weasel" Fratianno wanted to sell a questionable dental insurance plan to the Teamsters, he too had to see Korshak before he could get to Andy Anderson.[20] It didn't matter that Fratianno, the Cleveland thug who started out as a chauffeur at the old Mayfair Casino, had worked his way up the Mafia ladder with an impressive career in gambling, fraud, and murder. He still had to go through proper channels if he wanted to do business with the West Coast Conference of Teamsters. That meant paying homage to Sidney in the back booth at the Bistro.

"Mr. Korshak has strong ties to the Chicago Mob," Fratianno later explained to the House Select Committee on Aging during a hearing on Teamsters Union pension fraud. "He said he would take care of the problem with Anderson."

But he didn't. The Weasel never got to meet with Anderson or pitch his dental insurance. A few weeks later, Fratianno ran into Korshak in Vegas and reminded him of his promise in the only way he knew how: with a threat.

"The next thing I knew, I was summoned to Chicago," Fratianno testified.

There, Tony Accardo's top lieutenant, Joey Aiuppa, told Fratianno someone had put a dead fish in Korshak's mailbox. Fratianno did not deny that he might be the culprit. Aiuppa told him to lay off.

---

[20] In a 1979 FBI-wiretapped conversation between Teamsters Central States Pension Fund trustee Allen Dorfman and Chicago Mob lieutenant Joey "the Clown" Lombardo, Dorfman referred to Anderson as "absolutely an 18-carat cunt, but he belongs lock, stock, and barrel to Sidney." Five years later, former Teamsters president Roy Williams confirmed in testimony before the President's Commission on Organized Crime that Korshak "controlled" Anderson.

New York Times or no, Sidney still had the Mob's protection, at least for the time being. Nevertheless, the newspaper series had its impact.

In Saint Petersburg, Florida, a young assistant state's attorney named Marvin Rudnick clipped the Korshak series out of the paper and attached it to the side of his refrigerator where it remained until it yellowed and curled at the edges.

A bulldog prosecutor in the tradition of Leonard Posner, Rudnick marveled at Korshak's ability to slip through life unscathed as a high-priced bagman while lesser criminals were eventually caught and punished. As the years passed and Rudnick moved on, first to the U.S. attorney's office as a prosecutor and later to the Justice Department's Organized Crime Strike Force in Los Angeles, he took the newspaper clippings with him. They were a reminder of the beguiling face of Mob corruption—a face Rudnick swore to rub in the dirt.

THIRTY

The Acting President

1977–1980

O n October 2, 1977, the Glenville High Class of 1930 joined four other Glenville classes dating back to 1927 for one big fiftieth class reunion. People were dying off, and nobody was sure if enough were left for a single class reunion. As she had done in 1960 for the thirtieth reunion, Mollie Marshall again invited Lew Wasserman. This time he didn't even acknowledge her invitation.

The chairman of the board of MCA-Universal had far more important business to attend to in Washington, D.C., during reunion week. While old high school chums gathered at the Holiday Inn on the West Side of Cleveland, Lew was lunching with Hamilton Jordan, President Jimmy Carter's chief of staff. Half Lew's age, Jordan was lukewarm about meeting the legendary Hollywood mogul.

"Ham didn't even want to return Lew's phone calls," said Wasserman's son-in-law, Jack Myers, who became friendly with the Carters' son, Chip. "Carter's people didn't want anything to do with old party regulars like Lew. They'd rather meet Warren Beatty and get laid."

Not only did he represent an earlier era in Democratic politics, but Lew's reputation as a cold-blooded tyrant had preceded him. Nevertheless, Democratic National Committee treasurer Joel McCleary prevailed upon Jordan to give Lew "a few strokes" for the sake of the party. Wasserman would soon head up a $1,000-a-plate West Coast Salute to the President dinner, like the old President's Club Dinners that Lew and Arthur Krim had once hosted for Kennedy and Johnson. MCA no longer stood for Music Corporation of America; it meant Muscle, Cash, and Attorneys. McCleary wanted all the campaign cash that a rainmaker like Wasserman could command. He felt he had to caution Jordan about the importance of not insulting the sixty-four-year-old MCA chairman. "Contrary to the Hollywood legend," McCleary told Jordan, "Lew is really a very kind man and wants to help as much as he is physically able."

Jordan dutifully treated the MCA chairman with kid gloves. President Jimmy Carter himself understood that Wasserman had become a political power who was not to be taken lightly. As an early step in preparing to run for the 1976 Democratic presidential nomination, Carter had paid his respects to Lew Wasserman.

"I met him when I was still governor of Georgia," Carter said in a 1982 interview. "When I decided to run, Mr. Wasserman was one of the first out-of-state people I told. People respected his judgment in business, international affairs, and political affairs. When he let his friends know he had confidence in me, it was extremely helpful. He knows influential people on a worldwide basis. He generates confidence based on his sound judgments."

After eight years out of the White House loop, Wasserman desperately needed to back a winner in 1976. That would not be Senator Ted Kennedy, whose chances of ever occupying the Oval Office ended on the night of July 18, 1969, when he drove twenty-eight-year-old Mary Jo Kopechne to her death off the bridge at Chappaquiddick Island.[1] Senator Henry "Scoop" Jackson was another Wasserman favorite, until Lew calculated that post-Watergate America was in a populist mood and did not want a D.C. insider like Scoop in the White House.

If he had learned nothing else from fifty years in show biz, Lew Wasserman knew that you always sold the masses what they wanted, not necessarily what they needed—and after Richard Nixon, what America wanted was the illusion of an unsullied citizen politician from outside the Beltway. Lew saw the bandwagon and got on board. It was not the year of *The Last Hurrah* or *State of the Union*. It was the year of *Mr. Smith Goes to Washington*.

Wasserman hadn't been a complete stranger to the White House during the Republicans' reign. Through Secretary of State Henry Kissinger,[2] Lew finagled at least one presidential visit with Gerald Ford to talk about a favorite issue: the Middle East.

While President Ford didn't brush Wasserman off during their brief meeting, he was only dimly hopeful about the U.S. role in burying the hatchet between the Palestinian Arabs and Jews. Egypt's Anwar Sadat and Israel's Menachem Begin had been inching toward peace since the October War of 1973, Ford told Wasserman. But the two men and the warring factions they represented were still a long way from signing any treaty. That was not what Lew wanted to hear. After fifteen unsatisfying minutes together, President Ford offered Lew a consolation prize: an invitation to bring Edie to a state dinner at the White House, honoring the president

---

[1]   One of Kennedy's first phone calls following the accident, and before notifying the police, was to Jules Stein's son-in-law, William vanden Heuvel.

[2]   A favorite of the Wassermans despite his Nixon administration roots, Kissinger became a Hollywood devotee during the 1970s, partying with the movie crowd and even dating Korshak consort Jill St. John for a time.

of Zambia. The Wassermans accepted and sat among the hoi polloi at one of the outlying tables.

The following November the Wassermans cast their lot with Jimmy Carter. During the next four years they were assured of far better White House access whenever the subject of Israel arose, as well as first-rate seating at state dinners. During a prestigious bash for the Shah and Empress of Iran, for example, Jimmy and Rosalynn Carter sat with Lew and Edie. Unlike the Republican Fords, the Carters even asked the Wassermans to spend the night upstairs in the Lincoln bedroom when they happened to be in Washington. The Wassermans and Carters became so close that Jimmy personally wrote thank-you notes to Lew, just as LBJ had. Carter even made a point of calling Lew personally to wish him a happy sixty-fifth birthday on the evening of March 15, 1978.[3]

Rosalynn invited Edie to serve on the Committee for the Preservation of the White House. Edie responded by sending Rosalynn an orchid arrangement. Rosalynn sent Edie a pepper plant; Edie sent Rosalynn lilies.

The budding relationship between Carters and Wassermans almost smacked of déjà vu. Lew mailed videocassettes of old Universal movies to Jimmy, the way he had once regaled Lyndon and Lady Bird with eight-track stereo cassettes of MCA recording artists. Like LBJ, Jimmy even offered Lew a cabinet position, which would have required a full FBI background check. Lew graciously but regretfully declined.

The Wassermans extended their fondness to the younger Carter children, showering Amy and Chip with MCA-Universal products. Amy, who was just a year younger than Lew and Edie's beloved granddaughter Carol Ann Leif, responded:

> **Dear Mr. Wasserman, Thank you for sending me the [*Sgt. Pepper's Lonely Hearts Club Band*] T-shirt and album. I like them very much and can't wait to see the movie![4] Annette teases me that she is jealous, but I promised to let her tape my new record. It was nice of you to think of me. I'm glad we're friends,**
>
> **Love, Amy Carter**

---

[3]   According to official White House records, March 15, 1913, was Lew's birthday. In clearing the Wassermans for access to the White House inner circle, no one at the FBI, the National Security Agency, or the Executive Protective Section of the Secret Service had ever bothered to verify exactly where or when Wasserman was actually born.

[4]   A wretched screen adaptation of the Beatles' landmark concept album, *Sgt. Pepper*, starred Peter Frampton and the Bee Gees as Beatles substitutes. It tanked at the box office as well as in the record stores.

At the start of the 1978 fall TV season, Lew shipped off *Battlestar Galactica*[5] souvenirs to Amy and Chip Carter and got yet another strategic product off to her parents a few months later. Just as the prototype of MCA's DiscoVision was about to be test-marketed in the Carters' home state of Georgia, a disc player arrived on the White House doorstep.

Hooking the First Family on DiscoVision could be a ringing endorsement for the gadget that Lew envisioned as the ultimate weapon in the MCA arsenal. As early as 1970, MCA shareholders were told that because MCA Technology was developing a revolutionary new form of entertainment, the division might be running at a loss for a little while — unusual by MCA standards, to say the least. According to the annual report, MCA designers needed the red ink to create "a color videodisc recording and playback system…designed to show films on the home television screen by means of a playback device attached to the television set."

DiscoVision was Wasserman's ultimate vision. To Lew it represented the culmination of a lifetime dedicated to delivering to America the fastest, if not the finest, in entertainment. The kind of escapist diversion that Cleveland's poor working men and women had bought for a nickel in a movie palace in Lew's boyhood could now be reduced to a plastic disc and sold for $15.95.

"With DiscoVision, you'll have an amusement center tied in to each television set," Wasserman predicted. "It'll need programming — and MCA has the largest facilities to make film and the largest reservoir of film."

Indeed, MCA already had a library of 2,200 theatrical films and another 12,000 episodes of old TV shows, each of which could be repackaged and sold again on videodisc. The trick was to make American consumers believe that they could not live without it.

"I think its potential is literally mind-boggling," Wasserman told *Fortune* magazine writer Peter Schuyten. "I do believe that videodisc entertainment in the home will absolutely revolutionize the income of suppliers."

Lew loved repeating the story of how he got MCA immersed in the new technology. It began back in 1967 with MCA's purchase of Saki Magnetics, Gauss Electrophysics, and four smaller cutting-edge companies. He bought the companies to give Universal better access to the raw materials of filmmaking, including videotape and sound track technology. But when he paid a visit to the Saki labo-

---

[5]   The most expensive TV series up to its time, *Battlestar Galactica* was a special effects–laden rip-off of *Star Wars* and lasted little more than a year on ABC. The $3 million three-hour premiere was refashioned into a Sensurround movie shown overseas, but deemed too hokey for release in the United States. A live-action version of *Battlestar Galactica*'s evil Cylons outlived their TV incarnation by more than a decade as a bewildering stop on the Universal Tour. Most tourists had no idea what *Battlestar Galactica* or Cylons were, but they still had to sit through the ride.

ratories, he recognized that the tiny group of sound engineers were experimenting with something far more intriguing than hi-fi tape decks.

"The way Lew liked to tell it," recalled a Wasserman lawyer, "he was taking the tour of the place when he pointed at some closet down in the basement and asked, 'What's in there?' And the fellow taking him around answered, 'Oh, that's just old so-and-so. Kind of an eccentric.' Lew pressed for more. 'What's he do?' Well, it turned out the guy was experimenting with putting movies on LPs. Lew went nuts. He wanted to meet the guy right away."

While the closet story may be apocryphal, the relationship between Lew and physicist-entrepreneur Kent Broadbent was not. By playing to Wasserman's vanity as a media visionary, Broadbent persuaded him to finance an MCA laboratory in the Los Angeles suburb of Torrance. Lew learned soon enough that developing a product as sophisticated as movies on disc could not be done on the cheap. Trial and error was expensive: for every success, a hundred failures. There were simply no shortcuts.

Broadbent praised Lew as nothing less than the Thomas Edison of his time, but as the videodisc kept sucking cash from the company with no immediate prospect of earning it back, Lew turned his substantial spleen against Broadbent.

"The poor bastard would come in, flattering him with what a great visionary he was and Lew would scream at the guy, practically throw him out of his office," said one insider from that era.

By 1974, Dutch-owned Magnavox agreed to produce the disc player while MCA Technology concentrated on putting video on disc.

"We had the patents on the compact disc, if you really want to get down to it, and that became important in a lot of ways," said MCA vice president Al Dorskind.

Industry and government, particularly General Motors[6] and the Central Intelligence Agency, showed a marked interest in DiscoVision as a potential tool for information storage. If an entire motion picture could be reduced to a plastic circle, why not a multimedia auto sales pitch or a filing cabinet loaded with documents? But Wasserman never wavered from his primary goal. Mr. and Mrs. Average American wouldn't be able to grasp the importance of commercials on disc or CD information storage, but they *would* buy DiscoVision movies, perhaps by the millions. *That* was where the money was!

"I think Lew really wanted to stick to his way," said Dorskind. "He knew motion pictures, film, and television because he grew up with those."

What he did not count on was the Japanese coming up with a cheaper and more versatile video technology and blowing all other competition out of the

---

[6] General Motors bought 12,000 videodiscs for sales theaters around the nation, where prospective customers could get a rundown on the latest model cars.

water. First marketed in 1975, Sony's Betamax videocassette recording system was expensive, but it used tape instead of discs. Besides playing recorded movies, a Betamax could record shows right off the tube. When *The Godfather* first aired on television, one Sony dealer advertised: "NBC paid millions for *The Godfather*. You can have it for $14.99."

As sales increased, the prohibitive cost of Betamax recorders dropped. In 1976, MCA fought back. Universal and Walt Disney Productions sued Sony for copyright infringement, demanding a royalty on all blank videocassettes to defray losses each time Betamax owners taped a Disney TV special or an MCA dramatic series right off of their TV set. Calling it "my personal lawsuit," Sid Sheinberg preached that, unchecked, the VCR would promote movie piracy, allow viewers to zap out commercials, and bring economic ruin to Hollywood.

"We cannot accept technology taking our property, benefiting from it economically, and giving us nothing in return," he said.[7]

While the complex, costly lawsuit wound its way through federal court, Sony continued to sell VCRs. By 1979 an estimated 600,000 had been sold in the United States. That number doubled the following year. When Matsushita subsidiary JVC Electronics developed VHS recorders and began competing head-to-head with Betamax, prices fell even further. While neither as sophisticated as DiscoVision nor as high-quality as Betamax, VHS was more affordable and more readily available. VCRs promised to free America's TV audience from a network timetable and from the one-time cable broadcast, and give them the convenience of watching their favorite TV shows whenever they wanted to.

By the time Magnavision began test-marketing its new videodisc player in Atlanta on December 15, 1978, it was already too late. VCRs gripped America's TV addicts. At $500 for the disc player compared to $750 for the far more versatile VCR, Magnavision simply couldn't compete. Add the limited selection — only 200 MCA DiscoVision movies to choose from at $15.95 apiece — and the battle for the marketplace became a rout. VCR prices kept dropping. By 1981, Americans owned over 1 million VCRs, but only 35,000 Magnavision (renamed Laservision in 1980) players.

Bypassing its informal agreement with Magnavox, MCA teamed up with Japan's Pioneer Electronic Corporation to create Universal Pioneer Corporation in a final desperate attempt to mass-produce MCA's own videodisc player. The following year, MCA Technology and IBM formed DiscoVision Associates, a sepa-

---

[7]   Senator Dennis DeConcini of Arizona introduced a bill in 1981 that would let VCR owners tape for home use. Sheinberg indignantly howled that the bill "strips from authors and creators the rights to their property without just compensation." The bill passed. Three years later MCA and Disney lost their war of attrition with Betamax when the Supreme Court decided in Sony's favor. MCA's lawyers knew their case was doomed when they ran a warranty check on the nine justices and discovered that six of them were VCR owners.

rate joint venture to help defray the escalating Universal Pioneer production costs. Nevertheless, MCA wound up spending well over $100 million.

"There were many episodes where Lew didn't get it, but videodisc was probably the worst," said one former MCA officer, a twenty-year veteran of the Black Tower. "Lew wasn't that wealthy a person that he could just blow $300 million. What DiscoVison was really good for was a storage of knowledge. It would be like putting the entire Pentagon files on a single disc and then you can just burn all these ridiculous files.

"But Lew was convinced and Sheinberg was convinced that [the videodisc player] was going to outstrip VHS and Betamax, even when it was so obvious that the market was going to go to Betamax or whatever, but it *wasn't* going to be the videodisc. They didn't have any way to market it. In the few times that Lew ventured into the hardware delivery system, he got nailed."

By 1982, MCA had thrown in the towel. A terse item buried on the sixth page of the 1981 annual report to shareholders read, "In February 1982, your Company announced that DiscoVision Associates, an equally owned and controlled joint venture of your Company and IBM, had completed discussions with Pioneer Electronic Corporation enabling that company to become sole owner of Universal Pioneer Corporation."

MCA held on to its patents, but left the hardware to the Japanese.[8]

In the meantime, Lew and Sid quietly created a new division: MCA Videocassette. At the end of its first year of operation, Universal offered eighty movies for sale to the 4.5 percent of all U.S. homes that now had VCRs. In 1982 an MCA workout video from Olivia Newton-John, *Olivia Physical*, became the top-selling cassette in the country and won the Grammy for Video of the Year.

———∿∿∿———

WHILE DISCOVISION DRAINED the company coffers, the rest of the MCA machine did well. By 1978 the entertainment conglomerate employed over 18,000 people. On September 20 its stock split again, this time five shares for four. For the first time annual revenue topped the $1 billion mark and cash-rich MCA now had nearly $200 million in the bank.[9]

---

[8] Ironically, by the time MCA spun off DiscoVision in 1989, the division was profitable. Licensing MCA's patents over the better part of the decade, as audio CDs replaced the outmoded vinyl phonograph record, more than made up for the company's losses in developing its ill-fated videodisc.
[9] One windfall that contributed mightily to MCA's bottom line was a $34.5 million judgment MCA won against the IRS in 1979. For the years 1962 through 1970, auditors disallowed MCA's investment tax credits. The company sued for its money back and won, much to the delight of Jules Stein, who loved sticking it to the IRS.

"It obviously gives us a bit of an edge," Wasserman boasted in an interview with journalist Bob Gottlieb. "We don't have to worry about paying the 10.25 percent to borrow money."

With all that extra cash, Lew exercised his longtime desire to insinuate MCA into Broadway by backing plays like *Same Time Next Year* and the musical *The Best Little Whorehouse in Texas*. Once they finished their initial New York stage run, the idea was to spin them off as Universal pictures, with potential for cast albums, action figures, syndication, maybe even a TV series. In a giant step backward to the Leland Hayward era, Broadway became an MCA proving ground. Lew's idea of a Universal winner was a big-budget Broadway musical like *The Wiz*, an all-black update of *The Wizard of Oz*. Instead of looking to the future for Universal movies, Wasserman seemed to want to return to the past. He even entered talks with MGM's Kirk Kerkorian at one point about making a sequel to *Gone With the Wind*.

"He was very proprietary about the box office numbers for *The Wiz*," Gottlieb said. "He tapped his coat and said, 'I have the numbers right here in my pocket.' He is very focused. Like he has a handle on success based on accountants' ledgers."

But the movie version of *The Wiz*, starring Diana Ross as Dorothy and a young Michael Jackson as the Scarecrow, turned out to be an unmitigated disaster. It bombed at the box office and was stiffed at the Academy Awards. The best that could be said of *The Wiz* was that it preserved for future generations exactly what pop icon Michael Jackson looked like before plastic surgery. During an irony-filled interview on the eve of the film's premiere, Sheinberg pontificated, "You've got to believe in yourself, like Dorothy in *The Wiz*. You market your product aggressively, you go with your people, and you look at what happens in the long run." [10]

In the long run, hit movies did continue to turn up, courtesy of Universal president Ned Tanen, in spite of the recurrent bad judgment of Wasserman and Sheinberg. MCA's box office champ for 1978 was a sleeper comedy about college fraternity pranksters, *National Lampoon's Animal House*.[11] *National Lampoon* publisher Matty Simmons, who brought the idea to Universal, had never made a movie before in his life, but Tanen let Simmons produce, over Wasserman's misgivings. *Animal House* became the biggest-grossing comedy of all time.

Similarly, Tanen gave the green light to comedian Steve Martin's first starring role in *The Jerk* (1979), the offbeat comedy *Melvin and Howard* (1980), and the

---

[10] During an October 1978 tribute to Jules Stein by the Motion Picture Pioneers in the ballroom of the Waldorf-Astoria, Lew did not miss an opportunity to hype *The Wiz*. Diana Ross was dispatched to sing "Home," the movie's signature song. In her braless plunge-neckline blouse, she then led the crowd in a swaying, heart-tugging sing-along of "Take Someone's Hand."

[11] Typically, Universal tried to parlay *Animal House* into a weekly TV series called *Delta House*, just as it had done successfully with *Coogan's Bluff* (*McCloud*) but unsuccessfully with *Smokey and the Bandit* (*B.J. and the Bear*). ABC canceled *Delta House* after one season.

Loretta Lynn biopic *Coal Miner's Daughter* (1980) — all big moneymakers and/or Oscar winners for Universal, despite their untested talent, relatively modest production budgets, and lack of special effects.[12]

The Blues Brothers (1980) also did well at the box office, even though director John Landis let production costs balloon to more than $36 million, incurring Wasserman's wrath and turning Tanen into a nervous wreck. Wasserman and Sheinberg were far more tolerant of similar cost overruns on *1941* (1979), Steven Spielberg's all-star extravaganza about wacky wartime antics in southern California. Originally budgeted at $6 million, *1941* ultimately cost $31.5 million.

Another dark horse authorized by Tanen was a three-hour Vietnam War epic from neophyte Michael Cimino, who fast developed a reputation as an erratic, brilliant director and a profligate spender. Cimino had just a single credit, but that 1974 United Artists release was already regarded as a cult classic: the bittersweet buddy movie *Thunderbolt and Lightfoot,* starring Clint Eastwood and Jeff Bridges. *The Deer Hunter,* Cimino's new film for Universal, quickly went over budget. Once again, Tanen found himself refereeing a running feud between Lew and the free-spending director.

"Lew had one comment to make about *The Deer Hunter:* 'Cut the fucking thing,'" recalled a Black Tower executive from that time.

As in the case of *American Graffiti* and a dozen other films that Lew didn't like, Tanen's instincts prevailed over Wasserman's tantrums. *The Deer Hunter,* starring Robert De Niro, Meryl Streep, and Christopher Walken, and running over three hours, took five Oscars, including Best Picture.

But it was always television, never movies, that "paddled the company's canoe," according to Wes Whiteman, the First National Bank of Chicago's lending liaison with MCA. At the end of the 1970s, MCA had a combined revolving credit line with Bank of America, Crocker Bank, and Whiteman's bank that totaled half a billion dollars, and it was primarily television money that made it possible.

In a late attempt to break into cable, Universal joined Paramount, Columbia, Twentieth Century Fox, and Getty Oil to create the Premiere Channel.[13] The new pay TV operation was squarely aimed at unseating Time Inc.'s Home Box Office — which Sheinberg termed "arrogant" for foisting third-rate movies on its customers — as the cable leader. But before the Premiere Channel got on the air, Lew's old nemesis, the Justice Department Antitrust Division, cracked down. A consortium of four of the seven major movie studios and the nation's most suc-

---

[12] Five of Hollywood's ten largest-grossing films of 1980 came from Universal: *The Jerk, Smokey and the Bandit II, Coal Miner's Daughter, The Blues Brothers,* and *The Electric Horseman.*

[13] In addition to selling gasoline, Getty owned and operated ESPN, the most successful cable TV network through the early 1980s.

cessful cable operation could unfairly monopolize pay-TV, argued the Justice Department, and a federal judge in New York agreed.

The five Premiere Channel partners broke up, but three months later MCA joined Paramount and Time in a cable venture called the USA Network. Lew waited for the inevitable squawk from the Justice Department, but it never came. As Wasserman told Gottlieb, MCA was "primarily committed to be in all of the fields of communication," but he was still wary of buying broadcast stations. After the 1962 antitrust investigation, coupled with the Justice Department's defeat of the MCA-Westinghouse merger seven years later, Wasserman had no itch to get on the wrong side of the antitrust division or the FCC ever again.

Meanwhile, MCA's non-movie and non-TV enterprises were also growing. From its Atlantic City headquarters, Spencer Gifts now operated 414 stores in forty-six states. Denver-based Columbia Savings and Loan, after buying Pioneer Savings and Mutual Savings, now had forty-two branches.

After years of neglect, MCA also began moving vigorously back into the music business, buying both ABC Records and Infinity Records. MCA Records cut its own recording artist roster from three hundred to eighty, but the streamlined catalog included such moneymakers as Electric Light Orchestra, Barbara Mandrell, the Oak Ridge Boys, Rufus and Chaka Khan, Jimmy Buffett, B. B. King, Merle Haggard, Tanya Tucker, and Tom Petty and the Heartbreakers. Elton John and the Who, two MCA blue chips, quit for a Warner Communications record label run by former William Morris agent David Geffen, who had developed an uncanny knack for picking hits. Still, MCA Records, which had operated at a $10 million loss in 1979, showed a $15.9 million profit the following year.

Wasserman had also taken a personal interest in developing Universal City's commercial real estate. Like a realty agent working off commission, he proudly pointed out to anyone who asked that Universal's largely undeveloped 422 acres were just "nine minutes from downtown L.A. during the non–rush hour."

The Black Tower would soon be dwarfed by the $100 million thirty-six-story Getty Oil headquarters going up next door. In addition to the 500-room Sheraton Universal Hotel and seven office buildings, MCA planned a second 479-room Sheraton Premiere Hotel as well as three theme restaurants, including L.A.'s largest Chinese restaurant, right outside the gates of Universal Studios.

Despite its continuing success, MCA headed into the new decade with a troubling bottom line. While Universal income remained among the highest of any movie factory in Hollywood, MCA's consolidated revenues had eroded steadily: $243 million in 1978, $145 million in 1979, and a mere $31 million in 1980. Management blamed everything from the lengthy actors' strike to worldwide inflation, but Wasserman's beloved DiscoVision had to bear much of the blame.

TEN YEARS EARLIER, Lew had still had Jules to answer to, but by 1979 the ailing eighty-three-year-old founder of MCA was completely out of the loop. Lew controlled the empire.

Jules's fading impact could be measured by the odd irrelevance of his demands. He once sent a memo to every MCA employee extolling the benefits of dim lighting. In his role as Dr. Stein, Ophthalmologist, Jules argued that fewer lights meant less glare and better vision. Around the water cooler, cynics translated Stein's advice to mean that the stingy old fart wanted to save on MCA's electricity bill and, at the same time, boost admissions to his eye institute.

His younger sister, Ruth, had more clout in the Black Tower than Jules did. Ruth continued to invest the MCA portfolio for the profit-sharing plan, and she could be glimpsed wandering the corridors of power in the upper reaches of the Black Tower like a tiny waif whom the receptionist had misdirected. Although she looked out of place in the all-male empire, Ruth was one of only a handful who could walk into Lew's office unannounced while he was in the middle of one of his tirades, retrieve her paperwork, and walk back out as if nothing had happened.

Ruth also rode herd over MCA's bankers. "They were always doing tax loans with us and Ruth would want us to wire money," said First National Bank of Chicago's Wes Whiteman. "It could be twenty-two cents, and she'd *still* want us to wire it. But we never made a big deal about it. We just smiled and did what she asked."

Jules and Ruth shared office space in the sixteenth-floor penthouse of the Black Tower, with Lew, Sid Sheinberg, Ned Tanen, and executive vice president Tom Wertheimer one floor below. Elevators went only as high as the fifteenth floor and, as Jules became more frail, he had more and more trouble climbing the final flight of stairs to his office. Lew accommodated the old man by installing a one-person elevator between the top floor and the penthouse; it was hidden in the wall behind the desk occupied by Sid Sheinberg's secretary. Visitors waiting to see Sheinberg often gasped when the wall slid open to reveal the small, bent figure of Dr. Stein or his birdlike sister Ruth.

Jules now seemed to spend as much time in the hospital as he did at home. During one stay at UCLA Medical Center in 1979, he required an oxygen tent and round-the-clock attendants. When Jennings Lang heard that the old man's failing heart had taken a turn for the worse, he paid Stein a visit. After a few minutes at Jules's bedside, Lang ordered his nurses to take a hike. When the attending physician stormed into the room, demanding to know what was going on, Lang boomed, "Look, Doc, I absolutely fucking guarantee you that I can tell him something that'll have him up and out of that bed in three days."

While the doctor watched skeptically, just out of hearing range, Lang bent over the weak old man and whispered in his ear. Two days later Jules was up, taking nourishment, and ready to go home. When the doctor asked what he had said to bring Stein back from death's door, Lang grinned broadly and answered, "I told him, 'Jules! It's me: Jennings! When you get out of here, we'll get Doris out of the house and I'll bring in a broad who'll give you the greatest blow job you've ever had in your life!'" Lang later insisted that he'd tried to keep his promise, but Stein wasn't up to the offer.

Shirley Stein, who had married the son of Jules's cousin, recalled a drawn and sobered Dr. Stein who showed up for the 1980 MCA shareholders' meeting at Chicago's Drake Hotel.

"He seemed very sad and very alone," said Shirley. "Bitter, somehow. The one person he spoke enthusiastically about and whom he seemed to really care for was his granddaughter, Katrina [vanden Heuvel]. He was getting ready to take her to Europe and that was the bright spot in his life. And it made me think about my own father-in-law, who was Jules's cousin — how very fortunate he was because his children and grandchildren were all so devoted and loved him dearly. I thought, Poor Jules, with all your money…"

Jules had grown philosophical. He spent more time brooding, or so it seemed to those closest to him. Even his passion for antiques had waned. In the late 1970s, he sold Stair and Company to David Murdock, a fellow Republican millionaire and Reagan supporter.

During this period Jules developed a late-blooming interest in Roman Catholicism and began a running correspondence with a nun from his native South Bend, pondering grand questions of mortality and man's place in the universe.[14]

Mrs. Stein, on the other hand, was still very much grounded in the material world. She cared less about the meaning of life than she did about the eternal quest for the perfect martini. "She would go to the old Bistro, and they would have a martini waiting for her when she walked through the door," recalled John Maschio. "Doris used to tell my wife Connie [Moore], 'My God, I'm so rich!'"

In 1978, when the slightly less formal Bistro Garden opened a few doors down Canon Drive from the original Bistro, Doris toasted its inauguration repeatedly. She went there often with "the girls" — Betsy Bloomingdale, Connie Wald, Dolly Green, Constance Moore, Kitty LeRoy, and others — and drank Scotch for lunch and vodka straight up with a whisper of vermouth for dinner.

At home, Doris drank Scotch by the tumblerful so often that Jules threatened to leave her. Once he got as far as the penthouse of the Sheraton Universal, where he had his chauffeur bus his meals from Misty Mountain because he would not eat the hotel food. Doris browbeat the chauffeur, demanding to know where Jules was hiding out, but Stein's chauffeur refused to tell her. After three days, a tearful

---

[14] In his will, one of the few specific bequests Jules made was $5,000 to the American Society of the Most Venerable Order of the Hospital of Saint John of Jerusalem.

Doris vowed to drink nothing harder than wine in the future and persuaded Jules to come back home. Within a week, she was sneaking Scotch again.

As the years passed, Doris stood less and less on ceremony, unless she was intent on displaying her power. The older she got, the more often she let her guard down and behaved around those who knew her best just like the Kansas City housewife that she had once been. Although she was one of the richest women in Los Angeles, she constantly borrowed cash from her servants so she could tip waiters — never more than 5 percent — at the city's most elegant restaurants.

Nevertheless, Doris remained the dowager empress of Beverly Hills. In social settings she spoke in a whisper, forcing her subjects to lean in close to hear her. While Dr. Stein was just happy to wake up in the morning and eat cornflakes in the kitchen with his personal cook, Doris was never satisfied. She raced around the mansion like Cinderella's stepmother, torturing Charles Harris, the Steins' butler of forty years' standing, as well as the secretaries, gardener, chef, chauffeur, and upstairs and downstairs maids. In her eyes, the patio was always dirty, the food was always rancid, and the flower bed that spelled out her name in blooms was always full of weeds.

With each passing year, Doris grew more eccentric, filling her closets with every imaginable hat and the largest collection of costume jewelry in Beverly Hills. Like Hedda Hopper's, Doris's bizarre collection of *chapeaux* contained headgear made of everything from a bird's nest to pari-mutuel tickets. She bought her baubles and brooches from bazaars and street vendors as well as from the best designers on earth: Van Cleef and Arpels, Bulgari, Fulco di Verdura, Buccellati, and Cartier. When she donated her eclectic collection to the L.A. County Museum of Art, it became the opening exhibition of the museum's Doris Jones Stein Costume and Textile Design Center.

Doris made life hell for her servants, hiring, firing, and rehiring as she went from drinking binge to drinking binge. She was just as temperamental with her domestics in New York, in Paris, and at the Piccadilly apartment in London, which she and Jules still visited at least once a year.

Once, when she was in her cups during a London stay, she turned to Ziggy, the Steins' British butler, and said, "I'm just a drunken old bitch, aren't I?"

"Yes, madam," Ziggy answered fondly. "But you're *my* drunken old bitch.'"

—◊◊◊—

DESPITE THE PALESTINIAN Liberation Organization on one side and the Jewish Federation Council on the other, Jimmy Carter adopted Lew Wasserman's negotiating style in finally striking the first Arab-Israeli peace treaty. His Camp David agreement resembled a Hollywood contract, with both sides forced to accept elements they did not like. A Palestinian homeland provision especially galled Israel's Orthodox conservative minority. Had they lived to see the creation of Israel, Lew's own parents would likely have been among the treaty's critics.

But not Lew. He was as practical about Israel as President Carter was. When Jewish activists picketed Lew's fund-raisers for the president or tried to lobby with Lew personally against a Palestinian homeland, Wasserman barely contained his frustration.

"How you gonna convince anyone without talking to them?" he fumed during a 1978 interview with journalist Robert Scheer. "I never made a deal with an empty chair. I made deals with Harry Cohn and Jack Warner, Louis B. Mayer — I could give you thousands of people. Billions of dollars' worth of contracts I made. Never made one with an empty chair.... Well, there are a million Palestinian people, aren't there? You gonna pretend they're not there?"

On Sunday, March 25, 1979, Lew and Edie arrived by limo at the south portico of the White House to spend a couple of nights with their good friends Jimmy and Rosalynn Carter. While three years earlier Gerald Ford had spared Lew only fifteen minutes to discuss Middle East peace, Jimmy Carter offered the Wassermans the Lincoln bedroom and a front-row seat at the signing of the Camp David treaty.

Six months later Iranian fundamentalists stormed the American embassy in Tehran. On November 4, 1979, the militants took fifty-five Americans hostage. Carter pursued every possible means of freeing the hostages, including an abortive military rescue attempt in which eight American soldiers were killed, but nothing worked. Meanwhile, his domestic policy wallowed in economic torpor, heightened by a national gasoline shortage. Carter said the nation suffered from a "malaise."

Lew provided broad support of Democratic candidates and causes,[15] but his party was in for rough sailing in 1980. The tattoo from the Right was that Carter was too weak to resolve the hostage crisis, and long gas lines forming in front of American service stations spoke for themselves. To Lew, there was no small irony in the fact that Carter's chief critic as well as the GOP's 1980 candidate for president had been one of Wasserman's first Hollywood clients.

Of course, Ronald Reagan had been the Steins' candidate all along. After leav-

---

[15] According to his 1980 major donor statement, Wasserman contributed to state senators Diane Watson, Mike Roos, and Leo McCarthy; Los Angeles District Attorney John Van De Kamp, County Supervisor Yvonne Burke, and Mayor Tom Bradley; Californians against Proposition One and Californians for McCarthy; Friends of Barbara Klein, Californians for Brown, and Californians for a Bilateral Nuclear Weapons Freeze (Proposition 12); the David Cunningham Dinner Committee, Steve Afriat for Assembly, and Support Our Senate (Senate Majority Leader David Roberti). He also threw a reception for Jerry Brown's chief of staff, Gray Davis, catered with $2,084.24 worth of food from Chasen's.

ing the Governor's Mansion in Sacramento in 1974, Reagan and Nancy huddled often with Jules and Doris. The Steins did not stoop to circuslike stunts like the President's Club; they were above hosting $1,000-a-plate dinners in garish hotel ballrooms. They did, however, quietly marshal financial support for the Reagans — a fact that got scant attention during the 1980 campaign.

On August 1, 1980, the *Wall Street Journal* finally reported what no California newspaper had ever reported during Reagan's eight-year rein as governor, or during the six years that followed, when the former MCA client became a serious presidential hopeful. The *Journal* headline read, "Film Company Paid the Candidate a Steep Price for Some Steep Land to Make Him a Millionaire."

But the film company in question was Twentieth Century Fox, not MCA-Universal, and the studio spokesman who was raked over the coals for buying Reagan's Yearling Row Ranch at a grossly inflated price was a junior Fox executive, not Jules Stein or Lew Wasserman. Mention of Stein's role as the architect of Reagan's grand financial plan was buried at the bottom of the article, along with a sentence about his unreturned phone calls to *Journal* reporter Jim Drinkhall. Despite painstaking research into tax and property records detailing how Reagan managed to build a personal fortune out of questionable land speculation, the *Journal* failed to shine the spotlight on the financial wizard behind the rise of Ronald Reagan.[16] For the remainder of the 1980 campaign, Reagan's campaign managers, William Casey and Paul Laxalt, made certain that the issue of their candidate's personal finances was dwarfed by the Iranian hostage crisis.

On October 2, 1980, in a final gesture of gratitude to the Democratic Party's Hollywood Santa Claus, President Jimmy Carter nominated Lew Wasserman to sit on the board of the Kennedy Center for the Performing Arts.

One month later, Ronald Reagan was elected fortieth president of the United States.

---

[16] The *Journal* also failed to note that the Fox executive who signed the bill of sale in the Yearling Row Ranch land transaction was Richard F. Zanuck, who left Fox for Universal a year later, launching a new independent production company with partner David Brown.

THIRTY-ONE

Death of a Salesman

1980–1982

I n June 1980, *On Golden Pond* began shooting at Universal, a month before the biggest actors' strike since Ronald Reagan's SAG presidency. A ten-week walkout of 60,000 began July 21, paralyzing the town, and it was followed less than a year later by a thirteen-week strike of Hollywood writers as well as a musicians' walkout.

While Wasserman was lauded for restoring order to an industry beset by the chaos of divvying up proceeds from videocassettes, pay TV, and other new sources of revenue, the fractious negotiations took their toll on the great peacemaker. Lew was the very picture of sanguine composure at the bargaining table, but he was utterly volcanic when alone with his staff. In public he sang the guilds' praises as the unappreciated little people who constituted the backbone of the industry. In private he snarled at the ungrateful bastards who owed their jobs to the good graces of Universal. Following the musicians' strike, MCA's framed number one charter membership, signed by James C. Petrillo himself more than a half century earlier, disappeared from Lew's office wall.

Once President Reagan took office, antiunion sentiment swept the nation as well as Hollywood. In a highly publicized attack on organized labor, the Reagan administration deliberately broke a strike by the Professional Air Traffic Controllers Organization. That action signaled a decade of decline for organized labor, save the handful of unions that had endorsed the Reagan presidency — notably, the International Brotherhood of Teamsters. Angry SAG members tried to revoke Reagan's SAG membership in symbolic support of the traffic controllers, but they were overruled by SAG's national board.

The always practical Lew Wasserman cared less about Reagan's new antilabor philosophy than he did about completing movies before picket lines surrounded Universal. During the Screen Actors Guild strike, MCA got a waiver to finish *On*

Golden Pond because star Henry Fonda was old and ailing, but the rest of the studio's film operations slowly ground to a halt as picketers began showing up each morning at six o'clock outside the Universal gates. While most AFL-CIO unions sympathized with the striking actors, the Teamsters worked to defeat SAG. At one point, members of Teamsters Local 399 parked thirty trucks in front of the Hollywood Bowl to tie up traffic for a SAG benefit that featured Robin Williams, Waylon Jennings, and Lily Tomlin.

For its part, Universal put the best face on all the work stoppages, both in 1980 and in 1981. As the largest maker of TV programs and the second-largest feature-film producer after Warner Communications, MCA squirmed at every quirk and grumble of its thirty-seven unions, especially the high-profile guilds.

Still, Sid Sheinberg maintained that the 25,000 visitors who took the Universal Tour each weekday were never dissuaded by the eighty-five-day SAG strike or the others that followed. MCA even opened its successful new Castle Dracula for summer visitors in 1980.

"Our concern is more in the area of public safety," Sheinberg told reporters with characteristic sarcasm. "We probably get ten thousand tourist cars a day, and God forbid that an actor [on the picket line] be injured!"

Lew took his role as Hollywood's grand labor arbiter far more seriously. Shortly after the Writers Guild struck in April of 1981, Lew called a press conference. "I've been on the labor scene over forty years, and this is the first time I've asked anyone to attend a press conference," he announced dramatically in his deep, rumbling voice. While the gathered reporters held their breath, expecting to hear news of a breakthrough in negotiations, they learned that the momentous event that brought Wasserman voluntarily before the media for the first time in history had nothing to do with the strike. A rumor had circulated that Lew, having planned to abandon the pay-TV residuals issue during bargaining, had reversed himself and decided to keep pay TV on the bargaining table. Lew shook with fury when he heard this, because, he said, "I've lived in the community forty-two years, and I've *never* been told I'd changed my position."

With that, the briefing ended, leaving reporters scratching their heads as to why it had been called in the first place. There was no breakthrough. The strike continued for several more weeks. Lew had called the press conference simply because he could not bear to be labeled a waffler.

Esteem and ego had become increasingly important as Lew's evolution from flesh peddler to Beverly Hills Brahmin entered its fifth decade. As age weakened his eyesight, he took to wearing oversize black-framed glasses that contrasted dramatically with his gaunt scarecrow's face and shock of platinum hair. He looked like Moses on a hunger strike, posing as Cary Grant.

"I do believe he became the godfather of the film industry for many years," declared Charlton Heston, the movie version of Moses and Ronald Reagan's heir to the SAG presidency. "He knew where things were happening, and he knew how to control them. His influence depended primarily on the strength of his character."

Just as Jules had burnished his own image by reshaping his career for public consumption, so did Lew take his place as the unapproachable and unimpeachable beacon of Hollywood integrity. But Lew did not have the title "Doctor" to fall back upon. In its place, as he advanced toward his seventieth birthday, he became the industry spokesman—the graven image with the final word on any issue that impugned or impinged upon show biz.

Increasingly, when historians and journalists needed a few bons mots to summarize the mysteries and scandals that constituted the Hollywood hagiography, they begged a quote from Lew Wasserman. When he made a rare exception by granting a reporter an audience, as he did in 1982 with *Women's Wear Daily's* J. A. Trachtenberg, he spoke articulately and modestly, but in the blandest of generalities and absolutely without candor.

About his personal success, he said, "I don't take any credit at all for the growth of MCA. The company's success has come from the work of a great many people. Preserving our management group has been the most important part of my career, as opposed to any particular decision. I place the highest conceivable value on them. None of us are irreplaceable. None of us walk on water. As an executive, I've always tried to delegate responsibility. That's how you build an organization."

Regarding his conservative management style, Lew had this to say: "We don't have any debt, and we have a half-billion-dollar line of credit. Traditionally we haven't husbanded any money, although we have for the last several years. Unfortunately, I see no positive signs in the economy. Any time you have more than ten million Americans unemployed, you have a depression."

And on MCA's future: "We've had failures, yes, disappointments, yes, but those have always been within the context of life. Nobody sets realistic goals because nobody wants to fail. On balance, all you can do is hope your correct judgments outnumber the mistakes."

In his best-selling 1982 exposé *Indecent Exposure*, former *Wall Street Journal* reporter David McClintick revealed a side of Hollywood greed, power grabs, and deceit that had rarely been publicized. Then Watergate's own Bob Woodward turned the spotlight on Hollywood's widespread drug abuse in *Wired*, the *Washington Post* reporter's 1984 account of the events leading to the death of comedian John Belushi. Finally prodded into action, Wasserman lashed out at the press for trying to extend the reporters' revelations to every part of Hollywood.

"Why is it that when a particular person or company has a success, the coverage is confined to the specifics, but when something adverse occurs, it's the industry that's in trouble?" Lew complained. "There are some sixty thousand people who work here, but somehow the press has equated fifteen or twenty individuals with the entire film industry. Sure, there are beefs in this industry, but they are specific complaints about specific situations and ought to be kept in that proper perspective. But thousands of innocent people are being wronged."

Although the Belushi scandal had no direct effect on box office returns, the far more subtle impact of *Indecent Exposure* and other investigative reporting on the average American's impression of Hollywood immorality still enraged Lew Wasserman.

"I'm more concerned that some guy in Kansas City thinks that Hollywood is filled with crooks," he said with self-righteous annoyance. "It's just not true."

LITTLE MORE THAN a month after Ronald Reagan's election, marshals delivered convicted loan shark Walter Seifert to the federal correctional institute at Lompoc. According to Lew's son-in-law, Jack Myers, Wasserman began visiting Seifert a short time later.

Indeed, one MCA vice president remembered trying to contact Wasserman at least twice during that time, only to be told by Lew's secretary that the MCA chairman was away on business in Lompoc. Because prison business is about the only kind of business conducted in the tiny central California coastal community, the MCA vice president made a mental note of it. Neither he nor Myers understood why the most respected man in the entertainment industry would drive nearly 175 miles each way to visit a career criminal.

"Lew didn't confide in me," said Myers. "The only reason I know about it is because I knew someone [in prison at the same time] who saw him with Seifert in the visiting room."

Also known as Walter Stevens, the fifty-one-year-old New York extortionist and shakedown artist had a six-page FBI rap sheet that began with a two-year sentence back in 1955 for selling heroin. Since then Seifert had just about run the felony gambit: grand larceny, breaking and entering, bookmaking, armed robbery, battery, burglary, interstate transportation of stolen goods, securities, vehicle, and monies used in counterfeiting.

Still, Seifert was no garden-variety thug. Since he emigrated to California in 1962, he had developed surprising relationships within both the garment and entertainment industries. The strong-arm shakedown that had landed him in Lompoc was against a former talent agent named Ed Goldstone who had worked for Creative Management Agency before opening a West Hollywood restaurant called the Colony. Seifert showed up at the Colony one evening demanding $22,000 for a $3,000 loan Seifert had made seven years earlier to cover Goldstone's bookmaking debts. According to the court record, Seifert threatened to beat Goldstone and maybe shut down his restaurant if he didn't pay up.

Goldstone wasn't the only Hollywood denizen to seek gambling loans from Seifert. Goldstone had testified that actor James Caan, Warner Brothers production chief Guy McElwaine, and at least two other actors were among Seifert's bookmaking clientele.

There seemed to be no immediate explanation for Lew's relationship with Seifert, but Wasserman's fascination and familiarity with underworld characters was certainly not without precedent, given his friendship with Sidney Korshak and his early experiences with Moe Dalitz's Mayfield Road Gang.

Lew could be reduced to silence if a notorious name was uttered in his presence. "I mentioned Joseph 'Doc' Stacher to him once, and he turned absolutely white," recalled Myers. "Lew told me, *'Don't* ever mention that name *again!'*"

A New Jersey bootlegger who partnered with Abner "Longie" Zwillman in the nightclub, vending machine, and gambling trades during the 1930s, Stacher made his early reputation as an illegal importer of Bronfman whiskey across the Canadian border. Later on, he became a shadowy figure in Meyer Lansky's Cuba as well as in Miami, Las Vegas, and Hollywood. A Russian Jew whose U.S. citizenship had always been in question, Stacher's real name was Joseph Rosen. He was a Newark street thug who had graduated to casino skimming and murder. He was reportedly one of Johnny Rosselli's Stage Employees strikebreakers in the early 1930s as well as a silent partner in Harry Cohn's Columbia Pictures. He was also the first East Coast Mob representative to move into the Flamingo Hotel after Bugsy Siegel's untimely death in 1947.

As with Seifert, Jack Myers never understood how or why his father-in-law knew Stacher, who had died in 1977. Lew's friendship with Korshak, on the other hand, had become common knowledge in Beverly Hills. They remained close even after California Attorney General Evelle Younger released a report in May of 1978 naming Sidney as one of ninety-two Mob figures who plied their trade in the Golden State. Prominently featured among the dope dealers, pornographers, extortionists, and contract assassins, Sidney R. Korshak was anointed "a senior adviser to organized crime groups in Chicago, California, Las Vegas, and New York," according to the attorney general's report.

—◠◠◠—

IN THE 1980s, the Korshaks grew as close to the Sinatras as they had been to the Wassermans in the 1970s. Bea Korshak and Barbara Sinatra became best friends, shopping together at Gucci's, lunching at the chic restaurants along Rodeo, Robertson, and Canon, and traveling to Monaco for Princess Grace's annual Red Cross benefit and to Senegal to christen a new dispensary on behalf of the World Mercy Fund.

The Wassermans and Ziffrens remained part of the Korshaks' circle too, shuttling to and from each other's receptions, soirees, and benefits. Lew and Edie opened their home to David Janssen when he wed Buddy Greco's ex-wife, Dani, in 1975, and Korshak acted as Janssen's best man. Six years later, following Janssen's death, Dani was remarried to *Smokey and the Bandit* producer Hal Needham. Lew opened the gates to Universal so that Needham and his best man, Burt Reynolds, could arrive at the ceremony on horseback. Korshak gave the bride away on the set of a western movie while the Ziffrens, Wassermans, et al., witnessed the nuptials.

At the dawn of the eighties Universal belonged to Lew Wasserman, and he could invite anyone he pleased into his kingdom.

By 1981 every trace of the Jules Stein era at MCA had vanished forever.

—⁓—

AS HE APPROACHED his eighty-fifth birthday, Jules realized that he couldn't cheat death much longer. Virtually everyone who had helped him launch his beloved MCA way back in 1924 had joined the population of Forest Lawn. A few months after Taft Schreiber's peculiar death, George Campbell died in a mental institution. Both Charlie Miller and Guy Lombardo passed away the following year. Even Mae West, who had taught Jules how to shimmy in a South Side jazz lounge, had died the previous fall.

Aside from Jules and his sister Ruth, about the only survivors of Stein's earliest days in Chicago were Mickey Rockford, Sonny Werblin, and Maurie Lipsey. Jules could take some comfort in the fact that he had kept his promise to those who remained loyal to him and to MCA: they had all died rich. When Karl Kramer passed away on October 14, 1980, he left an estate worth $18,877,682.11—most of it in MCA stock.

First Jules, and now Lew, watched as the members of Hollywood's founding generation died off one by one. Following Charlie Miller's death, the MCA board no longer included a single pioneer; Lew Wasserman himself hadn't joined the company until twelve years after its birth. The agency once led by a cabal of hustlers, cardsharps, and sweet-talking con men was now a multinational conglomerate, overseen by outside directors from the East and West Coast establishments like Felix Rohatyn, general partner of the venerable investment banking firm of Lazard Freres; Southern California Edison president Howard P. Allen; Northrop chairman Thomas V. Jones; and former Democratic National Committee chairman Robert Strauss.

MCA was the Music Corporation of America in name only. Music had very little to do with the company Jules and Billy Stein had concocted fifty-seven years earlier, when they bought the name from Ernie Young and set up shop in a one-room office on Randolph Street. Thanks to Wasserman, MCA now stood for power, and Lew was final arbiter.

Jules held a grudging affection for his successor, in much the same way Dr. Frankenstein must have cared for his own creation. But there was something both covetous and extravagant about the lean and hungry youngster Stein had molded into his heir, some ineffable quality that nagged at Jules until he drew his final breath. Lew was just a little too self-righteous, a bit too solicitous, and an absolute tyrant behind closed doors—the perfect agent who was imperfect simply because he displayed no human flaws. In that way, Jules had taught his protégé almost too well. Lew was the paradoxical deal-maker, devoid of tears, and intent on negotiating even if the man across the table wore a black hood and carried a scythe.

When Death began showing up at the door to Jules's Fifth Avenue penthouse, Stein decided to flee back home to Misty Mountain. He paid for five tourist seats so that he could lie down, but negotiated to have the airline buy three of the seats back if the flight wasn't fully booked.

"When Father was dying of cancer, Wasserman offered to charter a jet," recalled Jean Stein. "That was the kind of thing Father would *never* do."

Two days after his eighty-fifth birthday, on Tuesday, April 28, 1981, Dr. Stein began complaining about a pain in his right side. Doris called a doctor, who diagnosed the problem as gallstones. Stein was rushed to UCLA Medical Center.

He was prepped immediately for removal of his gallbladder. For a younger man, the operation would have been almost routine. One quick incision beneath the rib cage and the gallbladder was gone. Since his first bout with cancer thirty years earlier, Jules Stein's long-standing bet on the wizardry of modern medicine had made him a winner. But winning streaks end. Following the successful removal of his inflamed gallbladder, Jules suffered a heart attack, and his legion of high-priced physicians and surgeons could do nothing to forestall the inevitable.

Shortly after midnight the universally acknowledged Caesar of the talent trade died.

A year earlier Jules had written six pages of meticulous instructions on how to conduct his public memorial service at his beloved eye institute. No one was to wear black, but neither was anyone to pay final respects in anything as casual as a sport coat. Jules demanded business suits, California champagne, French wine, and thirty-three of his favorite songs.

"This occasion, like all the important events in his life, was produced by my grandfather," said Katrina vanden Heuvel, the eldest of Stein's four grandchildren.

It was a spectacular affair costing over $100,000 and attended by more than 1,200, with the best parts of Jules's long and illustrious career on gaudy display. Henry Mancini flew in by chartered jet to play "Blue Skies" and "I Can't Give You Anything but Love" on the piano and to conduct a twenty-piece orchestra. Big band singer Helen O'Connell, whose vision had been saved at the Jules C. Stein Eye Institute, sang "I Remember You," "Tangerine," "Annapola," and "Green Eyes." Heading the list of seventy-six honorary pallbearers, President Ronald Reagan was unable to attend the memorial, but sent a telegram of condolence.[1]

"You might guess that all of us who flew here from the East for this weekend arrived on economy class," quipped Katrina vanden Heuvel, when it was her turn to step up to the lectern and speak about her grandfather.

And so it went with each person who spoke his or her memories of Jules: a light, often whimsical set of recollections about the paradoxical little Anglophile who loved fast cars, fine wine, and, finally, the future vision of the whole human race. Like that of the Roman statesman who was his namesake, the more ruthless side of his personality was interred with his bones. One wag at the funeral compared Stein's life to a shaggy-dog story: anyone who doesn't laugh at it while it's being told is sure to be disappointed with the punch line.

"Jules is up there now, handling Guy Lombardo, Tommy Dorsey, and Glenn Miller again," said George Burns. "He's starting all over."

A player to the very end, Stein left a watertight sixty-eight-page will written three weeks before his death, parceling out the bulk of his $200 million estate to three trusts: one for Doris, one for his daughters and grandchildren, and one for his eye institute. His son-in-law, Gil Shiva, whom he considered a ne'er-do-well, was pointedly left out of his will. But Stein left $150,000 to his sister Ruth and $100,000 to his brother David. He also rewarded the household servants with cash, beginning with Charles Harris, who was to receive $50,000, as long as he didn't displease Mrs. Stein until she too passed away.

Jules also settled any question about an heir taking over his precious MCA after he was gone. "I take special pride in the founding of MCA and building it with the assistance of my able and loyal associates into an immensely successful

---

[1] Stein's list of honorary pallbearers mixed familiar names with others that were obscure: Dr. William Adams, Venan Allessandroni, Dr. Leonard Apt, Dr. Aerol Arnold, Fred Astaire, Professor Joaquin Barraquer, Louis Blau, Alfred Bloomingdale, Campbell Bradt, Fred Brisson, Sidney Brodie, Al Burns, George Chasin, Dr. Robert Christensen, Herman Citron, Samuel Colt, William Conner, Albert Dorskind, Samuel Goldwyn Jr., Benny Goodman, Cary Grant, Henry Hathaway, Gavin Herbert Jr., William Hickey, Deane Johnson, Thomas V. Jones, Earle Jorgenson, Frank Kilroe, Tony Kiser, Dr. Carl Kupfer, Irving Lazar, Mervyn LeRoy, Maurice Lipsey, Dr. William Longmire, Richard Lowe, Henry Mancini, Dr. Edward Maumenee, Dr. Sherman Mellinkoff, Franklin Murphy, Dr. Frank Newell, Arthur Park, Dr. Thomas Pattit, Dr. David Patton, James C. Petrillo, Dan Ritchie, Mickey Rockford, Felix G. Rohatyn, Donald Rosenfeld, Herbert Rosenthal, Morris Schrier, Professor Gerd Meyer Schwickerath, Dr. William Scoville, Sidney Sheinberg, Norton Simon, Robert Six, Dr. Manfred Spitznas, Alistair Stair, Dennis Stanfill, Jay Stein, Herb Steinberg, Jimmy Stewart, Dr. Bradley Straatsma, Robert Strub, Ned Tanen, Charles Thornton, William vanden Heuvel, Hal Wallis, Dr. Stafford Warren, Lew R. Wasserman, Martin Webster, David Weeks, David Werblin, Thomas Wertheimer, René Wormser, and William Wyler.

public corporation," he wrote. "I adopted certain principles. One of these principles is avoidance of nepotism. I trust that this principle will be followed after my death; in particular, I would hope and expect that none of my issue or my wife's issue or their spouses or any other of my wife's relatives by blood or marriage shall be acquainted, retained, or elected as officers, employees, or directors of MCA."

Unlike the star-studded memorial service, Stein's funeral at Forest Lawn in Glendale was a small private affair. The family crypt at the very top of the hillside cemetery was located in a walled-in section called the Garden of Memory, where a heavy bronze door barred the entrance.

"You have to have a key to get in," said Charles Harris. "Why would anybody want to be buried behind a locked door? Were they afraid someone was going to come steal the headstone? The Steins were like that, though. I swear. These people..."

Inside the walls of this exclusive portion of Forest Lawn, the graves seemed pretty much like those of any other mortal, except for the names. Jules could count well-heeled industrialists and Hollywood stars among his eternal neighbors. Jules and Doris had picked out a well-tended corner of the Garden of Memory, located between family crypts for Mary Pickford and Earl Carroll. Jules specified in his will that his "casket be preferably of eighteenth-century English design," and he had a copy of his Jacques Lipchitz bust hoisted into a marble nook, overlooking his grave. A 50-foot eucalyptus towered overhead.

Ironically, the man who wanted to make certain that none of his children or his wife's children held any position of authority at MCA was buried in a plot occupied by his mother-in-law, father-in-law, brother-in-law, and a nephew from Doris's side of the family. All of Jules's family members were buried elsewhere.

And in a final cosmic joke upon the man whose whole life was based on selling music to the masses, a loudspeaker was mounted on a wall above Stein's grave. For eternity, incessant low-volume Muzak played to Jules and an audience of fellow patricians who were unable to hear a single note.

—◦◦◦—

ACCORDING TO MCA vice president Gene Brog, Jules's death fixed Lew's eyes on the ticking clock. He told his executive staff as much at the next meeting following Stein's funeral.

"If I last as long as Jules, that means you can look forward to seeing me around here for about another fifteen years," said Wasserman.

Under Lew's stewardship, the company seemed to be running just fine. During the previous decade, MCA's annual revenues had more than tripled, from $349.3 million in 1970 to $1.3 billion by 1980. Wasserman and Sheinberg began the new decade by stripping the company clean of any subsidiary that didn't directly feed its entertainment assembly line. They had already spun off the minibus-manufacturing subsidiary when the MCA board voted to dispose of MCA's Washington, D.C., and Mount Vernon tour franchises. Next, Wasserman laid plans to sell Columbia Savings and Loan. All proceeds went back into MCA's *raison d'être:* entertainment.

As an institution, Universal Studios transcended mere moviemaking. Neither the strikes nor the scandals of the early 1980s kept tourists or music fans away. Nearly 500,000 paid to see such varied performers as Bob Hope, Chuck Mangione, Jefferson Starship, and John Denver in concert at the Universal Amphitheatre. Commerce was so brisk at the theme park that Wasserman and Sheinberg began laying plans for the purchase of 306 acres near Orlando to build Universal Studios Movieworld, a rival to Florida's wildly successful Disney World. On July 24, 1981, MCA announced that it would spend $203 million to duplicate its Universal Studios Tour ten miles down the road from Disney's EPCOT Center.

Despite the corporate streamlining and a steady climb in stock value, MCA never produced handsome dividends. While Universal remained the most profitable film factory in Hollywood, it still operated with all the purported built-in black holes of any other studio: heavy script development costs, ballooning star salaries, and production schedule overruns. By 1981, Universal's movie advertising budget alone had skyrocketed to the highest level in its history: $80 million.[2] In addition, its television division suffered mightily with the departure of Frank Price. With only six shows left on the air, MCA's formidable TV revenues declined for the first time in nearly twenty years.

Wall Street blamed Wasserman for letting costs get out of control. With operating income falling two years in a row, Wasserman and Sheinberg ordered Universal production chief Ned Tanen to slash the feature budget by 30 percent, cutting the number of Universal movies from twenty-two to twelve a year. The ad budget was slashed by 25 percent.

Tanen did the best he could with the reduced budget. Despite the diminishing returns, Universal's top management insisted on making sequels. The wretched *Jaws 3-D* stank up theaters, and *Halloween III* turned in tepid box office results without the shrieking star presence of Wasserman's goddaughter, Jamie Lee Curtis. Universal also showed the chutzpah to cash in on *Psycho II* by resurrecting the hammy Tony Perkins as Norman Bates, fresh out of the asylum, and to make *Sting II* with Jackie Gleason and Mac Davis miscast as slapstick leads.

Universal was not without opportunities to make good films. Attorney Tom Pollock — one of a new breed of Hollywood lawyers who replaced agents as dealmakers — offered the studio George Lucas's latest project, about an archaeologist-

---

[2]   In 1980 fully one-tenth of that budget went into advertising Dino De Laurentiis's *Flash Gordon,* which laid an egg at the box office.

adventurer named Indiana Jones. But the creator of *Star Wars* demanded the kind of gross profit participation that Lew had once secured for filmmakers like Alfred Hitchcock. Sitting on the opposite side of the bargaining table, Lew was loath to give Pollock a dime.

"Within MCA, there was furious debate about whether to take this deal," reported one source. "But Lew and Sid, it drove them crazy. As far as they were concerned, that deal was asking for unheard-of pieces of profit and ownership. And they passed on it because it was something that went beyond their definition of how things should be."

Even though he was eventually able to restore peace between Lucas and Wasserman, Pollock failed to strike a bargain.[3] Pollock sold the Indiana Jones project to Paramount, where Lucas's pal Steven Spielberg directed, and *Raiders of the Lost Ark* became the biggest-grossing film of 1981.

Despite the niggardly policies handed him by his bosses, Ned Tanen still fought for his gems. *On Golden Pond* won the 1981 Academy Award for Best Screenplay and grabbed Best Actor Oscars for Henry Fonda and Katharine Hepburn while Meryl Streep took her second Oscar in 1982 for *Sophie's Choice*.

But the best news Universal had received in years was the return of Sid Sheinberg's prodigal son. After Steven Spielberg hit a home run at Paramount with *Raiders of the Lost Ark*, Sheinberg forgave his *1941* profligacy and invited him back home. Under Ned Tanen's watchful eye, Spielberg got a modest $10 million for a sci-fi feature. To keep labor costs down, he shot most of it at the nonunion Laird Studios in Culver City.

He called his movie *E.T. The Extra-Terrestrial*.

———∿∿∿———

WHAT WAS FOR years the biggest box office bonanza in history almost didn't make it to the screen as a Universal picture. Steven Spielberg, who still owed the studio one more feature following the *1941* debacle, originally planned to fulfill his contractual obligation with a sci-fi musical he called *Reel to Reel*. Sid Sheinberg made the difference.

"If Sid hadn't been at Universal, I would not have brought *E.T.* to MCA," Spielberg said in a 1984 interview. "I bring things to MCA because Sid is there."

E.T. The Extra-Terrestrial initially belonged to Columbia Pictures. The studio spent $1 million developing *E.T.*, first under the title *Night Skies* and later as *The Extra-Terrestrial*. But Columbia's newly ensconced production chief, former MCA

---

[3] According to one MCA executive, Lucas threatened to sue Universal for plagiarizing *Star Wars* in the obvious second-rate Universal rip-off, *Battlestar Galactica*. Lucas allegedly backed off only after he received a personal apology from Wasserman and Sheinberg.

vice president Frank Price, listened to his marketing people, who maintained that the public wasn't interested in a wimpy Disneyesque picture about a boy and his buddy from outer space. Price put *E.T.* into turnaround, meaning that Universal could go ahead and make the movie once it reimbursed Columbia for its development costs. Columbia retained a 5 percent share of *E.T.*'s net profits, which wound up resulting in a bigger bottom line than all the other films Columbia produced in 1982.

Over the years, critics, pundits, and journalists alike have dissected, explicated, and second-guessed the reasons for *E.T.*'s broad, unparalleled success. All agree that the movie transcended mere entertainment and reflected a restless alienation that troubled millions in Ronald Reagan's America. The favored explanation was that the country's divorce rate had hit the 50 percent mark by the early 1980s, and *E.T.*'s underlying autobiographical story of divorce in Spielberg's own family when he was growing up, touched the hearts of millions who had experienced similar suffering. E.T. represented everyone's inner child.

Lew Wasserman and Sid Sheinberg flew to Houston to join Spielberg for *E.T.*'s preview in the spring of 1982. They instantly recognized God and a gold mine flickering up on the screen. When the lights went up, Sheinberg and Spielberg were in tears.

"It truly was like a religious experience," Sheinberg rhapsodized in one interview. "It must be a little bit like the way people feel if they feel they've seen God."

Sheinberg had an E.T. clock, a film poster, and a life-sized facsimile installed in his office. Lew's handpicked successor, described by one journalist as "somewhat cold and crusty, hard-nosed, blunt, distancing himself from others in an intangible way," proudly proclaimed, "It was an incredible emotional experience. Steven and I ended up hugging each other."

Similarly, Tanen confessed to having seen *E.T.* more than twenty times and having cried like a baby each time. "It's getting to be silly," he said. "I think, Oh, my God! How do you follow this kind of success?"

On page 1 of the company's 1982 annual report to shareholders—ahead of every officer of the corporation, every member of the board of directors, and even Lew Wasserman himself—was a photo of MCA's Creature of the Year. Holding a bouquet of roses, the bug-eyed, pug-nosed visage of E.T. smiled shyly at the camera and the caption beneath his portrait told stockholders all they needed to know: "Steven Spielberg's E.T. *The Extra-Terrestrial* has been received with acclaim by audiences around the world. Since its release on June 11, 1982, this remarkably successful film has already earned the highest worldwide theatrical rentals of any film in history."

By comparison, news that MCA stock had split two for one again seemed ho-hum. During 1982, MCA netted a record $176.2 million on revenues of $1.59 billion. Losses from *1941* disappeared from all conversation, and Spielberg's chronic extravagance as a filmmaker became an irrelevant footnote in Universal history. Sheinberg did all in his power to keep his young genius shackled to MCA, even footing the $6 million to build the lavish adobe hacienda headquarters of Spielberg's Amblin Entertainment in the middle of the Universal lot. Like the comic strip character Richie Rich, Spielberg allowed Sheinberg to spoil him to the extent that he installed his own personal video game arcade at Amblin, and had "Steven Only" labels attached to his favorite desserts catered daily to Amblin.

Like a pair of sparring father figures, Sheinberg and Warner's Steven Ross spent most of the 1980s in a tug-of-war for Spielberg's services. Sheinberg paid $500,000 for the rights to a best-selling Holocaust saga called *Schindler's List* in the hope of persuading Spielberg to make it at Universal, but Spielberg went with Ross instead, after securing the rights to another best-seller, *The Color Purple*. He made his next three pictures for Warner Brothers, but his home was at Universal, where he ventured into television with *Amazing Stories* for three seasons, beginning in 1985.

And though he did not direct another feature for Universal until *Always* (1989), Spielberg did produce a string of minor hits for Universal: *The Money Pit* (1986), *An American Tail* (1986), and *Harry and the Hendersons* (1987). By the end of the decade it was clear that Sheinberg had won the war with Steve Ross for Spielberg's soul. Following the phenomenal success of *E.T.*, Sheinberg also took a stronger hand in running MCA. The company increased its credit line from $200 million to $375 million, and Sheinberg spoke of co-financing the new thirty-five-story Getty Oil building going up next door to the Black Tower. There were even rumors that Getty might buy MCA.[4]

Sid also raised his profile in the entertainment community, assuming Lew's former leadership role in the Association of Motion Picture and Television Producers. He chaired dinners for such industry institutions as the National Conference of Christians and Jews and the American Film Institute.

For all his bluster and tough talk, however, Sheinberg had obvious failings. "Sid could not read a financial statement or a balance sheet until Lew taught him," said one MCA vice president.

"I once heard that the difference between Lew and Sid was that Mr. Wasserman walks on water and Mr. Sheinberg never learned how to swim," said another.

In contrast to the angst that Lew and Jules poured into selecting their successors, Sid appeared almost oblivious of the notion that he might one day face retirement, or even his own mortality. Wasserman showed no signs of quitting, or even winding down, and Sheinberg had grown secure in his role as second banana.

Besides, who could he pick? The rising star among MCA executives was Tom Wertheimer, a Sheinberg hire and fellow Columbia University Law School grad-

---

[4] All talk of a Getty-MCA merger came to a halt at the beginning of 1984, when New York–based Texaco gobbled up the California oil company.

uate, but Wertheimer was only three years younger than Sheinberg. Like Sid, he had come to MCA early in his career and migrated from ABC's legal department in 1972 before moving up quickly to an MCA vice presidency two years later. By several accounts, Wertheimer was astute with numbers, pensive to a degree that dampened any natural spontaneity, and generally more polished in manners and style than either Sid or Lew. Having graduated from Princeton, he also had an Ivy League cachet both his bosses lacked.

But in comparison to MCA's dynamic chairman and its pit bull president, Wertheimer was a bland middle manager caught in a perpetual vise in the upper reaches of the Black Tower.

"He was not only Sid's outbox but Lew's punching bag for a while," said a former MCA executive.

Hammered from both ends of the fifteenth floor, Wertheimer was once rumored to have suffered a heart attack. Regardless of the chronic stress, Wertheimer ascended to executive vice president, and third-in-command behind Lew and Sid by the end of 1982. Any chance that Ned Tanen might have had of eventually running the company effectively vanished at the same time.

Despite his widely acknowledged genius as the MCA executive who had resurrected Universal as a critical and financial success during the 1970s, he would never measure up to the CEO standards of Lew's pretense.

Tanen had his final falling-out with Wasserman and, in December of 1982, resigned. Like most other studio heads, he pursued independent production, though his efforts proved to be far more successful than most.[5]

---

[5] Tanen went on to produce a string of teen hits, beginning with *Sixteen Candles* (1984) and followed by *The Breakfast Club* (1985) and *St. Elmo's Fire* (1985) before taking over as Paramount's production chief and spawning another series of hits that included *The Untouchables* (1987) and *Coming to America* (1988).

THIRTY-TWO

The Legacy

1983—1985

With Jules Stein's death, business underwent a subtle but distinct shift at 100 Universal City Plaza. It was as if an ocean liner that had been headed in the same direction for decades had lost its radar and quietly switched course, based on the whims of whoever was on the bridge at the moment.

When Sid Sheinberg named Frank Price as Universal's vice president for film production, for example, it marked a sea change in MCA's policy on rehiring ex-employees.[1] The very fact that the former Columbia Pictures chief returned at all to a company that traditionally shunned defectors astounded everyone.

"Lew made me *crawl* when I came back," recalled Harry Tatelman. "Frank just waltzed through the front gates."

Tatelman could take some solace in Price's short tenure. The studio executive's second time around ended abruptly with the 1986 super-bomb *Howard the Duck*. But the George Lucas–produced *Howard* was not the only Universal release to lay an egg in the mid-1980s. Since *E.T.*, much that MCA produced reeked, and not all of it could be blamed on Frank Price.

The TV division picked up the slack, producing more hits *(Simon & Simon; Gimme a Break!; Murder, She Wrote)* than flops *(Hawaiian Heat)*. Universal Television continued to spew hour-long dramas but could not deliver a single decent sitcom. Ridiculous but successful "dramas" like *Knight Rider*, about a crime fighter and his talking car, and *The A Team*, about three soldiers of fortune who behaved like high-tech Keystone Kops and got unintentional laughs, but MCA's

---

[1] As a fund-raiser for the Southern California Harvard Club, Price charged Harvard grads $150 a head to attend a reception at his home, noting on the invitation that Lew Wasserman would be there. As dozens lined up to personally meet the taciturn MCA chairman, it became clear that Price had pulled off one of the most successful fund-raisers in Harvard Club history.

idea of TV comedy continued in the vein of the unfunny *The Misadventures of Sheriff Lobo* and the short-lived *House Calls.* For authentic laughs, Universal bought Walter Lantz Productions in 1985, adding four hundred vintage Woody Woodpecker cartoons to its growing library.

MCA Records remained a major weak link, which Sheinberg proposed to fix by hiring Irving Azoff, a thirty-five-year-old dandy who first gained prominence in the 1970s as the manager of the Eagles. Azoff struck a distribution deal with Motown Records and hacked MCA's own artist roster from forty-three to seven,[2] brashly proclaiming his intent to rebuild the label with hot acts. His flamboyance and extravagance put off many of MCA's old guard, but Azoff appeared to produce results. The record division went from a 1983 operating loss of $7.97 million to a 1984 profit of $8.84 million.

Meanwhile, the USA Network floundered, and its chief proponent, Tom Wertheimer, got the blame. Wasserman derisively referred to MCA's sole cable venture as Wertheimer's "hobby" and regularly slammed the executive vice president for failing to make money off MCA's one-third share in the cable channel.

But it wasn't Wertheimer's fault. MCA lagged in the exploding broadcast field during the 1980s. While Fox toyed with the prospect of launching a fourth TV network and Warner quickly became the nation's second-largest cable system, MCA followed its conservative course and invested nothing in TV stations or cable.

Because Wasserman and Sheinberg worked in lockstep, fixing the blame was impossible, but one thing was certain: as show business evolved, MCA didn't. One filmmaker who worked closely with both executives posed the riddle of Lew Wasserman this way: "Where is he brilliant and visionary, and where do his tight-fisted instincts get in the way?"

"MCA looked for bargains that had no downside risk," one analyst told the *New York Times.* "Those are almost impossible to find. They were willing to put their foot in the door, but that was it."

At the time, Wasserman seemed far more interested in earning short-term profits at the expense of long-term investments. Instead of buying into a network, he milked the networks for all he could get. His shortsightedness was best illustrated by Lew's heavy-handed manipulation of Ronald Reagan in the so-called fin-syn wars.

Under the FCC's financial interest and syndication policy, only producers could own shows and collect rerun fees. Richard Nixon first established fin-syn in the early 1970s as a way of keeping the networks out of the rerun business. If the three networks controlled all the nation's programming, Nixon argued, they'd

---

[2]   One artist, singer Barbara Mandrell, sued MCA for $1.2 million in back royalties, claiming the company jacked up her albums' retail prices with no boost in her royalties.

become too powerful. Most network executives believed, however, that what the president *really* wanted was to punish his tormentors in the news divisions at CBS, ABC, and NBC by keeping the networks out of the most lucrative part of the television business: the recycling of old TV series.

Meanwhile, independent producers like Norman Lear (*All in the Family, Maude*) and Steve Bochco (*Hill Street Blues, L.A. Law*), along with old-guard studios like Universal, raked in millions. Universal's *Magnum, P.I.* showed the kind of money to be made. KTLA-TV in Los Angeles paid MCA $115,000 per episode for rebroadcast rights after the Hawaiian private eye drama went into syndication. Multiply such prices by 100 episodes in the 300 different TV markets that operate in the United States, and the sums generated by a single series could be staggering. As American entertainment became a global commodity, foreign syndication of *Magnum, P.I.* fetched even more—as much as $250,000 an episode. Ancient cop shows like *Columbo* and *Kojak* were now worth more than they'd ever been during their first TV run.

In 1981 the networks stormed Washington, D.C., assuming that Ronald Reagan, the champion of universal deregulation, would kill fin-syn and give them a share of the $1 billion-a-year syndication business. At first it appeared they were right. The Federal Trade Commission, the Commerce Department, and the Justice Department all approved the death of fin-syn. Even the FCC reversed its decade-old position that the policy was necessary.

But the studios, anchored by Wasserman, launched a counterassault. After the FCC voted to side with the networks, Lew personally complained to Reagan, who called his commissioners to the White House for a dressing-down. The deregulation president overruled his own FCC. The commissioners reconvened and reversed themselves. Fin-syn remained the law of the land.

"It was like we'd been mugged," a network lobbyist complained to *Regardie's* magazine reporter Alice Mundy. "We were in shock. We'd won every battle, but we'd lost the war."

During the Reagan presidency, partisan politics were less important than long-time loyalties. Thus, when called upon by old Hollywood cronies for a favor, Reagan listened and acted in their behalf whenever practicable. When it came to antitrust, the old rules that Leonard Posner used in 1962 to skewer MCA and grill Ronald Reagan before a grand jury were dead.

"Reagan changed everything," said Chuck Suber, a jazz historian and professor at Chicago's Columbia College who followed MCA's development over two generations, beginning with Suber's first job as a General Amusement Corporation band-booking agent in the 1930s.

"None of these mergers that are going on today would ever have happened in the years following the [1948] Paramount Decree," Suber continued. "Reagan's Justice Department let his old friends at General Electric buy NBC and didn't say boo about Warner merging with Time-Life. And Reagan was always beholden to MCA. After all, Wasserman gave him his start."

The antitrust posse that had finally reined in the Octopus in 1962 vanished in the age of Reagan. When Columbia Pictures bought control of the Walter Reade Organization, a small New York theater chain, the Justice Department said nothing. Studios, networks, theater chains, and cable companies merged and mingled as if the Sherman Antitrust Act had never existed. Whatever corporate Hollywood wanted, Reagan was more than happy to give.

Throughout his presidency, Reagan's Hollywood roots resonated in every White House decision. He even based his foreign policy on a book written by Larry W. Beilenson, the retired SAG-MCA attorney who had handled Revue Productions' controversial 1952 SAG waiver as well as Reagan's 1948 divorce from Jane Wyman. In 1969, Beilenson published *The Treaty Trap: A History of the Performance of Political Treaties by the United States and European Nations*, and the book became the cornerstone of Reagan's much vaunted "trust-but-verify" foreign policy with the Soviet Union. Simply put, *The Treaty Trap* said that nations keep treaties only when it's in their own best interests to do so. Otherwise, they break them without a second thought—not unlike talent agencies and movie studios.

———

IN LATE 1983 upstart gambling executive Steve Wynn began quietly acquiring the first of two million shares of MCA.

Wynn, a forty-two-year-old wunderkind who had purchased the Golden Nugget casino and taken Las Vegas by storm, apparently saw the same synergy between Las Vegas and MCA that rival gambling impresario Kirk Kerkorian recognized when he bought MGM. After Kerkorian dismantled the studio in the 1970s, the MGM Lion still roared along the Vegas Strip in the form of the MGM Grand Hotel. Perhaps Wynn saw an MCA Grand Hotel in the future.

But Wall Street theorized that Wynn might also be playing bluff poker. By July 1984, Wynn's publicly traded Golden Nugget had amassed nearly a 5 percent stake in MCA. MCA "didn't invite" Wynn to join MCA, Sid Sheinberg told the *Los Angeles Times*, and he didn't "see any commonality of interest with the Golden Nugget." But the cold reality remained: if Wynn bought enough shares, Wasserman might get so nervous he'd buy back Wynn's stake rather than risk a takeover— and pay a hefty price for his shares.[3] "I really don't want to speculate about what it means," Sheinberg said.

---

[3]   The ploy, known on Wall Street as greenmail, had worked for another high roller who made a similar play for Walt Disney Productions. Financier Saul Steinberg amassed an 11.1 percent stake before the Disney board bought his stock back at a sizable premium.

But Wasserman knew what it meant and exactly how to respond. At the annual board meeting in Chicago, he publicly declared that any purchase of 5 percent or more of MCA's stock would be regarded as a hostile act. He dispatched investigators to Nevada and New Jersey to dig up dirt on Wynn, and he increased MCA's credit line to $1 billion, invoking a "poison pill" policy that would flood the market with new stock to discourage raiders.[4]

By year's end, Wynn admitted defeat and sold off his MCA stock.

Unlike Jules Stein, Chairman Wasserman had no plans to step down—ever. He delivered his benediction to the Steve Wynn affair in three sentences: "I do not intend to sell. I do not intend to retire. And I do not intend to die."

But he also said he was not opposed to "any merger that's fair to all shareholders" and hoped that President Reagan's deregulation fever might finally allow MCA to sidestep antitrust law and unite with a TV network. "This company isn't up for sale, but I'm always open to anything that is good for the shareholders," Wasserman said.

Even before Steve Wynn made his move, Wasserman had put out feelers for a white knight who would protect MCA from raiders. While he had no interest in buying into cable or starting up his own network, Lew was not opposed to the right kind of merger with one of the Big Three. As early as 1982, he asked MCA board member—and Jules Stein pallbearer—Felix Rohatyn to arrange a meeting with Thornton Bradshaw, chairman of RCA, then the parent company of NBC.

"Talks? I don't know if 'talks' is the right word," Wasserman coyly told an interviewer. "Brad's a friend of mine; we shot the breeze. I wouldn't call them talks at that point in time."

But Wasserman did propose a deal in which he would run MCA and NBC while Bradshaw continued to chair RCA. As the major supplier of NBC shows, MCA seemed a perfect match. Bradshaw offered $90 a share for MCA while Wasserman demanded $120, and though that gap shrank over more than two years of talks, they ultimately failed to cement the deal.

"MCA pulled the plug on it," said Bradshaw.

"I just can't face putting my creative talent in the hands of engineers," explained Wasserman, who reportedly put his pen down just before signing.

General Electric picked up the pen a few months later. In 1985, RCA and NBC became General Electric subsidiaries in the largest non–oil company merger in history.

---

[4]   If anyone bought 10 percent of the company's stock, the "poison pill" plan would go into effect, allowing MCA shareholders to buy their own company's and the acquiring firm's common stock at an exceptionally low price, thereby making a hostile takeover prohibitively expensive.

SIX MONTHS AFTER Jules Stein's death, Doris began preparing her own legacy. As early as December 1981 she endowed the Doris Jones Stein Foundation with 9,610 shares of MCA Inc., then valued at $396,413. Jules had his monument at UCLA; Doris would leave hers right next door, in the form of a freestanding $9 million Doris Jones Stein Research Center. In addition to accommodating ophthalmology study, Doris filled her wing with Stein family memorabilia and furniture. Adams antiques, among the rarest and most fragile in Jules's collection, were housed in a special Doris Jones Stein reading room, away from the general public. Like Jules, Doris twisted arms to create her own foundation, which would perpetuate the Stein name for decades, perhaps centuries, after they had gone.

If any event hastened Doris's own passing, it was the premature death of her youngest child. Breast cancer claimed forty-seven-year-old Susan Rosa Shiva in January 1983. Within the year, Doris learned that she too had lymph node cancer. She hired round-the-clock nurses to care for her at Misty Mountain until her death on April 7, 1984.[5]

A week before she died, Doris named her surviving children coexecutors of her estate, along with her lawyer and Lew Wasserman. At her death, she held 2.7 million shares of MCA worth over $100 million, as well as the largest tract of land in New Mexico.[6] On her death certificate, her occupation was given as "rancher."

"Mother was an extremely forceful woman," eulogized Harold Oppenheimer during his mother's funeral. "Within our family we often joked that if she were only born a man she would have been commandant of the Marine Corps. She was one of the largest owners of livestock and ranch land in the United States...and was the leader of her family. She encouraged all family efforts to maintain the standards of excellence and good taste she represented all her life."

Beneath Doris's name on the family crypt was the inscription "Generous, Gracious, Lovely and Wise."

THE PASSING OF the Steins had as tangible an effect on Edie as it did on Lew. After years of playing second fiddle to Doris Stein, Edie burst into the society columns as Mrs. Stein's equal in all things philanthropic and chic. But there was a difference.

---

[5]   In 1986, News Corporation's Rupert and Anna Murdoch paid the Stein estate $5,312,000 for Misty Mountain and neighboring lots worth about $1.2 million each.

[6]   Doris was also the largest shareholder in Oppenheimer Industries, official owner of the 350,000 acre Armendaris Ranch, which her son, Harold, had purchased for cattle grazing in the 1960s. In 1991, Oppenheimer Industries declared Chapter 11 bankruptcy and had to sell the ranch at a loss to satisfy creditors.

"Jules and Doris wanted the world," said Leonora Hornblow. "Lew and Edie were satisfied with L.A."

Impressionist and post-Impressionist oils now graced the Wassermans' home — Degas, Vuillard, Matisse. Lew and Edie screened about two hundred films a year in their private projection room and threw regular Democratic fund-raisers at which MCA executives were expected to contribute generously. Edie loved to entertain.

"The only time I was out there and called Edith, we were invited over for cocktails," said Cleveland lawyer Robert Moss, who had graduated from law school with Edie's brother, Stanley Beckerman. "Lew was home but he never showed up during the cocktail hour, so I didn't see him. I saw Edith, and I will always remember that trip because my wife asked if they had a particular type of liquor and Edith said, 'Honey, we've got anything you could ask for. Whatever you want, we've got it.' It was quite a bar."

Edie discovered her favorite charity when her aged mother became too ill to care for herself. Her search for a suitable nursing home led her to the Motion Picture Country House and Hospital at the northern end of the San Fernando Valley.[7]

"I fell in love with the place and Lew said, 'If you like it so much, why don't you go on the board of trustees?'" Edie said, "So I did. And I decided to fix some things up."

Edie already sat on the board of Cedars-Sinai Medical Center, so she had some ideas as to how cash could be extracted from donors. Before Jules died, she and Lew had induced the Steins to give a $2 million maintenance endowment for the exclusive use of the home.

At home, Lew and Edie took care of their own too, as long as it was on their terms. The longtime breach between Lynne and her parents began slowly to close in the 1980s as Lynne became increasingly dependent on her parents' largesse. In one more attempt to win her father's approval, she returned to West Los Angeles College and earned enough credits to enter law school. In 1981 she took her degree cum laude from West Los Angeles University School of Law and passed the California bar. At the same time, her marriage to Jack Myers disintegrated. He accused her of gaining weight and of horrible hygiene. She accused him of adultery.

After divorcing in 1982, Lynne accepted a loan from Lew, secured by a trust deed on the house he'd bought for her nearly twenty years earlier. Though Lew

---

[7]   First opened September 27, 1942, the Woodland Hills retirement home for film veterans who had nowhere else to live out their declining years, was an outgrowth of the Motion Picture Relief Fund, which was created in 1921 by the four founding members of United Artists. In 1932, the studio bosses came to support the fund as an alternative to union demands for retirement benefits, establishing a rule that all employees had to have weekly contributions deducted from their paychecks.

would never give her a job at MCA, one of his former agents, producer Jerry Wein-traub, hired Lynne.[8] She went to work as senior vice president at the new Wein-traub Entertainment Group.

But Lynne never let her career overshadow motherhood. In apparent reaction to Edie's lack of interest in her own upbringing, Lynne was obsessed with her chil-dren. She did not entrust them to a nanny, and as they passed through adoles-cence, Lynne became an education activist, first with the Beverly Hills and Brentwood school systems and later as an appointee of Governor Jerry Brown to the California State University Board of Trustees. When her daughter, Carol, began college at Georgetown University in 1984, Lynne accepted a similar trustee-ship at the Washington, D.C., campus.

While parents and daughter achieved a degree of civility, the Wassermans' relationship with Lynne could never have been described as affectionate.

"They were kind of like the Addams family," said one intimate.

What emotional warmth remained in Lew and Edie they lavished on their two grandchildren. If either Carol or Casey phoned Lew at his office, Wasserman's sec-retaries had standing orders to interrupt whatever he was doing so he could take the call.

Dr. Donald Wexler, a Connecticut psychiatrist who was also Lew Wasserman's cousin, described Lew's behavior toward his grandchildren and his daughter as typ-ical, if extreme. Simply put, Dr. Wexler said Lew and Edie saw too many of their own flaws in Lynne while virtually overlooking them in their grandchildren.

The Wassermans were a textbook study in control and dysfunction. As they had with their own family, Lew and Edie behaved just as predictably toward Sid and Lorraine Sheinberg.

"The Jules and Doris shit, where the Steins were always looking down their noses at Lew and Edie?" recalled the Wassermans' former son-in-law, Jack Myers. "Well, Lew and Edie tried reenacting the same thing with Sid and Lorraine. But the difference was that Sidney is a very independent guy. He doesn't need Lew."

He did respect him, however. "I would characterize my relationship with Lew as extraordinarily close," said Sheinberg. "I see infinitely more of Mr. Wasserman than I do of my wife, my children, my dogs. In all candor, I don't believe I've ever tried to compete with him. I wouldn't deny that we are similar in some ways. But

---

[8]   Like Lynne's father, Weintraub had begun in show business as an usher in New York during the 1940s. He then worked as an NBC page and apprenticed in the mail room at William Mor-ris in the 1950s, stepping up to MCA in its waning days as a talent agency. Like other MCA agents left high and dry following the antitrust investigation, Weintraub quit Hollywood to hus-tle talent from Cherry Hill to the Catskills. In 1969 he returned, partnering with agents Bernie Brillstein and Marty Kummer in a music-movies-TV firm called Management III. With Robert Altman's *Nashville* (1975), Weintraub officially became a film producer.

he has capacities that I certainly don't have. I'd be the first to admit it. I don't have the ability to concern myself with the breadth of activities he's got. I don't know how he does it, and I don't know that anybody in the world knows how he does it."

For all of his filial affection for Lew, Sidney and his wife, Lorraine, stayed away from Mrs. Wasserman.

"Sid hated Edie," said Myers. "She used to give him a hard time, and he just shrugged her off, like 'Fuck you, lady!' Lorraine just didn't have anything to do with Edie at all. Or Lew."

Indeed, Mrs. Sheinberg had her own career.[9] Unlike Doris and Edie, actress Lorraine Gary refused to sit in the background. She demanded that her husband jettison the antiquated MCA nepotism policy and make her a star. When he balked, she systematically wooed his subordinates to get film and TV roles.

—◦◦◦—

WHEN JOHN BELUSHI died in January of 1983, Los Angeles Police Chief Daryl Gates appealed to Lew to help end the glorification of drug use in Hollywood.

"Hey, I'm all for it," Lew told Gates. "I'll do everything in my power to turn this around."

And Wasserman's power was substantial. His endorsement made Nancy Reagan's "Just Say No to Drugs" campaign a Hollywood mantra. He transcended the movies, having become a pillar of the community and a city father. Brandeis University and New York University awarded him honorary doctorates. Upon Jules's death, Lew assumed the chairmanship of Research to Prevent Blindness and carried on Stein's vision philanthropy. At UCLA he underwrote the Wasserman professorship of ophthalmology, the first chair ever endowed at the Jules Stein Eye Institute.

From Bunker Hill to Capitol Hill, Lew's political contributions paid off in a pinch, and every celebrity who ever whiffed scandal knew it. MCA's spin control was the finest that money could buy.

But during the same period that Lew was aiding the police by urging America's youth to say no to drugs, the LAPD's Organized Crime Intelligence Division was keeping tabs on his every move. In his autobiography, *Chief*, Chief Gates recalled Lew's reaction to the surveillance:

> "We knew every time you boarded a plane for Las Vegas."
> Lew was stunned. "But why?" he asked.
> "You're a major figure in Los Angeles and you're in a business that's highly

---

[9] For reprising her *Jaws* role as the police chief's wife in *Jaws 4: The Revenge* (1987), Lorraine Gary was paid $594,000.

attractive to organized crime. Many people get mixed up in organized crime, not because they want to, but because they become victims. We tried to make sure important people, good people like yourself, were protected and not preyed upon by the Mafia. We wanted to know who was running with whom."

Wasserman's obsession with secrecy and security intensified. While he had taken his own precautions, including the full-time staffing of a guard kiosk at the front driveway to his home, Lew could not protect himself against every potential threat. He had made enemies, and all the safety measures in the world could not ensure that they might not succeed in getting even.

———⁓⁓⁓———

ONE AFTERNOON IN the autumn of 1983, Brunswick Records president Nat Tarnopol walked and whispered with Teamsters associate Martin Bacow, speaking in snarls about killing Lew Wasserman.

Bacow was Teamsters president Jackie Presser's man in Hollywood. While some in law enforcement called him a labor fixer, Bacow called himself a rabbi — "Hollywood's man of mystery," he liked to say. And while some discounted the rabbi's alleged connections, they could not ignore his uncanny ability to get through to union leaders and production heads with a single phone call. Bacow seemed to be able to end wildcat strikes instantly.

At this particular moment, in a deserted corridor of McCarren Airport terminal in Las Vegas, Tarnopol was seething. He wanted Lew Wasserman dead, and he didn't mean figuratively. He wanted revenge, and he'd made the necessary calls to do it.

"They're gonna make a move on Lew Wasserman," Tarnopol said. "They're gonna hit him on a Sunday morning. That's when he usually goes to Nate 'n' Al's for breakfast."

"But why?" asked Bacow. "What's he done?"

"That rotten no-good motherfuckin' stool pigeon," snarled Tarnopol. "He's the one who caused all my problems. And you know some of the people I'm with. They lost a lot of money when I blew the record company. And you don't hurt people like that."

Bacow certainly did know the people Tarnopol was with. They had names like Gambino and Gotti. Some had become Tarnopol's silent partners after Brunswick left MCA in 1969. The label continued to prosper in the steady-selling R&B record market, and Tarnopol began distributing Brunswick through CBS Records, acquiring jazz legends like Louis Armstrong and Lionel Hampton along the way. Among recording executives, it was understood that Tarnopol owned Brunswick's biggest seller, legendary soul singer Jackie Wilson.

But six years after his break with MCA, federal prosecutors caught up with Tarnopol. On June 24, 1975, the U.S. attorney in Newark indicted Tarnopol and eighteen other record company executives for using threats and payola to get their records played on the radio. The federal payola sting, which also bagged Arista Records president Clive Davis, was the biggest music industry probe since the early 1960s, when legendary New York deejay Allen Freed and *American Bandstand*'s Dick Clark were accused of taking bribes to play records on the air.[10] But Tarnopol and the rest of the "Newark 19" were charged with far more serious offenses, including the use of cocaine and other drugs as payola, cheating their own artists out of record royalties, and threatening strong-arm tactics if deejays played the wrong records.

After two trials, Tarnopol went free — but not before his reputation and his record company were ruined.

"Who told you it was Wasserman who blew the whistle?" Bacow asked.

"I got it from a very reliable source," said Tarnopol. "A close friend. An FBI agent."

According to Tarnopol, Newark's U.S. attorney would not have been any the wiser about Tarnopol's threat and bribery tactics if MCA had not tipped off federal prosecutors.

"Nat, it's a bad move," said Bacow. "The first one they'll grab is you. And you need more grief? You haven't had enough?"

"But the prick has to pay," Tarnopol insisted.

While no fan of Lew Wasserman, Bacow later maintained that he talked Tarnopol out of the assassination attempt.

It was the first time Bacow had ever heard Wasserman's life threatened, but it would not be the last. Times were changing in Hollywood. The delicate balance of power among Mob, union, politicians, studios, and that most unpredictable element, the media, was wobbling with no fixmeister like Sidney Korshak anywhere in sight.

SEYMOUR HERSH'S ARTICLES about Korshak produced a delayed reaction. What the brash Chicago lawyer had once laughed off as character assassination unworthy of even minimal response became a recurring indictment. After California's attorney general, Evelle Younger, named Korshak among the state's top hoodlums, the media would not let Sid alone.

---

[10] Though he testified before the congressional committee investigating payola, Clark was never charged. Freed was convicted of accepting bribes, however, and died of alcoholism a few years after serving his prison sentence.

Korshak may have felt the heat, but he would not bow to it. He and Bea fearlessly made the party rounds, sitting with Frank and Barbara Sinatra, Ed and Victoria McMahon, or their old reliables, Lew and Edie. At one charity cocktail party, comedian Don Rickles kept calling Lew "Sid," prompting columnist James Bacon to write: "And then he wonders why he's not getting any offers from Universal."

But Sidney never had to fear an *"Et tu, Brute?"* from Lew. His betrayal came instead from Hilton Hotels chairman Barron Hilton who, in his vain attempt to build a casino in Atlantic City, effectively put Sidney out to pasture.

Twice in the last half of 1984 the New Jersey Casino Control Commission had interrogated Hilton over a $50,000-a-year retainer his company had paid Korshak for thirteen years, despite Korshak's well-known reputation as a Mob adviser. At first, Hilton stonewalled before the commission, but all that did was dredge up two other Hilton improprieties:

The first had occurred in 1975 when the Las Vegas Hilton cashed $100,000 in checks for lawyer Sorkis Webbe — checks that the government later proved to be kickbacks for construction of the Aladdin Hotel, which had been financed by the Teamsters' Central States Pension Fund. At Webbe's trial, Justice Department attorneys maintained that the Hilton had laundered Webbe's checks. Webbe was sentenced to prison in 1983 for concealing the kickbacks from the IRS, but he died before he could begin serving his sentence.[11]

The second impropriety went down in 1979 when the Justice Department filed criminal charges against the Las Vegas Hilton's executive vice president, Henri Lewin, and San Francisco Teamsters officer Rudy Tham, accusing them of Taft-Hartley Act violations regarding free lodging, meals, and drinks provided at the Las Vegas Hilton. U.S. District Judge Harry Claiborne in Nevada dismissed the charges on February 15, 1980, holding that Taft-Hartley did not cover "comps" that casinos give gamblers.[12]

On February 29, New Jersey authorities stunned Hilton by denying his company a casino license.[13]

For most who knew him, Korshak's friendship had become the mark of Cain. Nancy Reagan was among those who claimed ignorance of Sidney's Mob ties when she asked Kitchen Cabinet member Alfred Bloomingdale to solicit Korshak's help. She wanted him to settle a costly racetrack strike during Ron's first term as California governor, and Korshak obliged. Not only did he send striking pari-

---

[11] Former Saint Petersburg prosecutor Marvin Rudnick, who moved to the West Coast in 1980 to join the Department of Justice's Organized Crime Strike Force, prosecuted Webbe.

[12] Judge Claiborne was impeached in 1986 and sent to prison for accepting bribes in another case.

[13] Hilton had already built a $320-million casino hotel on the Atlantic City boardwalk, but he was forced to sell it to brazen New York real estate magnate Donald Trump, who was able to get a license. Hilton applied again in 1991 and was approved.

mutuel clerks back to work, but he also gave Governor Reagan a boost with the voters as the "great labor peacemaker."

"I just heard he had union connections," Mrs. Reagan later told reporters. "I've still never seen any proof that he's a Mob lawyer. And neither has Ron."

On June 9, 1984, Teamsters President Presser decided Sidney had become too hot. Presser, who had turned FBI informant, told his government contacts that the New York and Chicago families "are concerned about his image and want Korshak to 'phase out.'"

The last straw was a $60,000 organizing fee that the International Brotherhood of Teamsters sent to the West Coast once a month for two years to organize dockworkers. By 1983 the International had paid out $1.2 million. Out of this, Korshak took $800,000 for legal fees, according to Presser, only Korshak hadn't handled any cases and the dockworker organizing effort had brought in all of about two hundred new Teamsters. "That's nothing for all that money," said Presser.

"Korshak bullshitted around a lot of people," said Marty Bacow, Presser's right-hand man in Hollywood. "Everybody believed he had these Mob guys behind him and all of this. Well, they're all away [in prison] now. There is nothing left of them.

"When his name came up in my conversations, I said, 'Don't tell me about Sidney Korshak. He couldn't make a move without getting permission. He was an order taker.' And that was the end of it."

THIRTY-THREE

MCA and the Mob

1986–1987

When Ronald Reagan threw open the deregulation floodgates during his second presidential term, Wall Street became home to the largest concentration of perfectly coiffed cannibals ever to take part in a feeding frenzy. Everyone ate everyone else—except MCA, where circumspect Lew Wasserman was still in charge.

"To my mind's observation, there was never any question as to who was boss," said former MCA executive Sheldon Mittelman. "Always Lew. Always Lew."

Others weren't so sure. While he absolutely refused to ease himself out of the Black Tower as Jules had done in the 1970s, even Wasserman could not ignore nature. From an enlarged prostate to failing eyesight, age was catching up with him. He wasn't ready to retire and turn MCA over to junk bond maestros, but he was slowing down. The point at which Sidney Sheinberg's long apprenticeship ended and Lew passed the reins over came in the early months of 1986, according to several executives who witnessed the transfer of power firsthand.

"It happened with the sale of WOR," insisted one MCA vice president.

One of four so-called super stations that began broadcasting nationally over satellite as well as in their local markets in the early 1980s, WOR-TV Channel 9 was located in Secaucus, New Jersey, right across the Hudson River from Manhattan. The station served New York far better than it did New Jersey—a fact that did not sit well with the FCC, even under Ronald Reagan. In 1980 the FCC temporarily yanked WOR's license for pandering to Manhattan and failing to cover news about its own home state. In the ensuing six years, WOR's broadcasting hardly improved, and in 1986 the FCC forced its owner, GenCorp, to put the station up for sale.

Sheinberg was immediately interested. Outside of its one-third interest in the USA Network, MCA had no stake at all in broadcasting at a time when Reagan's

FCC had systematically destroyed virtually every government roadblock that sep-arated producers from broadcasters. Networks were gobbling up radio and TV sta-tions, studios were buying into cable, and an Australian billionaire named Rupert Murdoch was using his newly acquired studio, the venerable Twentieth Century Fox, as a launching pad for a fourth TV network.

As early as Operation Prime Time in 1976, Sheinberg had wanted to start his own quasi-network—a group of independent stations that could launch MCA pro-grams into syndication. Although Operation Prime Time fell apart in less than two years, Sheinberg never abandoned his dream. The opportunity to acquire a New York City powerhouse like WOR as MCA's flagship station seemed perfect.

Sheinberg was in New York two days before bids were due when he got a call from the company that had agreed to be MCA's acquisition partner, who said the asking price for WOR was simply too high. Sheinberg phoned Wasserman in a panic and asked what to do.

"It's your company," Wasserman said. "What do you want to do?"

Sheinberg wanted to buy the station outright, he said, partner or no partner.

"Well, do it," Wasserman said, and hung up.

On February 18, 1986, MCA paid $387 million for WOR-TV. The credit—or blame—for making the purchase was all Sheinberg's. It was Sheinberg who explained to shareholders the following June that MCA needed stations in large markets to ensure a rerun market for its programs. And it was Sheinberg who promised the citizens of New Jersey better coverage of Garden State news. Shein-berg also let it be known that he had his eye on KHJ-TV in Los Angeles as a pos-sible second jewel in the MCA network.[1]

After the WOR deal, MCA corporate policy underwent a subtle shift. Wasser-man retained control of three areas: labor, real estate, and tax matters. Everything else was Sheinberg's, and increasingly Sid relied for advice less upon Lew than upon his own cabal of eighteen senior executives.

—◈—

On July 5, 1986, Lew and Edie celebrated their fiftieth wedding anniversary with seven hundred of their closest Hollywood friends.[2]

On the Universal back lot where *To Kill a Mockingbird* (1961) and *Back to the Future* (1984) were filmed, a set was transformed to look like downtown Cleveland

---

[1] Westinghouse paid GenCorp $310 for KHJ, then sold it to Sheinberg's archenemy, Disney chairman Michael Eisner. Disney renamed the station KCAL and fashioned it into L.A.'s first prime-time all-news station.

[2] Neither the state of Ohio nor Cuyahoga County nor the city of Cleveland has any record of the Wassermans' marriage.

circa 1936. It featured the May Company, where Edie clerked; the Palace Theater, where Lew ushered; and the Mayfair Casino, where the Wassermans supposedly first met and became lifelong partners.

"It was a scene worthy of Francis Ford Coppola—the Godfather being feted by his friends and retainers," gushed a *Los Angeles Times* society columnist. "And at the center of it all was Wasserman himself: warm, solicitous, thinking not of himself but of the comfort of his seven hundred guests."

Chasen's provided its famous chili, and potatoes stuffed with Beluga caviar, while Rosemary Clooney and Sammy Kahn teamed up to serenade the Wassermans with a revised version of "My Way": "For fifty years, through laughs and tears, they did it their way."

Six months later Universal studio staff repeated the exercise, making over the "New York Street" on the back lot to look like 1936 Chicago, complete with gold curbs and Depression era automobiles. This time, the occasion was Lew's fiftieth anniversary with MCA. One building was even made over as the old Michigan Avenue headquarters where Lew first worked.

Johnny Carson emceed the gathering of thirteen hundred guests on Stage 12, cracking wise about how the black tie crowd was bound by "a common emotion— fear. I'm talking fear. Don't confuse shyness. Lew's tough. He's an agent."

Gladys Knight and the Pips performed in person. Frank Sinatra, Charlton Heston, Danny Kaye, Jimmy Stewart, and the recently deceased Cary Grant all sent greetings via videotape. Ron and Nancy Reagan couldn't make it in person, either, but they also agreed to deliver a video surprise.

In his original pitch to the White House, Universal's Irwin Rosten had asked that the first couple make their greeting "a happy celebration, not a eulogy." Rosten continued:

> Our theme is that although his business thrives on publicity, Mr. Wasserman is a private and modest man. Unlike earlier heads of motion picture companies, he is all but unknown to the public. (In researching the program, we were surprised to learn that the three television networks have no footage of him in their news files.) As a running gag there are several references to the paucity of Wasserman photographs.
>
> It would be fitting if the President and Mrs. Reagan would refer to their long relationship with Mr. Wasserman. Then the President might wish to express a thought like:
>
> "Lew, I know you're not an agent anymore, but in about two years' time I'll be at liberty again, and maybe..."
>
> Then, to pay off our running gag:
>
> "Oh, yes, and someday we'd like to take a *picture* with you."

The Reagans were busy, but they obliged Rosten. Sandwiched between tapings for the West Coast Ireland Fund Dinner and the Macy's Thanksgiving Day Parade, Ron and Nancy rushed through a scripted five-minute video commemorating Lew's golden anniversary with MCA.

Once the videos, paeans, and accolades ended, Lew finally spoke. His words of wisdom did not waver a jot from the workaholic ethic that had guided his own career for half a century:

"When I show up at work Monday and begin the first day of the next fifty years, I'll have the same eager anticipation of the future," he said. "Show up for work every day on time for fifty years and you will be rewarded."

———

ON SEPTEMBER 24, 1986, a letter postmarked from New York with no return address landed on the desk of federal prosecutor Marvin Rudnick in Los Angeles. Inside the envelope marked "Confidential" was a single sheet of folded paper that read:

> To whom it may concern:
> Wasserman wanted his daughter's boyfriend murdered.
> Sal Pisello committed the murder.
> Wasserman is now indebted to Sal Pisello.
> Wasserman gives orders to Azoff to allow Sal to move around freely.
> To keep Azoff quiet, Wasserman bought Azoff's company.

For the next two years those five anonymously typed lines haunted Rudnick and the L.A. branch of the federal Organized Crime Strike Force. The message led them on an elaborate and frequently dangerous chase of mafiosi, corporate criminals, labor racketeers, crooked cops, and all manner of wild geese. It was a hunting expedition that would involve hundreds of wiretapped conversations heard on dozens of telephones in sixteen states, and it would take a guerrilla army of dogged federal officials from the bottom-feeding world of pop music payola and cocaine trafficking to the halls of Congress and the White House itself. Careers would be ruined. Lives would be lost. And when it was over, the contents of the letter could not be proven, although no one could be absolutely certain just how much, or how little, the Phantom of the Black Tower had to do with any of it. In the end, the only thing proven in a court of law was that Sal Pisello didn't pay his taxes.

Identified by the FBI and DEA as a con artist, tax dodger, and international drug trafficker, Pisello had confounded investigators since the day he walked into MCA headquarters in 1983 and, with absolutely no previous experience in or connections to the music business, began selling millions of dollars' worth of records.

"He had the run of the place," one former MCA Records executive told *Los Angeles Times* reporter Bill Knoedelseder. "It was unprecedented in all my years at the company."

Pisello was a hustler and a street hood who had a history of running elaborate scams, from smuggling heroin into the country in shipments of frozen fish to getting naive investors to pour their cash into a phony beef export operation. He had bragged of executing his enemies but had never been charged with murder. Rudnick ultimately nailed Pisello on his failure to pay income taxes on the cash he took out of the Black Tower for record sales that were never made.

But Rudnick remained unsatisfied. A button-down outfit like MCA routinely checked the background of the lowliest clerk before offering him even a minimum-wage position. How could such a company have overlooked the neon-lit danger signs of a bona fide con man like Pisello? Despite his attempt to pressure Pisello into spilling his guts, Rudnick was never able to learn how the Gambino soldier got his foot in the door at the Black Tower. That was what made the mysterious five-line note from New York so irresistibly tantalizing.

The previous February, Rudnick had issued a grand jury subpoena, demanding all of MCA's documents involving Pisello and his record deals. Since then, the tension between the strike force and the Black Tower had systematically worsened. Why would MCA want to stonewall an investigation aimed at jailing a Mafia parasite who had already bilked the company of several hundred thousand dollars? The anonymous note made Rudnick wonder if he finally had the answer.

Indeed, three months earlier, MCA had exchanged about $30 million in stock to acquire all three of MCA Music President Irving Azoff's outside companies—somewhere between six and ten times their estimated market value.[3] And because the swap was in stock, the whole transaction was tax-free—a maneuver straight out of the Jules Stein school of tax avoidance. While Azoff had taken credit for turning MCA Records around since his elevation to the presidency of the music division in 1983, such a generous reward to one of its executives still seemed excessive, even by MCA standards.

The only detail in the anonymous letter that did not meet the basic plausibility test was the first line. Could Lew Wasserman actually have contracted for the murder of his daughter's boyfriend, and could such an execution have gone undetected and unreported?

Lynne Wasserman's history with men since her breakup with Jack Myers was uneventful. The couple separated in October of 1981, Lynne filed for divorce eighteen months later, and the divorce became final on December 30, 1983. She

---

[3] Azoff had incorporated Front Line Management (concert promotion), Full Moon Records (recording), and Facilities Merchandising (concert T-shirt licensing) while he was still managing rock acts like the Eagles and Linda Ronstadt during the 1970s.

had custody of both her children, who lived with her in her 5,500-square-foot home on Doheny Road, a couple of blocks from her parents' estate. The year following her divorce, she entered into a long-term relationship with attorney Michael Donaldson, who proposed marriage and accepted a loan from Lynne to buy a house in Beverly Hills.[4]

But during the period between leaving Myers and meeting Donaldson, she did date others. Rudnick turned to detectives Neil Kreitz and Herm Kaskowitz of the LAPD's Organized Crime Intelligence Division for help in scouring missing-persons reports and unsolved homicides during the early eighties to see if any could be linked to Lynne Wasserman. Then Rudnick set the letter aside. While never dismissing it out of hand as a crank note, he couldn't waste any more time trying to prove a murder if the police couldn't even locate a victim. He had a grand jury to attend to.

Rudnick had inherited the mantle of Leonard Posner as the Justice Department's chief bulldog. Something very wrong was going on at MCA, and he saw the Sal Pisello case as a way to get to the bottom of it. Rudnick became more and more certain that some of MCA's ranking executives would wind up being indicted right along with Sal the Swindler.

——◦◦◦◦——

DESPITE THE PURCHASE of WOR-TV, MCA's bottom line still depended on hit films and TV shows. During 1986, the year of *Howard the Duck*, and the disappointing debut of *Amazing Stories*, Steven Spielberg's NBC series, MCA earned an anemic $155.2 million on $2.44 billion in revenues.

But the company's asset base remained strong, especially its real estate: 420 acres in Universal City, now developed to include several office buildings, two hotels, and three dozen sound stages; and 435 newly acquired acres near Florida's Disney World, where a second Universal Studios Tour was scheduled to open in 1989 in partnership with the Toronto-based Cineplex Odeon theater chain.[5] Still in an expansive mood, MCA branched out into the toy business, paying $67 million for LJN Toys. The company also acquired a 9 percent stake in Coleco, the manufacturer of Cabbage Patch dolls.[6]

A second theme park, along with steady revenue from WOR and the perennially lucrative toy business, promised to reinvigorate MCA. Acquiring a chunk of

---

[4]   Lynne sued Donaldson for the repayment of the loan after they ended their engagement.
[5]   In 1986 the original Universal Studios Tour was the third largest tourist attraction in the United States, behind Disneyland and Disney World.
[6]   MCA threatened legal action over Coleco's use of the King Kong name in some of its products, and Coleco granted MCA equity in the toy firm in lieu of a settlement.

the booming Cineplex Odeon theater chain seemed like the next logical step — as well as potentially the biggest cash cow of all.

In less than a decade Cineplex Odeon had become the world's second largest film exhibitor. A slick young Canadian named Garth Drabinsky had opened the first of his multiplexes in 1979, and seven years later he and his partner, Myron Gottlieb, owned over 1,500 screens in more than 500 theaters scattered across North America. The chain's phenomenal growth so impressed Sheinberg and Wasserman that MCA bought a 49.7 percent stake for $219 million just three months after the close of the WOR deal. As long as the Reagan Justice Department didn't mind media monopolies, they reasoned, MCA would ignore the 1948 Paramount Decree and own its own theaters in addition to the movies those theaters screened. MCA started things off by opening its own eighteen-screen Cineplex Odeon complex in Universal City.

But replacing Frank Price as chief of the MCA motion picture division in September of 1986 didn't improve Universal's movie output much. Price's successor, attorney Tom Pollock, was a shrewd deal-maker, but he was close to only a few major stars and directors.[7] In a business where relationships and gut instinct are crucial, Pollock tended to rely upon logic. As a result, Universal had to depend for its hits on independents like Spielberg's Amblin Entertainment and on Imagine Films, cofounded by actor-turned-director Ron Howard.

And yet, by 1987, Universal did appear to be on the rebound with the mildly successful Dan Aykroyd–Tom Hanks version of *Dragnet* and a Michael J. Fox comedy, *The Secret of My Success*. Universal Television bounced back, too, claiming nine hours of prime time each week, including two new top ten Nielsen entries, *Murder, She Wrote* and *Miami Vice*.

MCA's other subsidiaries were also bouncing back.

All seemed well in Universal City on June 24, 1987, when Lew Wasserman entered Cedars-Sinai Medical Center to have a colon polyp removed. For a man of seventy-four, Lew was in splendid condition, and the polyp surgery was merely precautionary. There were no apparent signs of the cancers that had claimed his parents, and the worst that could be said about Lew's physical condition was that his knees were bad and his back was beginning to give him trouble. While the names of old friends kept popping up on the obituary pages of *Variety*, Lew himself felt fine.[8]

At Cedars-Sinai, where Edie sat on the board of trustees, the administration rolled out the red carpet for Wasserman while the nursing staff cringed. Lew had

---

[7] As Irving Azoff's attorney, Pollock arranged MCA's $30 million purchase of Azoff's three outside companies just three months before taking over as Universal production chief.

[8] On July 29, 1987, eighty-one-year-old George Chasin died of Parkinson's disease. Herman Citron died five months later, on November 18, 1987, of a brain tumor. He was eighty-two.

no particular aversion to doctors, but he had a reputation as an awesomely demanding patient.

Dr. Peter Fugeso vividly recalled Wasserman paying him an office visit in the early 1970s before embarking on an ocean voyage. At that time Lew was suffering from a kidney stone, which was extremely painful but not a major health threat. He wanted it removed. Immediately. "I leave on the QE2 from New York next Tuesday," he told Fugeso. "When I sail, I don't want this kidney stone."

Fugeso explained that kidney stone surgery was not worth the risk. With a little patience, some bed rest, and a lot of liquids, the stone would probably pass. Lew vetoed the idea. He demanded surgery. Now. When Fugeso tried logic, Lew simply countered with his own well-reasoned examples. "Unnecessary" surgery demanded by a patient took precedence over a physician's natural reluctance to cut the patient open, he said. As an example Lew pointed to a missionary headed to Africa for an indeterminate period. The missionary had every right to demand that his appendix be removed, because such "unnecessary" surgery might well be impossible in the event of an appendicitis attack somewhere in the Congo.

Wasserman's arguments were persuasive, but his natural dynamism was even more decisive. Fugeso had come highly recommended, but if he would not meet Lew's demands, Lew could find a surgeon who would. It didn't take long for the normally forceful physician to bend to his patient's will.

"I'm a lieutenant colonel in the army reserve, and I was called up during Desert Storm," recalled Fugeso. "I met Colin Powell and Norman Schwarzkopf, but neither of them had anywhere near the commanding presence of Lew Wasserman. When he said 'I want the stone removed,' I finally just said 'Yes, sir,' and I'd never said that before to *any* patient."

History repeated itself when Lew had the polyp removed from his colon. It was Lew, not his doctors, who called the shots. He did not want to waste time. He demanded that the procedure be executed quickly, quietly, and with minimal recovery time. He wanted to get in and out of the hospital and back to the Black Tower where he belonged.

All went according to Wasserman's timetable until he was wheeled out of the operating room, still groggy from the anesthetic. At one of the very few moments in his life when he was not in absolute control, disaster nearly struck.

"The head nurse put a thermometer in his mouth to take his temperature," recalled another former Cedars nurse who was assigned to the recovery area that day. "He bit it in two and swallowed it."

The nurse called for help and Lew was returned to surgery. Afterward his emergency set off an internal alarm within the hospital computer network, alerting everyone that the MCA chairman had been dispatched to a fifth-floor intensive care unit. Some veterans on the nursing staff remembered how Taft Schreiber had similarly checked in for routine surgery eleven years earlier at UCLA Medical Center and had not come out alive. Fear quickly spread that Lew might have swallowed mercury and could die in a similar freak manner. It didn't take long for that fear to leak to the Associated Press.

News reports set off a chain reaction on Wall Street. On the chance that Wasserman might not recover, MCA stock leaped from $48 to more than $60 a share—about 22 times its projected 1987 earnings. With Lew gone, his empire would be up for grabs. With more than 1.68 million shares changing hands, normally dormant MCA became the ninth-most-active issue traded on the New York Stock Exchange.

Sheinberg saw this as less than a ringing endorsement of his stewardship. While everyone from the board of directors to Lew himself openly acknowledged that MCA was now Sheinberg's company and that Sheinberg ran the show, the cold reality was that corporate America saw MCA as Lew Wasserman. Without him, MCA would cease to exist.

While MCA stock skyrocketed, Lew recovered. Unlike Taft Schreiber, he left the hospital alive after three weeks and began making the daily trek from Beverly Hills to the Black Tower. To quell speculation, he put in an office appearance each day, even though he was not fully recovered. "As someone who sees him six or seven hours a day, he appears vigorous and in great health," Sheinberg told the media.

Privately, Sheinberg and others feared permanent damage, including the permanent loss of Lew's voice. The emergency procedure to remove the broken glass and mercury from his throat had scarred his larynx, and even if his ability to speak returned, there would be no more of the legendary screaming tirades.

Two months after the accident, however, Wasserman's familiar guttural rhetoric could again be heard on the fifteenth floor, though it was barely above a whisper. Still, Lew showed enough of the old spark to allay any fears that MCA was in trouble. "If the stock gets too low," Wasserman joked with his subordinates, "just park an ambulance in front of my house."

—♦♦♦—

DARK VICTORY: RONALD *Reagan, MCA and the Mob* was published in the summer of 1986, and by the end of the year, investigative reporter Dan Moldea's chronicle of the rise of Lew Wasserman, Sidney Korshak, and Ronald Reagan had become required reading in Washington, D.C., and Hollywood. The exposé detailed Reagan's indebtedness to MCA and MCA's indebtedness to the Mob, dating back to the 1940s. But while it struck a home run with political and media insiders, *Dark Victory* didn't even get to first base with most of America. The names Wasserman, Korshak, and even MCA meant nothing to a middle class hypnotized by the Great Communicator.

Reagan had been dubbed "the Teflon president" because of his uncanny ability to drawl his way out of the stickiest scandal. Wasserman was the Teflon mogul. Publicly, both men ignored Moldea's scathing indictment, and the mainstream media let them get away with it. Instead of being reviled, Lew was exalted. When Pope John Paul II came to southern California for the first time in the fall of 1987, it was Lew who made arrangements for him to speak at one of Universal City's two hotels, and it was Lew who sat at the right hand of the pontiff while he delivered his sermon to the City of Angels.

"Lew was the one who entertained the pope," recalled *Los Angeles Herald Examiner* columnist Jim Bacon. "Imagine that. A nice Jewish boy like Lew."

Dan Moldea harbored darker sentiments. After the publication of *Dark Victory*, Moldea received a copy of the same anonymous letter that Marvin Rudnick had received during his MCA investigation of Sal Pisello. Moldea too was haunted by the damning first line of the letter. Could Lew have contracted a hit on his daughter's boyfriend?

Moldea's own underworld sources assured him that the letter writer was mistaken—but only on one crucial point. Based on their own wiretaps of mobsters' conversations, Moldea's sources had concluded that it was not Lynne's boyfriend who had been targeted. It was the boyfriend of Lynne's daughter, Carol Leif.

Since her graduation from Beverly Hills High School in 1985, Carol Leif had been living in a Georgetown condominium not far from Moldea's own Washington apartment. She was attending Georgetown University, and her doting grandfather was taking care of everything—her living expenses, her condo, and her tuition. Moldea spent several weeks following up leads he hoped would take him to her boyfriends or anyone else she knew who might have met with foul play. Moldea thought he was on to something when he followed up the mysterious death of a Washington disc jockey who might have known Carol, but that trail turned as cold as all the others.

Finally, in the spring of 1988, Moldea simply picked up the phone and called Carol Leif. He explained who he was and why he was calling. While she did not try to hide the consternation in her voice, Leif didn't lapse into hysterics. She was simply puzzled, somewhat taken aback, and told Moldea she would have to check into the allegations.

The next day, Moldea received a call on his answering machine from MCA security's second-in-command, Richard Sullivan. When Moldea returned the call, he also got a machine. He left his message and never heard from Sullivan or Leif again.

DURING THE YEAR following his own receipt of the anonymous letter, Marvin Rudnick called dozens of witnesses before the grand jury and built his case against Sal Pisello and MCA. The two detectives from LAPD's Organized Crime Intelligence Unit, who were assigned to investigate the allegations in the letter, never got back in touch with him, so he assumed they could find no victim who fit the description. In LAPD territory, at any rate, Lynne's boyfriends appeared to have survived dating her just fine.

While the letter continued to haunt Rudnick and his successors as the most logical explanation for the entire Pisello affair, none of its tantalizing contents could ever be proven.

But Rudnick had all but forgotten the letter by the autumn of 1987. The tedious process of building a grand jury indictment had gotten rocky after Rudnick subpoenaed MCA's four top music executives. To his astonishment, three of the four—MCA Records president Myron Roth, senior vice president Zach Horowitz, and controller Dan McGill—informed him that they intended to invoke their Fifth Amendment safeguard against self-incrimination if they were forced to testify without immunity. Only MCA Music Entertainment Group Chairman Irving Azoff agreed to speak without immunity and without taking the Fifth. With the *Los Angeles Times* now dutifully reporting every morsel that spilled from the Pisello investigation, the Fifth Amendment revelation was only the latest in a string of newspaper stories that Lew Wasserman himself labeled "the worst publicity this company has had in fifty years."

On September 9, 1987, Lew received the rudest shock yet when a workman discovered a wiretap in the basement of a building adjacent to the Black Tower. MCA security confirmed with Pacific Bell that it was an FBI wiretap, then notified MCA operations chief Dan Slusser, general counsel Bob Hadl, and Lew Wasserman.

Lew and his legal advisers immediately leaped to the conclusion that Rudnick had ordered the wiretap. They also believed that Rudnick had leaked a story to the *Times* about the MCA executives intending to take the Fifth Amendment because Rudnick was married to *Times* business writer Kathryn Harris.

The day after the wiretap was discovered, Wasserman's longtime personal attorney Allen Susman phoned Rudnick. "Mr. Rudnick, we want you to know that we are not happy with the way you're handling the Pisello case," he said.

"Oh, yeah?" said Rudnick.

"We have friends in the [federal] courthouse, too, you know," Susman continued. "We can make life very difficult for you."

After a long pause, Susman hung up, leaving Rudnick both troubled and puzzled. After more than a generation, Susman no longer represented MCA.[9] Two months earlier, Munger, Tolles and Olson had replaced Susman's firm as MCA's outside counsel. It was Dennis Kinnaird, a Munger, Tolles partner, who had taken up the official complaining about Rudnick, not Susman. Thus Rudnick could only assume that Susman's call had been an unofficial warning.

The official warning followed the discovery of the wiretap by less than a week. Kinnaird's complaint was a six-page letter to the Justice Department's Office of Professional Responsibility, accusing Rudnick of ordering illegal eavesdropping and literally being in bed with the media. Kinnaird said Rudnick must have lied to a judge in order to obtain permission for the wiretap and that his wife was leaking grand jury information to the *Times*. But Kinnaird had one overriding question: Is MCA under investigation or not?

His answer came three weeks later, from newly appointed strike force chief John Newcomer. As Rudnick's boss, Newcomer assured MCA's attorney that "neither MCA nor any of its employees or executives are the target of [the Pisello] case or its attendant investigation."

Then Newcomer called Rudnick into his office. "I want you to know that you're under investigation," he said.

"For what?" asked Rudnick.

For alleged professional misconduct, Newcomer answered in a chilly voice. From that day forward, Rudnick was instructed to stick to making a tax-evasion case against Pisello, and nothing more. Rudnick's investigation of MCA was over.

—◈—

MARVIN RUDNICK KNEW about the MCA wiretaps, but he did not authorize them, nor did he share any confidential information on the Pisello case with his wife or anyone else outside of the strike force and the grand jury. What MCA's top brass had yet to discover during the first few weeks of autumn 1987 was that Marvin Rudnick was not the only federal prosecutor who had run into peculiar and suspiciously schizophrenic behavior inside the Black Tower.

During the summer of 1987 the FBI had taps on telephones in Beverly Hills, Palm Springs, San Francisco, the San Fernando Valley, and dozens of other locations across the United States, from New York to Hawaii. The mosaic of overheard conversations the Bureau pieced together kept spelling MCA.

Also, as it turned out, Rudnick was not the only prosecutor who had received the anonymous letter about Pisello, Azoff, and Wasserman. Two doors down from

---

[9]   Since representing MCA during the 1962 antitrust case, Susman had risen to senior partner of the firm founded by Larry Beilenson, who died June 27, 1988. Subsequently known as Rosenfeld, Meyer and Susman, Beilenson's firm had been MCA's outside counsel for a generation.

Rudnick's office in the Los Angeles Federal Building, a second unit of the strike force knew about the letter and had begun forging its own case against MCA officials since December, 1986.

Headed by Richard Stavin, another seasoned prosecutor, this second probe had grown out of a low-level investigation of a Mob hit and mushroomed into the broadest investigation of the entertainment industry in southern California history. It included inquiries into possible labor racketeering, extortion, wire fraud, obstruction of justice, and insider stock trading. The information gathered from wiretaps of Teamster operatives, and a nationwide skein of mid-level mobsters soon led Stavin directly to the front door of 100 Universal Plaza.

With veteran FBI Agent Tom Gates doing much of the footwork, Stavin's investigation began to focus on Eugene F. Giaquinto, a native New Yorker who had risen through the ranks to become an MCA vice president and chief of Universal's $100-million-a-year home video division. Giaquinto had joined the company while still in college and had been a "loyal MCA soldier" and "stand-up company guy" for twenty-nine years, according to his friends.

But Giaquinto and Azoff squared off in a bitter struggle for control of the burgeoning home video division in 1985 — a civil war that would eventually cost both men their jobs. Azoff apparently fired the first shot, according to the wiretaps, when his executives sent Pisello to Giaquinto, asking him to channel some of MCA's videocassette duplicating business to a company that Pisello represented. Giaquinto refused.

But Giaquinto did *not* refuse to do business with a Clifton, New Jersey–based company that had Mob connections and had been gouging MCA for more than six years. Stavin wanted to know why Giaquinto continued to contract with North Star Graphics years after a reputed Pennsylvania Mafia boss had been caught and convicted of bilking Universal's home video division of thousands of dollars. As early as 1979, North Star had contracted for all of MCA's video printing and packaging, which eventually amounted to between $12 million and $15 million a year. Packaging for the hugely popular videotape of *E.T.* alone amounted to millions.

But in 1981 the government indicted Bufalino crime family underboss Edward M. "the Conductor" Sciandra in a false-invoicing scheme at North Star Graphics that had victimized Universal to the tune of several hundred thousand dollars. Even MCA's own internal audit had shown "irregularities" in dealings with North Star: payments of between $400,000 and $500,000 for work that was never done. MCA cooperated with the prosecution, supplying evidence against Sciandra. And yet, even after the seventy-year-old mafioso was convicted of tax evasion, Universal continued doing business with North Star.[10]

---

[10] The Pennsylvania Crime Commission identified North Star president Michael Del Gaizo as an associate of the Bufalino crime family.

The FBI fingered Giaquinto as Sciandra's Universal contact. The MCA executive had met at least twice with Sciandra since the mobster's conviction—once at a video convention in Florida and on another occasion at a Beverly Hills restaurant. In June of 1987, FBI Agent Gates placed a tap on Giaquinto's home telephone to see whether North Star had been funneling MCA money to the Bufalino family and whether Giaquinto knew about it. He expected to hear Sciandra threaten MCA if North Star's business was cut off.

What Gates heard, however, sounded far more disturbing than any double-billing video scam. Instead of discussing the fine points of fraud, Giaquinto spoke of his boyhood chum, Gambino crime family boss John Gotti, and how the nation's most powerful Mafia don had a "sit-down" with Sciandra to straighten him out.

But Gotti's help didn't end there. Based on the wiretaps, Gates concluded that Giaquinto had persuaded the Gambino capo to mobilize a Mafia militia in the summer of 1987—a squad to be dispatched to southern California to prevent the rival Genovese crime family from making a motion picture about the life of Meyer Lansky, the greatest mobster of them all.

—◈—

THE GREAT LANSKY film war was an object lesson in how modern-day mobsters infiltrate, cajole, boast, con, and wheedle their way into the movies—particularly if the movie is about one of their own.

The Lansky tale began with the success of *The Untouchables*, a 1987 Paramount remake of the story of Treasury Agent Elliot Ness's campaign against Al Capone. The Kevin Costner–Sean Connery gangster film became a surprise hit, coming in fifth among the year's top grossers, with nearly $75 million in domestic box office receipts. Suddenly mob movie projects, which had fallen by the wayside since *The Godfather* films of the early 1970s, were hot again, and the prospect of a Meyer Lansky biography became the hottest project of all. So hot, in fact, that four years after Lansky's death in a Miami hospital, the nation's two most powerful Mafia families squared off over who would bring Lansky's life story to the screen— and MCA was in the middle of the dispute.

First to come up with a script was Martin Bacow, a Hollywood jack-of-all-trades who began his career in southern California in 1948 as a boxing announcer and branched out over the next four decades to become an actor, screenwriter, labor negotiator, and B-movie producer.[11] A close associate of Teamsters President Jackie Presser, Bacow grew up in Detroit during the 1930s under the protection of the Purple Gang and remained an informal confederate of mobsters, Teamsters,

---

[11] Bacow produced *Jacktown*, *Tragedy USA*, *The Doctor*, and *Naked Road*, among others.

and moviemakers most of his adult life. In much the same way that Sidney Korshak had once fixed labor disputes, Bacow proved repeatedly that he too had the Teamster connections to start or stop a motion picture.

But while he had made a good living as the Teamsters' man in Hollywood, Bacow's real interest lay in making movies, not exploiting labor disputes. Thus, after Bacow launched his Lansky project, he broke the news to Hollywood via Jim Bacon's *Herald-Examiner* column. He told Bacon that Lansky himself had given him approval to write his life story. Armed with a finished script simply titled *Lansky*, Bacow sold MCA's Eugene Giaquinto on the idea. Giaquinto struck an agreement with Bacow to buy the video and pay-TV rights once Bacow's movie was made. Giaquinto cinched the deal with a tentative contract for $4 million.

But the wiretaps that the FBI's Tom Gates had installed on Giaquinto's home telephone indicated that Bacow and Giaquinto were about to get some unwelcome competition. In early July of 1987, actor James Caan had dinner at La Dolce Vita in Beverly Hills with several members of the Los Angeles Mafia and announced that he, not Bacow, would be making the Lansky movie.

Since his Oscar-nominated performance in *The Godfather*, Caan had developed a self-confessed fascination with career criminals—his twenty-five-year friendship with loan shark Walter Seifert being a case in point. In a subsequent interview about his client, attorney Donald E. Santarelli said that playing Sonny Corleone had changed Caan's life.

It got back to Bacow that Caan had told L.A. Mafia lieutenant Michael Rizzitello and several others that Caan had his own Lansky project, and Bacow's movie would never be distributed. Bacow might actually have secured Lansky's approval, but who could say for certain that he did? Lansky was dead, after all.

Caan, on the other hand, claimed to have consent for his project from Lansky's widow, Thelma, as well as from Lansky's second-in-command, Vincent "Jimmy Blue Eyes" Alo. Alo was eighty-five but still very much alive. The Genovese family capo was described by one Justice Department official as "one of the most significant organized-crime figures in the United States."

At Universal, Giaquinto began to worry whether Bacow actually "had permission" to make the Lansky movie, and Bacow went into a rage. "They'd have to be crazy to stop a picture," he said angrily.

He vowed to fight back, and Giaquinto offered to help. In a July 7 conversation, Giaquinto told Bacow that he'd had a meeting in New York with a representative of "Number One," and if Jimmy Alo's Genovese family wanted war, that's what they would get.

Bacow asked if Number One "was the G. guy," meaning Gambino capo John Gotti.

"Yes," Giaquinto answered.

The following day Bacow called again, and Giaquinto reassured him that both he and his liaison in New York had known Gotti all their lives. If necessary, Gambino soldiers could be dispatched to L.A. on a moment's notice. Giaquinto took the dispute seriously enough to discuss obtaining a concealed-weapon permit. While he had no immediate plans to have Gotti "call out the troops," Giaquinto said he didn't want to be alone and unprotected. He had a wife and kids.

Bacow scoffed that, if need be, he could protect himself. "I don't pull punches," he said. "Tough guys are worth the price of a bullet to me."

A week passed. Giaquinto's New York contact called to tell him that a Gotti representative was coming to Los Angeles to "get all the facts" and decide "what move to make." That was fine, Giaquinto said, but in the meantime Genovese family members were now "all over the place" in L.A.

"Shame on them, then," replied Giaquinto's contact.

Giaquinto next telephoned Bacow to relay the good news. "It will be resolved in one minute, no matter where the move [is] coming from," he said.

In a subsequent conversation with a man identified only as Tommy, Giaquinto boasted that Bacow's *Lansky* would be "the next *Godfather*" and that he would import thirty Gotti soldiers to squash any competition from James Caan, Jimmy Blue Eyes, or the Genovese mob.

———

As OFTEN HAPPENS with a hot Hollywood property, *Lansky* cooled. Neither version of the legendary Syndicate chairman's life story ever got off the ground at Universal, and the alleged bout between Gambinos and Genoveses apparently didn't get past the first round. The entire episode might never have come to light had Agent Tom Gates not been listening in.

Even so, more than a year passed before prosecutor Richard Stavin filed Gates's seventy-nine-page affidavit in federal court, detailing Giaquinto's and Bacow's threats and bluster.

"It was unsealed by accident," Stavin said years later. "It was not supposed to be public."

For his part, Giaquinto angrily denied any Mob involvement. "This is ridiculous," he said. "I don't work twenty-nine years for a company and all of a sudden become somebody that I'm not."

Bacow, who learned for the first time that he had been a key target of a Hollywood labor-racketeering investigation, was angriest of all. The FBI affidavit named Bacow as an extortion suspect in "threatening strikes" against movie and television production companies in exchange for "money or other things of value."

"They [the FBI] are trying to defame and frame me," Bacow said. "This is terrible. I've never been arrested. My name has been besmirched. All the studios are scared to even talk to me now."

Giaquinto, Bacow, and all the others whom Gates heard on the wiretaps in the summer of 1987 talked about much more than *Lansky*. They spoke about Lew Wasserman's health in the wake of the thermometer incident, and they discussed Sid Sheinberg's shaky future if they suspected an MCA takeover attempt. At one point in the wiretap transcript, Giaquinto told Bacow that Irving Azoff "was planning to take over the whole thing."

"It's warfare," Bacow replied.

If Azoff prevailed and Giaquinto lost his job, he vowed that MCA would be "in for trouble." Giaquinto had his own Mob contacts as well as Bacow's influence with the unions. He also had a secret weapon that Gates described in his affidavit as "an association with government employees in Washington who are furnishing [Giaquinto] with confidential law enforcement information."

But none of that helped the MCA executive when the *Los Angeles Times* broke the story of the Gates wiretaps on December 15, 1988. The newspaper reported the contents of Gates's affidavit, which had been unsealed the same week. It included details of the North Star swindle, including FBI suspicions that Giaquinto had funneled MCA money to Sciandra. The story also related Giaquinto's long-standing relationship with John Gotti, and the great Lansky film war. A shaken Giaquinto continued to put the best face on his worsening situation. "There's not going to be any indictment," he predicted.

MCA's outside attorney Ron Olson was less sanguine. He drew a distinction between MCA and any investigation of Giaquinto, distancing the company from its errant executive. "MCA has been advised repeatedly that it is not a target or a subject of this Department of Justice investigation," Olson said.

The day after the government unsealed Gates's affidavit, Sid Sheinberg put Giaquinto on a paid leave of absence. MCA general counsel Robert Hadl said the company was investigating Giaquinto, but none of its other employees. Echoing Olson, Hadl reiterated that MCA itself was not a target of the FBI.

Two months later, Sheinberg permanently replaced Giaquinto with Robert Blattner, president of RCA/Columbia Pictures Home Video. Giaquinto's wife divorced him and moved to New York. For the next several years he had trouble finding work in Hollywood.

But he was right about one thing: there were never any indictments.

THIRTY-FOUR

Cashing Out

1988–1990

In February of 1988, New York developer Donald Trump notified MCA that he owned 375,000 shares of its stock and that he planned to buy another 18.8 million—roughly 25 percent of the company's total worth. MCA immediately jumped 20 percent in value on the New York exchange. Three weeks after Trump's announcement, the investment newspaper *Financial World* summed up MCA as if it were a three-course dinner: $2.6 billion in annual revenues; real estate worth between $1.5 billion and $2 billion; 3,000 films and 12,500 episodes of TV shows valued between $2 billion and $3 billion.

Trump never followed through on his threat, but the fact that he could send stock soaring after buying one half of one percent of its 77.1 million outstanding shares was an uncomfortable reminder of MCA's spasms during Lew's hospital stay. For years analysts had labeled MCA one of the market's most undervalued issues. Conservatively, pundits guessed that a corporate dismantler like MGM's Kirk Kerkorian could sell off over $5 billion in MCA assets and still have the Universal logo to hang over the entrance to one of his Vegas hotels.

But Wasserman wasn't interested in liquidation.

"If somebody offered Lew $100 a share for MCA, there's no reason to think he'd take it," said PaineWebber analyst Lee Isgur. "If they offered $100 a share tax-free, he'd probably think about it."

Nor was Lew alarmed by the possibility of a hostile takeover. In addition to his own 7.1 percent stake, Wasserman controlled the 11 percent the Steins had left behind. Members of his management team and the MCA Inc. Profit Sharing Trust owned another 3.5 percent, which put Lew in control of more than 21 percent of MCA's total common stock. Because the board had changed the MCA bylaws after Steve Wynn's abortive takeover attempt, any management change had to be approved by a 75 percent vote of the shareholders.

Lew also had an added layer of protection in Washington. Former Democratic National Committee Chairman Robert Strauss had been on the MCA board since 1980, and former Senate Majority Leader Howard Baker was elected a director four years later. Baker sat on the board for three years before Ronald Reagan's Iran-Contra crisis called him to duty as White House chief of staff.[1]

"Remember, Lew is very pragmatic," said one MCA executive. "You'd ask him what to do about politics, and he'd say, 'If you think the train is going to leave the station, be on board.'"

His Democratic allegiance notwithstanding, Lew had quietly supported Reagan's reelection in 1984. When another senior Reagan adviser, Michael Deaver, resigned from the Ronald Reagan Presidential Foundation, Wasserman took his place and made the largest individual contribution — $517,969 — to the Reagan Library building fund.

"Lew's personal relationships are unequaled and can be brought to bear against an opponent," said another executive. Bottom line: Wasserman's old friend Ronnie Reagan could, and would, put any would-be corporate raider under a very uncomfortable regulatory microscope.

MCA was virtually takeover-proof. But Wasserman had other considerations beyond political string-pulling and junk-bond raids. At age seventy-five death and taxes loomed large. Lew faced crippling capital gains taxes on his 5.4 million shares if the company was ever sold in either a friendly bid or a hostile takeover.

When all eight MCA directors convened in Chicago on May 4, 1988, for the company's twenty-ninth annual meeting, Wasserman spoke of manpower. That was what MCA had always been about; that was what MCA would always be about while Lew was in charge. He proposed, and the board approved, golden parachutes for three hundred MCA executives. In the event of a management change, each executive could collect a lump-sum payment of up to three times his salary if he voluntarily quit within one year after the company was sold. If the top five highest-paid officers alone took the parachutes, it would cost MCA as much as $27 million.

Golden parachutes might be costly, but they had the same effect on migratory senior executives as had Stein's golden handcuffs policy in the past. Asked by one shareholder how he could justify so expensive a measure, Wasserman recalled his own hospitalization. "In July of 1987, with all of the rumors that were floating around, we had a great deal of concern and confusion in our executive ranks," Wasserman said. "We're in a very competitive business; we're in a very personal

---

[1]   During the first week of December 1986, Robert Strauss met with President Reagan, former Secretary of State William Rogers, and Deputy White House Chief of Staff Michael Deaver to beseech the president to fire Chief of Staff Donald Regan over Regan's poor handling of the Iran-Contra scandal. Two months later Reagan replaced Regan with Howard Baker.

business. We don't want our executive staff in a constant state of turmoil." MCA represented stability in a volatile industry.

Lew still staged all annual meetings in Chicago. Some said he did so for sentimental reasons, but a handful of shareholder dissidents maintained that holding the meetings in Chicago had the practical effect of discouraging the company's 16,800 employees from attending and raising hell over issues like the golden parachutes. Fewer than seventy attended the 1988 meeting, although it marked one of the largest turnouts in company history.

"I didn't even know they held [the meetings] here, and my father was on the board," observed Edward L. Heymann, son of First National Bank of Chicago's Walter M. Heymann.

What Wasserman did not tell the shareholders during the ninety-five-minute meeting was that—golden parachutes, poison pills, and political clout notwithstanding—he had seriously begun to think about selling the company. He quietly teamed MCA board members Felix Rohatyn and Robert Strauss with Wall Street merger attorney Martin Lipton to examine the possibilities.

It seemed likely that Wasserman wanted to settle the company in strong hands, as ABC chairman Leonard Goldenson had done when he merged his network with Capital Cities Communications. Lew made it clear after Steve Wynn and Donald Trump made their moves that the only merger prospects he found acceptable were blue-chip companies like RCA—which had recently been swallowed by General Electric. While GE or Walt Disney might have met the test, neither showed much interest in MCA.

Instead, potential suitors included Revlon chairman Ronald Perlman; former Twentieth Century Fox owner Marvin Davis; Nelson Peltz, head of Triangle Industries, the world's largest packaging company; and Coniston Partners, the New York investment group that broke up Allegis, the parent company of United Airlines. Lew regarded all of them as predators who might sell off MCA piece by piece.

A more likely match for America's most successful entertainment conglomerate might be found beyond the U.S. borders. When Sony blazed the way by paying $2 billion for CBS Records in November of 1987, it became clear that the Japanese had set their sights on Hollywood. MCA itself had recently formed its own joint venture with Nippon Steel to develop a Universal Studios theme park in Japan.

With the rumor that Felix Rohatyn's Lazard Frères was circulating an offering memorandum, MCA takeover rumors began anew. By October the *Wall Street Journal*'s widely read "Heard on the Street" column ran an article headlined "MCA Shares Up Once Again on Belief, Widespread on Street, of Inevitable Takeover." Whether a Japanese bankroller left MCA management to run the business or the company merged with a large U.S. firm, heavy speculative trading made a battle for MCA almost inevitable.

—◦ⵣⵣ◦—

IN APRIL OF 1988, Salvatore J. Pisello was sentenced to four years in prison for evading taxes on more than $400,000 in unreported income he'd earned from MCA Records between 1983 and 1985.

But Sal the Swindler's second tax-evasion conviction in as many years was a Pyrrhic victory for Marvin Rudnick. True to his word, L.A. Organized Crime Strike Force chief John Newcomer had narrowed Rudnick's two-year investigation of Pisello. MCA was no longer a target. Rudnick himself, in fact, was now under the microscope.

MCA retained yet another outside legal counsel in the closing months of 1987. The latest MCA lawyer invited onto the payroll was William Hundley, who had headed the Justice Department's organized crime division under Bobby Kennedy. In 1987, Hundley joined the Texas powerhouse law firm of Akin, Gump, Strauss, Hauer and Feld, and his first assignment as MCA board member Robert Strauss's newest law partner was to defuse the Pisello time bomb.

Hundley met in Washington with the two top officials of the very Justice Department division that he had once headed: Organized Crime Strike Force chief prosecutor David Margolis and his deputy chief, Michael DeFeo. He also met in Los Angeles with Rudnick's immediate boss, John Newcomer. In short order the Pisello problem had been handled.

Two months after Newcomer first warned Rudnick that he was under investigation by the Justice Department's Office of Professional Responsibility, Margolis and DeFeo called Rudnick back to Washington. They met in a conference room where Hundley's portrait hung on the wall, along with those of other former Justice Department officials. The two senior prosecutors ordered Rudnick not to embarrass MCA any further, in or out of the courtroom.

Several years later, Rudnick recalled Margolis putting his cowboy-booted feet up on his desk, leaning back in his chair, and pointing to Hundley's portrait before warning Rudnick: "Bob Strauss represents MCA. Bill Hundley is Bob Strauss's partner. If Bill Hundley starts complaining about you, you've got troubles."

After that meeting, Rudnick was constantly aware of the threat to his job. He documented and dated every phone call he received and secreted copies of his memos outside the office, where they could not be doctored or destroyed. He lived a paranoid professional existence, carrying a pocket notebook with him everywhere in order to record conversations with superiors whom he now believed to be in MCA's pocket.

By March of 1988, Newcomer was sitting with Rudnick every day of the Pisello trial, admonishing him like a schoolteacher each time the prosecutor's questioning veered too close to the subject of possible wrongdoing at MCA. As

Newcomer sternly reminded Rudnick, it was Sal Pisello who was on trial, not MCA. Nevertheless, with Newcomer gnashing his teeth at the prosecution table, Rudnick alluded to the possibility of a Pisello payoff in his closing argument. MCA contracted with Pisello, he said, "not because of his background in the record business but for some other unexplained series of events that cast a cloud over the testimony at this trial."

He never elaborated for the jury just what that series of events was. He named no names. For fear of his job, he maintained his silence about the anonymous letter he'd received eighteen months earlier, which—if true—traced the whole sorry story back to Lew Wasserman. It made little difference. Rudnick was considered a pariah following the trial—a loose cannon assigned low-level cases, shunned by his peers, and monitored constantly for fireable offenses. None could be found, but that didn't matter. Marvin Rudnick's days as a federal prosecutor were numbered.

—◦◦◦—

IN JULY 1988, nearly a month before the premiere of Universal's *The Last Temptation of Christ*, pickets appeared outside Lew and Edie's Foothill Drive estate. For months a Fundamentalist firestorm had been brewing over Martin Scorsese's dramatization of Nikos Kazantzakis's novel about a very human Messiah who brooded over being crucified, lusted after women, and generally behaved in a less than divine fashion. Because Lew was Jewish as well as CEO of the studio distributing the movie, he made a very convenient target.

When Baptist minister R. L. Hymers Jr. heard that Wasserman attended the Wilshire Boulevard Temple on the infrequent occasions when he and Edie visited a synagogue, Hymers set up a movie screen on the sidewalk outside. Then he phoned the media. While 150 members of his Fundamentalist Baptist Tabernacle congregation marched on the Temple, Hymers proclaimed, "These Jewish producers with a lot of money are taking a swipe at our religion." He slashed and spray-painted the movie screen just in time for the 6:00 P.M. newscasts and ominously warned reporters that "theater owners should think twice about showing this film."

Los Angeles Roman Catholic Archbishop Roger Mahoney, who'd befriended Lew when Wasserman helped arrange the 1987 papal visit, sprang to Wasserman's defense. "I strongly oppose the anti-Semitic implications that a few voices have raised in the matter, and I am hopeful that our excellent Jewish-Christian relationship will help diminish any suggestion that this film was produced to be anti-Christian," declared Mahoney. "Wasserman would not allow any film to be released through his studios that would be offensive to a large segment of the American film-going public."

The U.S. Catholic Conference Department of Communications did indeed brand *The Last Temptation of Christ* "morally offensive to everyone," but Mahoney hadn't seen the Scorsese film when he first came out in support of Wasserman. All he knew was that Lew was a generous donor to the Los Angeles archdiocese.

By the time the demonstrators carried their protest to Lew's doorstep, their numbers had grown. Recognizing the TV crews that waited for them, they gleefully crucified Christ in effigy and displayed posters that accused Wasserman of encouraging anti-Semitism and endangering Israel—again just in time for the evening news.

In August, the president of Edwards Cinemas, which operated dozens of theaters in southern California, became the first to announce a boycott of *The Last Temptation of Christ*. "We don't want to show a film that is in any way denigrating to the image of Christ," said Jim Edwards III who, like Archbishop Mahoney, had not yet seen the movie. Several other theater chains made similar boycott announcements, but Cineplex Odeon was not among them. The company, which was half owned by MCA, had co-produced the film, after all, and could not very well boycott its own movie.[2]

Three days before *The Last Temptation of Christ* opened in New York, Chicago, and Los Angeles, even Hollywood loyalists were turning on Wasserman. Actor Don Defore—best known as Shirley Booth's costar on the 1960s sitcom *Hazel*—imposed on his own thirty-year friendship with Ronald Reagan, begging the president to condemn MCA for releasing "the most vicious, diabolically anti-Christian film in the history of our industry."

Reagan apparently did not call Lew to ask his favor this time, and the din of protest grew louder. On August 11, the day before the movie's nationwide release, 25,000 protesters marched on Universal Studios. Most paid to park in the Universal garage, ate in the Universal restaurants, and sang "Onward, Christian Soldiers" when the TV news vans appeared.

Over the next several weeks a few theaters where *The Last Temptation of Christ* was shown were vandalized, but the groundswell of Christian outrage faded with the grosses. *The Last Temptation of Christ*, which was nearly three hours long, was preordained to sink quickly at the box office. While it was a labor of love for Scorsese—a lapsed Catholic who had once considered entering the priesthood rather than attending film school—it's familiar plot would have taken a miracle to compete with *Who Framed Roger Rabbit, Coming to America*, or any of the other escapist blockbusters of 1988.

The brief controversy worked better than any expensive ad campaign, how-

---

[2]   When Cineplex CEO Garth Drabinsky suggested that MCA might rerelease *The Last Temptation of Christ* to qualify for the Oscars, Wasserman flew into one of his patented tantrums, cursing the Canadian as an idiot who would bring anti-Semitic demonstrators again to his front door and falsely blaming Drabinsky for having given Scorsese the green light to make the movie in the first place. The film's sole Oscar nominee was Scorsese as best director.

ever. The movie had only cost $6.5 million to produce, and the curious who bucked the protests and paid to sit through it quickly earned Universal back its investment. What was more, a grateful Martin Scorsese was now scheduled to direct another film for Universal: a remake of the 1962 thriller, *Cape Fear*, which would become one of Hollywood's biggest hits in 1991. And the same Lew Wasserman whose name had been sullied for more than a year in the Organized Crime Strike Force investigations was now lauded for his strength of character, his grace under pressure, and his refusal to bend to the will of Fundamentalist censors.

In the end, for Wasserman and his studio, it couldn't have turned out better if Lew had planned it that way himself.

—◦◦◦—

IN THE FALL of 1988 strike force prosecutor Richard Stavin's grand jury investigation of Gene Giaquinto seemed to be moving right along unimpeded. Unlike the vanquished Marvin Rudnick, Stavin could not be labeled a loose cannon because he'd secured prior approval of his every move from the same strike force executives who had dressed Rudnick down for embarrassing MCA.

The picture Stavin painted for his grand jury was that of a band of gritty, streetwise hustlers who dressed as executives but behaved as gangsters. The Giaquinto wiretaps had revealed the possibility that money was being laundered through at least four unnamed motion pictures, that movie executives were targets of extortion, and that East Coast mobsters were expanding beyond the question of who would make the movie about Meyer Lansky to the question of who would succeed Sid Sheinberg as MCA president once Lew retired and Sheinberg stepped up to chairman. The obvious choice was Executive Vice President Tom Wertheimer, but wiretaps revealed that Giaquinto and Azoff were also contenders.

Stavin's cast of characters had grown to include the operator of a North Hollywood script service that Stavin and FBI agent Gates believed to be a front for drug sales; Harold Akimoto, a Honolulu gambler with a decade-long reputation as one of Hawaii's leading hoodlums; and Robert Booth Nichols, a shadowy figure straight out of a John le Carré novel who looked like Clark Gable, sold machine guns, and claimed to be a clandestine international agent for the intelligence community. At one point, Giaquinto introduced Nichols to Jack Valenti in an effort to get the Motion Picture Association president to hire Nichols as head of an international security unit aimed at preventing foreign piracy of American videos.

After one meeting, Valenti nixed the idea. "My instinct was I didn't feel comfortable about some of the things he was saying," Valenti said much later. "When a fellow tells you a lot of things are top secret…well, I know a lot about the CIA from my time in the White House."

But even as Richard Stavin's investigation gathered steam, his support from

L.A. Strike Force chief John Newcomer gradually disintegrated. In the manner of a disapproving schoolteacher, reminiscent of Newcomer's dealings with Rudnick, the strike force chief kept rejecting Stavin's prosecution memo, a lengthy document that distilled grand jury testimony into evidence aimed at securing indictments. By the beginning of 1989, Stavin's level of frustration had reached that of the chastened Marvin Rudnick.

Rudnick still worked down the hall from Stavin, but he now did little more than push papers from one side of his desk to the other. The two men rarely spoke. Stavin steered clear of his colleague outside of the office as well, for fear that Rudnick's taint might seep into Stavin's investigation of Mob infiltration of the motion picture business.

In a lengthy article entitled "Death of a Mob Probe" published in the previous summer's edition of *The American Lawyer* magazine, reporter Michael Orey had spelled out Newcomer's systematic destruction of Rudnick. Rudnick had been asked to resign, but he had refused. While Newcomer could not specify any misconduct on Rudnick's part, he had recommended to his own superiors back in Washington that Rudnick be fired. No cause could be given, so Rudnick stayed on. He came into the office each day—a living reminder of how even the most honorable government prosecutor could be dealt with if his zeal and outrage superseded an accurate perception of his foe's omniscience.

The mute fury of MCA was also manifesting itself at the *Los Angeles Times*, where reporter Bill Knoedelseder dutifully reported each episode of the MCA-Rudnick soap opera. During the first weeks of 1989, Knoedelseder's sources warned him to beware because the wiretaps that Stavin and Gates had authorized indicated that MCA's influence extended "all the way to the White House."

Indeed, the *Times* dutifully reported that Ronald Reagan's first luncheon date in California after George Bush's inauguration was with his former MCA agent, Lew Wasserman. Two months later the newspaper also reported Rudnick's indefinite suspension from the Justice Department. Pending a decision on his future with the strike force, Rudnick was no longer allowed to come to the office each day.

But as cynical as the Rudnick-Pisello story had made him, Knoedelseder thought he could carry on the investigative work that Rudnick had begun and publish his findings. He did not believe for a moment that MCA's tentacles could extend inside the *Los Angeles Times*. Others were not so sure. A knowledgeable *Times* insider maintained that *Times* publisher Tom Johnson owed allegiance to Wasserman after Johnson, who had been an LBJ aide, asked the former president to find him a job in 1970. According to Oates, Wasserman used his influence with the Chandler family to land Tom Johnson in the publisher's suite. As with every other allegation of influence-peddling that involved Wasserman, string-pulling could be strongly suggested but rarely proven.

Knoedelseder changed his mind about his newspaper's independence one day in the winter of 1989, when an anonymous caller phoned him at his desk on the third floor of the *Los Angeles Times* building. A gruff male voice told him to go to the window and look down at the intersection of First and Spring Streets. Then the caller hung up.

Knoedelseder went to the window and there, parked at the curb in front of the main entrance to the newspaper, was a waiting limo with the license plate number MCA 1. Somewhere in the plusher upper reaches of the *Times*, beyond the hardscrabble cubicles of the newsroom, Lew was enjoying lunch with the newspaper's executives.

A few weeks later, in May of 1989, Richard Stavin quit the Justice Department in disgust after John Newcomer refused to okay any of the proposed indictments Stavin had labored four years to develop.

In July, Marvin Rudnick was officially fired. Six months later, when *60 Minutes* reported on the aborted strike force investigations of MCA executives, correspondent Ed Bradley asked Justice Department criminal division chief Ed Dennis point-blank why Rudnick was fired. The only answer Dennis could give was "personality disputes."

At the same time, Knoedelseder's stories about MCA and the derailed Mob probe began to get rejected regularly by his editors. He was instructed to switch interests and write about something other than MCA for a change. Before the year was out, stories about MCA and the Mob ceased to appear in the paper at all, and Bill Knoedelseder quit his job at the *Times*.

———

SUING HAD BECOME such a regular way of doing business at MCA that Sid Sheinberg half-jokingly said that the legal department was one of MCA's biggest profit centers. One very unprofitable lawsuit, however, involved actor James Garner and his hit series, *The Rockford Files*.

In March of 1989, Garner settled a six-year-old fraud, deceit, and breach of contract suit against Universal for withholding his profits from the perennially popular 1970s detective series. Beginning in 1980, when *The Rockford Files* finished its first five-year network run, Garner was supposed to receive a 37.5 percent share of the net profits from syndication. While *The Rockford Files* earned (and still earns) millions in syndication, Garner never received a dime. After waiting three years, Garner did the unimaginable: he sued MCA. Some said he was committing professional suicide.

But times had changed and actors that onetime agent Lew Wasserman had helped free from the tyranny of the studios were now challenging Universal mogul Lew Wasserman on his own turf—and winning. After five years of legal wrangling,

MCA sent Garner a check for $607,000 in December of 1988. When Garner's lawyers pointed out to the court that *The Rockford Files* had grossed $125 million and that MCA's $607,000 was little more than an insult, MCA offered $6 million to settle the suit. Garner demanded $16.5 million.

For two months, while both sides deposed each other, investigators for Garner's attorneys made a damning discovery. According to TV station managers they interviewed, MCA had sold *The Rockford Files* as part of a package, though MCA salesmen were careful never to give it that name.

At one Seattle TV station the manager was told he could have *The Rockford Files* if he would also agree to buy reruns of the far less popular *Quincy*. When he received his invoices, the manager realized that *Quincy* cost more than twice what he was billed for *The Rockford Files*. Garner's lawyers believed that by undervaluing a popular series like *Rockford*, placing a premium price on a lukewarm series like *Quincy*, and selling them as a package, MCA had found a method of cheating its clients out of millions of dollars in profits. When they confronted MCA with this accusation, the company hastily agreed to settle out of court if Garner would seal the court record. Garner agreed.

While the exact dollar amount of the settlement was not officially disclosed, Garner walked away with over $14 million...and MCA no longer had the clout to ruin his career and make an example of him, as it had done with John Payne, Eddie Bracken, and others. In addition to an Oscar nomination for his role in *Murphy's Romance* (1985), Garner appeared in a half dozen other movies, including *Maverick* (1994), with Jodie Foster and Mel Gibson, a big-screen version of his best-known TV series. He also made dozens of TV appearances, including several new movie-of-the-week episodes of *The Rockford Files*. He eased into retirement both rich *and* famous.

"I became an actor by accident," Garner once remarked. "I am a businessman by design."

—⁓—

RONALD REAGAN WAS an actor by design and a businessman designed by MCA.

After leaving the White House, Reagan complained that he hadn't earned much money during all his years of public service. His presidential and gubernatorial pensions plus the income from the blind trust that Jules Stein had set up for him way back in 1966, simply hadn't kept pace with his and Nancy's lavish lifestyle. So the ex-president took up where he'd left off when he quit Hollywood: he went on the road as the highest paid public speaker in the world.

In October of 1989 a Japanese firm, described as the world's fourth-largest media conglomerate, asked Reagan to make an eight-day tour of Japan. While he was there, the ex-president spoke twice over Japanese TV for about twenty minutes each time, delivering the kind of scripted homilies about moral values that he loved to give. Afterward the audience applauded and asked no questions.

For his efforts, the ex-president was paid $2 million. "That's what was offered, and I didn't protest," Reagan said defiantly, "even though I knew there was an actor in Hollywood who got $3 million for just doing a Toyota commercial there. I just thought that in sixteen years I hadn't made any kind of money."

Until Reagan rewrote the rules, America's highest-paid public speaker had been comedian Bill Cosby, who charged as much as $300,000 for a single appearance. In the world of politics, Henry Kissinger and Colin Powell were the heavyweights, commanding $50,000 for each speaking engagement. Reagan's successor, President George Bush, refused to comment, but former President Jimmy Carter said: "If you hear of a deal like that, let me know." Reagan's $2 million was so far off the scale that it might have raised eyebrows as a post-presidential payoff if it had been made by a U.S. company.

But Nobutaka Shikanai, chairman of the Fujisankei Communications Group, gladly paid Reagan the $2 million in the hope that the former president would lend prestige to his company. Except for MCA, Reagan and Shikanai had little in common. Reagan was a former American president; Shikanai was a Japanese media baron. For years, Fujisankei was one of MCA's biggest overseas customers for syndicated TV shows, records, and movies, which were broadcast over Fujisankei's wholly owned Fuji Television Network and Nippon Broadcasting System.

The American reaction to Reagan's $2 million junket was muted and might have faded quickly from the headlines if Reagan hadn't predicted in one of his two Fujisankei speeches that Sony's $3.4 billion purchase of Columbia Pictures Entertainment from Coca-Cola would "bring back decency and good taste" to Hollywood. Until the Sony buyout was revealed in late September of 1989, Wall Street had been betting for more than six months that Sony was angling to buy MCA, not Columbia. In Hollywood, what Sony bought didn't matter so much as how the ex-president had slandered American show biz.

"What a person says in one country is often misinterpreted in another," Reagan said upon his return to the United States.

His excuse did not wash. He still owed Hollywood an apology. Addressing a thousand members of the Hollywood Radio and Television Society at the Beverly Wilshire Hotel a month later, Reagan pleaded foot-in-mouth disease. "I'm sorry I was a little tardy in getting here today," he began. "You see, my dentist was running late. He had a little difficulty in removing from my mouth the last piece of shoe leather I acquired in Japan. I'm glad he did, though. Otherwise I wouldn't be able to enjoy this wonderful lunch. There's nothing like crow soufflé followed by humble pie."

Nonetheless, he went on to blast "immorality" and "vulgarity" in many Holly-wood releases. While he'd seen nothing worth criticizing in *The Last Temptation of Christ* just one year earlier, Reagan reiterated his concern that the frayed Amer-ican moral fiber might be rewoven by the Japanese. He was especially indignant over foul language in U.S. films: "You can call me a blockhead or a prude if you want, but…if I was offered a script and told I had to say those words, I would have turned down the script."

He would not turn down good clean gifts, however, like the $1 million in video equipment that Sony offered to donate to his presidential library. Reagan said that Sony's gift had no more to do with his praise of the Japanese than did Fujisankei's $2 million speaking honorarium.

—⁓—

AT DECADE'S END the Universal Studios Tour topped 5 million visitors a year, still making it third among the nation's top attractions. Only Disney World and Dis-neyland were bigger, a fact that stuck in Sid Sheinberg's craw like a pair of undi-gested mouse ears.

Since moving from Paramount to Disney Studios at the end of 1984, CEO Michael Eisner officially heralded an end to Disney's traditional isolationism among major studios. With stillborn efforts like *Tron* (1982), *Trenchcoat* (1983), and *The Black Cauldron* (1985), Disney had just emerged from as bleak a decade at the box office as Universal Studios had experienced during the 1960s. In an address to the Academy of Television Arts and Sciences in January 1985, Eisner and his second-in-command, former Paramount production chief Jeffrey Katzen-berg, promised a new day at Disney. To begin with, he vowed to ally the moribund Burbank animation factory with Warner Brothers, Universal, Fox, and all three TV networks.

Despite his declaration of camaraderie, Eisner was soon at odds with Sid Sheinberg. Eisner carried a secret with him when he defected from Paramount — a secret that would mean war with MCA for the next decade. As a member of for-mer Paramount chairman Barry Diller's management team, Eisner had sat in on the proposed merger talks between Paramount and MCA in the late 1970s. He learned of the two studios' secret plan to build a second Universal Studios Tour near Orlando, where MCA could cash in on the national fascination with Walt Disney World in much the same way that Lew Wasserman had fed off the success of Disneyland in the early 1960s by reinventing Carl Laemmle's 1915 Universal Tours in order to lure Disneyland visitors to Universal City.

While Paramount dropped out of the Florida project in the early 1980s, MCA forged ahead. Then, in 1985, the men in the Black Tower got a rude shock. One of Eisner's first acts as Disney's new CEO was to announce that Disney would build its own behind-the-scenes studio theme park in partnership with MGM, right next door to Walt Disney World. Sheinberg immediately characterized Disney as "one large, ravenous rat."

"They invaded our home turf," Eisner responded. "We will not be intimidated."

Though Wasserman reassured him that it would never happen, Sheinberg lived in constant fear that Disney would grow large enough to tender an offer for MCA. Over the next few years, Sheinberg took potshots at Disney at every opportunity.

When three day-care centers near Walt Disney World painted Disney characters on the walls of their buildings, Disney charged copyright infringement and sued. Sheinberg heard about it, dispatched a band of MCA studio painters to the day-care centers, and replaced Mickey Mouse murals with MCA's newly acquired characters, the Flintstones.[3]

In early 1987, Eisner escalated the war to MCA's home turf. Disney asked the city of Burbank for permission to build its own $300 million studio theme park a few miles east of Universal City on a 40-acre site that MCA had been eyeing. Sheinberg's answer to Eisner's aggression was to sue the city of Burbank. Under the name "Friends of Burbank," MCA surreptitiously mailed anti-Disney pamphlets to Burbank residents. In April 1988, Disney threw in the towel. Plans for a Disney studio tour in Burbank were dropped, and so was MCA's lawsuit.

By the time the rival Florida studio tours finally opened, the war had cooled, but it was not over. During the months leading up to their respective grand openings — Disney in 1989 and Universal one year later — each theme park sent helicopters to carry out aerial surveillance on the other. Already a year late, Sheinberg ordered MCA's Orlando theme park to open prematurely, before all the rides were running properly, just to compete head-to-head with Eisner. The feud had become so public that Universal incorporated it into its tours. As their trams rolled by the set of *Jaws*, tour guides pointed out a pair of Mickey Mouse ears floating in the bloody waters.

But Bruce, the mechanical shark from *Jaws*, was unable to bare his teeth because of a technical glitch, and King Kong couldn't snarl as he rose up three stories to hurl tramloads of tourists to cushioned disaster. Disappointed thrill-seekers began demanding their money back. Media critics who had been observing the Eisner-Sheinberg feud for years, gave their approval to the Disney–MGM Studio Tour over Universal. *Time* magazine went so far as to dub the MCA theme park "Universal's Swamp of Dreams."

---

[3] Though they were licensed to Universal, the Flintstones belonged to Hanna-Barbera, which sold out to Turner Broadcasting in the early 1990s.

THE FINAL PRICE tag for Universal Studios Tour–Florida came to $700 million, but despite the expense and its rocky start, within three years the park was drawing more visitors than the Hollywood original.[4] Disney and MCA settled into a comfortable rivalry, and both theme parks succeeded — and even complemented each other as the dueling tourist attractions that turned Orlando into the world's leading vacation destination. Disney or no, Wasserman's Universal empire wasn't exactly floundering at the dawn of the 1990s.

Yet it wasn't surging forward into the computer age, either. Three times in three years, MCA stock moved from the low 40s to around 60, only to fade again to 40.

In November 1989, Wasserman made a rare televised statement about the future of MCA. He recited for CNN's Dan Dorfman his oft-repeated mantra that he would "consider anything in the best interest of my shareholders." Lew's casual remark carried the same weight with MCA stock that Federal Reserve chairman Paul Volker's utterances seemed to have on the general economy. Following the Dorfman broadcast, MCA stock rose $5.63 to close at $67.50 on the New York Stock Exchange. MCA's resistance to takeover appeared to be softening, and everyone wanted a piece of this California plum.

"It was inevitable that something was going to happen," said veteran MCA vice president Al Dorskind, who finally retired in 1989. "MCA was not keeping up and didn't realize that they were in the communication business as much as the motion picture business."

Universal Pictures continued to be a roller-coaster ride. While 1988 produced tepid box office results, 1989 turned out to be a banner year with bona fide hits like Born on the Fourth of July, Field of Dreams, Parenthood, and Back to the Future II, followed a year later by Back to the Future III, Kindergarten Cop, and several noteworthy stinkers: Havana, Ghost Dad, and Jetsons: The Movie.

"Movie attendance hasn't increased for twenty years," Sheinberg told Aljean Harmetz of the New York Times. "It's silly to argue whether it goes up a bit or down a bit any given year."

Universal Television was equally unspectacular. Tom Wertheimer's "hobby," the USA Network, began to show cable muscle with some original programming in addition to its broadcast of reruns. Otherwise, at the close of the decade, MCA's traditionally lucrative video arm registered no new hits akin to Murder, She Wrote or Miami Vice.

On the toy front, MCA got out of the business almost as quickly as it had got-

---

4   By 1994 some 5 million tourists had passed through the Universal City gates, and another 7 million had visited the Orlando park.

ten in. LJN Toys' first product for MCA, a paint gun called Gotcha!, had to be recalled because its paint pellets stuck in the gun barrel. Gotcha! got MCA for nearly $35 million before both LJN Toys and Coleco were sold off.

In June of 1988, MCA paid $61 million to acquire Motown Records. That was $34 million less than MCA had offered two years earlier for the rock-and-roll powerhouse, but Motown founder Berry Gordy muted the bargain by retaining its most profitable asset: Jobete Music, the publishing end of Motown, which held copyright to the valuable recordings of the Supremes, the Temptations, and other pop stars of the sixties and seventies.

By far the biggest coup for MCA Records was the acquisition of Geffen Records, but at a price far steeper than it paid for Motown. In March of 1990, with no advance warning, Sheinberg swung a deal to buy the most influential record label of the decade.

From Donna Summer to Guns N' Roses, former William Morris agent David Geffen had ridden the crest of every pop music fad since disco. He spotted Aerosmith, XTC, Nirvana, and dozens of other pop acts in their infancy and nurtured them to monied maturity and more than fifty gold record albums. In a reenactment of Decca's early Broadway successes, Geffen also reinvented the cast album, with hit recordings of *Miss Saigon, Les Miserables, Cats, Dreamgirls,* and *Little Shop of Horrors.* In 1989 alone, Geffen's worldwide record sales came to over $225 million.

But Sheinberg took note of the fact that Geffen had recently had a nasty falling-out with his distributor, Warner Brothers records. Geffen had offered Warner chairman Steve Ross his company for $50 million in 1986 and for $75 million in 1987. Both times Ross turned him down, implying that Geffen Records wasn't worth the asking price. Geffen next turned to Disney, where he had developed close social ties to Michael Eisner's production chief, Jeffrey Katzenberg. A deal simmered but never came to a boil.

When Sheinberg finally made him an offer, Geffen was ready to deal. And what an offer it was! Not since the stock swap to buy out Irving Azoff's companies in 1985 had MCA paid so dearly.

Geffen agreed to trade his company for 1 million shares of MCA preferred stock, convertible to 10 million shares of common stock. What made the deal even sweeter was that Geffen would stay on as CEO of Geffen Records while his sworn enemy in the music business, MCA Music chairman Irving Azoff, had resigned. Six months before Sheinberg offered to buy Geffen Records, the tiny (5 feet 4) Azoff resigned from MCA in the wake of the Pisello affair and started his own company, Giant Records.

The bad blood between Azoff and Geffen went back more than a decade. It had begun when Azoff managed the Eagles and the rock group became the first huge act that Geffen ever signed to his new record label. What started out as a friendship deteriorated quickly. Geffen called Azoff a back-stabbing liar and used the industry's nickname for Azoff: the Poison Dwarf. Azoff made cruel fun of Geffen's homosexuality, referring to the record executive as "she" and "her."[5]

Thus, for Geffen, the MCA deal was doubly delicious. In a single transaction, David Geffen replaced Azoff as the guiding force behind MCA Music. Furthermore, if he ever converted his preferred shares to common stock, he would become second only to Lew Wasserman himself as MCA's largest individual stockholder. On paper, at least, David Geffen would be worth twenty times as much as Irving Azoff.

Sheinberg had equal reason to savor the Geffen deal. Steve Ross, Sheinberg's longtime rival for the filial affections of Steven Spielberg, had lost out to MCA once again. He hadn't been able to persuade Spielberg to settle permanently on the Warner Brothers lot, and this time he had seriously underestimated the worth of David Geffen's record label. The fact that Sheinberg had also won Geffen Records over a possible Disney bid was just more icing on the cake.

But at the dawn of the 1990s, MCA represented even more than movies, TV, and pop music. Thanks to a comatose Justice Department antitrust division, Universal was also back in the exhibition business for the first time in sixty years. Lew and Sid held high expectations for Cineplex Odeon, even though it had cost MCA millions to seize control of the company and obliterate the nettlesome executive who had founded the theater chain in 1979.

Under Cineplex CEO Garth Drabinsky, Cineplex had expanded to 1,800 screens, branched out into film production — *Madame Sousatzka* (1988), *Talk Radio* (1988), and *Prancer* (1989) — and invested in Film House, a postproduction facility that competed with old-line Hollywood firms like Technicolor and Deluxe. With MCA as his chief investor, Drabinsky felt cocky enough to underwrite a portion of Universal's Florida theme park — and *really* get into bed with MCA.

"Orlando!" Drabinsky would write in his memoirs several years later. "It helped turn the ruler of the Black Tower, Lew Wasserman of MCA, into the Beast that Ate Drabinsky."

Sheinberg's war with Disney, coupled with huge cost overruns, turned Orlando into Drabinsky's worst nightmare. Cineplex cash came in at its many box offices — and went out again to pay for the long-delayed Universal Studios Tour in Orlando. But all the while that Cineplex poured money into the theme park, its theater chain was also growing, and the rapid expansion took its toll. Cineplex had become asset rich but cash poor.

When Drabinsky turned to cash-rich MCA for help, Wasserman told him to

---

[5] Joe Walsh, the irreverent lead guitarist for the Eagles, once carried the feud onstage when he wore a T-shirt that read "Who is Irv Azoff and why is he saying those terrible things about David Geffen?"

go borrow from a bank. He was just as brusque when Drabinsky asked him to sell MCA's shares back so that Cineplex could again be a private company. "We bought into a public company," Wasserman told Drabinsky, "and we want it to remain a public company."

Angered, Drabinsky struck a deal with the Bronfman family of Montreal to secretly buy back control of his company in spite of Lew Wasserman. The dynasty that owned the Seagram's liquor empire was the second largest Cineplex share-holder, with 30 percent of the stock, while Drabinsky and his partner, Myron Got-tlieb, came in third, with 8 percent. Under Canadian law, foreign corporations like MCA could control no more than one-third of the voting stock, which meant that Drabinsky and Gottlieb would run the company if they owned the Bronfmans' 30 percent stake, even though MCA owned nearly half of the Cineplex Odeon stock. It seemed like the perfect coup.

Sheinberg and Wasserman thought so too. The moment they got wind of the deal, they vowed revenge. Sheinberg flatly accused Drabinsky of trying to steal the company.

MCA sued to block Drabinsky's $1.1 billion bid for the Bronfman shares on grounds that the Bronfmans could not sell exclusively to Drabinsky. Under U.S. Securities and Exchange Commission rules, the Bronfmans had to offer their stock to *all* bidders, including MCA. At first, Drabinsky wasn't worried. Technically, SEC rules did not apply in Canada, where Cineplex was headquartered. But Dra-binsky did not count on the fact that Seagram was incorporated in the United States as well as in Canada, and the Bronfmans didn't want to upset the American authorities. They feared SEC reprisal if they did not buckle under to U.S. law.

Ultimately the Bronfmans canceled their deal with Drabinsky and it was only a matter of time before MCA would wreak its final revenge. Within a year, Shein-berg had forced Drabinsky's resignation from the Cineplex board. By December of 1989 MCA was back in control.

Meanwhile, Cineplex stock plummeted from $16 to $2 a share.

But that didn't matter to Sid and Lew. It was a small price to pay for van-quishing the Canadian imp who had dared to challenge the supremacy of MCA.

—◁∾▷—

IN MARCH OF 1990, Lew's old friend and ally Eugene Klein died. The former chairman of National General Corporation and owner of the San Diego Chargers, who had helped Wasserman organize the first President's Club Dinner for John F. Kennedy in 1962, was sixty-nine when he suffered a fatal heart attack. At the funeral, held in the Cinerama Dome on Sunset Boulevard, seventy-seven-year-old Lew Wasserman delivered Klein's eulogy.

As the years passed, Lew found himself delivering eulogies and attending funerals with disturbing regularity. In 1990 alone the death toll on a Hollywood where Wasserman once reigned as the preeminent power broker was staggering: Barbara Stanwyck, Greta Garbo, Ava Gardner, Paulette Goddard, Sammy Davis Jr., Rex Harrison, Irene Dunne, and Joel McCrea. The French actress Capucine, a personal favorite of Lew's, committed suicide, and Joan Bennett, the femme fatale whose tryst with Jennings Lang had once sparked the biggest scandal in Beverly Hills, also died.

Times had changed, and so had Hollywood. Adultery scandals like the Bennett-Lang affair seemed to have migrated east, where they were now grist for the *Washington Post,* not the *Hollywood Reporter.* Even lusty, loud Jennings Lang had suffered a stroke and been reduced to a wheelchair. When Lew and Edie ran into him and his wife, Monica Sellers, at Dan Tana's or some other old-line Beverly Hills restaurant, they stopped to say hello, but they never invited the Langs over to dinner anymore.

As if Lew needed even more reminders of his mortality, his older brother, Bill Wasserman, died on September 29, 1989, in a condo near Palm Springs where he and his wife of fifty-nine years had retired after Bill spent thirty years on the outskirts of Hollywood, scratching out a living as a film stock salesman. Throughout their lives, Lew and his brother had remained estranged. Bill received the arm's-length treatment even after he died. Lew and Edie had purchased exclusive family plots for themselves and their parents at Hillside Cemetery in Culver City, but Bill was buried by himself in a San Fernando Valley cemetery 30 miles to the east.

For Lew, the clock was ticking. The stock was high. And while he could never consciously admit it to himself, Lew's executive actions were not those of a man who had made even a token surrender of the reins of power. He never contradicted or gave the impression that he would override a decision made by Sidney Sheinberg, but something kept him from passing the torch to his handpicked successor.

"Jules Stein programmed Lew," said Jack Myers. "He's afraid not to stay programmed because he is afraid he might lose it. If he tries to venture out on his own in some new area and get creative, he may just lose it all. He *knew* he had to sell that company! Somebody who is brilliant builds a pyramid-shaped organization. It is real deep underneath him. You see that in Japanese corporations. They have no trouble passing the reins down because they are trained for it. They prepare for it. Lew didn't."

One agent, a man who had patterned his whole career after Wasserman's, sensed Lew's hesitation. He saw Hollywood's *éminence grise* wrestle with MCA's suitors and the prospect of saving face once the shaky promise of Sheinberg's succession became reality. He observed, he probed, and he knew something wasn't quite right.

But then, Michael Ovitz was not just any agent. As head of Creative Artists Agency, he was the new Godfather in town. In its very first attempt to quantify power in the entertainment industry, *Premiere* magazine in May 1990 placed Ovitz at the top of its list of the 100 most powerful people in Hollywood. Wasserman was number two.

Ovitz controlled the A-list of talent, and talent ran the business—a principle Lew had understood half a century earlier. In fact, everything Ovitz did was patterned after Wasserman.

Since his college days as a Universal tour guide, Ovitz had been analyzing the master of the Black Tower in much the way that Plato must have studied Socrates. Perhaps the most valuable lesson he'd learned from Lew was timing. By his actions, Lew had taught that an agent—a wise agent—weighed every element of a deal and always waited until the time was right, and not a moment sooner. Then he acted swiftly, with dead aim, and no hint of misgiving.

In August 1990, Ovitz made the first phone call that would assure him of the top spot on the puerile *Premiere* power roster for years to come, while Wasserman slowly tumbled off of the list altogether. Like the Godfather whom the editors of *Premiere* perceived him to be, Mike Ovitz made Lew an offer he couldn't refuse.

THIRTY-FIVE

Banzai

1990–1993

For more than a decade Creative Artists Agency and its chairman, Mike Ovitz, dominated show business like no agency since the golden age of MCA. Thanks to Creative Artists, agencies were once again the stable generating power behind motion picture packaging, while temporal studio executives came and went, gnashing their teeth in a feeding frenzy for the superstars controlled by Ovitz and his foot soldiers.

"In the eighties, with the growth of the post-theatrical markets [videocassettes, cable, satellite, and so forth] and the huge increase in revenues coming to the film companies," said veteran Hollywood business reporter A. D. Murphy, "the agents reasserted themselves—principally CAA, with Ovitz modeling his every move on Lew Wasserman."

Ovitz spoke often and reverently of his role model and spoke of his early attempt to read everything he could find about Wasserman. While Ovitz was still an undergraduate at UCLA, he went through an exhaustive search of every card catalog, periodical directory, and microfilm index in the research library, searching for Wasserman's name. After coming up with virtually nothing, he'd learned his first lesson from Lew: No publicity is the best publicity.[1]

---

[1] The Joe Eszterhas affair in October of 1989 proved the practical truth of this principle when Ovitz—virtually unknown to the general public up to that time—exploded into print as an allegedly blackmailing tyrant who threatened to destroy the highly paid screenwriter if he quit CAA. In a widely reprinted letter, Eszterhas quoted Ovitz as threatening to sue him: "I don't care if I win or lose, but I'm going to tie you up with depositions and court dates so that you won't be able to spend any time at your typewriter. If you make me eat shit, I'm going to make you eat shit. I don't care if everybody in town knows. I want them to know. I'm not worried about the press. All those guys want is to write screenplays for Robert Redford. If somebody came into the building and took my Lichtenstein off the wall, I'd go after them. I'm going to go after you the same way. You're one of this agency's biggest assets." While the letter did little to damage

479

While he did his best to keep a low profile, Ovitz differed markedly from his idol in the ensuing years. To begin with, Lew and Ovitz were two generations apart and barely spoke to each other, even after Ovitz had risen to the presidency of CAA. After all, Lew was a mogul who had once been an agent while Ovitz was an agent who still coveted the idea of running his own studio.

Ovitz was as different from Wasserman as his airy, functional CAA headquarters was from MCA's Black Tower. Inside the CAA building, which rose up five stories at the junction of Wilshire and Santa Monica Boulevards, the ambience bespoke Zen minimalism instead of British rectitude. Furnishings were more likely to be futons than fine antiques—a further reflection of Ovitz's ongoing fascination with Far Eastern philosophy. The crisp, stark atmosphere was steeped in the Shinto philosophy of the samurai, not the Old Testament orthodoxy of immigrant Russian Jews.

Like Lew's MCA of the forties and fifties, Ovitz's CAA commanded the bulk of Hollywood's star clients in the eighties,[2] many of whom depended upon Ovitz to map out their careers. More than any other force in show business, Ovitz got the blame for inflating star salaries to a point where an Arnold Schwarzenegger could command $15 million a picture, with a private jet tossed in to sweeten the deal. The trend that Wasserman began with *Winchester '73* had evolved to a point where top CAA talent could usually count on a share of gross profits and residuals, all the way down to video sales in Afghanistan. And, like Lew, Ovitz hijacked other agencies' stars, precipitating a war with rivals William Morris and International Creative Management.

In Hollywood, where history enjoys the same respect as writers and carrion, Ovitz was even credited with creating an innovation called packaging. In *Rain Man* (1988), for example, CAA represented both of the stars, Tom Cruise and Dustin Hoffman, as well as Barry Levinson, who directed the Oscar-winning film after Steven Spielberg, Martin Brest, and Sydney Pollack all passed on it. In addition to negotiating sizable profit participation for his clients, Ovitz served as the glue that kept the troubled project from falling apart.

Like his role model, Ovitz had learned to balance his clients' insecurities with their greed, playing them like chess pieces in a constant match with the studios and rival agencies. Afraid of losing Ovitz's favor, CAA talent rarely made a move without first seeking his permission. A producer who fell out of favor with Creative

---

Ovitz, it did shift the public perception of him from no opinion at all to that of a potentially dangerous enemy.

[2]   Kevin Costner, Dustin Hoffman, Tom Cruise, Warren Beatty, Robert De Niro, Robin Williams, Michael Douglas, Sylvester Stallone, Sean Connery, Martin Scorsese, Oliver Stone, Francis Coppola, Tim Burton, Robert Redford, Barry Levinson, Steven Spielberg, Barbra Streisand, and others.

Artists Agency risked losing the relatively few stars that movie and TV audiences wanted to see.

But by the dawn of the 1990s Ovitz had moved beyond mere movie stars and studio executives. He was getting into the business of representing whole companies. Since Sony's purchase of CBS Records and Columbia Pictures, a rival Japanese electronics behemoth had developed its own appetite for Hollywood. Matsushita Electrical Company, manufacturer of television sets, VCRs, and all things Panasonic, approached the ersatz Zen master of Creative Artists Agency in the autumn of 1989 with its own agenda for buying a studio. The giant consumer electronics firm had $25 billion in cash and securities to spend. After discouraging Matsushita from going after Paramount and steering the company away from the nearly bankrupt Orion Pictures, Ovitz locked in on Universal.

But in the early months of 1990, MCA was once again immersed in its decades-old on-again, off-again talks of its own merger with Paramount Studios. Having slimmed down from its Gulf and Western days when the late Charles Bluhdorn had acquired everything from sugarcane fields to a chain of consumer lending agencies, the new Paramount Communications under chairman Martin Davis was strictly in the entertainment business, just like MCA. An alliance made sense, but oversize egos scotched the deal. Talks miscarried over the issue of Sheinberg and Davis acting as dual, and dueling, CEOs. Given the abrasive manner of both men, it was a marriage never meant to be.

When he heard that talks had collapsed, Ovitz made his opening gambit. He told Felix Rohatyn of Lazard Frères and Company about Matsushita's tentative interest. Rohatyn was not only MCA's financial adviser; he'd also been sitting on its board since 1979, and he'd taken many such offers to the Black Tower.

But this time things were different. Ovitz's timing was right. Matsushita was serious, and Lew was ready — even uncharacteristically anxious at times, according to those who had seen him enter into these corporate mating dances several times before. Ovitz arranged for Matsushita executive vice president Masahiko Hirata to meet Wasserman at his home, where Lew impressed the Japanese executive with his hospitality and his koi pond.

Lew told Sid about Hirata's visit, and Sheinberg shared the news with the MCA board as well as with MCA's newest major shareholder, David Geffen. It was only a matter of time before the information leaked to the *Wall Street Journal*. On September 25 the newspaper broke the story, and, in the parlance of 1980s arbitrage, MCA was suddenly in play. Matsushita takeover speculation became Hollywood's newest spectator sport, and MCA stock leaped 20 points overnight.

Matsushita accused MCA of leaking the news to inflate its stock value, but Wasserman accused Matsushita, figuring the leak was an attempt to force him to make a hasty decision. Even at this late date, Lew would not be forced to do anything he didn't want to do. The leak had only hurt MCA's chances of heading off opposition in Washington, where congressional jingoists had been grumbling about the "Japanese invasion" ever since Sony swallowed Columbia Pictures.

Lew turned to another MCA board member, Robert Strauss, to clear the way past lawmakers and the Federal Communication Commission—two possible stumbling blocks. Strauss had added cachet because he also represented Matsushita's interests in Washington, D.C. Dating all the way back to the OPEC embargoes of the 1970s when the Japanese turned to Strauss to keep their oil flowing, Matsushita's hierarchy had been impressed with the lawyer.[3]

During the long weeks that followed, the only real contact the two companies had with each other was through Ovitz and Strauss. Following the incendiary *Wall Street Journal* leak, Ovitz kept the principals apart as long as possible while Strauss, who had a history with both sides, would be able to act as a crucial back channel in a pinch.

Matsushita took the first step in smoothing over the distrust caused by the *Journal* leak with a show of good faith. For the record, the company stated up front that it was not interested in buying an MCA that did not include Wasserman and Sheinberg at the helm. Through Ovitz, Matsushita invited the two top executives to name their own salaries under the new regime. Wasserman asked for $3 million a year for five years to continue as CEO, and the Japanese did not quibble.

Price discussions were not so cordial. As negotiations got under way in New York in late November, Ovitz began by floating a figure of $75 to $90 a share— Wasserman's initial asking price. Matsushita offered $60 in cash, plus an equity stake in WOR. Lew rejected the offer without coming down a dime.

Ovitz felt he had to educate the Japanese by emphasizing the fluctuation in movie stocks and pointing to the fact that MCA had traded as high as $70 earlier in the year. Slightly pacified, Matsushita upped its bid to $64, and once again Wasserman rejected the offer. With that, the very serious matter of saving face entered into the negotiations. As Matsushita's chief representative at the New York talks, executive vice president Hirata refused to go any higher. Even though Matsushita could easily have paid as much as $100 a share, to do so would have been to bow to MCA's wishes—a breach of honor and an indelible sign of shame in the eyes of the Japanese.

Neither side budged, the talks teetered, Ovitz flew home to Hollywood for Thanksgiving, and yet another MCA courtship appeared headed for breakdown. It was then that Matsushita asked Strauss to step in and mediate. While the Japanese had expressed early confidence in Ovitz's shuttle diplomacy, they had not entered

---

[3]   President Jimmy Carter named Strauss his special trade representative as a reward for his work as Democratic National Committee chairman.

upon so keen a game of corporate seduction without reserving a player who really *knew* Lew Wasserman and could act as middleman in a clutch.

After dinner at Manhattan's "21" the night before Thanksgiving, Strauss pressed Wasserman. What would it take? he wanted to know. Lew casually mentioned that an extra $2 or $3 per share might sufficiently sweeten the pot. That was the signal Matsushita had been waiting for. Over the Thanksgiving weekend the company made its third and final bid for MCA: $66 a share, plus an equity stake in WOR worth a little over $5 a share.

But there remained one final problem, for which Matsushita had found an ingenious solution: an appeal to Lew's personal greed.

Lew owned 5 million shares of MCA for which he had paid an average price of three cents per share decades earlier. If he died, his heirs would face an inheritance tax bill so mammoth that they would have to flood the market with MCA stock just to pay it. If Lew sold out to the Japanese, however, his capital gains bill would be about $110 million of his $327-million windfall. Either way, the dread taxes, which Jules Stein had taught him all his life to avoid, would reduce Lew's wealth from gargantuan to merely spectacular.

Sensing Lew's love of money and his unwillingness to part with even a dime of his personal fortune, Matsushita proposed a special deal for MCA's three largest shareholders. Instead of cash, Wasserman, Sheinberg, and David Geffen would each be allowed to exchange their MCA shares for tax-free preferred Matsushita stock. While the stock would pay hefty dividends, it could not be redeemed for years—but neither could it be taxed.

Of the three who were offered the deal, only Wasserman agreed. Geffen, who held MCA stock valued at $540 million, opted to cash out. So did Sheinberg, to whom the Japanese paid an extra $21 million just to get him to tender his shares.

But Lew's deal called for a far more elaborate execution. He insisted that his Matsushita preferred stock be secured by letters of credit from top banks. The stock would then be held in a newly formed Matsushita subsidiary called MEA Holdings, which would pay Wasserman a guaranteed annual dividend of 8.75 percent—roughly $28 million a year. The stock that the new Matsushita subsidiary held would not be redeemable until either Lew or Edie died, at which time it could be sold for fair market value.[4]

The one clear point in the very complicated deal was that, as long as he and Edie were alive, Lew could absolutely count on growing richer with each passing year while paying minimal taxes and *still* retaining control of MCA! It was the kind of deal that would have made Dr. Stein proud of his favorite disciple.

Lew told Matsushita yes.

---

[4]   Should the banks fail, Wasserman was empowered under the agreement to seize MEA Holdings, appoint a new MCA board, and take whatever steps were necessary to get his money.

Ironically, the man who had once fired an executive for failing to know the definition of "fiduciary" made certain that his own nest was better-feathered than that of any other MCA shareholder before recommending the Matsushita sale to his board. All of this notwithstanding, on the day the deal was to be signed, Wasserman balked and a satellite news conference from Matsushita's company headquarters in Osaka was briefly put on hold. Lew was uncomfortable with the fact that one of the banks issuing his letters of credit was Japanese. A last-minute accommodation was made, and the sale went ahead.

At 9:15 A.M. eastern standard time on November 28, 1990, Matsushita agreed to pay $6.13 billion for MCA—50 percent more than all of Hollywood had grossed at the box office the previous year and the largest show business acquisition in history up to that time. Wasserman took $352 million in Matsushita preferred stock out of the MCA sale while David Geffen netted $710 million in cash and Sheinberg got $92 million. Matsushita also assumed $1.36 billion in MCA debt.

There was one final obstacle to the sale. The day after the September 25 *Wall Street Journal* report, angry MCA shareholders—including Lew's old agency sparring partner, Irving "Swifty" Lazar—began suing. This first wave of suits argued that negotiating exclusively with Matsushita squelched any shot at getting a better price from a higher bidder.

Following the consummation of the deal, a second wave of lawsuits hit the courts, spearheaded by Walter J. Minton, former president of G. P. Putnam's Sons. Minton held 180,000 shares of MCA stock, which left him with a hefty tax bill. Thus he asked Matsushita for the same preferred stock exchange that Wasserman had received, but Minton was turned down. He sued in federal court under Securities and Exchange Commission Rule 14d-10, which requires a company offering more than one type of payment in a takeover to give all shareholders the right to choose among them.[5]

Shareholder suits similar to Minton's followed, but by mid-December most of them had been folded into a single class action demanding an injunction that would void the Matsushita sale. On the evening of December 28, hours before the expiration of a thirty-day deadline that Matsushita had placed on its tender offer, U.S. District Judge Manuel Real ruled against the shareholders.[6] He had no power

---

[5]   Sheinberg and Wasserman had used this same "all-holders, best-price" rule two years earlier to defeat Garth Drabinsky's attempt to wrest control of Cineplex Odeon away from MCA. When Drabinsky offered to buy the Bronfman family's 30 percent stake in Cineplex for $1.1 billion without opening the bidding to majority shareholder MCA or at least making MCA the same offer that Drabinsky made to the Bronfmans, MCA threatened suit. Drabinsky backed down and eventually lost the company.

[6]   Appointed to the bench by Lyndon Johnson in 1966, Judge Real earned a reputation among L.A. attorneys as an often erratic courtroom tyrant whose decisions were controversial and frequently reversed on appeal.

to force Matsushita to offer common shareholders the same deal as Wasserman, he said. For the time being, the dissident shareholders had been defeated.

When Matsushita's tender offer expired at 12:01 A.M. on December 29, 1990, owners of 91 percent of MCA's common stock tendered their shares; at 12:05 A.M. Matsushita accepted those shares for payment; and at 1:25 A.M., Matsushita exchanged Wasserman's shares for MEA Holdings preferred stock. And MCA, Inc. — the Music Corporation of America — ceased to exist.

For his role in the negotiations, Bob Strauss walked away with a commission of more than $8 million for his law firm.[7] Felix Rohatyn earned $16 million for Lazard Frères, and Mike Ovitz, as master architect of the deal, came away with $40 million.

When it came to running his own studio, however, Ovitz remained a brides-maid and seemed destined never to become a bride. During the long weeks of negotiation, he had let it be known that he might like to run the studio, but no one asked. Wasserman still ran MCA, and Sheinberg was still his heir apparent. Ovitz appeared to have unwittingly helped the wily old wizard of the Black Tower find a way to keep his studio and cash out, too.

———

IN A DECEMBER 25, 1990, article about the MCA buyout, *Financial World* writer Geoffrey Smith offered "a moment of sympathy for the Japanese." Matsushita pres-ident Akio Tanii had naively figured that the synergy of marrying American soft-ware to Japanese hardware would earn back his $6.13 billion in no time. After all, wrote Smith, "experts" predicted that booming world markets could mean a return on motion picture investments of as much as 50 to 75 percent.

But, as Smith wryly observed, such returns rarely seemed to filter down to the bottom line in Hollywood. Instead, they vanished into unforeseen expenses, star perks, studio overhead, and bloated movie budgets.

"Hollywood accounting is one of the most permissive art forms ever used to count beans," Smith wrote. What was more, it was Lew Wasserman's army of attor-neys who had turned the art form into a science. MCA's net profit contracts, used to fleece even the most sophisticated actors, directors, and writers, were prototypes for contracts used throughout the industry.

"It's a sucker's game, Tanii-san, trust me," Smith warned.

Warnings were wasted on the sixty-two-year-old Matsushita chief executive. In keeping with his imperial position as the conqueror of MCA, Tanii had attended none of the New York negotiating sessions in November. But he and his executive

---

[7]   Strauss also resigned from the MCA board, cashed in about $100,000 worth of MCA stock, and became President George Bush's ambassador to the Soviet Union.

entourage deigned to survey their newest outpost during the second week of January. Significantly, they made their first stop at the Beverly Hills offices of Creative Artists Agency. Only after they had paid their respects to Mike Ovitz, the most powerful man in Hollywood, did the Matsushita cortege move on to Universal City where they were mildly amused by the thrills and spills of the VIP studio tour.

That evening, Tanii dined with the Wassermans at their Beverly Hills home. According to executives whom Wasserman and Sheinberg debriefed following that dinner, MCA was to continue operating as it always had—independently and expansively. Matsushita assigned a single senior vice president to oversee its new MCA subsidiary, but he rarely visited Hollywood and did not even maintain an office in the Black Tower.

The first two years of the Matsushita era can be accurately described as an extended honeymoon, with only a few notable examples of Japanese meddling. Late in the first year, the *New York Times* published a front-page account of the production of Universal's *Mr. Baseball* (1992), a comedy about an American baseball star (Tom Selleck) who is traded to a Japanese team and must learn how to tone down his celebrity arrogance so he can become a true team player. According to the reporter's sources, Tanii himself pushed for a movie depicting humility, group effort, and other Japanese values—a claim that the proud executives of MCA vehemently denied for fear that they would be seen as mere pawns of Matsushita.

American hysteria over Japan's economic invasion also manifested itself at Yosemite National Park. Shortly after the buyout, the Interior Department notified MCA that it could no longer operate Yosemite Park and Curry Company because the Music Corporation of America was now a Japanese subsidiary and was therefore American in name only. Interior Secretary Manuel Lujan Jr. asked MCA to donate Yosemite Park and Curry Company to the American people, but Lew refused.

Congressional hearings subsequently confirmed that MCA would indeed have to sell the concession, but because MCA's contract with the National Park Service was due to expire in 1993 anyway, Matsushita was allowed to wait three years and sell Yosemite Park and Curry Company to the nonprofit National Park Foundation for $49 million.

Fears of a Japanese conquest slowly subsided, however, and the reality predicted by *Financial World*'s Geoffrey Smith set in. MCA-Universal motion pictures, television, and music seemed to cost nearly as much to produce as they earned. In its quarterly reports, Matsushita showed MCA profit margins were around 5 percent, not the 50 percent range that the optimistic Hollywood "experts" had predicted.

Sheinberg and Wasserman saw no problem with the company's doldrums. They had cashed out and were now just high-priced hired hands. In the early 1990s, Sid Sheinberg's cabal of about two-dozen senior MCA executives who ran the day-to-day operations described the post-buyout atmosphere in the Black Tower as "collegial." For the first time in many years, it was actually fun to go to work there. Reverting to adolescence as he never would have dared to do in earlier years, Sheinberg went to the door of his office each afternoon, peered out, looked left, looked right, and then howled like a wolf.

After a long, lingering decline, the infamous MCA dress code, too, finally died. Paisley ties and blazers were as prevalent in the upper reaches of the tower as the all-black undertakers' duds that Lew required of his executives in the early days. Wasserman himself was spotted one Saturday at a labor negotiating session wearing a red sport coat. Sheinberg even wore a kimono once at the Black Tower — a facetious tip-of-the-hat to his Japanese overlords.

—◦◦◦—

FOLLOWING THE COLLAPSE of the Pisello and Giaquinto investigations, former federal prosecutor Richard Stavin went to work in a law office in West Los Angeles. While he hadn't forgotten the bitter lessons of his MCA grand jury investigation, he did move on, as had Marvin Rudnick, who opened his own thriving practice in Pasadena. The two men never spoke and paid scant attention to MCA after the Matsushita buyout. Then, in the first week of August 1991, Stavin got a telephone call that would draw Rudnick, FBI Agent Tom Gates, and all the others who were involved in the Pisello-Giaquinto affairs back to MCA like moths to the light.

A gushing forty-four-year-old journalist named Danny Casolaro called Stavin with a fantastic tale about MCA, international arms dealing, and the Iran-Contra scandal. For the better part of an hour, Casolaro explained to Stavin how Ed Meese, the former attorney general, had attempted to cover up the Justice Department theft of a sophisticated $10 million computer database program and how Casolaro's subsequent investigation led him into every government conspiracy, real or imagined, of the past decade.

One of these alleged conspiracies was the October Surprise allegations that the 1980 Reagan-Bush campaign had cut a deal with the Iranian government to delay the release of American hostages until after President Jimmy Carter had lost the presidential election. Another was the collapse of the Bank of Credit and Commerce International (BCCI), which had become the bank of choice during the 1980s for international arms dealers, drug barons, renegade intelligence agents, and corrupt politicians. A third involved the Inslaw case, in which a small husband-and-wife computer software firm claimed — and some courts had confirmed — that the Justice Department stole its PROMIS software package in order to use it to break into private and foreign computer databases.

Stavin listened skeptically but with growing interest — especially after Casolaro told him that a peripheral figure in the Giaquinto investigation was one of his prime sources. Casolaro told Stavin that Robert Booth Nichols had assured him that MCA was connected to all of these scandals.

Stavin recalled Nichols as the Clark Gable look-alike[8] who had hit up Giaquinto and Jack Valenti with the idea of an antipiracy security force to prevent international counterfeiting of MCA-Universal videos. In the wiretaps that Agent Gates had placed on Giaquinto's phones and others, Nichols boasted of his long-standing ties to the CIA, the National Security Council, and other government spook operations.

The effervescent Casolaro bubbled over with cloak-and-dagger enthusiasm for a book he said he was writing about the whole fantastic story. He called it *Behold a Pale Horse*, though the single word that he used to describe the international net-work of double agents and double dealers would have been just as good a title. "He kept calling it the Octopus," Stavin recalled. "He said it over and over. The Octopus."

Casolaro signed off by telling Stavin that he planned to meet with Nichols soon and would keep Stavin posted. A week later, on August 10, a maid found Casolaro's naked body in a bathtub at the Sheraton Hotel in Martinsburg, West Virginia, sixty miles from Washington. His wrists had been slashed ten to twelve times. The local police, who found no signs of struggle or forced entry, declared Danny Casolaro a suicide.

THERE WAS NO question that fear played a recurring role in Lew's life. Even as he approached his eightieth birthday, Wasserman—the shrewd, revered, and rich embodiment of all the rewards that motion pictures are supposed to provide—lived like a besieged general, constantly aware of nameless danger.

In the days following the August 22, 1989, shotgun slayings of home video executive José Menedez and his wife, Kitty, Wasserman and Sheinberg ordered security beefed up around the clock at their Beverly Hills homes. For several weeks, police speculated that the Menendezes might have been executed in a Mob reprisal somehow linked to José's connection to the entertainment business.

According to a former MCA security guard, Lew and Sid were so shaken by the killings that they ordered their own surveillance of the Menendez residence, which was located just a few blocks away from their own homes. While José Menendez didn't work for Lew, the company he chaired, LIVE Entertainment, had recently made a distribution deal with MCA. Whoever shot him might strike again, Lew reasoned. Descriptions and license plate numbers of all automobiles

---

[8]   In 1992, Nichols had a cameo role in Steven Seagal's high-seas thriller, *Under Siege*.

parked near the Menendez house, as well as descriptions of everyone who came and went, were cataloged and carried back to MCA.

While the Menendez murders were later revealed to have been committed by the couple's own two sons, the paranoia that the sensational killings reignited in Lew did not fade. His fear of robbery, kidnapping, or worse dated back at least to the 1976 disappearance of Jimmy Hoffa, and now it was back.

During the 1984 Los Angeles Olympic Games, Lew discouraged his grandson, Casey, from carrying the Olympic torch as part of the citywide celebration — a privilege for which Lynne's fiancé had paid $3,000. Lew objected, fearing tragedy might befall his only grandson. Indeed, twice-divorced Lynne Wasserman who lived a block away from her parents' estate, was not protected by security personnel, as her parents were. Thieves had broken into her home more than once. In one instance, burglars made off with all of her family's passes to the Summer Games. In another instance, according to her former husband, Jack Myers, Lynne and Casey hid in a closet while a burglary was under way.

"What upset Big Lew most wasn't the Mafia," said one former MCA security official. Organized crime can be controlled, he explained. On the other hand, terrorists — acting on their own without any bosses, *capos* or *consiglieres* to answer to — are far more frightening.

"They [Wasserman and Sheinberg] were afraid of Aryan hate crimes," said the security official.

Just before the Matsushita buy out, an arsonist allegedly translated threats into action by setting fire to the Universal Studios back lot in November 1990, causing $25 million in damage to the so-called New York Street movie set. Around the same time, another zealot trying to get inside the Universal gates shot two MCA security guards.

Another zealot, fired MCA janitor Bruce Breitstein, sued MCA for wrongful termination and vowed personal revenge against Wasserman and Sheinberg. Diagnosed by MCA corporate psychiatrist Norman Barr as "homicidal," Breitstein claimed to be a munitions expert who threatened "to kill up to eighty of the top executives," according to Dr. Barr. A former MCA security official said Breitstein never made good on his death threats, but did mail a severed pig's head to Sid Sheinberg's Beverly Hills home. Breitstein later committed suicide.

In the 1990s, Lew made a practice of hiring retired LAPD officers to watch out for him and his family. According to a former security guard, the driver of his car had a concealed-weapon permit, was trained in antiterrorist driving school, and knew by heart which of the labyrinthine roads through the Santa Monica Mountains and Hollywood Hills were the best and fastest escape routes in the event of high-speed pursuit.

But terror in the nineties had evolved beyond the neat, predictable violence of organized crime, as Lew learned shortly after 10:00 A.M. on April 20, 1993. That morning, former Universal studio driver John Brian Jarvis drove his station wagon to a spot directly across Lankershim Boulevard from the Black Tower, loaded his hunting rifle, and began firing at the fifteenth floor. Before he was arrested in a nearby park a few minutes later, the fifty-eight-year-old former studio driver fired off more than thirty rounds.

Sobbing, he told police that MCA had ruined his life. Since his dismissal in 1986 he had rarely been able to find work. He had moved in with his mother in the northern California town of Pleasanton, and after her death a few weeks earlier Jarvis had resolved to even the score.

Jarvis had shot and wounded two employees and injured six others with flying glass, but none of them was even close to Wasserman. According to his executives, Lew demonstrated genuine grace under fire during the shooting spree. Instead of holing up in his office, he rode the elevator up and down the Black Tower, checking on the safety of his employees on each floor.

In his *Variety* column the following day, Army Archerd wrote: "As Universal employees lunched Tuesday in the commissary alongside toppers Lew Wasserman and Sid Sheinberg, the consensus was movies seemed unimportant—for a while.[9] And, as one executive told me, 'You had the feeling people are concerned beyond the deal as they came face to face with today's mortality—and insanity.'"

—◦◦◦—

DURING THE MATSUSHITA honeymoon, Lew was absent with increased frequency. He actually spent time away from the office, chiefly with his grandchildren.

Following her graduation from Georgetown University, Carol Ann Leif moved back to Los Angeles, bought a condo, and began a career as a stand-up comedienne. While it might not have been the career Lew would have selected for her, he did not stand in her way. On her twenty-first birthday he had made her independently wealthy with a trust worth millions. She and her fastidious grandfather occasionally had words over Carol's sloppy housekeeping, but she didn't take his kvetching with the same troubled gravity that her mother once did. Generally, Carol and Lew remained close.

Lew, however, lavished most of his affection on Carol's younger half brother, Casey Myers. An undergrad at UCLA, Casey became the son Lew never had. They shopped, screened movies, and ate breakfast together every Saturday morning at Nate 'n' Al's Deli in Beverly Hills. Lew encouraged his grandson's entrepre-

---

[9]   Smelling ratings, NBC replaced *Trapped*, a scheduled earthquake movie-of-the-week, with *Terror in the Towers*, a hastily made TV movie about a sniper shooting at an office building, just in time for the May sweeps ratings period a month after the actual sniper incident took place.

neurial zeal when nineteen-year-old Casey partnered with a classmate to retail novelty T-shirts and baseball caps. Any other pair of college freshmen might have been laughed out of so keenly competitive a field, but Casey had a secret weapon: his grandfather knew everyone. The witchcraft of the Wasserman name carried Casey past dozens of executive secretaries who would normally have protected their bosses from a teenage businessman wanna-be.

Lew had mellowed to the degree that he occasionally wore brown sport jackets to the office and rarely went through the Rolex-removing, fingernail-tapping spit fits that were once his despotic trademark. He hadn't lost interest in MCA, but the company was now totally in Sheinberg's hands.

Lew showed no sign of scaling back his enthusiasm for politics, however. In 1992, he adopted another southern governor as one of his projects. In August of 1991, Arkansas Governor Bill Clinton was just one of half a dozen Democratic presidential hopefuls who attended a fund-raiser at the Wassermans' Beverly Hills home. There Clinton witnessed the Wasserman money magic up close. The event raised more than $1 million for the Democratic National Committee—the most cash that a single homespun soiree had ever earned for the party. Wasserman contributed the $82,969 that it cost to put on the event, as well as another $100,000 that he gave directly to the Democratic National Committee the following week.[10]

Lew's ability to twist arms was legend. During a 1992 banquet honoring Fox Network owner Rupert Murdoch as the National Conference of Christians and Jews' twenty-ninth annual Entertainment Industry Humanitarian, Wasserman chaired the $500-a-plate dinner committee and raised nearly $1 million. Like the Democratic National Committee fund-raiser the Wassermans had staged at their home, the Murdoch banquet was the most financially successful affair in the organization's history.[11]

"One reason is we had a great honoree," Lew said at the time.

"And the other is you had Lew Wasserman raising the money," interjected Edie.[12]

---

[10] Lew also contributed $77,730 to the Democratic Congressional Campaign Committee in 1992 and MCA-Universal gave the committee an additional $10,000.

[11] As the new master of Misty Mountain, Murdoch invited the Wassermans to a reception for his daughter Elisabeth's September 1993 wedding—one of the few times both Lew and Edie had been invited to Jules Stein's hilltop mansion since Doris's death ten years earlier. Other guests included the Ronald Reagans, the Michael Ovitzes, and the Sidney Sheinbergs.

[12] No slouch herself as a fund-raiser, Edie Wasserman was honored at a June 24, 1993, benefit premiere of *Sleepless in Seattle*, which netted $2.5 million for the Motion Picture and Television Fund. Recuperating from hip surgery, Edie hobbled to the party leaning on a cane.

"The best thing I've ever done is to work for the Motion Picture Country Home," she declared. "It's a marvelous place, and I love the work that is done there. We've always felt this is a way of returning something to the community."

The Wassermans had already given $5 million to the Motion Picture Home, their favorite charity.

Through Lew, Bill Clinton made the acquaintance of Barbra Streisand, Michael Eisner, Steven Spielberg, and a host of other Hollywood high rollers who helped him on his way to the Democratic nomination. Like every other presidential hopeful since Franklin Roosevelt, Bill Clinton was fascinated by the movies and the people who made them. On August 13, 1992, almost exactly one year after Governor Clinton attended his first Wasserman fund-raiser, Edie and Lew threw a $5,000-per-person reception for Democratic presidential candidate Bill Clinton.

Three months later, following Clinton's triumph over George Bush, the Wassermans hosted a victory party for the new president. For two hours following that party, Steven Spielberg bent the president-elect's ear. When *Variety's* Army Archerd asked Spielberg what they talked about, Spielberg answered, "He spoke to me about movies, and I spoke to him about politics. Then he spoke to me about politics, and I spoke to him about movies!"

Having his very own Democrat back in the White House did not end Lew's politicking. For the next year, he and Edie hosted fund-raiser after fund-raiser for Senator Ted Kennedy, Majority Leader George Mitchell, and various members of California's congressional delegation.

On the occasion of Lew's eightieth birthday on March 15, 1993, Senator Dianne Feinstein[13] read a paean to Wasserman into the *Congressional Record*:

> In my opinion, he is one of this Nation's most clever and innovative business leaders. Lew's nearly five decades of service and unprecedented commitment to the film industry has led him to accomplish feats which would take many of us several lifetimes to achieve. A pioneer of the film industry we know today, Lew embodies strength, ingenuity, drive, and motivation — he is a role model for us all to follow. Hollywood's power and prestige would not have reached the heights it has today without Lew Wasserman's stalwart dedication.

President Clinton was in absolute agreement. Once again, Lew and Edie were getting the red carpet treatment at the White House, and Bill Clinton was getting the same from the Wassermans. The president put in a return appearance at the Wassermans' home the following autumn for an October 4, 1993, "Salute to California's Congressional Committee Chairmen." Clinton had a standing invitation to spend the night at Lew's house whenever he visited California, and whenever Lew and Edie went to Washington, the president let them stay at his house.

Lew even stayed in the picture when the president had his photograph taken, and he welcomed the prospect. The man who had once spurned photo opportu-

---

[13] In an August 5, 1996, analysis of Hollywood political contributions, *Los Angeles Times* staff writer Robert Welkos reported that Senator Feinstein was the largest recipient of Hollywood money ($589,609) and Wasserman was the second-largest contributor ($507,833).

nities and public speaking began to appear with some regularity at media events. During the first week of December, Lew made a rare televised appearance as a presenter at the annual Kennedy Center Honors, giving the lifetime achievement award to former *Tonight Show* host Johnny Carson.

And when newly confirmed Supreme Court Justice Ruth Bader Ginsburg presented a commemorative medal to the widow of Oskar Schindler at the Holocaust Museum in Washington, D.C., Lew was on hand to do what he did best: combine show biz with politics. As he and Edie stood by with the Clintons, TV news cameras panned from Justice Ginsburg and Oskar Schindler's widow to Sidney Sheinberg and Steven Spielberg, whose Universal production of *Schindler's List* would premiere the following evening at Universal's Cineplex Odeon theater in downtown Washington.

Just as Bill Clinton represented Lew Wasserman's ultimate triumph in politics, Steven Spielberg represented Sid Sheinberg's ultimate triumph in the movie business. As it turned out, 1993 was not only Bill Clinton's first year as president, it was also *the* pivotal year in Spielberg's career.

Sheinberg's best-known protégé cinched the 1993 box office sweepstakes with the release of *Jurassic Park*, which supplanted *E.T.* as the highest-grossing movie of all time. By summer's end, Universal's ultimate dinosaur romp had earned over $400 million and boosted MCA's revenues to $4.1 billion, giving it the highest operating margin of any of Matsushita's divisions.

When the owlish forty-seven-year-old director stepped to the podium at the Sixty-sixth Annual Academy Awards the following April to accept his award as Best Director of 1993 for *Schindler's List*, his passion to sell emotion as well as popcorn was at its peak. By all rights, Sid Sheinberg, Lew Wasserman, and their Japanese owners ought to have been as jubilant as Steven Spielberg.

But they were not. As the third anniversary of the Matsushita takeover loomed, MCA management and Matsushita's conservative hierarchy could agree on almost nothing. Increasingly, Sheinberg's rants and Wasserman's restrained outrage punctuated their confrontations with Matsushita's stolid Japanese bureaucracy.

The honeymoon was over.

THIRTY-SIX

The End

1994—1995

Trouble surfaced as early as 1992, when Matsushita tightened its creative and financial hold on MCA, ordering a freeze on executive salaries and year-end bonuses. Wall Street wondered if, and when, Wasserman, Sheinberg, and perhaps David Geffen would admit that they had made a mistake and buy MCA back.

But Hollywood veterans predicted a different outcome.

"[Wasserman's] moment passed when he sold his company," perennial studio executive Barry Diller recalled in later years.

When he was younger, Lew might have relished the scheming that it would require to retake his company, but now he was just too tired for that sort of confrontation.

"I think if he had sold the company twenty years ago, when he was more full of piss and vinegar, he could have handled Matsushita," said former United Artists executive Max Youngstein.

But Sid Sheinberg, who was not yet sixty, was not too old. He slowly worked himself into permanent petulance over the differences that had arisen between the Japanese manufacturing giant and its new American subsidiary. MCA made movies, TV, and music while Matsushita made everything else.[1] The Japanese could not understand why making a movie was any more or less profitable than making hand saws or patio furniture. Shortly after buying MCA, Matsushita executives suggested that the company make more hit movies and stop making flops,

---

[1] Matsushita products included TVs, VCRs, soldering equipment, radios, toaster ovens, stereos, cameras, tape machines, planes, kitchen cabinets, books, loose-leaf binders, china, plumbing fixtures, earthenware fittings, bathroom accessories, welding torches, computers, computer peripherals, microwave ovens, office machines, vending machines, air conditioners, heaters, refrigerators, motors, generators, household cooking equipment, home and farm freezers, washing machines, can openers, etc.

as if there were a quality-control system as suitable to fabricating films as there was for VCRs. All of Sheinberg's explanations fell on deaf ears.

One Matsushita executive traced the schism to the Japanese business principle of *kaizen*, or incremental improvement. Like all movie companies, MCA had bad years followed by good, and nothing short of an oracle would change that. At the beginning of 1994, for example, no sober studio executive could have predicted that movies about a a good-natured dimwit *(Forrest Gump)*, a pair of philosophical hit men *(Pulp Fiction)*, and a spy who spends too much time away from home *(True Lies)* would be among the year's biggest hits.

The Universal Pictures slate for 1994 looked far more promising. Among other releases, Sheinberg and production chief Tom Pollock had approved *The Little Rascals*, a movie based on the perennial kids' TV series; *Junior*, a topical turn-the-tables comedy starring the always bankable Arnold Schwarzenegger as a man who becomes a mom; *The Paper*, a tough newspaper drama directed by the highly respected Ron Howard; *The Shadow*, starring Alec Baldwin as the classic radio superhero; and *The Getaway*, a surefire remake starring Baldwin and Kim Basinger.

All five movies tanked. MCA's big hit for the year was a live-action version of the long-running animated TV series, *The Flintstones*. By year's end, that unlikely jewel in the Universal crown had taken in over $260 million at the box office. In the movie and TV business, *kaizen* clearly didn't work.

The music business was almost as unpredictable, but Sheinberg's answer was as old as the Music Corporation of America itself: buy the competition and expand the market share. When Britain's Virgin Records, home to the Rolling Stones and Janet Jackson, came on the market at the end of 1992, Sheinberg saw a chance to expand the MCA Music Group beyond its growth in the 1980s, when MCA had acquired ABC, Infinity, Motown, and Geffen Records. But when he asked for $600 million to start the bidding, Matsushita declined. Virgin, which could have made MCA a global power in the record business, went instead to Britain's Thorn-EMI for $973 million.

Following the Virgin Records snub, Sheinberg got worse news: Matsushita switched management.

At the end of 1993 falling sales and bad loans forced Matsushita President Akio Tanii and his executive vice president for financial affairs, Masahiko Hirata, to resign. The two men most responsible for Matsushita's 1990 acquisition of MCA were replaced by Yoichi Morishita—a far more conservative corporate president handpicked by the company's legendary archconservative chairman, Masaharu Matsushita—and Mamoru Furuichi, a senior vice president who did not understand, or care to understand, the idiosyncracies of doing business in Hollywood.

Most outsiders would have guessed that MCA was running at the time like a fine-tuned racing engine. While other California corporations were downsizing during the region's worst recession in more than a decade, MCA seemed to weather it quite well. At Universal City headquarters, the hugely popular Universal City-Walk opened next door to the eighteen-screen Cineplex Odeon, the country's most successful theater complex. A new office building went up, a 3,000-car parking garage was added, and four more acres were prepared for a second CityWalk.

In Orlando the studio tour drew 7.4 million visitors a year, prompting MCA to announce plans for a second Florida theme park. This one would be populated by Marvel Comics characters like the Incredible Hulk and X-Men, and would include a new thrill ride based on Spielberg's *Jurassic Park*. With five new hotels, the entire project was estimated to increase the MCA workforce in Florida from 4,000 to 18,000.

Yet Matsushita remained as obdurate as a stone Buddha when it came to the big-business crapshoots that Lew and Sid wanted to make. Still licking their wounds over the lost chance to acquire Virgin Records, Wasserman and Sheinberg decided to try making their case once again in Osaka—this time to Chairman Matsushita himself. Matsushita's new management team aside, their Japanese sovereigns could not argue with the bottom line. Spielberg's hits and the tourism surge in Orlando proved that MCA was on a roll.

The time was ripe to make a pitch for a TV network. If he and Sheinberg pulled it off, Lew's long-held dream of running every element in the entertainment food chain—studio, theaters, *and* a network—would be the crowning achievement in his remarkable career. The largest share of an American network that the FCC would allow a foreign-owned corporation like Matsushita to own was 25 percent, but that would be more than enough for MCA's purposes.

By 1994, Universal Television's original TV production had shrunk to *Coach* and *Murder, She Wrote*. Once its premier cash cow, TV now represented a trickle.[2] Competition stiffened once Ronald Reagan left the White House and the Financial Interest and Syndication rules that kept networks out of the production business were finally put to death. With the demise of fin-syn, NBC, ABC, and CBS began producing their own programs or striking partnerships with independents, squeezing Universal out of the market.

Fox, Warner, and Paramount fought back by creating their own networks. Disney made the boldest move of all when Sheinberg's nemesis, Michael Eisner, bought ABC. Of the major studios, MCA alone had no guaranteed network outlet for its programs. Without it, MCA was severely handicapped, if not irreparably crippled in the rapidly evolving mass media business.

---

[2]   Within a year, MCA-TV would hit the lowest ebb in its history. Spielberg's *SeaQuest DSV*—the most expensive TV series in history at $2 million per episode—hadn't found an audience after two seasons, and MCA's other new offerings, NBC's *Earth 2*, Fox's *Partners* and *Sliders*, and CBS's *American Gothic*, sank before half the season was over. *Coach* and *Murder, She Wrote* were canceled, and MCA was reduced to producing two off-network hits, *Hercules: The Legendary Journeys* and *Xena: Warrior Princess*.

Thus, when they heard that CBS might be for sale, Lew and Sid rose to the occasion like a pair of aging foxhounds. At the beginning of 1994 they set out to find an investment partner. Then they prepared to joust with the Japanese for the cash they would need to buy the late Bill Paley's broadcast network.[3]

—*~~*—

NEARLY EVERY DAY for more than twenty years, Sid Sheinberg and Lew Wasserman lunched together at the Universal commissary. As with Lew and Jules before them, their public personas evolved into good cop–bad cop, and Lew had finally settled into the role of good cop after serving for nearly a generation as Jules Stein's bad cop.

"Sid Sheinberg has acquired this reputation as the MCA tough guy, but when it's time to get tough, it's still up to Lew," one unnamed MCA "insider" told *Variety* editor Peter Bart.

Except on the rarest of occasions, Lew had abandoned his tantrums. He no longer raved or roared or fired pencils across his desk like poison darts. Yet he remained the unchallenged master of instilling fear in foes.

"The most chilling thing that Lew could say to you was that you had disappointed him," said one of his closest confidants. Those who disappointed Lew once never had an opportunity to do so a second time. Indeed, Wasserman could leave scorched earth where more reasonable men would leave bygones.

For nearly a generation the American Film Institute suffered Lew's wrath because its president, George Stevens Jr., had disappointed him. The institute had been created in 1967 under President Johnson at the urging of Wasserman and Jack Valenti. Its mandate included the preservation of historic films. Less than a year after Stevens became its first president, staff archivist Sam Kula came to him with a copy of *The King of Jazz*, an extremely rare documentary featuring orchestra leader Paul Whiteman. Filmed under the auspices of Carl Laemmle's Universal in the late 1920s, *The King of Jazz* had long been believed lost. But a British collector contacted Kula and offered to give the Film Institute his copy of the movie, provided the collector remained anonymous.

When Lew heard the story, he demanded the collector's identity. The man had somehow acquired Universal property, Wasserman argued, and should at the very least be questioned by MCA lawyers. Stevens refused. If the collector hadn't voluntarily turned over the film, he said, *The King of Jazz* never would have been

---

[3] Brothers Laurence and Preston Tisch took control of CBS in 1986, sold off all but its TV and radio divisions, and stole David Letterman from NBC in 1993 in a drive to rebuild the third-place "Tiffany" network into a broadcasting power again.

preserved at all. Stevens saw to it that *The King of Jazz* became a permanent part of the Library of Congress.

While Stevens won his point, the American Film Institute lost the backing of Lew Wasserman. He didn't hate Stevens or speak ill of him, but he never let Stevens forget that he was disappointed in him. Until Stevens left the AFI presidency in the 1980s to assume an executive position with the Kennedy Center in Washington, D.C., Wasserman refused to help the institute.

"Lew and I were always friends," said Stevens, son of the Oscar-winning director of *A Place in the Sun* and *Giant*. "But Lew compartmentalizes his thinking. He never held the same attitude toward the Kennedy Center, when I took over, that he did about AFI. He believed he was right about this one thing on *The King of Jazz*, and he never forgot."

Similarly, Wasserman did not easily forgive a snub by the Los Angeles Music Center president Esther Wachtel. Whether by accident or by intention, Wachtel neglected to publicly recognize Lew as the founding president of the Music Center Theater Group during its twenty-fifth anniversary celebration in 1992. To the horror of many patrons, Lew turned his back on the Music Center.

A similar faux pas nearly cost UCLA Lew's patronage when Wasserman believed that he had not been accorded the proper respect. Bill Sheinberg, the younger of Sid Sheinberg's two sons, wanted to attend UCLA Law School in the early 1980s, but he had neither the test scores nor the grades to qualify. Sheinberg persuaded Lew to lobby UCLA Chancellor Charles Young on his son's behalf, but Young left the task of calling Lew with the disappointing news to Susan Prager, the law school dean.

Lew blew up. As a major UCLA supporter, he expected personal attention from the highest levels, not from Prager. Through former chancellor Franklin Murphy, who had become chairman of Times Mirror, Lew let Young know just how disappointed he was. He then resigned from the university's planning committee. Despite a chastened Chancellor Young's pleas for understanding, Lew turned his back on UCLA for several years.[4]

Meanwhile, Sid's younger son went elsewhere to law school.[5]

---

[4] Lew began to soften by 1992, when he and Edie established the Wasserman Film Production Fellowships for UCLA film students. Two years later, the couple funded the Wasserman Scholars Endowment at the school and, in March 1998, they pledged $10 million to UCLA, chiefly for undergraduate scholarships. They also gave their Palm Springs home to the university for retreats, conferences, and meetings. Showing their appreciation, university officials conferred the UCLA Medal on Lew in 1996, during the same graduation ceremonies at which grandson Casey received his bachelor's degree.

[5] Sid's elder son, on the other hand, risked going to jail. During early negotiations for the Matsushita buyout, Jonathan Sheinberg passed the news to friends who, like Jonathan, bought MCA stock while its price was still languishing around the forty-dollar mark. Following the *Wall Street Journal* revelation that Matsushita was negotiating, MCA stock shot up more than twenty dollars

BY THE SPRING of 1994, newspapers were already having a field day with Universal's *Waterworld*, a postapocalyptic fantasy pitting good Kevin Costner against evil Dennis Hopper on a floating man-made atoll. Everything about the Universal epic was big—especially its production budget. Leaks from its shooting location in Hawaii had already put *Waterworld*'s budget way beyond $100 million. Repeated disasters with a sinking set threatened to push both the shooting schedule and the costs ever higher.

Sid Sheinberg spoke about the movie almost philosophically, treading a delicate line between defending *Waterworld* and distancing himself from it. "I don't think anyone should make pictures that cost this much money," he told the *Hollywood Reporter* before catching himself and adding, "I think we have a good picture."

But *Waterworld* became far more than a picture, good or bad, during the summer of 1994. It became the latest symbol of Hollywood excess—a monstrously sprawling film that cost too much to begin with and continued to suck off more cash every day. Meanwhile, the daily rushes were less than spectacular, and its predicted reputation as the largest neutron bomb in film history swelled each time another news report nudged the production budget a little higher. Not since *Heaven's Gate* in 1980 had a movie seemed so out of control or so preordained to fail. With *Waterworld*, Sid and Lew were able to send a not-so-subtle message to Osaka: if you can't afford the stakes, get out of the game.

"You know why *Waterworld* cost so much money?" said one of Wasserman's former confidants. "They wanted to make the Japanese say uncle and sell MCA back to them real cheap. That was their first ploy. When that didn't work, they started insulting them. And Matsushita said, 'You don't understand our culture. We lose face, that is very bad thing. You cause us to lose face, bye-bye! You will see a new game.'"

Indeed, the *Waterworld* debacle didn't erupt overnight. Sheinberg's hierarchy had learned that the only way it could reasonably expect to get Matsushita to reinvest in MCA was to spend the dollars that each division spit out rather than send them back to their absentee Japanese landlord.

MCA-TV, for example, took in about $700 million in 1994. Nearly $100 million of that $700 million gross represented pure syndication profit from renting out the vast MCA television library. And yet at year's end, MCA-TV showed abysmal earnings of only $5 million. To Matsushita's auditors, the huge operating overhead made no sense at all.

---

a share. Jonathan and friends sold out quickly, making a killing, and were later fined by the SEC for trading on insider information.

Against such a background, the spiraling *Waterworld* budget of the Universal Pictures division was not merely excessive; it was insulting.

It was in this toxic climate that Wasserman and Sheinberg flew to Osaka in September 1994 to discuss their latest proposal. They wanted to join with ITT in a joint bid to acquire CBS Television. At Matsushita headquarters, the two top MCA executives were shown into a conference room where several polite but lower-level executives awaited them. Like a pair of screenwriters making a pitch to executives who had no power to green-light a movie, Lew and Sid spent the next two humiliating hours rehearsing their CBS proposal with vice presidents who could not have approved such a plan even if they'd wanted to. Finally, just before lunch, Matsushita's president, Yoichi Morishita, entered the room and said, "I see you have been told."

"Told what?" Sheinberg wanted to know.

"You mean you haven't told them yet?" asked Morishita, panning the conference table with a mildly reproving look at his subordinates. The CBS acquisition, he announced, had been rejected — a decision that had been made before Sheinberg and Wasserman ever set foot on the airliner that brought them to Japan.

"Sid was livid," recalled an MCA vice president. "He got up, stormed out, got on a plane, and flew home. Practically said, 'Fuck you.'"

Sheinberg wrote Morishita a bitter letter upon his return to Los Angeles. He demanded another opportunity to make the case for buying CBS as well as any other properties that he and Wasserman deemed beneficial to MCA's continued growth. When they'd made the original deal to sell MCA, it was with the clear understanding that Lew and Sid would operate autonomously. Matsushita now seemed intent on violating that understanding.

On October 18, 1994, Lew and Sid again met with a Matsushita delegation. This time President Morishita and his subordinates flew to San Francisco, where they listened to Sheinberg and Wasserman for five hours before again saying no.

Following that meeting, Sheinberg went public. "He bashed the bejesus out of Matsushita in an interview he gave the *New York Times*," said one former MCA executive. "I doubt Sid did it without strategizing with Lew."

In this high-stakes game of bluff and bluster, Sheinberg's ace in the hole was Steven Spielberg. The director's dinosaurs, sharks, and cuddly extraterrestrials were at least as popular in Japan as they were in the United States. Even the harshest of Sheinberg's many Matsushita critics knew that Spielberg had been absolutely loyal to Sid. Alienating Sheinberg could mean alienating Spielberg as well.

Thus when Steven announced that he and a couple pals wanted to start their own movie studio, the revelation had repercussions far beyond any novelty news value.

The same fateful week that Lew and Sid first flew to Osaka with their ill-fated CBS bid, Spielberg, David Geffen, and Jeffrey Katzenberg held a press conference to announce the creation of DreamWorks SKG, the first attempt to start a brand-new studio since Francis Coppola's ill-fated Zoetrope Studio of the early 1980s. One of Spielberg's initial proposals was to dissolve his Amblin Productions and establish DreamWorks on a 35-acre site on Universal's back lot, a move that underscored his long-standing loyalty to Sid.

Wall Street immediately speculated that DreamWorks would align with Sheinberg, thus helping Lew's perpetual heir apparent raise financing to buy back part — or perhaps all — of MCA. But an equity stake wouldn't come cheap. Earlier in the year Viacom's chairman, Sumner Redstone, had engaged in a bidding war with QVC Television's Barry Diller to acquire Paramount Studios. Every day the bids and counterbids boosted the price higher. When the smoke cleared, Redstone won with a bid of $10 billion. For months afterward the value of entertainment companies hit the moon.

If Lew and Sid wanted MCA back, the scuttlebutt on Wall Street was that Matsushita would make them pay nearly twice the $6.7 billion that the Japanese had spent in 1990. With all his contacts and clout, even Wasserman couldn't conjure up that kind of money.

The Matsushita buyout had made Lew one of the richest men in the country, according to *Forbes* magazine's annual tabulation of the 400 wealthiest Americans. But it also bound him to the Japanese. Even if his $450 million net worth had not been tied up in Matsushita preferred stock, it would have paled next to the billions generated by his Matsushita taskmasters.

It would take someone with a lot more assets than Lew Wasserman to buy MCA. Someone with an ego as large as Lew's, a taste for the ups and downs of show business, and a bottomless pool of capital — the kind of money only oil, drugs, or booze seemed capable of generating.

—⁓—

WHEN LEW WAS still a little boy, Sam Bronfman sold hooch to Moe Dalitz and the Mayfield Road Gang to lubricate their casinos on the outskirts of Cleveland. Seagram kept America tipsy during Prohibition, and once it was over, Sam cut his best bonded whisky with grain alcohol and marketed it legitimately as blended booze, commanding premium prices both in the United States and around the world. Sam tempered his natural tendency toward greed by giving generously to both politicians and charitable causes. He taught his children to do the same. Sam Bronfman would always be labeled an avaricious rumrunner, but his progeny didn't have to be.

As chairman of the World Jewish Congress, Sam Bronfman's eldest son had erased the stench of the founding father's career as deftly as the Kennedy family once had done. The personal fortune of Edgar Bronfman, one of the world's richest men, was estimated at $2.5 billion in 1994, but he was recognized as much for his activism on behalf of Israel as he was for his role as the world's largest purveyor of whiskey.

Edgar rediscovered Judaism in a big way after he celebrated his fiftieth birthday. He endowed a chair in Jewish studies at Columbia University and another at New York University, he established the Edgar Bronfman Center for Jewish Life in New York, and he donated with equal generosity to the Jewish Museum. But it would have been a mistake to interpret his faith and philanthropy as softheaded sentiment. When it came to making deals, Edgar Bronfman Sr. was every bit his father's son.

Beginning with his 1968 purchase of a 15 percent stake in MGM, Edgar had tasted all the glamour of Hollywood that he wanted. His brief tenure as a pretender to Louis B. Mayer's empty throne, plus his subsequent creation of Sagittarius Productions, sated Bronfman's appetite for gala movie premieres, Beverly Hills air kissing, and the empty exercise of dating starlets.

While he had matured to a more sophisticated game of international finance, his son, Edgar Miles Bronfman Jr., was still young and somewhat callow. Like his father before him, Edgar Junior had chased the Hollywood rainbow since his teens. He dutifully worked his way up the management chain in the family business,[6] but continued to lust after show business. Besides working for producer David Puttnam[7] and later producing on his own (*The Border* [1982]), Edgar Junior considered himself a serious songwriter. Under the pen name Junior Miles (a combination of "Junior" and his middle name), he composed tender love songs.

Dionne Warwick sang Bronfman's "Whisper in the Dark" on one of her albums, and the titles of many of his other songs reflected the dreamy sentimentality of a young romantic: "In Your Arms," "Our Love Affair Is Over," "When Love Goes," "The Man Who Loves You," "Quiet Sound of You and I," and "If I Didn't Love You." Edgar Junior told interviewers that his favorite composers were Cole Porter and Stephen Sondheim, while his favorite movie was *Cabaret*.

When pop singer Bruce Roberts—Bronfman's longtime songwriting partner—landed an Atlantic Records contract, Bronfman cowrote three of the offerings on his debut album, *Intimacy*. In the album's liner notes, Roberts thanked "Effer" and his Boozetunes music publishing company.

For a couple of years, Effer's father had been looking to diversify. The Seagram's chairman thought about buying into the perfume or fashion industry,

---

[6]   Edgar Bronfman Jr. was named Seagram CEO in June 1994, after serving for five years as the company's chief operating officer.

[7]   At fifteen, Bronfman apprenticed himself to Puttnam during the making of *Melody* (1970). At that time, Brits were being urged to eat more eggs via an advertising campaign called Eggs for Breakfast. The phrase "E for B" soon became a national slogan. Since those letters were Bronfman's initials, Puttnam began calling him "Effer"—a nickname that stuck for life.

but when it came time to get serious, he returned to show business. He tested the waters by acquiring Time Warner shares in 1993,[8] eventually investing $2.17 billion. Despite building a 14.9 percent stake in the company, however, Edgar Bronfman Sr. was never able to land a seat on the Time Warner board of directors.

As much for his son as for the future of Seagram, Edgar Bronfman Sr. listened once more to the sirens of Hollywood. In the closing days of 1994 rumor had it that Michael Ovitz was once again shuttling in and out of Osaka, and all anyone had to do to see that all was not well between MCA and Matsushita was to pick up the *New York Times*. If someone could come up with enough cash, and if the whole thing was kept very quiet, Bronfman concluded that MCA might be had for a bargain-basement price.

Besides, running a studio like Universal might get Hollywood out of Effer's system, and when it came down to cases, Edgar cared as much about his son as he did the future of Seagram. Edgar Bronfman's entire life did not revolve around his company, as did Lew Wasserman's. He had been divorced and remarried, and he understood the value of family.

It was quiet testimony to the warm bond between father and son that one of Effer's many unrecorded love songs was titled "Dad."

—◦◦◦—

Marvin Rudnick had never heard of Danny Casolaro or the Inslaw affair until a pair of congressional investigators asked him for a deposition on his ill-fated investigation of Sal Pisello and MCA.

James Lewin and John Cohen worked for Representative Jack Brooks, a tough Lyndon Johnson Democrat from the Texas Gulf Coast whose powerful House Judiciary Committee began looking into allegations of wrongdoing and cover-up in the Justice Department as early as 1992. While the probe was initially based on Casolaro's purported suicide and the pirated software from the Inslaw company, it quickly branched out to encompass all that Casolaro had been investigating before his death: Iran-Contra, BCCI, the October Surprise, the Octopus....

An octopus also seemed to have poisoned Rudnick's own career.

"It's my understanding that you believe MCA had something to do with your demise," Lewin said to Rudnick during his deposition.

"Somehow," said Rudnick.

"Why didn't you sue them?"

"I didn't want to spend the money and time and effort to go ahead and fight a lawsuit," said Rudnick. "I had to go and start a law practice. It's a fair question,

---

[8]   Shortly thereafter, Bruce Roberts won his contract with Atlantic Records, a Time Warner subsidiary.

though. I will tell you another thing. They're a big company. They have all the resources in the world. I would be spending all my time in answering interrogatories and going through depositions....I mean, they would just tear me apart."

Rudnick had already had his fill of MCA. He'd lost his livelihood, been followed by MCA goons, made an appearance on *60 Minutes* during which both he and Stavin laid out all that they knew—or thought they knew—about Ronald Reagan's Justice Department and its systematic dismantling of any investigation that might implicate MCA.

Nothing made any difference. The Black Tower remained unassailable. Shortly after Rudnick left, the Justice Department even dissolved its Organized Crime Strike Force. Bobby Kennedy's thirty-year-old experiment in trying to tame the Mob was as dead as Danny Casolaro, but the only thing that had happened to Lew Wasserman was that he'd hoodwinked the Japanese into buying MCA, making himself even richer and more powerful in the process.

Rudnick had concluded that poking around MCA was not only futile; it could also be hazardous to one's health. In his deposition, Rudnick said he had even heard that the mysterious Robert Booth Nichols, who purported to work for MCA, had threatened to sue, then kill, the FBI's Tom Gates if Gates persisted in digging through MCA's dirty laundry.[9] Nothing would surprise Rudnick...or at least he didn't think it would.

"We have been informed by FBI officials that several volumes of the MCA investigation are missing," Lewin said.

"From?" Rudnick asked incredulously, sitting forward in his chair.

"From several locations, including the FBI offices here."

"About the strike force?" Rudnick persisted.

"Yes, sir."

"*That's* missing too?"

"I don't have any specificity, other than apparently it's several volumes. Would this be unusual?"

Rudnick collapsed back in his chair, shaking his head as if he'd just had his face slapped, hard. "Oh, I should hope so," he said slowly. "I find that very significant, if it is missing."

"I said *may* be missing," said Lewin. "They don't know."

"Well, either they have it or they don't," said Rudnick. "I mean, the FBI keeps track. That's what they do. They keep files on people. They don't seem to want to lose files."

---

[9]   Nichols did sue Gates for defamation—twice in U.S. District Court where the case was dismissed, and once in Los Angeles Superior Court, where it went to trial and Nichols lost. As of this writing, Gates is retired from the FBI and is serving as a security executive for Orion Scientific Systems in Irvine, California...but he's very much alive.

The MCA files never materialized. Without them, Lewin and Cohen ran into the same brick walls that Rudnick, Stavin, and FBI Agent Gates had hit years earlier. In writing about the Brooks Committee probe in the spring of 1993, *Mother Jones* magazine's Steve Pizzo spelled out the investigators' frustrations in an editorial titled "The Long Arm of the Lew." Everyone Lewin and Cohen contacted seemed to have another MCA horror story. Rudnick's just happened to be the latest.

Lewin and Cohen completed their report, finding that ranking members of the Justice Department had indeed systematically broken the law, but the missing FBI files never did turn up. Months later, Representative Jack Brooks himself sent his personal thanks to Rudnick: "This report concludes that the Department of Justice misappropriated Inslaw's Promis software and used its considerable litigative resources to legitimize and cover up its misdeeds. The report recommends that the attorney general appoint an independent counsel to conduct a full and open investigation of the entire matter including Inslaw's allegation that high-level officials within the department conspired to steal and distribute Inslaw's Promis software domestically and internationally."

Attorney General Janet Reno did not appoint an independent counsel, nor did the Justice Department admit any wrongdoing. The Inslaw affair was dismissed as inconclusive and slowly faded from the nation's headlines. Despite Representative Brooks's angry accusations of a further Justice Department cover-up, the Judiciary Committee was forced to move on to other matters.

By Election Day 1994 the strange death of Danny Casolaro and the Inslaw affair meant as little to the voters of Jack Brooks's south Texas congressional district as did the names Sal Pisello, Eugene Giaquinto, and Lew Wasserman. The grizzled old legislator who had enjoyed Lew Wasserman's political support in the past, all the way back to the days of Lyndon Johnson's presidency, suddenly found himself on his own. After more than thirty years in Congress, Brooks lost to a Republican challenger who had no interest in pursuing Inslaw, Casolaro, or MCA.

—◦◦◦—

DURING A CASUAL phone conversation one morning in January of 1995, Seagram's chief financial officer Stephen Banner mentioned to a low-level Matsushita executive that the Bronfmans might be interested in buying MCA. Within days that conversation escalated.

Matsushita was fed up. In the final quarter of 1994, Matsushita's total profits had nearly quadrupled while entertainment sales at its MCA subsidiary had grown a paltry 5 percent. With the cost of *Waterworld* shooting toward the $200 million mark, earning a decent profit from MCA seemed out of the question for the near future.

Meanwhile, Lew and Sid refused to give up their pursuit of Matsushita capital. In January of 1995 they set out once more for Japan in yet another pitch for project funding. On the table as well was renewal of their five-year management contracts, which were due to expire at the end of 1995. And there was also the prospect that DreamWorks might indeed be setting up permanent headquarters on the Universal lot.

"Conversation [about DreamWorks] awaits other decisions," Sheinberg told reporters cryptically, just before he and Lew left for Osaka. "The first thing on the agenda that the dream team [Spielberg, Geffen, and Katzenberg] wants to know is whether we'll be here."

Upon their return, Sid had nothing to report. His spirits were not so dampened that he did not celebrate his sixtieth birthday with an expensive bash at trendy Spago restaurant. The Wassermans seemed equally upbeat and untroubled; they staged a charity Valentine's Day dinner at the Motion Picture and TV Country Home, with Chasen's catering.

The Wassermans' beloved restaurant was due to close on April 2, prompting Edie to insist on eating there often. Two days after Valentine's Day, Lew and Edie attended a dinner party at Chasen's honoring former British Prime Minister Margaret Thatcher. A few days after that, they were spotted sharing a booth with Johnny and Alex Carson.

At the Black Tower, it was business as usual. Along with other leaders of the Hollywood community, Sid Sheinberg flew to Washington, D.C., in March to testify before Congress on an entertainment industry tax matter. Lew stayed home for a change, leaving the lobbying to his second-in-command in what some interpreted as a sign that he might finally be relinquishing the reins to Sheinberg. Lew celebrated his eighty-second birthday without fanfare or flourishes. All the discussions with Matsushita aside, life was good. With nearly half a billion dollars in Matsushita stock, Lew still felt confident that he held the winning hand. The Japanese might be stubborn for the moment, but they could not hold out against him forever. To Lew, who had never lost when his hand was finally called, the power politics with Matsushita now became a waiting game.

While Sheinberg was away in Washington, Edgar Bronfman Jr. paid a visit to Osaka. He wanted a commitment from Matsushita President Morishita that Seagram's would have an exclusive negotiating agreement before he and Morishita got down to business. The Matsushita-Seagram talks were to be top secret. Bronfman didn't want another bidding war like the one that had driven the price of Paramount all the way up to $10 billion.

Within weeks they had a deal. Matsushita agreed to sell Seagram's an 80 percent share of the entertainment conglomerate for a reported $5.7 billion.[10]

---

[10] Edgar Bronfman Sr. put the final price Seagram's paid for MCA at $7.059 billion.

Because of its preferred stock obligation to Wasserman, Matsushita retained 20 percent. The Japanese manufacturer would continue to pay Lew his 8.5 percent annual dividend of $28 million, but it would no longer have to put up with him or his bumptious second–in–command. So anxious were the Japanese to rid themselves of Wasserman and Sheinberg that they agreed to accept a $1.9-billion loss[11] over what they had originally paid for MCA.

As icing on the cake, Matsushita agreed to eat most of *Waterworld*'s burgeoning production costs. The *Waterworld* clause in Bronfman's contract stipulated that Seagram's was to get all the assets of MCA, debt-free, retroactive to January 1, 1995. That meant Matsushita had to write off everything it had already spent on the $200 million Kevin Costner boondoggle.

Touted as the most expensive movie ever made, *Waterworld* had to become one of Hollywood's all-time biggest hits just to break even,[12] yet Seagram's would make money on the movie. Bronfman's sole obligation was $50 million for *Waterworld*'s prints and publicity. Matsushita would absorb the rest. "We paid wholesale," Bronfman would boast later.

Both Effer and his father knew the risks in buying MCA. Since the beginning of the 1990s, five major companies had bought large studios and the stock prices of each company had slid without a rebound, most notably, Columbia-Tristar whose Japanese parent, Sony, would incur a disastrous $2 billion write-off in 1996.

But the deal Matsushita offered was too good. President Morishita wanted out, Effer wanted in, and the price was a bargain. If Effer got bored with moguldom in a few years, father and son could be assured of getting out without losing, even if they had to sell MCA off piece by piece the way Kirk Kerkorian had disposed of MGM. MCA's hard assets alone — its library, theme parks, and real estate — were easily worth $5.7 billion.

And the best part was they had pulled the whole thing off without a single leak. Even as Edgar Bronfman shook Yoichi Morishita's hand and sealed the deal, neither Wasserman nor Sheinberg had an inkling that they were about to have the Black Tower sold right out from under them.

—◊◊◊—

THE LAST WEEK of March 1995 began like any other on the fifteenth floor of 100 Universal City Plaza. Lew's driver ferried him in from Beverly Hills while Executive Vice President Tom Wertheimer drove in from Santa Monica. Sid was usu-

---

[11] Based on an adjusted purchase price, given the Japanese yen's increase in value over the dollar since the 1990 buyout.

[12] In 1998 director James Cameron's *Titanic* exceeded *Waterworld*'s free-spending record by nearly $100 million, but far from dying at the box office, *Titanic* was on its way to becoming the highest-grossing movie of all time just a few weeks into its release.

ally first in his office, having bypassed morning freeway traffic by zipping over back roads in the Hollywood Hills—a trick Jennings Lang had taught him decades earlier.

Universal production chief Tom Pollock commuted all the way from Montecito some 100 miles north of Universal. He was invariably the last to arrive, but he kept on top of things via mobile phone as he tooled down the freeway. His customized van was even outfitted with a fax so that he was just one phone connection away from Universal's grosses, internal bulletins, and general gossip, like the recurring nonsense that Matsushita might put the company on the auction block.

It was inconceivable to Pollock that the four men who directed MCA's operations would not know about such a move. It was especially laughable that Lew Wasserman, the unchallenged master of the inside scoop, could be kept in the dark. That simply would not happen. Ever.

Thus when friends, business acquaintances, and journalists began to besiege the MCA executives about a Seagram buyout, Pollock and the others maintained absolute ignorance.

But the day before April Fool's Day, either the *Wall Street Journal* printed the biggest front-page mistake in its 136-year history or all the rumors were indeed 100 percent, 24-karat true. Seagram's was buying MCA from the Japanese for $5.7 billion, the newspaper reported.

And while the eighty-two-year-old MCA chairman remained as mute on the subject as a pillar of salt, the hushed talk around the fourteenth and fifteenth floors was that Lew Wasserman hadn't even gotten a courtesy call from Matsushita.

"The Seagram deal was made without the knowledge of any of the MCA executives," said MCA Music chief Al Teller. "We were told about it after the fact, then asked to participate in that process. If you look at the various stories which emerged at the time, it's clear that Lew Wasserman and Sid Sheinberg were not consulted about any of this, and that reflects the difficulty of the relationship with Matsushita."

Pollock and others concurred: Lew had been clueless until the very end.

On April 5 the Bronfmans agreed to buy 80 percent of MCA. On his HBO comedy show two days later comedian Dennis Miller deadpanned that it was the first time Seagram's had ever left a fifth on the table. Little more than a week after word first leaked, Chairman Edgar Bronfman Sr. and President Edgar Bronfman Jr. flew to Los Angeles to sign a 147-page contract with Matsushita.

To pay for the deal, the Bronfmans sold Seagram's 25 percent stake in Du Pont Chemical, netting $7.7 billion the same week that they negotiated the agreement to buy MCA. It was the largest such transaction in Wall Street history and brought on harsh criticism from Seagram's shareholders, who remained skeptical about trading in the blue-chip security of Du Pont for a feast-or-famine film company. The Bronfmans shook off the grievances. They both knew a steal when they saw it.

Lew's shock dissipated slowly. He had to take some small solace in the fact that he still held a minority stake in the company he had helped create. By taking stock instead of cash in the 1990 buyout, Matsushita guaranteed that MCA could not be sold without including Lew as part of any deal.

Any insult he endured during the first few humiliating days of the takeover dissipated after he and Sheinberg met with Edgar Bronfman Jr. Two weeks after the news was announced, they dined at Morton's, the power brokers' restaurant of choice in West Hollywood, and certainly the proper venue for such a meeting. Edgar showed the proper deference, handing Lew a courtesy copy of the Matsushita contract, which Wasserman took home to study over the weekend.

Wasserman might have fought. His preferred Matsushita shares would have gotten him a court hearing at the very least. The friendly political appointees who sat on the benches of the Los Angeles courts — many of whom knew Lew personally and felt an allegiance if not an obligation to him — could probably have been counted upon to stop the sale with a temporary restraining order. It would have bought Lew and Sid some time to make a countermove.

But in the end, against foes as powerful as Matsushita and the Bronfmans, resistance probably would have just created bad blood and only postponed the inevitable. Lew was eighty-two and tired. Sid was sixty and quite capable of leaving the MCA nest. It was time.

"I told Edgar [Junior] that I would do anything he asks," Lew said in his first public statement following the announcement. "This is my life, this company."

Then he waxed philosophical — his version, perhaps, of Jimmy Stewart in *It's a Wonderful Life* bidding adieu to Bedford Falls in the sequel, *It's a Wonderful Life II*, when an aging George Bailey's wonderful life nears its inevitable end.

"There's nothing so permanent as change," Wasserman told *Variety*. "As tempting as it is to reflect on the past, I've always had a tendency to look toward the future. The only reason I wish I were younger is because this is just the beginning of this industry. The possibilities are limitless. I wish I could be around to see all these changes."

EPILOGUE
1995–1998

Hollywood is a place for very, very old people to go and die. Everything

is imitation except the cemeteries. They are the only real thing.

Evelyn Waugh

The Lion in Winter

The curtain did not fall abruptly on Wasserman's reign at MCA. Just as he could not easily find, groom, and hand over his throne to a successor, Lew was reluctant to surrender his company to the Bronfmans. Displaying none of the weakness of a desperate or more reasonable man, Lew went about his business as usual.

Because he was still a large minority shareholder through his Matsushita holdings, Lew could not simply be shown the door following the Seagram sale. He had to be eased out by inches. When it came to ribbon cuttings, receptions, and other public ceremonies, he continued to behave as if he owned the place.

On June 1, 1995, Lew showed up at the Flintstones Theater on the Universal lot for the unveiling of the U.S. Postal Service's commemorative Marilyn Monroe postage stamp on what would have been the actress's sixty-ninth birthday. Backstage, Lew chatted politics, predicting that California governor Pete Wilson would stand a better chance of robbing Bill Clinton of a second presidential term than did Senator Bob Dole. With the 1996 campaign just about to get under way, Lew's money was very much riding on President Clinton.

Lew hadn't given up on politics inside the Black Tower, either. In the months following the Seagram takeover, he helped broker Sid Sheinberg's move from the MCA presidency to a lucrative independent production deal. Incorporated as the Bubble Factory, President Sid joined his two sons in a family business actually making motion pictures, not just passing judgment on them, as Sheinberg had done in his previous incarnation as a studio executive. Not only would his Bubble Factory have offices and staff, but his MCA exit agreement also provided for Universal to act as the Bubble Factory's exclusive distributor. It was the richest independent production deal ever made in Hollywood. As a producer, Sid had every advantage that Lew's substantial weight could swing for him.

Wasserman also played his trump card against Michael Ovitz. As the story of

Seagram's silent coup began to unfold, it soon became apparent that Ovitz had been instrumental in selling MCA out from under Lew. The quiet necromancer in the Seagram-Matsushita deal turned out to be Lew's own best student. Just as Lew might have done in a previous era, Ovitz put a ready seller and willing buyer together even more quietly than when he'd swung the original Matsushita-MCA deal five years earlier.

Edgar Bronfman Jr.'s hope of replacing Wasserman with Ovitz was not so secret, however, and both Sheinberg and Wasserman were outraged.

"They made it clear that if Ovitz was to get the job, they would be our enemies forever," Edgar Bronfman Sr. wrote in his memoirs. Before negotiations broke down, Ovitz made the cover of *Newsweek* as the probable new chairman of MCA. Within days the talks ended and Ovitz began looking elsewhere, eventually winding up as Michael Eisner's second-in-command at Disney.

Seagram's official story was that Ovitz had demanded too much—a $250-million-plus pay package—and that Hollywood's top agent was just too reluctant to leave Creative Artists Agency. Unofficially, Black Tower sources told the trade press that Wasserman had threatened to quit if Ovitz got the job.

Lew was delighted with Ovitz's snub. At a Universal luncheon for Bronfman three days after the news broke, Wasserman said, "I have not spoken to everybody in this room, but I think it is fair to say that everyone here is not unhappy with the turn of events." Privately he told friends, "I'm eighty-two years old, and this is the happiest day of my life."

While strategically and practically Wasserman's resignation would have mattered little—might, in fact, have been a blessing to the Bronfmans—Hollywood's sentimentalists would have raised hell about shutting poor Lew out of the very business that he'd helped to create.

Indeed, during a stylish Manhattan dinner party some months later, one of the guests expressed disgust for the deluge of "poor Lew" comments making the rounds among the New York power elite. In a weird twist of logic, Lew's supporters spoke of Wasserman as Snow White and Edgar Bronfman as the Evil Stepmother who was casting poor Lew out of the Black Tower. Prince Rupert Lowenstein, a suavely intimidating German financial consultant who counted the Rolling Stones among his clients, asked his fellow dinner guests to consider what they would do if they had purchased Lew's Beverly Hills home from him. Would they be obligated to keep one of the rooms made up for Lew to stay in? Not likely.

In contrast to Lew's glee, Edgar Bronfman Jr. was not happy at all about losing Ovitz. He had no CEO, and Sheinberg began moving out of the fifteenth floor as soon as he got his Bubble Factory. By midsummer Sheinberg's heir apparent, executive vice president Tom Wertheimer, had also tendered his resignation. Only Bronfman and Lew remained at the pinnacle of the Black Tower. With no CEO buffer between them, it took no time at all for Effer and Lew to become known around the Universal lot as the fifteenth-floor Odd Couple.

Bronfman's respectful deference to Lew wore off quickly once he'd lost Ovitz. He wanted more room in the Black Tower, and so he banished the entire motion picture department to a new building on the north end of the lot. Then he went on a spending spree, remodeling the top three floors at an estimated cost of $7 million. Effer thereafter did business out of a down-home living room with elegant wood paneling, couches, coffee table, big-screen TV, and stereo system, in contrast to the austere museum display that was Lew's office. Unlike previous occupants of the fifteenth floor, Effer had no obligation to trek in to see Lew for advice and consent on every major decision, so he didn't. Relations remained cordial, but they were cooling.

With Bronfman tightening his grip at the office, Lew seemed to get out and about more. During the first week of July he was spotted in team owner Peter O'Malley's box at Dodger Stadium, taking in a ball game while socializing with Warner Brothers production chief Bob Daly. He and Edie celebrated their fifty-ninth wedding anniversary that same week at fashionable Drai's restaurant in Beverly Hills, flanked by Lynne, Casey, and Carol. Following his anniversary dinner, Lew left for Washington, D.C., with Sheinberg and Tom Pollock for a July 8 White House preview screening of Universal's summer offering, *Apollo 13*.

During his White House stay, Lew was told he would be honored that fall along with eleven other distinguished Americans. In another high-profile veneration of the godfather of Hollywood, he was to receive the nation's highest civilian award: the Presidential Medal of Freedom — the same medal that Gerald Ford had once denied Dr. Jules Stein.

When he presented Lew with the medal later that year, President Clinton praised Wasserman for carrying on Dr. Stein's work with Research to Prevent Blindness and commended him as the living incarnation of the American dream, a Hollywood Horatio Alger if ever there was one.

At the beginning of August, Effer named Lew MCA's chairman emeritus and appointed him the sixteenth member of Seagram's board of directors. Following the announcement, Bronfman offered to throw him a congratulatory party. Lew declined.

Three days later, Wasserman attended funeral mass for Eva Gabor at the Church of the Good Shepherd in Beverly Hills. Yet another old friend had passed on.

"Wasserman told me every time the phone rings, it's 'Who died?'" former MCA vice president Lou Friedland said at the time. "I think he is finally becoming conscious of his mortality."

—⁓⁓—

THE GROUND FLOOR of the tenement building where Lew grew up at the corner of Garfield and East 105th Street became the Holy Tabernacle Store in the 1990s. The rate of violent crime in that part of Cleveland was among the highest in all of Ohio. It was now a neighborhood where neither WASPs nor Jews dared to venture after dark. Glenville High had been replaced decades earlier by a newer version of the school in a different part of town, and the Mayfair Casino on Playhouse Square had become a genuine playhouse—the Ohio Theater, where road-show performances of New York stage plays made their stops after finishing their Broadway runs.

Up on the hill, in Cleveland Heights, Edie's girlhood home was also still standing. Gleaming white and well tended, her old house rose two stories above a tree-shaded avenue in a neighborhood that remained affluent three-quarters of a century after Henry Beckerman's arson trial. Unlike her husband, Edie stayed close to her roots. She called one childhood friend in particular at least once each week to catch up on the gossip.

Lew had no such use for family nostalgia and cheap sentiment. "Lew always treated his family with a great deal of kindness, but always at arm's length," said Joan Golden, the widow of a Wasserman cousin. "Sometimes we'd see him at funerals, but he'd always slip in late and slip out early."

Golden recalled one relative who had been in a terrible automobile accident. Lew wrote a check as his way of showing sympathy. Former MCA executives spoke of Lew's generosity toward janitors, valets, and secretaries. He once quietly paid the college tuition for his manicurist's daughter, according to a former vice president. But Lew's ex-son-in-law Jack Myers viewed Wasserman's charity as a crass attempt to avoid intimacy and still absolve himself of his sins.

"He had no feelings," said Myers. "That's what came of shutting off his family. He lost that part of his emotional capability. The truth is that the people he was dealing with, from the Cleveland boys to Jules Stein, all had a pretty good sense of family. It was part of their breeding. Any of the underworld or whatever you want to call it, they all have a strong, strong sense of family. Lew didn't."

Former United Artists executive Max Youngstein, who was born on the same date as Wasserman and had known him for nearly fifty years, saw Lew's checkbook compassion in a far kinder light. "If somebody was in trouble, Lew would give huge sums of money to help," said Youngstein. "He and Edie have given more to the motion picture home than anyone else. You might think that such a man would be very generous with his employees on health and welfare, and yet he would sit down at the bargaining table and cut such a tough deal with the unions. This is not one man. This is a complex human being with many very good sides."

A MONTH AFTER his protracted effort to hire Ovitz, Effer invited Ovitz's longtime Creative Artists partner Ron Meyer to dinner at his Manhattan town house and offered him the MCA presidency. On July 11 word leaked that Meyer would get the job. A short time later, Effer hired O. J. Simpson's original defense lawyer, Howard Weitzman, to act as Meyer's chief operating officer.[1] Six months after buying the company, Bronfman was finally putting his own team in place.

His efforts to coexist with the former MCA hierarchy, both inside and outside the Black Tower, changed from day to day. As 1995 rolled to a close, more and more followed Sheinberg's and Wertheimer's lead, handing in their resignations before they were asked to leave.

Bronfman's public face in Hollywood remained placid, even congenial. With a boost from Sid Sheinberg, Effer and his wife, Clarissa, made their show-biz community debut by chairing a Human Rights Watch dinner on December 13, 1995. Wasserman cohosted the evening.

But the surgical removal of Lew's top executives continued. On March 13, 1996, Tom Pollock pulled out of Universal. Within a month, Bronfman replaced him with former Viacom president Frank Biondi, completing his post-MCA management team of Ron Meyer, Howard Weitzman, and Sandy Climan, a former Creative Artists Agency executive whom Bronfman named executive vice president to replace Wertheimer.

"This represents the final takeover of MCA by Seagram," a Universal producer told *Variety*'s Anita Busch. "This is the last piece of familial ties being broken at MCA. Today it is now truly a new company."

In 1996, Effer retired the MCA name. Except for the record label and music publishing divisions, everything that had once been known as a subsidiary of MCA became Universal. In deference to Lew, the Black Tower was rechristened the Lew Wasserman Building.

Former MCA executives like Sheldon Mittelman attributed the changes to Bronfman's pragmatism: "Seagram is a public brand name, and that's what the company is concerned with—public associations. They have their liquor brands, they have their soft drink brands—everything is branded to the public. Universal was known to the public. MCA was not. I never spoke to Mr. Wasserman about this, but my feeling is that he must have been terribly hurt when they changed the name."

The Bronfmans were not nearly so circumspect with Wasserman as they had been in the beginning. Slowly the kid gloves had come off.

At a tribute marking Lew's sixtieth year at MCA, Edgar Bronfman Jr. went through the ritual of toasting Wasserman while Angela Lansbury, Charlton Hes-

---

[1] On April 6, 1998, Weitzman resigned from Universal.

ton, Peter Falk, John Forsythe, Jamie Lee Curtis, Steven Spielberg, and Fay Wray, all stepped up to the lectern and sang Lew's praises. But later, during the dinner on Soundstage 28, Edgar Bronfman Sr. was heard hollering at his son from several tables away, "Effer! What are all these people doing in *our* room?"

At the same time he was firing and hiring, the younger Bronfman began carefully laying out his own vision of Universal's future. He bought 50 percent of Interscope Records, vowing to play down the label's very lucrative but widely condemned gangsta rap. He also okayed two new theme parks: a new $2 billion park in Universal City, Florida, and a $1.6 billion Japanese effort scheduled to open in Osaka in 2001.

"I believe that Universal will have 70 percent to 80 percent of its revenue — like our spirits business — coming from outside of North America. That may take us ten years, but that's the way it should go," he said.

Still in his early forties, Edgar Bronfman Jr. had global plans for his company — plans that would transform Universal Studios into a truly universal communications, media, and entertainment conglomerate. In a highly publicized battle with Viacom's Sumner Redstone, he bought out Paramount's one-third share of the USA Network, giving Seagram's a solid platform from which to launch made-for-TV movies and new series, including *The Big Easy, Silk Stalkings, Pacific Blue,* and *La Femme Nikita.*

In a semi-merger move, he invited QVC's Barry Diller to take over the entire Universal television operation in late 1997. With his track record as the founding executive of the Fox Television Network, Diller appeared to be preparing Seagram's to make Lew's long-held dream of a Universal TV network a reality — but without Wasserman.

Effer wiped out the last vestige of Lew's regime on Friday, June 13, 1997, when he gave Sid Sheinberg and sons their walking papers. After three bombs in a row (*Flipper, McHale's Navy,* and *That Old Feeling*), Lew's heir apparent severed his last tie with Universal. Amid much rancor and Sheinberg's characteristic invective, the Bubble Factory was ordered off the lot and relocated in a Wilshire Boulevard high-rise in Beverly Hills, ten blocks southeast of MCA's very first building on Burton Way.

For his part, Bronfman had no ill words to aim at Sheinberg. He simply would not tolerate repeated failure, and that was what the Bubble Factory had given him.

In a corner of his Manhattan office overlooking Park Avenue, Effer kept a photo of his grandfather, Sam Bronfman. In the photo, the irascible old bootlegger glared at the camera over a hand of solitaire, a glass of whiskey to one side and, posted nearby, a quotation from Sam that Effer read to himself every day: "Shirtsleeves to shirtsleeves in three generations. I'm worried about the third generation. Empires have come and gone."

OCTOGENARIAN RICHARD GULLY, a Hollywood gossip maven since the 1930s who once palled around with Jules and Doris Stein's faux royalty, and gangsters like Bugsy Siegel, wrote sadly of Sidney Korshak's funeral.

The weekly throwaway tabloid *Beverly Hills 213*, itself testimony to a Hollywood that few people cared much about anymore, still printed Gully's kind of gossip. The great middle class, which once paid premium prices to get the inside dope on Hollywood's elite, had switched to TV's *Hard Copy* and trashy talk shows for its daily dose of scandal. In February of 1996, Gully's glamour dirt was distributed free from door to door in the tonier neighborhoods of West Los Angeles. There, aging show-biz pioneers still lived who might recall that MCA was once an agency, Lew Wasserman its master, and Sidney Korshak the suave but sinister mouthpiece for the Mob in Hollywood.

Korshak's passing left Gully chilly and cheerless about a Hollywood that had drawn to a close and would not return.

"The entertainment industry has changed," said attorney Don Wager, reflecting on Korshak's death. "I get the feeling that organized crime is not what it once was, and it's because it was concentrated in labor. When organized labor was big, organized crime was big. But neither of them have much clout anymore. They say there's no business like show business, and that's absolutely true. There is no business quite like it. Or, at least, there *was* no business like it."

Sidney's wasn't the only funeral the Wassermans had missed in recent years. There had just gotten to be too many, beginning with their old crony Paul Ziffren, who died in 1991 of a heart attack. Sonny Werblin died the same year at eighty-one, and Milt Rackmil passed away in a New York nursing home the following year after suffering a stroke. Rackmil was eighty-six, the same age as tough little Swifty Lazar when kidney failure claimed his life.

David, the last of Jules Stein's brothers, died on the Spanish island of Ibiza in July of 1993, leaving an estate worth $3.8 million. Ruth Stein Cogan was the only one of Jules's siblings left, and she spent most of her remaining days in a Santa Monica convalescent home. Ruth was only three years older than Lew.

Although they weren't able to attend Sidney Korshak's funeral, Lew and Edie planned to spend eternity nearby. They purchased their own "family estate" in the upper reaches of Hillside Cemetery and had already moved their parents in. Edie imported Henry Beckerman's remains from Cleveland to join Tillie, whose coffin had already made the short trip to Hillside from its first resting place in Glendale. The same month that Korshak died, Lew had Isaac and Minnie Wasserman disinterred and hauled over from their twin graves at Hollywood Memorial Park. The immigrant Orthodox Jews who had brought Lew into the world were re-interred next to the upper-crust Beckermans. The plan was for Lew and Edie eventually to join them in Hillside's exclusive Land of Canaan lawn crypts.

——◦◊◦——

WASSERMAN'S FORCED RETIREMENT from the film business did not end his political life. He might be emeritus in the Black Tower, but Lew was still a player in Washington. According to the 1995 report of the Center for Responsive Politics, Wasserman personally gave $223,249 to Democrats, and his protégé, Sheinberg, gave even more: $249,000. Other big contributors included the three founders of DreamWorks: David Geffen ($268,120), Steven Spielberg ($228,850), and their Disney sidekick, Jeffrey Katzenberg ($150,620).

Edgar Miles Bronfman Jr. gave $154,500.[2]

The following year, when Clinton ran for his second term, history nearly repeated itself. Along with Lew and Sid, Hollywood's top five contributors to the Democratic Party in 1996 were the three DreamWorks founders, followed by Edgar Bronfman Jr.[3] The top ten Democratic recipients of Hollywood's largesse included six senators and two congressmen as well as President Clinton.[4] By comparison, Senator Robert Dole's entire campaign for the Republican nomination took in a paltry $55,250 from show-biz contributors in 1996. Dole ranked twenty-seventh among the beneficiaries of Hollywood contributions — just slightly ahead of Bush-Quayle in 1992.

The Associated Press postmortem on the 1996 Clinton campaign ranked Lew as the fourth largest individual donor. With campaign finance reform making a brief appearance as the issue *du jour* on the 1997 Washington carousel, the nation's TV news commentators and newspaper editorial writers registered a jaded kind of shock that contributors like Wasserman were invited to spend the night in the Lincoln bedroom — a routine quid pro quo that Lew and Edie had been enjoying since the days of LBJ. Following fizzled congressional hearings during the summer of 1997, campaign financing continued unchanged, Wasserman contin-

---

[2]   Covering both parties just as Schreiber and Wasserman had done for a generation, Edgar Bronfman Sr. was a major contributor to the GOP, donating $200,000 in the 1992 campaign.

[3]   The top five were David Geffen, $575,697; Lew Wasserman, $507,833; Steven Spielberg, $503,123; Jeffrey Katzenberg, $408,320; and Sidney Sheinberg, $321,362. Bronfman gave $318,000.

[4]   California's two Democratic senators, Dianne Feinstein ($589,609) and Barbara Boxer ($442,777), were Hollywood's biggest beneficiaries, followed by former West L.A. Congressman Mel Levine ($401,625), Senator Ted Kennedy ($247,371), West L.A. Congressman Howard Berman ($143,150), Massachusetts Senator John Kerry ($123,400), Connecticut Senator Christopher Dodd ($114,900), and Nebraska Senator Bob Kerrey ($107,000). President Clinton's campaign received $381,649 in 1992 and $381,390 in 1996.

ued to give generously wherever he thought it would promote his personal political agenda, and the Clintons continued to put Lew and Edie up for the night whenever they came to the White House.[5]

Lew and Edie reciprocated. Whenever Bill Clinton was in southern California, he had a standing invitation to drop by for the evening. On Saturday, July 26, 1997, President Clinton bunked in at the Wassermans' after having dinner with Barbra Streisand, Michael Eisner, and Warren Christopher. Beverly Hills motorcycle cops were stationed at every corner along Sunset Boulevard while the Secret Service whisked the president into the Wassermans' driveway. Once inside, he was as safe as if he were in the White House.

—◦◦◦—

LEW STILL DROVE, or was driven, each workday to the Black Tower, which now bore his name. He ate lunch at the Universal Studio Commissary at the same table near the rear of the restaurant and always at the same time. While chatting with one executive or another, he surveyed the room like a bored but dutiful sovereign, and when he finished, he'd disappear through a rear door. More than once Lew had to fight off producers and starlets who wanted to get near enough for a photo opportunity.

Lew had become a god in Hollywood, but an old and tired god. The restless, hungry young hustler from the Mayfair Casino, who had been mistaken in the early days as the MCA mail boy, had been transformed into a figure straight out of the Old Testament—the kind of ancient prophet that Wasserman had once shrugged off as a vestige of his parents' shtetl folklore.

Lew was not the kind and ceaselessly forgiving God of the New Testament, but rather Yahweh, the God whose name dared not be spoken. An avenging God. A hard-nosed God who sat in judgment and grudgingly dispensed kindness and compassion to those few who passed His special kind of muster.

"While we all worked with and admired Lew Wasserman, I don't think any-

---

[5]   One event that came under congressional scrutiny was a June 11, 1996, Democratic fundraiser that Lew threw at his home. Among the guests were Leung Chun Fat, a Hong Kong businessman who wanted to export U.S. movie videos. Fat and his wife paid $20,000 to dine at the Wassermans'—a price investigators believed to be the cost of doing business with MCA and the Clinton administration. Investigators were wrong on both counts. The $20,000 was the cost of playing politics, and the payment was apparently perfectly legal under the loosely interpreted federal election laws. In addition to leading the West Coast campaign fund-raising for the president, Lew and Edie each gave $1,000 to the Presidential Legal Expense Fund to help Clinton defray the cost of defending himself against Paula Jones's sexual harassment lawsuit and the various legal actions stemming from the Whitewater investigation. The Bronfmans and Barbra Streisand also contributed.

one could honestly say that they knew him that well," said former MCA executive Sheldon Mittelman. "He kept his private life separate from his business, and he didn't discuss it."

At a United Jewish Appeal dinner held in May 1996, Lew Wasserman joined both Bronfmans in honoring the memory of Time Warner chairman Steve Ross, who had died of prostate cancer in 1992. For weeks Lew had been advertised as the host of the event, while Edgar Junior was to be the recipient of the United Jewish Appeal's very first Steve Ross Humanitarian Award.

Prior to the dinner, David Geffen praised Bronfman for "making all of the right decisions. He has a love for this business, and he wants to grow with it. He's the next Steve Ross."

Sitting alone at a table near the front of the Waldorf-Astoria ballroom, his hawklike glare reduced to a ghostly pair of pupils behind his massive trademark horn-rims, Lew was a relic in a room crowded with Manhattan's power elite. The tall, imposing figure that Lew had once cut now seemed shrunken and bent inside his tuxedo. When approached by a reporter looking for a few quotes from the past grand master of Hollywood, however, he lit up and was all smiles until she asked him, "Is Edgar Junior a protégé?"

"Not of mine," he said, his voice instantly chilled.

"Well, then, whose would he be?" the reporter persisted.

"His father's."

"Why did you decide to be host of this event?"

"I didn't decide," Lew answered testily, his scowl signaling that the interview was over. "The organization decided, and then they asked me to help."

Across the room, well-wishers mobbed Bronfman. When asked if Lew was a mentor, he would only say, "I'm really here just to have a good time, not to talk to the press."

During the lead-in to the presentation of the Steve Ross Humanitarian Award, the usual parade stepped up to the lectern to praise the late Time Warner chairman for his warmth and his charisma. Ross was the kind of boss who listened to his stars and executives and lavished personal attention on them, the audience was told. He pampered people and, in return, received the kind of loyalty no one since had equaled.

The fact that some looked to Bronfman to try to fill Ross's shoes was evidence of how badly show business missed Ross. Bronfman was "talent friendly"—a breath of fresh air in Hollywood.

When Lew made it to the lectern, he extolled the United Jewish Appeal for bringing dignity to people, but he did not mention Ross or Edgar Bronfman Jr. Keeping his remarks pointedly general, he ended by asking the audience to "Join me in applauding the values for which the United Jewish Appeal stands."

Later still, after Lew had turned over the microphone to Nobel laureate Elie

Wiesel, who was to make the formal award presentation, Wiesel turned to Edgar Bronfman Jr. and said, "In a way I feel sorry for you. This is just the beginning."

—◈—

"To BE ON your job and be there right up until the end, whatever that means, is a mitzvah," said actor Tony Curtis. "Whatever else you might say about Lew, he's got that."

Lew took enough time off from work to join the Hillcrest Country Club, following the Seagram takeover — not for himself, he told friends, but for Casey. He wasn't encouraging his grandson to take up the frivolous game the way Casey's golf-obsessed father, Jack Myers, had done. Rather, Lew wanted to put the boy in contact with show-biz movers and shakers.

The prevailing notion in the industry was that Lew was grooming Casey to become the next Mike Ovitz.

Lew always wanted a son, so he drafted Casey, according to Jack Myers. "My son changed his name to Wasserman," said Myers.[6] "I said, 'Casey, first of all everyone will think you're a fool if you do that. You look like an idiot. If you wanted to change your name, you should have done it twenty years ago. It doesn't do anything for you now. It just makes you look weak.'"

"He can go into business with that name," said Berle Adams. "It's still a big name. Casey Wasserman sounds pretty good, eh?"

Following Jack Myers's conviction for acting as courier in a 1989 money laundering scheme,[7] Casey repudiated his father. At twenty-four, he told friends that Lew was more a father to him than Myers.

"We have a lot of the great things about a father-son relationship," he told W's Tim Street-Porter in December 1997. "But I didn't live with him, so we didn't have to go through the problems."

In Casey's eyes, his grandparents were unostentatious and "low key." When he went shopping for a VCR, Lew took him to an Adray's discount outlet to get him the best deal. When Edie needed toiletries, she picked them up herself at Thrifty Drug Store or Ralph's supermarket. "My grandfather wouldn't even get in a limousine," Casey said. "He still drives himself around in a Lincoln Town Car."

But if Casey was disingenuous about his grandparents being just plain folks, he

---

[6] Casey Myers applied to formally change his name to Casey Wasserman on June 5, 1995, nineteen days before his twenty-first birthday.

[7] In exchange for three years' probation, Myers testified against former Governor Jerry Brown's chief of staff Richard Silberman, the millionaire husband of San Diego County supervisor Susan Golding. Silberman was sentenced to forty-six months in federal prison and fined $50,000 for directing a scheme to launder $300,000 that an undercover FBI agent identified as the profits of Colombian cocaine dealing.

found out otherwise when Lew handed over to him the presidency to the Wasserman Foundation. A successor to a charity created in the name of Edie's father, the Wasserman Foundation had assets of more than $65 million by 1995.[8] As president, Casey handed out checks totaling $4.8 million to seventy-five charities, ranging from a lavish $1.5 million for the Survivors of the Shoah Visual History Foundation to a paltry $320 for the Los Angeles Music Center Theater Group.

Dubbed by W's Street-Porter as "the JFK Jr. of Los Angeles," Casey lived in a 4,400-square-foot mansion on the rim of Gilcrest Drive overlooking Los Angeles, within jogging distance of both his mother's home and his grandparents' estate. He and Paul Ziffren's granddaughter Laura had already been anointed L.A.'s hottest new golden couple in an "Around Town" item in the May 15, 1996, edition of *Beverly Hills 213*: "Did you know that Ken Ziffren's daughter and Lew and Edie Wasserman's grandson are going together? I just love it. Just think of the potential Wasserman-Ziffren dynasty."

Like his older half sister, Carol, Casey got access to a trust fund on his twenty-first birthday. He had no plans to go into the movie business, though. Instead, he asked his grandfather to help him buy a sports team — perhaps an NFL franchise in football-starved Los Angeles.

"Sports are tangible," he told W. "You win or you lose. There are only thirty teams in the world. But someday they'll be playing football in Los Angeles."

Jack Myers said his son was spoiled and confused and had no idea what kind of a man his grandfather really was. Berle Adams, Lew's old adversary, knew what kind of man Casey's grandfather was, though. "Without bragging about anything, he doesn't have the family life that I have," said Adams. "He doesn't have the relationship that I have with my children or my grandchildren, and he certainly doesn't have the wife that I had. His wife is a pain in the ass, to start with. He didn't talk to his daughter for years. Whether he sees Carol or not, I don't know. Casey is the only one he has."

—∿∿—

ON JANUARY 15, 1997, the last of Jules Stein's siblings passed away. Neither *Variety* nor the *Hollywood Reporter* noted Ruth Stein Cogan's passing at the age of eighty-six. The *Los Angeles Times* merely made note of it in a small paid obituary, which said, in part, that "business associates at MCA, Inc., where she worked for forty years... remember her for her financial acumen, compassion and generosity."

---

[8]   Lew and Edie rolled over the $22,430 in capital of the Henry B. Foundation into their new Wasserman Foundation in 1963. According to trust documents, the Henry B. Foundation was first registered in California in June 1958 with $15.15. By 1997 the foundation's assets had risen to $78 million, and contributions totaled $5.8 million. Casey's annual salary as president was $36,000.

"Nobody ever knew it, but she was one of the most powerful people at MCA for close to half a century," said Art Heisman, an auditor who worked for Jules, Ruth, and the entire Stein family.

In addition to comanaging the trusts that Doris and Jules left behind,[9] Ruth had been one of the founding partners of a mysterious general partnership called Emseeay and Company, which Lew reorganized four months after Jules's death. The only clue as to what Emseeay did was found in the original filings, which said that any of the partners could "convey title to real property standing in the partnership name." According to Seagram's spokesperson Deborah Rosen, Emseeay was created in 1956 as part of the executive profit-sharing plan and was due to be dissolved by the end of 1998. Emseeay had been conducting unspecified business in the Black Tower for more than a generation with only one of the original partners still listed on its 1997 legal filing with the Los Angeles County recorder. That partner was Lew Wasserman.

While Lew was still among the *Forbes* 400 richest Americans in 1997, his legal battle over the Matsushita deal that had put him on the list was still not over. The MCA shareholder lawsuit, which U.S. District Judge Manuel Real had dismissed the day before it was supposed to go to trial in 1992, had been appealed and appealed again.

At one point, the three-judge panel of the Ninth Circuit Court of Appeals in San Francisco overturned Real's decision and found that Matsushita had violated U.S. securities law by giving Wasserman his special stock deal. Jane Rockford, daughter and executor of MCA pioneer Mickey Rockford, said in her deposition that all she wanted from Matsushita was the same deal for her MCA stock that Lew had gotten: no capital gains taxes and a guaranteed 8.5 percent annual dividend for life.

The ruling from the Ninth Circuit could have cost Matsushita as much as $2 billion in damages, but the company appealed to the U.S. Supreme Court, which reversed the ruling and sent it back to the Ninth Circuit.[10]

Aside from his occasional court skirmishes and the incessant funerals, political fund-raisers, or Industry award ceremonies he attended, Lew's life had not seemed to evolve a jot since the Seagram takeover. In all his life he had never made a movie and did not feel compelled to make the same mistake as Sheinberg and start at so late a date. Asked if he might finally be interested in retiring and

---

[9] As of June 1995, the trusts' assets were worth over $250 million. The dollar value of the Jules and Doris Stein Foundation alone totaled $58,070,834, but the endowment the Steins had created chiefly for the operation of Research to Prevent Blindness was worth nearly four times as much. The foundation also financed the Oppenheimer-Stein Sculpture Garden at Johnson County Community College in Overland Park, Kansas, and the Jules and Doris Stein UCLA Support Group.

[10] In the spring of 1998 the appeal was still under review by the Ninth Circuit.

writing his memoirs, he answered, "I was trained by Jules Stein who looked on clients as a doctor looks on patients. I couldn't sleep at night if I were to write about who was sleeping with whom." With unspoken irony, Universal honored him on the occasion of his eighty-fifth birthday by creating a living history program in his name at UCLA. In March 1998, the Lew Wasserman Oral History program began underwriting filmed interviews of film pioneers at the Motion Picture Home about their lives and experiences in the movie business, to be housed in the UCLA library system. But there was nothing in the Universal or UCLA press releases that indicated that Wasserman himself would be among the interview subjects.

Lew had memories, of course, but no one he could really share them with. All he really had was the Black Tower, and in the end, that turned out to be as big an illusion as flickering images on a motion picture screen.

Herbert Coleman, associate producer on *Vertigo*, traveled to Universal City in the spring of 1997 for the fortieth anniversary of the premiere of the Hitchcock classic. While he was there, he got a summons to visit Wasserman in the Black Tower. Recalling the days when such a summons usually augured disaster, the ninety-year-old filmmaker felt a twinge of anxiety as he took the elevator to the fifteenth floor.

"Turned out he just wanted to reminisce," said Coleman. "We remembered stories and people. Actually, I remembered a lot more than Lew did. He seemed hazy on things—got a lot of the dates and people wrong."

During the first week of June 1997, Max Youngstein called Wasserman's office to ask a business favor. A friend was coming to town who needed entrée to Universal to talk business. "Melody, his secretary, said [Lew] hardly ever comes into the office at all anymore," said Youngstein.

Nonetheless, Lew granted Max's favor immediately and asked nothing in return. Max, who lived in a modest apartment near the La Brea Tar Pits, was always amazed that Lew, the most successful person ever to come out of Hollywood, did not forget old friends who were a little down on their luck.

"I consider Lew like the hub of a wheel," said Youngstein. "The whole story of the industry could be told around him, but it would always come back to Lew as its centerpiece."

Three weeks after Lew granted Max's favor, Youngstein died of heart failure.

—◦◦◦—

ON FEBRUARY 4, 1998, in his regular quarterly report to shareholders, Seagram's Chairman Edgar Bronfman Sr. announced that Lew Wasserman had resigned from the Seagram's board. Lew kept his fifteenth-floor office in the Lew Wasserman Building. He also got to keep his secretary and his driver, and he acquired a new title: honorary chairman emeritus of Universal—since MCA, Inc. no longer existed.

"Although we will miss his active participation a great deal, we look forward to continuing to seek his counsel," said Bronfman.

Then he went on to the numbers.

Seagram's entertainment division was doing splendidly, thanks to the video release of *The Lost World: Jurassic Park*. Pretax earnings for Universal, Seagram's filmed entertainment unit, had nearly doubled to $113 million. Music division earnings had climbed $2 million to $47 million....

Liquor sales had fallen off in Asia, but it looked like another great year in show business.

ACKNOWLEDGMENTS

Thanks to the dozens who spoke to me anonymously. You know who you are, but what you might not know is that every one of you contributed mightily and materially to the telling of this very difficult tale. Because Lew Wasserman's power flourished in the dark substrata of Hollywood, and depended upon the silence of its users, abusers, and victims, the men and women who broke their silence and spoke to me helped shine a long-needed antiseptic glare on Wasserman's Hollywood sausage factory. Lew understood that autocracy—whether exercised benevolently or with cruel finality—feeds on information. Like the Florentine prince that Niccolò Machiavelli once counseled on the art of governance, Lew Wasserman wielded facts and fictions like darts and cudgels.

While understandably not yet ready to speak the truth with their own names attached to it, these anonymous sources deserve credit for at least breaking the silence and pointing the way. They might not have been able to shout from the rooftops that the emperor wasn't wearing Armani, but they mustered enough courage to say as much to me.

My front-line support stems from a family of stubborn strong-willed men and women who believe as passionately as I do in getting at the truth, and damn the obstacles: Sharon McDougal; Amy and Kate McDougal; Jennifer, Megan, and Bobby Cole; Mike Randolph; Tim, Austin, Cody, and Andrea Conklin; David and Sheila Murphy; Neal, Erin, and Jamie McDougal; Mike Riley; Donald McDougal; Shelley, Mindy, Pat, and Lynne McDougal; Colleen, Doojie, Jessica, Allie, and Michelle; and Fitz. Carl and Lola, my loving, supportive, hardworking parents, taught me through example that the only rule anybody ever really has to follow is the Golden one.

Thanks to Berle Adams, who lost a company but gained his soul; to Marvin Rudnick, who lost a career but kept his honor; to Mr. Roadhouse, who walked me through the fifteenth floor in the powerhouse years; to Mr. Trani, who took me up the Black Tower elevator during the long, painful decline; to Tom Gates and Richard Stavin, who revealed MCA's final secret, suffered the wrath of a dying beast, and lived to tell about it; and to all the other men and women who suffered the whims of Wasserman with dignity and good purpose, never trading their integrity for power, puffery, or pieces of silver.

Thanks to Julie Payne, a daughter of Hollywood who not only became my researcher but also shaded the nuances of show-biz society; J. L. "Cerulean" Fernandez, compatriot and computer whiz; Diane Goldner, who helped me stay in touch with my best sources; Brian Zoccola, who trudged through the tedious transcription process while constantly offering kind and encouraging words, a dual task that can only be performed by a saint; Steve Bowie, a breathing encyclopedia of movie and TV trivia; and David Levinson, whose blue pencil and breadth of knowledge are matched only by his bemused wit.

I am always pleasantly startled and buoyed up by the unexpected friendships that develop in the course of a project like *The Last Mogul.* Among the friends I've made this trip are Harold Jovien, Joan and Bill Luther, Marty Bacow, Cynthia Lindsay, Bob Patton, Susan Deutsch-Carroll, Tom Gray, the late great Max Youngstein, Jack Myers, and Herb and Katie Rosenthal.

My pals and international support system include Susan Daniels in Cleveland; Deborah Caulfield Rybak in Minneapolis; Bill Steigerwald in Pittsburgh; Toni Cook in South Bend; Jim Agnew, Ira Abrams, Pam Pierce, Larry Finley, John O'Brian, Gina Richardson, and J.C. in Chicago; Chuck Suber in New Orleans; Justin Coffey in Laramie, Wyoming; Avis Layman in Maine; Steve Hough in Kansas City; David Johnston, David Crook, and Larry Josephson in New York City; Carol Vogel in Reno; Judy Hansen in Las Vegas; Michael Bygrave in London; Dan Moldea in Washington, D.C.; Keith Carter and Mike and Frances Meenan in Palm Springs; Dwight and Julia Whitney in San Francisco; the Fictionairres of Orange County; and Dorothea and the late Bruce Campbell in Elroy, Wisconsin.

And the list continues: Jeff Abraham, Gary Abrams, Jerry Adler, Dr. Mark Alpert, James Bacon, Bob Balaban, Elmer Balaban, Dorothy Barton, Marty Beck, Jim Bellows, Lowell Bergman, Eames Bishop, Peter Biskind, Judy Bloom, Ernest Borgnine, Phil and Sylvia Borkat, Eddie Bracken, Howard Brandy, Judy Brennan, David Brenner, Roy Brewer, Gene Brog, Peter Harry Brown, Charles Champlin, Michael Cieply, Jim and Tish Coblenz, Herbert Coleman, Scott Collins, Ned Comstock, Vince Cosgrove, Tony Curtis, Frank Dana, Bill Davidson, Ivor and Sally Davis, Henry Denker, Al Dorskind, Lois Draegin, George Duning, Dominick Dunne, Tim Fall, Dave Farmer, Will Fowler, Ralph Frammolino, Dave Fulton, Roy Gerber, Marcus Gilbert, Mark Gladstone, Joan Golden, Bill and Sandy Goodheart, Billi Gordon, Bob Gottlieb, Beverly Grossman, Richard Gully, Ed Guthman, Katie Harris, Seymour Heller, Nat Hentoff, Alida Herrera, Seymour Hersh, Charlton Heston, Leo Hetzel, Robin Hinch, Leonora Hornblow, Barbara Howar, Marsha Hunt, Chuck Isaacson, Merle Jacobs, Bill and Michelle Katz, Bill and Bryn Knoedelseder, Neal Koch, indomitable Dot Korber, Boris Kostelanetz, Irv Kupcinet, Aaron Latham, Janet Leigh, David Leanse, Shawn Levy, Danny Lewis, Richard Lewis, Lillian Lipsey, Lee Loevinger, Betty Lukas, Malcolm MacArthur, Gisele MacKenzie, Peggy Madden, Michael Martin, Jamie Masada, John and Connie Maschio, Chet Migden, Sheldon Mittelman, Ed Muhl, Jim Murray, Jim Neff, Mary Neiswender, Stewan Ng, Russell Nype, Pierce O'Donnell, Sergio Pestos, Rudy Petersdorf, Paul Peterson, Marty Plotnick, Zazi Pope, Cheryl Pruitt, Michael Pye, Vera Hruba Ralston, Frances Raskin, Dave Robb, Frank Rose, Deborah Rosen, David and Margo Rosner, Don Roth, Marvin Rudnick, Peter Safir, Ed Sallee, Gunther Schiff, David and Joanna Shear, Tom Pollock, Bill and Mimi Silverman, Ira Silverman, Johnny Singer, Bob Sipchen, Ron Soble, Lisa Sonne, Jim Spada, Violet Spivack, Cameron Stauth, Dorothy Stevens, George Stevens Jr., Jill Stewart, Bella Stumbo, Norton Styne, Karen Sullivan, Tom and Donna Szollosi, Brian Taggert, Joe Takamine, Al Teller, Harry Tessel, Bob and Esther Thaller, Nick Tosches, Don Wager, Marc Wanamaker, Irwin Warsaw, Tom Weaver, David F. Weeks, Steve Weinstein, Jeff Wells, Dr. Donald Wexler, Weston Whiteman, George Williamson, John Wilson, Michelle Winterstein, Tracy Wood, Marcie Wright, Francine York, and Bill Zehme.

Farewell and much thanks to the late Julian Blaustein, Charles Harris, Bob Hussong, Paul Jarrico, George Murray, Harry Tatelman, and Jack Tobin. Your contribution was real and your absence sorely felt.

Thanks to my remarkably patient and supportive editor, Karen Rinaldi, and her assistants, Lara Webb and Panagiotis Gianopoulos; Steve Weissman and his able legal staff at Random House; Donna Ryan, my terrific copy editor; Alice Martell, the world's only wolverine disguised as Annette Funicello; and Irv Schwartz, a creature of Hollywood who somehow avoided infection.

I am also indebted to the staffs of the Chicago Crime Commission; Chicago Historical Society; Cleveland Public Library; Western Reserve Historical Society; Pacific Pioneer Broadcasters; Cuyahoga County Archives; Saint Joseph County Public Library; Margaret Herrick Library of the Academy of Motion Picture Arts and Sciences; Chicago Public Library; Lake Forest Historical Society; Highland Park Public Library; University of Chicago Library; Billy Rose Collection of the New York Public Library; Louis Mayer Library of the American Film Institute; California State Archives; Stanford University libraries; Los Angeles Public Library; UCLA libraries and archives; Bancroft Library of the University of California at Berkeley; Riverside County Public Library; Orange County Public Library; Los Angeles County Hall of Records and Archives; Beverly Hills Public Library; USC film and television library; Columbia University libraries and archives; the U.S. Securities and Exchange Commission; the FBI; Steve Allen and his personal organized crime library; the U.S. State Department; the National Archives; the Harry Ransom Center of the University of Texas at Austin; the Kansas City Public Library; the University of Wyoming library; Boston College library; Long Beach Public Library; Los Angeles County Public Library; and the University of Wisconsin libraries.

And, of course, Irv Letofsky — the last real newspaper editor that the *Los Angeles Times* Sunday Calendar seems ever destined to have had.

BIBLIOGRAPHY

Books

Allyson, June, with Frances Spatz Leighton. *June Allyson*. New York: G. P. Putnam's Sons, 1982.

Anderson, Clinton H. *Beverly Hills Is My Beat*. Englewood Cliffs, N.J.: Prentice-Hall, 1960.

Anger, Kenneth. *Hollywood Babylon*. New York: Dell Publishing, 1975.

———. *Hollywood Babylon II*. New York: E. P. Dutton, 1984.

Arce, Hector. *The Secret Life of Tyrone Power*. New York: Bantam Books, 1979.

Asbury, Herbert. *Gem of the Prairie*. New York: Alfred A. Knopf, 1940.

Auletta, Ken. *Three Blind Mice*. New York: Random House, 1991.

Austin, John. *Hollywood's Unsolved Mysteries*. New York: Shapolsky Publishers, 1992.

Bacon, James. *Made in Hollywood*. Chicago: Contemporary Books, 1977.

Baker, Carroll. *Baby Doll*. New York: Dell Publishing, 1984.

Balaban, Carrie. *Continuous Performance: Biography of A. J. Balaban*. New York: A. J. Balaban Foundation, 1964.

Bart, Peter. *Fade Out*. New York: William Morrow, 1990.

Baxter, Anne. *Intermission: A True Story*. New York: Ballantine Books, 1976.

Benny, Mary Livingstone, and Hilliard Marks with Marcia Borie. *Jack Benny*. Garden City, N.Y.: Doubleday, 1978.

Bergreen, Laurence. *Capone: The Man and the Era*. New York: Simon & Schuster, 1994.

Berman, Susan. *Lady Las Vegas*. New York: TV Books, 1996.

Bernstein, Matthew. *Walter Wanger, Hollywood Independent*. Berkeley: University of California Press, 1994.

Billman, Larry. *Betty Grable: A Bio-Bibliography*. Westport, Conn.: Greenwood Press, 1993.

Biskind, Peter. *Easy Riders, Raging Bulls: How the Sex-Drugs-and-Rock 'n' Roll Generation Saved Hollywood*. New York: Simon & Schuster, 1998.

Black, Shirley Temple. *Child Star: An Autobiography*. New York: Warner Books, 1988.

Block, Alex Ben. *Outfoxed*. New York: St. Martin's Press, 1990.

Bogdanovitch, Peter. *Who the Devil Made It*. New York: Alfred A. Knopf, 1997.

Boyer, Jay. *Bob Rafelson: Hollywood Maverick*. New York: Twayne Publishers, 1996.

Brady, Kathleen. *Lucille: The Life of Lucille Ball*. New York: Hyperion Press, 1994.

Brill, Steven. *The Teamsters*. New York: Pocket Books, 1978.

Bronfman, Edgar M. *Good Spirits: The Making of a Businessman*. New York: G. P. Putnam's Sons, 1998.

Brooks, Tim, and Earle Marsh. *The Complete Directory to Prime Time Network TV Shows: 1946–Present*. New York: Ballantine Books, 1985.

Brown, David. *Let Me Entertain You*. New York: William Morrow, 1990.

Brown, Gene. *Movie Time*. New York: Macmillan, 1995.

Brown, Peter Harry. *Kim Novak: Reluctant Goddess*. New York: St. Martin's Press, 1986.

———, and Patte B. Barham. *Marilyn: The Last Take*. New York: E. P. Dutton, 1992.

Brownstein, Ronald. *The Power and the Glitter: The Hollywood-Washington Connection*. New York: Vintage Books, 1992.

Bruck, Connie. *Master of the Game*. New York: Simon & Schuster, 1994.

Cahn, Sammy. *I Should Care: The Sammy Cahn Story*. New York: Arbor House, 1974.

Caine, Michael. *What's It All About?* New York: Ballantine Books, 1992.

Cannon, Lou. *President Reagan: The Role of a Lifetime*. New York: Simon & Schuster, 1991.

———. *Ronnie and Jesse: A Political Odyssey*. Garden City, N.Y.: Doubleday, 1969.

Cassini, Oleg. *In My Own Fashion*. New York: Pocket Books, 1987.

Castle, Charles. *The Folies-Bergère*. London: Methuen, 1982.

Caute, David. *Joseph Losey: A Revenge on Life*. London: Faber & Faber, 1994.

Cohen, Mickey, as told to John Peer Nugent. *Mickey Cohen: In My Own Words*. Englewood Cliffs, N.J.: Prentice-Hall, 1975.

Collins, Joan. *Past Imperfect*. New York: Berkley Books, 1985.

Condon, Eddie, and Hark O'Neal: *The Eddie Condon Scrapbook of Jazz*. New York: St. Martin's Press, 1988.

Considine, Shaun. *Bette and Joan*. New York: Dell Publishing, 1989.

Corio, Ann, and Joseph DiMona. *This Was Burlesque*. New York: Madison Square Press, 1968.

Crane, Cheryl, with Cliff Jahr. *Detour: A Hollywood Story*. New York: Arbor House/ William Morrow, 1988.

Crowther, Bosley. *Hollywood Rajah*. New York: Dell Publishing, 1960.

Curcio, Vincent. *Suicide Blonde: The Life of Gloria Grahame*. New York: William Morrow, 1989.

Curran, Bob. *The $400,000 Quarterback*. New York: Macmillan, 1965.

Curtis, Carlo. *Skouras: King of Fox Studios*. Los Angeles: Holloway House, 1967.

Curtis, Tony, and Barry Paris. *Tony Curtis: The Autobiography*. New York: William Morrow, 1993.

Dannen, Fredric. *Hit Man*. New York: Times Books, 1990.

David, Saul. *The Industry: Life in the Hollywood Fast Lane*. New York: Times Books, 1981.

Davidson, Bill. *The Real and the Unreal*. New York: Harper & Brothers, 1961.

Davis, Bette, with Michael Herskowitz. *This 'n' That*. New York: G. P. Putnam's Sons, 1987.

Davis, John H. *The Kennedys: Dynasty and Disaster 1848–1984*. New York: McGraw-Hill, 1984.

Dean, John W. *Lost Honor*. Los Angeles: Stratford Press, 1982.

Demaris, Ovid. *The Boardwalk Jungle*. New York: Bantam Books, 1986.

———. *Captive City: Chicago in Chains*. New York: Lyle Stuart, 1969.

———. *Dirty Business: The Corporate-Political Money-Power Game*. New York: Harper's, 1974.

———. *The Last Mafioso*. New York: Times Books, 1981.

Denker, Henry. *The Kingmaker*. New York: Pocket Books, 1978.

Dewey, Donald. *James Stewart: A Biography*. Atlanta: Turner Publishing, 1996.

Dmytryk, Edward. *It's a Hell of a Life But Not a Bad Living*. New York: Times Books, 1978.

Douglas, Kirk. *The Ragman's Son: An Autobiography*. New York: Simon & Schuster, 1988.

Drabinsky, Garth, with Marq de Villiers. *Closer to the Sun*. Toronto: McClelland & Stewart, 1995.

Dunne, George H., S.J. *King's Pawn*. Chicago: Loyola University Press, 1990.

Dunning, John. *Tune in Yesterday*. Englewood Cliffs, N.J.: Prentice-Hall, 1976.

Durso, Joseph. *The All-American Dollar: The Big Business of Sports*. Boston: Houghton Mifflin, 1971.

Eastman, John. *Retakes: Behind the Scenes of 500 Classic Movies*. New York: Ballantine Books, 1989.

Easton, Carol. *The Search for Sam Goldwyn*. New York: William Morrow, 1976.

Edwards, Anne. *Early Reagan: The Rise to Power*. New York: William Morrow, 1987.

Eells, George. *Hedda and Louella*. New York: G. P. Putnam's Sons, 1972.

Eisenberg, Dennis, Uri Dan, and Eli Landau. *Meyer Lansky: Mogul of the Mob*. New York: Paddington Press, 1979.

Evans, Robert. *The Kid Stays in the Picture*. New York: Hyperion Press, 1994.

Faber, Harold, ed. *The Kennedy Years*. New York: Viking Press, 1964.

Farber, Stephen, and Marc Green. *Outrageous Conduct: Art, Ego, and the Twilight Zone Case*. New York: Arbor House, 1988.

Fein, Irving A. *Jack Benny: An Intimate Biography*. New York: G. P. Putnam's Sons, 1976.

Firestone, Ross. *Swing, Swing, Swing: The Life and Times of Benny Goodman*. New York: W. W. Norton, 1993.

Fisher, Eddie. *Eddie: My Life, My Loves*. New York: Harper & Row, 1981.

Fishgall, Gary. *Against Type: The Biography of Burt Lancaster*. New York: Charles Scribner's Sons, 1995.

Flower, Joe. *Prince of the Magic Kingdom: Michael Eisner and the Re-Making of Disney*. New York: John Wiley & Sons, 1991.

Flynn, Errol. *My Wicked, Wicked Ways*. New York: Buccaneer Books, 1959.

Fordin, Hugh. *Getting to Know Him: A Biography of Oscar Hammerstein II*. New York: Random House, 1977.

Fox, Larry. *Broadway Joe and His Super Jets*. New York: Coward, McCann, 1969.

Franco Joseph, with Richard Hammer. *Hoffa's Man*. New York: Prentice Hall Press, 1987.

Freedland, Michael. *Gregory Peck*. New York: William Morrow, 1980.

———. *The Two Lives of Errol Flynn*. New York: William Morrow, 1979.

Freeman, David. *The Last Days of Alfred Hitchcock*. Woodstock, N.Y.: Overlook Press, 1984.

Fried, Albert. *The Rise and Fall of the Jewish Gangster in America*. New York: Holt, Rinehart & Winston, 1980.

Friedrich, Otto. *City of Nets*. New York: Harper & Row, 1986.

Gabler, Neal. *An Empire of Their Own: How the Jews Invented Hollywood*. New York: Crown Publishers, 1988.

Gage, Nicholas. *Mafia, U.S.A.* Chicago: Playboy Press, 1972.

Gaither, Gant. *Princess of Monaco*. New York: Hillman Books, 1961.

Gartner, Lloyd P. *History of the Jews of Cleveland*. Cleveland: Western Reserve Historical Society and the Jewish Theological Seminary of America, 1983.

Gates, Daryl F., with Diane K. Shah. *Chief: My Life in the LAPD*. New York: Bantam Books, 1992.

Gehman, Richard. *Sinatra and His Rat Pack*. New York: Belmont Books, 1961.

Geist, Kenneth L. *The Life and Films of Joseph L. Mankiewicz*. New York: Charles Scribner's Sons, 1978.

Giancana, Sam, and Chuck Giancana. *Double Cross: The Explosive, Inside Story of the Mobster Who Controlled America*. New York: Warner Books, 1992.

Gitlin, Todd. *Inside Prime Time*. New York: Pantheon Books, 1983.

Goodman, Ezra. *The Fifty Year Decline and Fall of Hollywood*. New York: Simon & Schuster, 1961.

Goodwin, Betty. *Chasen's: Where Hollywood Dined, Recipes and Memories*. Los Angeles: Angel City Press, 1996.

Gottlieb, Robert, and Irene Wolt. *Thinking Big: The Story of the Los Angeles Times, Its Publishers, and Their Influence on Southern California*. New York: G. P. Putnam's Sons, 1977.

Graham, Sheilah. *Hollywood Revisited: A Fiftieth Anniversary Celebration*. New York: St. Martin's Press, 1984.

Green, Abel, and Joe Laurie Jr. *Show Biz: Variety from Vaude to Vid*. New York: Henry Holt, 1951.

Grobel, Lawrence. *Conversations with Brando*. New York: Hyperion Press, 1991.

Grover, Ron. *The Disney Touch*. Homewood, Ill.: Business One Irwin, 1991.

Gunther, John. *Taken at the Flood: The Story of Albert D. Lasker*. New York: Harper & Brothers, 1960.

Halberstam, David. *The Powers That Be*. New York: Alfred A. Knopf, 1979.

Halliwell, Leslie. *Halliwell's Film and Video Guide*, 6th ed. New York: Charles Scribner's Sons, 1987.

——. *Halliwell's Filmgoer's and Video Viewer's Companion*, 9th ed. New York: Harper & Row, 1990.

Hamilton, Ian, *Writers in Hollywood, 1915–1951*. New York: Harper & Row, 1990.

Hamilton, Nigel. *JFK: Reckless Youth*. New York: Random House, 1992.

Hanna, David. *Ava*. New York: G. P. Putnam's Sons, 1960.

Harmetz, Aljean. *Rolling Breaks and Other Movie Business*. New York: Alfred A. Knopf, 1983.

Harris, Jay S., ed. *TV Guide: The First 25 Years*. New York: Simon & Schuster, 1978.

Hayward, Brooke. *Haywire*. New York: Alfred A. Knopf, 1977.

Head, Edith, and Paddy Calistro. *Edith Head's Hollywood*. New York: E. P. Dutton, 1983

Heimel, Paul W. *Eliot Ness: The Real Story*. Coudersport, Penna.: Knox Books, 1997.

Henreid, Paul, with Julius Fast. *Ladies' Man: An Autobiography*. New York: St. Martin's Press, 1984.

Hersh, Seymour. *The Dark Side of Camelot*. New York: Little, Brown, 1997.

Hinckle, Walter. *If You Have a Lemon, Make Lemonade*. New York: G. P. Putnam's Sons, 1974.

Hirschhorn, Clive. *The Universal Story*. New York: Crown Publishers, 1983.

Hoopes, Roy. *When the Stars Went to War*. New York: Random House, 1994.

Hopper, Hedda, and James Brough. *The Whole Truth and Nothing But*. Garden City, N.Y.: Doubleday, 1963.

Hostetter, Gordon L., and Thomas Quinn Beesley. *It's a Racket*. New York: R. R. Donnelley, 1929.

Hotchner, A. E. *Doris Day: Her Own Story*. New York: William Morrow, 1975.

Hudson, Rock, and Sara Davidson. *Rock Hudson: His Story*. New York: William Morrow, 1986.

Hunt, Marsha. *The Way We Wore*. Fallbrook, Calif.: Fallbrook Publishing, 1996.

Huston, John. *An Open Book*. New York: Alfred A. Knopf, 1980.

Johnston, David. *Temples of Chance: How America Inc. Bought Out Murder Inc. to Win Control of the Casino Business*. New York: Doubleday, 1992.

Kaganoff, Benzion C. *Dictionary of Jewish Names and Their History*. New York: Schocken Books, 1977.

Kefauver, Estes. *Crime in America*. Garden City, N.Y.: Doubleday, 1951.

Keith, Slim, with Annette Tapert. *Slim: Memories of a Rich and Imperfect Life*. New York: Simon & Schuster, 1990.

Kelley, Kitty. *His Way: The Unauthorized Biography of Frank Sinatra*. New York: Bantam Books, 1986.

——. *Nancy Reagan: The Unauthorized Biography*. New York: Simon & Schuster, 1991.

Kennedy, Robert F. *The Enemy Within*. New York: Harper & Row, 1960.

Kipps, Charles. *Out of Focus: Power, Pride, and Prejudice—David Puttnam in Hollywood*. New York: Silver Arrow Books, William Morrow, 1989.

Knoedelseder, William. *Stiffed: A True Story of MCA, the Music Business, and the Mafia*. New York: Harper Collins, 1993.

Kobler, John. *Capone*. New York: G. P. Putnam's Sons, 1971.

Kohner, Frederick. *The Magician of Sunset Boulevard*. Palos Verdes, Calif.: Morgan Press, 1970.

Kupcinet, Irv. *Kup's Chicago*. Cleveland: World Publishing, 1962.

——, with Paul Neimark. *Kup: A Man, An Era, A City—Irv Kupcinet's Autobiography*. Chicago: Bonus Books, 1988.

Lacey, Robert. *Little Man: Meyer Lansky and the Gangster Life*. Boston: Little, Brown, 1991.

LaGuardia, Robert. *Monty: A Biography of Montgomery Clift*. New York: Arbor House, 1977.

Lait, Jack, and Lee Mortimer. *Chicago Confidential*. New York: Crown Publishers, 1950.

Lane, Abbe. *But Where Is Love?* New York: Warner Books, 1993.

Lasky, Jesse L., with Don Weldon. *I Blow My Own Horn*. Garden City, N.Y.: Doubleday, 1957.

Layman, Avis. *From Moose to Mousse*. Portland, Me.: Partridge Island, 1987.

Lazar, Swifty, with Annette Tapert. *Swifty: My Life and Good Times*. New York: Simon & Schuster, 1995.

Leigh, Janet. *There Really Was a Hollywood*. New York: Doubleday, 1984.

Lernoux, Penny. *Cry of the People: The Struggle for Human Rights in Latin America*. New York: Penguin Books, 1982.

LeRoy, Mervyn, as told to Alyce Canfield. *It Takes More Than Talent*. New York: Alfred A. Knopf, 1953.

——, as told to Dick Kleiner. *Mervyn LeRoy: Take One*. New York: Hawthorn Books, 1974.

Levy, Shawn. *King of Comedy: The Life and Art of Jerry Lewis*. New York: St. Martin's Press, 1996.

Lewis, Judy. *Uncommon Knowledge*. New York: Pocket Books, 1995.

Liberace. *Liberace: An Autobiography*. New York: G. P. Putnam's Sons, 1973.

Logan, Josh. *Movie Stars, Real People and Me*. New York: Delacorte Press, 1978

Lombardo, Guy, with Jack Altshul. *Auld Acquaintance*. New York: Ballantine Books, 1975.

Los Angeles Times staff. *Understanding the Riots*. Los Angeles: Los Angeles Times, 1992.

MacLaine, Shirley. *My Lucky Stars: A Hollywood Memoir*. New York: Bantam Books, 1995.

Madsen, Axel. *Stanwyck: A Biography*. New York: Harper Collins, 1994.

Manso, Peter. *Brando: The Biography*. New York: Hyperion Press, 1994.

Marx, Arthur. *Everybody Loves Somebody Sometime*. New York: Hawthorn Books, 1974.

McBride, Joseph. *Steven Spielberg*. New York: Simon & Schuster, 1997.

McClintick, David. *Indecent Exposure*. New York: Dell Publishing, 1982.

McCrohan, Donna. *Prime Time Our Time*. Rocklin, Calif.: Prima, 1990.

McNeil, Alex. *Total Television*. 4th ed. New York: Penguin Books, 1996.

McPhaul, John J. *Johnny Torrio, First of the Gang Lords*. New Rochelle, N.Y.: Arlington House, 1970.

Messick, Hank. *The Beauties and the Beasts: The Mob in Show Business.* New York: David McKay, 1973.

——. *Lansky.* New York: G. P. Putnam's Sons, 1971.

——. *The Silent Syndicate.* New York: Macmillan, 1967.

Mitgang, Herbert. *Dangerous Dossiers.* New York: Donald J. Fine, 1988.

Moldea, Dan E. *Dark Victory: Ronald Reagan, MCA, and the Mob.* New York: Viking Press, 1986.

——. *The Hoffa Wars: Teamsters, Rebels, Politicians, and the Mob.* New York: Paddington Press, 1978.

——. *Interference: How Organized Crime Influences Professional Football.* New York: William Morrow, 1989.

Mollenhoff, Clark. *Tentacles of Power: The Story of Jimmy Hoffa.* Cleveland: World Publishing, 1965.

Molyneaux, Gerard. *Gregory Peck: A Bio-Bibliography.* Westport, Conn.: Greenwood Press, 1995.

Mordden, Ethan. *The Hollywood Studios.* New York: Fireside, 1989.

Morella, Joe, and Edward Z. Epstein. *Jane Wyman: A Biography.* New York: Delacorte Press, 1985.

——. *The Adventurous Life of Paulette Goddard.* New York: St. Martin's Press, 1985

Murphy, George, with Victor Lasky. *Say...Didn't You Used to Be George Murphy?* New York: Bartholomew House, 1970.

National Security Archive. *The Chronology: The Documented Day-by-Day Account of the Secret Military Assistance to Iran and the Contras.* New York: Warner Books, 1987.

Neff, James. *Mobbed Up: Jackie Presser's High Wire Life in the Teamsters, the Mafia, and the FBI.* New York: Atlantic Monthly Press, 1989.

Newman, Peter C. *The Bronfman Dynasty: The Rothschilds of the New World.* Toronto: McClelland and Stewart, 1978.

New York Times. *The New York Times Directory of the Theater.* New York: Quadrangle, New York Times, 1973.

Niven, David. *Bring on the Empty Horses.* New York: Dell Publishing, 1975.

Noguchi, Thomas T. *Coroner.* New York: Simon & Schuster, 1983.

O'Donnell, Pierce, and Dennis McDougal. *Fatal Subtraction: How Hollywood Really Does Business.* New York: Doubleday, 1992.

Oppenheimer, Harold L., and James D. Keast. *Cowboy Litigation.* Danville, Ill.: Interstate Printers & Publishers, 1968.

Parrish, Bernie. *They Call It a Game.* New York: Dial Press, 1971.

Pero, Taylor, and Jeff Rovin. *Always, Lana.* New York: Bantam Books, 1982.

Perry, Jeb H. *Universal Television: The Studio and Its Programs, 1950–1980.* Metuchen, N.J.: Scarecrow Press, 1983.

Pestos, Spero. *Pin-Up: The Tragedy of Betty Grable.* New York: G. P. Putnam's Sons, 1986.

Peterson, Virgil. *Barbarians in Our Midst.* Boston: Little, Brown, 1952.

Phillips, Julia. *You'll Never Eat Lunch in This Town Again.* New York: Random House, 1991.

Pollock, Dale. *Skywalking: The Life and Films of George Lucas.* New York: Harmony Books, 1983.

Pourroy, Janine. *The Making of* Waterworld. New York: Boulevard Books, 1995.

Preminger, Otto. *Preminger: An Autobiography.* Garden City, N.Y.: Doubleday, 1977.

Pye, Michael. *Moguls: Inside the Business of Show Business.* New York: Holt, Rinehart & Winston, 1979.

Quigley, Martin. *International Motion Picture Almanac*. New York: Quigley Publishing, 1936–1995.

——. *International Television Almanac*. New York: Quigley Publishing, 1956–1995.

Quine, Judith Balaban. *The Bridesmaids*. New York: Pocket Books, 1989.

Rappleye, Charles, and Ed Becker. *All-American Mafioso: The Johnny Rosselli Story*. New York: Doubleday, 1991.

Reagan, Maureen. *First Father, First Daughter, A Memoir*. Boston: Little, Brown, 1989.

Reagan, Ronald. *An American Life: The Autobiography*. New York: Simon & Schuster, 1990.

——, and Richard G. Hubler. *Where's the Rest of Me?* New York: Best Books, 1965.

Reid, Ed. *The Grim Reapers*. New York: Bantam Books, 1970.

——, and Ovid Demaris. *The Green Felt Jungle*. New York: Pocket Books, 1964.

Richman, Saul. *Guy: The Life and Times of Guy Lombardo*. New York: RichGuy Publishing, 1978.

Roemer, William F. Jr. *Accardo: The Genuine Godfather*. New York: Donald I. Fine, 1995.

——. *The Enforcer*. New York: Donald I. Fine, 1994.

——. *Roemer: Man Against the Mob*. New York: Donald I. Fine, 1989.

Rogers, Henry C. *Walking the Tightrope*. New York: William Morrow, 1980.

Rose, Frank. *The Agency: William Morris and the Hidden History of Show Business*. New York: Harper Collins, 1995.

Rosenberg, Bernard, and Harry Silverstein. *The Real Tinsel*. London: Collier-Macmillan, 1970.

Rosenstein, Jaik. *Hollywood Leg Man*. Los Angeles: Madison Press, 1950.

Sale, Kirkpatrick. *Power Shift: The Rise of the Southern Rim and Its Challenge to the Eastern Establishment*. New York: Vintage Books, 1976.

Sanello, Frank. *Spielberg: The Man, The Movies, The Mythology*. Dallas: Taylor Publishing, 1996.

Saxton, Martha. *Jayne Mansfield and the American Fifties*. Boston: Houghton Mifflin, 1975.

Schary, Dore. *Heyday: An Autobiography*. Boston: Little, Brown, 1970.

Schatz, Thomas. *The Genius of the System*. New York: Pantheon Books, 1988.

Scheim, David E. *Contract on America: The Mafia Murder of President John F. Kennedy*. New York: Shapolsky Publishers, 1988.

Scheuer, Steven H., ed. *Movies on TV and Videocassette, 1989–1990*. New York: Bantam Books, 1989.

Schickel, Richard. *The Stars*. New York: Bonanza Books, 1962.

Sciacca, Tony. *Who Killed Marilyn?* New York: Manor Books, 1976.

Segaloff, Nat. *Hurricane Billy: The Stormy Life and Films of William Friedkin*. New York: William Morrow, 1990.

Sheridan, Walter. *The Fall and Rise of Jimmy Hoffa*. New York: Saturday Review Press, 1972.

Shulman, Arthur, and Roger Youman. *How Sweet It Was—Television: A Pictorial Commentary*. New York: Bonanza Books, 1966.

Silver, Phil, with Robert Saffron. *This Laugh Is on Me*. Englewood Cliffs, N.J.: Prentice-Hall, 1973.

Simon, George T. *The Big Bands*. New York: The Macmillan Company, 1967.

Sinatra, Nancy. *Frank Sinatra, My Father*. New York: Pocket Books, 1985.

Singular, Stephen. *Power to Burn: Michael Ovitz and the New Business of Show Business*. New York: Birch Lane Press, 1996.

——. *The Rise and Rise of David Geffen*. New York: Birch Lane Press, 1997.

Sklar, Robert. *Movie-Made America*. New York: Vintage Books, 1975.

Slater, Robert. *Ovitz*. New York: McGraw-Hill, 1997.

Slatzer, Robert F. *The Marilyn Files*. New York: S.P.I. Books, 1992.

Smith, Alson J. *Syndicate City*. Chicago: Henry Regnery, 1954.

Smith, Sally Bedell. *In All His Glory: The Life and Times of William S. Paley and the Birth of Modern Broadcasting*. New York: Simon & Schuster, 1990.

Smoodin, Eric, ed. *Disney Discourse: Producing the Magic Kingdom*. London: Routledge, 1994.

Spada, James. *Grace: The Secret Lives of a Princess*. New York: Dell Publishing, 1987.

———. *More Than a Woman*. New York: Bantam Books, 1993.

———. *Peter Lawford: The Man Who Kept the Secrets*. New York: Bantam Books, 1991.

Spoto, Donald. *The Dark Side of Genius: The Life of Alfred Hitchcock*. Boston: Back Bay Books, 1993.

———. *Marilyn Monroe*. New York: Harper Collins, 1993.

Stans, Maurice H. *The Terrors of Justice: The Untold Side of Watergate*. New York: Everest House, 1978.

Stein, Jean, and George Plimpton. *American Journey: The Times of Robert Kennedy*. New York: Harcourt Brace Jovanovich, 1970.

Stine, Whitney. *Stars and Star Handlers*. Santa Monica, Calif.: Roundtable Publishing, 1985.

———, with Bette Davis. *Mother Goddam*. New York: Hawthorn Books, 1974.

Strait, Raymond, and Terry Robinson. *Lanza: His Tragic Life*. Englewood Cliffs, N.J.: Prentice-Hall, 1980.

Taylor, John Russell. *Hitch: The Life and Times of Alfred Hitchcock*. New York: Da Capo Press, 1996.

Teichman, Howard, and Henry Fonda. *Fonda: My Life*. New York: New American Library, 1981.

Thomas, Bob. *Joan Crawford: A Biography*. New York: Bantam Books, 1978.

———. *Thalberg: Life and Legend*. Garden City, N.Y.: Doubleday, 1969.

Thomas, Kenn, and Jim Keith. *The Octopus: Secret Government and the Death of Danny Casolaro*. Portland, Ore.: Feral House, 1997.

Thompson, Robert J. *Adventures on Prime Time: The Television Programs of Stephen J. Cannell*. New York: Praeger, 1990.

Tosches, Nick. *Dino: Living High in the Dirty Business of Dreams*. New York: Doubleday, 1992.

Trumbo, Dalton. *Additional Dialogue: Letters of Dalton Trumbo, 1942–1962*. Edited by Helen Manfull. New York: M. Evans, 1970.

Valenti, Jack. *A Very Human President*. New York: W. W. Norton, 1975.

Van Doren, Mamie, with Art Aveilhe. *Playing the Field*. New York: Berkley Publishing, 1988.

Wakeman, Frederic. *The Hucksters*. New York: Rinehart, 1946.

Walker, Alexander. *Hollywood England: The British Film Industry in the Sixties*. London: Michael Joseph, 1974.

———. *Joan Crawford: The Ultimate Star*. New York: Harper & Row, 1983.

Walker, Leo. *The Wonderful Era of the Great Dance Bands*. Berkeley, Calif.: Howell-North Book, 1964.

Walley, David G. *Nothing in Moderation: A Biography of Ernie Kovacs*. New York: Drake Publishers, 1975.

Warner, Jack L., with Dean Jennings. *My First Hundred Years in Hollywood*. New York: Random House, 1965.

Wayne, Jane Ellen. *Gable's Women*. New York: St. Martin's Press, 1987.

Weissman, Steve, ed. *Big Brother and the Holding Company: The World behind Watergate*. Palo Alto, Calif.: Ramparts Press, 1974.

Wertheim, Arthur Frank. *Radio Comedy*. New York: Oxford University Press, 1979.

Westmore, Frank, and Muriel Davidson. *The Westmores of Hollywood*. Philadelphia: J. B. Lippincott, 1976.

Whalen, Richard. *The Founding Father: The Story of Joseph P. Kennedy*. New York: New American Library, 1964.

White, Theodore H. *Breach of Faith: The Fall of Richard Nixon*. New York: Atheneum Publishers, 1975.

Wiley, Mason, and Damien Bona. *Inside Oscar: The Unofficial History of the Academy Awards*. New York: Ballantine Books, 1986.

Wills, Garry. *The Kennedy Imprisonment: A Meditation on Power*. Boston: Little, Brown, 1981.

Wilson, Earl. *Show Business Laid Bare*. New York: Signet, 1974.

Winter-Berger, Robert N. *The Washington Pay-Off: A Lobbyist's Own Story of Corruption in Government*. Secaucus, N.J.: Lyle Stuart, 1972.

Winters, Shelley. *Shelley*. New York: Ballantine Books, 1980.

Woodward, Bob. *Wired: The Short Life and Fast Times of John Belushi*. New York: Simon & Schuster, 1984.

WPA Federal Writers' Project. *Chicago and Suburbs 1939*. Evanston, Ill.: Chicago Historical Bookworks, 1991.

Wynn, Ned. *We Will Always Live in Beverly Hills*. New York: Penguin Books, 1992.

Yamashita, Toshihiko. *The Panasonic Way: From a Chief Executive's Desk*. Translated by Frank Baldwin. Tokyo: Kodansha International, 1987.

Yule, Andrew. *Fast Fade: David Puttnam, Columbia Pictures, and the Battle for Hollywood*. New York: Delacorte Press, 1989.

Zeller, F. C. Duke. *Devil's Pact: Inside the World of the Teamsters Union*. New York: Birch Lane Press, 1997.

Zimmerman, Paul. *The Last Season of Weeb Ewbank*. New York: Farrar, Straus & Giroux, 1974.

Zolotow, Maurice. *Billy Wilder in Hollywood*. New York: Limelight Editions, 1987

———. *Marilyn Monroe: An Uncensored Biography*. New York: Bantam Books, 1960.

Periodicals

Akst, Daniel, and John R. Emshwiller. "MCA Inc. Is Battling Accounts Linking It to Organized Crime." *Wall Street Journal*, Sept. 12, 1988.

Bart, Peter. "Still Standing Tall." *Variety*, Mar. 15, 1993.

Beck, Roger, and Howard Williams. "Giant Agency Runs Show Business." *Los Angeles Mirror News*, Nov. 10–12, 1958.

Benedict, John. "Who Controls the Whiskey Trust?" *American Mercury*, Dec. 1959.

Berges, Marshall. "Lew and Edie Wasserman: The Movie Usher Grew Up to Be Chairman of the Board." *Los Angeles Times*, Dec. 2, 1973.

Block, Alex Ben. "Father of the Bride." *Forbes*, Sept. 23, 1985.

Boyer, Peter. "Hollywood's King Cashes Out." *Vanity Fair*, Feb. 1991.

Bruck, Connie. "The World of Business." *New Yorker*, Sept. 9, 1991.

Business Week staff. "How MCA Gets Its Teeth into Profits." *Business Week*, Aug. 18, 1975.

——. "Reshaping a Sluggish MCA." *Business Week*, Aug. 10, 1981.

Capeci, Jerry. "Hollywood Executive Asked Alleged Mob Boss Gotti to Block Film, FBI Says." *Daily News* (New York), Apr. 12, 1990.

Cieply, Michael. "MCA's No. 2 Tower of Power." *Los Angeles Times*, Aug. 12, 1987.

Citron, Alan, and Leslie Helm. "MCA Parent's New Role." *Los Angeles Times*, June 4, 1992.

Corn, David. "The Dark World of Danny Casolaro." *The Nation*, Oct. 28, 1991.

Davenport, Walter. "Heat Wave." *Collier's*, Mar. 10, 1934.

Davidson, Bill. "MCA: The Octopus Devours the World." *Show Magazine*, Feb. 1962 and Mar. 1962.

Deutsch, Susan. "Lew!" *California*, Mar. 1985.

Dunne, Dominick. "The Last Emperor." *Vanity Fair*, Apr. 1996.

Egan, J. "A Hollywood Thriller: MCA v. the Sharks." *U.S. News & World Report*, Sept. 7, 1987.

Fabrikant, Geraldine. "Chairman Holds Key to MCA's Sale." *New York Times*, Oct. 1, 1990.

Fadiman, William. "Blockbusters or Bust!" *Frontier*, Nov. 1962.

Galluccio, N. "MCA's Big Gamble." *Fortune*, Apr. 14, 1980.

Gelman, David, and Alfred G. Aronowitz. "MCA: Show Business Empires." *New York Post*, June 4–10, 1962.

Goldberg, Michael. "Grand Juries Investigate Mob Ties to Record Biz." *Rolling Stone*, June 2, 1988.

——. "Independent Promotion: The Inside Story." *Rolling Stone*, Apr. 24, 1986.

Goodwin, Fritz. "Colossus of the Entertainment World." *TV Guide*, July 25, and Aug. 1, 1964.

Gottlieb, Bob. "Wasserman." *Los Angeles*, Jan. 1979.

Grover, Ronald. "MCA: A Rift Runs Thru It." *Business Week*, Oct. 31, 1994.

——. "Trump Sends a Mash Note to MCA." *Business Week*, Feb. 29, 1988.

Gubernick, Lisa. "Carry On, Mr. Sheinberg." *Forbes*, July 18, 1994.

Haber, Joyce. "Jules Stein: Eye Doctor, Movie Visionary." *Los Angeles Times*, May 26, 1974.

Harmetz, Aljean. "Hollywood's Video Gamble," *New York Times*, Mar. 28, 1982.

Hersh, Seymour M., with Jeff Gerth. "Double Life of Sidney Korshak," *New York Times*, June 27–30, 1976.

Hyams, Joe. "MCA in the Computer Age." *New York Herald Tribune*, Nov. 10, 1963.

Johnston, Alva. "Hollywood's Ten-Per Centers." *Saturday Evening Post*, Aug. 8, 15, and 22, 1942.

Kelly, John Redmond. "Singin' Sam Does the Jersey Bounce." *New Jersey Independent*, Mar. 1959.

Knight, Arthur. "New Life for the New Wave." *Saturday Review*, Aug. 20, 1966.

Knoedelseder, William K., Jr. "Salvatore Pisello: A Shadowy Figure in Records Deals." *Los Angeles Times*, May 4, 1986.

Lalli, Frank. "The Korshak Series: Firecrackers, Not Dynamite." *New West*, Aug. 2, 1976.

Latham, Aaron. "MCA's Bad Cop Shoots from the Hip." *Manhattan, Inc.*, July 1988.

Ludwig, Steven. "MCA Inc.'s Sidney Jay Sheinberg." *Executive L.A.*, May 1981.

Maisel, Albert Q. "The Four Careers of Jules Stein." *Reader's Digest*, Jan. 1974.

McPhee, John. "New Kind of King." *Time*, Jan. 1, 1965.

Moldea, Dan. "MCA and the Mob." *Regardie's*, June 1988.

Mulgannon, Terry. "When Ronnie Played Vegas." *Los Angeles*, Apr. 1983.

Mundy, Alice. "Jack Valenti." *Regardie's*, Jan. 1991.

Munroe, Keith. "Leland Hayward." *Life*, Sept. 20, 1948.

Orey, Michael. "Death of a Mob Probe." *American Lawyer*, July-Aug. 1988.

Pizzo, Stephen. "The Long Arm of the Lew?" *Mother Jones*, May-June 1993.

Pye, Michael. "What Made Jules Run?" *Sunday Times* (London), June 17, 1973.

Ridgeway, James, and Doug Vaughan. "The Last Days of Danny Casolaro." *Village Voice*, Oct. 15, 1991.

Rockaway, Robert. "Mobsters for Zion." *Detroit Jewish News*, June 29, 1990.

Rose, Frank. "The Last Mogul." *Los Angeles Times*, May 25, 1995.

——. "What Ever Happened to Mike Ovitz?" *Fortune*, July 7, 1997.

Rosenbaum, Ron. "The Strange Death of Danny Casolaro." *Vanity Fair*, Dec. 1991.

Scheer, Robert. "Jews of L.A." *Los Angeles Times*, July 30, 1978.

Smith, Geoffrey. "Land of the Ganef." *Financial World*, Dec. 25, 1990.

Stewart, James. "James Stewart Tells His Own Story." *Saturday Evening Post*, Feb. 11, 18, and 25, March 4 and 11, 1961.

Thompson, Edward T. "There's No Show Business like MCA's Business." *Fortune*, July 1960.

Tobias, Andrew. "The Hidden Fight That Finally Made MCA the Greatest." *New West*, Apr. 26, 1976.

Trachtenberg, J. A. "The Most Powerful Man in Hollywood." *Women's Wear Daily*, Oct. 1, 1982.

Trebay, Guy. "Stein's Way." *Vanity Fair*, July 1991.

Turner, Richard. "Steven Spielberg: His Stories Aren't Amazing Enough…Yet." *TV Guide*, Aug. 2, 1986.

Velie, Lester. "Capone Gang Muscles into Big-Time Politics." *Collier's*, Sept. 30, 1950

Walter, Lyle. "Taxes and Entertainment." *Show Business Illustrated*, Oct. 31, 1961.

Weinraub, Bernard. "Bombs Away." *New York Times*, June 16, 1997.

Weinstein, Henry, and Paul Feldman. "Trial Offers Murky Peek into World of Intrigue." *Los Angeles Times*, Mar. 21, 1993.

Weisberg, Jacob. "A Strauss Waltz: Matsushita-MCA Takeover Greased by Robert Strauss, Other High-Powered Lobbyists." *New Republic*, Jan. 28, 1991.

Whitney, Dwight. "The Octopus." *Time*, April 23, 1945.

Wittels, David G. "The Star-Spangled Octopus." *Saturday Evening Post*, Aug. 10, 17, 24, and 31, 1946.

Zeitlin, D. "Meanwhile Back in Hollywood, Efficiency Takes Over." *Life*, Dec. 20, 1963.

Court Cases

Bracken v. MCA, Los Angeles Superior Court, Civil Action No. C-503177.

Brandt v. MCA, Los Angeles Superior Court, Civil Action No. C-461677.

Breitstein v. Sheinberg et al., Los Angeles Superior Court, Civil Action No. WEC-137749.

Cardinal Pictures Inc. v. MCA, Los Angeles Superior Court, Civil Action No. C-558647.

Finley v. MCA et al., U.S. District Court, Southern District of California, Central Division, Civil Action No. 4328-M.

Hitchcock, Alfred J., Los Angeles Superior Court Probate Action No. P-656507.

Hitchcock, Alma Lucy, Los Angeles Superior Court Probate Action No. P-675073.

Holden v. MCA et al., U.S. District Court, Southern District of California, Central Division, Civil Action No. 4583.

Hover v. MCA et al., U.S. District Court, Southern District of California, Central Division, Civil Action No. 18159-HW.

Jarsen v. MCA, Los Angeles Superior Court Civil Action No. C-102609.

Kramer, Karl F., Los Angeles Superior Court Probate Action No. P-660082.

Lazar et al. v. MCA Inc. et al., Los Angeles Superior Court Civil Action No. BC-11305.

Leif v. Leif, Los Angeles Superior Court Divorce Action No. WED-12939.

MCA, Inc. v. Cary Grant, Los Angeles Superior Court Civil Action No. C-958895.

MCA v. Liberace, Los Angeles Superior Court Civil Action No. C-845094.

Penthouse International Ltd. v. Dalitz, Los Angeles Superior Court Civil Action No. C-162233.

Penthouse v. Rancho La Costa, Los Angeles Superior Court Civil Action No. C-124901.

Schreiber, Taft B., Los Angeles Superior Court Probate Action No. P-623149.

Spielberg v. Hoffman, Los Angeles Superior Court Civil Action No. C-37860.

Stein, Doris, Los Angeles Superior Court Probate Action No. P-689513.

Stein, Herman David, Los Angeles Superior Court Probate Action No. BP-24430.

Stein, Jules, Los Angeles Superior Court Probate Action No. P-664540.

Stein, William H., Cook County Probate Court Action No. 43 P-4114.

Stone v. MCA, Los Angeles Superior Court, Civil Action No. BC-455796.

U.S. v. Campagna et al., 146 F. 2d 524 (New York, 2d Cir., 1944).

U.S. v. MCA et al., U.S. District Court, Southern District of California, Central Division, Civil Action No. 62-942-WM.

U.S. v. Paramount Pictures, Inc., et al., 334 U.S. 131, 92 L ed 1169, 68 Ct. 915.

U.S. v. Parvin Dohrmann et al., U.S. District Court of New York, Southern District, 69 Civ. 4543.

U.S. v. Seifert, U.S. District Court, Southern District of California, Central Division, Criminal Action No. 80-838-LTL.

Wanger v. Wanger, Los Angeles Superior Court, Divorce Action No. D-590279.

Wasserman v. Donaldson, Los Angeles Superior Court Civil Action No. C-559339.

Other Documents

Academy of Television Arts and Sciences. *12th Annual Hall of Fame Program*. North Hollywood: ATAS, 1996.

Adams, Berle. *A Sucker for Talent*. Unpublished memoirs, 1996. Courtesy of the author.

Bacow, Martin. *Man in the Middle*. Unpublished memoirs, 1996. Courtesy of the author.

Celebrity Directory. 6th ed. Ann Arbor, Mich.: Axiom Information Services, 1996.

Cinebooks Motion Picture Guide. CD-ROM. New York: News America Publishing, 1995.

Committee on the Judiciary, U.S. House of Representatives. Washington, D.C.: 1992 (Brooks Committee Hearings on the Inslaw Affair).

Dales, Jack. *Pragmatic Leadership: Ronald Reagan as President of the Screen Actors Guild*. Oral history. Interviewed by Mitch Tuchman, 1981. UCLA Oral History Program.

Dunne, George H. *Christian Advocacy and Labor Strife in Hollywood*. Oral history. Interviewed by Mitch Tuchman, 1981. UCLA Oral History Program.

Encore Media Corporation. *The Universal Story*. Videotape. Englewood, Colo.: Encore Media, 1996.

The Forbes 400. New York: Forbes, 1987–1997.

Foundation of the Motion Picture Pioneers. *1978 Pioneer of the Year Program*, honoring Dr. Jules C. Stein.

Goe, Robert. *Emissary from Chicago*. Unpublished manuscript, 1960. Courtesy of Dave Robb.

Hollywood Reporter. *Universal 75th Anniversary Salute Special Issue*. Los Angeles: Hollywood Reporter, June 1990.

Kent, Martin, Ray Loynd, and David Robb. *Hollywood Remembers Ronald Reagan*. Unpublished manuscript, 1983. Courtesy of David Robb.

Lewis, Jon. "Disney after Disney." In *Disney Disclosure: Producing the Magic Kingdom.* Edited by Eric Smoodin. New York: Routledge, 1994.

Mallory, Mary Elizabeth. *Agent Provocateur: The Tradition and Influence of Myron Selznick on the Motion Picture Talent Agency Business.* Master's thesis, University of Texas, 1990.

Newell, Frank W. "The Origins of the National Eye Institute 1933–1968," *The Fifth Charles B. Snyder Lecture,* read at the annual meeting of the Cogan Ophthalmic History Society, National Library of Medicine, Mar. 16, 1994.

Peterson, Virgil W. "Historical Background of Organized Crime Prior to 1967." Paper presented to the National Conference on Organized Crime, University of Southern California, Nov. 8, 1979.

Radio Ink. *75th Anniversary Collector's Edition.* West Palm Beach, Fla.: Streamline Publishing, 1995.

Raskin, Hyman. *A Laborer in the Vineyards.* Unpublished memoirs, 1994. Courtesy of author's widow.

Regents, University of California. *Jules Stein Eye Institute: The Initial Years,* 1978.

——. *Jules Stein Eye Institute: 1980–1981.* Annual report.

——. *Jules Stein Eye Institute: 1984–1985.* Annual report.

Rudnick, Marvin. Sworn Statement on Behalf of the Committee on the Judiciary, U.S. House of Representatives. Washington, D.C.: 1992 (Brooks Committee on the Inslaw Affair).

Securities and Exchange Commission. Form 10-K. MCA Inc., 1960–1989.

——.Form 10-K/A, 10-Q. Seagram Company, 1995–1997.

Select Committee on Assassinations, U.S. House of Representatives. Washington, D.C.: 1979 (Stokes Committee Hearings).

Select Committee on Improper Activities in the Labor or Management Field, U.S. Senate. Washington, D.C.: 1960 (McClellan Committee Hearings).

Select Committee on Public Lands, National Parks and Forests, U.S. House of Representatives. Washington, D.C.: 1991 (Yosemite Hearings).

Select Committee to Investigate Organized Crime in Interstate Commerce, U.S. Senate. Washington, D.C.: 1951 (Kefauver Committee Hearings).

Select Committee to Study Governmental Operations with Respect to Intelligence Activities, U.S. Senate. Washington, D.C.: 1975 (Church Committee Hearings).

Sorrell, Herbert Knott. *You Don't Choose Your Friends: The Memoirs of Herbert Knott Sorrell.* Oral history. Interviewed by Elizabeth I. Dixon, 1963. UCLA Oral History Program.

State of New Jersey Casino Control Commission. "Plenary Licensing Hearing of Hilton New Jersey Corporation," 1984.

Time 1947: The Year in Review. New York: Time, Inc., 1947.

United Jewish Appeal–Federation of New York, Entertainment and Music Industries Division. *Steven J. Ross Humanitarian Award Dinner Program.* New York: 1996.

Universal Studios. *Universal City Studio Story: Yesterday, Today and Tomorrow.* Brochure. Los Angeles: Universal Studios, 1965.

INDEX

A&M Records, 324–325n
ABC, 238–239
Accardo, Tony, 221
Adams, Berle, 4, 12, 13, 22–23, 119–120n,
    131, 132, 149, 161, 163–164, 167, 168,
    186, 197, 203, 207, 220, 243, 324–325,
    332, 336, 340–341, 342, 346, 350, 359n,
    368, 523, 524
  coup attempt against Wasserman,
    351–352, 354–356, 357–358, 359
  departure from MCA, 364–365
Adams, Lucy, 356, 358
Adler, Buddy, 237, 238, 284n
Adler, Jerry, 192–193, 314, 331, 344
Ahmanson, Howard F., 330
Airport (film), 362–363
Aiuppa, Joey, 399
Akimoto, Harold, 466
Alexander, Willard, 32, 71, 175
Alfred Hitchcock Presents (TV show),
    252–253
All About Eve (film), 115
Allen, Howard P., 421
Allenberg, Bert, 229–230, 247
Alliance of Television Film Producers, 186
Alliance of Theatrical Stage Employees, 377,
    380–381
Allyson, June, 179
Alo, Vincent "Jimmy Blue Eyes," 457
American Federation of Musicians, 16–17,
    38, 70, 123
American Federation of Television and
    Radio Artists, 165
American Film Institute, 497–498
American Graffiti (film), 370–372
American Jewish Committee, 383
Amos 'n' Andy (radio show), 162–163

Amusement Enterprises, Inc., 160, 162–163
Anderson, Andy, 399
Anderson, Eddie "Rochester," 80
Andorn, Sidney, 60
Andrews, Dana, 309–310
Andrews, Julie, 346–347, 348
Apartment, The (film), 173–174
Archerd, Army, 198, 490, 492
Argyle, duchess of, 197
Arkoff, Sam, 380, 381
Armstrong, Louis, 13, 19
Arnaz, Desi, 233, 291
Arthur, Robert, 339
Arvey, Jacob, 141, 142
Associated Booking Corporation, 140–141
Association of Motion Picture and Television
    Producers (AMPTP), 331, 376–379,
    380, 428
Astaire, Fred, 193
Aubrey, James, 291, 394
Azoff, Irving, 431, 446, 447, 449n, 453, 455,
    459, 466, 474–475

Bacall, Lauren, 211
Bacon, James, 69, 152, 357, 358, 441, 452,
    457
Bacow, Martin, 264, 439, 440, 442,
    456–459
Baker, Carroll, 292
Baker, Howard, 461
Balaban, Barney, 173, 231, 280, 346n
Ball, Lucille, 233, 291
Banner, Stephen, 505
Barker, Jess, 98
Barnett, Larry, 123, 125, 129, 206, 224–225,
    297, 299, 301
Barr, Norman, 489

Bart, Peter, 497

Bartlett, Sy, 229

Bartok, Phil, 51

Barton, DeArv, 44, 63–64, 65

Barton, Dorothy, 63, 64, 100

Battlestar Galactica (TV show), 404*n*, 426*n*

Bautzer, Greg, 327

Bazelon, David, 141

Beatty, Warren, 302

Beck, Johnny, Jr., 81

Beckerman, Henry A., 52–54, 61–62, 121, 221*n*

Beckerman, Stanley, 60, 61, 62, 121*n*

Beckerman, Tillie, 221

Begelman, David, 301

Beilenson, Larry, 186, 187, 190, 267, 268, 300, 433

Belafonte, Harry, 258

Bennett, Constance, 92

Bennett, Herman, 124, 127

Bennett, Joan, 170–173

Benny, Jack, 113, 160–164, 282–283, 292, 315, 316

Benson, Edgar, 13

Bergen, Edgar, 70–71, 113, 118

Bernstein, Jay, 337

Beutel, William, 302

Beyond the Forest (film), 115

Billings, Carter, 245

Biondi, Frank, 517

Bishop, Eames, 123, 128–129

Blackburn, Norman, 178

Blacker, Fred "Bugs," 40–41

Blattner, Robert, 459

Blaustein, Julian, 238

Bloomingdale, Alfred, 441

Bluhdorn, Charles, 2, 366–367, 368, 393*n*, 397, 481

Bob Hope Presents the Chrysler Theater (TV show), 313–314

Bogart, Humphrey, 32*n*

Borgnine, Ernest, 314

Boyle, Mike "Umbrella," 23*n*

Bracken, Eddie, 110–112, 166

Bradley, Ed, 468

Bradshaw, Thornton, 434

Brando, Marlon, 169–170

Breitstein, Bruce, 489

Brennan, Hank, 284

Brenner, Herb, 301, 302*n*

Brenner, Temme, 91, 171

Broadbent, Kent, 405

Brog, Gene, 424

Brolly, Brian, 324

Bronfman, Edgar, Jr., 2–3, 394, 502–503, 506–507, 508, 509, 514–515, 517–518, 520, 522

Bronfman, Edgar, Sr., 367*n*, 393–394, 501–503, 506*n*, 508, 514, 518, 526–527

Bronfman, Sam, 144, 394*n*, 501, 518

Bronfman family, 143–145, 476

Brooks, Jack, 503, 505

Brown, David, 370, 380, 387–388, 415*n*

Brown, Edmund G. "Pat," 331

Brown, Jerry, 316*n*, 397*n*, 437

Brown, Peter Harry, 303

Bruce, Lenny, 249–250

Busch, Anita, 517

Caan, James, 420, 457

Cahn, Sammy, 165

Calgush Oil Company, 113*n*

Call, Asa V., 332

Campanella, Joseph, 336*n*

Campbell, Bruce, 66, 159, 192, 201, 209, 259, 306–307

Campbell, Dorothea, 66, 122

Campbell, George, 4, 20, 37, 64*n*, 66, 159, 259, 301, 421

Camp David peace agreement, 413–414

Candidate, The (film), x

Cannon, Lou, 191, 333

Caplan, Derrick, 49

Capone, Al, 11, 23*n*, 34, 35, 40

Carson, Jack, 98

Carter, Amy, 403

Carter, Jimmy, 2, 397, 401–403, 413–414, 415, 482*n*

Carter, Rosalynn, 403

Casolaro, Danny, 487–488, 503

Castro, Fidel, 304

CBS, 24, 30, 81, 162–163
    MCA's proposed purchase of, 496–497, 500

Central Intelligence Agency, 340*n*

Champlin, Charles, 309, 379

Chandler, Dorothy Buffum, 342–343, 396–397

Chaplin, Charles, 348

Chasin, George, 137, 156, 193, 203, 297, 299, 301, 302*n*, 306–307, 368*n*, 449*n*

Chávez, Cesar, 398–399
Cimino, Michael, 409
Cinema International Corporation, 366, 368–369
Cineplex Odeon, 6, 448–449, 465, 475–476, 484n
Citron, Herman, 137, 177–178, 222n, 297, 301, 449n
Citron-Park-Chasin Agency, 301, 385
Claiborne, Harry, 441
Clare, Ralph, 280
Clayton, Eddie, 226, 290, 291, 292, 294
Clift, Montgomery, 259–260, 303
Climan, Sandy, 517
Clinton, Bill, 2, 491, 492, 493, 513, 515, 520–521
Cobb, Lee J., 152
Cogan, Ruth Stein, 35, 43, 411, 423, 519, 524–525
Cohen, John, 503, 505
Cohen, Mickey, 146, 147–148
Cohn, Harry, 46, 96, 146, 184, 264, 284n
Coleman, Herbert, 526
Columbia Pictures, 426–427
Columbia Savings and Loan, 316, 425
Colyer, Ed, 280
Communist witch–hunts, 139
Como, Perry, 63–64
Contemporary Artists Management, 276–277
Coogan, Jackie, 80
Coppola, Francis Ford, 371, 372
Corday, Eliot, 355, 362, 365, 390
Correll, Charles, 162
Corwin, Sherill, 222
Costello, Frank, 144, 277n
Cotten, Joseph, 286
Countess from Hong Kong, The (film), 348
Courtright, Hernando, 354n
Cowan, Warren, 251–252
Crawford, Joan, 114, 156, 387
Creative Artists Agency, 4, 385–386, 479, 480–481
Creative Management Associates, 385
Crutcher, Robert Riley, 111
Cukor, George, 104, 303
Cummings, Bob, 292
Cunningham, James D., 267–268
Curtis, Jamie Lee, 135
Curtis, Tony, 135, 151–152, 156, 165, 166, 205, 248, 250, 292, 302, 310, 311, 335, 352, 523

Daillard, Wayne, 108–109
Dales, Jack, 184, 185, 186, 187, 262, 264
Dalitz, Moe, 221–222, 329n
D'Amato, Skinny, 176
Daniels, Clifton, xi, 381
Dark Victory: Ronald Reagan, MCA and the Mob (Moldea), x–xi, 451
Davenport, Walter, 39
David, Saul, 349–350, 352, 359
Davidson, Bill, 131, 157, 237, 252, 259
Davies, Marion, 76, 77
Davis, Bette, 86–87, 92–93, 95, 98, 114–115, 116, 165, 387
Davis, Martin, 481
Davis, Marvin, 2
Day, Doris, 251–252
Deaver, Michael, 461
Decca Records, 43, 241–242, 323–324
  MCA's purchase of, 296–297, 298, 299, 300
Deer Hunter, The (film), 409
DeFeo, Michael, 463
Defore, Don, 465
DeHaven, Gloria, 179
De Laurentiis, Dino, 397–398
Del Gaizo, Michael, 455n
DeMille, Cecil B., 45–46, 177–178
DeMotte, David, 393
Denker, Henry, ix–x, 185, 189, 331
Dennis, Ed, 468
Desilu Productions, 233, 291
Deutsch, Susan, 151, 170
Deverich, Nat, 104, 106
Diller, Barry, 393, 494, 501, 518
DiMaggio, Joe, 215–216
DiscoVision, 404–407, 410
Distillers Company Limited, 145
Dmytryk, Edward, 236–237
Donaldson, Michael, 448
"Doonesbury" (comic strip), 397n
Dorfman, Allen, 399n
Dorfman, Dan, 393, 473
Doris Jones Stein Foundation, 435
Dorsey, Tommy, 17, 69, 93–94
Dorskind, Albert, 219, 244, 254, 317, 321, 336, 351, 352, 357, 359, 365, 374, 405, 473
Dot Records, 231n
Douglas, Donald W., Jr., 330
Douglas, Kirk, 242–243, 252
Drabinsky, Garth, 449, 465n, 475–476, 484n

DreamWorks SKG, 500–501
Drinkhall, Jim, 415
Duel (TV movie), 387
Duke, Patty, 337
DuMont Television Network, 188*n*
Dunfee, Jack, 197
Duning, George, 67–68
Dunne, Dominick, 61, 164, 396*n*
Dutton, Fred, 319
Dykstra, Peter, 391

Earthquake (film), 372–373
Edwards, Blake, 257
Edwards, Jim, III, 465
Edwards, Ralph, 202–203
Ehrlich, Jake, 171
Eisner, Michael, 393, 471–472, 514
EMKA Corporation, 232
Emseeay and Company, 525
Enemy Within, The (Kennedy), 279–280, 304
Englander, Maurice, 56
Escovar, Martin, 120
Eszterhas, Joe, 479*n*
E.T. The Extra-Terrestrial (film), 426–427
Evan Picone clothing label, 368
Evans, Robert, 346*n*, 367–368, 389, 393*n*

Factor, John "Jake the Barber," 222, 279*n*
Falk, Peter, 338
Famous Artists Agency, 214, 287
Farnsworth, Arthur, 93
Farnsworth, Philo T., 117–118
Fat, Leung Chun, 521*n*
Faulkner, William, 281
Federal Bureau of Investigation (FBI), 5,
    96*n*, 124, 139, 188*n*, 286, 454, 458,
    504–505
Federal Communications Commission
    (FCC), 81, 266–268, 283, 287, 431,
    432, 443
Feinstein, Dianne, 492
Feldman, Charles, 92, 104, 134, 135, 153,
    185, 213–216, 287
Felsman, H. H. "Bob" and Max, 61–62
Fields, Freddie, 176–177, 259, 301, 385
Finley, Larry and Miriam, 108–109, 110,
    123, 125, 128
Fiorito, Ted, 17, 79
Firestone Tire and Rubber, 359
Fischer, Clifford C., 36

Fischetti, Charlie, 146
Fisher, Eddie, 291
Flaherty, George, 306
Fleming, Rhonda, 183
Flynn, Errol, 93, 98, 116, 386
Flynt, Elmo, 129
Folies-Bergère, 36–38
Fonda, Henry, 117
Ford, Frederick W., 268
Ford, Gerald, 381, 389, 402–403
Ford, Tennessee Ernie, 113*n*, 292
Ford Startime (TV show), 282
Forman, Milos, 372*n*
Fortune magazine, 265, 266
Four Star Productions, 230
Fratianno, Aladena "Jimmy the Weasel," 58,
    399
Fricano, John, 245, 292, 293–294
Friedkin, William, 391–392*n*
Friedland, Lou, 158, 231–232, 306*n*, 357,
    515
Friedman, Harry, 193–194, 302
Fugeso, Peter, 450
Furuichi, Mamoru, 495

Gable, Clark, 156, 194, 303
Garfield, Harry, 324
Garfield, John, 86, 95, 116, 386
Garland, Judy, 291, 361*n*
Garner, James, 468–469
Gary, Lorraine, 374*n*, 388, 437, 438
Gates, Daryl, 438–439
Gates, Tom, 455–456, 459, 466, 487, 504
Gazarra, Ben, 337
Gazley, Al and Kathy, 32, 33
Geffen, David, 410, 474–475, 481, 483, 484,
    500–501, 520, 522
Geffen Records, 474–475
General Amusement Corporation, 287
General Electric Theater (TV show),
    189–191, 261
Gershwin, Jerry, 373
Gerth, Jeff, 396, 397
Getty Oil, 428
Giancana, Sam, 146, 221, 304, 305, 329*n*,
    395
Giaquinto, Eugene, 455–456, 457–459, 466
Glaser, Joe, 19, 71, 140–141
Gleason, Jackie, 207
Gobel, George, 203–205
Goetz, William, 154, 155, 200, 242*n*

Goldblatt, Joel, 140
Golden, Joan, 516
Goldenson, Leonard, 230, 239
Goldhammer, Leonard, 51
Goldstone, Ed, 419
Goldwyn, Samuel, 45–46, 92, 182,
    212–213
Goldwyn, Samuel, Jr., 319
Gollob, Herman, 168
Goodheart, Bill, III, 29, 31, 71
Goodheart, Billy, Jr., 15–16, 17, 18, 20, 28,
    30, 31, 32–33, 39, 64n, 69, 71, 72, 83,
    175, 237–238
Goodman, Benny, 17, 71
Gordy, Berry, 474
Gosden, Freeman, 162
Gotti, John, 456, 457–458
Gottlieb, Bob, 408, 410
Gottlieb, Myron, 449, 476
G. P. Putnam's Sons, 369
Grable, Betty, 79–81, 92, 98–100, 209–210,
    211–213, 286, 386
Gradle, Harry S., 12, 15, 19, 42, 100, 149
Graham, Sheilah, 99
Grant, Arnold, 222
Grant, Cary, 201, 205, 250–251, 260–261,
    292, 314n, 322
Grauman, Sid, 92
Green, Levis, 133–135
Greenberg, Alex Louis, 37, 141
Greene, Milton, 216, 217–218
Greshler, Abner J., 174–180, 236–237
Grossman, Harry, 374n
Gulf and Western Industries, 367, 393
Gully, Richard, 519

Haber, Bill, 386
Haber, Joyce, 396
Hackett, Harold, 32, 129, 237
Hadl, Robert, 453, 459
Halley, Rudolph, 147–148
Hamer, John W., 290, 292, 293
Hamm, Fred, 12
Hammerstein, Dorothy, 75
Hardy, Ed, 369
Harlow, Jean, 146
Harmetz, Aljean, 473
Harris, Charles, 11, 27, 28, 77, 413, 423,
    424
Harris, Kathryn, 453
Hartman, Don, 238

Hays, Will, 52n
Hayward, Brooke, 104, 107
Hayward, Leland, 4, 103–108, 109, 122,
    186n, 195, 300
Hayward, Susan, 97–98
Hayworth, Rita, 149–150, 153n, 292
Hazen, Joe, 178, 180–181
Head, Edith, 346
Hearst, William Randolph, 77–78
Hefner, Hugh, 398
Heidt, Horace, 17, 41, 160
Heisman, Art, 525
Heller, Seymour, 59
Henreid, Paul, 88–89
Henry, Edd, 346, 347, 357, 372
Hentoff, Nat, 136
Hepburn, Audrey, 197–198, 292
Hersh, Seymour, 395–396, 397
Heston, Charlton, 130, 373, 417–418
Heymann, Edward L., 462
Heymann, Walter M., 316n, 352
Hilton, Barron, 441
Hinshaw, Gerry, 344
Hirata, Masahiko, 481, 482, 495
Hitchcock, Alfred, 205, 252–254, 275, 291,
    334, 346–347
Hockey, televised, 159
Hoffa, James R., 222, 279, 280, 395
Holiner, Mann, 111
Hollywood Canteen, 95–98, 99
Hollywood Palladium, 93–94
Hollywood shakedown scandal, 141n, 146
Hope, Bob, 49, 107n, 264, 288
Hopper, Dennis, 371n
Hopper, Hedda, 77, 211, 212, 224
Hornblow, Leonora, 220, 276, 436
Horowitz, Zach, 453
House Un-American Activities Committee
    (HUAC), 139, 143
Hover, Herman, 224–226
Hronek, Frank, 328–329
Hucksters, The (film), 127–128
Hudson, Rock, 245–246, 252, 292, 338
Hughes, Howard, 93, 222, 233
Hundley, William, 463
Hunt, Marsha, 139
Hunt, Sam "Golf Bag," 23
Hunter, Ross, 363n
Hussong, Bob, 81, 335, 346, 356, 358
Hyams, Joe, 335
Hyde, Johnny, 150, 153n, 210, 214, 247
Hymers, R. L., Jr., 464

Ice Follies, 78, 159
Industry, The (David), 349–350
International Alliance of Theatrical Stage
    Employees, 263
International Creative Management, 385n,
    480
Isadora (film), 351
Isgur, Lee, 460
It's a Wonderful Life (film), 117

Jackson, Michael, 408
Jacobs, Merle, 44, 60, 64, 65, 175
James, Harry, 99–100, 209, 212, 286,
    386
Janssen, David, 421
Jarvis, John Brian, 490
Jasinski, Bernard, 294
Jaws (film), 387–389
Jewish Mob, 143–145
Johnny Staccato (TV show), 257
John Paul II, Pope, 452
Johnson, Erskine, 115
Johnson, Lady Bird, 2, 319, 330
Johnson, Lyndon, 231, 318, 319–320,
    330–331, 344–345
Johnson, Stephen, 389
Johnson, Tom, 467
Johnson, Van, 106n, 171
Johnston, Alva, 86
Jolson, Al, 23
Jones, Carolyn, 258–259
Jones, Geoffrey, 27
Jones, Mary Gardiner, 330n
Jones, Merle, 233
Jones, Thomas V., 421
Jordan, Hamilton, 401–402
Jukebox Jury (TV show), 203
Jules and Doris Stein Foundation,
    525n
Jules Stein Eye Institute, 333–334,
    438
Jurassic Park (film), 493
Juro, Monte, 111
Justice Department, 5, 124, 129
    illegal activities, alleged, 487–488,
        503–505
    MCA-organized crime investigations,
        446–448, 453–456, 458–459, 463–464,
        466–468
    See also antitrust actions *under* MCA

Kalmbach, Herbert, 344
Kansas City Night Hawks, 13–14, 18–19, 25
Kanter, Jay, 161, 169–170, 172, 173, 217,
    218, 231, 248, 278n, 297, 347–348,
    350–351, 352, 371n, 373
Kapp Records, 324
Kaskowitz, Herm, 448
Katzenberg, Jeffrey, 471, 474, 500–501, 520
Kaufman, Joseph (doctor), 389
Kaufman, Joseph (producer), 156
Kaye, Danny, 247–248, 292
Kefauver, Estes, 58, 142–144
Keith, Brian, 219
Kelly, Grace, 278
Kelly, Pat, 192
Kennamer, Rex, 355, 356, 361, 397
Kennedy, Joe, 277–278, 279
Kennedy, John F., 226, 278–279, 285,
    303–305, 317–318
Kennedy, Robert F., 226, 279–280, 318, 344,
    345
    antitrust actions against MCA, 277,
        280–284, 288, 295, 299, 306
    Monroe and, 304, 305
Kennedy Center for the Performing Arts,
    318n, 415
Kerkorian, Kirk, 368–369, 394, 408, 433
Khan, Aly, 149–150
Kid Stays in the Picture, The (Evans), 368
Killers, The (film), 332n
King, Wayne, 19, 41, 160
King Kong (film) (1976), 397–398
Kingmaker, The (Denker), ix–x
Kings Row (film), 84–85
Kinnaird, Dennis, 454
Kintner, Robert, 238–240, 257, 331
Kissinger, Henry, 402
Klein, Gene, 317, 329n, 358, 366, 476
Knoedelseder, Bill, 447, 467–468
Korshak, Marshall, 141, 327
Korshak, Sidney, 4–5, 140–141, 280, 346n,
    358n
    Bluhdorn and, 367
    death of, 519
    Evans and, 368, 393n
    exposé on, 395–397
    friends of, 326–328
    organized crime and, 142–143, 179n,
        279n, 328–329, 395–396, 399–400, 420,
        440–442
    RKO purchase attempt, 222–223

Korshak, Sidney (*cont.*)
  SAG strike, 263–264
  United Farm Workers and, 398–399
  Wasserman's relationship with, 395–396,
    397–398, 420–421
Kramer, Karl, xi, 4, 20, 37, 64*n*, 105, 118,
    122, 129, 158, 161, 168, 202, 204, 206,
    301, 421
Krasna, Norman, 228
Kreitz, Neil, 448
Krim, Arthur, 318, 319
Kubrick, Stanley, 347
Kuencer, Walter, 226–227, 292
Kula, Sam, 497
Kupcinet, Irv, 223, 326, 396
Kyser, Kay, 67–68, 113–114, 160

Ladd, Alan, Jr., 371*n*
Laemmle, Carl, 78–79, 321
Lalli, Frank, 397
La Mare, Rufus, 238
Lamarr, Hedy, 97
Lancaster, Burt, 363*n*
Landmark Services, 345
Lang, Jennings, 161, 167, 207–208, 257, 314,
    337, 338*n*, 344, 357, 372, 375, 411–412,
    477, 508
  shooting scandal, 170–174
Lang, Pamela, 167, 171–172, 173
Lansky, Meyer, 146, 328–329, 358*n*
  proposed film about, 456–458
Lanza, Mario, 152, 220
Lasker, Albert, 31*n*
Lasky, Jesse, 45–46
Lastfogel, Abe, 69, 71, 247–248, 267, 385
Last Movie, The (film), 371*n*
Last Temptation of Christ, The (film),
    464–466
Laughton, Charles, 252, 267
Lawford, Peter, 286, 303
Lazar, Irving "Swifty," 32, 72, 136–137, 213,
    291, 484, 519
Leanse, David, 141, 142
Leave It to Beaver (TV show), 204
Leeds Music, 325
Leif, Carol Ann, 360, 384, 437, 452, 490
Leif, Ronnie, 276–277, 360, 384
Leigh, Janet, 133–135, 274, 302, 311
LeRoy, Mervyn, 92, 183, 264, 347
Levee, Mike, Jr., 297
Levitt, Harold, 275

Levy, Shawn, 179
Lewin, Henri, 441
Lewin, James, 503, 504, 505
Lewis, Jerry, 147, 174–181, 234–235
Lewis, Judy, 199
Linsk, Lester, 87, 279
Lipsey, Lillian, 206
Lipsey, Maurie, 4, 20, 24, 29, 122, 129, 206,
    343, 421
Lipton, David, 136, 158, 309, 354, 356
Lipton, Martin, 462
Lockhart, June, 264
Loder, John, 97
Loevinger, Lee, 285–286, 288, 294, 296,
    297–298, 299
Logan, Josh, 259
Lombardo, Guy, 17, 21–25, 30–31, 296, 421
Lombardo, Joey "the Clown," 399*n*
Loos, Anita, 383
Los Angeles Music Center, 342–343, 498
Los Angeles Times, 396–397, 467–468
Losey, Joseph, 348*n*
Lowenstein, Rupert, 514
Lucas, George, 370, 371, 372, 425–426
Luft, Sid, 291
Lytess, Natasha, 217

MacArthur, Malcolm, 256, 295, 307
MacDonald, Arthur D., 393
MacKenzie, Gisele, 291, 301
MacLaine, Shirley, 226, 235, 356–357
MacMurray, Fred, 174
Madden, Marguerite, 29, 64, 72, 198
Made-for-TV movies, 338
Magnin, Edgar, 383
Magnum, P.I. (TV show), 432
Mahoney, Roger, 464–465
Mailer, Norman, xii*n*
Majors, Lee, 337
Maloney, George, 23–24
Mandrell, Barbara, 431*n*
Mankiewicz, Joseph, 101–102
Mannix, Eddie, 134, 135
Mannix (TV show), 336–337
Mansfield, Jayne, 218–219
Margolis, David, 463
Marshall, Mollie, 51, 273, 401
Martin, Dean, 64, 147, 174–181, 234–235,
    236–237, 363*n*
Marx, Zeppo, 101
Maschio, John, 106, 210, 412

Maschke, Helen, 60
Maschke, Maurice, 52–53, 54
Maschke, Maurice, Jr., 221*n*
Mason, Sully, 68
Massengale, Sarah, 381
Matsushita, Masaharu, 495, 496
Matsushita Electrical Company, 1, 3, 4, 406,
    481–487, 493, 494–497, 499, 503,
    505–507, 525
Mayer, Louis B., 46, 78, 80*n*, 117, 155, 157,
    163, 284*n*
Mayfair Casino, 56, 57–60, 62–65
MCA
  acquistions of rival agencies, 20, 81–82,
      101, 104–106, 150
  actors' power, promotion of, 116–117,
      152–157
  Adams's departure, 364–365
  agents' treatment within, 131–132,
      192–195
  antitrust actions against, 5, 108–109,
      123–125, 127, 128–129, 224–229,
      232–234, 245, 255, 256–259, 277,
      280–284, 286, 288, 289–294, 294–295,
      296, 297–301, 305, 306, 307, 353–354,
      358–359, 409–410
  bait-and-switch tactics, 257
  band-booking business, 16–17, 18–25,
      29–31, 43–44, 67–68, 71, 108–109, 123,
      220
  Beverly Hills headquarters, 75–76, 306
  Black Tower headquarters, 306, 315,
      335–336, 517
  board of directors, 330, 351–352, 421,
      460–461
  bookkeeping, 35
  branch offices, 70, 125, 339–340*n*
  broadcasting operation, 443–444
  Bronfman regime, 513–515, 517–518,
      526–527
  cable television ventures, 409–410, 431,
      473, 518
  casting decisions of studios, influence on,
      228, 235–237
  CBS, proposed purchase of, 496–497, 500
  class action suit against, 484–485, 525
  Communist witch-hunts and, 139
  conspiracies, alleged involvement in,
      487–488, 503–505
  contract renegotiations, 178–179, 180–181
  coup attempt against Wasserman, 350,
      351–352, 354–360, 361
  Decca Records, purchase of, 296–297,
      298, 299, 300
  Disney's war with, 471–472
  established stars, focus on, 161
  European production of films, 150–151,
      156*n*
  executives in entertainment industry,
      influence with, 238–240
  executive vice presidential triumvirate,
      336, 359
  fashion standard for employees, 107–108,
      135–136, 487
  FCC investigation of television, 266–268,
      287
  fictionalized portrait of, 127–128
  film library, 230–233, 298, 306, 431
  financial situation, 202, 310, 353,
      362–364, 369, 391, 392, 407–408, 410,
      424, 448, 460
  financial success of cooperative clients,
      155–156, 160–161, 204–205
  Firestone's takeover bid, 359
  firing of clients, 152, 165–166
  firing of employees, 379
  Folies-Bergère, 36–38
  founding of, 12, 14–16
  full-service agency for nightclubs, 39–40
  global predicaments, 339–342
  golden parachutes for executives, 461–462
  gross profit deals for clients, 152–156
  Hollywood Canteen, 95–98
  hostile takeover, protection against, 394,
      433–434, 460–461
  hotel business, 354
  ice shows, 20, 78, 159
  incorporation of, 35
  incorporation of clients, 116, 160,
      162–163, 180
  initial public offering, 254
  as Jewish company, 64
  labor relations, 16–17, 29–30, 37–38,
      376–379, 380–381, 416–417
  Lang shooting scandal, 170–174
  Las Vegas bookings, 220
  legal actions by clients, 93–94, 111–112
  legal department, 71
  literary agencies, 151*n*
  London headquarters, 197
  magazine business, 393
  Matsushita's ownership of, 3, 4, 485–487,
      493, 494–497, 499, 503, 505–507
  Matsushita's purchase of, 481–485, 525

MCA (*cont.*)

MCA name, retirement of, 517

media relations of, 125–127, 265, 266, 284, 310

merchandising division, 392

Michigan State Fair of 1937, 66–67

movie theater business, 448–449, 475–476, 484*n*

music division, 323–325, 363, 392, 410, 431, 474–475, 495

NBC's proposed merger with, 434

nepotism by Stein, 20, 276

New York headquarters, 196, 307

New York office, opening of, 28–29

organized crime and, x–xi, 38, 328–329, 366*n*, 419–420, 438–439, 446–448, 451–459, 463–464, 466–468

packaging practices, 67–68, 70, 109, 110, 227–228

Paramount's proposed merger with, 393, 481

"piece of talent" attitude toward clients, 259–261

public relations responsibilities, 92–93, 99–100, 194

publishing business, 369

quid pro quo deals, 31, 108

race relations, 329–330

real estate and oil speculation, 113, 410

reorganization of 1959, 254

ruining of rebellious clients' careers, 110–112, 258–259

SAG strike of 1960, 262–263

SAG waiver, 184–187, 190–191, 229–230, 287, 293–294

as satirical target, 248–250, 336–337

Seagram's purchase of, 1–3, 503, 505–509

shareholders, 4, 206–208, 253*n*, 391, 475, 484–485, 525

Sheinberg's exit agreement, 513

social ecology of clients, 199, 201

star leverage used for blackmail, 282–283

stealing clients from rival agencies, 167, 174–180, 214–216, 218, 245–248, 258

syndication of TV shows, 431–432, 468–469

talent agency business, 69–70, 79–85, 86–89, 104–106, 110–112, 116–117, 150, 152–157, 160–161, 174–181, 204–205, 209–219, 245–248, 258–261, 287–288, 296, 297, 299–302, 306–307

television productions, 157–160, 184–191, 202–205, 219–220, 230, 243, 257, 282–283, 287–288

terrorist attacks on, 489–490

theater productions, 70, 106, 314–315, 408

tour business, 321–323, 345, 369, 392, 486

toy business, 448, 473–474

training program for new agents, 167–170

under–the–table payments, 207–208

video technology program, 404–407, 410

Wasserman's election as chairman and CEO, 374

Wasserman's fiftieth anniversary with, 445–446

Wasserman's hiring, 44, 63, 65

Wasserman's management style, 135–137

Wasserman's promotion to president, 121–122, 126–127, 129, 130

Wasserman's relations with clients, 89, 151–152

Wasserman's successor as president, 336, 364, 373–374

Wasserman's transfer of power to Sheinberg, 443–444

Werblin's departure, 325–326

Westinghouse's takeover bid, 353–354, 358–359

wives' involvement, 91–92

writings about, ix–xiii

See also Universal Studios

McBride, Joseph, 322

McCleary, Joel, 401

McClure, Doug, 338–339

McCoy, Horace, 90

McDaniel, Ron, xiii

McElwaine, Guy, 420

McGill, Dan, 453

McGowan, Everett, 78

McHale's Navy (TV show), 314

McPhee, John, 310

McPherson, Harry, 330

MEA Holdings, 483

Meany, George, 263

Medallion Theatre (TV show), 189

Meese, Ed, 487

Meiklejohn, William, 81–82

Melcher, Marty, 251–252

Menendez murders, 488–489

Merrick, David, 315

Meyer, Ron, 386, 517

MGM, 157, 394, 433

Michigan State Fair of 1937, 66–67

Migden, Chet, 187
Miller, Adelaide Stein, 20, 43
Miller, Arthur, 217
Miller, Charles, 4, 20, 28, 122, 129, 206, 301, 343, 352, 364, 421
Mills Music, 324
Mining, Lou, 32
Miniseries, 338
Minow, Newton, 283–284
Minton, Walter J., 484
Misfits, The (film), 303
Mr. Baseball (film), 486
Mitchum, Robert, 194
Mittelman, Sheldon, 443, 517, 522
Moguls: Inside the Business of Show Business (Pye), x
Moldea, Dan, x–xi, 263, 451, 452
Monroe, Marilyn, 210–212, 214–218, 219, 226, 248, 278, 302–305
Montagne, Eddie, 314
Moore, Constance, 102
Moretti, Willie, 146
Morishita, Yoichi, 495, 500, 506, 507
Moss, Robert, 436
Motion Picture Association of America, 320
Motion Picture Country House and Hospital, 436, 491n
Motown Records, 474
Moyers, Bill, 319
Muhl, Ed, 205, 241, 242, 243, 244, 339, 347, 373
Mundy, Alice, 432
Murdoch, Rupert, 435n, 491n
Murdock, David, 412
Murphy, A. D., 363, 479
Murphy, Franklin, 334, 362, 498
Music Corporation of America. *See* MCA
Myers, Casey. *See* Wasserman, Casey
Myers, Jack, x, 156n, 200, 215, 221, 360, 361, 373, 384–385, 401, 419, 420, 436, 437, 477, 489, 516, 523, 524

Nate, Rowena, 171
National Eye Institute, 345n
National Lampoon's Animal House (film), 408
National Telefilm Associates, 230–231
Nazi Germany, 83
NBC, 178–179, 239–240, 257, 282
  MCA's proposed merger with, 434
Needham, Hal, 421

Nelson family, 249
Newcomer, John, 454, 463–464, 467, 468
Newman, Paul, 261, 292
New York Post, 296
New York Shakespeare Festival, 382
New York Times, 295, 395
New York Titans, 325–326
Niblo, Fred, 90
Nichols, Robert Booth, 466, 488, 504
Niebahr, Eddie, 16
1941 (film), 409
Nitti, Frank "the Enforcer," 34, 69
Nixon, Richard, 344, 345, 377, 431
Northcross, Sam, 257
North Star Graphics, 455–456
Nype, Russell, 132–133

Obringer, Roy, 138
O'Hara, Ray, 20
Oliver, King Joe, 13
Olson, Ron, 459
O'Malley, David, 204–205
O'Malley, Walter, 327n
Onassis, Jacqueline Kennedy, xii, 285
One Flew Over the Cuckoo's Nest (film), 372n
Oppenheimer, Gerald, 27
Oppenheimer, Harold (father), 26, 27, 28
Oppenheimer, Harold (son), xii, xiii, 27, 34, 435
Orey, Michael, 467
Organized crime, 519
  cooperation by mobsters, 38
  income tax evasion and, 34
  Jewish Mob, 143–145
  Kefauver investigation, 142–148
  Kennedys and, 277n, 304–305
  Korshak and, 142–143, 179n, 279n, 328–329, 395–396, 399–400, 420, 440–442
  Lansky film war, 456–458
  Las Vegas ventures, 221–222
  MCA and, x–xi, 38, 328–329, 366n, 419–420, 438–439, 446–448, 451–459, 463–464, 466–468
  motion picture industry and, 69, 145–148
  in nightclub business, 19, 22–24, 57–58
  Ross and, 366
Orsatti, Frank and Victor, 79–80

O'Shea, Daniel, 233–234
Ovitz, Michael, 4, 323, 385–386, 477–478, 479–481, 482, 485, 486, 503, 513–514

Pacific Coast Hockey League, 159
Paley, William, 24, 30, 162–163
Papp, Joseph, 382
Paramount Pictures, 2, 82, 367, 368, 501
    King Kong affair, 397–398
    MCA's proposed merger with, 393, 481
    sale of film library to MCA, 230–232
Park, Arthur, 112, 137, 182, 227, 301
Parsons, Louella, 78, 82, 100, 129, 181, 224, 241
Payne, John, 98
Payne, Julie, 384
Peck, Gregory, 203
Perkins, Rowland, 386
Perry, Lou, 176
Pesci, Joe, 324n
Peter Gunn (TV show), 257
Peterson, Virgil, 221
Petrillo, James, 17, 23, 29–30, 38–39, 70, 81, 123
Pickford, Mary, 78–79
Pickman, Milton, 32
Picone, Joe, 367
Pidgeon, Walter, 187, 262
Pioneer Electronic Corporation, 406
Pirchner, Herman, 56, 57, 62
Pisello, Sal, 446–447, 448, 452, 453, 455, 463–464
Pizzo, Steve, 505
Plimpton, George, xii
Polan, Barron, 106
Pollock, Tom, 425–426, 449, 495, 508, 517
Posner, Leonard, 165, 226–229, 231, 232–234, 245, 249, 256–259, 277, 281–284, 286, 288, 289–290, 294, 296, 297, 299–300, 305, 307–308
Potter, Peter, 203
Power, Tyrone, 156
Powolny, Frank, 99
Prager, Susan, 498
Preisler, Eddie, 51–52
Premiere Channel, 409–410
Presser, Jackie, 439, 442
Price, Frank, 425, 426–427, 430
Propper, Harry, 57, 59, 65
Prostitution, 278n
Pryor, Tom, 235

Psycho (film), 253–254
Puttnam, David, 394, 502
Pye, Michael, x, 87

Quodbach, Al, 22–23, 24–25

Rackin, Martin, 238
Rackmil, Milton, 241–242, 243, 244, 254, 262, 274, 285, 317, 366n, 373, 519
Raft, George, 146, 147
Ragle, Ruth, 294
Raiders of the Lost Ark (film), 425–426
Rand, Sally, 36, 37, 38
Randall, Tony, 236–237
Randle, Bill, 67
Raskin, Hyman, 188n
Ray, Nicholas, 200
Raymond, Julie, 322
Reagan, Maureen, 83, 276
Reagan, Nancy Davis, 183, 354, 438, 441–442, 446
Reagan, Ronald, ix–xi, 2, 5, 354, 423, 467
    acting career, 82, 84–85, 116–117, 182–183, 332n
    antitrust actions against MCA, 293–294
    criticism of Hollywood, 470–471
    draft status, 83–84
    governorship of, 331–333, 441–442
    as Las Vegas headliner, 184n
    liberal activism, 138–139
    marriages, 82, 183
    as MCA partner, 191
    presidency of, xi, 386–387, 414–415, 416, 432–433, 461
    SAG leadership, 138, 139, 182, 186–187, 190n, 262, 265
    SAG strike, 262, 263, 264–265
    speaking engagement in Japan, 469–471
    television career, 188–191, 261–262
    trust fund for, 333, 415
    Wasserman's fiftieth anniversary with MCA, 445–446
Reagan Library, 461
Real, Manuel, 484
Redstone, Sumner, 501, 518
Reinfeld, Joe, 144n
Reischauer, Edwin, 341
Reno, Janet, 505
Research to Prevent Blindness, Inc., 265–266, 438

Residual payments, 186, 187, 262–265
Revue Productions, 158, 185, 187–191, 204, 219–220, 229, 243, 244, 287–288
Reynolds, Burt, 350, 392, 421
Reynolds, Debbie, 326n
Rickles, Don, 394n, 441
Ritchie, Daniel, 336, 351, 352, 353, 359, 364n
Rizzitello, Michael, 457
RKO Radio Pictures, 222–223, 233–234, 277–278, 397
Roach, Hal, 186–187
Robb, Dave, 294
Rockford, Jane, 525
Rockford, Mickey, 4, 20–21, 40, 64n, 122, 129, 159, 161, 166, 206, 301, 343, 421
Rockford Files, The (TV show), 468–469
Rockwell, Tommy, 140
Rogers, Henry, 114
Rohatyn, Felix, 421, 434, 462, 481, 485
Rollins, Jack, 258
Rooney, Mickey, 264–265
Rose, Marianne, 50
Rosen, Deborah, 525
Rosenfeld, Michael, 386
Rosenstein, Jaik, 302
Rosenthal, Herb, 4, 83, 91–92, 122, 129, 137, 161, 206, 207, 301
Rosenthal, Jerry, 251n
Ross, Brian, 398
Ross, Diana, 408n
Ross, N. Joseph, 180
Ross, Steve, 366, 428, 474, 475, 522
Rosselli, Johnny, 146, 304, 395
Rosten, Irwin, 445
Roth, Myron, 453
Roth, Otto, 18–19
Royal, John, 49
Rozelle, Pete, 358n
Rubin, Howard, 301
Rudnick, Marvin, 400, 441n, 446, 447, 448, 453–454, 463–464, 467, 468, 487, 503–505
Russell, Jane, 152
Russell, Rosalind, 198, 292
Rutkin, James "Niggy," 144
Ryan, Ray, 222

Sacks, Manie, 32, 71, 100, 239
Safier, Gloria, 132
Sahl, Mort, 249

St. John, Jill, 218, 402n
Salinger, Pierre, 284
Salkind, Marty, 324
Sanders, Coon, 13–14, 19, 25
Sands, Tommy, 249
Santarelli, Donald E., 457
Saphier, Jimmy, 107n, 288
Sarnoff, David, 117, 118, 163, 239, 277, 278n
Sarnoff, Robert, 239, 240, 258
Saturday Evening Post, 86, 124, 125–127, 128
Schary, Dore, 155n, 157, 238
Schatz, Tom, 245, 253
Scheer, Robert, 383, 414
Schenck, Joe, 141n, 210–211, 284n
Schenck, Nick, 157
Schiff, Gunther, 186n
Schiff, Hans, 152n
Schindler's List (film), 493
Schlesinger, Arthur, 304
Schreiber, Rita, 391
Schreiber, Taft, 4, 20, 28, 35, 43, 83, 89, 105, 114, 118, 129, 130–131, 132, 158, 161–163, 188n, 195, 206, 243, 244, 250n, 274, 333, 351, 366, 369
    Adams's departure from MCA, 364–365
    art collection, 122, 343
    coup attempt against Wasserman, 351–352, 355–356, 357, 359
    death of, 389–391
    FCC investigation of television, 266–268, 287
    political involvement, 331, 332, 344, 381
    power base within MCA, 343–344
    star leverage, theory of, 283
Schrier, Morris, 71, 122, 125, 129, 207, 208, 245
Schumach, Murray, xi–xii, 228, 295, 306, 381–382, 383
Schuyten, Peter, 404
Schwab, Betty, 200
Schwartz, William D., 391, 392
Sciandra, Edward M. "the Conductor," 455–456
Scorsese, Martin, 464, 465, 466
Scott, Rick, 171
Scoville, William, 382
Screen Actors Guild (SAG), 96, 117, 179, 182, 190n, 299, 378
    MCA's waiver, 184–187, 190–191, 229–230, 287, 293–294

Screen Actors Guild (SAG) (*cont.*)
  Reagan's leadership, 138, 139, 182,
    186–187, 190*n*, 262, 265
  strike of 1960, 262–265
  strikes of 1980 and 1981, 416–417
Seagram Corporation, 1–3, 145, 476,
    501–503, 505–509
Secret Ceremony (film), 348*n*
Seifert, Walter, 419–420, 457
Selznick, David O., 92, 155*n*, 184, 233, 245,
    284*n*
Selznick, Myron, 103–104
Sensurround special effect, 372–373
Setnick, Al, 50, 51
Seven Year Itch, The (film), 213–216
Seymour, Whitney North, 297–298, 299
Shearer, Norma, 134, 368
Sheinberg, Bill, 498
Sheinberg, Jonathan, 498–499*n*
Sheinberg, Sidney, 344, 352, 357, 363, 365,
    406, 407, 408, 409, 417, 424, 425, 430,
    431, 433, 451, 459, 468, 471, 472, 473,
    474, 475, 476, 488, 489, 494, 496, 499,
    500, 506, 507–508, 509, 514, 517, 520
  independent production company, 513,
    518
  Matsushita's purchase of MCA, 481, 482,
    483, 484, 485, 486–487
  MCA presidency, appointment to, 374
  Spielberg and, 387–388, 426, 427, 428,
    493
  Wasserman's relationship with, 331,
    374–375, 437–438, 497
  Wasserman's transfer of power to, 443–444
Sheraton Universal Hotel, 354
Sheridan, Ann, 337
Shiffrin, Bill, 218
Shikanai, Nobutaka, 470
Shiva, Guedaliahou "Gil," 383, 423
Shoriki, Nobutu, 342
Shurr, Louis, 81
Siegel, Benjamin "Bugsy," 146, 147
Silent Syndicate, 57–58, 147, 221, 222
Silvers, Chuck, 322
Silvers, Phil, 201, 227
Simmons, Matty, 408
Sinatra, Frank, 94, 146, 147, 163, 224,
    235–236, 286, 302
  Wasserman's conflict with, 165–166
Singer, Johnny, 60, 164–165
Skelton, Red, 160
Skouras, Spyros, 211–212, 279

Skullduggery (film), 349–350
Slow Fade to Black (TV movie), 338–339
Slusser, Dan, 453
Smith, Geoffrey, 485
Smith, Lillian, 258
Smokey and the Bandit (film), 392
Sokolov, Harry, 287–288
Some Like It Hot (film), 247–248
Song, Mickey, 304
Sony, 406, 470, 471, 507
Spada, James, 304
Spartacus (film), 242–243, 252, 285
Specktor, Fred, 268–269
Spielberg, Steven, 322–323, 366, 387–389,
    409, 426–428, 475, 492, 493, 500–501,
    520
Stacher, Joseph "Doc," 144*n*, 420
Stanfill, Dennis, 380
Stans, Maurice, 344
Stark, Ray, 392
Stars Over Hollywood (TV show), 158
Star Wars (film), 371*n*
Stavin, Richard, 455, 458, 466–467, 468,
    487–488, 504
Steiger, Paul, 396
Stein, Bill, 4, 10, 12–13, 15, 16, 21, 22, 23,
    43, 44, 65, 66, 70, 100, 101, 161
Stein, David, 43, 119, 423, 519
Stein, Doris Jones, 41, 42, 90, 126, 182, 198,
    354, 356, 357, 362, 364–365, 415, 422,
    423
  death of, 435
  eccentricity in old age, 412–413
  Hollywood Canteen, 95, 97
  Jewish identity, 383
  marriage of, 26–28
  memoirs, xii–xiii
  as mother, 77
  philanthropic activities, 266, 334
  social life, 29, 102, 197, 199, 201
Stein, Jean, xii, xiii, 41, 77, 91, 198–199, 281,
    382, 422
Stein, Jules, 4
  antique collection, 10, 42, 75*n*, 149,
    196–197
  autobiography, xi–xii, 381–382
  awards and honors, 381
  band-booking business, 11–12, 13–14
  clothing preferences, 14
  death of, 422–424
  early years, 9–10
  education, 10–11, 12

as father, 77, 382–383
fictionalized portrait of, ix–x
flying paranoia, 195–196
Friedkin and, 391–392n
furniture boutique business, 197
gambling by, 92
graphology, interest in, 63n
Hayworth and, 149–150
"head of the family" status, 100–101
health problems, 265, 362, 365, 411–412
homes of, 41–42, 90–91, 237n
Hopper and, 371n
investing by, 41
irrelevance in old age, 411–412
Jewish identity, 65, 383
Kennedys and, 285
kidnap threats against, 39, 40
marriage of, 26–28
media coverage of, 109–110, 125–127
medical career, 12–13, 16, 151
Nype and, 132–133
philanthropic activities, 265–266, 333–334, 345n, 381
physical appearance, 10
political involvement, 331, 333, 344, 415
Reagan trust fund, 333, 415
schmoozing strategy with clients, 87
Schreiber's death, 390
social life, 77–78
stinginess of, 89, 195, 196
vanden Heuvel and, 281
Wasserman's relationship with, 65, 89, 101, 351
will of, 412n, 423–424
See also MCA
Stein, Louis, 9–10, 100–101
Stein, Rosa Cohen, 9–10, 43
Stein, Shirley, 412
Stein, Susan, 41, 77, 91, 198–199, 382–383, 435
Steinberg, Herb, 322, 323
Sterling, Robert, 136
Stevens, George, Jr., 497–498
Stevens, Inger, 258
Stevens, Stella, 179n
Stewart, James, 83, 117, 151, 152–155
Sting, The (film), 370
Stompanato, Johnny, 146–147
Straight, Charlie, 19
Strauss, Robert, 2, 421, 461, 462, 482–483, 485
Street-Porter, Tim, 523, 524

Strickling, Howard, 194
Strong, Edwin P., 53, 54, 121n
Styne, Jule, 21n
Styne, Norton, 21
Suber, Chuck, 36, 38, 43, 69, 432–433
Sugarland Express, The (film), 387
Sullivan, Richard, 452
Sunday, Billy, 10
Susman, Allen, 297, 298, 453–454
Susskind, David, 257, 291
Sweet Charity (film), 354, 356–357
Syndication of TV shows, 431–432, 468–469

Tanen, Ned, 324, 350, 365, 371–372, 373, 376, 392, 394n, 408–409, 425, 426, 427, 429
Tanii, Akio, 485–486, 495
Tarnopol, Nat "the Rat," 366n, 439–440
Tatelman, Harry, 83, 131, 132, 338–339, 346, 430
Teagarden, Jack, 109
Teamsters Union, 221, 222, 279, 280, 327n, 377, 380, 399, 416, 417, 442
Teller, Al, 508
Temple, Shirley, 152
Tennant, Cecil, 150
Thalberg, Irving, 79
Tham, Rudy, 441
Thau, Benny, 134, 135
This Is Your Life (TV show), 202–203
Thomas, Bob, 79, 311
Thompson, Edward, 266
Thompson, Robert J., 313
Thornton, Charles "Tex," 306n, 352
Thoroughly Modern Millie (film), 348
Tierney, Gene, 106n
Time magazine, 108, 109–110, 309–310
Tobias, Andrew, 359–360
Tobin, Jack, 328
Tolson, Clyde, 188n
Tormé, Mel, 249
Torn Curtain (film), 346–347
Torrio, Johnny, 38
Touhy, Roger, 40
Trachtenberg, J. A., 418
Treaty Trap, The (Beilenson), 433
Truman, Harry S, 141
Trump, Donald, 460
Turner, Lana, 146–147, 251
Twentieth Century Fox, 2, 81, 243, 333, 415
2001: A Space Odyssey (film), 347

UCLA, 333–334, 498, 526
Unger, Oliver, 231
UNI Records, 324
United Farm Workers, 398–399
United Jewish Welfare Fund, 200
United States Information Agency, 340
Universal City, 6, 242, 243, 315–317
Universal City Plaza, 354
Universal CityWalk, 6, 496
Universal Studios, 3, 78, 138, 154, 170, 205
    actors' treatment at, 337
    bad films of late 1960s, 345–348, 349–351
    business-oriented approach to filmmaking,
        312–313
    commissary, 317
    European distribution venture, 366, 368
    financial problems in 1958, 241–243
    hits and misses of 1990s, 495, 499
    independent filmmakers, rise of, 363
    King Kong affair, 397–398
    land acquisition and development,
        315–317
    MCA's purchase of Decca-Universal,
        296–297, 298, 299, 300
    MCA's purchase of facilities, 243–244
    missteps of 1980s, 425–426, 430, 449,
        473
    New Talent division, 313
    SAG strike of 1960, 262–263
    Spielberg's career, 387–389, 409, 426–428,
        493
    strikes of 1980 and 1981, 416–417
    successful films of 1970s, 362–363,
        369–373, 387–389, 391–392, 408–409
    television productions, 313–314, 337–339,
        363, 425, 430–431, 449, 473, 496
    turnaround under Wasserman's direction,
        250–254, 285
Universal Studios Tour, 3, 321–323, 369,
    397, 398, 417, 448n, 471
Universal Studios Tour—Florida, 425, 472,
    473, 475, 496
USA Network, 410, 431, 473, 518
Ustinov, Peter, 252

Valenti, Jack, 1, 318, 319–320, 376, 378, 466,
    497
Vallee, Rudy, 109
Vance, Cyrus, 2, 232, 256, 319, 367n
Vanden Heuvel, Katrina, xin, 412, 422, 423

Vanden Heuvel, William J., 281, 382, 402n
Video technology, 404–407, 410
Viner, Mort, 217

Wachtel, Esther, 498
Wager, Don, 519
Wagner, Robert, 249
Wakeman, Frederic, 127
Wald, Jerry, 114, 157, 217, 279
Wallis, Hal, 178, 179, 180–181
Wall Street Journal, 415, 481, 508
Walpaw, Eddie, 60
Walsh, Richard, 263
Walt Disney Productions, 406, 471–472
Walter Lantz Productions, 431
Wanger, Walter, 170–173
Ward, George, 82
Warner, Jack, 84–85, 93, 96, 114–115, 116,
    138–139, 182, 184, 241, 245n, 261,
    290–291
Warner Brothers, 50, 84, 366, 428, 474
Warsaw, Irwin, 276
Wasserman, Casey, 384, 437, 489, 490–491,
    498n, 523–524
Wasserman, Edie Beckerman, 6, 75, 196,
    215, 220, 221, 276, 319, 322, 338, 341,
    354, 355, 358, 360, 365, 403, 492, 506,
    515, 516
    cemetery plot, 519–520
    early years, 53, 54–55
    family life, 5, 100, 164, 310–311, 384,
        436–437
    fiftieth wedding anniversary, 444–445
    Hollywood Canteen, 96, 97
    Jewish identity, 199–200, 383
    marriage of, 60–61, 62
    philanthropic activities, 436, 491n, 498n,
        524
    romantic involvements, 98, 164–165, 166,
        200, 258n, 384
    social life, 76–77, 91, 119, 199, 274,
        435–436
    tropical plants, fondness for, 275
    as Wasserman's adviser, 205–206
Wasserman, Isaac, 46–47, 119, 120, 121
Wasserman, Lew
    aging, sense of, 268–269
    AMPTP leadership, 331, 376–379
    anger of, 192–195, 379–380, 497–498
    anonymity, preference for, 309, 479
    assassination plot against, 439–440

awards and honors, 370, 438, 498n, 515, 526

barbituate use, 360–361

birth date, 47n

California, move to, 72, 75

cemetery plot, 519–520

checkbook compassion, 516

clothing preferences, 1, 136

color-blindness, 136

draft status, 83

drinking by, 48

early years, 45, 47–52

family life, 5–6, 100, 119–121, 164, 310–311, 360–361, 436–437, 490–491, 516, 523–524

as father, 6, 276, 383–384

fiftieth wedding anniversary, 444–445

financial situation, 274, 359n, 483

gambling by, 92, 220

"god" status, 521–523

health problems, 59, 449–451

homes of, 90, 91, 274–276

investments, 118–119

Japan visit, 341–342

Jewish identity, 65, 199–200, 383

junk food, love for, 378n

Korshak's relationship with, 395–396, 397–398, 420–421

marriage of, 60–61, 62

media coverage of, 126–127, 266, 284, 295–296, 309–312, 395–396, 418–419, 473, 492–493

memoir-writing, disinterest in, 525–526

mogul status, 366, 417–419

movie theater work, 49–51, 56

murder contract rumor, 446, 447–448, 452

paranoia of, 488–490

philanthropic activities, 342–343, 438, 491, 498n, 524

political involvement, 5, 52, 142, 182, 317–320, 330–331, 344–345, 401–403, 413–414, 415, 461, 491, 492, 513, 520–521

portrait of, 275

power of, 2, 6, 122, 274, 290

publicist career, 56–57, 59–60, 64–65

safe of, 384–385

schmoozing strategy with clients, 87

Schreiber's death, 390

self-image, 273–274

Sheinberg's relationship with, 331, 374–375, 437–438, 497

Sinatra's conflict with, 165–166

sleeping problem, 50

social life, 274

speech problem, 51–52

Stein's relationship with, 65, 89, 101, 351

workaholic nature, 164

written record, avoidance of, 245

See also MCA; Universal Studios

Wasserman, Lynne Kay, 6, 76, 91, 200–201, 221, 276, 360–361, 383–385, 436–437, 447–448, 489

Wasserman, Max, 47–48

Wasserman, Minnie, 46, 49, 119, 120

Wasserman, William Isaac, 47, 48, 119–121, 275n, 477

Wasserman Foundation, 524

Waterfield, Bob, 152

Watergate scandal, 344

Waterworld (film), 3, 499–500, 505, 507

Watson, Philip E., 333

Weaver, Sylvester "Pat," 204, 227, 239, 291

Webb, Jack, 219

Webbe, Sorkis, 441

Weems, Ted, 19

Weintraub, Jerry, 437

Weis, Don, 339

Weisenberg, Nate, 64

Weisl, Ed, Jr., 232

Weisl, Ed, Sr., 188n, 231, 232, 256, 317, 318–320, 367

Weitzman, Howard, 517

We Just Kept Going (Stein), xii–xiii

Welk, Lawrence, 31

Welkos, Robert, 492n

Weller, Fred, 225, 226

Wells, Frank, 380, 381

Werblin, David "Sonny," 4, 31–33, 71–72, 83, 89, 105, 121, 126, 129, 130, 131, 132, 161, 166, 176, 195, 202, 204, 206, 232–233, 238, 239, 240, 257, 274, 282, 325–326, 421, 519

Wertheimer, Tom, 411, 428–429, 431, 466, 473, 507, 514

West, Mae, 11, 421

Westinghouse Electric, 353–354, 358–359

Westmore, Perc and Frank, 322

Wexler, Donald, 437

Whiteman, Weston, 316n, 409, 411

Whitney, Dwight, 108, 109–110

Whittinghill, Charles, 256

Wilder, Billy, 173, 198, 213, 215, 247, 248, 249, 295n, 302

Wilkerson, Billy, 147
Wilkins, Roger, 382
William Morris Agency, 43, 69–70, 71,
    229–230, 247–248, 287, 385, 480
Williams, Andy, 286n
Williams, Paul Revere, 76
Williams, Roy, 399n
Wills, Garry, 191, 279
Willson, Henry, 245–246
Winchester '73 (film), 152–155
Wittels, David, 125–126, 127
Wiz, The (film), 408
World's Fair of 1933, 36–38
WOR–TV, 443–444
Wrestling, televised, 159
Writers Guild of America, 187, 287,
    417
Wyman, Jane, 82, 83, 84, 137, 171
Wynn, Steve, 433–434

Yorty, Sam, 329
Yosemite Park and Curry Company, 369,
    392, 486
Young, Charles, 498
Young, Ernie, 12, 13, 14–15
Younger, Evelle, 420, 440
Young Lions, The (film), 235, 236–237
Youngstein, Max, 146n, 258n, 326, 335, 370,
    386, 494, 516, 526

Zanuck, Darryl, 81, 182, 184, 210, 211, 212,
    214, 241, 368n
Zanuck, Richard, 333n, 387–388, 415n
Zeitman, Jerry, 229, 302
Ziffren, Paul, 141–142, 182, 278n, 318, 343,
    519
Zwillman, Abner "Longie," 144, 146, 263